Operations & Supply Chain Management: World Class Theory and Practice

Operations & Supply Chain Management: World Class Theory and Practice

Rohit Verma
School of Hotel Administration and The Johnson Graduate School of Management, Cornell University

Kenneth K. Boyer
Fisher College of Business, Ohio State University

SOUTH-WESTERN
CENGAGE Learning™

Australia • Brazil • Japan • Korea • Mexico • Singapore • Spain • United Kingdom • United States

***Operations & Supply Chain Management: World Class Theory and Practice*, First Edition**
Rohit Verma and Kenneth Boyer

Senior Acquisitions Editor: Charles McCormick, Jr.
Senior Development Editor: Julia Chase
Editorial Assistant: Bryn Lathorp
Media Editor: Chris Valentine
Marketing Manager: Bryant T. Chrzan
Marketing Communications Manager: Libby Shipp
Marketing Coordinator: Suellen Ruttkay
Senior Content Project Manager, Editorial Production: Shelley K. Dickerson
Art/Design Manager: Jill Haber
Senior Art Director: Stacy Jenkins Shirley
Cover Design: Paul Neff
Print Buyer: Miranda Klapper
Senior Rights Acquisition Accounts Manager: Katie Huha
Text Permissions Editor: Tracy Metivier
Senior Photo Editor: Jennifer Meyer Dare
Cover Image: © Brand X Pictures, Inc.
Compositor: NK Graphics

Library of Congress Control Number: 2008943088

For product information and technology assistance, contact us at
Cengage Learning Academic Resource Center, 1-800-423-0563
For permission to use material from this text or product,
submit all requests online at **www.cengage.com/permissions.**
Further permissions questions can be e-mailed to
permissionrequest@cengage.com

International Student Edition:

ISBN-13: 978-0-324-83487-1

ISBN-10: 0-324-83487-X

Cengage Learning International Offices
Asia
cengageasia.com
tel: (65) 6410 1200

Australia/New Zealand
cengage.com.au
tel: (61) 3 9685 4111

Brazil
cengage.com.br
tel: (011) 3665 9900

India
cengage.co.in
tel: (91) 11 30484837/38

Latin America
cengage.com.mx
tel: +52 (55) 1500 6000

UK/Europe/Middle East/Africa
cengage.co.uk
tel: (44) 207 067 2500

Represented in Canada by Nelson Education, Ltd.
nelson.com
tel: (416) 752 9100 / (800) 668 0671

Cengage Learning products are represented in Canada by Nelson Education, Ltd.

For product information: **www.cengage.com/ international**
Visit your local office: **www.cengage.com/global**
Visit our corporate website: **www.cengage.com**

Printed in China by China translation & Printing Services Limited
1 2 3 4 5 6 7 12 11 10 09

ROHIT

For Amita, Pooja, Rishi, and my parents Prem Chandra and Urmila Verma

KEN

For Mary, Graham, Julia, and Caesar Boyer

Brief Contents

Contents

PART II TOOLS AND TACTICAL ISSUES

CHAPTER 4 Process Design and Analysis 102

CHAPTER 5 Forecasting 144

PART III THE EXTENDED ENTERPRISE

CHAPTER 12 Lean Enterprise 447

CHAPTER 13 Technology and Integrated Supply Management 476

CHAPTER 14 Global Supply Chain and Service Integration 508

Preface

THE IMPORTANCE OF OPERATIONS/ SUPPLY CHAIN MANAGEMENT

WHAT is operations management, and why do we care? Consider a product or service that you have bought recently—a cell phone, perhaps. Why did you choose this particular product or service rather than a competitor's? Was it better quality? Less expensive? More convenient? More attractive? Whatever the reason, the company or organization that provided the product or service had numerous decisions to make before that product or service got to you—decisions regarding where and how to produce it, what it should include, how it should be delivered, and so on. Let's examine a few examples from a "typical" day for the reader of this book:

Breakfast: Whether you had a Kellogg's Eggo Waffle, a quick bagel from the corner bakery, or simply a piece of fruit, someone had to (1) grow the ingredients, (2) purchase and acquire the ingredients and packaging, (3) produce the product (bake the bagel or waffle), and (4) deliver the product to you, the store, or the restaurant . . .

Transportation: How did you get to school or work today? Someone had to design and produce the car, bike, or train you probably traveled on . . .

Clothing: Where did the clothing you are wearing come from? Did you sew it yourself? Did you buy it online or in a store? How was it made? Who chose the sizes it would be produced in? Who chose what styles and colors would be made?

These are the types of decisions and issues on which this text will focus. **Operations management** consists of the processes that effectively produce, transform, and deliver a product or service. As Figure A.1 illustrates, every organization must transform inputs such as labor, materials, machinery, and equipment into outputs such as a car, a computer, a sandwich from a fast-food restaurant, or a medical diagnosis from a doctor. Let's consider an example. Budweiser sells many types of beer—in fact, its market share of all U.S. beer sales is approximately 50 percent. *Inputs* to make beer include materials such as water, barley, hops, and yeast, and also include the machinery and equipment used to produce the beer, such as the vats in which the beer is fermented and the machines that fill bottles or cans with beer. Human labor is involved in handling raw materials, maintaining equipment, moving the finished product, and so on. The *transformations* that Budweiser makes include not only the physical process of transforming raw materials into finished beer, but also the transportation of the beer from the manufacturing plant to the store where it is sold, the advertising and promotion for the beer, and other such actions. Finally, the *output* is both the bottle or can of beer and the choice of location where it is sold.

- **Operations management** the processes that effectively produce, transform, and deliver a product or service

In general, operations management refers to processes within a single firm or organization, whereas **supply chain management (SCM)** refers to processes and exchanges across multiple organizations. Over the past 10 to 20 years, companies have increasingly integrated their operations and information flows with those of their suppliers, distributors, and customers. Leading proponents of a supply chain approach to managing value-added activities

- **Supply chain management (SCM)** the organization of supply chain activities, including purchasing of raw materials and components from suppliers, distribution of parts and finished goods, and administration of the relationship with customers, in order to maximize customer value and maximize competitive advantage. SCM involves a coordinated effort by a group of organizations to manage the supply chain from raw material to finished product or service in the most efficient way possible.

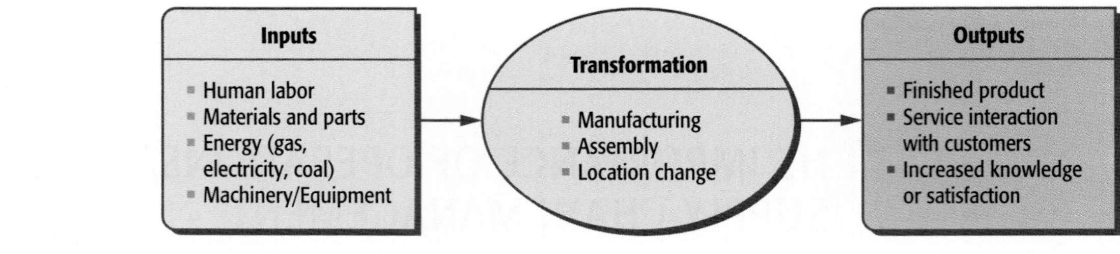

FIGURE A.1 Transformation Processes

across multiple organizations include companies such as Wal-Mart, Procter & Gamble, Cisco Systems, and Apple.[1] Supply chain management is the organization of supply chain activities, including purchasing of raw materials and components from suppliers, distribution of parts and finished goods, and administration of the relationship with customers, in order to maximize customer value and maximize competitive advantage. SCM involves a coordinated effort by a group of organizations to manage the supply chain from raw material to finished product or service in the most efficient way possible.

Every product or service involves some type of transformation, as illustrated in Figure A.1. Services such as FedEx or Deutsche Post may not physically transform a product, but instead change its location—i.e., picking the package up from your home or place of business and delivering it across the country or world to another location or person. A doctor's office also involves a transformation: from a sick, worried patient to a healthy, calm patient. Throughout the book, we will examine various transformation processes and the associated decisions regarding how to design them. For now, consider the following:

- Describe the types of inputs, transformations, and outputs that occur in manufacturing an airplane.
- Describe the types of inputs, transformations, and outputs that occur in producing a movie.
- Describe the types of inputs, transformations, and outputs that occur in building a large new building, such as a 90-floor skyscraper.
- How might the inputs, transformations, and outputs for producing beer differ if you were brewing small batches at home versus producing 3 million cases a year?

OUR PHILOSOPHY AND APPROACH

LEARNING and education form the foundations of the emerging knowledge-based society of the twenty-first century. Technology has revolutionized much of the way business is done around the world. One of us was recently talking to a colleague who said, "I remember teaching next to you back in 1994 and you were using this new thing called the Internet." We (the authors)

[1] AMR Research published an annual Value Chain Strategies Report titled "The AMR Research Supply Chain Top 25 for 2007" by Tony Friscia, Kevin O'Marah, Debra Hofman, and Joe Souza.

have each been teaching for approximately 15 years—the same length of time the Internet has been around. While we are relatively aware of the opportunities technology offers for education, we are not, nor will we ever be, as completely immersed in it as the generation of college students today that has grown up with Facebook and MySpace.

As teachers, we all use the Internet now for a huge variety of purposes—*but do we use it well?* There is a variety of learning styles as well as a variety of pedagogical approaches for teaching. We believe that there is some type of repository for standard, accepted knowledge central to all learning in an organized university-level course. We have been disappointed over the last decade by the relatively slow rate at which new technology has been embraced to revolutionize education. Thus, we embarked on a project to develop a new approach to teaching operations and supply chain management: an approach which places equal emphasis on technology and text. We view the tangible textbook as a necessary but insufficient component of the educational package. The online learning management system (CengageNow) and premium web site should be the order winner—the tool that really engages students and facilitates learning in a multi-dimensional, interactive manner that is far richer than a traditional textbook. As such, when we started this project three years ago, we started with a blank slate as opposed to many of the existing textbooks where the book preceded the web site/technology. What we offer here is a pull-based learning package—one that is developed to pull students in and encourage them to play and explore the core topics while using technology. This is in contrast to textbooks of the last 10 years, which have used a push approach—put enough content on the web and someone will use it. Thus, this text focuses on the following concepts, starting with a highly interactive web interface.

Strategy

While much of operations and supply chain management is very tactical and detail oriented, there is an increasingly strategic aspect to it. Much of the rising interest in this area over the past decade is due to the ability to pursue different strategies to achieve success—think of a responsive organization such as Zara versus a low-cost organization such as Wal-Mart. The first chapter offers an overview of operations/supply chain management along with a strategic framework. This material is based on one of the authors' 15 plus years of teaching an elective in operations strategy and is presented in a manner so that it is broadly applicable to many situations. Strategy then serves as an overarching framework throughout the book for considering alternative approaches to specific challenges or decisions.

Service Operations

Service operations are of increasing importance since well over 80 percent of jobs worldwide are in this sector. Even the biggest manufacturing companies these days have extensive customer support, product development, service activities, etc. In contrast to many existing textbooks, we're starting with a clean slate, bringing over 15 years of experience in both teaching and researching service operations to this book. Every chapter has service examples woven in as part of its foundation rather than as an add-on to what started as a manufacturing operations book 10-plus years ago. Our choice of American Express as one of our exemplary companies profiled throughout the book is intended to underscore the importance of and commitment to service operations management.

Global Supply Chain

The past decade has seen an explosion in world trade and the outsourcing of many manufacturing and service activities to countries globally. It is fairly routine for major corporations to have both suppliers and customers in scores of countries. While the fundamental principles for managing operations and the broader supply chain have not changed radically due to this growth in global interconnectedness, the need to be aware of cultural and communication differences is of dramatic importance. To highlight the advantages and disadvantages of global supply chains, Chapter 14 (Global Supply Chain and Service Integration) is devoted solely to this topic. In addition, every chapter includes at least one example from a non-U.S. company or organization.

Exemplary Companies

Three organizations—the Kellogg's Company, Sony, and American Express—represent excellent examples of what we consider to be "world class" operations and supply chain management. Each of these three organizations is examined thoroughly and from multiple perspectives throughout the book. Each is the subject of an opening case or featured example for every chapter—the goal being to illustrate how the principles discussed in the chapter are implemented in an actual company. These companies have been chosen because

- they are familiar to many readers.
- they illustrate the various supply chain principles we will be examining throughout the book.
- the companies are international in terms of the breadth of their operations and sale of their products.
- the cases provide examples of three different product/service mixes—Kellogg's is primarily a product-centric firm in that it sells very tangible products; Sony offers a mix of products and services; and American Express is primarily a service provider.
- these companies offer a fresh perspective from the typical examples of Wal-Mart, Toyota and Dell, all of which are often overused in many textbooks. We still refer to these when appropriate, but the use of Kellogg's, Sony, and American Express offers a fresher perspective.

Technology Interface: The Online Learning Management System (CengageNow)

The optional textbook online learning management system is intended as a highly interactive, pull-based repository of OM knowledge. It has the usual push-oriented content: videos, PowerPoints, Excel spreadsheets, audio summaries and quizzes, and more. The order winner is that these features have been set up so that instructors can assign a percentage of their grade for students to utilize these technologies. Once an instructor assigns the homework, the system will automatically track student usage and scores for the various elements. These include watching videos (with questions asked to ensure that students watch the videos), working with spreadsheets, and completing homework (both from end-of-chapter content and unique content). In addition, some basic content can be found on the textbook companion web site. Beyond the basic companion web site, we offer the premium, protected web site that contains a wealth of valuable student assets. The web site access code is free for all students purchasing a new textbook. We believe that leveraging the power of the Internet to allow students to interact online with the material and each other is a key to twenty-first-century learning, and it allows the instructor to teach groups of students as if teaching a course with an enrollment of one. Rather than explaining in great detail here—in a twentieth-century manner—we encourage you to go online and find out for yourself!

ORGANIZATION OF THE TEXT

OUR goal is to examine key tools, techniques, and practices in operations as they revolve around three themes: strategy, global supply chain, and service operations. Strategy is a key theme because, while there is a set of generally sound principles of operations, companies will make different decisions based on their operations strategy. As seen in Chapter 1, a low-cost-focused firm or supply chain will make fundamentally different choices than a company or supply chain focused on flexibility. We will examine strategy throughout the book as a driving force behind decision making. Second, global supply chain is a focus because of the growing interconnectedness of companies and customers around the world. As technology increasingly lowers barriers to communication and travel across the globe, so too are barriers for free trade lowered. As such, it is important to examine operations and supply chain in a global context. To that end, we try to present examples from companies from different regions of the world and companies that are truly worldwide in their operations. Finally, services are an increasing proportion of global output. The product service bundle must be managed carefully; thus, service operations are a central theme of the book.

In terms of organization, the book is divided into three parts: Strategic Operations Management, Tools and Tactical Issues, and The Extended Enterprise.

• Part I: Strategic Operations Management

The primary emphasis in Part I will be on how individual company operations (i.e., manufacturing, services, logistics, purchasing) contribute to a company's success or failure. Chapter 1 introduces operations strategy as a guide to positioning the organization. Supply chain is introduced as an important concept, but one that in many ways is an extension of operations management within a single firm. In other words, we focus on operationally managing a single organization but provide a quick introduction to the idea of linking multiple organizations in a broader supply chain. Thus, students will be expected to master internal operations as a primary goal, but develop an understanding of broader supply chain issues as a secondary goal. Quality and Six Sigma constitute the second chapter because they are the foundation of so much of business and form a key strategic component. In the third chapter, product and service innovation discussions provide a review of the challenges of developing and keeping products and services fresh.

Chapter 1: Operations and Supply Chain Strategy. This chapter introduces our three exemplary organizations: Kellogg's, Sony, and American Express. Operations strategy is presented as the foundation framework for understanding and linking together the numerous operational decisions any organization must make. The text illustrates how different strategies can be used to achieve success. Supply chain strategy is presented as an extension to operations strategy within a single firm.

Chapter 2: Quality Management. This chapter discusses the meaning of quality in both goods and services. The teachings of gurus including Deming, Crosby, Feigenbaum, and Juran are examined. ISO 9000, ISO 14000, and the Malcolm Baldrige Criteria are examined in depth. Six Sigma is described and calculation of sigma level is demonstrated.

Chapter 3: New Product Development. This chapter describes the new product development process, the product life cycle, and strategies and tradeoffs in product innovation. This chapter includes a special emphasis on concepts such as enhancing the customer experience, mass customization, and virtual reality. Design techniques covered include customer choice analysis, product reliability analysis, and quality function deployment.

Part II: Tools and Tactical Issues

Part II contains a series of chapters that provide in-depth discussion of various tools, techniques, and concepts necessary for day-to-day operations management. Each chapter provides basic concepts and necessary mathematical derivations, but the emphasis is on application/illustration of techniques for solving "real-world" OM problems. This part examines the core principles of operations, including process design and analysis, inventory management (including forecasting, independent demand, and dependent demand), project management, and quality improvement tools.

Chapter 4: Process Design and Analysis. This chapter leads off with the service-process matrix to emphasize service operations differences, before examining the product-process matrix for manufacturing. The text examines the interaction of strategy with process choice while highlighting the impact of technological evolution. Process analysis techniques including break-even, flowcharting, and bottleneck identification are presented, and several numerical examples are worked.

Chapter 5: Forecasting. This chapter examines the basic principles of forecasting. Specific methods covered include moving average, exponential smoothing with and without a trend, seasonal forecasting, and linear regression. Methods of assessing forecast accuracy including MAD, MAPE, and MSE are illustrated with numerical examples. A discussion of the broader supply chain and the ability to be responsive is offered.

Chapter 6: Independent Demand Inventory. This chapter covers the reasons for and against holding inventory. Basic inventory types including cycle, safety stock, anticipation, work-in-process, remanufactured/reconditioned, and pipeline are explained. Two basic inventory systems, continuous and periodic review, are explained in detail and illustrated with solved examples. Quantity discounts are discussed and a model presented. The role of technological applications—including ERP, RFID, and VMI—is discussed.

Chapter 7: Dependent Demand. This chapter explains the inputs and outputs of an MRP system. Single-level MRP records are discussed and the solution method illustrated. Multiple-level MRP records are then examined, and solved examples are presented. This chapter has numerous spreadsheet examples on the web that illustrate the dynamic nature of MRP and the linked nature of inventory transactions. The chapter concludes with a discussion of dependent demand in services and the role of technology, including a McDonald's illustration.

Chapter 8: Project Management. This chapter describes the steps involved in managing a project and explains the role of a project manager. This chapter discusses various project management tools and techniques such as work breakdown structure, critical path method, program evaluation and review technique, cost and time tradeoff analysis, recourse management, and risk analysis. Finally the chapter discusses success factors and how to avoid project failures.

Chapter 9: Optimization and Simulation Modeling. This chapter focuses on two important decision-making techniques for operations and supply chain managers. The first technique, known as linear programming, is used to optimize (or find the best solution) under given constraints. Second, computer simulation models can characterize the complexities of an operations system that contains a lot of variability. This chapter describes different types of simulation modeling approaches and provides several real-world examples.

Chapter 10: Capacity Planning. This chapter describes methods of measuring capacity, planning capacity, and calculating capacity utilization. Capacity strategy at an aggregate level is discussed and a methodological approach to evaluating the need for capacity expansion/contraction is presented. Also included is an examination of several factors that impact capacity considerations (economies of scale and scope, experience curves, and complementary products). The chapter also includes a special section on factors unique to services and an examination of yield management.

Chapter 11: Quality Improvement Methods. This chapter discusses both qualitative and quantitative quality and process management techniques. The qualitative quality improvement tools discussed include brainstorming, affinity diagrams, interrelationship diagrams, tree diagrams, process decision program charts, flowcharts, cause-and-effect diagrams, failure modes and effects analysis, and mistake-proofing. The quantitative quality improvement tools include inspection and sampling, check sheets, Pareto analysis, histograms, scatter diagrams, process capability analysis, run charts, and statistical process control charts.

Part III: The Extended Enterprise

Increasingly, competition is occurring across supply chains of multiple organizations. This is due to several factors, including lean production, technology, and increasing globalization. Part III examines these three factors as individual chapters. Lean production is examined as a philosophy and as a set of tools for not only reducing inventory and waste, but also for linking together separate organizations in a supply chain. Technology is examined both as a means of making operations more efficient, agile, or capable, and as a means of linking together organizations and providing visibility across the entire supply chain. The final chapter examines the challenges inherent in operating across borders, including global sourcing and international transportation.

Chapter 12: Lean Enterprise. This chapter describes the concepts of lean production and lean thinking. It explains how lean thinking can eliminate different types of waste present in a production (either manufacturing or a service). It discusses the essential components of a lean production system (such as just-in-time inventory) and describes new advances such as Lean Six Sigma. Lean methods are also described for application across the broader supply chain and within services.

Chapter 13: Technology and Integrated Supply Management. This chapter provides an overview and description of the role of technology in improving operations/supply chains. Key types of service and manufacturing technologies are discussed. Supply chain technologies that help link organizations are examined, with particular emphasis on methods of reducing the bullwhip effect.

Chapter 14: Global Supply Chain and Service Integration. This chapter discusses various issues related to the globalization of industries and its impact on operations and supply chain management. The chapter describes why firms globalize and establish production facilities. It also compares the positive and negative impacts of outsourcing and off-shoring production.

KEY FEATURES IN THE TEXT

THE text is formatted with some key features to underscore points of interest.

Learning Objectives. Every chapter starts with key objectives in a numbered list. These objectives are then matched to a summary explanation at the end of each chapter.

Opening Vignette. A company example, most often from one of our three exemplary companies, leads off each chapter. These vignettes provide a contextual illustration of several key principles of the chapter.

Key Terms. Every key term and definition is included in the margin. Key terms also appear in bold within the paragraphs.

Solved Examples. Within each chapter, problem statements, along with step-by-step illustrations for every key quantitative technique, are included.

Best Practices in Operations Management. These boxed inserts illustrate examples of companies employing practical and effective practices.

Technology in Operations Management. These boxed inserts highlight companies and organizations using technology applications and cover the associated people/work force decisions.

Case Studies. Every chapter includes a short closing case that can be used in the classroom as a discussion and application tool.

End-of-Chapter Problems. At the end of chapters with quantitative material, there are several problems with at least one of each type presented in the chapter. Additional problems are available on the text web site.

Web Site Material. Anywhere the @ symbol appears signals that there is accompanying material on the online learning management system (CengageNow) and/or on the premium web site.

SUPPLEMENTS DESIGNED TO AID STUDENT SUCCESS

Web Sites. The companion textbook web site offers a plethora of assets, including flashcards, learning objectives, chapter outlines, and chapter summaries. The premium web site contains games, quizzes, Excel spreadsheets, and additional content referenced in the text. An access code comes free with each new text. Go to **www.cengage.com/login** to register your premium access code. If you have purchased a used text, you will not receive the access code free with your book. To purchase an access code, please visit **www.ichapters.com**.

SUPPLEMENTS DESIGNED TO AID INSTRUCTORS

Text Web Site. Key instructor ancillaries (Instructor's Manual, Test Bank, ExamView, PowerPoint slides, and Classroom Response System content) are provided at **www.cengage.com/international,** giving instructors the ultimate tool for customizing lectures and presentations.

- *Instructor's Manual.* Designed to provide support for instructors new to the course as well as innovative materials for experienced professors, the Instructor's Manual includes Learning Objectives, a Teaching Note for the Opening Vignette, a Detailed Lecture Outline, Notes on the Solved Problems and End-of-Chapter Problems, Suggested Answers to Case Questions, and Additional Exercises.
- *Test Bank.* Scrutinized for accuracy, the Test Bank includes over 1,000 questions. Question types include true/false, multiple choice, short answer, and problems. Page references are indicated for every question.
- *ExamView.* ExamView contains all of the questions in the printed Test Bank. This program is easy-to-use test creation software compatible with Microsoft Windows. Instructors can add or edit questions, instructions, and answers, and they can select questions (randomly or numerically) by previewing them on the screen. Instructors can also create and administer quizzes online, whether over the Internet, a local area network (LAN), or a wide area network (WAN).
- *PowerPoint Lecture Presentation.* The PowerPoint Lecture Presentation enables instructors to customize their own multimedia classroom presentation. Containing approximately 500 slides, the package includes figures and tables from the text, as well as outside materials to supplement chapter concepts. Material is organized by chapter, and can be modified or expanded for individual classroom use. PowerPoint slides are also easily printed to create customized Transparency Masters.
- *Classroom Response System Content.* Using state-of-the-art wireless technology and text-specific content, a Classroom Response System (CRS) provides a convenient and inexpensive way to gauge student comprehension, deliver quizzes or exams, and provide "on-the-spot" assessment. Ideal for any classroom, a CRS is a customizable handheld response system that will complement any teaching style. Various answering modes, question types, and display options mean that a CRS is as functional as you want it to be. As a testing platform, as an assessment tool, or simply as a way to increase interactivity in the classroom, a CRS provides the technology you need to transform your lecture into a dynamic learning environment.

DVD Video Package. You can find exciting and engaging video clips for your students on this comprehensive DVD. Topics from the text are expanded upon to "show" rather than "tell" your students about the many complex operations management concepts.

SUPPLEMENTS DESIGNED TO AID STUDENTS AND INSTRUCTORS

CengageNow™. You envisioned it, we developed it. Designed by instructors and students for instructors and students, CengageNow for Verma/Boyer, *Operations & Supply Chain Management: World Class Theory and Practice* is the most reliable, flexible, and easy-to-use online suite of services and resources. With efficient and immediate paths to success, CengageNow delivers the results you expect.

- *Personalized learning plans.* For every chapter, personalized learning plans allow students to focus on what they still need to learn and to select the activities that best match their learning styles.
- *More study options.* Students can choose how they read the textbook—via integrated digital eBook or by reading the print version.

ACKNOWLEDGMENTS

WRITING a textbook has been an enormous lesson in project management. As with many projects, we had only a vague understanding of the scope of the challenge when we started. Fortunately for us, we also had a team of talented and dedicated people to guide, advise, and support us.

Lisé Johnson first approached us about writing a book, then spun a wonderful story about the joys of textbook writing and finally was ever ready with a sunny email or phone call to encourage us during the demanding or frustrating periods. **Julia Perez Chase,** our developmental editor, always kept us on schedule (sort of) and on task; she was instrumental in keeping us enthusiastic and moving forward. This was in addition to getting married and giving birth to a lovely daughter during the book development process. **Mike Schenk** and **Charles McCormick, Jr.,** acquisitions editors, were the overall project managers who helped create, manage, and deliver our vision. **Shelley Dickerson,** our content project manager, kept the process of putting the final text together running and caught the hundreds of loose ends that inevitably occur. **Ann Marie Radaskiewicz,** copyeditor, always found the slightly better way to phrase everything and never lost the ability to give the text "one more close read!" **Karen Lindsay,** art editor, helped add jazz to the written content. **Lisa Jelly Smith,** photo researcher, was instrumental in finding just the right pictures to illustrate key concepts. **Randy Byrd,** VP Convenience Foods Manufacturing for Kellogg's, provided a managerial touchstone and helped with getting permission to show Kellogg's operations. **Moe Izadpanah,** web guru, provided web site development expertise and interactive learning acumen. **Tom Gattiker,** Boise State University, wrote the Instructor's Resource Manual. **Patrick Penfield,** Syracuse University, developed the PowerPoints to match with the text. **Earl L. Wiese, Jr.,** DeVry University, developed mp3 audio summary and quiz scripts. **Lori Cook,** DePaul University, developed student quiz questions and classroom response system questions. **Matt Lindsey,** University of Texas at Tyler, wrote the Test Bank. **Andrea Prud'homme,** Ohio State University; **Liana Victorino,** University of Victoria; **Amita Verma,** Cornell University; and **William Colley,** MBA Michigan State University, read the initial drafts of the book and provided important interjections of "What are you trying to say here?"

In addition to these talented and dedicated people, we also had a team of reviewers and advisory board members who read the various drafts of the chapters. The following people provided excellent critical commentary and constructive comments that have strongly shaped the finished product: Miguel Anjos, University of Waterloo; Robert Banis, University of Missouri–St Louis; Hooshang Beheshti, Radford University; Walid Belassi, Athabasca University; Bill Bleuel, Pepperdine University; Injazz Chen, Cleveland State University; Wen-Chyuan Chiang, The University of Tulsa; Rex Cutshall, Indiana University; Ajay Das, Baruch College; Richard Dawe, Golden Gate University; Ping Deng, Maryville University of St. Louis; Keli Feng, St. Cloud State University; Warren Fisher, Stephen F. Austin State University; Theodore Glickman, George Washington University; Karolina Glowacka, University of Pittsburgh; Elkafi Hassini, McMaster University; Xin James He, Fairfield University; John Hebert, University of Akron; Craig Hill, Georgia State University; Eric Huggins, Fort Lewis College; Basheer Khumawala, University of Houston; Srimathy Mohan, Arizona State University; Jaideep Motwani, Grand Valley State University; David Olson, University of Nebraska; Patrick Penfield, Syracuse University; Anand Paul, University of Florida; Pedro Reyes, Baylor University; Edward Rosenthal, Temple University; Marc Schniederjans, University of Nebraska–Lincoln; Natalie Simpson, University at Buffalo; V. Sridharan, Clemson University; Ahmad Syamil, Arkansas State University; Thomas Patrick Waite, DeVry University; John Wang, Montclair State University; Larry Weinstein, Wright State University; Lifang Wu, Xavier University; and Qingyu Zhang, Arkansas State University.

Last and, in contrast to the saying, certainly most important, we would never have been able to do this without the love and support of our families. They are the ones who calmed us down when we ranted about the many hurdles involved. They are the ones that reminded us to take some time off and play some baseball or just hang out. They are the ones who hung in through the years of writing, and both of us changing universities during this process. They are the ones who provided constant support and encouragement.

As a version of the American Express slogan goes ". . . . Don't leave home without it!"

We couldn't have written this without you! Thank you all!

About the Authors

Rohit Verma

Rohit Verma is an Associate Professor of Service Operations Management at Cornell University, School of Hotel Administration. He is also a Visiting Associate Professor at the Johnson Graduate School of Management at Cornell University. Prior to his current appointment, he was the George Eccles Professor of Management, David Eccles School of Business at the University of Utah. He has also taught MBA and executive development classes at DePaul University, Chicago; University of Sydney; Norwegian School of Logistics; Helsinki School of Economics; and Indian School of Business.

He has published over 50 academic and managerial articles in prestigious business journals, such as *California Management Review, Cornell Hospitality Quarterly, Decision Sciences, Journal of Operations Management, Journal of Product Innovation Management, Journal of Service Research, MIT Sloan Management Review, Production and Operations Management,* and other journals. His research has been supported by numerous well-respected organizations around the world, such as Fairmont/Raffles/Swissôtel (Singapore); Hammerson, NCR Knowledge Lab (United Kingdom); Citycon (Finland); Siemens, Fraport (Germany); Wiener Konzerthaus (Austria); and, in the United States, American Express, Calvin Klein, eBay, First Chicago, Neiman Marcus, and the U.S. Forest Service.

Verma has received several teaching and research awards, including the Skinner Award for Early Career Research Accomplishments from the Production and Operations Management Society; the Sprit of Inquiry Award, the highest honor for scholarly activities within DePaul University; Teaching Innovation Award, DePaul University; and Doctoral Faculty Teaching Award, University of Utah.

Ken Boyer

Ken Boyer is a Dean's Distinguished Professor of Operations Management at the Fisher College of Business, Ohio State University. Dr. Boyer is co-Editor in Chief of the *Journal of Operations Management.* He previously was a professor of supply chain management at the Broad College of Management, Michigan State University, from 2000 to 2008. Prior to that, he was an assistant/associate professor at DePaul University, from 1995 to 2000. He earned a B.S. in mechanical engineering from Brown University, and an M.A. and Ph.D. in Business Administration from Ohio State University. In addition, Dr. Boyer worked as a project engineer with General Dynamics Electric Boat Division in Groton, Connecticut.

Dr. Boyer's research interests focus on the strategic management of operations, electronic commerce, and the effective use of advanced manufacturing technologies. He has published articles in *Management Science, Sloan Management Review, Decision Sciences, Journal of Operations Management,* and *Business Horizons,* among others. His research received the 1997 Chan Hahn award, the 1996 Stan Hardy award, and the 2004 Wick Skinner award. Dr. Boyer received the 2007 John D. and Dortha J. Withrow Teacher-Scholar Award at Michigan State University. He co-wrote the book *Extending the Supply Chain: How Cutting-Edge Companies Bridge the Critical Last Mile into Customers' Homes,* American Management Association, 2005. He is a member of the Academy of Management, Decision Sciences Institute, and the Production and Operations Management Society.

CHAPTER 1

Operations and Supply Chain Strategy

LEARNING OBJECTIVES

1 Discuss the importance of operations/supply chain management.
2 Describe the history and development of three exemplary organizations to be used as examples throughout this book.
3 Explain how single organizations can follow different competitive strategies to be successful.
4 Illustrate the differences and similarities between manufacturing and service activities.
5 Characterize supply chain strategy within a single organization and across multiple organizations.

Kellogg's Company: They Taste Grrreat—All Over the World!

This maker of popular cereal, breakfast, and snack products, such as Kellogg's Corn Flakes, Rice Krispies, Raisin Bran, Pop-Tarts, Eggo Waffles, and Nutri-grain bars, was founded in 1906 in Battle Creek, Michigan, by W. K. Kellogg. Much of the company's early success was based on its superior quality and consistency in making a "ready-to-eat" cereal product that replaced the heavy, fat-laden breakfasts of the early twentieth century. Kellogg's triumphed over 42 other cereal makers that began in Battle Creek by adhering to strong quality standards and developing new technologies, such as Waxtite wrappers to keep cereal fresh for long periods of time.

Kellogg's developed an international presence early in its existence, opening its first foreign cereal facility in 1914 in Canada, followed by exports of cereal to England in the early 1920s and the opening of another cereal plant in Sydney, Australia, in the late 1920s. Today, Kellogg's products are sold around the world in millions of locations; as shown in Figure 1.1, 33.1 percent of the company's sales come from locations outside the United States. Europe is Kellogg's second largest market with 19 percent of sales. The supply chain consists of 27 manufacturing plants in the United States and 19 plants in 15 countries around the world, including Australia, Mexico, India, Brazil, and Japan.

Key supply chain decisions must be made throughout Kellogg's network of plants. The product mix to be manufactured at each plant must be decided—for example,

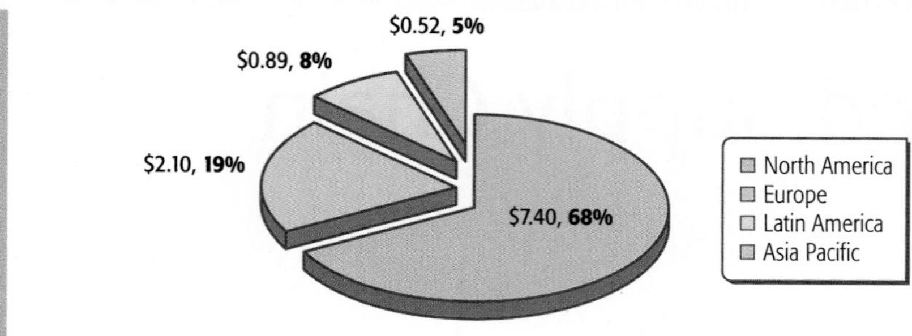

FIGURE 1.1 Kellogg's 2006 Sales Around the World (in $ billions)

should every plant make every product, or should plants be specialized and focus on a smaller subset of the company's products? The network of suppliers must be determined—is it better for Kellogg's to work with smaller, local suppliers for each plant or with larger, national or international suppliers? Inventory decisions and policies must be set for each plant, each distribution center, and each retailer that Kellogg's runs, works with, or sells to. These inventory decisions need to be linked to forecasting and production planning.

Sony—Electronics and Entertainment Provider to the World

Rice cookers similar to Sony's first product.

Sony Corporation is likely to be familiar to most readers because of its fabulous electronic products, including cameras, video cameras, computers, games, and other fun and useful electronic items, and its entertainment, including television programs, movies, and music. The company was founded as "Tokyo Tsushin Kenkyujo (Totsuken)," or "Tokyo Telecommunications Research Institute," on May 7, 1946, immediately following the end of World War II, by Masaru Ibuku and Akio Morita. Founded in the ruins of postwar Japan, Sony's (renamed in 1958) initial operations were under constant pressure. The first revenues were generated by repairing radios that had been damaged during the war. The first new product was an electric rice cooker that was developed to take advantage of an availability of excess electricity. Unfortunately, the cooker tended to severely under- or overcook rice—fortunately for Sony, its later products achieved a much higher degree of success!

Sony's first successful products were a power megaphone and a magnetic tape recorder. The company continued to innovate and soon needed to expand its facilities, opening a second manufacturing plant in Tagajo, Japan, in 1954; a color TV assembly plant in Bridgend, Wales, in the U.K. in 1974; and an audio/video product assembly plant in Colmar, Alsace, France, in 1986. These are just a few of the manufacturing plants and facilities opened worldwide to support the rapidly growing array of new products, including the first direct-view portable TV (1960), the first home-use open reel video TV recorder (1965), the Trinitron color TV (1968), the first personal headphone stereo, the Walkman (1979), and the world's first CD player (1982). Today, Sony operates offices in scores of countries around the world and sells products to a large percentage of the world.

Sony Vaio computers in store display.

Deriving a complete supply chain map for Sony's operations is very difficult, but we can illustrate the geographic dispersion of manufacturing for a single product category—electronics. Figure 1.2 illustrates two things. First, Sony produces around the world, with 50 percent of total electronics production occurring in Japan and the remainder in China, the rest of Asia, and the Americas/Europe. Second, Sony also sells products around the world. Interestingly, the majority of the products made in Japan, China, and the rest of Asia are for export. Figure 1.2 shows the percentage of all electronics production occurring in a given area along with the proportion destined for export. Notice that the Americas and Europe have zero exports. This is because while 22 percent of electronics are produced in these regions, 73 percent of all products are sold in these regions. In other words, the core of Sony's production is in Asia, but the core of Sony's markets is in the Americas and Europe.

Two key supply chain decisions can be inferred from the data in Figure 1.2. First, much of Sony's manufacturing capacity is situated in Asia. The large amount of capacity in Japan is due to the company's Japanese heritage and its having its home base in Japan. The relatively high amount of production in China and the rest of Asia is due to two factors. First, this approach takes advantage of low labor rates in these areas relative to those in Japan. Second, these areas' relative proximity to Japan makes the management of relationships fairly easy. In contrast, the 22 percent of production that is done in the Americas and Europe is likely to be substantially more expensive, but it has the advantage of being close to its market, allowing for faster delivery and quicker response to changes in demand. The second major decision that can be inferred from Figure 1.2 is that Sony must use a great deal of logistics service providers to ship product between its manufacturing plants and the end product markets. This requires a careful assessment of costs for various types of transportation (plane, ship, rail, and truck) and for different sizes of shipments or order sizes. Sony must also make decisions about speed of delivery, whether to have distribution centers to store

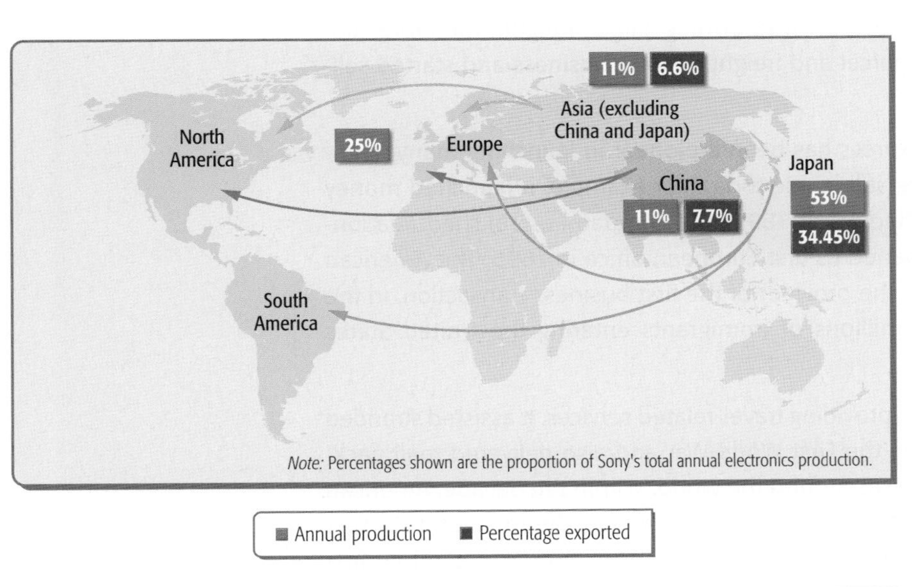

FIGURE 1.2 Sony Electronics Production by Geographic Region

products, and whether to ship products directly to retailers through a distribution center run by Sony, a third party, or the customer.*

Today, Sony is a thriving corporation with roughly 160,000 worldwide employees and sales of 7.5 trillion Japanese yen (roughly $65 billion).

American Express—Financial Services Worldwide: Worldwide Premier Provider of Personal Credit Cards, Travel, and Financial Services for Consumers, Small Businesses, and Merchants

American Express credit card.

American Express Company (AMEX) is one of the world's largest and most prestigious financial and travel services companies. The company serves individual customers, small businesses, and merchants by providing a variety of credit cards, banking and financial services, and travel-related services. Its 2007 annual revenue was in excess of $24 billion, and it employed over 65,000 employees in several countries around the world.

American Express was founded in 1850 in New York and was among the first and most successful of the express delivery companies that were formed during the westward expansion of the United States. Intrepid expressmen, typically on horseback or driving stagecoaches, traveled from the eastern cities to the western frontier, transporting correspondence, parcels, freight, gold, and currency, among countless other goods. During its early years, American Express was not a financial services company, but its largest clients were banks. Delivering the banks' typically small parcels of such things as stock certificates, notes, currency, and other financial instruments was considerably more profitable than transporting larger freight. Therefore, the company soon scaled down its parcel and freight delivery business and started selling its own financial products.

Since its early days, American Express has been a pioneer in launching many financial products, some of which are still in use today. For example, it launched money orders in 1882 and travelers' cheques in 1891. The company established relationships with foreign banks and opened its first European office in 1895. The American Express teller window was often the provider of the first business transaction, in the form of currency exchange, to millions of immigrants entering the United States through Ellis Island.

In 1915, American Express started providing travel-related services. It assisted stranded tourists in returning home during the First World War and also delivered mail packages to governments and businesses around the world. Within the decade, American Express started undertaking tours to Europe, South America, the Far East, the West Indies, and other destinations around the globe. American Express issued its first charge card in 1958. Currently, AMEX offers a variety of charge and credit cards to its

*Source: All information is either from 2005 annual report or www.Sony.net.

customers, including the BLUE card for students, various co-branded cards that provide bonus points to their users (e.g., JetBlue, Hilton, and Costco co-branded cards), and Platinum and Centurion cards for high-end customers.

The year 1986 was very special for AMEX, as its earnings exceeded $1 billion for the first time in history. During recent years, building relationships with merchants has become the company's top priority, along with increasing acceptance of the American Express Card across a wide range of industries and geographical markets. The company also began forming a number of strategic partnerships with selected airlines, banks, retailers, and other key businesses around the world. These alliances have proved highly successful and have enabled American Express and its partners to leverage their brands and business strengths efficiently while providing premium products and services to their mutual customers.

Today, American Express is a world leader in providing charge and credit cards to consumers, small businesses, and corporations. It is the world's largest travel agency, offering travel and related consulting services to individuals and corporations around the world. American Express is routinely recognized as one of the best companies to work for in America, is highly profitable for its shareholders, and strives to provide the highest level of products and services to its customers.

While American Express is primarily a service company, the range of supply chain decisions it must make is relatively similar to that faced by Sony and Kellogg's. For example, managers must decide where to locate branch offices to meet customer needs and must determine where to locate corporate offices for processing checks and financial transactions. The size of various offices must be determined, and decisions as to what tasks will be handled at each office must be made. For example, American Express has several dedicated call centers, each of which employs several hundred representatives to answer customer calls. A single call center may handle calls from numerous countries regarding numerous products. Other decisions include what suppliers to work with; in this context, a supplier might be a manufacturer of credit cards, a processor of bills, or an IT firm that provides software or services for routing financial transactions. ■

OPERATIONS STRATEGY WITHIN A SINGLE ORGANIZATION

KELLOGG'S, Sony, and American Express are companies that we will examine and follow throughout this text. For this chapter, they each present a different approach to operations strategy. Thus, we turn to a discussion of operations strategy. For now, we focus on the strategy followed by a single organization. There is more than one strategic approach that can be successful—one company might offer a lower-priced product made with a minimal quality level, while another company offers a very high quality product at a very high price. The ultimate goal is to convince customers to buy a product so that the company will make larger profits than its competitors. Thus, it is possible that either the low-price or the high-quality company could be more profitable. It is also possible that neither company is profitable—particularly if they do not manage their operations well.

What is the difference between buying a Rolex watch and a Casio? A meal at McDonald's or a meal at a five-star restaurant? Price and quality, among many other things. Companies follow different strategies to compete for customers, and these strategies depend on their operations being able to support them. Companies can emphasize one of four broad categories of competitive priorities, as shown in Table 1.1.

We focus first on operations strategy within a single organization. In this case, the choice of which competitive priorities to emphasize is entirely under the control of company management. Toward the end of the chapter, we will examine supply chain strategy involving networks of more than one company that work together to jointly deliver a product or service. While the principles of operations strategy within a single organization broadly hold true, developing a supply chain strategy is somewhat more complicated because of the multiple parties involved.

Competitive Priorities versus Capabilities

- **Competitive priorities** the relative rankings of what the company would like to achieve
- **Competitive capabilities** the relative effectiveness that the company is able to actually achieve

Competitive priorities are the relative rankings of what the company would like to achieve. **Competitive capabilities** are the relative effectiveness that the company is able to actually achieve. Competitive priorities provide a guide for what the company is aiming for—for example, which is more important, achieving low cost or achieving high quality? While both may be important, companies are most successful if they focus their efforts on one category at a time. Competitive capabilities are a measure of what the organization can actually achieve. Compare this to competing in a decathlon, which consists of 10 events. While most athletes would love to be the fastest, strongest, highest jumping, and so on, they realize that it is impossible to be "world class" in multiple events. Thus, an Olympic-level decathlete is very good at all 10 events relative to 99 percent of the athletes in the world, but is not of Olympic caliber in any single event. The decathlete will work on improving all areas of his or her performance, but will prioritize (i.e., set a competitive priority on) one area over others.

By extension, setting a competitive priority does not automatically ensure that a company will be capable of achieving that goal. As Olympic athlete want-to-be's, you and I may dream of high-jumping seven feet, but setting a priority of

TABLE 1.1 Competitive Priorities

Cost • Low-cost operations
Quality • Consistent quality • Superior quality
Time/delivery • On-time delivery • Delivery speed • Product development speed
Flexibility • Range of products/customization • Variety • Volume flexibility

achieving that goal is ridiculous if we do not have the athletic skills to do so. Table 1.2 lists some examples of companies with different competitive priorities.

We will focus on competitive priorities because they are the goals that an organization seeks to achieve. Capabilities will occur if the priorities are chosen well and if operations are managed well to match these priorities.

Cost

Cost is often the first thing that companies think of when they are developing an operations strategy. Lowering prices is the easiest reason to communicate to customers why they should buy a particular product or service. Unfortunately, simply lowering prices will lead to reduced profits or even losses; therefore, a company must simultaneously reduce its operating costs. **Low-cost operations** seek to provide a product or service that is less expensive than similar products or services offered by competitors. This can be done by investing in new equipment that runs faster, by reducing scrap, or by eliminating waste or unused capacity. Companies must use rigorous process analysis and consistent corporate management to consistently find ways to reduce costs.

● **Low-cost operations** provide a product or service that is less expensive than similar products or services offered by competitors.

Quality

Many companies seek to move away from an overarching emphasis on low cost by offering products or services with improved quality. Quality involves offering a product or service that is superior to the alternatives in the eyes of the customer. There are numerous aspects of quality, but for the sake of simplicity, we will discuss two key aspects.

Consistent quality involves meeting the product specifications and the promises made to customers with high reliability. The product does not necessarily have to be superior to another, but customers must have a high degree of confidence that what they are buying will perform as promised. For example, McDonald's may not offer the best-quality hamburger, but hamburgers purchased in Beijing, Stockholm, and Sydney are likely to be almost identical. Offering consistent quality of products is one of the foundations that has led McDonald's to operate 30,000 restaurants in 119 countries around the world. Competing based on consistent quality involves continually monitoring and evaluating processes to minimize errors. Thus, one of the key factors in McDonald's success is the adherence to a single system for operating every restaurant around the world.

● **Consistent quality** meeting the product specifications and promises made to customers with high reliability

Superior quality is a term describing a product or service that clearly is better than another in one or more aspects. A luxury car drives more smoothly, feels or looks better, or is faster than a lower-quality car. A five-star hotel has nicer furniture, more service, and better facilities than a lower-cost hotel. Superior quality

● **Superior quality** a term describing a product or service that clearly is better than another in one or more aspects.

TABLE 1.2 Examples of Companies with Different Operations Strategies

Competitive Priority/Capability	Company
Low cost	Wal-Mart, Taco Bell, Southwest Airlines
Superior quality	Rolex, BMW, Singapore Airlines
Delivery speed	FedEx
Customization flexibility	Dell, Land's End (custom khakis), wedding planner

involves offering something that customers will pay a premium for, something that outshines the competition. With tangible products, superior quality is often achieved by having more or nicer features, such as a finer-quality fabric in clothing. The difference between a $155 Hermès tie and a $35 tie available from almost any retailer is astounding—you can feel the difference in your fingers (and your wallet).

Time/Delivery

The speed and reliability with which a product or service is delivered is another area in which companies can distinguish themselves. Time/delivery refers to the gap between when a customer orders a product and when he or she receives it.

● **On-time delivery** delivering a product when promised, but not necessarily quickly

On-time delivery involves delivering a product when it is promised, but not necessarily quickly. A computer manufacturer that requires microprocessor chips for each of the computers it builds is very concerned about the supplier's ability to deliver those chips when promised—after all, a computer without its core processor is not particularly useful. Most mail organizations, such as the U.S. Post Office or the Royal Mail in the U.K., compete based on on-time delivery—a letter will get there with high reliability (>99.5 percent of the time), but may take three

BEST PRACTICES IN OPERATIONS MANAGEMENT

Rolex: No Copying the Original

In almost any major city in the world, you can find someone on a busy street corner selling fake Rolex wristwatches. Everyone knows that these are cheap imitations, but two questions come to mind. First, why is Rolex so widely copied? The answer is that Rolex has been making premium watches with the utmost quality since Hans Wilsdorf established the firm in London in 1905. Second, how can you tell the difference between a knockoff and a true Rolex? Rolex sells watches only through carefully licensed dealers—not over the Internet. Rolex exerts great control over its dealers and is very careful to ensure that each represents the ultimate in quality and professionalism. This fact is clearly conveyed by the large legal notice that comes up when you first visit the Rolex web site. Watches also go through extremely thorough testing during development, including tests for clasp fatigue, corrosion, bracelet fatigue, case waterproofness, agitation, and torsion. Every watch has a unique serial number, which allows instant traceability of it and the conditions in which it was manufactured. Watch movements are tested individually for precision and accuracy after every single operation. Thus, a timepiece that has received final quality certification has been examined hundreds of times. Rolex has a motto that "perfection is the fruit of time." Clearly, Rolex has tremendous quality, which comes at a price. The watch may cost several months' salary, but it will last a lifetime. In summary, Rolex makes the following operational decisions in order to ensure a superior-quality final product:

- Certification and monitoring of approved dealers
- Extensive testing for durability and quality during product development
- An individualized serial number and matching database to allow the life history of the watch to be traced
- Selection of suppliers that use superior materials and production methods
- Manufacturing watches by hand with highly trained craftspeople rather than on a high-volume production line

More information is available at www.rolex.com.

to five days. In contrast, companies such as FedEx, DHL, or Airborne compete based on delivery speed.

Competing on **delivery speed** means that a corporation offers to deliver a product or service faster than a competitor. Getting something quickly has obvious appeal. Pizza delivery, emergency rooms, and overnight package delivery provide examples of companies that get products or services to the customer quickly. Many customers will pay a premium for speed—consider a dry cleaner that will clean a garment in one hour for a higher price than if it is to be picked up the next day.

- **Delivery speed** when a corporation offers to deliver a product or service faster than a competitor

Product development speed refers to the time between generations or major changes to a product. Manufacturers who can develop a product and make substantial changes in it can sell the product as new and different. Product development speed is important to just about any business, but it is particularly important in dynamic industries such as electronics, computers, and fashion. As illustrated in Figure 1.3, Apple* has introduced seven different versions of its popular iPod music player in a span of little more than 4½ years. This willingness to innovate and create new products allowed Apple to sell over 1 billion songs from iTunes by October 2005 and reach 1 million video downloads in just 19 days following the launch of the video iPod.

- **Product development speed** the time between generations or major changes to a product

Flexibility

Flexibility is another way for companies to differentiate their offerings from those of companies that emphasize low cost. **Customization** is the ability to make a product to exactly fit customer needs. A hand-sewn dress shirt from a tailor is completely customized and is likely to fit better than the off-the-shelf alternative that comes with a preconfigured neck, chest, and arm size. Dell Computers also offers custom products, allowing customers to select one of several hard drive capacities, processor chip speeds, computer models, and so on. Each choice involves only a few (three to five) options, but when these choices are all combined, each individual computer is highly differentiated. Dell and other companies offer customization by capitalizing on **postponement,** which involves keeping products in a standard format and then adding unique components for the individual customer at the last possible moment.

- **Customization** the ability to make a product to exactly fit customer needs

- **Postponement** keeping products in a standard format and then adding unique components for the individual customer at the last possible moment

Customization is most often applied in low-volume settings where the product commands a premium price. However, new technologies such as the Internet and computer-aided technology are increasingly allowing **mass customization,** the process in which products are produced in high volume at roughly the same cost as standard products, but are customized to individual customer tastes. A critical element when pursuing a customization strategy is involving the customer at appropriate points in the design and production process.

- **Mass customization** the process in which products are produced in high volume at roughly the same cost as standard products, but are customized to individual customer tastes

iPod	iPod Mini	iPod Photo	iPod Shuffle	iPod Mini 2nd Generation	iPod Nano	iPod Mini 5th Generation with Video	iPhone
Oct. 1, '01	Jan. 1, '04	Oct. 1, '04	Jan. 11, '05	Feb. 23, '05	Sept. 7, '05	Oct. 2, '05	Jun. 29, '07

FIGURE 1.3 Apple iPod New Product Timeline

*Apple, iPod, iTunes, and iPhone are trademarks of Apple, Inc., registered in the United States and other countries.

BEST PRACTICES IN OPERATIONS MANAGEMENT

Apple: Maintaining a Steady Supply of Innovation

Never Stand Still

Looking back today, Apple's iPod has clearly revolutionized the digital music industry—creating its own term: podcasts. Yet this success was not preordained. When the first iPod debuted in November 2001, the entire computer industry was in a major slump, and Apple was infamous for its failed Newton—an early PDA device that never took off. The initial price for an iPod was $399, roughly twice that of similar products from other companies. At the time, Apple President Steve Jobs said, "Our strategy is making Macintosh a digital hub, to make the way we do movies and image viewing and music to a point where you can't live without them."

The success of the iPod resulted from its sleek design and its ability to hold a lot of music. The original iPod was about the size of a pack of cigarettes and held 1,000 songs—several times the number held by similar-size devices at the time. These advantages and some savvy marketing allowed iPod to overcome its price disadvantage and its limited market, as at first it was usable only by owners of Apple PCs (of which there were only 7.5 million in 2001). All of this was powered by Apple's drive to steadily introduce new versions of the iPod and create a buzz around the product. The original iPod was the result of an eight-month crash development project. As shown in the timeline in Figure 1.3, Apple has kept up a steady stream of new versions and products—including a new iPhone released June 29, 2007—intended to broaden its early lead in the digital entertainment business. The iPhone was greeted by waiting lines to get one of the first in cities around the world. Early estimates were that 500,000 phones were sold in the first week following release. As of January 22, 2008, Apple had already sold approximately 5 million iPhones (2.3 million in Q1 of 2008) and was selling iPods at the rate of 22 million per quarter.

● **Variety** the ability to handle a wide range or assortment of products without undue costs

Variety is the ability to handle a wide range or assortment of products without undue costs. With variety, the product is not customized to individual specifications, but instead numerous choices are offered. A retailer offering a T-shirt in small, medium, large, or X-large offers more variety than a one-size-fits-all retailer, but the product is still far from custom. A manufacturer that produces plastic toys may make 10 to 20 thousand different toys, but these toys are all produced in a repetitive, fairly large-volume process. Typically, variety is forecast and pushed to the customer, who makes his or her selection only at the point of purchase rather than earlier in the process, as with customization.

● **Volume flexibility** the ability to adjust production volume either up or down to meet fluctuations in demand

Volume flexibility is the ability to adjust production volume either up or down to meet fluctuations in demand. Volume flexibility is important when supporting delivery speed and when demand is fairly unstable. Restaurants must have high volume flexibility to deal with large swings in demand between lunchtime highs, midafternoon lulls, and dinnertime increases in demand. Service-sector businesses often place a high premium on volume flexibility because of their inability to inventory products as a buffer against demand fluctuations.

Operations' Role Within Business Strategy

● **Business strategy** defines the markets, products, and target customers and sets both short- and long-term objectives for the company

While operations is extremely important to the success of the organization, it remains one of many functional areas that must be integrated and coordinated if overall success is to occur. The entire company is generally guided by a **business strategy** that defines the markets, products, and target customers and sets both short- and long-term objectives for the company. A company's business strategy sets the broad guide for what the company will be doing for the near future (the next 6 to 18 months), the mid-range future (the next 2 to 5 years), and the distant future (5 or more years from the present). A mission statement is often used to summarize the business strategy. A **mission statement** defines why a company exists, outlines its core values, and seeks to position the company within the larger market.

● **Mission statement** a statement that defines why a company exists, outlines its core values, and seeks to position the company without the larger market.

Examples of mission statements include the following:

- The mission of Southwest Airlines is dedication to the highest quality of Customer Service delivered with a sense of warmth, friendliness, individual pride, and Company Spirit.
- Establish Starbucks as the premier purveyor of the finest coffee in the world while maintaining our uncompromising principles while we grow.
- Ford: We are a global family with a proud heritage passionately committed to providing personal mobility for people around the world. We anticipate consumer need and deliver outstanding products and services that improve people's lives.

As can be seen by these examples, mission statements tend to sound very nice and positive, but they do not offer much prescriptive guidance. This is because companies are faced with a large amount of uncertainty, and predicting the future is difficult; thus, building flexibility into the mission statement allows a company to adapt and react to changes in its environment.

More specific details are provided by breaking the high-level business strategies into **functional strategies,** which specify the core goals of areas such as operations, marketing, finance, IT, R&D, and so on. This is the level at which strategy starts to become more detailed and tactical in nature. It is important that each functional area within a company has a clearly articulated strategy and that these strategies are integrated to jointly support the overall business strategy. Figure 1.4 illustrates the basic relationships among three functional areas chosen to highlight the way functional strategies should be integrated and work together. The functional strategies shown are not more or less important than other functional strategies; we have chosen them simply because operations is the focus of this book, and marketing and finance are two functions that are often involved in situations where their goals are in conflict with those of operations.

● **Functional strategies** specify the core goals of areas such as operations, marketing, finance, IT, R&D, and so on.

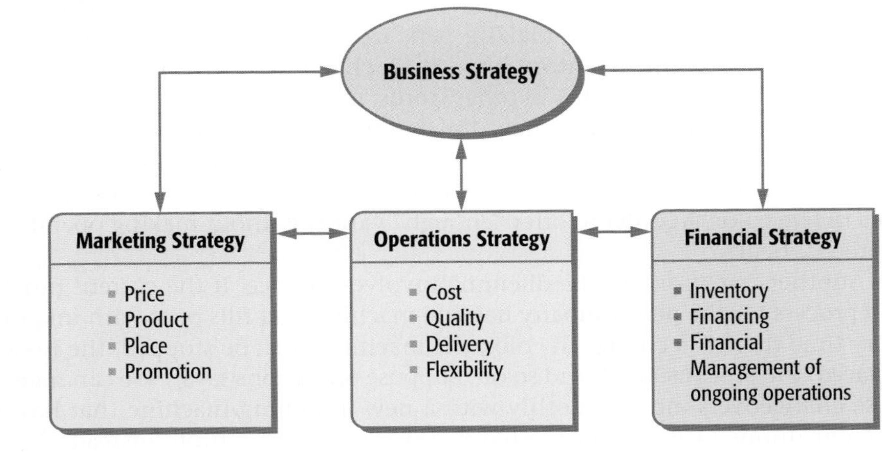

FIGURE 1.4 Relationships Between Business Strategy and Functional Strategies

Let's start with marketing. You may be familiar with the four Ps of marketing: price, place, product, and promotion. While these are easy to remember because of their alliterative naming, they represent the yin to the yang of operations' competitive priorities. Price is the level at which a product or service will be sold, including various discounts for buying in bulk or other incentives that a company offers to get customers to buy. Numerous companies advertise low prices as a way of luring customers—the problem is that this must be matched operationally with low cost. To compete with Wal-Mart in the summer of 2001, Kmart tried to promote in its "Bluelight Always" campaign that it had low prices. The problem was that Kmart did not have the operational system to support the low prices with low costs—which led to the company's bankruptcy in January 2002.

From a marketing perspective, product is the type, range of choices, and features for a given item or service. Generally, more is better—a product with more features is likely to sell better than a product with fewer features (assuming that the prices are the same). The operations equivalent is quality—the more products a firm offers from a marketing perspective, the more difficult it is for operations to track and monitor quality.

In marketing, place means where and how the product will be sold. In other words, in how many stores will it be sold? On the Internet? Only in certain types of stores? As with the product/quality relationship, marketing generally wants products to be sold at more places, yet this means that operations must deal with more deliveries.

Marketing defines promotion as comprising the advertising, sales force, public relations, and direct marketing that support a product. In terms of operations, flexibility can be considered complementary to promotion, although it is not as directly related to promotion as price is to cost.

In short, there is a natural tension between functions such as operations, marketing, and finance. Each has its unique objectives, which may be somewhat at odds with the objectives of the other functions. The most successful companies manage to balance this tension to achieve the best overall results for the company as a whole. Consider an example. Suppose you manufacture ballpoint pens—a fairly simple product. These pens can be sold with the exact same structure and parts, but with different colors of ink (and maybe the cap of the pen in a matching color). Would you rather sell the pen in ten different colors (say blue, red, black, green, purple, pink, aquamarine, magenta, brown, and indigo) or in two colors (black and red)? Most people will instinctively pick ten colors—more choice should result in more sales. From a marketing perspective, more choice (i.e., more product) is almost always better, but from an operations perspective, this requires more flexibility. Making pens in ten colors requires ten different forecasts, ten different inventory quantities, changing over the ink-filling machine for each different color—in other words, more work. So, the average operations manager would prefer to make the pen in only two colors.

So who is right? Probably neither side. The best answer for the business involves balancing the concerns of the two sides. It might be best to make pens in five colors in order to offer "enough" variety without making operations' job too difficult.

Another "solution" to the dilemma involves finance. If the current production process for the pen company has one machine that fills pens with ink, then every time there is a change in color, the machine must be stopped, the inkwell replaced, the pipes cleaned, and so on. Suppose operations says, "We can manage these changeovers more smoothly with a new ink-filling machine that has ten different drums of ink and can change ink colors in 1 minute instead of 20"? What is finance's typical response? "What is the payback period, and why do you need to replace the existing machine if it is not 100 percent utilized?" However, the strategic choice for finance may be to realize that given the tension between marketing's desire for ten pen colors and operations' desire for two, buying a machine that facilitates quick changeover may offer the best of both worlds: increased product/flexibility with little increase in cost/price.

Operational Decision Areas

We turn now from an examination of *what an organization wants to achieve* (i.e., competitive priorities) to *how it can achieve* those capabilities. The competitive priorities of an organization are like the needle on a compass; they show us the direction in which to go, but they are not sufficient by themselves. Knowing that quality is the most important competitive priority points the organization and its employees in a general direction. **Operational decision areas** are the tactical tools that allow an organization to achieve its priorities. Operational decision areas are similar to the hiking shoes, hiking stick, backpack, and other equipment that are invaluable on a challenging hike to supplement the guidance provided by a compass. An organization is faced with hundreds or thousands of operating decisions that must be made on a daily basis. These decisions can be classified in two categories. **Structural decisions** are long-term, high-capital-investment decisions that occur less frequently but have a lasting impact on the organization. Once made, these decisions are difficult to change or modify. **Infrastructural decisions** are shorter-term, more frequent, less capital-intensive,

● **Operational decision areas** the tactical tools that allow an organization to achieve its priorities

● **Structural decisions** long-term, high-capital-investment decisions that occur less frequently but have a lasting impact on the organization

● **Infrastructural decisions** decisions that are shorter-term, more frequent, less capital-intensive, and easier to change or modify

TABLE 1.3 Operational Decision Areas

Structural Decisions	
Capacity	**Facilities**
• How much? • When to grow/shrink? • How to grow/shrink?	• Where/how many? • Layout/design? • Local/global?
Technology	**Vertical Integration/Sourcing**
• What kind? • How often updated?	• What suppliers? • Type of relationship with suppliers? • Number of suppliers?
Infrastructural Decisions	
Work Force	**Quality Systems**
• How many workers of each type? • What skills?	• What metrics? • How to assess and check quality?
Production Planning/Scheduling	**Organization**
• What quantities should be produced? • In what order?	• How many levels in the organization? • Who makes decisions in each area?

and easier to change or modify. Table 1.3 provides an overview of the types of decisions and an illustration of different decisions that must be made. We simply want to introduce the idea here—each of these specific areas will be covered in much more detail throughout the remainder of the book. For now, just remember that a company that is focusing on low-cost operations will make substantially different decisions from one that is focusing on high flexibility.

As an illustration of how operational decisions can differ, let's examine two restaurants: a McDonald's like the one within a few miles of your home and an upscale restaurant such as Charlie Trotter's in Chicago. McDonald's competes on a combination of cost, flexibility, and delivery. It offers low-cost meals, delivered within a couple of minutes, with a medium degree of flexibility or product choice. Notice that McDonald's does not try to offer the "best" products available—i.e., performance quality is not a competitive priority, but conformance quality is important (the French fries you get in Omaha, Nebraska, are identical to those you could get in Shanghai, London, or Mumbai/Bombay). In contrast, Trotter's competes on offering top-notch performance quality. It is a five-star restaurant, and its meals are excellent—but not cheap. Dinner for two can easily run higher than $250.

In order to support their respective strategies, McDonald's and Trotter's make very different operational decisions. For example, the two handle their sourcing in very different ways. McDonald's has developed a network of suppliers that produces its food to exacting specifications. Simplot is a $3 billion per year firm that supplies French fries to McDonald's. In the 1960s, Simplot developed a method for flash-freezing French fries that preserved their flavor. McDonald's buys mostly frozen food because it keeps better and provides excellent conformance quality. In contrast, Trotter's buys its food from local producers and farmers' markets. This method of procurement is substantially more expensive, particularly in terms of the restaurant labor involved in acquiring ingredients, but it provides much higher quality food. Table 1.4 shows other differences in operational decisions between these two restaurants. Can you think of others?

The remainder of this book deals with the operational decision areas shown in Table 1.3. Each will be examined in depth, and decision-making techniques and tools for that decision area will be explained.

TABLE 1.4 Comparing McDonald's and Charlie Trotter's

McDonald's	Charlie Trotter's
Price of meal: $3–$7	Price of meal: $30–$150
Primary competitive priority: Cost and delivery	Primary competitive priority: Quality, customer experience
Sourcing: Contracts with a few suppliers for very standardized, consistent ingredients	Sourcing: Dynamic relationship with local farmers and farmers' markets to get the freshest and best-quality produce, meats, and dairy
Work force: Low-skilled, interchangeable. Seeks to standardize jobs and skills so that one employee can perform multiple tasks	Work force: Highly skilled and specialized
Facilities: Designed primarily for efficiency. Easy to clean. Spartan, efficient	Facilities: Designed primarily for customer benefit. Extra capacity. Very plush

SERVICES

THE operations strategy principles that we have examined are universal across businesses, yet it is important to understand the particular subcontext of services. Business processes can be categorized as primarily manufacturing or primarily services. Manufacturing processes create tangible products like cars, tables, toys, and bikes. Services create more intangible offerings that may include a tangible product, but that also include an intangible offering. More than 80 percent of the jobs and sales in developed countries are in services. Thus, while manufacturing goods is important, providing services is just as, if not more, important. Increasingly, businesses are selling a product bundle that includes both tangible products and less tangible but very valuable services. Many businesses use services as a way to differentiate their products. In addition, many service enterprises in such areas as consulting, software development, medical care, project management, and education are very knowledge intensive and challenging to manage. In what has been called the postindustrial economy of the twenty-first century, managing services is seen by many as being critical to the success of individual nations, industries, and businesses. Therefore, services will be a major focus throughout this book.

Differences Between Services and Manufacturing

It is important to distinguish between services and manufacturing because they have three fundamental differences:

1. The nature of their output—tangible vs. intangible
2. The degree of customer contact and co-production
3. Simultaneous production and consumption

Manufacturing processes convert raw materials and inputs into finished products that have a physical, tangible form. For instance, an assembly line produces a Sony Playstation 3, a batch production process produces cookies at a bakery, and a shipyard manufactures ferryboats. The manufacturing process consists of one or more of the following transformations of the input materials:

1. Physical properties
2. Shape
3. Fixed dimension
4. Surface finish
5. Joining parts and materials

If a process does not make one of the five changes listed here, it is considered to be a service process. Services generally produce more intangible, perishable outputs. For example, a restaurant produces not only food but also the service of the food. A store provides the service of selling the physical items manufactured by other companies. A hairstylist provides a haircut. A lawyer provides legal advice or representation. While each of these may involve some tangible components, the bulk of the service is intangible. The **service bundle** is defined as all the value-added physical and intangible items that an organization provides to the customer. The following are three key ways in which services differ from manufacturing.

● **Service bundle** all the value-added physical and intangible items that an organization provides to the customer

Services Are Intangible

A service may include tangible goods as some of its components, such as food in a restaurant, a seat on an airplane flight, or medical equipment in a physician's office. However, the overall product offering, such as a dining experience in a restaurant or medical advice from a physician, is primarily intangible.

This intangibility adds subjective considerations to the design and development of new services. Furthermore, because of this intangibility, two customers cannot be expected to evaluate a service in the same manner. This makes quality more difficult to assess and measure for services than for manufactured products.

Customer Co-production

Perhaps the most distinctive feature of a service is the involvement of the customer in the production process. While most goods can be produced in factories far away from customers, services require the participation of the customer in the production process. Since customers are part of the service production process, the degree of variability in the quality of services provided is considerably higher than that for manufactured goods. Therefore, mass customization of many new services and evaluation of quality are relatively difficult and subjective. The type of service offered has a large impact on how the service is designed and the amount of co-production with customers. For example, the design and development of a *low-contact service* (e.g., a call center, check processing center, or Internet retailer) is typically driven by operational efficiency considerations (similar to those involved with the goods manufactured in factories). In contrast, the design and development of a *high-contact service* (e.g., a doctor's office or full-service restaurant) is driven by marketing and customer-preferences-related considerations. Similarly, site selection and layout for low- and high-contact services are directed by proximity to customers or efficiency/cost considerations.

Customer contact is both good and bad. In manufacturing, less customer contact is good in that processes can be more standardized without customers getting in the way. Customers tend to complicate things by wanting small differences in their orders and by introducing variability into the process. On the other hand, many services capitalize on customer involvement by encouraging customers to "have it their way" and customizing the service bundle. This helps create a more satisfied customer who is willing to pay a premium for that service.

Simultaneous Production and Consumption

Because services cannot be delivered without customer involvement, they are produced and consumed at the same time (a dining experience is *produced* while customers in the restaurant *consume* the service at the same time). Therefore, it is almost impossible to inventory services the way one can store finished goods (e.g., a psychological counseling session cannot be inventoried in advance). Furthermore, because many services are consumed at the point of "production," they lack transportability (e.g., to have the experience of staying in an "Ice Hotel" in Norway, the customer has to visit the facility in Norway). Nevertheless, because of technological advances, one could argue that the portability of many services is becoming similar to that of manufactured goods (e.g., videoconferencing might allow a surgeon to participate and advise during a surgery without being physically present in the hospital).

Furthermore, production capacity in many services is also perishable (e.g., an airline seat has no value after the airplane takes off). Because services cannot be inventoried, the issue of perishability is even more crucial in services than in goods. Hence, the simultaneous production and consumption and the perishable nature of a service mean that the strong link between features of the service observed by the customer (e.g., waiting time) and operational processes (e.g., labor schedules and capacity) must be considered carefully in service development efforts.

Other Operational Considerations

Services in general are more labor-intensive than the production of goods. However, for certain services (e.g., customer service call and e-mail centers), technological advances are reducing the percentage of capital spent on labor in favor of technology and automation. Customers evaluate services on both tangible and intangible features; therefore, it is relatively difficult to measure productivity in service processes.

The differences between services and manufacturing are not entirely consistent. Many manufacturing processes include substantial service components, while many services include substantial manufacturing components. Manufacturing cars has a large tangible component, but there is also a large service component involved in selling the car, providing warranty support, designing new cars, and so on. Similarly, a credit card company such as American Express provides a service, but the company also has employees or contractors that manufacture and process the physical credit cards that customers carry in their wallets and handbags. What is most important is that we recognize that the degree of customer contact varies between manufacturing and services; therefore, we must seek to design processes accordingly.

Similarities Between Services and Manufacturing

While it is useful to recognize key differences between services and manufacturing, it is also important to recognize similarities. While service firms generally cannot inventory their finished product (such as a haircut or a legal opinion or a medical diagnosis), they do inventory the supplies they need for providing this service (hairspray and scissors; computers and office supplies; stethoscope and tongue depressors). Some manufacturing firms—such as Airbus, which produces planes to a specific customer order, or Dell—do not inventory finished goods.

It is best to look at the process level rather than the organization level. Most manufacturing firms have substantial service components. Most service firms have some tangible components. At the process level, it is clearly important that a Four Seasons hotel provide a clean, nicely appointed room (i.e., manufacturing), but it is also important that it provides top-notch, superior-quality service. Similarly, Toyota must not only provide a well-made car, but also provide good service for warranty repairs if something goes wrong. Thus, we will examine individual processes as components of the overall manufacturing or service enterprise. While it may be unclear whether a company such as Toyota, McDonald's, Four Seasons, or a medical office is a service firm or a manufacturing firm, the distinction is much less ambiguous at the individual process level. Furthermore, almost all companies have a combination of services and manufacturing; thus, they must be good at both.

SUPPLY CHAIN STRATEGY

TO this point, we have primarily examined operations strategy as it applies to a single organization. Now we turn to the broader application of supply chain strategy across a linked set of multiple organizations. No business operates completely independently—all have trading partners at multiple levels—and thus we examine how businesses interact with others in a structured fashion. Supply chains have existed since trading routes were developed to allow the different peoples of the world to exchange goods. The driving forces behind the greater emphasis on supply chain management recently are the development of information technologies that allow quick and inexpensive communication between multiple parties and the globalization of world trade, which has accelerated the exchange of goods across borders. Thus, in examining supply chain strategy, we first examine the nature of global supply chains, then we examine the nature of supply chain management within a single organization, and finally we look at supply chain management across multiple organizations.

The Global Nature of Supply Chains

As shown in the descriptions of Sony, Kellogg's, and American Express at the beginning of the chapter, each of these organizations has operations in multiple countries and deals with suppliers and customers in almost every country around the world. This is typical of most large and many smaller companies in today's business environment. Many companies have increased their offshore sourcing of parts, components, and finished goods and must manage multiple suppliers and shippers. According to the World Trade Organization, world merchandise exports have risen from $157 billion in 1963 to $8.907 trillion in 2004, an increase of 57 times. Much of this growth has occurred in Asia, specifically China. China's trade with the United States has grown from $5.7 billion in 1981 to $286 billion in 2005. At the same time, China imported $660 billion from other countries in 2005, while its total exports were $762 billion.

While China is the focus of a great deal of attention because of its phenomenal growth and size, it is one of many countries experiencing similar globalization. The Council of Supply Chain Management Professionals (CSCMP) estimates that logistics costs represent 7.15 percent of European GDP on average, 9.5 percent of U.S. GDP, 17 percent of India's, and 22.3 percent of China's. Clearly, supply chain management plays a critical role in managing the manufacture and flow of goods around the world. The numerous challenges in managing that global supply chain include differing laws and regulations, different languages, cultural barriers, and political strife. While the rise of the global village is generally viewed as a positive development, managing these challenges is essential for the long-term success of countries, supply chains, and individual organizations.

Supply Chain Within a Single Organization

Many companies have elevated the importance of supply chain management over the past 10 years, both in terms of managing across multiple organizations and in terms of managing the supply chain within a single organization. Many large companies signal the importance of supply chain management by appointing a vice president or director of supply chain management, as shown in Figure 1.5. Typically, this person will be responsible for three areas of supply chain management: operations, sourcing/purchasing, and logistics. While supply chain management often refers to coordinating multiple organizations, it can also refer to managing operations within a single organization. Each of our three exemplary organizations (Sony, Kellogg's, and American Express) operates numerous manufacturing or service centers around the world. Each of these companies also manages distribution centers and other facilities, and tracks logistics among these various facilities. The coordination of multiple facilities is a common challenge in large organizations and is one of the reasons why the role of supply chain manager has been elevated to the vice presidential level, as shown in Figure 1.5.

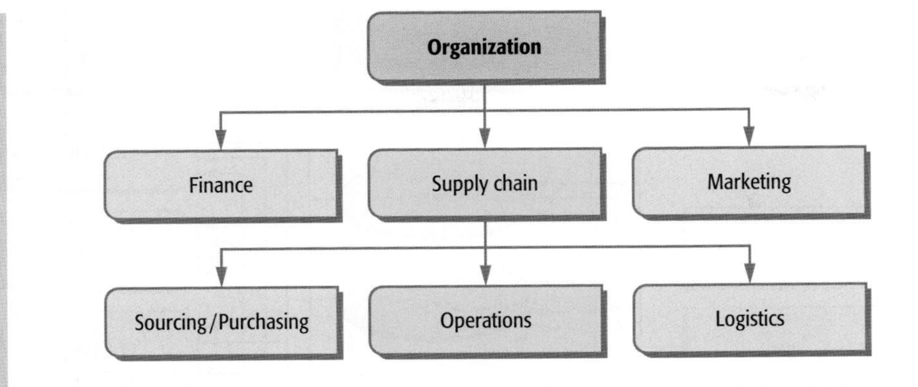

FIGURE 1.5 Organizational Structure with Detail on Supply Chain Positions

We have already discussed and defined operations management. **Sourcing/purchasing** includes the processes associated with identifying material and service needs, locating and selecting suppliers, negotiating contract and payment terms, and tracking to assess supplier performance. In the example on Maple Leaf and food supply chain traceability challenges on page 21, sourcing/purchasing would take the lead role in selecting suppliers of ingredients and equipment, as well as auditing and assessing their safety records. **Logistics** plans, implements, and manages the efficient, effective flow and storage of goods and services from the point of origin to the point of end consumption. In the Maple Leaf example, logistics is in charge of managing and coordinating shipments of ingredients and equipment from suppliers to Maple Leaf's various manufacturing plants, storing input materials and finished goods, and shipping finished goods to customers.

● **Sourcing/purchasing** the processes associated with identifying material and service needs, locating and selecting suppliers, negotiating contract and payment terms, and tracking to assess supplier performance.

● **Logistics** the function that plans, implements, and manages the efficient, effective flow and storage of goods and services from the point of origin to the point of end consumption.

Supply Chain Across Multiple Organizations

While every company wants to design its operations to be as effective as possible and to give itself a competitive advantage, increasingly businesses are very interconnected through their supply chains. A **supply chain** is a network of organizations that work together to convert and move goods from the raw materials stage to the end customer. These organizations are linked together through physical, information, and monetary flows. Figure 1.6 shows a simplified supply chain for personal computers. Companies such as Intel, AMD, and Microsoft make components or parts (including software) that are assembled by various companies such as HP, Sony, Apple, and Dell. The end product is shipped to various stores around the world, including Best Buy, Circuit City, Tesco, Globus, and Wal-Mart. The end customer thus has a choice of numerous similar products from similar retailers provided through different supply chains. Put another way, supply chains are multiple-company linkages of the operations of individual companies. The goal of individual companies is to manage their supply chain upstream (the part that supplies components/parts/inputs) and downstream (the part that distributes outputs) so that it provides a competitive edge that makes the company's product or service superior to that of another producer.

● **Supply chain** a network of organizations that work together to convert and move goods from the raw materials stage to the end customer. These organizations are linked together through physical, information, and monetary flows.

We will examine principles throughout this book at both the individual company level and the supply chain level. In general, many of the same principles apply to both individual companies and supply chains, but there are also substantial differences. For example, companies would generally like to minimize or reduce inventory if it is possible to do so without decreasing customer service. So would supply chains. However, it is often difficult to coordinate relationships

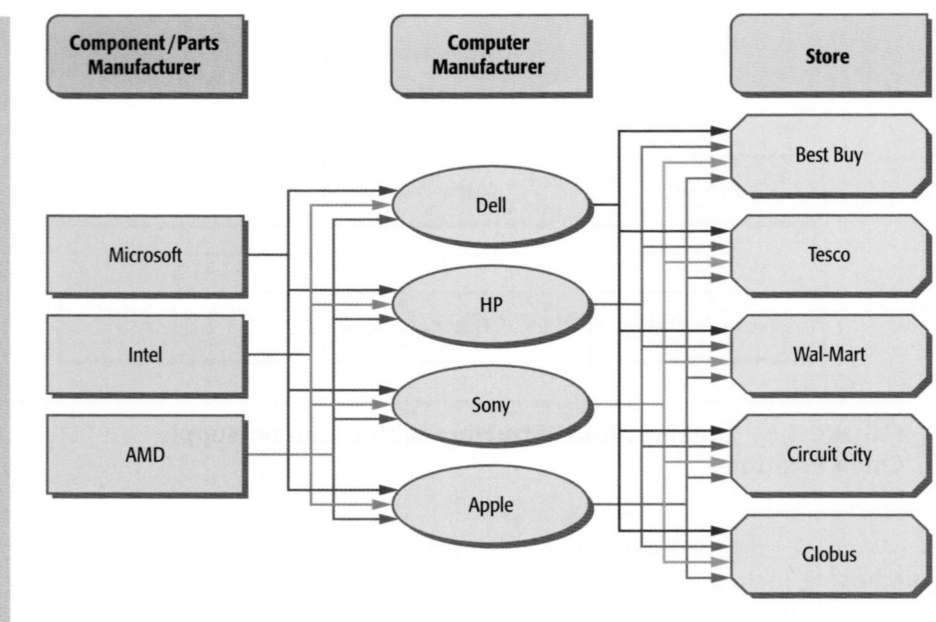

FIGURE 1.6 A Supply Chain View of Personal Computer Production and Sales

between companies, with the result that one company ends up holding a disproportionate share of inventory or bearing a disproportionate share of costs or risks.

There are a number of challenges in managing a supply chain across numerous organizations. These include conflicting objectives, mismatched communication systems, differences in organizational culture and national culture, competitive pressures, lack of trust, and government regulations. Despite these challenges, companies have seen a huge return on investments in broadening their focus to the entire supply chain rather than limiting it simply to operations within their firm. One of the primary reasons that supply chain management has increased recently is the improved capabilities of computers and information technology to facilitate information sharing and cooperation among numerous organizations. Many companies now routinely share information across numerous levels of a supply chain; for example, in the supply chain in Figure 1.6, Wal-Mart can share forecast and sales information with Dell, HP, Sony, and Apple, and also with their suppliers (Intel, AMD, and Microsoft). Throughout this book, we will provide examples of how interorganizational communication provides the foundation for effective supply chain management.

ORGANIZATION OF THIS BOOK

HAVING introduced basic operations and supply chain concepts, we now turn to a discussion of the purpose and organization of this book. Our goal is to examine key tools, techniques, and practices in operations as they revolve around three themes: strategy, global supply chain, and service operations. Strategy is a key theme because while there is a set of generally sound principles of operations, companies will make different decisions based on their operations strategy. As seen in this chapter, a firm or supply chain that is focused on low cost will make fundamentally different choices from those made by a company or supply chain

TECHNOLOGY IN OPERATIONS MANAGEMENT

Supply Chain Challenges in Tracing Food

It seems like every day there is an announcement or news item about some type of food poisoning or *E. coli* problem in a fast-food restaurant or in an item sold in your local grocery store. Most of these problems are attributable to the complex supply chain for food products in the developed world. Suppose a single package of bagels at your local grocery store is found to be contaminated. How worried should you be about other purchases you have made at the store? Who is at fault for the problem—the grocery store? The distributor of the bagels? The manufacturer? One of the scores of providers of raw ingredients and supplies? Traceability in the food supply chain is an issue of increasing importance.

One company that is focusing on this problem is Maple Leaf Foods, a Canadian $5.5 billion producer of fresh and frozen baked goods, pasta, and pasta sauces. Maple Leaf has the goal of making food purchases traceable from concession to consumption, farmer to consumer, farm to fork. This can be quite a challenge: The company's fresh bakery group operates 22 bakeries and employs 5,200 people, and this is less than 20 percent of the entire company. Each of the bakeries deals with scores of suppliers and scores of customers. Thus, tracing the complete history of any single product can be exceedingly difficult. To assist with this task, Maple Leaf has come up with a "40 steps to food safety program." Maple Leaf communicates across the entire supply chain to verify and encourage a consistent approach to food safety. This includes auditing supply chain partners to verify compliance with government regulations and encouraging suppliers to implement third-party audits. The program also involves operators from different plants visiting other facilities and studying safety procedures.

A technology that shows a lot of potential for increasing traceability is radio frequency identification (RFID). While bar codes require a direct line of sight to be read and generally require human hands to physically scan the items, RFID can allow indirect reading and allow multiple items to be read seemingly simultaneously. The second major advantage of RFID is its ability to carry substantially more information than most bar codes, as well as the capability to both read and write information on a tag. For these reasons, many food producers such as Maple Leaf are experimenting with RFID as a means of better tracking and tracing the movement of food products through the supply chain.

The need for increased traceability and security of the food supply chain became abundantly clear in the first half of 2007. Contaminated pet food using raw ingredients from China resulted in the deaths of over 4,000 pets. The Chinese companies added the chemicals melamine and cyanuric acid to wheat products to boost the apparent protein content and the price. While the pet food contamination made headlines, there were numerous other incidents; one estimate is that 76 million illnesses and 5,000 deaths from food poisoning occur in the United States each year. The system of inspecting and tracing food shipments is under great stress; imports of food were more than 9 million shipments in 2006, double the number in 2002. The resource-limited U.S. Food and Drug Administration (FDA) is able to inspect less than 1 percent of imports. This led the U.S. Senate to rush to pass a bill, by a vote of 94-0, giving the FDA more responsibilities, including creating databases of adulterated food. The FXA Corporation offers a software system, the OpsSmart Traceability Solution (see Figure 1.7) that delivers online traceability for the food industry by tracking product safety, quality, and origin at any point across the supply chain, from farm to table.

Food producers have realized the need to gain control over their supply chains. For example, ConAgra Foods Inc. was forced to recall Peter Pan peanut butter because of salmonella contamination resulting from a leaky roof in a Sylvester, Georgia, plant that allowed peanuts to get wet and bacteria to grow. The company spent $15 million to fix the plant and hired a top food safety expert. Like Maple Leaf, many other companies are investing in systems that will trace shipments back to their original sources rather than simply buying from middlemen and taking their word for it. According to Sean McBride, spokesperson for the Grocery Manufacturers Association, "This has forced our companies to go back and double-check their suppliers."

Sources: "Maple Leaf Foods: Stepping Up the Focus on Food Safety," *Canadian Grocer,* 120, no. 2 (March 2006): 20–21 and www.mapleleaf.com; J. Carey, "How Safe Is the Food Supply? The Hamstrung FDA May Be Unable to Prevent a Contamination Crisis," *BusinessWeek*, no. 4035 (May 21, 2007): 40.

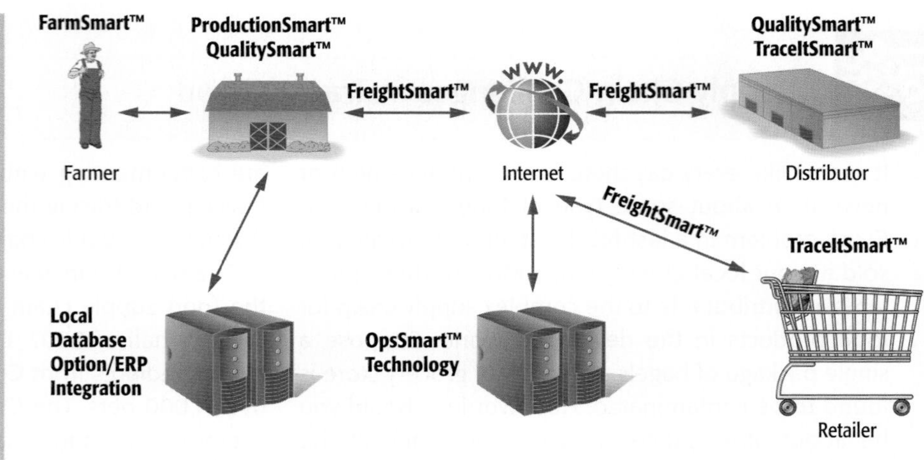

FIGURE 1.7 Increasing Food Traceability—The OpsSmart™ Traceability Solution

Source: Copyright © FXA Group. Reprinted with permission.

that is focused on flexibility. Throughout the book, we will examine strategy as a driving force behind decision making. Second, global supply chain is a focus because of the growing interconnectedness of companies and customers around the world. As technology increasingly lowers barriers to communication and travel across the globe, barriers to free trade are also lowered. As a result, it is important to examine operations and supply chain in a global context. To that end, we try to present examples from companies from different regions of the world and companies that are truly worldwide in their operations. Finally, services are an increasing proportion of global output. The product/service bundle must be managed carefully; thus, service operations are a central theme of the book.

In terms of organization, the book is divided into three parts: Strategic Operations Management, Tools and Tactical Issues, and the Extended Enterprise. An outline by chapter is given here, and a description of each of the three major parts follows the outline.

Part 1: Strategic Operations Management

1 Supply Chain Strategy

2 Quality Management

3 New Product Development

Part 2: Tools and Tactical Issues

4 Process Design and Analysis

5 Forecasting

6 Independent Demand Inventory

7 Dependent Demand Inventory

8 Project Management

9 Optimization and Simulation Modeling

10 Capacity Planning

11 Quality Improvement Methods

Part 3: The Extended Enterprise

12 Lean Enterprise

13 Technology and Integrated Supply Management

14 Global Supply Chain and Services Integrations

Part 1: Strategic Operations Management

The primary emphasis in this part will be on how individual company operations (manufacturing, services, logistics, and purchasing) contribute to a company's success or failure. We will introduce operations strategy as a guide to positioning the organization. The supply chain is introduced as an important concept, but one that in many ways is an extension of operations management within a single firm. In other words, we will focus on operationally managing a single organization but provide a quick introduction to the idea of linking multiple organizations in a broader supply chain. Thus, students will be expected to master internal operations as a primary goal, but develop an understanding of broader supply chain issues as a secondary goal. Quality and Six Sigma are the focus of the second chapter because this is the foundation of so much of business and forms a key strategic component. The third chapter, on product and service innovation, provides a review of the challenges of developing products and services and keeping them fresh.

Part 2: Tools and Tactical Issues

This part contains a series of chapters that provide an in-depth discussion of various tools, techniques, and concepts necessary for day-to-day operations management. Each chapter will cover basic concepts and necessary mathematical derivations, but the emphasis will be on application/illustration of techniques for solving "real-world" operations management problems. This part examines the core principles of operations, including process design and analysis, inventory management (including forecasting, independent demand, and dependent demand), project management, and quality improvement tools.

Part 3: The Extended Enterprise

Increasingly, competition is occurring across supply chains of multiple organizations. This is due to several factors, including lean production, technology, and increasing globalization. This part examines these three factors in individual chapters. Lean production is examined as both a philosophy and a set of tools for not only reducing inventory and waste, but also linking together separate organizations in a supply chain. Technology is examined both as a means of making operations more efficient, agile, or capable and as a means of linking together organizations and providing visibility across the entire supply chain. The final chapter examines the challenges inherent in operating across borders, including global sourcing and international transportation.

SUMMARY

1. Discuss the importance of operations/supply chain management.

- Operations management consists of the processes that produce, transform, and deliver a product or service.
- Supply chain management is the organization of supply chain activities, including purchasing of raw materials and components from suppliers, distribution of parts and finished goods, and administration of the relationship with customers, in order to maximize customer value and maximize competitive advantage. Supply chain management involves a coordinated effort by a group of organizations to manage the supply chain from raw material to finished product or service in the most efficient way possible.
- All products or services involve operations and supply chain management to be produced or delivered.

2. Describe the history and development of three exemplary organizations to be used as examples throughout this book.

- The Kellogg's Company was founded in 1906 in Battle Creek, Michigan, and has grown into a company with over $10 billion in annual sales and supply chain facilities in 15 countries around the world.
- Sony Corporation was founded in 1946 in Japan and has grown into a company with sales of over $65 billion that produces electronics and entertainment. Sony employs 160,000 people worldwide.
- American Express was founded in 1850 in New York and has grown into one of the world's leading financial and travel services companies.
- Each of these organizations uses many of the techniques and tools described in this textbook, and all three will be used as illustrations throughout the text.

3. Explain how single organizations can follow different competitive strategies to be successful.

- Competitive priorities are the relative rankings of what the organization would like to achieve with respect to its operations, while competitive capabilities are what the organization is able to achieve. The four types of priorities/capabilities are cost, quality, delivery, and flexibility. Companies can be successful by placing primary emphasis on any of these competitive priorities if appropriate matching operational decisions are made.
- Operations strategy must fit with the overall business strategy and link with other functional strategies, such as those of marketing and finance. No single functional strategy takes priority over another; instead, all the functional strategies must be meshed and developed in concert.
- Operational decision areas consist of structural and infrastructural decisions. Structural decisions are generally long-term and expensive investments in facilities, capacity, vertical integration/sourcing, and technology. Infrastructural decisions are shorter, more frequent, and less expensive investments in the work force, production planning/control, quality systems, and organization.

4. Illustrate the differences and similarities between manufacturing and service activities.

- Services represent 80 percent or more of the economies of most developed nations, and thus managing them well is essential.
- Two essential differences between manufacturing and services are that services are generally more intangible and have a more direct, interactive relationship with the customer. The intangible nature of services presents challenges in measuring productivity and quality and prevents businesses from stocking inventory to manage fluctuations in demand. The greater interaction with customers presents challenges in dealing with customers on a real-time basis, but also presents opportunities to develop strong relationships with customers.

- While there are some clear differences between manufacturing and services, on an organizational level, almost all businesses involve elements of each. The operations strategy process of matching competitive priorities with appropriate operational decisions is appropriate for either. Examining things at the individual process level rather than the more general organizational level helps identify an individual process as a manufacturing process or a service, thus making decision making clearer.

5. Characterize supply chain strategy within a single organization and across multiple organizations.

- Managing supply chain strategy within a single organization involves linking decisions by operations, purchasing, and logistics to maximize the effective productivity across multiple facilities within a single organization.
- Managing supply chain strategy across multiple organizations involves linking decisions by operations, purchasing, and logistics across numerous organizations. The linkage of multiple organizations is challenging because of the organizations' different goals, policies, and procedures. While information technology has greatly facilitated the ability to exchange information seamlessly and at low cost, developing trust and a culture of sharing across multiple organizations remains a fundamental barrier to successful supply chain strategy.

QUESTIONS

1. Describe several structural decisions that a low-cost manufacturer of computers would have to make. Describe infrastructural decisions that such a company would make. How would the decisions made in each of these areas compare to the decisions made by Dell Computer? Define Dell's operations strategy and its key competitive priorities.
2. EXERCISE: Choose two restaurants with substantially different operations strategies. For each restaurant, discuss its competitive priorities—what is *most* important to it. Allocate 100 points across each of the four competitive priorities (e.g., the most important might get 40 points, the next most important might get 25, and so on). For each restaurant, list four or five operational decisions/investments that the restaurant manager must make. These decisions should fit within one of the eight categories in Table 1.3. Compare decisions for the two restaurants—how do they differ?
3. Describe several structural decisions that a low-cost hotel such as a Days Inn would have to make. Describe infrastructural decisions that such a hotel would make. How would the decisions made in each of these areas compare to the decisions made by a high-quality hotel like a Four Seasons?

CASE STUDY

Natural Designs Inc.

Natural Designs manufactures a variety of bird feeders, garden accessories, and other items intended to help people get in touch with and observe nature. Founded in 1995 by Jim McMaster in LaGrange, Illinois, the company started when he was working as a fourth-grade teacher. Presentations to students on birds and wildlife had a way of capturing their enthusiasm; thus, McMaster started offering presentations to other schools in the greater Chicago area. Within a few years, McMaster was so busy doing presentations at various schools, as well as running nature camps from his home, that he quit his full-time job as an elementary school teacher to form Natural Designs. At first, Natural Designs was mostly Jim and his wife giving presentations and running camps, but gradually the company expanded to sell some of the bird feeders and other nature devices featured in his class talks. Today, the company has sales of $2 million per year, most of which comes from physical products sold to outdoor, nature, and bird stores such as Wild Birds Unlimited.

In the first few years of operation, Jim McMaster and his wife, Sheila, produced bird feeders and other products in their garage. In 1997, however, the operation became too large for their garage, so they rented a 4,000-square-foot facility for production and distribution purposes. They also hired two employees to manage these two functions so that the McMasters could continue giving school talks. Today, Natural Designs has 15 employees, 2 of which are focused solely on giving nature talks and selling the products to retailers interested in reselling Natural Designs products. The product range consists of 500 stock-keeping units (SKUs).

One of the challenges faced by Natural Designs involves its customized bird feeders. This operation allows customers to get one of the 10 made-to-stock bird feeders and have it customized with their name or address carved in the wood, plus painting in any of 10 color schemes. This portion of the business has been growing by 50 percent per year and now represents $100,000 per year in sales. A customer order is taken over the Internet and promised for delivery within one week. Then the item is pulled from stock, carved with the appropriate name and address, and painted. Finally, the item is shipped directly to the customer's home. While this product has been wildly popular with customers, Jim McMaster has two major concerns. First, he is not sure that the customization is profitable—he charges an additional $10 per bird feeder, but he is not sure exactly how much extra labor is involved in fulfilling the customization portion of the order. Second, despite assigning an employee to the custom bird feeder operation full time, lead times on orders have gradually increased from an average of 4.5 business days to 9.2 business days. This prevents Natural Designs from meeting its promised lead time of one week or less. In addition, during peak periods (early spring and early fall), the lead time can stretch to three or four weeks.

As Jim McMaster reviews the current state of Natural Designs, he is pleased to note that sales are continuing to grow overall at a rate of 10 percent per year. Furthermore, his work force is generally happy, and the business is profitable. However, his accountants have been telling him that profits are declining as a percentage of sales and that the number of customer returns of items and complaints has increased by over 30 percent in the past year. The capacity of the existing facility is extremely tight, and Jim is considering either adding a second facility or moving to a larger 8,000-square-foot facility.

QUESTIONS

1. What types of decisions must Jim McMaster make on a daily basis for Natural Designs to run smoothly? What kind of decisions must he make on a long-term basis?
2. Describe the operations strategy for Natural Designs. Has this strategy changed as a result of the custom bird feeder operation? If yes, how?
3. What might have been done differently to facilitate the offering of custom bird feeders?
4. How should McMaster analyze the alternative expansion options? Which would you recommend: a second facility or a move to a single, larger facility?

Quality Management

LEARNING OBJECTIVES

1 Define the meaning of *quality*.
2 Explain why it is necessary to improve the quality of goods and services.
3 Define the components of quality in goods and services.
4 Summarize the history of quality management.
5 Summarize the teachings of quality gurus W. Edwards Deming, Philip Crosby, Armand Feigenbaum, Kaoru Ishikawa, Joseph M. Juran, Genichi Taguchi, and Walter Shewhart.
6 Describe commonly used quality management approaches, such as total quality management (TQM), the ISO 9000 and ISO 14000 standards, and the Malcolm Baldrige Criteria for Performance Excellence.
7 Describe the Six Sigma quality management approach and the steps in implementing it.

Many Facets of Quality Management at American Express

American Express (AMEX) provides a variety of services to its customers, such as credit cards, travelers' checks, and other financial services. Although they are not apparent to users, a number of quality improvement processes, policies, and procedures are in place to ensure that AMEX delivers high-quality service to its customers. This feature describes some of the challenges associated with delivering high-quality service to AMEX customers.

Let's take the example of the credit card services provided by AMEX. First, each application for a credit card goes through a structured review process (see Chapter 4 for a simplified flowchart of the credit card approval process). Accuracy in the credit card application review process ensures that each applicant who meets the established criteria gets approved for a specific type of credit card. Various quality control checks are conducted at each stage to ensure error-free processing.

Once an application is approved, the AMEX factory produces a custom credit card with the customer's name and his or her unique account number. Again, the information encoded on the credit card is checked to ensure that a wrong card does not reach a customer.

After the customer receives the new credit card in the mail, he or she is instructed to call a specified toll-free phone number to activate the card. The activation process

A new credit card activation may require further quality checks by the AMEX operator.

may be automatic or may require further quality checks by the AMEX operator. Once the card is activated, the customer can use it for financial transactions, such as booking an airline ticket, reserving a hotel room, or purchasing products at a shopping center.

For the AMEX credit card to work reliably for each customer in virtually every country in the world, all aspects of the processes just described need to be executed perfectly, millions of times every few minutes. For example, the physical product (the credit card itself) should have no errors (e.g., the magnetic strip at the back of the card should contain the accurate account information). Similarly, AMEX's information systems and the entire worldwide financial services network need to contain accurate information about the account. If the card information is not accurately stored on the system, then it is possible that use of the card will be denied, resulting in a dissatisfied and sometimes very angry customer.

American Express also needs to ensure that its employees answering telephone calls at the customer service centers are trained to provide the highest-quality service. Providing high quality at a telephone customer service center includes ensuring the lowest possible wait time, the politeness and helpfulness of the customer service agent, speed and accuracy in taking care of customers' requests or problems, and so on.

As described in this example, American Express has to ensure that the quality of its goods (the credit card) and services (the telephone call center) meet customer expectations. Therefore, the company takes elaborate steps and uses a variety of quality improvement concepts and tools in its operations. ■

In the increasingly global business environment, quality is no longer considered a *nice-to-have* luxury but is acknowledged as a necessary requirement for successfully competing and surviving in the marketplace. While the concepts, tools, and procedures of quality improvement are now universally recognized and firmly in place in a large number of high-performing organizations around the world, this was not always the case. The importance of quality in business organizations has gone through a complete cycle. In this chapter we will discuss the history, major themes, concepts, and frameworks of quality improvement.

DEFINING QUALITY

● **Quality** the ability of a product (a good or a service) to consistently meet or exceed customer expectations

BROADLY speaking, **quality** means the ability of a product (a good or a service) to consistently meet or exceed customer expectations. A few of the words in this definition of quality need further elaboration.

- *Ability* refers to the competence, either native or acquired, that enables one to do something well. For example, Sony's video game console Playstation has a high-speed computing ability that allows very sharp displays and a fast gaming environment. The Nintendo Wii console, on the other hand, has an innovative remote control device that gives a player the ability to move his or her body parts as in the real world while playing a video game.

THREE STEPS OF SERVICE

1
A warm and sincere greeting. Use the guest name, if and when possible.

2
Anticipation and compliance with guest needs.

3
Fond farewell. Give them a warm good-bye and use their names, if and when possible.

"We Are Ladies and Gentlemen Serving Ladies and Gentlemen"

THE EMPLOYEE PROMISE

At The Ritz-Carlton, our Ladies and Gentlemen are the most important resource in our service commitment to our guests.

By applying the principles of trust, honesty, respect, integrity and commitment, we nurture and maximize talent to the benefit of each individual and the company.

The Ritz-Carlton fosters a work environment where diversity is valued, quality of life is enhanced, individual aspirations are fulfilled, and The Ritz-Carlton mystique is strengthened.

THE RITZ-CARLTON®

CREDO

The Ritz-Carlton Hotel is a place where the genuine care and comfort of our guests is our highest mission.

We pledge to provide the finest personal service and facilities for our guests who will always enjoy a warm, relaxed yet refined ambience.

The Ritz-Carlton experience enlivens the senses, instills well-being, and fulfills even the unexpressed wishes and needs of our guests.

Source: © 1992–2008 The Ritz-Carlton Hotel Company, L.L.C. All rights reserved. Reprinted with the permission of The Ritz-Carlton Hotel Company, L.L.C.

- *Consistently* refers to a reliable or steady pattern of performance. For example, Motorola and GE are highly regarded for developing and manufacturing products that are highly consistent.
- *Expectations* refers to a state of anticipation about a future outcome. For example, Ritz-Carlton and Four Seasons hotels are well known for working hard to meet the expectations of each and every customer.

BEST PRACTICES IN OPERATIONS MANAGEMENT

The Evolving Definition of Quality at Ritz-Carlton

Ritz-Carlton, a two-time winner of the Malcolm Baldrige National Quality Award (the highest honor for performance excellence, awarded by the U.S. Department of Commerce) is internationally known for its commitment to the highest level of quality and service for its guests. The foundations of Ritz-Carlton's quality management practices are quite accurately captured in its motto, credo, and three steps to service.*

For more than two decades, 20 rules based on Ritz-Carlton's quality management philosophy were followed by each employee. These rules included a description of the firm's credo, motto, and employee promise and a set of instructions for providing highest-quality service to the customer. They included such things as "escorting guests to another location in the hotel" rather than just pointing directions, maintaining uncompromising cleanliness, taking pride in personal appearance, keeping track of customers' individual preferences, and using proper vocabulary, such as "good morning," and so on.

Recently, however, the 20 rules were replaced by 12 "service values" that provide broad guidance to employees rather than specific instructions. These values include statements such as, "I am always responsive to the expressed and unexpressed wishes and needs of our guests," "I own and immediately resolve guest problems," and "I have the opportunity to continuously learn and grow."

So while Ritz-Carlton's credo and motto remain the same as before, its implementation of its quality management philosophy has evolved from a *formal* approach to a *broader* definition of elegance and luxury. Its typical guests are no longer limited to middle-aged male business travelers and wealthy individuals, but may include a 30-year-old in a T-shirt and jeans fiddling with a BlackBerry smart phone or a 20-something listening to an iPod. The definition of quality at this two-time winner of the Malcolm Baldrige National Quality Award continues to evolve as customers' needs and expectations change with the passage of time.

---

*See Ritz-Carlton web site—Gold Standards page (http://corporate.ritzcarlton.com/en/About/GoldStandards.htm).
Source: "Takin' Off the Ritz—a Tad—Chain Relaxes Service 'Rules' to Rely on Workers' Judgment; No More Escort to Restroom," *Wall Street Journal*, June 23, 2006.

The AMEX example presented at the beginning of this chapter illustrates various components of the definition of quality. This example demonstrates how the meaning of quality and its implementation vary in different aspects of the production process. The Ritz-Carlton example later demonstrates how the meaning of quality and its implementation change with evolving customer needs and expectations. An example about Motorola, also described later in this chapter, will discuss the importance of building core capabilities within the organization that lead to the production of consistent and error-free products and services.

WHY FIRMS IMPROVE QUALITY

FIRMS undertake quality and process improvement efforts to achieve multiple goals, such as cost reduction, customer satisfaction enhancement, increased customer loyalty, and improvement of financial and market performance. These four reasons for quality improvement are discussed in the next sections.

Cost Reduction

In 1979, Philip B. Crosby authored the book *Quality Is Free,* which emphasized that doing things right the first time adds nothing to the cost of a product or a service. Dr. W. Edwards Deming, in his teachings, also emphasized that improving quality means reducing the cost of rejects and rework, warranty expenses, and loss of goodwill. (Additional details about the teachings of Deming, Crosby, and other quality gurus are provided later in this chapter.)

These reductions in costs, in the long run, lead to an increase in profitability and therefore assist the company in surviving and prospering in the competitive marketplace. Nevertheless, quality improvement does not happen automatically. It requires effort and investment in better employees, raw materials, production processes, and all support activities. In the long run, however, these investments lead to cost reductions and enhanced profitability.

The different types of costs associated with quality improvement can be classified in four broad categories:

- *Internal failure cost.* If a defective good (or service) is produced, but the error is caught before the product leaves the production facility, then all costs associated with rework, scrap, and lost production time are classified as **internal failure cost**. For example, suppose that a customer ordered a thin-crust pizza with only vegetarian toppings. Let's assume that the pizza delivery company made a mistake in the order-taking process and produced a pizza with a thick crust and a pepperoni topping, but caught this mistake before the driver could deliver the pizza to the customer. All the costs associated with this mistake (i.e., the waste of a fully cooked pizza and the equipment and employee time used in the production of the wrong pizza) will be classified in the internal failure cost category.

● **Internal failure cost** the cost of poor quality if the error is caught within the production facility

- *External failure cost.* If the error is found after the customer has purchased the product or service, then the associated costs are classified as an **external failure cost**. For example, assume that the wrong pizza described in the previous paragraph is delivered to the customer. The customer might return the pizza, which will require the company to produce and deliver another pizza. In addition, this error might lead to loss of the customer's goodwill and also negative word of mouth.

● **External failure cost** the cost of poor quality if the error is caught after the product has been sold to the customer

- *Assurance costs.* The costs necessary to ensure that the product or service meets quality standards (e.g., cost of sampling and inspection) are classified as **assurance costs**. These costs may include the salary of quality inspectors, costs of purchasing and using the necessary tools and equipment for quality checks, costs of conducting customer surveys for postsale quality assessment, and so on.

● **Assurance costs** the cost of sampling and inspection

- *Prevention costs.* All costs and efforts associated with preventing quality problems are classified as **prevention costs**. For example, to ensure that the wrong pizza is not delivered to a customer, the restaurant may provide additional training to the employees and may also install a computerized sale and order-tracking system. The costs of doing these things will be included as part of prevention costs.

● **Prevention costs** all costs and efforts associated with preventing quality problems from occurring

Figure 2.1 shows how the four categories of costs change when the quality of products and services is increased. As quality increases, both internal and external failure costs decrease, whereas assurance and prevention costs increase.

From looking at Figure 2.1, a casual reader might conclude that a company needs to improve its quality only up to the point where the total costs are at a minimum. However, we must realize that the definition of quality changes over time as customer needs change and evolve. Therefore, the lowest-cost point in Figure 2.1 changes with time, and companies must strive for continuous quality improvement.

Customer Satisfaction Enhancement

The quality of products and services can have a big impact on customer satisfaction, which is an indication of the long-term profitability of a company. For example, a research project initiated at the University of Michigan tracks customer satisfaction for major competitors in 43 different industries within the United States (www.theacsi.org). Figure 2.2 shows plots of the **American Customer Satisfaction Index** (scaled between 0 and 100) for major companies in the personal computer and airline industries. The figure shows that Southwest

● **American Customer Satisfaction Index (ACSI)** an ongoing index for tracking customer satisfaction for a wide range of products and services in the United States

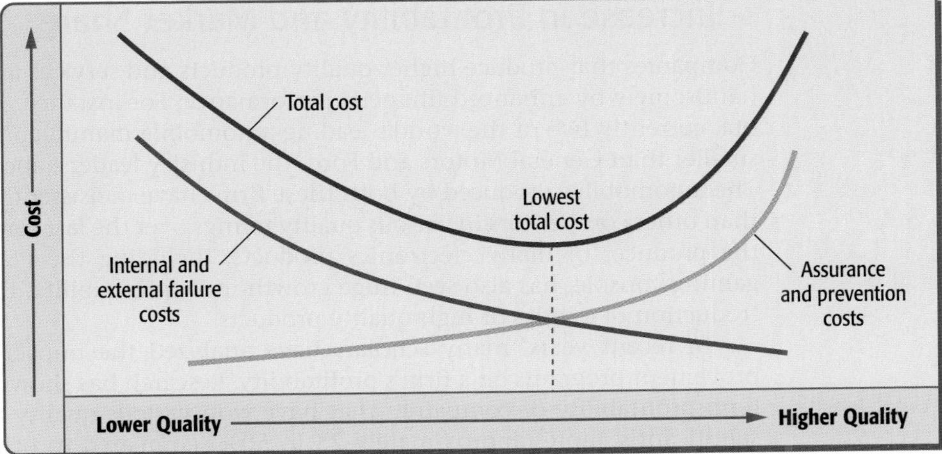

FIGURE 2.1 The Costs of Quality

Total costs of quality include internal and external failure costs, assurance costs, and prevention costs.

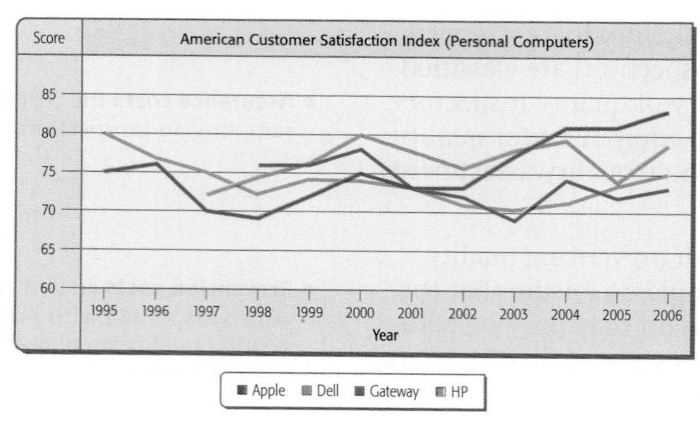

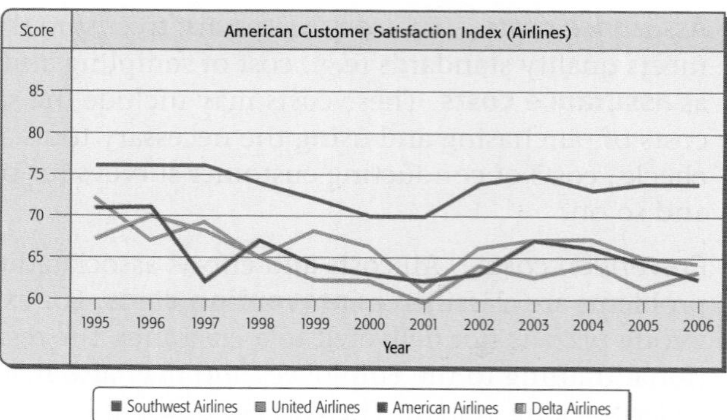

FIGURE 2.2 American Customer Satisfaction Index

This figure shows American Customer Satisfaction Index scores for major competitors in the airline and personal computer industries.

Source: These plots are based on data from http://www.theacsi.org.

Airlines has consistently scored much higher than its close competitors over the last 10 years. Within the personal computer industry, Dell scored highest for several years, but Apple has taken the lead in customer satisfaction during the last few years. Accordingly, revenue for Apple has grown faster than its competitors during recent years.

Customer Loyalty, Word of Mouth, and Enhancement of the Firm's Reputation

Research over a long period has shown that it is less costly to continue serving existing customers than to increase market share. Companies that continue to provide high-quality products and services realize high customer loyalty. A customer who is satisfied and more loyal to a company is also likely to spread positive word of mouth and therefore create additional goodwill in the marketplace. On the other hand, lower-quality offerings lead to negative word of mouth and lower customer loyalty.

Increase in Profitability and Market Share

Companies that produce higher-quality products and services are also rewarded handsomely by enhanced financial performance. For instance, Honda and Toyota, currently two of the world's leading automobile manufacturers, were much smaller than General Motors and Ford, the industry leaders, about 25 years ago. The automobiles produced by both these firms have consistently ranked higher than other competitors in various quality ratings over the last several years. Sony, the producer of many electronics products, including the Playstation videogaming console, has also seen huge growth in its profitability, thanks to the introduction of a series of high-quality products.

In recent years, many scholars have analyzed the impact of quality improvement programs on a firm's profitability. Research has shown that the long-term profitability of companies that have won various quality awards increase significantly more (approximately 25 to 50%) compared to other firms in the same industry.

DETERMINANTS OF QUALITY

DETERMINING the underlying components of quality can be difficult because customers often think of many different characteristics of a good or a service when they think about quality. Therefore, product (goods and service) quality is considered to have several dimensions.

Quality of Goods

The quality of a good is determined by the following dimensions:

- *Performance.* This refers to the primary purpose of a tangible good.
- *Special features.* Special features are additional characteristics of a tangible good that enhance the value or usefulness of the primary purpose of the product.
- *Reliability.* Consistency in the performance of a good is measured by its reliability. A good with higher reliability is considered to have higher quality than a good with lower reliability.
- *Conformance.* Conformance is the degree to which a good matches the prespecified standards or guidelines.
- *Durability.* Durability refers to the useful life of a good. The longer the useful life, the higher the quality.
- *Serviceability.* The ability of the good to perform with ease is also a measure of its quality.
- *Aesthetics.* A good's appearance is often considered to be a dimension of its quality.
- *Brand equity or reputation.* Often customers associate the quality of a good with the image of the company, its brand name, or its past reputation. These indirect measures of quality are collectively called brand equity.

Service Quality

A product often contains both a tangible good (e.g., a mobile phone from Motorola or Nokia, the bed in a Marriott or Hilton hotel room) and a service (e.g., telecommunications service provided by AT&T or T-Mobile, concierge or room service in a hotel). Like the quality of tangible goods, the quality of a service is also determined by multiple dimensions:

- *Reliability.* Like reliability of tangible goods, service reliability is a measure of consistent performance and dependability.
- *Responsiveness.* This is the willingness of the service provider to assist customers.
- *Competence.* This covers the knowledge and skills of the provider needed to perform the service.
- *Access.* This is the approachability and the ease of contacting the service provider.
- *Courtesy.* Services providers' politeness, respect, consideration, and friendliness are also measures of their service quality.

- *Communication.* Communication means using language that customers can understand so that they can understand different facets of the service.
- *Credibility.* A service provider is expected to keep customers' best interests at heart. Therefore, a service provider's trustworthiness, believability, and honesty, collectively known as its credibility, are important measures of its service quality.

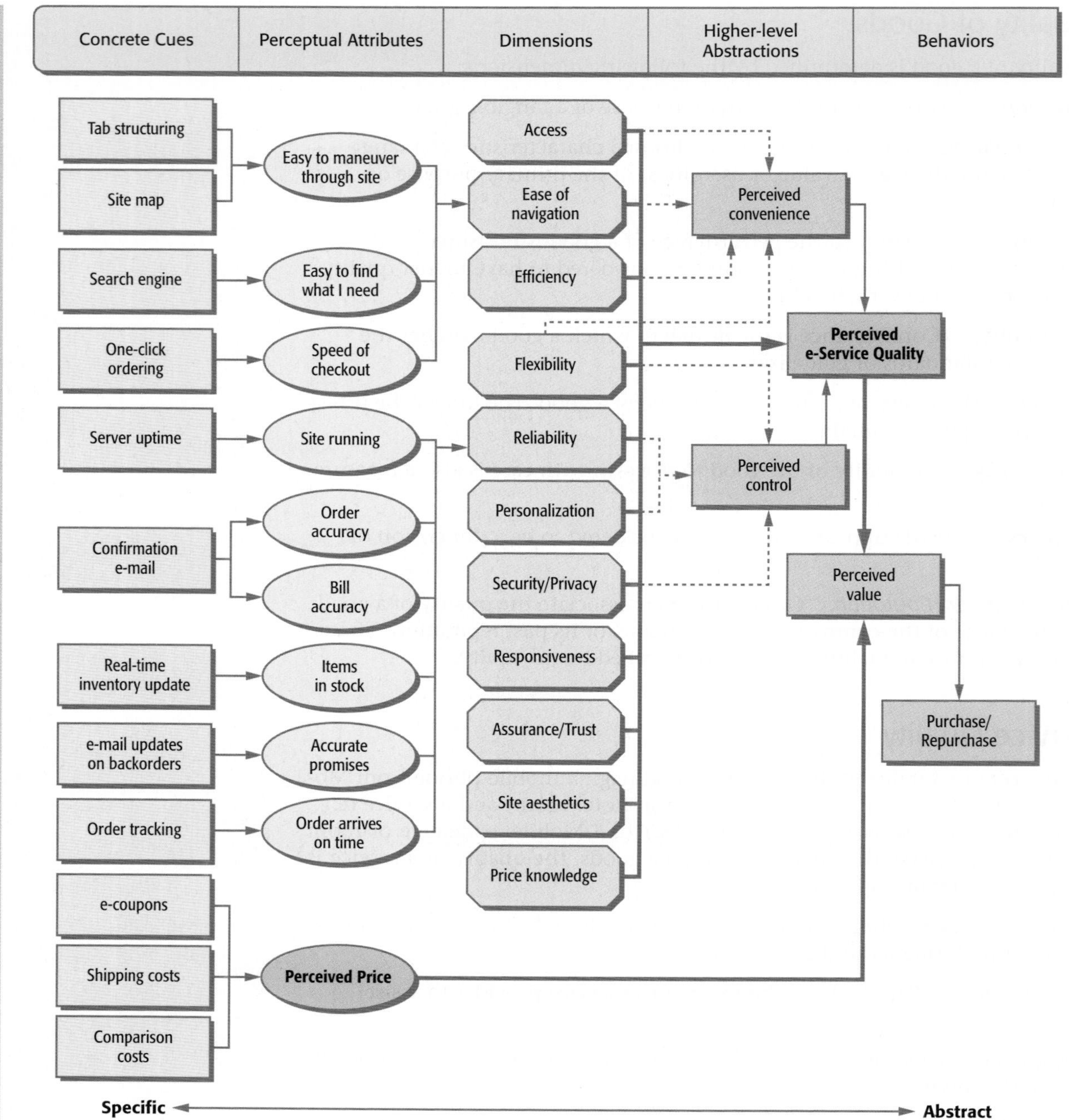

FIGURE 2.3 A Model of e-Service Quality

Source: A. Parasuraman, Valarie A. Zeithaml, Arvind Malhotra, "A Conceptual Framework for Understanding e-Service Quality: Implications for Future Research and Managerial Practice," *Journal of Service Research*, Vol. 7, Issue 3, p. 21. Copyright © by SAGE Publications. Reprinted by Permission of SAGE Publications.

- *Security.* Confidentiality and personal and financial security are important components of service delivery and measures of its quality.
- *Understanding/knowing the customer.* A provider's efforts to understand the needs of its customers (e.g., listening to customers' specific requirements, providing individualized attention, and recognizing regular customers) are also a measure of its service quality.
- *Tangibles.* Finally, the physical characteristics (e.g., facilities, appearance of personnel) of the service are also indicators of its quality.

The dimensions of service quality described here are generally common to a variety of industries. However, with the Internet playing a big role in service delivery, more specialized models for service quality have recently been proposed. One such model that describes the components of e-service quality (or service quality in electronic services) is shown in Figure 2.3.

Customer Expectations

While understanding the dimensions just discussed is important when measuring product quality, we must also remember the role that customer expectations play in the assessment of quality. Recall that "quality is the ability of a product or service to meet or exceed customer expectations."

Customer expectations are influenced by many different factors, such as personal needs, word of mouth or the reputation of the company, and individuals' own past experiences. Therefore, a customer compares the **objective quality** of a product based on the dimensions described earlier with his or her expectations. Based on such comparisons, the **perceived quality** of the product is thought to be higher or lower than expectations (Figure 2.4). Therefore, quality

- **Objective quality** the quality of a good or a service based entirely on its determinants
- **Perceived quality** the quality of a product or service as perceived by the customer

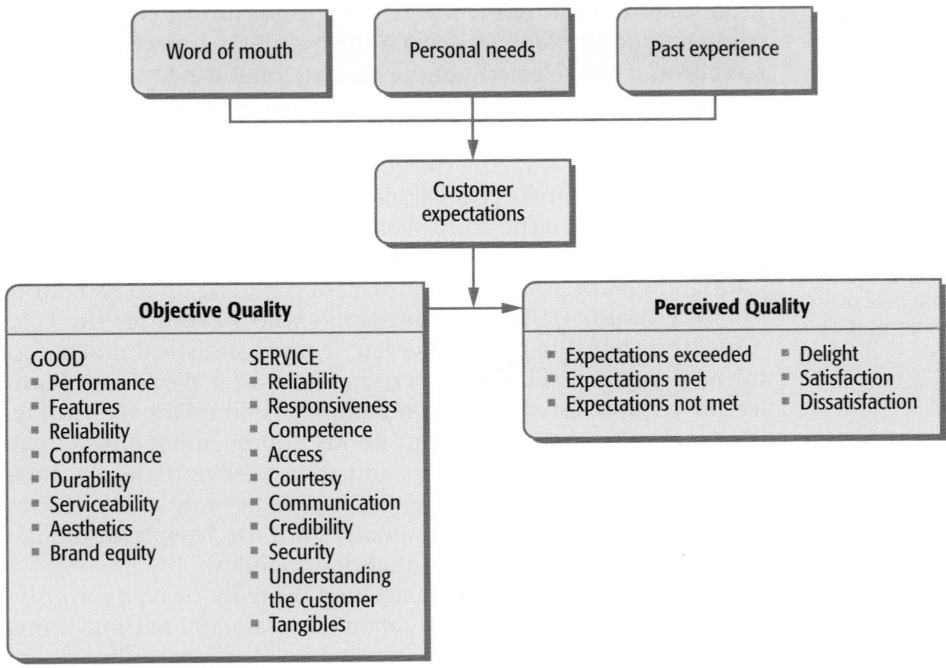

FIGURE 2.4 Objective and Perceived Quality Compared to Customer Expectations

The customer is delighted, satisfied, or dissatisfied based on a comparison between objective quality and perceived quality derived from expectations.

Source: Adapted from Parasuraman, Zeithaml, and Berry (1985).

excellence means improving the dimensions of both objective and perceived product quality.

HISTORY OF QUALITY MANAGEMENT

CONTEMPORARY quality management frameworks and techniques are based on decades of knowledge and experience on the part of practicing managers and scholors. In this section, we briefly describe the historical developments that have shaped modern quality management practices.

Early Development of Quality Management

Humans have always sought to improve the outcome of their efforts, whether in agricultural production or in modern industrial and service-based economies. During the preindustrial periods, however, the practice of quality management was quite different: Craftsmen were generally in direct contact with their customers, and products were created based on specifications provided by individual customers to local producers.

However, the practice of quality management changed dramatically starting in the early twentieth century because of industrialization and the growth of mass production. Factories and production facilities started manufacturing large volumes of products, and quality standards were developed based on broad market requirements.

While standards are important in delivering products with consistent quality, the task of ensuring that each product meets the established guidelines became more difficult as production volume grew during the early part of the twentieth century. Because it is impossible for a quality inspector to check each individual product to ensure that it meets the specifications, companies gradually started using **sampling** plans to select a few products from the production line for **inspection**. If the selected sample met the established specifications, then the entire production batch was assumed to have acceptable quality. If the sample did not meet the established specifications, then the entire batch was rejected.

- **Sampling** the selection of a few randomly selected products from the production line for quality checks
- **Inspection** the process of comparing a sampled product with established guidelines
- **Statistical process control (SPC)** a statistical technique for determining whether the quality of a production process is in control

In the 1920s, realizing the deficiencies of quality management systems based on sampling and inspection alone, Walter A. Shewhart, a statistician at Bell Laboratories, developed the control charts and principles of modern **statistical process control**. Shewhart's statistical principles were used in American companies during the 1920s and 1930s, in the period leading up to and during World War II.

W. Edwards Deming, a statistician who worked for the U.S. Department of Agriculture and the Census Bureau, learned statistical process control principles from Shewhart. Dr. Deming went to Japan after World War II and was invited to lecture to Japanese scientists and engineers on quality control techniques. Deming taught the concepts of continuous improvement and statistical process control techniques to the Japanese and advised them to apply these concepts in all aspects of management if they wished to become a "world-class" producer. At about the same time, another quality guru, Dr. Joseph M. Juran, was also invited by the Japanese to lecture on quality principles.

The teachings of Deming and Juran were followed rigorously by the Japanese companies, leading "Made in Japan" to gradually become a mark of excellence within the next two decades. To recognize the extraordinary efforts of Dr. Deming in overhauling the state of Japanese companies, the **Deming Prize** was established; it is given to companies that have exerted a substantial influence, directly or indirectly, on the development of quality control/management in Japan.

- **Deming Prize** one of the highest honors for quality achievement, given to a company by the emperor of Japan

In contrast to the heavy emphasis on quality in Japan, the booming demand for products manufactured by American companies during the period following

World War II (the 1950s and 1960s) meant that the focus on quality took a back seat to speed of production, marketing, and financial activities. As a result of the quality revolution in Japan while western companies had focused their attention elsewhere, U.S. companies were caught off guard when high-quality Japanese products started gaining market share in many different industries.

Recent Advances in Quality Management

The quality movement went through a rebirth in American companies during the 1980s. A TV documentary, "If Japan Can, Why Can't We?" broadcast during the early 1980s is often credited with making American executives aware of structured quality management practices in Japanese firms. American companies, alarmed by their loss of market share, refocused their attention on strategic, organizational, and statistical concepts related to quality management.

The **Malcolm Baldrige National Quality Award** (www.baldrige.org) was created by the U.S. government in 1987 to help improve the quality and competitiveness of American companies by recognizing the highest-performing organizations in the manufacturing, service, healthcare, education, and small business categories. The American Society for Quality (www.asq.org) promoted quality through its journals, conferences, magazines, and seminars.

● **Malcolm Baldrige National Quality Award** highest honor for quality and performance excellence for a United States–based manufacturing, service, small business, education, or healthcare organization.

With the formation of a common economic market within the European Union, **ISO 9000** standards were created that certify companies based on their adherence to quality management principles through their use of documented operational procedures. Later, a second set of standards (**ISO 14000**) was also developed to certify companies based on their commitment to environmental quality management. Detailed information about these international quality management standards is presented later in this chapter.

● **ISO 9000 and ISO 14000** international standards for quality and environmental management

During the last two decades, quality management concepts and techniques have become widely recognized as an essential requirement for competing in the global marketplace. First under the umbrella of total quality management (TQM) and then as Six Sigma quality, high-performing companies around the world now actively pursue quality-related best practices in the management of their daily operations.

More recently, with the increase in the role of services in the marketplace, companies are also paying greater attention to service quality, customer satisfaction, and customer loyalty. There is also a renewed focus on the continuous improvement and capability enhancement tools and techniques that facilitate the production of high-quality products and services. Firms now realize that the teachings of the quality gurus (described in the next section) and various quality management frameworks (e.g., TQM and Six Sigma) are equally applicable to both manufacturing and service industries.

TEACHINGS OF QUALITY GURUS

AS mentioned earlier, modern quality management techniques are based on the core teachings and philosophies of several pioneers who have influenced practice over the last several decades. Therefore, we will briefly review the core concepts introduced by some of these quality gurus. We will first describe the teachings of Dr. W. Edwards Deming, who had perhaps the most significant impact on the practice of quality management around the world. Following the discussion of Deming's philosophies, we will briefly describe the teachings of other significant quality management pioneers, such as Crosby, Feigenbaum, Ishikawa, Juran, Shewhart, and Taguchi, in alphabetical order.

W. Edwards Deming

● **Continuous improvement philosophy** an approach involving continuously searching for ideas for improving the quality of goods and services

Deming is often considered the father of modern quality management. He emphasized the philosophy of **continuous improvement**. He taught that the quest for quality is a never-ending journey. Deming also created simple-to-understand examples and visuals for teaching quality management concepts. For example, he summarized his teachings in 14 points, which continue to be used as a guide for quality management by practicing managers (Table 2.1). He summarized his continuous improvement philosophy using a simple diagram of a wheel with four activities: Plan, Do, Check, and Act (Figure 2.5). Deming was trained as a

TABLE 2.1 Deming's 14 Points for Quality and Process Improvement

1. Create constancy of purpose toward improvement of product and service, with the aim to become competitive and to stay in business and to provide jobs.
2. Adopt the new philosophy. We are in a new economic age. Western management must awaken to the challenge, must learn their responsibilities, and must take on leadership for change.
3. Cease dependence on inspection to achieve quality. Eliminate the need for inspection on a mass basis by building quality into the product in the first place.
4. End the practice of awarding business on the basis of price tag. Instead, minimize total cost. Move toward a single supplier for any one item, with a long-term relationship of loyalty and trust.
5. Improve constantly and forever the system of production and service to improve quality and productivity, and thus constantly decrease costs.
6. Institute training on the job.
7. Institute leadership. The aim of supervision should be to help people and machines and gadgets to do a better job. Supervision of management is in need of overhaul, as well as supervision of production workers.
8. Drive out fear, so that everyone may work effectively for the company.
9. Break down barriers between departments. People in research, design, sales, and production must work as a team to foresee problems of production and in use of the product or service.
10. Eliminate slogans, exhortations, and targets for the work force asking for zero defects and new levels of productivity. Such exhortations only create adversarial relationships, as the bulk of the causes of low quality and low productivity belong to the system and thus lie beyond the power of the work force.
    - Eliminate work standards (quotas) on the factory floor. Substitute leadership.
    - Eliminate management by objective. Eliminate management by numbers, numerical goals. Substitute leadership.
11. Remove barriers that rob the hourly worker of his right to pride of workmanship. The responsibility of supervisors must be changed from sheer numbers to quality.
12. Remove barriers that rob people in management and in engineering of their right to pride of workmanship. This means abolishment of the annual or merit rating and of management by objective.
13. Institute a vigorous program of education and self-improvement.
14. Put everybody in the company to work to accomplish the transformation. The transformation is everybody's job.

Source: Deming, W. Edwards, *Out of the Crisis*, pp. 23–24, "14 Points for Quality and Process Improvement," © 2000 Massachusetts Institute of Technology, by permission of The MIT Press.

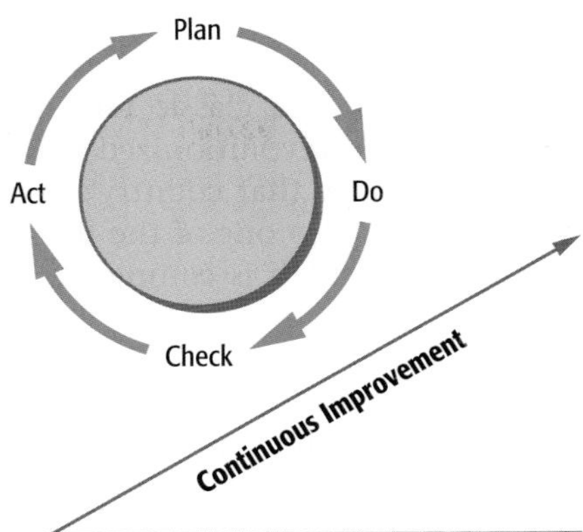

FIGURE 2.5 Plan-Do-Check-Act (PDCA) Cycle

Deming's PDCA cycle illustrates the continuous improvement philosophy.

Source: Deming, W. Edwards, *Out of the Crisis,* 1 figure: Plan-Do-Check-Act, page 88, ©2000 Massachusetts Institute of Technology, by permission of The MIT Press.

statistician and was also instrumental in teaching statistical quality control (SPC) to managers.

Philip Crosby

Crosby is perhaps most widely known for his easy-to-read management book entitled *Quality Is Free*. Crosby's ideas came from his experiences as a quality inspector on an assembly line in a factory. He proposed that if management does not create a system in which zero defects are the objective, then employees are not to blame when things go wrong and defects occur. The benefit of such a system for companies is a dramatic decrease in wasted resources and time spent producing goods that consumers do not want.

Crosby defined quality as containing four absolutes: (1) Quality is defined as conformance to requirements, not as "goodness" or "elegance"; (2) the system for causing quality is prevention, not appraisal; (3) the performance standard must be zero defects, not "that's close enough"; and (4) the measurement of quality is the price of nonconformance, not indices.

Armand Feigenbaum

Feigenbaum, another early pioneer of quality, is the author of a book on quality control published in 1951. In this textbook, he developed the concept of total quality control (TQC), which later evolved as part of total quality management. Feigenbaum believed that the management of a company must always strive for quality excellence. He also believed that everyone in the organization must commit to quality.

Kaoru Ishikawa

Ishikawa created a **cause and effect diagram** (also known as a *fishbone diagram*) that allows a user to visualize all possible causes of a result and hopefully find the root cause of process imperfections. Additionally, Ishikawa explored and popularized the concept of *quality circles*. A **quality circle** is a small group of employees who are responsible for similar or related work functions. This volunteer group meets regularly to identify, analyze, and solve quality and production problems related to its work.

● **Cause and effect diagram** a diagram that visually displays all possible causes of a quality problem, with the goal of finding the reasons for the imperfections

● **Quality circle** a small group of employees who are responsible for similar or related work functions. This volunteer group meets regularly to identify, analyze, and solve quality and production problems related to its work

Joseph M. Juran

Juran's *Quality Control Handbook* is a classic reference work for quality engineers. Along with Deming, Juran revolutionized the Japanese practice of quality management and helped shape that country's economy into the industrial leader that it is today. Juran was also one of the first to incorporate the human aspect of quality management, which is commonly referred to as total quality management.

Juran summarized his quality teachings as (1) quality planning, (2) quality improvement, and (3) quality control. **Quality planning** includes activities such as identifying the customer, determining customer needs, translating customer needs into production language, and optimizing product features to meet customer needs. **Quality improvement** means developing and optimizing a process that is able to produce a specified high-quality product. **Quality control** means proving that the process can operate under normal conditions without the need for inspection. Juran is also credited with identifying the four *costs of quality* (internal and external failure costs, assurance costs, and prevention costs) described earlier in this chapter.

- **Quality planning** activities such as identifying the customer, determining customer needs, translating customer needs into production language, and optimizing product features to meet customer needs
- **Quality improvement** developing and optimizing a process that is able to produce a specified high-quality product
- **Quality control** proving that the process can operate under normal conditions without the need for inspection
- **Quality loss function** a mathematical formula for determining the cost of poor quality
- **Robust quality** an experimental design and statistical analysis approach for identifying the optimum product design configuration

Genichi Taguchi

Taguchi is credited with creating the **quality loss function**, which is a mathematical formula for determining the cost of poor quality. The quality loss function estimates how much revenue a company is losing because of variability in the production process. He is also credited with developing the principles of **robust quality** by isolating the causes of the randomness or noise in the production process. Robust quality is an experimental design and statistical analysis approach for identifying the optimum product design configuration. Robust quality principles are now routinely used in identifying the optimum design of product components for many complex industries.

Walter Shewhart

No discussion of quality management can be complete without highlighting the contributions of Shewhart, who is also known as the grandfather of quality management. The earliest notions of quality and continuous improvement principles can be traced back to this former Bell Telephone employee. One of W. Edwards Deming's teachers, he preached the importance of adapting management processes to create profitable situations for both businesses and consumers, promoting the utilization of his own creation: statistical process control (SPC) charts. Additional details about SPC charts are provided in Chapter 11.

QUALITY MANAGEMENT FRAMEWORKS

OVER the years, both scholars and practicing managers have refined the concepts and frameworks of quality management. In this section, we briefly describe major themes that have affected the practice of quality management.

- **Total quality management** a quality management framework that addresses all areas and all employees of an organization, emphasizes customer satisfaction, and uses continuous improvement tools and techniques

Total Quality Management

Total quality management is an umbrella term used to describe a quality management system that addresses all areas and employees of an organization, emphasizes customer satisfaction, and uses continuous improvement tools and techniques. The TQM approach builds on the Japanese quality improvement

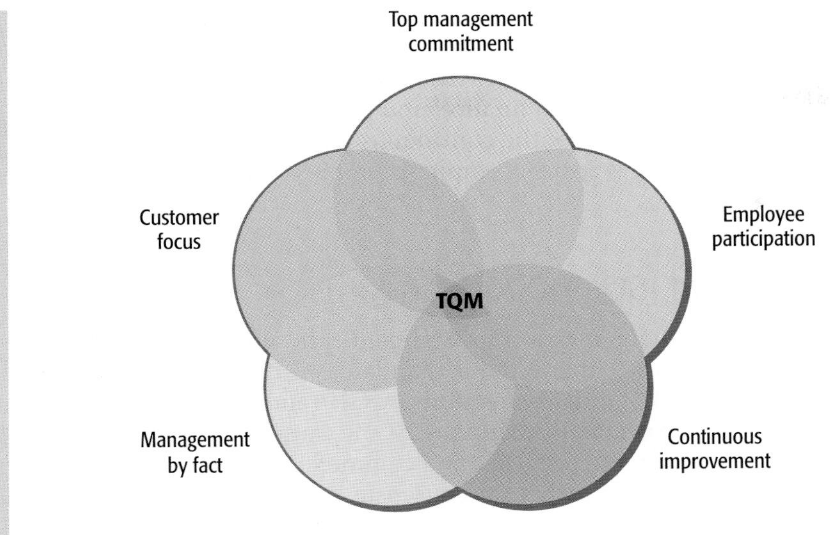

FIGURE 2.6 Components of Total Quality Management

practices and also encompasses many of the teachings and techniques of the gurus described in the previous sections.

The essential elements of TQM (Figure 2.6) can be described as:

- *Top management commitment.* TQM advocates support and commitment from the highest level of management. It requires personal involvement from the top management in clearly deploying values and goals that are consistent with the objectives of the company and in creating and deploying well-defined systems, methods, and performance measures for achieving those goals.
- *Employee participation.* A successful TQM environment requires a committed and well-trained work force that participates fully in quality improvement activities. Such participation is reinforced by reward and recognition systems that emphasize the achievement of quality objectives. Employees are encouraged to take more responsibility, communicate more effectively, act creatively, and innovate.
- *Customer focus.* The definition of quality within the TQM framework comes from the customer; therefore, achieving the highest levels of customer satisfaction is considered to be the highest priority. Customer focus means understanding the needs of customers, translating those needs into specific product and service design requirements, designing products and delivering services that satisfy customer needs, and developing processes that support all related production activities. TQM encourages extending the same principles to supplier and partner firms that participate in the production process.
- *Management by fact.* TQM emphasizes the need for using objective data rather than subjective perceptions when making managerial decisions. It advocates the use of statistical techniques such as statistical process control and the design of experiments for collecting and analyzing data.
- *Continuous improvement.* The underlying philosophy of continuous improvement lies at the heart of all TQM activities. Given that customer needs evolve over time and competitive offerings constantly emerge in the marketplace, continuous improvement of the quality of the product or service is seen as the only way to maintain a high level of customer satisfaction. Since

the quality of market offerings is linked to production, a focus on the continuous improvement of processes is also necessary. Improvement cycles are encouraged for all the company's activities, such as product development, support services, marketing and finance, and production. Elimination of waste is a major component of the continuous improvement approach. Furthermore, there is also a strong emphasis on prevention rather than detection.

ISO 9000 and ISO 14000 Standards

The ISO (International Organization for Standardization) is a nongovernmental organization encompassing the national standards institutes of 157 countries. The American National Standards Institute (ANSI) represents the U.S. government, businesses, and consumers within the ISO. Because of a partnership among the public sector, government agencies, and commercial enterprises, the ISO acts as a bridging organization in which a consensus can be reached on standards that meet the requirements of different segments of the society.

The ISO develops standards that have technical, economic, and social impact around the world. The primary objective of ISO standards is to make the development, manufacturing, and supply of products and services more efficient, safer, and cleaner. Furthermore, ISO standards also protect the users of products and services and make their lives simpler (Table 2.2). Some examples of widely used ISO standards are included in Table 2.3.

TABLE 2.2 How ISO Standards Help Everyone

According to the ISO, its standards help different segments of society in the following manner:
For businesses, the widespread adoption of international standards means that suppliers can base the development of their goods and services on specifications that have wide acceptance in their sectors.
For customers, the worldwide compatibility of technology achieved when goods and services are based on international standards brings them an increasingly wide choice of offerings, and they also benefit from the effects of competition among suppliers.
For governments, international standards provide the technological and scientific bases underpinning health, safety, and environmental legislation.
For trade officials negotiating the emergence of regional and global markets, international standards create a "level playing field" for all competitors in those markets.
For developing countries, international standards that represent an international consensus on the state-of-the-art advances are an important source of technological know-how.
For consumers, conformity of products and services to international standards provides assurance of the quality, safety, and reliability of those products and services.
For everyone, international standards can contribute to the quality of life in general by ensuring that the transport, machinery, and tools that we use are safe.
For the planet we inhabit, international standards on air, water, and soil quality and on the emissions of gases and radiation can contribute to efforts to preserve the environment.

Source: Adapted from http://www.iso.org/iso/en/aboutiso/introduction/index.html.

The *ISO 9000* and *ISO 14000* families are among the ISO's most widely known standards. ISO 9000 has become an international benchmark for assessing quality requirements, and ISO 14000 helps organizations with environmental quality management. Both ISO 9000 and ISO 14000 are known as "generic management system standards" because they are not specific to a particular product, process, or material. Instead, these two standards provide guidelines for certification that are applicable to a wide range of organizations (manufacturing, service, education, and healthcare organizations and government agencies).

ISO 9000 standards consist of a series of documents that describe the requirements and guidelines for quality improvement. Organizations that wish to be certified as ISO 9000–compliant prepare their own documents (e.g., a quality manual) describing how their business practices comply with the guidelines provided by ISO 9000. Accredited auditors then evaluate the organization's documents and practices, and if the organization passes, it is certified. Periodic audits and compliance with standards are necessary to maintain certification. The

TABLE 2.3 Some Examples of ISO Standards

Standard Number	Where It Is Used
ISO 31	Basic units of measurement
ISO 3591	Wine tasting glass
ISO 4217	International currency codes
ISO 7010	Graphical symbols
ISO 7810	Physical characteristics of credit cards
ISO 8120	Safe toys for children
ISO 9000	***Quality management***
ISO 9241	Computer display screens
ISO 9660	CD-ROMs
ISO 10002	Customer satisfaction and complaint handling
ISO 14000	***Environmental management***
ISO 15707	Identification of musical works
ISO 16104	Classification of environmentally dangerous substances
ISO 17363 to ISO 17367	Radio frequency identification (RFID) for supply chain management
ISO 17799	Electronic data and e-commerce
ISO 22000	Food safety management
ISO 22222	Personal financial planning
ISO 28000	Security standards for supply chains

Source: http://www.iso.org/iso/en/commcentre/isocafe/index.html.

guidelines for ISO 9000 standards are based on the following eight principles (Figure 2.7):

- Customer focus
- Leadership
- Involvement of people
- Process approach
- System approach to management
- Continual improvement
- Factual approach to decision making
- Mutually beneficial supplier relationships

Ever since their inception, ISO standards have been widely popular, and well over 500,000 organizations worldwide in many different industries have taken the certification.

ISO 14000, which is structured very similarly to ISO 9000, is also gaining broad acceptance as a measure for achieving higher environmental quality standards within the production process. The focus of ISO 14000 standards is on minimizing the harmful effects on the environment caused by an organization's activities and on achieving continual improvement in environmental performance.

Many scholars, however, believe that while ISO 9000 can assist companies in achieving minimum acceptable standards, it does not help them to achieve excellence or the highest quality levels. Because ISO 9000 requires companies to "document what they do and do what they document," critics argue that these standards are simply a tool for document management, nothing else. Research

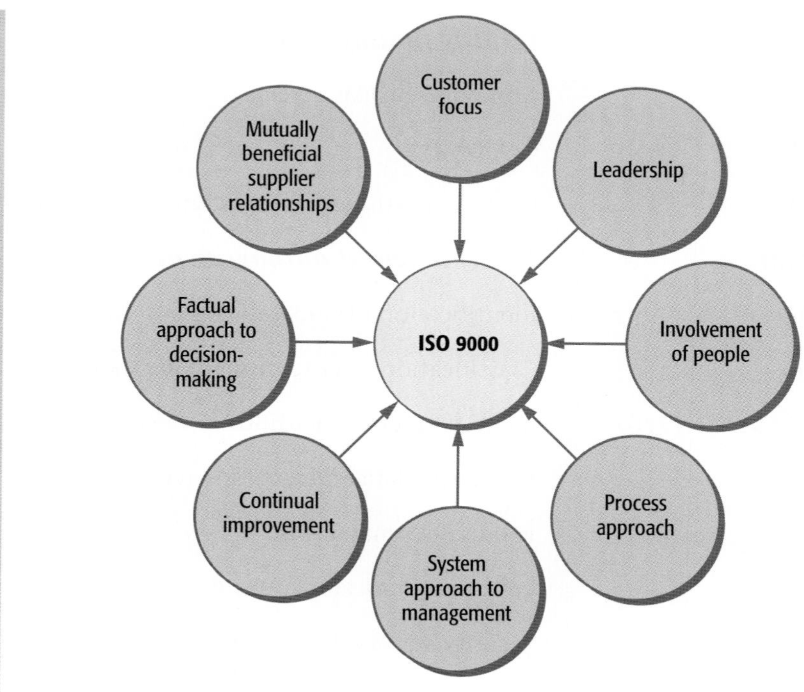

FIGURE 2.7 The Basis of ISO 9000 Standards

has shown that ISO 9000 certification does improve a firm's competitiveness and financial performance. While the ISO 14000 standards are still in their early growth phase, their positive impact on environmental quality practices has also been starting to show.

France has a long and fascinating heritage of setting the standard for the highest-quality wine among all wine-producing countries.

Baldrige Framework for Performance Excellence

The Malcolm Baldrige National Quality Award (MBNQA) is an annual award given to high-performing organizations within the United States (http://www.baldrige.gov). The MBNQA was created by Public Law 100-107, signed into law on August 20, 1987. The award is named for Malcolm Baldrige, who served as the U.S. secretary of commerce from 1981 to 1987.

The MBNQA recognizes the highest-performing organizations in six categories: manufacturing, service, small business, healthcare, education, and not-for-profit. The award is administered by the National Institute for Standards and Technology (NIST) and the American Society for Quality (ASQ). The award structure is built on the premise of active collaboration between private-sector companies and government agencies to help achieve performance excellence in U.S. organizations. The board of examiners and panels of judges for the awards consist of scholars and leading experts from U.S. businesses. Table 2.4 shows the names of the winning organizations from 1988 to 2007.

BEST PRACTICES IN OPERATIONS MANAGEMENT

Setting High Quality Standards for French Wine

When many consumers around the world think of *high-quality wine,* they think of *France*. France has a long and fascinating heritage of setting the standard for the highest-quality wine among all wine-producing countries.

The Greeks and Romans are credited with planting and growing the early vineyards. Over the next several centuries, French vineyards gradually started to become known for their high-quality grapes and wines. During the nineteenth century, however, many French vineyards became infected by a disease caused by a small insect that destroyed the roots of vines. Furthermore, France also suffered economically during the two world wars, and this also significantly affected the quality and production of wines.

In part to regain its reputation as the producer of the highest-quality wine and in part to standardize, a system of "regulated origin names" for French wine was developed. The A.O.C. standards for wines defined and regulated grape-growing regions as well as protected the quality of wines. (The *Appellation d'Origine Contrôlée* [A.O.C.], which translates as "term of controlled origin," is the French certification granted to geographical indications for wines, cheeses, butters, and other agricultural products.) The A.O.C. helped to reclaim the country's wine reputation and determined guidelines for quality and consistency within the French wine market.

Today it is estimated that France has around 150,000 grape growers, producing about 1.5 billion gallons of wine per year. There are many recognized wine-growing regions in France, spanning north to south and east to west. Alsace, Beaujolais, Bordeaux, Burgundy, Champagne, the Loire Valley, and the Rhone Valley are the big producers. French wines continue to serve as the standard by which modern wines worldwide are evaluated.

TABLE 2.4 Winners of Malcolm Baldrige National Quality Award

Year	Award Winners and Categories
1988	Motorola (manufacturing); Westinghouse Electric Corporation Commercial Nuclear Fuel Division (manufacturing); Globe Metallurgical (small business)
1989	Milliken & Company (manufacturing); Xerox Corporation, Business Products & Systems (manufacturing)
1990	Cadillac Motor Car Company (manufacturing); IBM Rochester (manufacturing); Federal Express Corporation (service); Wallace Co. (small business)
1991	Solectron Corporation (manufacturing); Zytec Corporation (manufacturing); Marlow Industries (small business)
1992	AT&T Network Systems Group Transmission Systems Business Unit (manufacturing); Texas Instruments Incorporated Defense Systems & Electronics Group (manufacturing); The Ritz-Carlton Hotel Company (service); AT&T Universal Card Services (service); Granite Rock Company (small business)
1993	Eastman Chemical Company (manufacturing); Ames Rubber Corporation (small business)
1994	AT&T Consumer Communications Services (service); Verizon Information Services (service); Wainwright Industries (small business)
1995	Armstrong World Industries (manufacturing); Corning Incorporated, Telecommunications Products Division (manufacturing)
1996	ADAC Laboratories (manufacturing); Dana Commercial Credit Corporation (service); Custom Research (small business); Trident Precision Manufacturing (small business)
1997	3M Dental Products Division (manufacturing); Solectron Corporation (manufacturing); Merrill Lynch Credit Corporation (service); Xerox Business Services (service)
1998	Solar Turbines Incorporated (manufacturing); Boeing Airlift and Tanker Programs (manufacturing); Texas Nameplate Company (small business)
1999	STMicroelectronics, Inc.—Region Americas (manufacturing); The Ritz-Carlton Hotel Company (service); BI (service); Sunny Fresh Foods (small business)
2000	Dana Corporation—Spicer Driveshaft Division (manufacturing); KARLEE Company (manufacturing); Operations Management International (service); Los Alamos National Bank (service)
2001	Chugach School District (education); Pearl River School District (education); University of Wisconsin-Stout (education); Clarke American Checks (manufacturing); Pal's Sudden Service (service)
2002	SSM Health Care (healthcare); Motorola Commercial, Government & Industrial Solutions Sector (manufacturing); Branch-Smith Printing Division (small business)
2003	Community Consolidated School District 15 (education); Saint Luke's Hospital of Kansas City (healthcare); Baptist Hospital (healthcare); Medrad (manufacturing); Caterpillar Financial Services Corporation (service); Boeing Aerospace Support (service); Stoner (small business)
2004	Kenneth W. Monfort College of Business (education); Robert Wood Johnson University Hospital (healthcare); The Bama Companies (manufacturing); Texas Nameplate Company (small business)
2005	Jenks Public Schools (education); Richland College (education); Bronson Methodist Hospital (healthcare); Sunny Fresh Foods (manufacturing); DynMcDermott Petroleum Operations Company (service); Park Place Lexus (small business)
2006	North Mississippi Medical Center (healthcare); MESA Products (manufacturing); Premier (service)
2007	PRO-TEC Coating Co (small business); Mercy Health System (healthcare); Sharp Health Care (healthcare); City of Carol Springs (nonprofit); U.S. Army Armament Research, Development and Engineering Center (nonprofit)

Source: http://www.baldrige.gov/.

While it is great to recognize the high achievers, the real impact of the MBNQA has been as a guiding framework for performance excellence. For example, a number of other quality awards, including local and state awards and awards in some other countries, have been modeled after the MBNQA. Furthermore, the web site for the MBNQA (http://www.baldrige.gov) contains many freely downloadable documents, including *The Criteria for Performance Excellence*; profiles of past award winners; and other supporting information that assists companies in enhancing their quality, profitability, and competitiveness.

The guiding framework of MBNQA can be considered an excellent model for implementing TQM and the teachings of quality gurus. The Baldrige framework is based on 11 core values and concepts, which are summarized in Figure 2.8.

Based on the core values and concepts just described, a set of *Criteria for Performance Excellence* has been developed (Figure 2.9). The criteria have seven categories: leadership; strategic planning; customer and market focus; measurement, analysis, and knowledge management; work force focus; process management; and results. Additional information about the Baldrige Award and its underlying quality management framework is available at http://www.baldrige.org.

The MBQNA trophy.

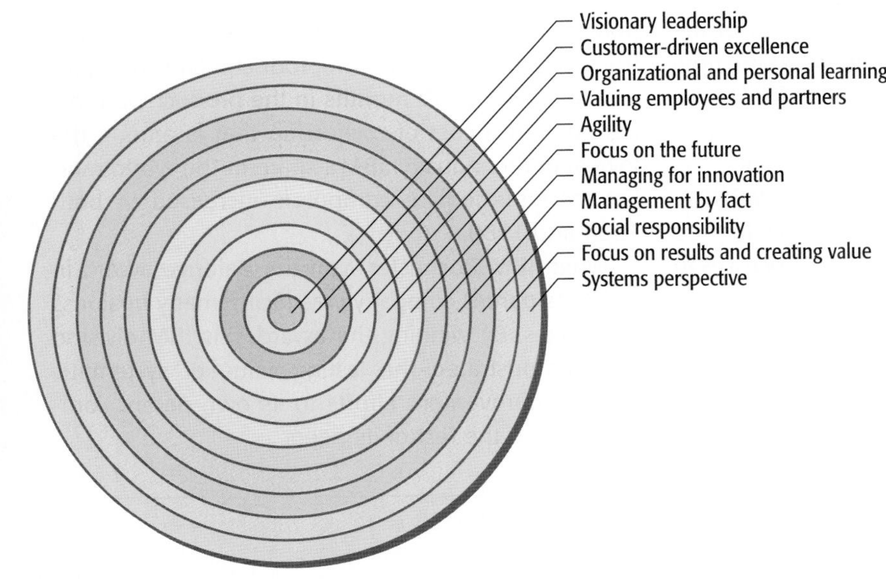

FIGURE 2.8 Malcolm Baldrige Award: Core Values and Concepts

Source: The figure is based on information included within the 2007 Criteria for Performance Excellence (http://www.baldrige.gov/).

FIGURE 2.9 Framework for the Malcolm Baldrige National Quality Award

Source: 2007 Criteria for Performance Excellence (http://www.baldrige.gov/).

BEST PRACTICES IN OPERATIONS MANAGEMENT

Profile of a Baldrige Award Winner: IBM Rochester

IBM Rochester was one of the early winners of the Malcolm Baldrige National Quality Award. At the time it received this award in 1990, this IBM facility exported more than $501 million worth of computer hardware and electronic assemblies worldwide.

During the years prior to its winning the MBNQA, the IBM Rochester quality culture was transformed from one that relied on *technology-driven processes* to one that used *market-driven processes* that directly involved suppliers, business partners, and customers in delivering innovative solutions. A 30 percent improvement in productivity occurred between 1986 and 1989. Product development time for new mid-range computer systems was reduced by more than half, while the manufacturing cycle was reduced 60 percent from the 1983 level. Customers benefited from a threefold increase in product reliability, an increase from 3 to 12 months in the product warranty period, and a cost of ownership that is among the lowest in the industry. IBM's share of the world market for intermediate computers increased in both 1988 and 1989.

When IBM Rochester won the Baldrige award in 1990, its parent company was facing many business challenges. By winning the award, this IBM division has demonstrated the lasting value of systematic quality improvement efforts to its own parent company and to the rest of its peers.

Source: www.baldrige.org.

High-degree-of-quality processes are necessary for computer manufacturing.

SIX SIGMA

DURING the last decade, Six Sigma, an approach that is based heavily on statistical and fact-based data and tools, has rapidly emerged as the dominant quality management framework used in manufacturing and service organizations. While Six Sigma is also based on the philosophies of gurus (Deming, Juran, and others) and has aspects in common with TQM and the Baldrige Framework, it heavily emphasizes the structured use of quantitative and data-driven quality improvement techniques. As mentioned earlier in this chapter, Six Sigma was originally developed as a framework for implementing quality improvement approaches at Motorola. Since that time, GE, Allied Signal, American Express, and a wide range of other companies in the United States and abroad have adopted the Six Sigma approach to quality and process improvement.

Six Sigma can be defined as "[a] comprehensive and flexible system for achieving, sustaining, and maximizing business success. Six Sigma is uniquely driven by close understanding of customer needs, disciplined use of facts, data, and statistical analysis, and diligent attention to managing, improving, and reinventing business processes."

The Six Sigma way of thinking is organized around **DMAIC**, which stands for Define, Measure, Analyze, Improve, and Control. The "sigma" refers to standard deviation, a measure of variation from the perfect outcome. The number six refers to the objective that no measure should be more than six standard deviations from the desired standard to achieve almost perfection (99.9997 percent error-free

- **Six Sigma** a comprehensive and flexible system for achieving, sustaining, and maximizing business success. Six Sigma is uniquely driven by a close understanding of customer needs; disciplined use of facts, data, and statistical analysis; and diligent attention to managing, improving, and reinventing business processes
- **DMAIC** the acronym for define, measure, analyze, improve, and control, the five-step plan of a Six Sigma approach

products). Later in this section, we describe both DMAIC and the calculation of the sigma level of a production process in additional detail.

The Conceptual Framework of Six Sigma

The major themes of the Six Sigma approach can be summarized as follows:

- There is a genuine focus on understanding the *needs and preferences of the customer.* Customers' definition and assessment of quality are central to the Six Sigma approach. Therefore, the Six Sigma approach advocates a periodic and scientific approach to assessing customer satisfaction and feedback about product and service offerings.
- *Management by fact* is a necessary requirement for a Six Sigma approach. This emphasis requires that companies use only relevant and objective data collected from the process to make decisions and refrain from basing decisions on preconceived subjective judgments.
- The unit of analysis within a Six Sigma approach is a *process.* A process consisting of a sequence of activities is necessary for producing goods and services that satisfy the needs of the customer. Therefore, by improving the quality of processes, the Six Sigma approach can automatically enhance the quality of the products and services that are delivered to customers.
- Six Sigma emphasizes the need for a *proactive management style.* Rather than waiting for a quality problem to occur, management should focus on identi-

BEST PRACTICES IN OPERATIONS MANAGEMENT

Motorola and the Genesis of Six Sigma

Motorola, one of the world's leading manufacturers of cool mobile phones, is credited with the development of the quality management process known as *Six Sigma*. The original plan to develop almost error-free products (99.9997 percent, or approximately 3.4 defects in a million) was proposed by Bill Smith, a senior engineer and scientist at Motorola under CEO Robert Galvin. The use of Six Sigma concepts contributed heavily to Motorola's winning the Malcolm Baldrige National Quality Award in 1988. Now an integral part of Motorola's management practice, Six Sigma concepts are embedded in all its processes, including research and development, product design, production, and support services.

The impact of the Six Sigma process on improving business performance has been dramatic and well documented by other leading global organizations, such as General Electric, Allied Signal, American Express, and many other manufacturing, service, and not-for-profit organizations around the world.

Six Sigma requires almost perfect products in processes.

Source: Roger O. Crockett and Jena McGregor, "Six Sigma Still Pays Off at Motorola: The Company Is Thriving, with a Culture That Lets Left-Brain and Right-Brain Types Coexist," *BusinessWeek,* December 4, 2006, p. 50; Tom McCarthy, "Six Sigma at Motorola," Motorola Inc., http://www.motorola.com/mot/doc/1/1736_MotDoc.pdf (December 3, 2006); GE web site, http://www.gewater.com/who_we_are/we_believe/six_sigma.jsp (November 16, 2006).

fying the root causes ahead of time so that problems do not occur in the first place.

- Active cooperation and collaboration between employees working within different functional areas in a firm is a must if the Six Sigma approach is to be successful. *Teamwork* at different levels and across the organization therefore requires breaking down barriers based on hierarchy and/or different functional areas.
- Finally, Six Sigma *strives for perfection*. The term *Six Sigma* itself refers to a statistical term meaning 3.4 defects in a million opportunities. If we assume that a process is behaving according to the normal distribution, then the area under the curve can be determined by the distance in terms of number of standard deviations (σ) from the mean (μ). As shown in Figure 2.10, a distance of one standard deviation (or 1 σ) from the mean value gives an area of approximately 68.27 percent under the normal distribution curve. Similarly, distances of two and three standard deviations give areas of 95.45 percent and 99.73 percent under the normal distribution curve. Later in this chapter, we describe how the normal distribution is used to identify the sigma level of a production process.

The technical goal of Six Sigma is to ensure that the variations that are present within a product process, a product, or a service become so small that the distance of six standard deviations to either side of the mean (μ) is still within the **acceptable quality range**. The acceptable quality range can be specified by a variety of sources, such as the customers, government regulations, industry standards, competition, or the organization itself.

- **Acceptable quality range** the range of values that represents good quality

The acceptable quality range is usually represented by **upper and lower tolerance limits** (UTL and LTL). These two values represent the highest and the lowest value that a product, service, or process can have and still be considered to have acceptable quality. Once the tolerance limits are set, the quality of the process on the sigma scale can be calculated by comparing the distance between the tolerance limits and the actual standard deviation of the process.

- **Upper and lower tolerance limits** two values that represent the highest and the lowest value that a product, service, or process can have and still be considered to have acceptable quality

A Six Sigma quality thus means that the distance from the mean value of the process to both the LTL and the UTL is six standard deviations.

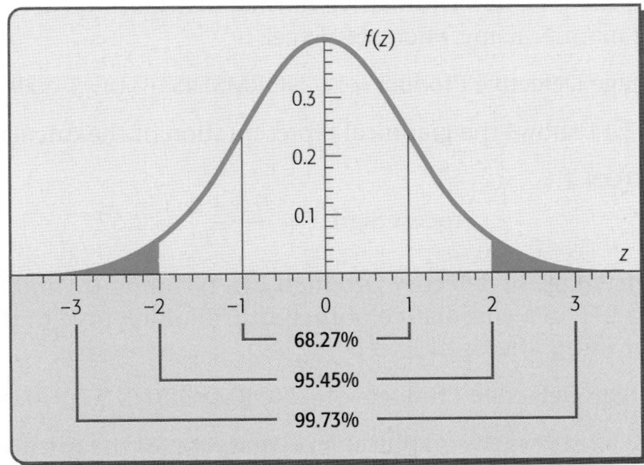

FIGURE 2.10 Percentage of Area Under the Normal Distribution Curve Based on a 1, 2, and 3 σ Distance from the Mean

The Six Sigma Level of a process can be calculated by dividing the distance from the tolerance limits (either LTL or UTL) to the mean by standard deviation (assuming μ represents mean and σ represents standard deviation).

$$\text{Process Sigma} = \frac{UTL - Mean}{\sigma} \text{ or } \frac{Mean - LTL}{\sigma} \qquad \text{(Equation 1)}$$

The percentage of defective products can be calculated by using the normal distribution curve included in the Appendix at the back of this book or by computer (Equation 2 can be used in Microsoft Excel).

% of defictive products = 1 – NORMSDIST (Process Sigma) (Equation 2)

Equation (2) represents the area under the tail of the normal distribution curve (see Figure 2.10). If LTL is used to calculate Process Sigma, then Equation (2) calculates the area of the left tail. When UTL is used to calculate Process Sigma, then it calculates the area of the right tail. It is up to the practicing manager to decide which of the two (or both) tolerance limits are important to consider in a given situation.

A simple example of the calculation is presented in Example 1.

Solved Example 1: Calculation of Sigma Level and Percentage of Defective Products

Xeta Manufacturing Company (XMC) produces electronic components for a number of partner companies. The products need to be manufactured using strict tolerance limits specified as follows: UTL = 10 and LTL = 2. Past data shows that the mean for the production process is 6.5 and the standard deviation is 1.75.

Question 1: Calculate the Sigma Level and percentage of defective products for the process considering UTL.

Question 2: Calculate the Sigma Level and percentage of defective products for the process considering LTL.

SOLUTION 1

$$\text{Process Sigma} = \frac{10 - 6.5}{1.75} = 2.0$$

The percentage of defective products can be found by finding the area beyond the UTL in a cumulative normal distribution curve in the following manner using Microsoft Excel.

Percentage Defective Product = 1 – NORMSDIST(2.0) = 1 – 0.9772 = 0.0228

Figure 2.11 shows the graphical representation of the calculations above.

SOLUTION 2

$$\text{Process Sigma} = \frac{6.5 - 2}{1.75} = 2.57$$

The percentage of defective products can be found by finding the area prior to LTL in a cumulative normal distribution curve in the following manner using Microsoft Excel.

Percentage Defective Product = 1 – NORMSDIST(2.57) = 0.0051

Figure 2.12 shows the graphical representation of the calculations above.

While the exact calculation of Process Sigma is given in Equation (1), in practice, managers like to account for an approximately 1.5 σ shift of the mean in ei-

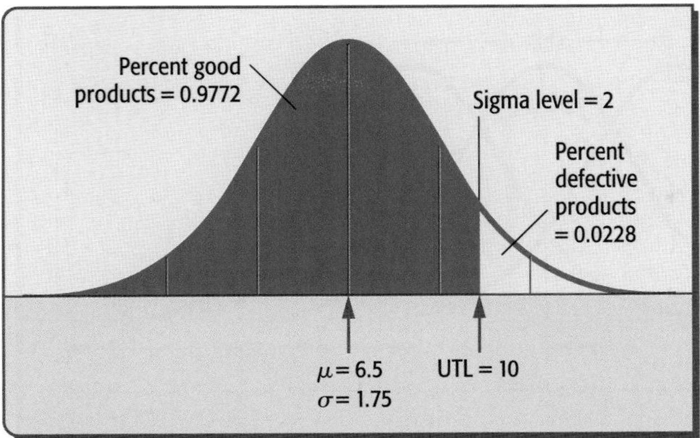

FIGURE 2.11 Calculation of Sigma Level and Percentage Defective Products Based on UTL

ther direction because of the natural variation that is present in any process. This allowance for a shift of the distribution is important because no process can be expected to be in perfect control and therefore have exactly the same mean value all the time. Therefore, in reality Six Sigma quality is equivalent to the LTL and the UTL being 4.5 standard deviations away from the extreme position of the mean on either side (Figure 2.13).

The calculations described above allow managers to calculate the impact of a low sigma quality level on a firm's operation. One can imagine how many airline flights would be delayed, how many computer game consoles would malfunction, and how many credit card transactions would be denied if companies like Southwest Airlines, Sony, or American Express operated at a low sigma level. Each of these companies is manufacturing products or delivering services to hundreds of thousands of customers, and therefore even a small error rate could mean a very large number of dissatisfied customers. Hence, the Six Sigma framework can also be a very useful tool for developing guidelines and goals for a quality improvement program.

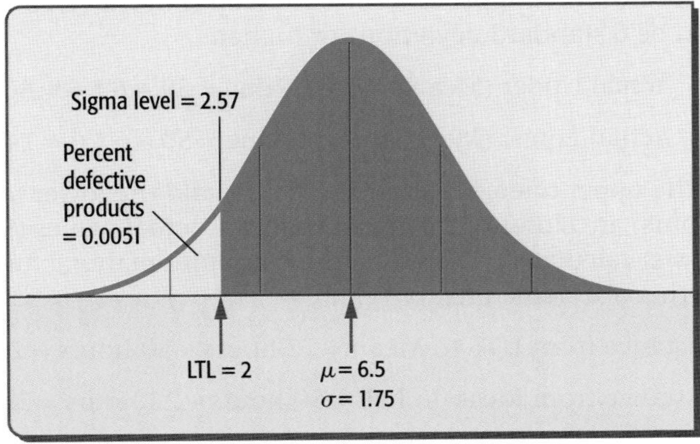

FIGURE 2.12 Calculation of Sigma Level and Percentage Defective Products Based on LTL

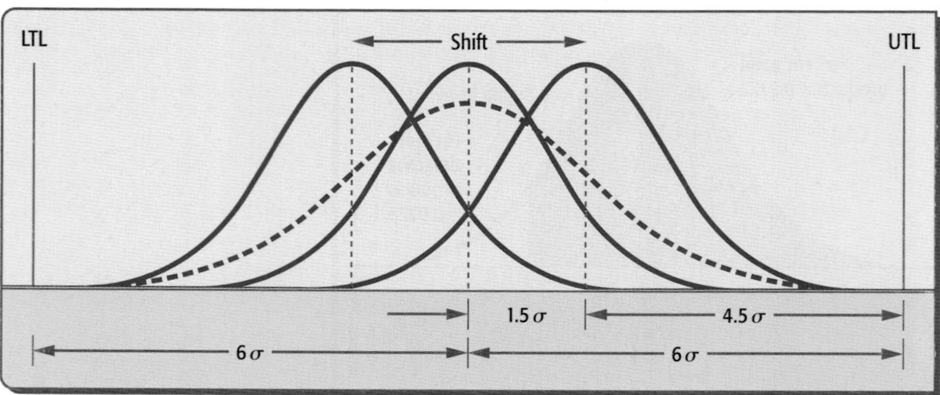

FIGURE 2.13 Six Sigma and Tolerance Limits

Solved Example 2

The Internet store of a computer manufacturer promises to ship all customer orders within 24 to 72 hours of receiving the order at its web site. Actual shipment data for all computers shipped during the past month showed that the average shipment time was 50 hours, and the standard deviation was 6 hours.

1. **Is the company delivering Six Sigma quality to its customers?**
2. **If not, then how much should the standard deviation of the process be reduced to get Six Sigma quality?**

SOLUTION

(a) Upper tolerance limit (UTL): 72 hours

Lower tolerance limit (LTL): 24 hours

Mean (μ): 50 hours

Standard deviation (σ): 6 hours

If the computer manufacturer is delivering Six Sigma quality, then the distance from the upper and lower tolerance limits (UTL and LTL) should be 6 standard deviations or higher.

Actual Upper (Mean + 6 * σ) Value = 50 + 6 * 6 = 86 hours

Actual Lower (Mean – 6 * σ) Value = 50 – 6 * 6 = 14 hours

Both the upper tolerance limit (72 hours) and the lower tolerance limit (24 hours) are closer to the mean than the actual values (86 hours and 14 hours) calculated. Therefore, the computer manufacturing is not delivering Six Sigma quality yet.

(b) Distance from UTL to Mean = 72 hours – 50 hours = 22 hours

Distance from Mean to LTL = 50 hours – 24 hours = 26 hours

For the manufacturer to deliver Six Sigma quality, both of the distances just calculated should be at least 6 standard deviations.

Therefore, the smaller distance of the two calculations will have to be reduced to equal 6 standard deviations.

$$6 * \sigma = 22 \text{ hours}$$

$$\sigma = 3.67 \text{ hours}$$

Therefore, the computer manufacturer will have to reduce its standard deviation from 6 hours to 3.67 hours to achieve a Six Sigma quality level.

Many products and services are produced in multistage processes, and mistakes can occur during each step. The sigma level (and corresponding quality) of the entire production process can be found by multiplying the percentages of good outcomes achieved at each stage of the production process. Examples of the calculations are presented next.

Solved Example 3: Sigma and Quality Level for a Multistage Production Process

A routine visit to a dentist's office could involve four process steps: (1) checking in at the reception desk, (2) getting dental x-rays taken by the nurse, (3) having teeth cleaned by a dental hygienist, and (4) being examined by the dentist.

Calculate the percentage of error-free outcomes for the entire process if the percentages of error-free outcomes for each step is as specified in (a) Figure 2.14 and (b) Figure 2.15.

SOLUTION

(a) The fraction of error-free outcomes for the entire production process is found by multiplying the percentage of error-free outcomes for each of the four production stages:

$$0.9332 * 0.9332 * 0.9332 * 0.9332 = 0.7584$$

$$= 75.84 \text{ percent error-free outcomes}$$

(b) The percentage of error-free outcomes for the entire production process represented in Figure 2.15 is

$$0.9938 * 0.9938 * 0.9938 * 0.9938 = 0.9754$$

$$= 97.54 \text{ percent error-free outcomes}$$

This example illustrates that by going from a lower (Figure 2.14) to a higher process (Figure 2.15) sigma level at each step, the overall quality improves from 75.84 percent to 97.54 percent—a significant improvement.

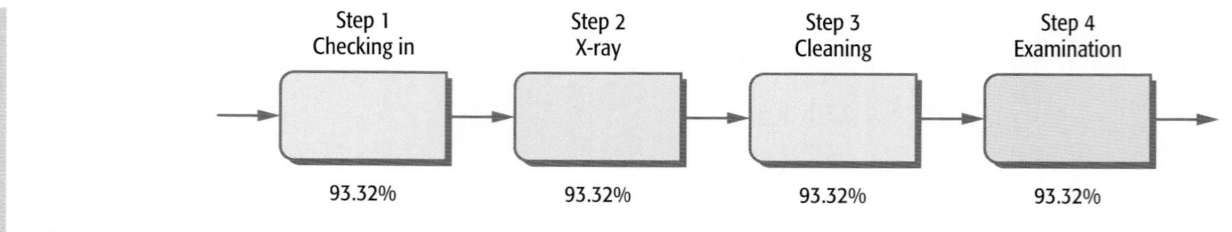

FIGURE 2.14 Percentage of Error-Free Outcomes at Each Step

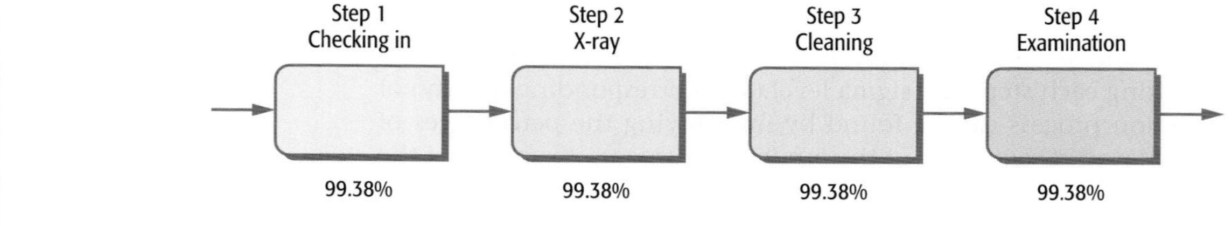

FIGURE 2.15 Percentage of Error-Free Outcomes at Each Step

Implementing Six Sigma

The Six Sigma approach described here is implemented using a structured five-step plan known as *DMAIC* (define, measure, analyze, improve, and control). DMAIC defines the steps that a Six Sigma practitioner is expected to follow, starting with identifying the problem and ending with the implementation of long-lasting solutions (Figure 2.16):

- *Define* a problem or improvement opportunity.
- *Measure* process performance.
- *Analyze* the process to determine the root causes of poor performance.
- *Improve* the process by attacking the root causes.
- *Control* the improved process to hold the gains.

The first three steps in the DMAIC plan are also called the *process characterization* phase because they provide descriptive information about the existing process. The remaining two steps are also known as the *process optimization* phase because they attempt to move the performance of the process to its best possible level.

Implementation of the Six Sigma approach goes beyond the quality improvement tools and steps outlined here. The improvement projects within an organi-

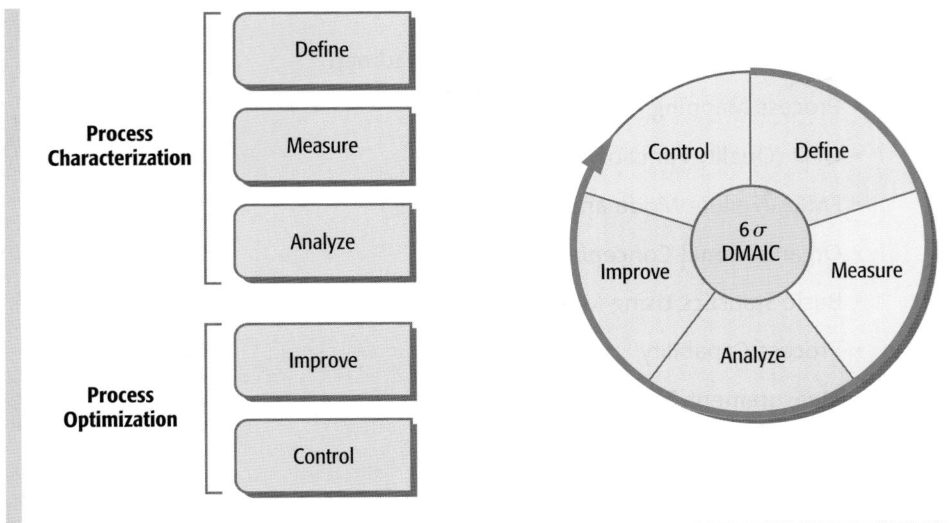

FIGURE 2.16 The DMAIC Methodology

zation must be carefully selected by the leaders to ensure that the outcome of the effort will have significant impact on key stakeholders such as customers, employees, and the company's shareholders and that it will positively contribute to the organization's financial and other goals.

Employees who are being trained in Six Sigma methodology go through a specified rigorous curriculum. While the curriculum and the corresponding training programs used by different companies differ based on each company's unique needs, the core elements of the program are essentially the same. They all focus on the quality improvement philosophies taught by quality gurus and TQM, and they use objective data and many advanced qualitative and quantitative techniques heavily. The individuals trained in the Six Sigma approach are certified as Green Belt, Black Belt, Master Black Belt, and Six Sigma Champions. Green Belts typically spend less than 25 percent of their time working on a Six Sigma project. Black Belts typically work full time on multiple Six Sigma projects and also advise Green Belts. A sample Black Belt curriculum is presented in Figure 2.17 on page 58.

WEEK 1
- Six Sigma Overview and the DMAIC Roadmap
- Process Mapping
- QFD (Quality Function Deployment)
- FMEA (Failure Mode and Effects Analysis)
- Organizational Concepts Effectiveness
- Basic Statistics Using Minitab
- Process Capability
- Measurement Systems Analysis

WEEK 2
- Review of Key Week 1 Topics
- Statistical Thinking
- Hypothesis Testing and Confidence Intervals (*F, t,* etc.)
- Correlation
- Multivariate Analysis and Regression
- Team Assessment

WEEK 3
- ANOVA (Analysis of Variance)
- DOE (Design of Experiments)
  Factorial Experiments
  Fractional Factorials
  Balanced Block Designs
  Response Surface Designs
- Multiple Regression
- Facilitation Tools

WEEK 4
- Control Plans
- Mistake-Proofing
- Team Development
- Parallel Special Discrete, Continuous Process, Administration, and Design Tracks
- Final Exercise

FIGURE 2.17 A Sample Six Sigma Curriculum

Source: R. W. Hoerl, "Six Sigma Black Belts: What Do They Need to Know," *Journal of Quality Technology* 33, no. 4 (2001), 391–406. Reprinted with permission from *Journal of Quality Technology*.

SUMMARY

1. Define the meaning of *quality*.

- High quality implies having the capability to consistently produce products that satisfy or exceed customer needs.
- While the implementation approaches might be different, the meaning of quality is the same for both manufacturing and service organizations.

2. Explain why it is necessary to improve the quality of goods and services.

- High-quality products and services are necessary for the survival, growth, and competitiveness of an organization.
- Quality improvement efforts reduce overall production cost within an organization. In the long run, by investing in prevention costs, a firm can reduce both internal and external failure costs and assurance costs, thereby reducing the overall cost.
- In the long term, higher customer satisfaction, positive word of mouth, good reputation, increased market share, and profitability are results of an organization's quality improvement efforts.

3. Define the components of quality in goods and services.

- Quality in tangible goods can be determined by eight dimensions: performance, special features, reliability, conformance, durability, serviceability, aesthetics, and brand equity.
- Service quality is measured by ten determinants: reliability, responsiveness, competence, access, courtesy, communication, credibility, security, understanding/knowing the customer, and tangibles.
- Many determinants of quality for Internet-based goods and service offerings have been proposed. They include access, ease of navigation, efficiency, flexibility, reliability, personalization, security/privacy, responsiveness, assurance/trust, site aesthetics, and price knowledge.

4. Summarize the history of quality management.

- The increase in mass-produced products in the early twentieth century meant that the responsibility for maintaining quality was delegated to the "quality inspector" at the end of the production process.
- Japanese managers learned the concepts of quality management from western gurus Deming and Juran after the Second World War. The Japanese companies implemented comprehensive quality improvement plans that led to *made in Japan* changing from a term implying cheaply made products to one that was known as the measure of excellence around the world within three decades.
- Quality management concepts have regained their importance in western companies during the last three decades. The teachings of quality gurus, the total quality management framework, and Six Sigma concepts are now widely used in all high-performing organizations.

5. Summarize the teachings of quality gurus W. Edwards Deming, Philip Crosby, Armand Feigenbaum, Kaoru Ishikawa, Joseph M. Juran, Genichi Taguchi, and Walter Shewhart.

- Deming, known as the father of modern quality management, went to Japan at the conclusion of the Second World War and revolutionized the practice of quality management. Deming emphasized the philosophy of continuous improvement. His 14 points and the Plan-Do-Check-Act cycle provide guidelines for implementing quality improvement plans.
- Crosby's quality improvement ideas came from his experiences as a quality inspector on an assembly line in a factory. He defined quality as containing four absolutes: (1) Quality is defined as conformance to requirements, not as "goodness" or "elegance"; (2) the system for causing quality is prevention,

not appraisal; (3) the performance standard must be zero defects, not "that's close enough"; and (4) the measurement of quality is the price of nonconformance, not indices.

- Feigenbaum developed the concept of total quality control (TQC), which later evolved as part of total quality management (TQM).
- Ishikawa created a cause and effect diagram (also known as a fishbone diagram) that allows a user to visualize all possible causes of a result and hopefully find the root cause of process imperfections. He also popularized the concept of quality circles.
- Juran has made many contributions to the field of quality management. His *Quality Control Handbook* is a classic reference for quality engineers.
- Taguchi is credited with creating the quality loss function, which is a formula for determining the cost of poor quality. He is also credited with developing the principles of robust quality by isolating the causes of the randomness or noise in the production process.
- Shewhart is also known as the grandfather of quality management. One of W. Edwards Deming's teachers, he preached the importance of adapting management processes to create profitable situations for both businesses and consumers.

6. Describe commonly used quality management approaches, such as total quality management (TQM), the ISO 9000 and ISO 14000 standards, and the Malcolm Baldrige Criteria for Performance Excellence.

- Total quality management (TQM) is an umbrella term that is used to describe a quality management system that addresses all areas and employees of an organization, emphasizes customer satisfaction, and uses continuous improvement tools and techniques. The components of TQM include top management commitment, employee participation, customer focus, management by fact, and continuous improvement.
- The ISO develops standards that have technical, economic, and social impact around the world. Both ISO 9000 and ISO 14000 are known as "generic management system standards" and are not specific to a particular product, process, or material. Instead, these two standards provide guidelines for certification that are applicable to a wide range of organizations.
- The Malcolm Baldrige National Quality Award (MBNQA) is an annual award given to high-performing organizations (manufacturing, service, small business, healthcare, education, and not-for-profit) within the United States. However, the real impact of MBNQA has been as a guiding framework for performance excellence.

7. Describe the Six Sigma quality management approach and the steps in implementing it.

- The Six Sigma approach is also based on the philosophies of gurus (Deming, Juran, and others) and has aspects in common with TQM and the Baldrige framework. However, it heavily emphasizes the structured use of quantitative and data-driven quality improvement techniques.
- The Six Sigma way of thinking is organized around DMAIC, which stands for Define, Measure, Analyze, Improve, and Control.
- Employees who are being trained in Six Sigma methodology go through a specified rigorous curriculum. The individuals trained in the Six Sigma approach are certified as Green Belt, Black Belt, Master Black Belt, and Six Sigma Champions.

SOLVED PROBLEMS

Solved Problem 1

A food processing company wants to ensure that the taste of its very popular frozen low-fat dinner entrée meets the Six Sigma quality standards. The manufacturing engineers believe that the taste is strongly related to the percentage of a secret spice (known as *Alpha-Omega 1001*) that is added during the production process. A number of consumer taste tests were conducted, and it was found that all samples of entrées that were rated "excellent" contained between 1.5 and 3.25 percent *Alpha-Omega 1001*. If the mean percentage of *Alpha-Omega 1001* falls in the middle of the identified limit, calculate the standard deviation necessary to achieve Six Sigma quality.

SOLUTION

Upper tolerance limit = 3.25

Lower tolerance limit = 1.5

Mean (middle of the upper and lower tolerance limits) = $\frac{1.5 + 3.25}{2} = 2.375$

For Six Sigma quality, the distance from the mean to the upper and lower tolerance limits should be at least 6 standard deviations (σ). Therefore,

$$6 * \sigma = (3.25 - 2.375) = 0.875$$

Therefore

$$\sigma = 0.146$$

Answer: To ensure Six Sigma quality, the mean should be 2.375 percent and the standard deviation should be 0.146 percent of *Alpha-Omega 1001* in each packet of the frozen low-fat dinner entrée.

Solved Problem 2

A bank uses outside contractors to complete two process steps for home mortgage applications. The bank auditors have noticed that the timeliness of the first step (application screening) is at 93.32 percent, and the timeliness of the second step (property assessment) is at 97.72 percent. The third step (mortgage underwriting) is done in-house, and the timeliness of this step has been found to be at 99.38 percent.

What is the timeliness of the entire home mortgage application process?

SOLUTION

Figure 2.18 shows the three process steps and corresponding fractions of good outcomes (in this case a "good" outcome refers to its timeliness).

The fraction of good outcomes for the entire home mortgage application process is

$$0.9332 * 0.9772 * 0.9938 = 0.9062$$

Therefore, the timeliness of the home mortgage process is at 90.62 percent.

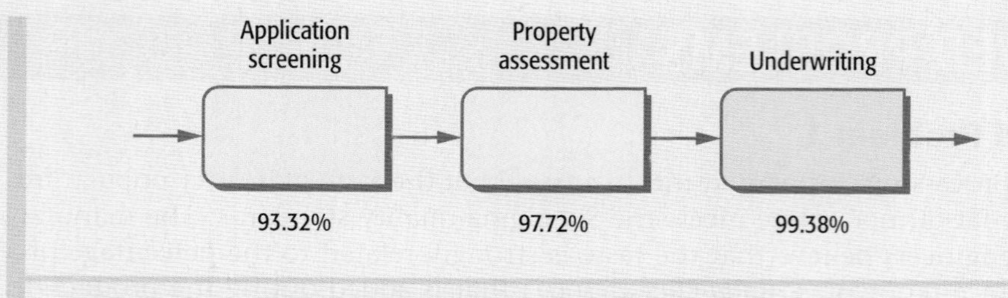

FIGURE 2.18 Process Steps and Good Outcomes

PROBLEMS

1. Table 2.5 shows the temperature of a sample of coffee served by a café located in a shopping center's food court. The café manager wants to ensure that the coffee temperature in each cup meets established federal guidelines of 160 to 180 degrees Fahrenheit. Based on the information provided, what can you conclude about the sigma level?

TABLE 2.5 Temperature (degrees Fahrenheit)

162	166	173	173	168	168	159	166
159	181	169	175	177	168	171	162
172	172	181	166	173	172	172	181
168	174	178	169	172	169	179	175
159	166	168	170	180	160	180	168

2. Assume that the four-step process described in Problem 8 is replaced by a three-step process with the same sigma level. Find the sigma level for each of the three steps.

3. A customer service center wants to answer all calls within 30 seconds to 90 seconds with Six Sigma quality. Table 2.6 shows waiting time (in seconds) for a random sample of 50 customers for a customer service call center. Based on the information provided, what can you conclude?

TABLE 2.6 Customer Waiting Times (in seconds)

58	54	67	68	55	51	54	67	69	59
63	52	53	56	70	54	51	50	55	62
54	67	69	64	55	69	53	64	60	65
69	62	65	67	65	67	56	63	58	51
57	69	68	69	65	59	51	50	60	57

4. A manufacturing facility uses a four-step process to assemble an automotive component. The quality auditors have noticed that the quality of the first step is at the 4.5 sigma level, and the quality of the second step is at the 5 sigma level. Both the third and fourth steps are at the 5.5 sigma level. What is the sigma level of the entire process?

5. A pizza delivery company promises to deliver all customer orders within one hour of receiving an order at one of its stores. Actual data for all pizza delivered during the past week showed that the average delivery time was 40 minutes and the standard deviation was 10 minutes.

   (a) Is the company delivering Six Sigma quality to its customers?

   (b) If not, then how much should the standard deviation of the process be reduced to get Six Sigma quality?

6. A quick service restaurant is considering changing the number of process steps necessary in assembling a burger. Currently the burger assembly process requires four steps, each of which operates at the 4 sigma quality level. It is expected that after increasing the number of process steps to eight, the quality level will increase to a 5.5 sigma level. Calculate the net gain or loss in the final quality level if the restaurant proceeds with the change in the number of process steps.

7. An Internet book retailer promises to ship all customer orders within 24 to 36 hours of receiving an order at its web site. Actual shipment data for all computers shipped during the past month showed that the average delivery time was 30 hours, and the standard deviation was 4 hours.

   (a) Is the company delivering Six Sigma quality to its customers?

(b) If not, then how much should the standard deviation of the process be reduced to get Six Sigma quality?

8. The production process for an electronic product has 12 major steps. If each of the first six production steps is at a 5 sigma quality level and the remaining steps are at a 5.5 sigma quality level, calculate the total percentage of error-free products manufactured.

9. Zeta Automotive Limited (ZAL) has designed a new engine component (code name *FE73*) that can potentially increase the fuel efficiency of a car to approximately 72 miles per gallon. ZAL supplies its components to automotive assembly plants. The automotive assembly plants want assurance that each *FE73* can provide fuel efficiency of between 70 and 75 miles per gallon at the Six Sigma quality level.

   What should be the standard deviation for *FE73* to achieve Six Sigma quality?

10. The production process for a video game console has 10 major steps. If each production step is at a five sigma quality level, calculate the total percentage of error-free products manufactured.

CASE STUDY

The Case of the Complaining Customer

In an effort to improve service, Presto Cleaner installed a new computer system, designed to cut the customers' waiting time and simplify the drop-off and pickup processes. But the system was only a few months old when Mr. J.W. Sewickley, the company president, received an angry letter from Mr. George Shelton, whose laundry had been lost by the new system. Mr. Shelton's letter described his experience with Presto Cleaner's complaint-handling operations and demanded compensation and an apology. To respond to the complaint, Mr. Sewickley sent the letter to his customer complaint office, asking for more information. The answer came back from Paul Hoffner. He explained that there were extenuating circumstances and suggested that some customers may not be worth keeping. Is the customer always right? Where should a company draw the line on compensation and service? What is the best way to handle cases of complaining customers?

Letter from George Shelton to J.W. Sewickley

Mr. J.W. Sewickley
President
Presto Cleaner

Dear Mr. Sewickley: October 14, 1989

My wife and I are angry, frustrated, and disappointed ex-customers. We weren't always that way. In fact, for a year prior to the recent set of events, we were exceptionally pleased with your service. When you opened your store at the intersection of Adams and Broadway, we were delighted. Even though you're not exactly the least expensive dry cleaner in the area, my wife and I felt that the convenience of the location, the extra early and late hours of operation, and the helpfulness of the staff more than made up for the cost.

That was before you installed your computerized system. The following set of facts will tell you why we are not doing business with Presto Cleaner and what you need to do to get us back as satisfied customers.

July 28: I dropped off some laundry at the store, and the counterperson introduced me to the new computer system. I filled out a "preference card" (light starch for my shirts, folded in a box, and so on) that was entered into the computer. I selected an identification number. The bag was only $3, no big deal. Ideally, the next time I had laundry, all I would have to do was put my laundry in a bag and drop it off. No waiting in line, no waiting for a receipt, the computer knew what I wanted done. When it came time to pick it up, I would just pay, get the laundry, and go. Easy, convenient, time saving. *Supposedly.*

August 4: My wife stopped in to pick up the July 28 order and dropped off the bag with the new laundry (4 of my shirts, 2 blouses, 1 suit, 1 skirt). The counterperson had her fill out her own preference card and entered that information into the computer.

August 10: On the way home from work, I stopped in to make a drop-off and a pickup. Guess what, Mr. Sewickley? I needed to buy a second special bag if I wanted to use the new system every time. I had to stand in line and wait my turn and finally give my order to the person behind the counter. It took forever. The great new system required the counterperson to enter every item, its color or other distinguishing feature, and also what operation I wanted done (clean, press, and so on). It took more than ten minutes. The old system was actually faster.

Then when I finished with the drop-off, I told the counterperson I also had an order to pick up. She asked me for the receipt. I explained that I had used the new computerized system with the bags, so I didn't have a receipt. She asked for my identification number. When she punched it into the computer, it said that my wife had picked up the order earlier in the day.

When I got home, I asked my wife if she had picked up the order. She said she had a business meeting the next day and needed a suit that was at the cleaners. I asked about the bag, and after looking everywhere, including the backseat of the car, we finally determined that she had picked up a previous order and definitely not the order with the special bag. Missing were 4 shirts, 2 blouses, 1 suit, and 1 skirt.

August 11: I called the store from work and explained the problem. The counterperson was very courteous, apologized, and said that the store would be searched for the missing items.

August 14: I went to the store to pick up the last order. I stood in line, waiting for roughly 15 minutes for the two people in front of me to struggle through the computer system. I finally got my order and asked about the lost clothing. After a lot of asking around, the counterperson finally determined that the clothes had not turned up at the store. We next tried to locate the order in the computer, only to discover that when my wife and I had chosen identification numbers, she had used our home phone number and I had used my business number. After searching the computer using both numbers, we still turned up nothing. The counterperson said he would put a tracer on the order back at the plant.

August 15: My wife left work early to take our next laundry order to one of your competitors that has a store near our house. It's open only until 5:30, but there's less nonsense.

August 19: I picked up the order from the nearby Kwik N' Klean on my way to my favorite men's store to buy four new shirts. I didn't have enough shirts to make it through two weeks of work because of the four that were still missing. I am enclosing the sales slip for the four new shirts. I fully expect you to reimburse me for these shirts.

August 25: I called the store again. It had heard from the plant, and the plant did not have the clothing. Why, Mr. Sewickley, did they not call me? I asked how to pursue a claim for lost items and learned that I should call a Mr. Paul Hoffner at the office. I immediately called Mr. Hoffner and was told that he was not available. I left a message for him to call back as soon as possible.

August 26: I called back again. Mr. Hoffner was not available. I left the same message.

August 27: I called back again. Mr. Hoffner was not available. I asked if there was anyone else who could handle a claim for lost items and was told that only Mr. Hoffner could do that.

August 31: Mr. Hoffner called. I told him that I wanted to put in a claim. He was totally unaware of the situation, so I had to explain it to him. He suggested that he call the store and the plant to find out if there was any progress. I got the distinct impression that he didn't believe me and that he felt he needed to check with the store to make sure that I really was a customer and that there really was missing laundry. I assured Mr. Hoffner that I was a real customer. In fact, for more than a year, my wife and I have averaged between $20 and $30 worth of dry cleaning every week. Despite my assurances, Mr. Hoffner insisted that he had to check before anything could happen. When I pushed to find out what the process was, Mr. Hoffner said that if the clothing really was lost, I could fill out a claim form and apply for compensation.

September 7: A week had passed with no word from Mr. Hoffner. I called. He wasn't available. I left a message.

September 11: Still no word from Mr. Hoffner. I called and miracle of miracles, he answered the phone. After all that time, the only thing he could tell me was that neither the store nor the plant could find the clothes. I asked him to send the claim form.

September 18: No claim form had yet arrived in the mail, so I called Mr. Hoffner again. I got him and asked about the form. He said he had delayed sending it because he was sure that the clothes would be found. I insisted that he send the form immediately.

September 21: The claim form arrived, and I discovered that it required that I attach both the original purchase receipt for the clothes and the counter receipt for the laundry order. Mr. Sewickley, do you keep your year-old receipts for clothing? And with the new computer system, there are no counter receipts!

It took two more calls to get through to Mr. Hoffner to complain about these requirements. He said that they were necessary to guard the company against fraud. He did acknowledge that since your own system no longer produced counter receipts, I couldn't be expected to send them in. But as far as the receipts for the clothes were concerned, he suggested that I go back through our charge card records to come up with the proof of purchase. I flatly refused. I told Mr. Hoffner that we have done more than $1,000 worth of business with Presto Cleaner over the past year and that we were not in the business of extorting money from dry cleaners. Further, I told him that if my word wasn't good enough for him, he could kiss our business good-bye, along with that of our friends and colleagues at work, who would soon hear all about the Presto Cleaner way of doing business.

September 22: Having had a terribly busy week, we forgot that my wife needed a dress cleaned for a business function Saturday night. Since it was Friday morning when we discovered this, our only real option was for my wife to drop off the dress at Presto Cleaner in the morning.

September 23: I went in to pick up the dress. The woman behind the counter recognized me and told me that the store had found our lost clothes. Apparently, they had been mysteriously included in another customer's order and only just now returned. She had no clue how this could have happened with the new system. She was, as usual, cheerful, apologetic, and polite about the mix-up. I paid for the order, picked up the dress, and went home.

September 25: Since there was no way to call your office over the weekend, I waited until Monday to try to reach Mr. Hoffner. He was again unavailable, so I left him the last message he will ever get from me: the clothes were found, but I would still like to talk to him.

Mr. Sewickley, that was more than two weeks ago, and I still haven't heard from Mr. Hoffner. I am outraged by this entire episode, by the way your company treats customers, by Mr. Hoffner's conduct, by the lack of communication, and by the ridiculous system you introduced. I am particularly incensed at having to pay for clothes that were delivered almost two months late and by having to purchase new clothes to cover your company's mistake.

I expect the following: a full refund for the order that was lost, full payment for the four shirts that I had to buy to make up for the lost order, and a full apology from Mr. Hoffner. If all of those are forthcoming, I might consider giving your company another chance at my business. Otherwise, my wife and I will never patronize your company again.

Sincerely,
George Shelton

Memo
To: JWS Oct. 29, 1989
From: Paul Hoffner
Re: Customer Complaint

This is in response to your memo requesting background information to respond to the customer complaint of Mr. George Shelton. I have reviewed his letter as well as our own file concerning this matter. I am convinced that we did make a good-faith effort to do right by Mr. Shelton, although he may not recognize it as such. Nevertheless, should you wish to mollify the customer, I would be perfectly happy to play the role of fall guy if it would help. As far as extending compensation to the customer is concerned, his demands seem to me far in excess of any real liability: he did get his clothes back, he will keep the four new shirts and use them, as well. I would certainly extend an apology to him—if he would like it from me, fine; I assume that it would be even more satisfactory coming from you, along with an offer to clean his next order free of charge.

Having said this, there are some mitigating circumstances that you should be aware of. I would not share these with the customer, but I present them to you so that you will understand more accurately and fully what really happened, rather than what this one customer says happened. Again, that does not mean that a mistake was not made; there was a mistake, and we should take responsibility for that. But we acted in a way consistent with company policy and operations. Let me describe what really happened:

1. The customer dropped off his clothing on literally the first day of operation of the new computerized system—a system that everyone at headquarters agrees is the key to our future success. Everyone also agrees that there will be problems, including, unfortunately, some lost customers. Mr. Shelton may be one such example. As you remember, because of delays with the system vendor and the software, we had only one week to train our people on the new system. Also, as I'm sure you're aware, not all of our store personnel are great at using this technology. It has taken more time than expected to get them to understand all of the steps they have to take to prevent mistakes.
2. As I suspected all along, the real problem in this case was that the clothing was picked up by another customer. This is not that unusual. When it happens, we must rely on the goodwill of our customers to return what is not theirs. This time, because the customer was an infrequent user of our service, it took him more than four weeks to bring the clothes back in. Also, he dropped the clothes off at a different store. Unfortunately, we have more than one case of lost clothes at a time (please note all the letters of complaint that you don't have, proof that the system works most of the time), so we cannot call every customer and ask him or her to come in and identify the clothes. Our policy, therefore, is simply to wait for customers to come in and then offer them a chance to identify the clothes.

3. Much of Mr. Shelton's gripe concerns the early period (approximately August 12 through August 25) during which time he felt he was kept in the dark. But as you know, our process is designed to get the stores and the plant to figure out problems. My written record shows that the plant did two thorough searches before reporting the lack of results to the store. It's hard to fault it for thoroughness. Apparently, the store also delayed referring the customer to me, probably thinking that the clothes would turn up and, perhaps, not wishing to have to report bad news concerning our new computer system. The process also may have taken this much time because of our standing company policy that requires all reports between stores, the plant, and the office to be in writing.
4. After I spoke with the customer, I spent the next ten days or so checking with the store and the plant in an attempt to determine what exactly had happened and to locate and identify the clothes. By the end of the first week, I felt sure that the clothes had mistakenly gone to another customer. But there was no way to retrieve them, other than to wait for them to turn up. I did not tell the customer this, of course; after years of experience, I have found that customers only get more upset at the idea that a stranger has their clothes.
5. Unbeknownst to me, the missing clothes were returned to the Adams and Broadway location on September 14. The customer who had mistakenly received the clothes dropped them off at one of our suburban locations, which then forwarded them to the plant. The plant used our standard identification process, sent them to the Adams and Broadway store, and then wrote me a memo, which I received on September 23. Before I could call the customer and inform him, he had picked up his clothes. I did get one more very angry message from the customer, which I decided not to return, since further communication would unlikely be of any benefit.
6. Mr. Shelton's letter has several misstatements of fact. While there is no point in disputing these points with him, you should know the following:
   (a) I did not delay in sending him a claim form. I sent the form after he requested it and do not know why it was not received. When he called back on September 18, I sent another form. I did not tell him that I had delayed in sending the form. I told him we were trying to locate and identify his clothes.
   (b) When I spoke to the customer regarding the standard claim form, I did not tell him to produce proof of purchase. I told him it would be helpful to us if he could get a good estimate of the value of the items.
7. As you can tell from the tone of Mr. Shelton's letter, he is a very demanding, persistent individual. What his letter does not tell you, however, is that he inundated us with the sheer volume of his calls. Given the number and frequency of his calls, there was no way for me to demonstrate progress on his problem before he called again. When he writes that he "left a message," you should know that his "messages" were usually cryptic. He often did not leave a phone number and, on more than one occasion, even refused to leave his name. For example, he would say, "You know who this is." My secretary found all of this quite distressing. Moreover, I've never run into a customer so anxious to be compensated.

This brings up several interesting questions: How do we make up for the mistake we made without being browbeaten into excess compensation? For example, his four shirts would cost us more than $200; refunding his order would add another $35; if I had swiftly processed his original claim, it would have come to over $600.

In other words, despite Mr. Shelton's threats, I think our system worked. Although we did misplace his clothes, he got everything back, and we avoided a major expense. Now some restitution, such as one free order and a written apology, should be enough. If that is not good enough for Mr. Shelton, it seems to me we should ask, "Aren't there some customers we are better off losing?" Maybe this is a customer that Kwik N' Klean deserves!

Source: Reprinted by permission of HARVARD BUSINESS REVIEW. From "The Case of the Complaining Customer," by Dan Finkelman and Tony Goland.

QUESTIONS

1. Why is Mr. Shelton upset? What should be done to address his complaint?
2. Based on the information presented in the case, develop a comprehensive quality improvement plan for Presto Cleaner.

CHAPTER 3

New Product Development

LEARNING OBJECTIVES

1 Describe the importance of new product development to a firm's success or failure.

2 Describe the new product development process, the product life cycle, and different strategies and tradeoffs in product innovation

3 Learn different concepts in new product development, such as designing for enhanced customer experience, mass customization, virtual reality, rapid prototyping, environmentally friendly design, modular design, concurrent engineering, product platforms, group technology, and reverse engineering

4 Learn important new product development analysis techniques, such as customer choice analysis, reliability analysis, product-complexity index, and quality function deployment.

Development of a New Pharmaceutical Drug

While no monetary value can be assigned to saving a human life, developing a new pharmaceutical drug costs somewhere between $800 million and $2 billion, and the process often takes more than 10 years. A pharmaceutical company may test up to 30,000 different drug formulations before one can be successfully introduced into the market as an approved medicine for human use. Development of a new drug is a long, difficult, expensive, and high-risk undertaking for a pharmaceutical company. The major steps associated with the development of a new drug are described here.

Once researchers understand how a disease works, the first step in developing a new medicine is to identify a specific molecule that could play a crucial role in combating that particular disease. Teams of chemists, pharmacologists, and biologists then screen thousands of chemically or genetically engineered compounds, considering a number of issues such as potential effectiveness, manufacturability, and cost. Once a potential drug candidate has been identified in the laboratory, it undergoes three to six years of intensive testing. The tests start with a series of laboratory animal studies, which are conducted to evaluate the drug's safety and to demonstrate that it has biological activity against the disease. After the successful completion of this stage, the company files an investigational new drug (IND) application with the U.S. Food and Drug Administration (FDA) prior to initiating human trials.

During clinical trials, teams of physicians carry out prespecified studies designed to determine if the drug is safe for humans and if it is an effective treatment for the disease. There are three phases of clinical trials. During *Phase I,* the medicine is tested in a small group (up to 100) of healthy volunteers, often in a hospital setting, to determine its safety profile, including the safe dose range. During *Phase II,* placebo-controlled trials are conducted for up to 500 volunteer patients who have the disease. The goal of this phase is to establish the "proof of concept"—i.e., that the medicine treats the disease effectively. During *Phase III,* the medicine is tested in large, randomized, placebo-controlled trials with a much larger number of patient volunteers (up to 5,000) in hospitals, clinics, and/or physicians' offices to generate statistically reliable data. Researchers closely monitor patients at regular intervals to confirm that the drug is effective and to identify side effects. While Phase I and Phase II studies can take six months to one year, Phase III studies can take from one to four years to complete, depending on the disease, the length of the study, and the number of volunteers.

At the conclusion of all the tests and analyses, the pharmaceutical company has to complete and submit an elaborate, comprehensive, and complex application (typically 100,000 pages or longer) to the FDA for approval. The application contains all of the information about preclinical testing, clinical trials, dosage information, manufacturing details, and proposed labeling for the new medicine. During this final stage, the FDA scientists review all the results from all the studies carried out over the years and determine whether those results show that the medicine is safe and effective enough to be approved. It takes about one and a half years for the FDA to review each medicine.

Even after FDA approval, the development and innovation process continues because a much larger group of patients may now begin using the medicine. The FDA requires firms to continue to submit periodic reports, including any cases of side effects or complications. Sometimes the FDA may require a company to conduct additional studies. Known as Phase IV or "postmarketing" studies, they evaluate the medicine's long-term safety or generate more data about how the medicine affects a particular group of patients (e.g., children or the elderly). The stages of a typical new drug development project described here are summarized in Figure 3.1. ■

A potential drug undergoes three to six years of laboratory testing.

This chapter provides a review of the major concepts, tools, and trends in new product development for manufacturing and service industries. We discuss why it is necessary for firms to establish effective product development processes to permit their long-term survival and growth in a highly competitive marketplace. We highlight major trends such as continuous and disruptive innovation, customer experiences, concurrent engi-

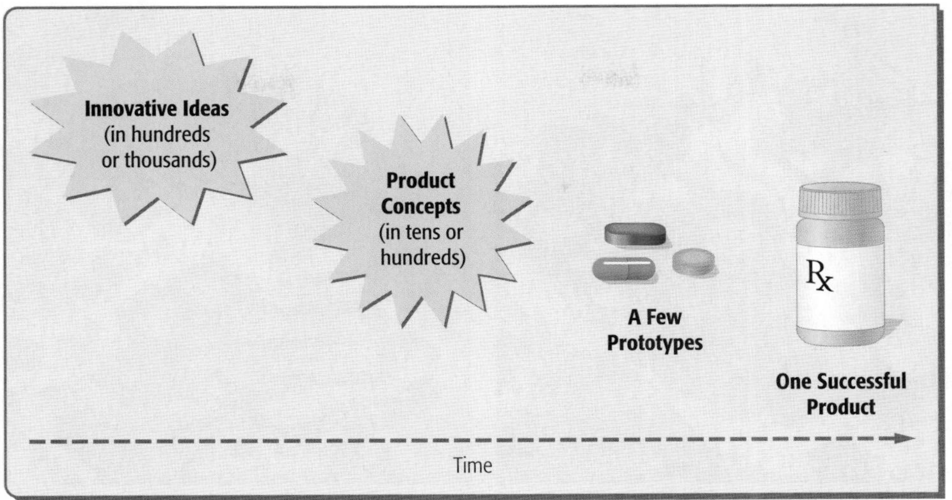

FIGURE 3.1 Stages in the Development of Pharmaceutical Products

neering, time-based competition, mass customization, and so on. Finally, this chapter describes commonly used and emerging tools and methods used in new product development.

● **New product** a good, a service, or a good/service bundle that was previously not available to customers

WHAT IS NEW PRODUCT DEVELOPMENT?

New product is a loosely used term that can be defined as a good, a service, or a good/service bundle that was previously not available to customers. However, from the perspective of a specific firm, a new product can also be defined as an offering that the firm has not produced before. For example, consumers around the world are very familiar with mobile phones, but the iPhone was a completely new product for Apple Computer. Similarly, the development of theme parks based on the popular LEGO toys was a completely new undertaking for the LEGO Corporation, which now operates LEGOLANDs in Denmark, Germany, the United Kingdom, and the United States.

The iPhone, Apple's new mobile phone, combines the elements of existing phones with the functionalities of an iPod.

The Product Development and Management Association (PDMA) defines **new product development** as the overall process of strategy, organization, concept generation, product and marketing plan creation and evaluation, and commercialization of a new product (http://www.pmda.org). Leading companies in many different industries (such as 3M, Abbott Laboratories, Sony, American Express, Kellogg, Toyota, and others) employ structured new product development processes to enable them to constantly innovate and produce new market offerings.

Chapter 1 describes some common differences between manufactured goods and services. Because of increased use of technology, globalization, and interdependence of industries, many differences between goods and services are disappearing. Therefore, large firms often design, develop, and produce both goods and services. For example, motorcycle manufacturer Harley-Davidson is also known for having the highest-quality customer service. Similarly, while McDonald's is generally considered

LEGOLAND is an adventure theme park based on and inspired by a variety of LEGO toys.

● **New product development** the overall process of strategy, organization, concept development, marketing plan creation and evaluation, and commercialization of a new product (good or service)

a quick-service restaurant company, it also operates highly advanced manufacturing plants that produce highly standard and consistent food products such as French fries and burger patties. Therefore, the term *new product development* is applicable to both manufacturing and services industries.

Why New Products Fail

While there are many advantages to undertaking new product development efforts, a large percentage of new products are not successful. For example, a typical supermarket introduces more than 5,000 new products to its customer base every year, and as many as 80 percent of those products are commercially unsuccessful. Many failed efforts are simply misunderstood by consumers. Other products fail for a variety of unexpected reasons. Some common reasons for new product failure are as follows:

- Failed new products are based on poor market research.
- Failed products can also be closely associated with problems or defects.
- Some new products are based on inferior designs; therefore, they do not succeed.
- Sometimes products fail because of the poor timing of their introduction.
- Products can fail if the company does not undertake effective communication to make potential customers aware of their benefits relative to those of the competition.
- If the new product is introduced with costs higher than expected compared to the benefit derived, then its sales are lower.
- Often products fail because other companies introduce a superior product.
- Finally, products can fail because of a number of operations considerations, such as an ineffective supply chain or inventory policy, which make it difficult for the product to be available to the customer at the right place, at the right time, and at the right price.

Why Firms Develop New Products

Even though new products may fail, it has also been observed that in many industries, the development and introduction of new products can make the difference between a company's success and its failure to survive. Some specific reasons why firms undertake systematic new product development efforts are discussed here.

Sources of Competitive Advantage

Firms innovate and develop new products because the products offer them unique opportunities for competitive advantage. For example, many critics agree that the successful development of the iPod was instrumental in the survival and emergence of a stronger and more competitive Apple Computer. Pharmaceutical companies often undertake the development of multiple new products because their existing drugs no longer enjoy patent protection. The early movers also have the advantage of taking a leading role in setting industry standards for the emerging product categories.

Market Share Gain

New products introduced in the marketplace provide additional "first mover advantages" to the company. By developing new products, a company can quickly capture a big share of the market before competitive products are introduced. For example, Toyota's successful introduction of the Prius hybrid car prior to its competitors' development of such a car has allowed the company to establish a dominant position in the emerging market segment of fuel-efficient and environmentally friendly automobiles.

Higher Profitability

During the early stages, a new product faces less competition than a product in a mature market; therefore, its profitability tends to be higher (Figure 3.2). As the market becomes saturated with several competitive products, prices start falling, and profit margins decrease. This general trend is observed in many industries.

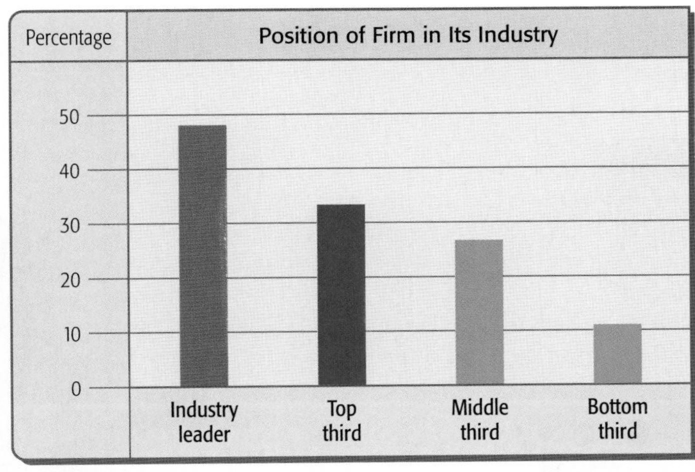

FIGURE 3.2 Relative Profitability of Early Movers Versus Later Entrants in New Product Markets

Because of its higher quality and attractiveness, the Aeron chair commands much higher prices than other office chairs.

The Aeron chair produced by Herman Miller is a great example of a highly profitable office chair. While a typical office chair sells for $200 or less, Aeron chairs cost close to $800.

Enhancement of Corporate Image and Brand Name

The development of innovative and creative new products is a very powerful source of goodwill and creates a positive corporate image. It is difficult to assign a monetary value to the goodwill associated with the enhanced corporate image that results from new product development. At the same time, **brand equity** measures used in marketing show that firms with more successful new product development efforts command higher respect from customers, which leads to enhanced long-term profitability.

● **brand equity** the monetary or relative value of a brand perceived in the marketplace by its customers

Faster Competitive Response

A company that has a systematic process for new product development in place can introduce new products quickly after a competitor's product is launched. A classic study of the worldwide automobile industry, summarized in the bestseller *The Machine That Changed the World,* showed that Honda and Toyota were roughly three times better than General Motors, Ford, and Chrysler Corporations in terms of time to develop new products (Womak, Jones, and Roos, 1990). Therefore, they were able to introduce new products quickly as consumer tastes and preferences changed and competitors launched new products (e.g., minivans and trucks).

Operating Cost and Capacity Utilization

Firms that constantly innovate also identify better approaches for producing products. The product development effort is often closely linked with process development. Therefore, over a period of time, production cost is reduced, leading to enhanced profitability. Furthermore, new products provide the opportunity for

From left to right, Sony's Playstation 3, Microsoft's X-Box, and Nintendo's Wii compete fiercely in the video-game industry. Each company tries to quickly introduce new products to compete with others.

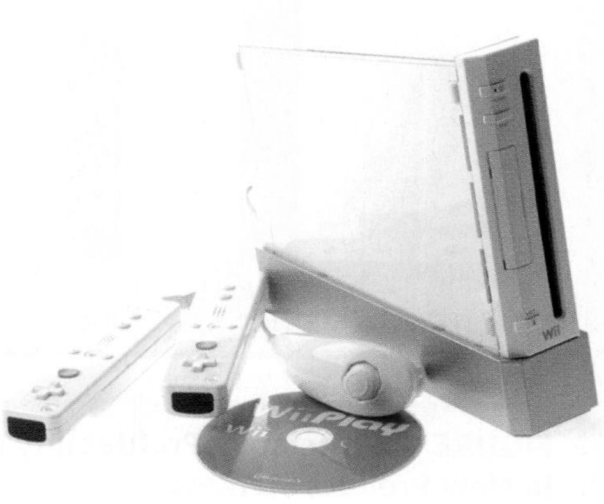

enhanced sales, as the demand for older products decreases over time. Therefore, a company can continue to operate at a similar capacity (both labor and equipment) if it continues to innovate and introduce new products.

THE NEW PRODUCT DEVELOPMENT PROCESS

THE **new product development process (NPD process)** can be defined as a disciplined and definite set of tasks and steps that describe the normal means by which a company repetitively converts embryonic ideas into saleable products or services.

● **New product development process (NPD process)** a disciplined and definite set of tasks and steps that describe the normal means by which a company repetitively converts embryonic ideas into saleable products or services

The NPD process in goods production industries has been studied extensively. Over the years, a number of NPD process frameworks have been proposed. Two commonly used NPD process models are described here:

- A five-stage framework linking new product development opportunity to design, testing, information, and profit management.
- The stage-gate system that recognizes the importance of cross-functional teams, parallel processing in activities, and up-front predevelopment activities in the NPD process.

The new product development processes for tangible goods described here are summarized in Figure 3.3. While the individual steps in the proposed approaches appear to be different, they all follow the same general pattern.

At the strategic level, the concepts, tools, and techniques used in the development of new goods and services remain very similar. However, at the operational level, differences between manufacturing and services need to be explicitly considered to effectively develop new market offerings. Therefore, a number of frameworks for establishing a systematic new service development process have been proposed. They are summarized in Figure 3.4.

Regardless of the framework used to describe new product development for goods and services, for a specific company, or a context, they all include several common elements:

- The generation of innovative new ideas is very difficult. Development of a successful idea requires input from several different sources, including customers, competitors, suppliers, employers, and also other industries.

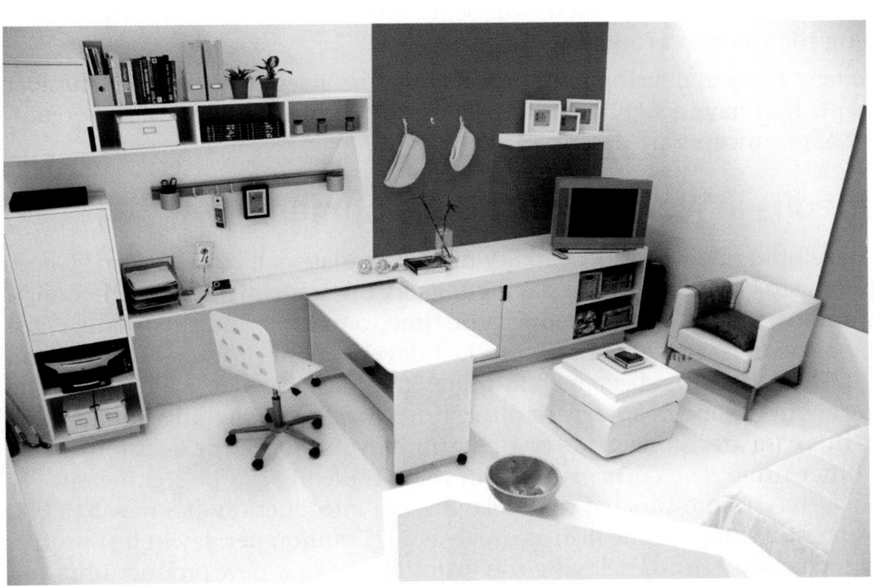

IDEO's full-scale prototype of a new guest room for Marriott TownePlace Suites. Many corporations get assistance with new product development from professional design companies such as IDEO. This example shows IDEO's design of the workspace for an extended-stay hotel suite for Marriott.

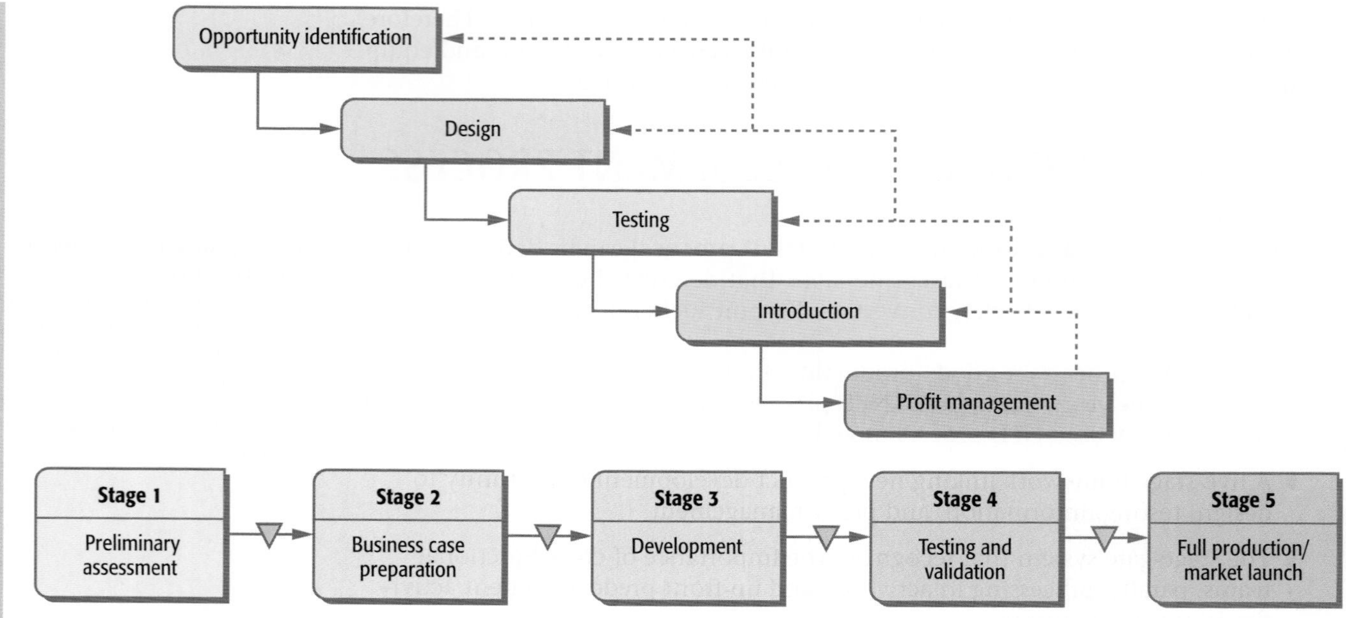

FIGURE 3.3 Two Commonly Used NPD Process Models Primarily for Tangible Goods

Source: **Top portion:** Urban & Houser, *Design and Marketing of New Products,* First Edition, © 1980. Electronically reproduced by permission of Pearson Education, Inc., Upper Saddle River, New Jersey. **Bottom portion:** Cooper, R. G., S. J. Edgett, and E. J. Kleinschmidt, "Optimizing the Stage-Gate Process: What Best-Practice Companies Do—II," *Research Technology Management,* 45 (5), 21–27. Copyright © 2002 by Industrial Research Institute. Reprinted with permission.

Therefore, the idea development part of an NPD process is also known as the "fuzzy front end."

- The NPD process involves multiple and sometimes overlapping steps. At various stages of new product (goods or services) development, the company needs to evaluate whether the idea should be dropped or developed further during the next phase.
- The NPD process requires participation and input from multifunctional teams. It is necessary for members of the marketing, engineering, operations, research and development, and corporate departments to share ideas early and often. Active collaboration ensures that the most promising ideas, considering multiple points of view, will be incorporated in NPD, thereby increasing the chances of success.

The new product development process in a firm needs to consider a number of concepts that have a significant impact on the competitiveness of the organization. These concepts are described next.

Tradeoffs in New Product Development

When developing new products, many project managers have a saying: "Good, fast, and cheap—pick two!" This saying reflects the tradeoffs among the design quality and performance of a product, the time to market, and the product cost that managers must make in a new product development process (Figure 3.5 on page 76) These tradeoffs become still more complicated when we consider the dynamic environment created by multiple firms that are developing similar products. In this case, decisions made by one firm may influence the decisions made by the other firms. The costs involved in these tradeoffs can be significant. For example, it has been estimated that delaying the introduction of a new $15,000 car could cost an automobile firm as much as $1.5 million per day in lost profits. In high technology firms, delaying the introduction of a new product imposes, on average, a penalty of approximately $120 million on firms' market value.

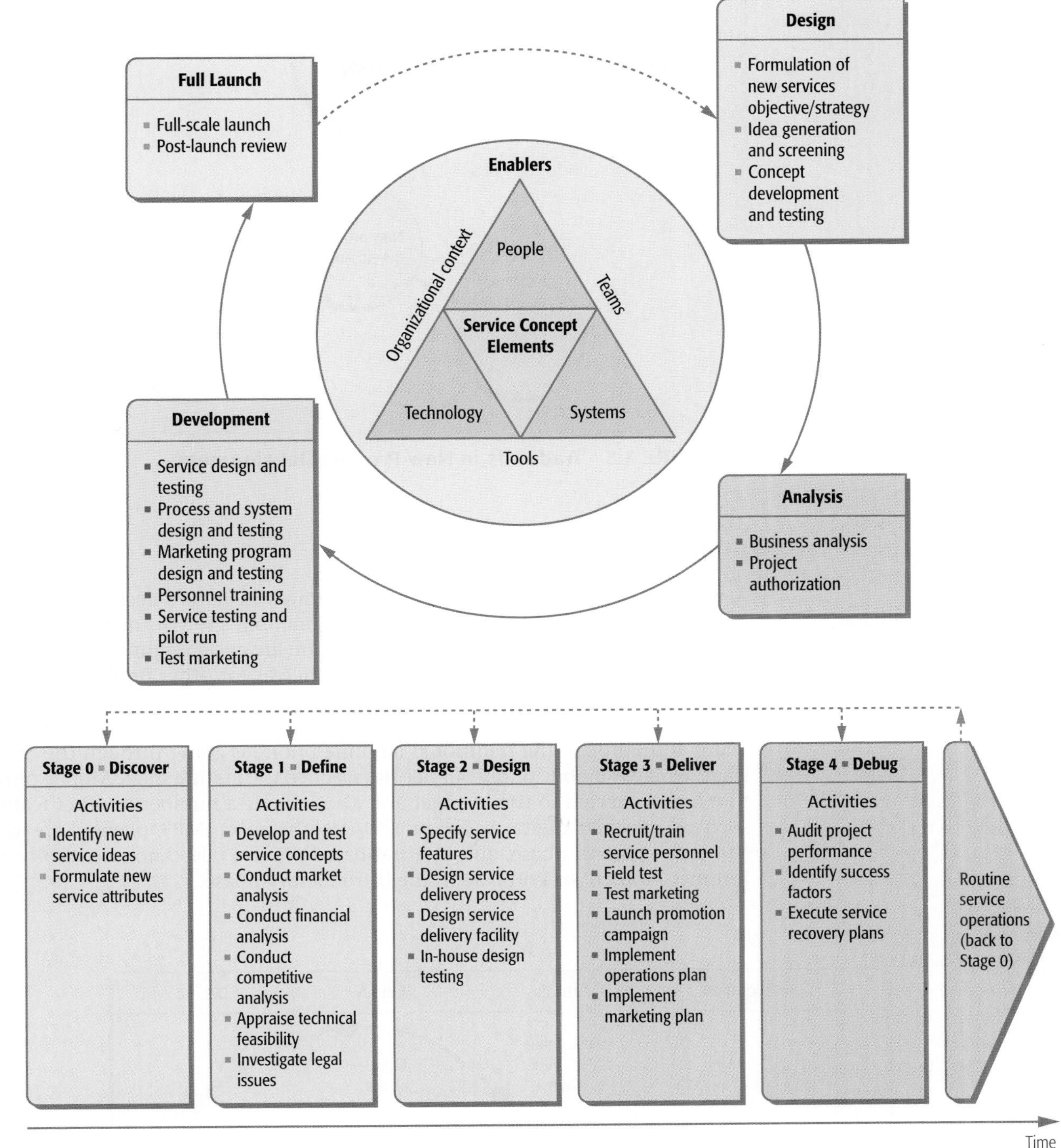

FIGURE 3.4 Selected Models Primarily for New Service Development

Source: **Top portion:** Reprinted from *Journal of Operations Management,* 20 (2), Menor, L. J., M. V. Tatikonda, and S. E. Sampson, "New Service Development: Areas for Exploitation and Exploration," 135–157, Copyright © 2002, with permission from Elsevier. **Bottom portion:** This figure was published in *Handbook of New Product Development* by Tsai W., G. Schmidt, and R. Verma, Copyright © Elsevier, 2007. Reprinted with permission.

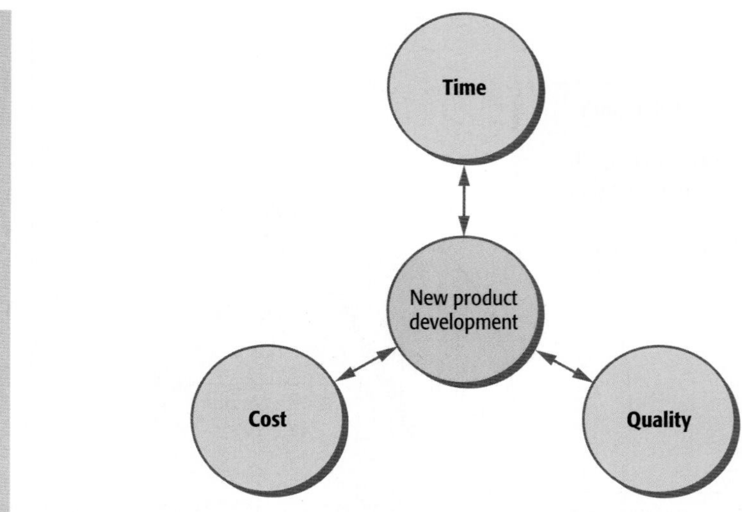

FIGURE 3.5 Tradeoffs in New Product Development

Product Life Cycle

● **Product life cycle** the four stages that a product typically goes through in its life cycle: introduction, growth, maturity, and decline

A typical new product goes through four stages in its life cycle. These stages, known as the **product life cycle,** are introduction, growth, maturity, and decline. For some products, the four stages of the life cycle might be over within a few weeks of the product's initial launch, whereas for other product categories, the life cycle could last for several years. Figure 3.6 shows the four stages of the product life cycle for phone services. In many parts of the world (e.g., the United States and Europe), the traditional landline phone is going through the decline stage, whereas mobile phone service has reached the mature stage. Mobile phones that are connected to the Internet and also include a number of other features, such as personal digital assistant (PDA) software or MP3 players, are going through a growth phase, and Internet-based phones (also known as Voice over Internet Protocol or VoIP) are in the introductory phase.

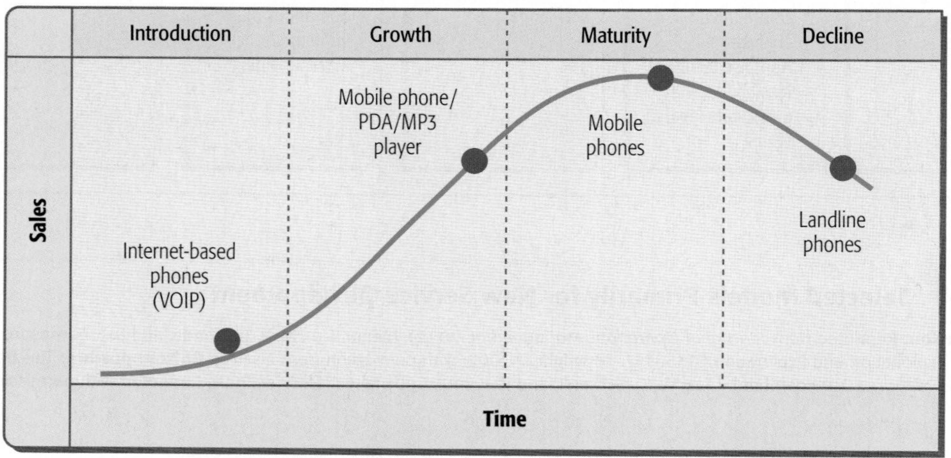

FIGURE 3.6 Product Life Cycle

The characteristics of a product, its demand, competitive pressures, and costs change as it goes through its life cycle. Therefore, different operating decisions become important during different stages, as described here.

Introduction Stage

During the introduction stage, a product is still being fine-tuned and its design is undergoing revisions based on evolving customer feedback and evolving preferences. Typically, the sales revenue for the product is very low during this phase; therefore, the company incurs a net loss on the product. During this period, the manufacturing or the service delivery of the product is still being adjusted, and most processes are not standardized. The competition starts to grow, but there are only a few viable alternatives to the products in the marketplace. The demand has to be created, and potential customers have to be encouraged to try the new product.

Growth Stage

The product design begins to stabilize during the growth stage. The unit cost starts decreasing because production processes have been standardized and because of economies of scale. Sales of products start increasing rapidly, and the firm starts generating additional profits. At the same time, the firm needs additional capital and production resources to cope with the higher demand. Competitive pressures within the marketplace start increasing because several companies start offering competing products.

Maturity Stage

During a product's maturity stage, the production or service delivery processes are standardized; therefore, the unit costs become lower. Sales volume reaches its maximum potential, and there is increased competition, often leading to lower prices for the customer. Competing firms try to differentiate their product offerings from others so that they can increase their market share at the expense of competitors.

Decline Stage

During the decline stage, a product's sales start decreasing, and the firm has to start preparing for its end. The price of products falls because there are many competitors; therefore, firms start divesting resources to other emerging products.

Because most products that companies introduce go through the four life-cycle stages just described, a worthwhile strategy for firms is to continuously innovate so that they always have products at different stages in their sales and growth. This approach ensures that the firm can use its production resources and capacity effectively, as shown in Figure 3.7.

Time-Based Competition

The term **time-based competition** was originally coined by George Stalk Jr. in a 1988 *Harvard Business Review* article entitled "Time—The Next Source of Competitive Advantage." Time-based competition is a broad-based competitive strategy that emphasizes time as the major factor for achieving and maintaining a sustainable competitive advantage. The objective is to significantly compress the time required to propose, develop, produce, market, and deliver products. In other words, the firm needs to develop the ability to minimize the time required

● **Time-based competition** a broad-based competitive strategy that emphasizes time as the major factor for achieving and maintaining a sustainable competitive advantage

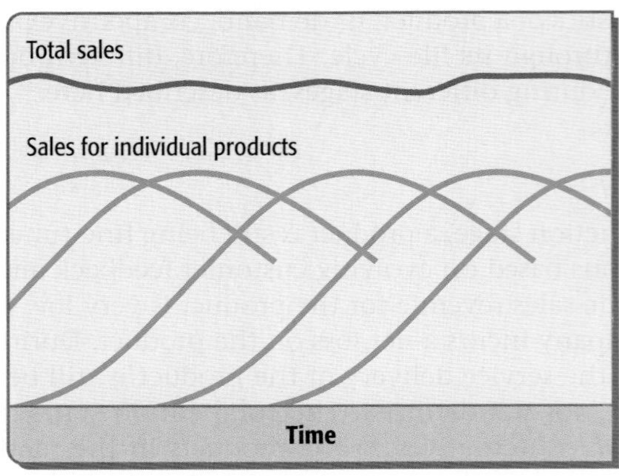

FIGURE 3.7 Multiple Product Life Cycles

to develop new products or make rapid design changes. As product life cycles in many industries are getting shorter, the need for faster product development is increasing. Therefore, time-based competition has become the rule rather than the exception.

Industry Clock Speed

● **Industry clock speed** a measure of the speed of innovation within an industry

The concept of **industry clock speed** suggests that industries evolve at different rates, or "clock speeds," depending on differing opportunities for innovation and competition. For example, high-clock-speed industries, like electronics, see multiple generations of products within short time periods, perhaps even within 12 months. In low-clock-speed industries, like the chemical industry, a generation of products may last as long as five or even ten years. Whether industry clock speeds are slower (e.g., for steel) or faster (e.g., for Internet-based services), any competitive advantage that a company attains is only temporary because each product eventually matures and declines. The faster the industry clock speed, the more temporary the advantage of a firm. Therefore, a company must constantly innovate to maintain its leadership position within the marketplace.

Continuous, Radical, and Disruptive Innovation

The types of new product innovations in both manufacturing and service firms can be classified into three broad categories: continuous, radical, and disruptive innovation.

Continuous Innovation

● **Continuous innovation** a product modification that allows improved performance and benefits without changing either consumption patterns or behavior

The term **continuous innovation** typically refers to a product modification that allows improved performance and benefits without changing either consumption patterns or behavior. The product's general appearance and basic performance do not functionally change. Examples of continuous innovations include adding variety to Kellogg's existing cereal line, adding new menu items in a restaurant, and using a slightly different mix of components for a laptop computer. Continuous innovation might also mean repositioning an existing product for a new market (e.g., vegetarian burgers for McDonald's restaurants in India). A vast majority of new products introduced by companies are the result of a form of incremental or continuous innovation.

Radical and Disruptive Innovation

A new product, generally containing new technologies, that significantly changes behaviors and consumption patterns in the marketplace is known as a **radical innovation.** For example, with the development of the Internet, many consumers are shopping for a variety of products online (e.g., booking a hotel room or purchasing an airline ticket) rather than visiting a store (e.g., a travel agent).

The term **disruptive innovation** is associated with a new product that is initially introduced at a lower quality level along some established criteria but a much superior quality level along a new dimension. For example, mobile phones provide higher mobility than traditional landline phones, but initially they had lower voice quality. Over a period of time, disruptive new products slowly increase their quality along the traditional dimension as well. Research shows that when established companies ignore disruptive innovation, the result is long-term, significant loss of sales and market share. Even if a disruptive innovation is recognized, existing businesses are often reluctant to take advantage of it because it would involve competing with their existing (and more profitable) technological approach. Existing firms should watch for these innovations, invest in small firms that might adopt these innovations, and continue to push technological demands in their core market so that their performance stays above what disruptive technologies can achieve. Several examples of disruptive new products are listed in Table 3.1.

- **Radical innovation** a new product, generally containing new technologies, that significantly changes behaviors and consumption patterns in the marketplace
- **Disruptive innovation** a new product that is initially introduced at a lower quality level along some established criteria but a much superior quality level along a new dimension

TABLE 3.1 Some Examples of Disruptive New Products

Industry	Existing Product	Disruptive Product
Transportation	Horse-driven carriages	Automobiles based on gasoline-powered engines
Transportation	Automobiles based on gasoline-powered engines	Automobiles based on hybrid (gasoline + electric battery) engines
Computers	Mainframe computers	Laptop computers
Computers	Laptop computers	Palm-top computers
Retailing	Shopping center	Internet retailer
Hotels	Large convention and standard hotels	Boutique hotels
Restaurants	Traditional quick-service (or fast-food) establishments	Gourmet, organic, and health food–based restaurants
Communication	Landline phones	Mobile phones
Communication	Mobile phones	Internet-based phones (VoIP)
Photography	Camera using film	Digital cameras
Music	Audio cassettes	Compact disk players
Music	Compact disk players	MP3 players

Red Ocean Strategy	Blue Ocean Strategy
Compete in existing market space	Create uncontested market space
Beat the competition	Make the competition irrelevant
Exploit existing demand	Create and capture new demand
Make the value-cost trade-off	Break the value-cost trade-off
Align the whole system of a firm's activities with its strategic choice of differentiation *or* low cost	Align the whole system of a firm's activities in pursuit of differentiation *and* low cost

http://www.blueoceanstrategy.com © Kim & Mauborgne 2005

FIGURE 3.8 Red and Blue Ocean Strategies of Innovation

Source: © Kim & Maugorgne 2005, www.blueoceanstrategy.com

Blue Ocean Strategy of New Product Innovation

● **Blue ocean strategy** a strategy that suggests that companies should innovate not to compete with products from other companies, but to try to make the competitive products irrelevant

Another concept related to radical or disruptive innovation is commonly known as the **blue ocean strategy.** The premise of this approach to innovation is that companies should innovate not to compete with products from other companies, but simply to try to make the competitive products irrelevant. The "blue oceans" are untapped and uncontested markets that provide little or no competition for anyone who dives in because the markets are not crowded. A "red ocean," on the other hand, refers to a saturated market in which there is fierce competition because it is already crowded with people (companies) providing the same type of services or producing the same kind of goods. Major differences between the two strategies are highlighted in Figure 3.8.

MAJOR CONCEPTS IN NEW PRODUCT DEVELOPMENT

BECAUSE of its extreme importance to businesses, the topic of new product development has been studied extensively and includes a number of concepts, tools, and techniques. In this section, we briefly describe some of the major concepts commonly used in product development.

Product Development for Enhanced Customer Experience

● **Experience economy** the economic progression from commodities to goods, services, and experiences as the main driver of competitive advantage

In recent years, companies in both goods- and service-producing industries have been paying increased attention to the logic of **experience economy** when developing new market offerings. The term *experience economy* was introduced by Pine and Gilmore (1998), who described the economic progression from commodities to goods, services, and experiences as the main driver of competitive advantage. These differences are shown in Figure 3.9.

Economic Offering	Commodities	Goods	Services	Experiences
Economy	Agrarian	Industrial	Service	Experience
Economic function	Extract	Make	Deliver	Stage
Nature of offering	Fungible	Tangible	Intangible	Memorable
Key attribute	Natural	Standardized	Customized	Personal
Method of supply	Stored in bulk	Inventoried after production	Delivered on demand	Revealed over a duration
Seller	Trader	Manufacturer	Provider	Stager
Buyer	Market	User	Client	Guest
Factors of demand	Characteristics	Features	Benefits	Sensations

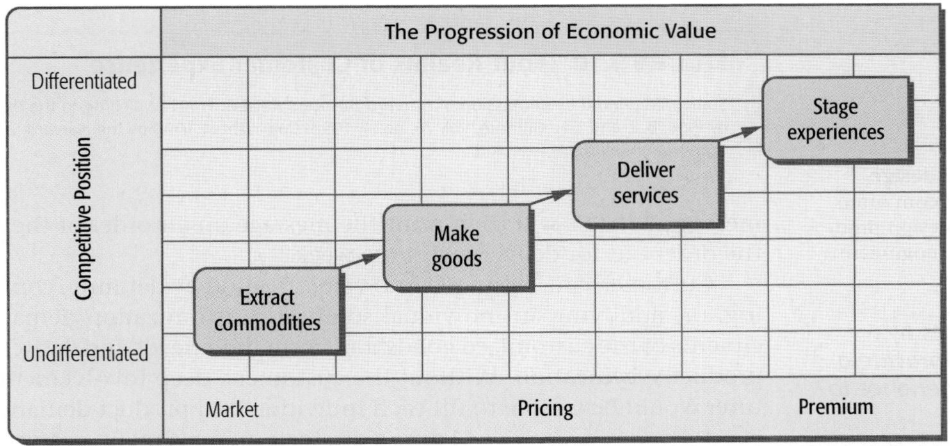

FIGURE 3.9 Economic Progression from Commodities to Goods, Services, and Experiences

Source: Reprinted by permission of *Harvard Business Review.* From "Welcome to the Experience Economy," by Pine, B. J. and J. H. Gilmore, Vol. 76, no. 4, 1998.

Successful experiences are those that the customer finds unique, memorable, and sustainable over time; would want to repeat and build upon; and enthusiastically promotes via word of mouth. But experiences are inherently emotional and personal, so product innovators acknowledge that many of the factors involved are beyond the control of management (e.g., personal interpretation of a situation based on cultural background, prior experience, mood, sensation-seeking personality traits, and many other factors). The key dimensions of customer experiences are described in Figure 3.10.

Mass Customization

Mass customization refers to a process in which individual customers codesign products and services that meet their needs with regard to certain product features. Using advanced technology, all operations are performed within a predefined solution space, characterized by stable but still flexible and responsive processes. As an example, M&M's offers the opportunity to put your own message on the famous candy. Customers can go to the web site (http://www.mymms.com/) and choose from several colors, while typing in a short, customized

● **Mass customization** a process in which individual customers codesign products and services that meet their needs with regard to certain product features

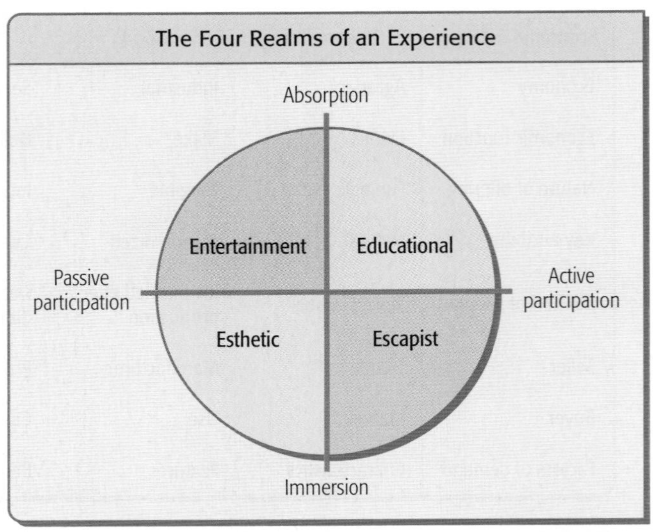

FIGURE 3.10 Four Realms of Customer Experience

Source: Reprinted by permission of *Harvard Business Review.* From "Welcome to the Experience Economy," by Pine, B. J. and J. H. Gilmore, Vol. 76, no. 4, 1998. Copyright © 1998 by the Harvard School Publishing Corporation; all rights reserved.

● **Computer-aided design (CAD)** the use of computers to interactively design products and prepare engineering documentation

message. M&M's will then print the message on an order of the candy and ship the order out for delivery within a week.

Customers are integrated into value creation by defining, configuring, matching, or modifying an individual solution. Customization demands that the recipients of the customized goods transform their needs and desires into a concrete product specification. Without the customers' deep involvement, the manufacturer would be unable to fill each individualized product demand adequately.

Live performances by Cirque du Soleil provide a multisensory experience to the audience.

From a strategic management perspective, mass customization is a differentiation strategy. From a managerial point of view, customization can be carried out with regard to fit, style, and functionality. At the same time, the space within which a mass customization offering is able to satisfy a customer's needs is finite. A successful mass customization system is characterized by stable but still flexible and responsive processes that provide a dynamic flow of products.

Research shows that the customers for mass-customized products are frequently willing to pay a price premium to reflect the increment of value that they gain from having a product that better fits their needs. At the same time, if the price of customization becomes too high, then customers are likely to stay with the standard product.

Computer-Aided Design (CAD) and Virtual Reality

Computer-aided design (CAD) is the use of computers to interactively design products and prepare engineering documentation. CAD software allows designers to save time and money by shortening development cycles for virtually all products. The speed and ease with which sophisticated designs can be manipulated, analyzed, and modified with

BEST PRACTICES IN OPERATIONS MANAGEMENT

Boutique Hotels by Joie de Vivre Hospitality

Hospitality firms, such as hotels, are an ideal example of an industry that could benefit from enhanced customer experiences. The emergence of "boutique" hotels during recent years is an excellent example of an innovative offering in an otherwise standardized industry. The boutique hotel typically features a contemporary or minimalist décor while also offering many additional lifestyle amenities. Hotel guests tend to perceive boutique hotels as stylish locations for which they are willing to pay premium room rates.

Each of the boutique hotels by Joie de Vivre Hospitality in San Francisco and the northern California region provides unique experiences to its customers. The company's mission statement (related to the company name), "creating opportunities to celebrate the joy of life," is demonstrated very clearly by each hotel it operates. Each of the hotels has unique visual styles, uncompromising design principles, one-of-a-kind amenities, and personalized service. For example, the Phoenix Hotel is designed according to a "rock 'n' roll" theme.

The company was started by its current CEO, Chip Conley, when he opened the rock 'n' roll–themed Phoenix Hotel in San Francisco in 1987. Over the last two decades, Phoenix Hotel has regularly hosted many well-known celebrities, such as Norah Jones, Red Hot Chili Peppers, and Keanu Reeves, among others. Now the company has grown considerably, operating 25 boutique hotels and various restaurants, bars, and spas. Its sales were well over $140 million in 2006.

The hotel's innovative goal of providing a unique customer experience can be clearly seen at the company's reservation web site, http://www.jdvhospitality.com/. Here potential customers who want to book a hotel room meet Yvette, the "Hotel Matchmaker." She asks them a number of questions, such as: "What kind of people do you most connect with?" (answers could be fun-loving, active, serene, gentle, charming, professional, or urbane) and "What would best describe your outside interests?" (answers could be romantic, sophisticated, family oriented, and so on). Based on the responses to five questions for which customers select up to two answers each, Yvette recommends hotels that best meet the customer's psychographic profile. Furthermore, the reservation web site also features comments from past visitors and local residents and a list of activities available at the recommended hotel. This approach ensures that the recommended hotel will make a strong emotional connection with the customer.

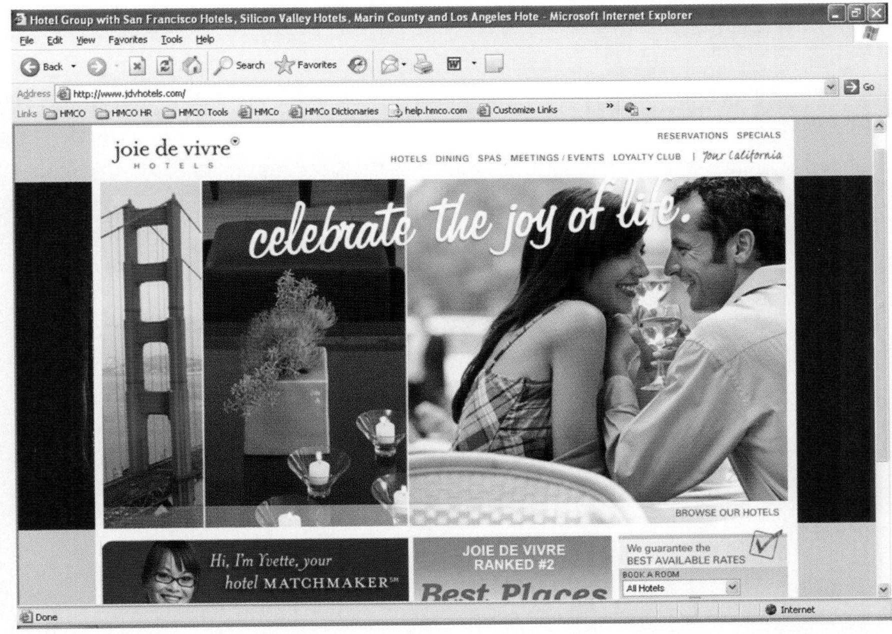

The Joie de Vivre Hospitality reservation web site features Yvette, the "Hotel Matchmaker," plus comments from local residents, recommended activities for guests, and an offer to join the loyalty program known as the "Joy of Life Club."

TECHNOLOGY IN OPERATIONS MANAGEMENT

Mass Customization by Lands' End

A good example of both mass customization and personalization is provided by Lands' End, a catalog retailer. The company is a pioneer in exploring personalization techniques on the Internet and has been using a virtual model and recommendation service on its web site since 1999. The system would recommend a customized bundle of standard mass products that match one another and the customers' style profiles. This service provided customers with a set of coherent outfits rather than with isolated articles of clothing. But each product was still a standard product.

Starting in 2001, Lands' End also introduced mass customization for its customers. Now customers can order made-to-measure trousers and shirts. All products are made to order in a specially assigned factory. The company offers a substantial number of design options and varieties. A customer specifies details such as style, waistline, and length on the Lands' End web site. The specifications are submitted electronically to the factory, which produces the clothes and ships them directly to the customer.

CAD makes the review of numerous options possible before final commitments are made.

CAD also allows designers to quickly investigate many alternatives and consider their potential problems. These efforts make the design cycle shorter and therefore provide the company with an additional competitive advantage. During recent years, CAD techniques have expanded to the world of virtual reality.

● **Virtual reality** a visual form of communication in which images substitute for the real thing but still allow the user to respond interactively

Virtual reality is a visual form of communication in which images substitute for the real thing but still allow the user to respond interactively. The roots of virtual reality technology in operations are in computer-aided design. Once design information is in a CAD system, it is also in digital form for other uses. Virtual reality is also being used to develop 3D layouts of everything from restaurants

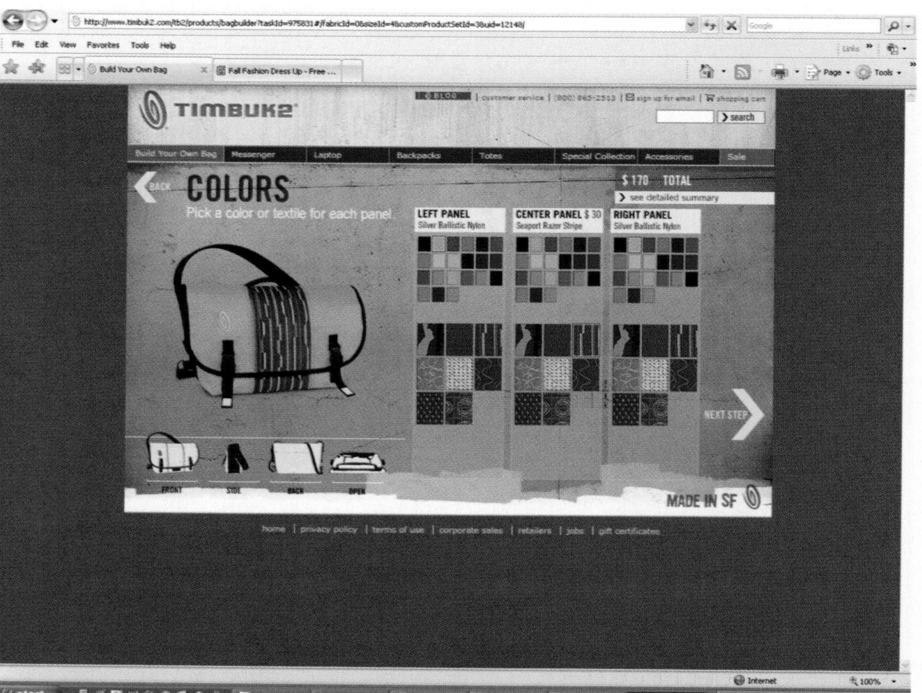

Similar to Land's End, the Timbuk2 web site offers the company's customers many customization options for their orders.

to amusement parks. Changes in a car, restaurant, or ride are made much less expensively at this design stage than they can be later. For example, several products have recently been launched for testing by potential customers at Second Life (www.secondlife.com), a virtual reality–based Internet site. Another example of a virtual reality platform is Google Earth, an example of which is shown in Figure 3.11.

CAD allows designers to view the product in three dimensions and predict its performance and potential failure points.

Design for Production (Manufacturability) and Rapid Prototyping

New product developers can use a variety of components, raw materials, and engineering designs during the design process. However, to ensure that the new product is easy to produce, the designers try to keep the number of parts and components as low as possible. Computer-aided design (CAD), virtual reality, and computer-aided manufacturing (CAM) techniques are utilized to explore various alternatives. These technqies together are known as **design for manufacturability** (DFM).

Furthermore, firms also use an approach known as **rapid prototyping** (RP). RP is a technique for quickly building physical prototypes from the computer-aided design (CAD) data files used to develop three-dimensional drawings while also considering production constraints.

- **Design for manufacturability** the use of a variety of computer-based techniques, such as CAD, virtual reality, and CAM, to develop products that can be manufactured effectively
- **Rapid prototyping** a technique for quickly building physical prototypes from the computer-aided design (CAD) data files used to develop three-dimensional drawings while also considering production constraints

Environmentally Friendly Designs

During recent years, there has been increased awareness of the environmental impact of human progress. The careless use of natural resources can result in irreversible damage to the earth's environment and its habitats. Therefore, there is increased pressure on new product developers to consider the environmental

FIGURE 3.11 Google Earth: Virtual Reality Web Site

This screenshot from Google Earth shows a 3D image of lower Manhattan—the Statue of Liberty can be seen on the lower left-hand side.

impact of any new innovation. At the same time, it is also essential for companies to make customers aware that environmentally friendly new product designs may cost slightly more, at least in the short run.

The good news is that a number of companies in both goods and services industries have started developing new products that are based on environmentally sound practices. For example, in recent years a number of automobile models, such as the Toyota Prius, that use electric and gasoline hybrid engines have appeared in the marketplace. The hybrid engines regenerate power when the car is decelerated or goes down a hill or when the driver applies the brakes. The regenerated power is used to charge a high-capacity battery. The battery power is used when it is inefficient to use the gasoline engine (e.g., when the car is waiting at a stoplight). Therefore, the car uses less gasoline, produces less exhaust, and releases fewer greenhouse gases into the atmosphere. Another example of environmentally friendly design is the use of paper cups and plates (often partially made from recycled paper) instead of Styrofoam at quick-service restaurants.

- **Green production** techniques that include reducing wastes and emissions during production and assessing the total impact of a good or service on the environment, taking into account every activity associated with the production and supply of that good or service
- **Design for disassembly** designing products so that they are easy to take apart once they're discarded

However, environmentally friendly new product design means more than just the features of the goods produced or the service delivered. It also means reducing the product's impact on the environment by practicing "green production" techniques. **Green production** techniques include reducing wastes and emissions during production and assessing the total impact of a good or service on the environment, taking into account every activity associated with the production and supply of that good or service. Chapter 2 describes an industry standard known as ISO 14000, which is used to certify companies that have achieved high environmental quality standards. Another concept is known as **design for disassembly** (DFD), which means that products should be designed so that it is easy to take them apart once they're discarded. This approach allows the usable parts of the product to be recycled and only the unusable parts to be discarded. For example, many computer ink-jet printer cartridges are now designed so that they can be refilled, thus eliminating the need for discarding a used cartridge's shell.

Modular Design

- **Modular design** products designed as independent subproducts that are attached to create a final product

Some products are designed as independent subproducts that are attached to create a final product. This approach is known as **modular design.** A modular design enhances the efficiency and flexibility of both the production and the marketing functions. For example, in designing computers, Dell uses the concept of modular design to keep a minimum inventory of raw materials and components but still rapidly satisfy the needs of its large number of customers. The concept of product modularity also assists in the development of an efficient supply chain for the products. For example, Dell assembles the finished products (computers), but the individual modules used (e.g., the hard disk, DVD-ROM, microprocessor, and display panels) are finished products from its suppliers. Because of modular design, Dell is able to directly assemble the products made by its suppliers according to the configurations specified by its customers (Figure 3.12).

The Toyota Prius runs on a hybrid engine that regenerates power when the driver brakes or decelerates.

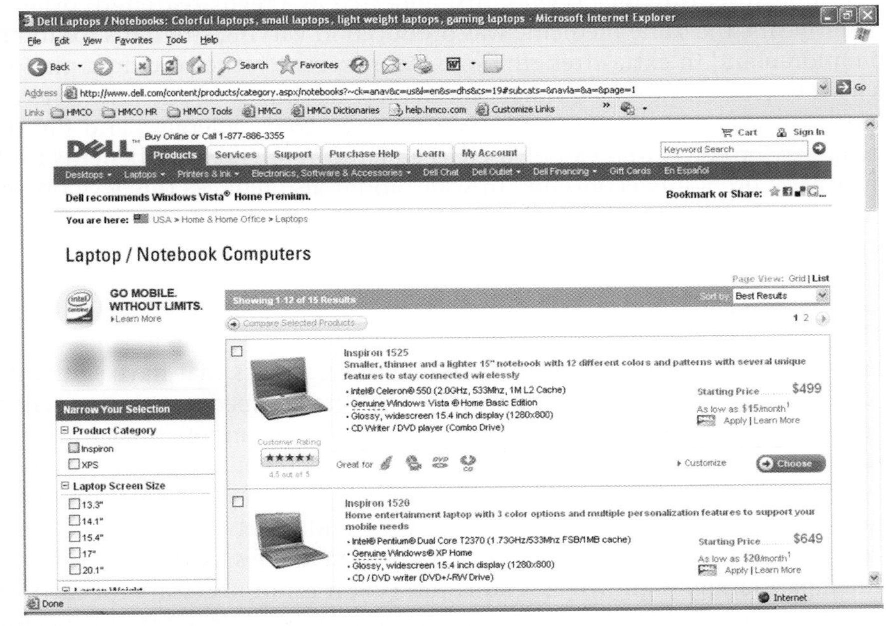

FIGURE 3.12 Dell Ordering Web Site

Dell uses the principles of modular design to assemble final products quickly and ship them to its customers within a few hours.

Concurrent Engineering

● **Concurrent engineering** the practice of designing products and developing the production process concurrently in an integrated fashion, using a cross-functional team, rather than having them performed sequentially by separate functions

The practice of **concurrent engineering** (CE) implies that product design and production process development occur concurrently in an integrated fashion, using a cross-functional team, rather than being performed sequentially by separate functions. CE is intended to facilitate the development team in considering all elements of the product life cycle from conception through disposal, including quality, cost, and maintenance, from the project's outset. Bose Corporation, the manufacturer of high-quality speakers and audio systems, takes the concept of concurrent engineering one step further by actually allowing the employees of its suppliers to have offices at Bose facilities and participate in its product development efforts. Such collaboration allows Bose engineers to identify design problems early in the development process and also come up with more effective design ideas.

Product Platforms

● **Product platform** a commonly used technique for developing a variety of products based on common structures or basic architectures

A **product platform** is a commonly used technique for developing a variety of products using common structures or basic architectures. These platforms are the basis of a series of products that may be commercialized over a number of years. For example, the painkiller Tylenol first appeared as a regular-strength drug. After a few years, the same medicine was produced in varying strengths for infants and children and in extra-strength doses. More recently, the core drug platform was used to create a variety of other products for treatment of other illnesses that appear along with headache and body pain (e.g., colds, allergies, and flu). Designing new products that can be used as a platform offers many benefits to the company by providing economies of scale, and it also reduces the development life cycle of subsequent products. Several examples of product platforms are presented in Figure 3.13.

Group Technology

● **Group technology** an approach in which product parts that have similarities (in shape, usage, and/or manufacturing process) are grouped together to achieve a higher level of integration between the product design and manufacturing

● **Part family** a group of similar parts

● **Machine cell** the group of machines used to process an individual part family

● **Cellular manufacturing** the type of manufacturing in which a part family is produced by a machine cell

Group technology is an approach in which product parts that have similarities (in shape, usage, and/or manufacturing process) are grouped together to achieve a higher level of integration between the product design and manufacturing. GT is based on the general principle that many product design and production problems are similar. By grouping parts with similar problems, a single solution to these problems can be found, thus saving time and effort. The group of similar parts is known as a **part family,** and the group of machines used to process an individual part family is known as a **machine cell.** It is not necessary for each part in a part family to be processed by every machine in the corresponding machine cell. This type of manufacturing, in which a part family is produced by a machine cell, is known as **cellular manufacturing.**

Reverse Engineering

● **Reverse engineering** the process of discovering the technological principles of a new product through the analysis of its structure, function, and operation

Reverse engineering (RE) is the process of discovering the technological principles of a new product through the analysis of its structure, function, and operation. It often involves taking the new product apart and analyzing its components and functionalities in detail, usually to try to make a new device or program that does the same thing without copying anything from the original.

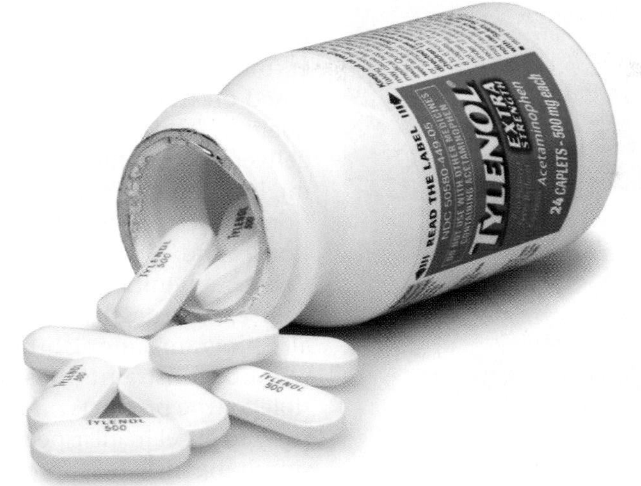

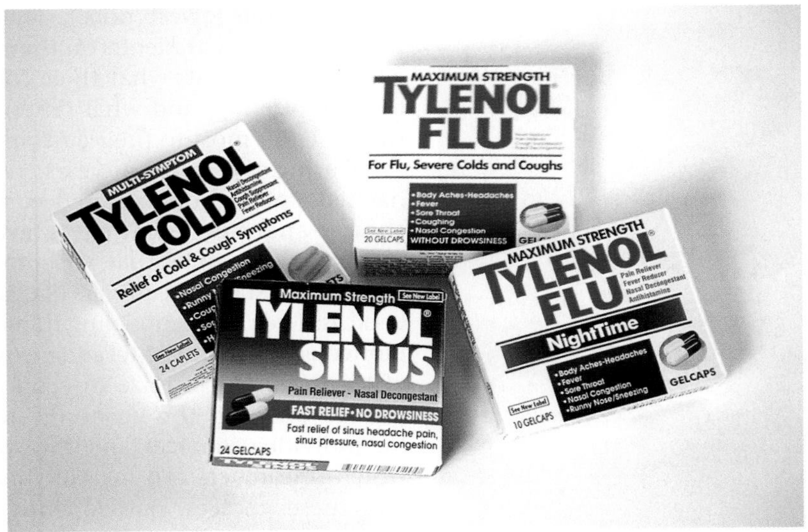

FIGURE 3.13 Example of a Product Platform

ANALYSIS TOOLS FOR NEW PRODUCT DEVELOPMENT

AS discussed earlier in this chapter, new product development in the manufacturing and service industries is an important but very wide and diverse topic. Therefore, companies use a number of tools and techniques to undertake their new product development efforts effectively. This section describes some of the commonly used techniques in NPD.

● Customer Choice Analysis

Incorporating customer preferences and choices into new product development decisions is extremely important for most competitive businesses because

Can the apparent similarities between fiercely competing products such as the Honda Accord (top) and Ford Taurus (bottom) be explained by the use of reverse engineering by one of the competitors?

● **Customer choice analysis** an experimental approach to identify the relative importance of various product features for customer choices

their customers evaluate them on more than one criterion. For example, customers might choose fast-food establishments based on their cost, service quality, food quality, food variety, and/or speed of delivery attributes. Similarly, customers might choose a hotel based on its location (close to the airport, tourist attractions, and downtown), brand name, various amenities (swimming pool, golf course, or fitness center), price, and loyalty program, among other things. Given resource constraints, it is virtually impossible for the products offered by one company to excel in all aspects of the product simultaneously (e.g., provide the highest quality, the fastest delivery, and the most variety at the lowest price). Therefore, firms must make tradeoffs on the basis of what they do best, what their competitors are offering, and what criteria they think matter most to their customers.

During the last few years, research has redefined a sophisticated **customer choice analysis** tool that is available to those companies that wish to accurately understand the drivers of customer choices. The choice modeling framework, pioneered by Daniel McFadden (winner of the 2000 Nobel Prize in economics), focuses on both the economic reasons for individual choices and the ways in which researchers can measure and predict these choices. Subsequently there have been many diverse applications of this tool, such as design and development of new products and services, transportation and logistics planning, evaluation of alternative pricing strategies, financial services design, and supplier selection, among others.

The customer choice modeling approach requires a representative sample of customers to make choices in simulated situations derived from realistic variations of actual product offerings. The process typically comprises three broad steps

First, using qualitative market assessment, customer interviews, case studies, industry data, focus groups, and other information sources, a list of drivers that are believed to influence customers' buying decisions is compiled. For example, for a food-service operation at an airport terminal, the relevant product features might be type of food (Italian, Chinese, Mexican, deli, or hot dog), variety, waiting time, brand name, and price. For an upscale hotel operation, the relevant drivers might be brand name, personalization and customization options, amenities (spa, golf course, swimming pool, and fitness center), office facilities, and so on. Once the list of choice drivers is finalized, sophisticated experimental design techniques are used to develop many realistic versions of product offerings.

The next step involves constructing "choice experiments" that ask respondents to select one out of two or more services available to them in a series of "choice sets." In the final phase, econometric models based on responses from a representative sample of customers (or potential future customers) are used to identify key patterns in the survey responses, providing a relative weighting for each market driver and for interactions among drivers. Managers can then select the optimal combination of operations and market drivers in order to develop a profitable and sustainable value proposition that, given normal competitive constraints, will maximally leverage their available resources. The resulting models are used to calculate **willingness to pay** and **desirability** for new product features and also to conduct many "what-if" types of analysis. Two examples of spreadsheet models based on customer choice studies for the restaurant and hotel industries are described in Figure 3.14 on pages 92–93.

- **Willingness to pay** the amount a customer is willing to pay for a new product configuration
- **Desirability** the relative attractiveness of a new product offering

Product Reliability Analysis

Product reliability analysis is an approach for assessing the overall integrity of a product based on the configuration of its components. For example, while a large commercial airplane may have four engines, it can still fly a full load of passengers and cargo with only two or three engines, although not at the same speed. Therefore, the addition of the third or fourth engine not only enhances the performance of the airplane, but also increases its reliability.

- **Product reliability analysis** an approach for assessing the overall integrity of a product based on the configuration of its components

Product reliability analysis is a detailed science that is built heavily on probability, statistics, and uncertainty theories. A care analysis of product design is conducted throughout the development stage to identify the potential failure points and possible solutions. Reliability analysis begins with the development of a model of the proposed new product, using block diagrams and fault trees to provide a graphical means of evaluating the relationships between different parts of the system. Such a model incorporates predictions based on parts-count failure rates taken from historical data. While the predictions are often not accurate in an absolute sense, they are valuable for assessing relative differences in design alternatives.

One of the most important design techniques is **redundancy.** This means that, if one part of the system fails, there is an alternative success path, such as a backup system. Redundancy significantly increases system reliability and is often the only viable means of doing so. However, redundancy is difficult and expensive and is therefore limited to critical parts of the system.

- **Redundancy** the use of backup components and systems to enhance the reliability of a product

Another related concept is known as **robust design.** This means that the product is designed so that small variations in production or assembly do not adversely affect the quality of the product. Many of the commonly used robust design techniques were pioneered by Taguchi, who used advanced statistical concepts such as experimental design and loss functions to assess and enhance product reliability.

- **Robust design** a design approach that ensures that small variations in the production process do not adversely affect the quality of the product

Product-Complexity Index

The **product-complexity index** is the critical parameter that a firm needs in order to estimate the design levels and prices for a new product. Research has shown that the product-complexity index is equal to the maximum price/cost ratio multiplied by a "difficulty scale." Some examples of a product-complexity index are given in Table 3.2. This index is used to assess the relative ease or difficulty in developing a product.

- **Product-complexity index** the critical parameter that a firm needs in order to estimate the design levels and prices for a new product

Quality Function Deployment

Quality function deployment (QFD) has been recognized as an effective method for integrated product and process development. QFD is a structured approach

- **Quality function deployment** a structured approach for systematically integrating customer requirements into every aspect of product development, from planning to the production floor

Competitors	Alpha	Beta	Gamma	Delta
Type of restaurant	Burger	Pizza	Hot Dog	Deli
Brand name	2	2	1	1
A local chain (1)				
A national chain (2)				
Variety	2	1	1	3
Low (1)				
Medium (2)				
High (3)				
Wait time to order	2	3	1	3
0–2 mins (1)				
3–4 mins (2)				
5–6 mins (3)				
Service wait	2	2	1	3
0–2 mins (1)				
3–4 mins (2)				
5–6 mins (3)				
Picture display of menu items	2	2	1	3
None (1)				
For a few special items (2)				
For all popular items (3)				
Price of a combo meal	2	3	1	3
$4 (1)				
$5 (2)				
$6 (3)				
$7 (4)				
$8 (5)				

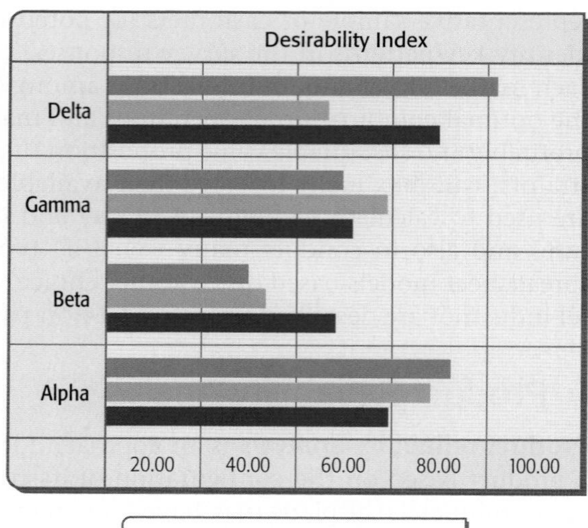

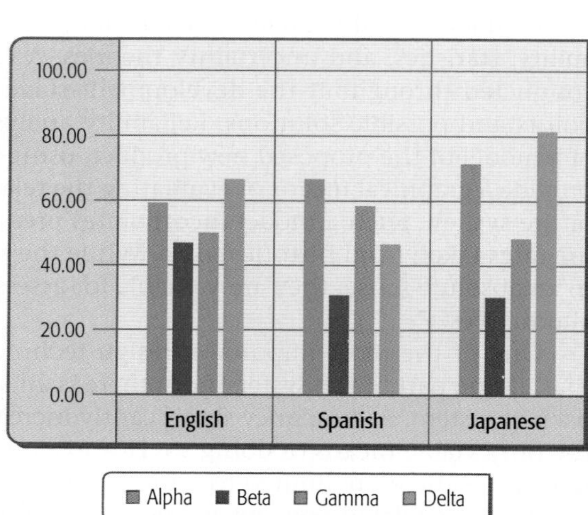

FIGURE 3.14 Product Design Decision Support Simulator

Spreadsheet-based decision-support simulation models are derived from customer choice analysis to prioritize and make tradeoffs among features in new product development. (Note: The interactive version of these decision-support simulations is available at the textbook web site, www.cengage.com/management.)

Type of Hotel	Economy	Midrange	Upscale
BUSINESS travelers	$43.15	$105.71	$170.05
LEISURE travelers	$43.51	$105.97	$164.57
Loyalty program	1	2	2
None (1)			
1FF mile/$ spent (2)			
2FF miles/$ spent (3)			
3FF miles/$ spent (4)			
Check-in/check-out options	1	1	1
Check-in 3 pm; check-out noon (1)			
Any 24-hour cycle (2)			
Room personalization options	1	1	2
Not available (1)			
Available for frequent guests (2)			
Pet policy	2	2	1
Pets not allowed (1)			
Small pets allowed (2)			
High speed internet access	3	2	1
Available for $10.00/day (1)			
Available for $5.00/day (2)			
Available for free (3)			
Business center	1	2	4
Not available (1)			
A centrally located business center (2)			
Multiple business kiosks located throughout the facilities (3)			
Mini-business center (printer, fax, etc.) available in room (4)			
Restaurant facilities	1	2	3
None on site (1)			
In-house casual dining facilities (2)			
In-house casual and formal dining facilities (3)			
Swimming pool	1	2	3
None on site (1)			
Outdoor pool (2)			
Indoor heated pool (3)			
Childcare facilities	2	2	3
Not available (1)			
In-room nanny facility at extra charge (2)			
In-room nanny facility and kids' club (6–12 yrs.) at extra charge (3)			
In-room kitchen facilities	1	2	2
Coffeemaker only (1)			
Coffeemaker, fridge, and microwave oven (2)			
A complete small kitchenette (3)			
Airport shuttle service	1	2	3
Not available (1)			
Airport shuttle available for extra charge (2)			
Free shuttle to airport (3)			
Fitness center	1	2	3
Not available (1)			
Access to on-site facility for extra charge (2)			
Free on-site fitness center (3)			

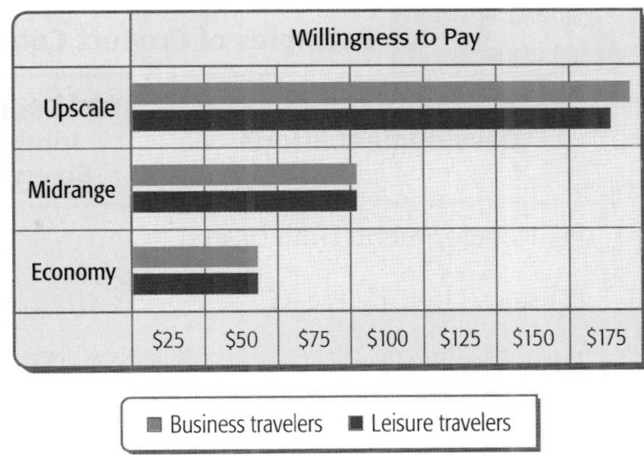

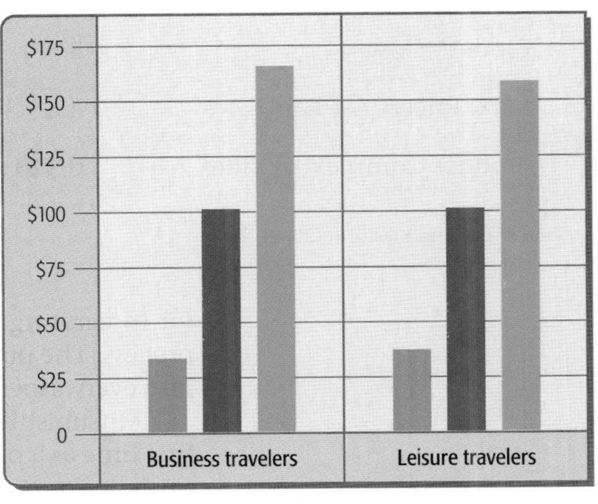

FIGURE 3.14 Product Design Decision Support Simulator (*continued*)

TABLE 3.2 Examples of Product Complexity Index

Development Efforts	Stanley Jobmaster Screwdriver	Volkswagen New Beetle	Rollerblade In-Line Skate	Hewlett-Packard Desk-Jet Printer
(1) Development Time (years)	1	3.5	2	1.5
(2) sales Lifetime (years)	40	6	3	2
Difficulty Scale = (1)/(2)	0.025	0.583	0.667	0.75
Sales Price	$3	$17,000	$200	$300
Max. Sales Price	$4.5	$25,500	$300	$450
Product Cost	$1	$9,550	$80	$84
Max. Price/Cost Ratio	4.5	2.67	3.75	5.36
Product Complexity Index	0.113	1.56	2.51	4.02

Source: Tsai and Klastorin (2004).

for integrating the voice of the customer into the product design/development process. The purpose of QFD is to ensure that customer requirements are factored into every aspect of product development, from planning to the production floor.

Mitsubishi's Kobe shipyard is credited with developing and using QFD for the first time as a product/process design tool in 1972. Shortly thereafter, building on earlier efforts at Mitsubishi, Toyota developed advanced QFD concepts and has used the technique since 1977, with very impressive results. Since then, a number of companies in Japan, the United States, Europe, and the rest of the world have implemented QFD, with good results. Xerox and Ford initiated the use of QFD in the United States in 1986. Recently, leading companies including General Motors, Motorola, Kodak, IBM, Procter & Gamble, AT&T, and Hewlett-Packard have successfully used QFD for product/process design and development. An overview of the QFD process is presented in Table 3.3.

QFD uses a series of matrices, which look like houses, to deploy customer input throughout the design, manufacturing, and delivery of products. The premise is that cooperation and communication among marketing, manufacturing, engineering, and R&D lead to greater new product success.

The first QFD matrix, called the *House of Quality,* links the voice of the customer to the product design attributes (*voice of the engineer*). The second matrix (*Design Matrix*) of QFD links the design attributes to the product components or features. The *Operating Matrix* further links the product components to process decisions. Finally, the *Control Matrix* links the operating processes to production planning and control decisions. Completing all four matrices will allow managers to identify and control the critical process parameters and therefore lead to effective product and process development. Figure 3.15 shows the relationship among the four QFD matrices. The QFD concepts presented in Table 3.3 and Figure 3.15 can be implemented for almost any good or service.

TABLE 3.3 The Quality Function Deployment (QFD) Process

Step 1	Identification of customer needs and preferences
Step 2	Relationship between customer needs and engineering design characteristics
Step 3	Interrelationships among the engineering design characteristics
Step 4	Competitive evaluation of competing products and targets for design attributes
Step 5	Linking engineering design characteristics and component characteristics
Step 6	Linking component characteristics and the process operations
Step 7	Linking the process operations and control parameters
Step 8	Implementation and continuous improvement

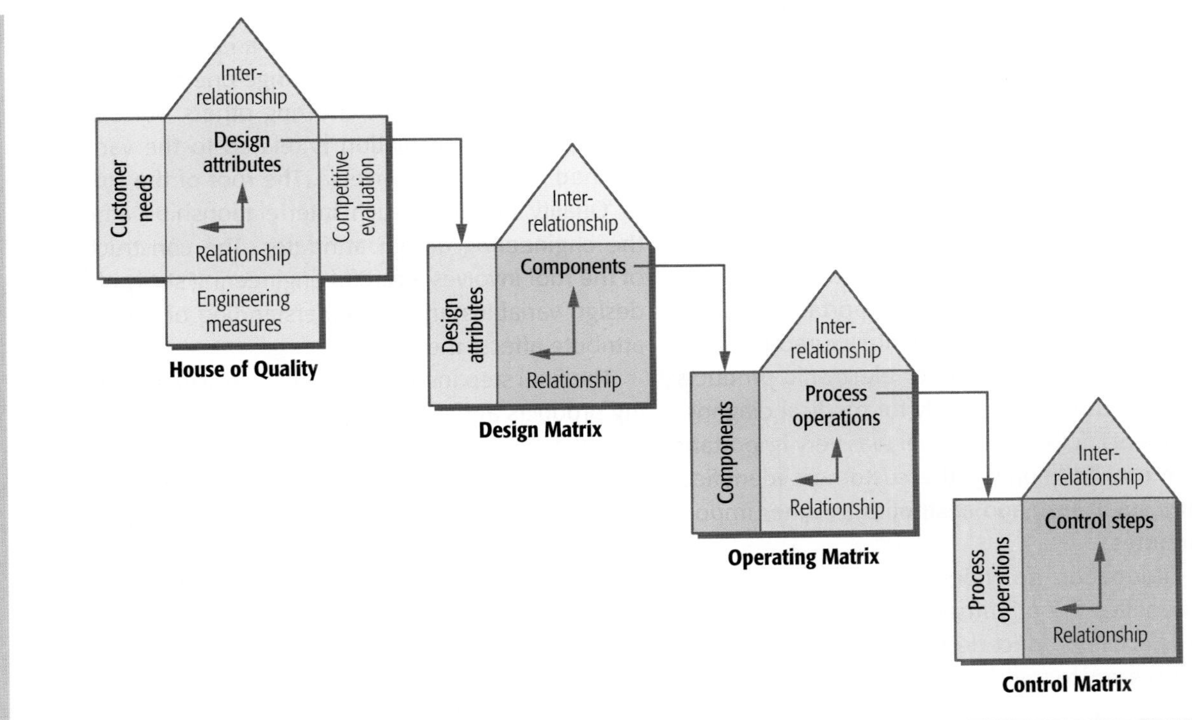

FIGURE 3.15 The QFD Process

BEST PRACTICES IN OPERATIONS MANAGEMENT

Use of Quality Function Deployment in the Design, Development, and Production of Electrical Transformers

Here we present a quality function deployment example for the design and manufacturing of electrical transformers by HighTrans Inc. (the actual name of the company is disguised for confidentiality reasons).

Constructing the House of Quality

Figure 3.16 (on page 98) shows a completed House of Quality for HighTrans Inc.. The next paragraphs describe various components of the construction of the House of Quality.

Customer needs were determined jointly by the staff members in marketing, sales, and engineering because all three groups interact with the customer. The information was obtained through interviews, surveys, and brainstorming over several months. One production manager was responsible for information collection and for the development of the four QFD matrices, while other members of the organization provided feedback (in individual or group settings) whenever necessary. The customers identified cost and product reliability as the two most important attributes of the transformers. They emphasized that the transformers should be reliable and should meet the legal regulations at the lowest possible cost. They also regarded on-time delivery as very important. A low rate of temperature rise in a transformer was identified as another important product attribute. Conforming to industrial and professional standards was also considered to be very important. Because several types of transformers manufactured by HighTrans Inc. are installed in other electronic products (for example, the power supply for medical diagnostic equipment), a low noise level was very important to customers. Additionally, the customers identified efficiency, small size, and aesthetics as other important attributes.

The information described in the previous paragraph identifies the prioritized needs of the customers. For effective product design and development, it is also necessary to translate those customer requirements into the relevant engineering design attributes of the product. Therefore, the next task was to identify the engineering design attributes of the transformers that are linked to customer needs.

An electrical transformer consists of metallic coil(s) (mostly copper or copper alloys) that are tightly wound over a stack of metallic lamination sheets. The finished transformer is used as a device for controlling electric current and/or voltage in the power module for various products (audio systems, medical equipment, and power supply lines). Even though the exact engineering specifications are different for different types of transformers, the following six product elements were identified by the engineering staff as being most important for all types of transformers: wire size, number of wire turns, lamination stack size, varnish method, insulation type, and design for manufacturability. The wire size, the number of turns, and the lamination stack directly affect the properties of the electromagnetic field generated in the transformer. The varnish and insulation processes are required for controlling the quality of the transformer properties. Finally, it is necessary for the transformer design to be manufacturable.

For a complex product such as an electrical transformer, it is often difficult to change one engineering design attribute without affecting others. For example, transformer insulation is related to the varnish method used, and vice versa. The roof of the House of Quality identifies such interrelationships among the engineering design attributes. The construction of the roof involves a careful engineering study of the design variables and an understanding of how one attribute affects the others.

The final step involves identifying existing competing products and evaluating them in terms of each of the customer preferences. Such evaluation helps in highlighting the relative strengths and weaknesses of the current product offerings and provides the product development personnel with directions for improvement. It also provides an opportunity for identifying the "selling points."

For example, the right side of Figure 3.16 shows the competitive evaluation of transformers for HighTrans Inc. (marked as X) and two of its major competitors (A and B) on a scale of 1 to 5 (5 = best; 1 = worst). The competitive evaluation of customer requirements was conducted by feedback received from customers

(continued)

by sales, engineering, and quality control staff. The evaluation of the technical requirements was completed by performing a benchmarking study as well as by obtaining customer feedback. The transformer manufactured by HighTrans Inc. is better than its competitors on almost all customer-based attributes except cost and efficiency. The delivery performance and low noise level for HighTrans Inc.'s transformers are much better than those of its competitors and therefore are selling points for the company. Because HighTrans Inc.'s transformers have better quality than the competitors' on more than one dimension, it can target its products to the high end of the market.

The "basement" of the House of Quality presents the engineering targets for process improvement. This space can also be utilized to develop a competitive evaluation of the competing products on the basis of engineering design attributes. Often this step involves benchmarking and/or reverse engineering the competitors' products. The target levels and competitive engineering evaluation provide further guidelines for translating customer information to the rest of the product/process development process.

Constructing the Other Three QFD Houses (or Matrices)

The previous section described the construction of the first QFD matrix: the House of Quality. The remaining three houses in QFD connect the product engineering characteristics to individual components, production processes, and control parameters.

The second QFD matrix, the Design Matrix, links the engineering design attributes to the individual components of the product. This matrix can be constructed either for all engineering design attributes from the House of Quality or for a selected few important attributes. Like the House of Quality, the Design Matrix requires a careful analysis of the product, its components, and the manufacturing processes. The roof of the design matrix presents the interrelationships among the component characteristics. As in the House of Quality, the basement of the Design Matrix can be used for engineering targets for the components.

The third QFD matrix, the Operating Matrix, connects the components to key process operations. The role of the fourth QFD matrix, the Control Matrix, is to develop specific quality control plans for key operating processes (from the Operating Matrix). Developing control parameters for the key process operations is necessary for effective operations management because these processes manufacture the components for the products that satisfy customer needs.

Detailed descriptions of the Design Matrix, Operating Matrix, and Control Matrix for HighTrans Inc. are presented at the textbook website. @

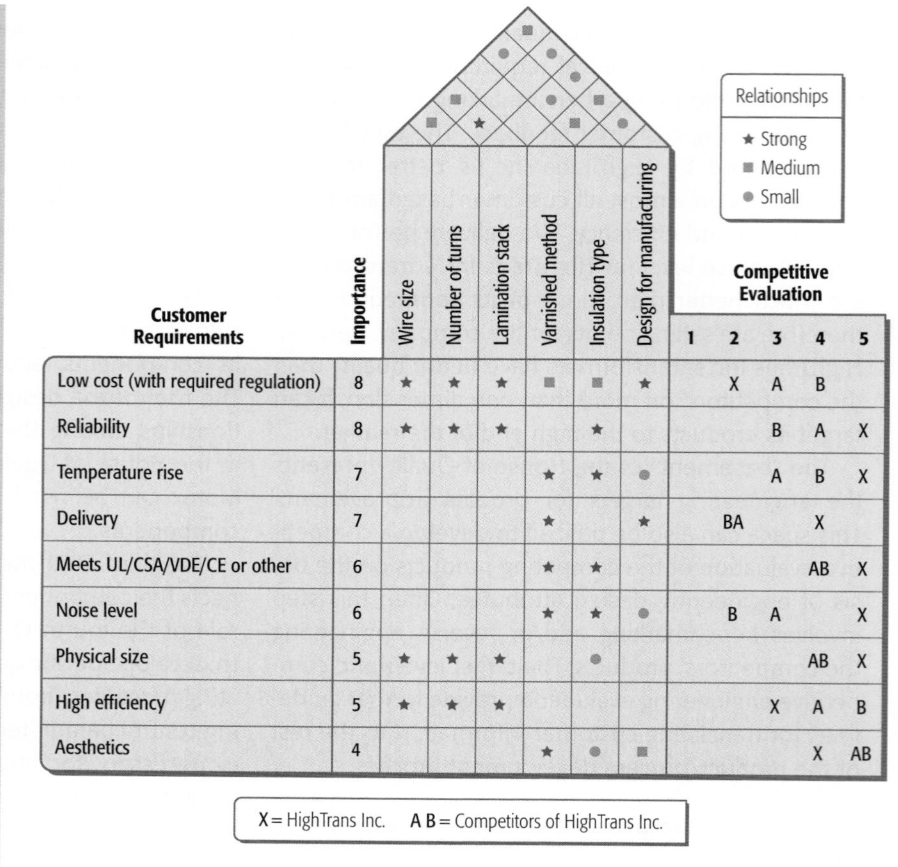

Customer Requirements	Importance	Wire size	Number of turns	Lamination stack	Varnished method	Insulation type	Design for manufacturing	1	2	3	4	5
Low cost (with required regulation)	8	★	★	★	■	■	★		X	A	B	
Reliability	8	★	★	★		★				B	A	X
Temperature rise	7				★	★	●			A	B	X
Delivery	7				★		★		BA		X	
Meets UL/CSA/VDE/CE or other	6				★	★					AB	X
Noise level	6				★	★	●		B	A		X
Physical size	5	★	★	★		●					AB	X
High efficiency	5	★	★	★						X	A	B
Aesthetics	4				★	●	■				X	AB

FIGURE 3.16 The House of Quality

SUMMARY

1. Describe the importance of new product development to a firm's success or failure.

- New products fail for a variety of reasons, such as poor market research, product defects, poor timing of introduction, ineffective marketing campaigns, higher than expected costs, supply problems, and competition.
- Manufacturing and service companies invest resources in new product development because it can provide opportunities for additional competitiveness, revenue, and market share and enhance the corporate image.

2. Describe the new product development process, the product life cycle, and different strategies and tradeoffs in product innovation.

- The new product development process involves multiple and sometimes overlapping steps. At various stages of new product (goods or services) development, the company needs to evaluate whether the idea should be dropped or developed further during the next phase.
- The NPD process needs to consider the tradeoff among cost, timing, and quality.
- There are several different strategies for new product innovation, such as radical or disruptive innovation and the blue ocean strategy. Therefore, a firm needs to consider the life cycle of its products, the industry clock speed, and other characteristics unique to its own environment when developing a new product.

3. Learn different concepts in new product development, such as designing for enhanced customer experience, mass customization, virtual reality, rapid prototyping, environmentally friendly design, modular design, concurrent engineering, product platforms, group technology, and reverse engineering.

- Successful experiences are those that the customer finds unique, memorable, and sustainable over time; would want to repeat and build upon; and enthusiastically promotes via word of mouth.
- Mass customization allows companies to create products based on unique customer needs without significantly high costs.
- Computer-based techniques such as rapid prototyping, CAD, and virtual reality allow firms to evaluate complex product design alternatives successfully.
- Firms use a number of complementary approaches, such as modular design, product platforms, group technology, and reverse engineering, to develop new products effectively.

4. Learn important new product development analysis techniques, such as customer choice analysis, reliability analysis, product-complexity index, and quality function deployment.

- Customer choice analysis allows firms to assess the desirability of and willingness to pay for potential new product offerings.
- Reliability analysis and the product-complexity index are used to assess the robustness of the design and its relationship with costs in the new product development process.
- The four houses of quality function deployment connect customer needs with engineering design characteristics, components, production processes, and associated control parameters.

QUESTIONS

1. Compare and contrast continuous innovation, radical innovation, and the blue ocean strategy of product innovation.
2. Describe how new products can be introduced to enhance customer experiences within the following industries:
   (a) A fast-food store
   (b) A retail store
   (c) An airline terminal
   (d) A dentist's office
   (e) A bank branch
3. Describe a few products that are in the different stages in their life cycle within the following industries:
   (a) Pharmaceutical
   (b) Computer
   (c) Automobile
   (d) Hotel
   (e) Healthcare
   (f) Entertainment
4. Give two examples, one from manufacturing and the other from a service industry, of companies or products that use the following concepts:
   (a) Mass customization
   (b) Computer-aided design or virtual reality
   (c) Environmentally friendly design
   (d) Modular design
   (e) Product platform
5. Identify a successful good and a successful new service that were recently introduced in the marketplace. Also identify a failed new good and a failed new service that were recently introduced in the marketplace. List the reasons for the successes and failures of these four new products.

Note: The textbook website will contain additional questions for customer choice analysis, reliability analysis, product-specific index, and QFD. @

CASE STUDY

Boutique Hotels

Currently, there is no one definition of a boutique hotel; however, most people think of a boutique hotel as a small, upscale hotel with a hip environment where the customers feel connected to the staff.

> The beauty of the boutique segment is that it provides a wide range of opportunity for developers. Unlike the name implies, boutique properties no longer have to be small to fit into the category; they can have hundreds of rooms. What hotels do need to have to enter into the expanding segment is panache, some roster of unique features, services, or amenities that sets them apart and easily confirms that sense of exclusivity upon guests by association.
>
> —*Stefani C. O'Connor, Executive News Editor,* Hotel Business, *10/06*[1]

Even though people seem to disagree on the definition of boutique hotels, most commentators agree that they have four major defining characteristics.

First, as a general rule, boutique hotels put more emphasis on design and architecture than traditional chain hotels.[2] Incorporating cutting-edge design and décor and featuring celebrity architects and designers' work, boutique hotels look very distinctive inside and outside. These interior and exterior designs create the "personality" or "identity" of each hotel.[3] For example, each guest room in Library Hotel in New York City has a different theme, such as romance and music. The goal of these hotels is to create a unique, intimate, and stylish environment that makes every single stay different, even for repeat guests. Boutique hotels try to entertain their guests by creating a theatrical atmosphere that attracts all the senses though the use of design, color, lighting, aroma, and music.[4]

The second common feature is superior personal service.[5] Intimacy and familiarity between hotel staff and guests are emphasized; for example, a warm, caring attitude on the part of management and staff is encouraged, and staff members acknowledge guests by name.[6] Also, boutique hotels are known to provide a higher quality and wider range of guest amenities; such hotel properties surpass the standard amenity set by providing whimsical offerings such as stuffed goldfish, pillow menus, and complimentary candies and nuts. Technology is also widely used to enhance the cutting-edge design, fashionable image, and convenience. Every room has high-speed Internet access, a flat-screen TV, a DVD player, and other latest technological gadgets.[7]

The third feature is the number of rooms. Most commentators agree that boutique hotels should not exceed 150 rooms to maintain the intimacy between the guests and the hotel staff, and the personalized attention by the staff. Recently, however, there seems to be no upper limit on the maximum number of rooms; for example, among properties operated by Ian Schrager, Paramount Hotel has 594 rooms, and Hudson Hotel has 821 rooms.[8]

The last characteristic is the market that is attracted to boutique hotels. These hotels generally target customers who are in their early twenties to mid-fifties, in the mid- to upper-income brackets. Also, these hotels' corporate accounts include media, fashion, entertainment, and advertising companies that are attracted to the trendy design and lively atmosphere.[9]

Although boutique hotels might vary in many aspects, they can be grouped into two types based on their location.[10]

The first type is city destination hotels. These hotels are in urban edgy and chic neighborhoods in major cities like New York, London, San Francisco, and Miami. However, even though many boutique hotels are still located in major cities, more companies have recently been targeting less cosmopolitan

[1] Richard Miller and Kelli Washington, *Hotels and Reports 2007*, (Georgia: Richard K. Miller & Associates, 2007).

[2] Lucienne Anhar, "The Definition of Boutique Hotels," HVS International, December 13, 2001, January 29, 2008; http://www.hospitalitynet.org/news/4010409.print.

[3] Jones Lang Lasalle Report.

[4] Anhar, "The Definition of Boutique Hotels."

[5] Paula Drayton and Kristy Rodwell, "Boutique Hotels: An Australian Perspective," September 2001, January 29, 2008; http://www.hotel-online.com/Trends/Andersen/2001_BoutiquePerspective.html.

[6] Harry Nobles and Cheryl Thompson, "What Is a Boutique Hotel?" December 2001, January 30, 2008; http://www.hotel-online.com/News/PR2001_4th/Oct01_BoutiqueAttributes.html.

[7] Peter Jones, "Boutique Hotels," October 18, 2004, March 2, 2008; http://hotel-online.com/Views/1000.html.

[8] Ibid

[9] Jones Lang Lasalle report.

[10] Anhar, "The Definition of Boutique Hotels."

cities. Unlike traditional hotels, proximity or convenience is irrelevant for boutique hotels, but they are often located in cities with vibrant economies that are media or big fashion capitals to best attract their target market.

The second type is resort destination hotels. Located in well-hidden deserted corners of islands or mountains tucked away from the world, these hotels are smaller, more intimate, and less technology-focused. Unlike city destination hotels, the guest experience is based not on having cutting-edge technology, but on excluding it. Also, the more difficult it is to reach the destination, the more fashionable the location is considered. The goal of these hotels is to provide the ultimate "get away from it all."

QUESTIONS

1. What are the operational challenges associated with developing new boutique hotels?
2. What can we learn from the mass customization of tangible goods (e.g., Lands' End or Dell) that can be applied to the mass customization of services (e.g., boutique hotels)?
3. How can boutique hotels maintain a consistent/standard level of service without compromising their unique/personalized service mission?

Source: This case study was developed by Melissa Reich and Ho Jung Kim under the guidance of Rohit Verma.

CHAPTER 4

Process Design and Analysis

LEARNING OBJECTIVES

1. Describe the service-process matrix for service organizations. Identify the key differences between and the advantages and disadvantages of each process type.
2. Describe the product-process matrix for manufacturing organizations. Identify the key differences between and the advantages and disadvantages of each process type.
3. Explain the three physical types of layouts and describe the advantages and disadvantages of each type.
4. Characterize how strategic goals should be matched with appropriate process choices. Explain the effects of computerized technologies, including the Internet, on traditional product/process relationships.
5. Understand process analysis techniques, including break-even analysis, reengineering, flowcharting, from-to charts, and process simulation. Identify process bottlenecks in terms of human, equipment, or demand limitations.
6. Describe the nature of the process swamp and the need to improve processes that matter to customers.

Pop-Tart line at Kellogg's.

Pop-Tart Production at Kellogg's: Millions per Day

Kellogg's produces more than 10 million Pop-Tarts per day. It does this using the highly automated line process shown in the flowchart on the next page. Each step has specially designed equipment that often costs a quarter million dollars or more. For example, the mixer is not the same as your ordinary home mixer, or even the same as the larger mixers seen in commercial bakeries. The mixer for Pop-Tarts at Kellogg's mixes thousands of pounds of dough at a time. Similarly, the icing machine that follows baking in the oven is specially designed to lay sheets of icing or other decorations on a continuously moving series of precut and baked Pop-Tarts. The end result is a process that turns out thousands of Pop-Tarts per hour at a very low cost per Pop-Tart. The drawback to this process is that setting up for each individual order (e.g., chocolate or strawberry) takes quite a bit of time and wasted production. Thus, Kellogg's tries to minimize the inefficient down-

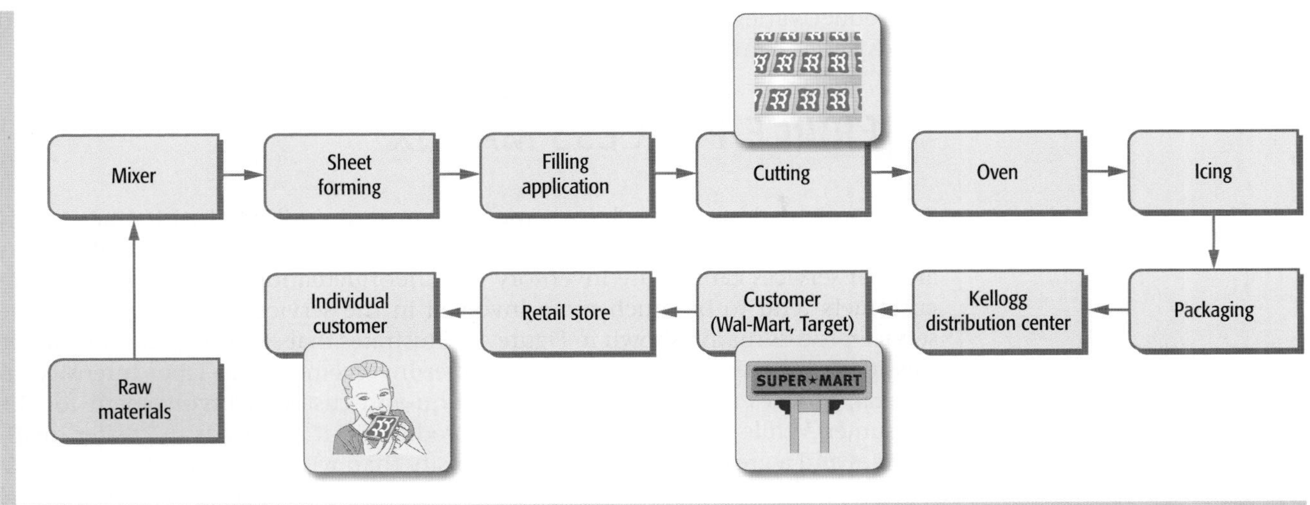

Kellogg's Production Line

time. Kellogg's cannot change any part of this system without changing all the remaining parts to ensure that they are adequately matched and paced.

A commercial bakery may also make pastries similar to Pop-Tarts using a process that can be diagrammed similarly, yet the equipment and techniques used to make the pastries will be quite different. The filling application, cutting, icing, and packaging will all be done using general-purpose equipment that can be used for multiple types of products. For example, the oven in a commercial bakery can be used for any type of baked product, but it will be less efficient than that at Kellogg's, as the pastries will have to be loaded, unloaded, and checked for doneness manually, rather than being fed through the oven automatically on a moving line. The end result is much more flexibility, but a penalty in terms of cost per pastry. ■

Choosing appropriate processes is a fundamental step in developing the ability to deliver products and services most effectively, in a manner that best reduces costs, most improves delivery flexibility or speed, or maximizes quality, depending on the strategic objective that is of foremost importance. The bakery example just described illustrates that processes must be chosen to fit the goals of the business. Often, a product or service can be provided using several different processes, but generally there is one process that fits best.

Process choice involves numerous decisions regarding the relationships among workers, technology, raw materials, and job assignments. On a macro level, service processes and manufacturing processes can each be grouped into several aggregate types. We focus on services first because they represent well over 80 percent of the economy of industrialized nations such as the United States, Japan, Great Britain, and Germany. Service-oriented businesses typically experience a tradeoff between the degree of sales opportunity and production efficiency. The service-process matrix shown in Figure 4.1 illustrates the four general types of service processes. These differ along two dimensions: the degree of labor intensity and the degree of customer involvement. Similarly, manufacturing processes can be described on a continuum where the volume for each type

● **Process choice** a procedure involving numerous decisions regarding the relationships among workers, technology, raw materials, and job assignments

of product varies from low to high while the flexibility to produce customized goods varies conversely from high to low.

SERVICE-PROCESS MATRIX

Service-oriented businesses have some fundamental similarities with manufacturing, but they also differ in critical ways. Two of the most fundamental differences are that services cannot use inventory to buffer fluctuations in demand and that customers tend to be much more involved in the service delivery process. The service-process matrix shown in Figure 4.1 illustrates that service operations can be classified along the dimensions of customer involvement and labor intensity. In general, services allow greater customization and customer involvement for the consumer. While this results in a better product fit, it also leads to greater inefficiencies and a greater degree of labor intensity than with the production of physical goods, as human labor is required to provide the flexibility needed to increase customization. As customers become more involved with a service process, they generally receive a more customized product, but at the expense of a loss in production efficiency, thus increasing delivery costs. Thus, one of the key challenges for service processes is to retain the ability to customize and encourage customer involvement without greatly inhibiting production efficiency.

● **Customer involvement** the degree to which customers are involved in shaping the end service/product that they receive

● **Labor intensity** the amount of labor needed to provide a service relative to the total amount of physical resources needed

As shown in Figure 4.1, service processes can be categorized along two dimensions: customer involvement and labor intensity. **Customer involvement** is the degree to which customers are involved in shaping the end service/product that they receive. For example, customers (patients) are typically quite involved in the service provided by physicians—patients must interact with the physician to tell him or her what symptoms they have, what medications they are taking, and numerous other pieces of information. This two-way exchange of information is important for providing the appropriate care. In contrast, customers have relatively little involvement in determining what types of products a retail store will carry. **Labor intensity** is the amount of labor needed to provide a service relative to the total amount of physical resources needed. To illustrate, auto repair shops have relatively low labor intensity because of the large amount of physical resources

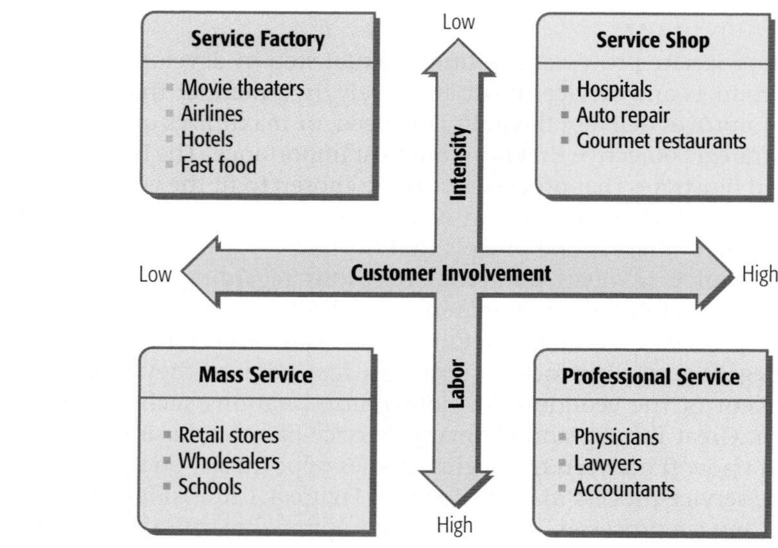

FIGURE 4.1 Service-Process Matrix

Source: Reprinted from "How Can Service Businesses Survive and Prosper," by Schmenner, R. W., *MIT Sloan Management Review,* Spring 1986, p. 25.

(hydraulic lifts, tools, parts, and other equipment) necessary to repair automobiles. In comparison, a lawyer's office has high labor intensity because the amount of physical resources required is relatively low compared to the need for the lawyer's time. As shown in Figure 4.1, there are four specific types of services, with each type being discussed in greater detail in the following sections.

Service Factories

Services with both low customer contact/customization and a low degree of labor intensity are classified as **service factories**. The facilities and equipment account for a large fraction of the costs of these services (the same is true of line-type processes in manufacturing). Much of the transportation industry (airlines, trucking companies), hotels, and fast-food establishments can be classified as service

● **Service factories** services with both low customer contact/customization and a low degree of labor intensity

BEST PRACTICES IN OPERATIONS MANAGEMENT

Outsourcing Scallion Production—Efficient or Dangerous?

With over 5,800 restaurants in the United States and thousands more worldwide, Taco Bell is an excellent example of a service factory. Each restaurant is designed to keep labor costs as low as possible, with very little customer contact. Jobs in a Taco Bell restaurant are very specialized and repetitive. Technology is used to standardize workers' jobs as much as possible; specialized tools for preparing tacos, burritos, and nachos have been developed, and counters, storage equipment, and wrapping are custom-designed. Taco Bell utilizes training videos and manuals to standardize the steps that are followed for almost every aspect of the product or service experience. The goal is to make the restaurant function efficiently using very low-skilled (and low-paid) employees, without compromising the speed or quality of service. Customers are typically not highly involved—they simply place an order at the counter or drive-through and receive a finished product that is the same every time a customer orders that product.

One way in which fast-food restaurants and other service factories try to cut costs is through outsourcing. In Taco Bell's case, much of the food preparation work is moved to outside facilities, where food can be processed in larger, more efficient volumes than would be possible in the restaurant. This approach is known as Taco Bell's K-minus strategy (for kitchen outsourcing). For example, scallions can be cut, cleaned, and bagged at a high-volume processing facility for less than 50 percent of the cost of performing these same operations in an individual Taco Bell restaurant. Taco Bell buys precut scallions from a number of vendors, including McLane Food Service.

Outsourcing of food preparation in this manner significantly reduces costs, but this longer supply chain does come with some risks. In December 2006, more than 60 customers became sick because of *E. coli* in Taco Bell restaurants. FDA investigators traced the problems to scallions delivered by third parties such as McLane Food Service. Both Taco Bell and McLane tried to place the blame on other parties. Taco Bell president Greg Creed published an open letter to customers in *USA Today,* the *New York Times,* and other newspapers on December 12, 2006, stating that Taco Bell food was safe. Furthermore, a Taco Bell spokesman promoted the idea that the problem with scallions was not limited to Taco Bell and that there was a need to ensure a safe supply of food from the farm to the table. Similarly, Bart McKay, associate general counsel for McLane, claimed that McLane employees handle only sealed boxes; thus, any contamination of scallions occurred at the supplier. In short, something as seemingly simple as scallions can be managed as a service factory, but also comes with a surprising degree of complexity in its supply chain.

Sources: Karen Robinson-Jacobs, "Carrollton's McLane Foodservice Drawn into Taco Bell Inquiry," *Knight Ridder Tribune Business News,* Washington, D.C., December 7, 2006; Alex Veiga, "Taco Bell Ad Blitz Says Food Is Safe," *Lansing State Journal,* December 13, 2006, p. 8A.

factories because of their low customer contact and customization and low labor intensity. Consider a major airline such as Delta. Customers tend not to be highly involved in the process of selecting flight times or options. While they may be able to choose either the 9 a.m. flight or the 11:30 a.m. flight from New York to Chicago, individual customers do not have input regarding the exact time a flight will be scheduled to leave. Similarly, customers do not have input regarding what type of aircraft will be used, what amount of individual seat space will be provided (much to many passengers' chagrin!), or what meal will be served when. While service factories have a fairly high amount of labor content relative to manufacturing enterprises, the degree of labor intensity is fairly low compared to other service businesses. For example, airlines average around $250,000 to $500,000 revenue per employee, which is much higher than the level for mass services, which have much lower revenue per employee.

Service Shops

● **Service shops** services with low labor intensity but high customer contact or customization

Services with low labor intensity but high customer contact or customization are classified as **service shops**. Service shops can provide various types of customized services for their customers (as is also true of job shops in manufacturing industries). Note that labor intensity is measured with respect to capital investment. Hospitals and auto and other repair services are excellent examples of service shops because, while labor is a critical component, the capital investment in equipment and capacity is relatively higher than the cost of labor. Service shops tend to focus on issues such as employee scheduling, work control, and technology selection. Because the range of jobs is so large, the control and scheduling of work is a critical component. The amount of capital investment required can be considerable. For example, the equipment in a hospital can cost millions of dollars for things like MRIs, x-ray equipment, operating rooms, and so on.

● **Mass services** services with low customer contact or customization in combination with high labor intensity

● **Professional services** services with both high customer contact or customization and a high degree of labor intensity

Mass Services

Mass services have low customer contact or customization in combination with high labor intensity. Retail companies, wholesalers, and schools are examples of mass services. Consider a large retail store such as a Target. Transactions are fairly standardized, with customer contact for the most part involving only entering price and item information and ringing up a bill of sale. A primary goal in this setting is to minimize the number of exceptions, such as returned items, irate customers, or out-of-stock items, because of the disruptions to standard business that these exceptions cause.

A Target store.

Professional Services

Professional services have both high customer contact or customization and a high degree of labor intensity. Services provided by doctors, lawyers, accountants, and architects all have very high labor costs because of the large amount of education associated with these professions. In addition, these services tend

BEST PRACTICES IN OPERATIONS MANAGEMENT

Process Management at American Express

American Express uses a variety of processes in conducting its business. The approval process for a new credit card or financial product is a professional service involving both a high degree of customer contact and a high degree of labor intensity. Figure 4.2 provides a flowchart of the basic credit card approval process. As can be seen in the flowchart, there are numerous steps involved in approving a credit card account; in particular, there are steps where different actions need to be taken based on the outcome of a check of the fraud database or a person's credit score. Consider the diamond marked "Meets credit requirement." A high credit score results in an approval and a low score results in a denied request, but a score in the middle is put in the marginal category. This means that the customer may be eligible for a credit card with different features, such as a higher interest rate or a lower credit limit. While companies such as American Express try to automate this process as much as possible, there is still a need for substantial human intervention on the part of both employees and customers.

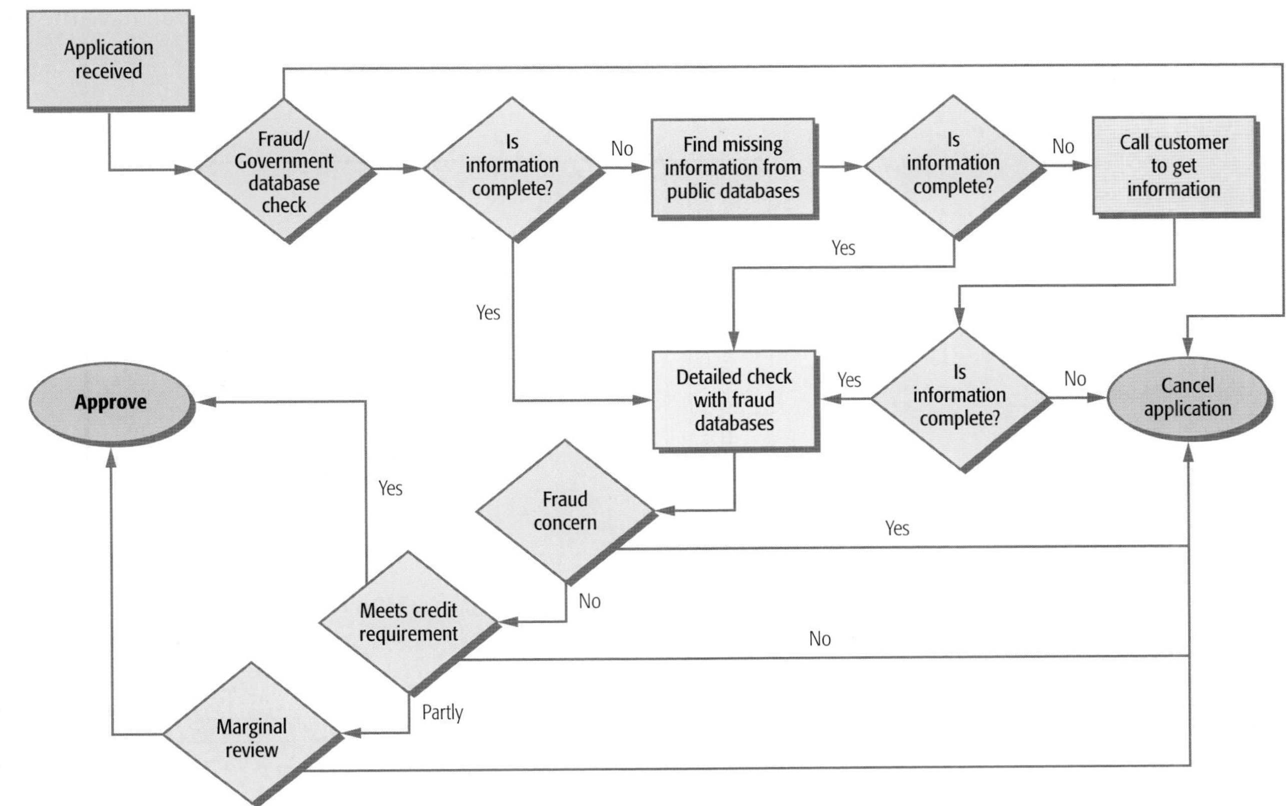

FIGURE 4.2 Credit Card Approval Process at American Express

Source: This flowchart represents an overview of the process followed by American Express as reported by a former employee and excluding company confidential information.

Credit card production.

to be highly customized according to the particular situation or need of each customer. A common approach to managing these services is to separate the business into front-office operations that have close contact with customers (e.g., doctors examining patients) and back-office operations that deal with ancillary issues that do not require such high skills. For example, physicians' offices typically have a group of clerks whose primary job is to file insurance papers, send and receive patient bills, and schedule and monitor appointments. While these tasks are certainly of critical importance, they generally require less skill and are compensated at a much lower level. Back-office operations can be standardized to a greater extent because of staff members' more limited contact with customers.

In contrast to American Express's credit approval process, the process of actually issuing the credit card is highly automated, taking the form of a line process. Physical cards are printed out at a central facility in batches of thousands at a time; then they are inserted into an envelope with the matching letter to the customer and mailed out. This process is used for both new cards and renewals of expired cards. This is done to minimize costs because the cards all have the same or very similar production steps.

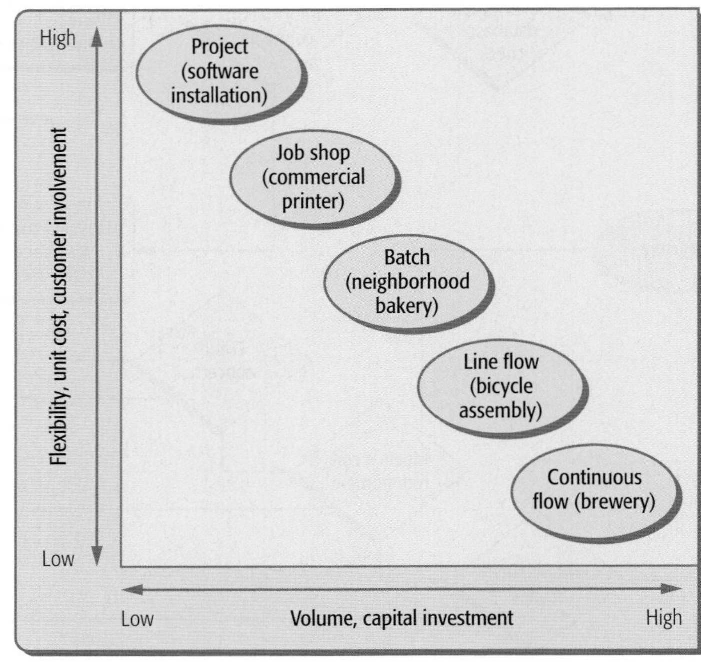

FIGURE 4.3 Product-Process Matrix

Source: R. Hayes and S. Wheelwright, *Restoring Our Competitive Edge: Competing Through Manufacturing* (New York: John Wiley & Sons, 1984). Reprinted with permission of John Wiley & Sons, Inc.

PRODUCT-PROCESS MATRIX

The **product-process matrix** was originally developed to match the product life-cycle stage (ranging from low volume–low standardization products to high volume–high standardization commodity products) with the appropriate choice of production process. The matrix shows that there is a tradeoff between high-volume standardized products that get produced for a low per-unit cost and low-volume customized products that have a high per-unit cost. Other tradeoffs exist between the degree of capitalized investment and customer involvement, and between generalized and specialized equipment. Each of the five process types shown in Figure 4.3 is discussed in detail in the following sections.

● **Product-process matrix** matches product characteristics with the appropriate choice of production process

Projects

The first process type examined is a project. Examples of projects include constructing a hospital, developing or installing a new software program, organizing a party, or developing and introducing a new product or service such as the Sony Playstation 3. A **project process** has a high degree of customization, a large scope, a high degree of customer involvement, and the use of primarily generalized tools and equipment. The exact composition and sequence of the tasks required vary widely from project to project because of the high degree of customization. There are typically numerous interrelated tasks (often hundreds) that must be completed in a sequential order and that involve workers from very different areas of the organization. Thus, a critical characteristic of projects is the requirement for close coordination among the various people and organizations involved with the project. This coordination can be primarily within a single organization, but it increasingly involves the exchange of information and resources across several different businesses. An example of a huge project is the coordination of an Olympic Games, which involves construction of facilities, coordination of thousands of people and supplies, and innumerable important details. The 2008 Summer Olympics held in Beijing involved over 10,000 athletes, 37 competition venues, and over 70,000 volunteers. The photos shown here and on page 110 are of two of the iconic buildings from the 2008 Beijing Olympics (the Beijing Olympic Swimming Center, or "Water Cube," and the Olympic Stadium, or "Bird's Nest," which hosted the opening and closing ceremonies). The construction of each facility was a project that took many years and millions of Chinese yuan to complete.

● **Project process** a type of process that has a high degree of customization, a large scope, a high degree of customer involvement, and the use of primarily generalized tools and equipment

● **Job Shop** a type of process that provides high flexibility to produce a variety of products in limited volumes

Job Shop Processes

Examples of job shop processes include a bakery with a large variety of breads and desserts, a plumber, airplane manufacturers, custom furniture manufacturers, or a machine shop. A **job shop** process provides high flexibility to produce a variety of products in limited volumes. Customization tends to be high, although not as high as for projects, while volume per product is fairly low. Workers' skills tend to be broad, and equipment tends to be general purpose. For example, a commercial printer might have a printer

Beijing Olympic Swimming Center and Olympic Stadium under construction: the Olympic Swimming Center (a.k.a., the Water Cube) is in the foreground, and the main Olympic Stadium (the Bird's Nest) is in the background.

and binder that can handle a wide variety of items. Workers in this situation must have a broad variety of skills in order to set up the equipment for a variety of orders. The printer and binder in the photo below is a good example of general-purpose equipment that has the flexibility to do many jobs, but at a cost per unit that is fairly high because of the need to specifically set up the printer and binder for each new job.

Finished Olympic Stadium.

Companies that use a job shop process must often bid against competitors for work, as products are typically produced in response to a specific order rather than being produced ahead of time for inventory or based on demand forecasts. Most resources are organized around common processing characteristics rather than around a given product. For example, a bakery would most likely have an area for mixing and assembling ingredients, a separate area for baking, a separate area for finishing goods (like putting icing on cakes), and another area for cleaning pans and equipment. This organization is appropriate because different products will flow through the system in different ways. For example, a cake might require 15 minutes of mixing and 15 ingredients, whereas a certain type of bread might need only 5 minutes and 6 ingredients. However, the bread needs time to rise between mixing and baking; thus, a storage area is required. While many of the tools and equipment for making bread and cakes are similar, the amount of time and the specific steps and ingredients required for each will be quite different.

Batch Processes

● **Batch process** a higher-volume job shop, in which the same or similar products are produced repetitively

Batch process examples include commercial printers that produce brochures or advertisements, car loan processing, the production of parts or components to feed an assembly line, or the production of swimsuits. A **batch process** is essentially a higher-volume job shop, in which the same or similar products are produced repetitively. The variety of products in a batch process operation is significantly lower than in a job shop, with variety being achieved primarily through an assemble- or make-to-order approach (in which components or parts are assembled from inventory in the appropriate combinations for each order). The variety remains too large for resources to be dedicated to a single product or family of products. Products are produced in moderate-size batches (typically from 10 to 1,000 units per batch); once one batch is finished at a location, then a batch of another product is made. Flow through the plant is still jumbled, with different batches requiring unique processing steps, but dominant patterns begin to emerge.

Commercial printing as a line process.

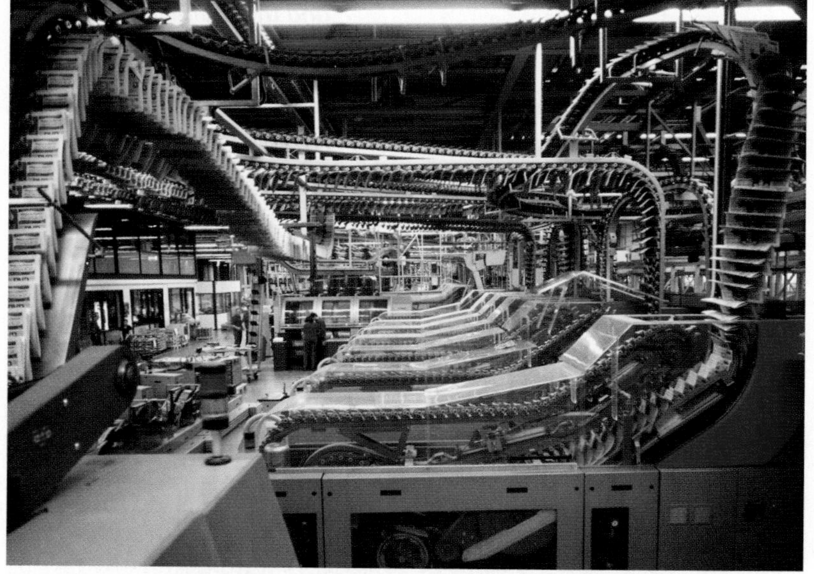

Line Processes

Examples of line processes include computer assembly, food production (such as Kellogg's Corn Flakes), book printing, or umbrella production. **Line processes** have high volumes, standardized products, and dedicated resources. The flow of products is organized around a single product (or a few products). The steps are arranged in a linear sequence and broken up into the smallest pieces possible. Workers specialize in a single task, and equipment may be designed to perform a single action. For example, Pop-Tarts are produced at Kellogg's with a dedicated set of resources that (1) shapes the raw Pop-Tarts, (2) bakes the Pop-Tarts, (3) applies the icing, and (4) packages the Pop-Tarts, all with minimal human intervention. This equipment is specifically designed for making Pop-Tarts and represents a fairly large fixed investment (several million dollars). However, it is well suited for its high-volume task and can produce thousands of Pop-Tarts per hour, thus making the per-unit cost only a few pennies per Pop-Tart.

● **Line processes** processes that have high volumes, standardized products, and dedicated resources

Every step in the process is performed repetitively, over and over, with very little variation in the products. The advantage of this approach is that both equipment and workers can be very specialized. One major disadvantage is that workers tend to become bored or do not have a good understanding of the final product because they perform only one small step out of hundreds or thousands. Line processes typically employ a make-to-stock approach, producing items not for individual customer orders, but to be held in inventory and used to fill future orders. A limited degree of variety can be introduced through careful design. For example, Pop-Tarts can be modified somewhat by having the roller cut different shapes (say, triangles instead of rectangles) or by applying a different color of filling. Similarly, the Patmont Motor Werks assembly line pictured here can supply thousands of vehicles per year in numerous colors. As shown in the photo, every scooter is the same—except for a few minor changes, such as the color of the scooter.

Continuous Processes

Examples of continuous processes include soda production, chemical production, brewing beer, and sugar and paint production. **Continuous processes** have high volume and low flexibility, and work with nondiscrete items that are not divided into their final packages until the very end of production. For example, beer is brewed in a series of very large containers and pipes, and it is not until the brewing process is complete that the beer is poured into bottles, cans, or kegs for final delivery to the end consumer. Occupying an extreme on the product-process matrix, continuous processes are extremely capital intensive, very standardized, and very inflexible. They tend to be operated 24 hours a day to recoup the huge investment in equipment. These processes are tremendously efficient, but the cost of any disruptions of production resulting from broken equipment, defective raw materials, or worker error is enormous, often running into tens of thousands of dollars per hour of lost production. Thus, worker skills tend to be focused on maintaining and repairing the equipment, fixing problems, and the design of the system. A continuous process for beer will make several thousand

● **Continuous processes** processes that have high volume and low flexibility, and that work with nondiscrete items that are not divided into their final packages until the very end of production

Push scooter assembly at Patmont Motor Werks in Minden, Nevada.

PART II Tools and Tactical Issues

cases of beer per hour at a very low per-unit cost, but will not have the same flexibility to change cans or types of beer as a craft production process. Thus, a large manufacturer such as Budweiser or Miller will employ a continuous process to produce beer. In contrast, a craft brewer such as Fat Tire will use a smaller batch process to make more styles of beer with a higher level of quality, but in much smaller quantities.

Using Technology to Move Off the Diagonal

The process types just described follow a pattern from the upper left to the lower right corner of the product-process matrix. In general, there is a tradeoff between high flexibility and high volume/low cost per unit. Process types such as project or job shop are good at providing a high degree of flexibility and producing a variety of end products, but this comes at the cost of limited volume and a relatively high cost to produce each unit. In contrast, line and continuous processes are at the other end of the diagonal—they are generally limited in their flexibility, but very good at producing high volumes of product at a low cost per unit.

While there is generally a tradeoff between high flexibility and low cost per unit, the use of advanced manufacturing technologies (AMTs) can allow firms or parts of firms to move "off the diagonal" and achieve a balance between these two. Similarly, computers and the Internet allow some opportunities to achieve both high flexibility and low cost per unit in a service environment. One example is painfully familiar to most e-mail users—spam. Computer software allows spammers to customize e-mail offers to millions of recipients at a low cost per unit by creating a form or mail merge letter. When technology is used properly, computers facilitate increased flexibility without increasing costs because they can be programmed to make changes without the need for human beings to set up new equipment. This type of technology is covered in more depth in Chapter 13.

LAYOUT TYPES

Up to this point, we have been describing process types, or general ways of organizing work in a manufacturing or service process. The general process types for services and manufacturing involve many decisions, including order size, method of organizing work, and types of equipment, among others. We now turn to a more focused examination of how work centers are physically laid out. Here the main decision is where to locate specific pieces of equipment, people, and work centers. Departments or work centers within an organization are defined by the general pattern of work and material flow. The three basic layout types are process, product, and fixed-position. Hybrid layouts (either group technology or cellular) combine features of these basic layouts. There are many variations on these basic types of layouts, but the general features of each generally match with one or more of the specific types of process discussed earlier.

Process Layout

● **Process layout** a layout that groups together machines, equipment, or people with similar functions or goals

A **process layout** groups together machines, equipment, or people with similar functions or goals. A bakery typically has a mixing/assembly area, a baking and decorating area, and a sales/packaging area, with similar types of equipment in each area. Similarly, a copy shop might have all the copiers in one area, the computers in another, and the faxes and scanning machines in still another. Parts or jobs travel from area to area, depending on what machines or work centers are required for that part or job. This type of layout is used when there is a large degree of variety in the jobs and no standard set of equipment is required for each job. Because demand for each product is fairly low, it is not economically feasible to dedicate either equipment or people to a single task. The flow tends to be jumbled in a process layout because of the varied paths taken by different jobs or products. Figure 4.4A shows the use of a process layout in a neighborhood bakery. While many products share usage of the same equipment (e.g., cookies and bread both need to have dough mixed and be baked), the order and length of processing at various steps will differ. Thus, Figure 4.4A illustrates that while the flow of products through a process layout can be shown fairly clearly for each individual product, when all the products the bakery makes are shown, things look more hectic or jumbled.

One of the challenges with process layouts is the scheduling of orders to be processed at each machine or work center. For example, in Figure 4.4A, there are likely to be multiple orders to be processed at the rolling station, multiple orders at the baking station, and so on. Sequencing rules such as first come, first served (FCFS) or shortest processing time (SPT) are used to schedule individual jobs either in order of arrival or in increasing order of time to process, respectively.

For an illustration of the application of scheduling rules in a process layout, please go to the course web site.

Product Layout

Product layout a layout that dedicates equipment and workers to specific products on a linear route

A **product layout** dedicates equipment and workers to specific products on a linear route. When volumes for a particular product are high, resources can be specialized and designed for a specific product. A good example is the making of lunches for a school picnic: Students might be lined up at a counter and assigned repetitive tasks. The first student would apply mayonnaise or mustard to the bread, the second would add the meat, the third would add lettuce and/or tomatoes, and the fourth would put the sandwiches in bags. Product layouts can be

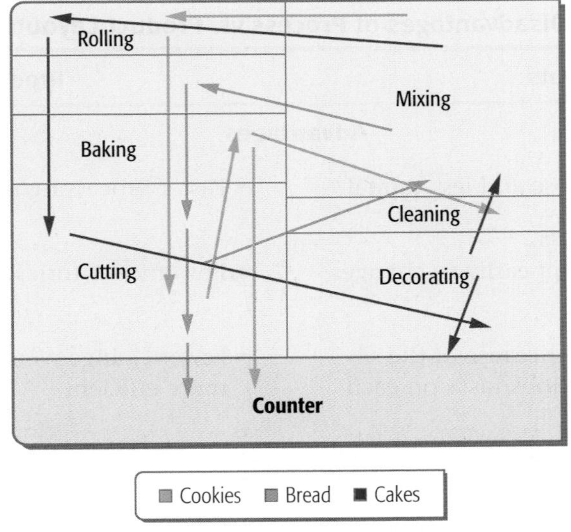

A. A Process Layout at a Neighborhood Bakery

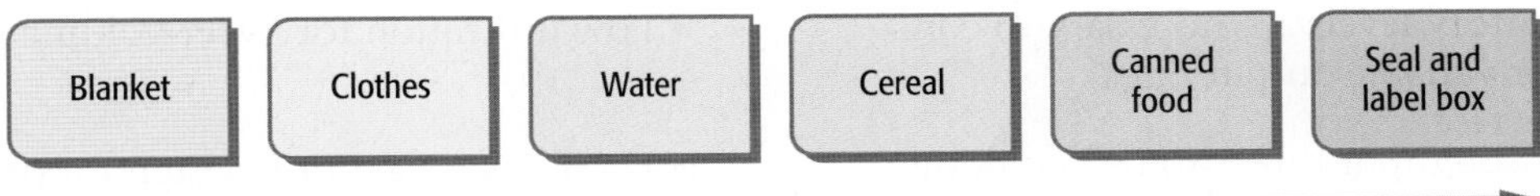

B. A Product Layout (Assembly Line for Filling Disaster Relief Boxes)

FIGURE 4.4 Comparing Process and Product Layouts

dedicated to a single product or can be mixed-model lines (in the case of the sandwich line, each sandwich can be made a little different by choosing rye, whole wheat, white, or peasant bread at the beginning, adding catsup or mayonnaise at stage 1; and adding pastrami, chicken, or beef at stage 2, for a total of $4 * 2 * 3 = 24$ sandwich combinations). Product lines are often in a straight line, but can also follow an L, O, S, or U shape. Figure 4.4B shows the product layout for filling disaster relief boxes.

In setting up any type of assembly line, one of the challenges is ensuring that there is an even flow of work. In other words, a balanced assembly line is one in which each work station has approximately the same amount of work. If an assembly line has four stations with 30 seconds, 40 seconds, 60 seconds, and 30 seconds of work, respectively, the station with 60 seconds of work will be the bottleneck that limits production because it takes longer than the other stations. It would be preferable to rearrange the work allocation so that each station had 40 seconds of work (i.e., total work = 30 + 40 + 60 + 30 = 160 seconds; divided by 4 stations = 40 seconds work per station). **Assembly line balancing** is the technique of assigning work to individual stations so that the variability across all stations in an assembly line is minimized.

● **Assembly line balancing** the technique of assigning work to individual stations so that the variability across all stations in an assembly line is minimized

For an illustration of the application of assembly line balancing techniques in a product layout, please go to the course web site.

Table 4.1 summarizes the relative advantages and disadvantages of process versus product layouts. In general, product layouts tend to be used for higher-volume situations (line or continuous flow for manufacturing, or service factory or mass services), while process layouts work best for low-volume situations (job shop or batch for manufacturing, or service shop for professional service). Hybrid layouts that seek to combine the advantages of both product and process layouts will be discussed later.

TABLE 4.1 Advantages/Disadvantages of Process vs. Product Layouts

Process Layouts	Product Layouts
Advantages	
• Resources are general purpose and less capital intensive	• Faster processing rates
• Flexibility is high—can adapt easily to changes in product mix or volume	• Lower inventories (and faster throughput)
• Capacity utilization is high because of the ability to perform multiple jobs/tasks on each piece of equipment	• Fewer changeovers, less material handling, more efficient
Disadvantages	
• Frequent changeovers result in lost production time	• Low flexibility
• High inventory levels are necessary to compensate for variable output rates	• Low utilization for lower-volume products
• Product throughput time can be very long	• High risk of layout redesign for products/services with uncertain life cycles
• Production planning and control is challenging	

Fixed-Position Layout

A **fixed-position layout** requires the product (because of its extreme weight or size) to remain at one location. The equipment required for each step must be moved to the site. Construction sites, shipyards, movie studios, airplane plants, and road construction typically use fixed-position layouts. One of the primary challenges of this type of layout is scheduling workers and equipment so that they don't conflict or bump into each other. Thus, this layout type is most often associated with a project.

● **fixed-position layout** a layout that requires the product (because of its extreme weight or size) to remain at one location

Hybrid Layouts

Hybrid layouts attempt to combine the advantages of process and product layouts by grouping disparate machines into work centers or cells to work on products that have similar shapes and processing requirements. **Group technology** is an approach in which the product parts having similarities (shape, usage, and/or manufacturing process) are grouped together to achieve a higher level of integration between the product design and manufacturing. Families may be based on size, shape (all parts are round or square), demand, or manufacturing or routing requirements. A family represents a set of products with similar processing requirements, and the goal is to minimize the need for changeovers and setups. The production of sandwiches at a Subway is a form of group technology—the resources are devoted to producing a family of sandwiches that have a degree of variation but are fundamentally similar in the steps needed for their production.

● **Hybrid layouts** layouts that attempt to combine the advantages of process and product layouts by grouping disparate machines into work centers or cells to work on products that have similar shapes and processing requirements

● **Group technology** an approach in which the product parts having similarities (shape, usage, and/or manufacturing process) are grouped together to achieve a higher level of integration between the product design and manufacturing

THE IMPACT OF STRATEGY AND TECHNOLOGY ON PROCESS CHOICE

Process Strategy

While it is important to understand the available choices regarding strategy type, it is equally important to carefully consider the organization's operations strategy and how it fits with process choice. Matching the strategy that an organization follows with an appropriate process choice is a significant decision. Typically, companies that focus primarily on a large range of product or service choices will focus on processes in the upper left quadrant of the product-process matrix in Figure 4.3, such as project, job, or batch. In contrast, companies that focus on achieving the lowest possible cost per unit are more likely to standardize their operations and use either a line or a continuous flow process. The example in Figure 4.2, in which the credit card approval process is compared to the process for issuing the physical card, illustrates how companies try to match the processes used with the objectives.

Comfort Inn and Four Seasons hotels provide another example of differing processes. While the two chains operate in the same industry and largely employ the same basic processes, there are numerous areas in which they have different processes to support strategic differences. Comfort Inn focuses primarily on low cost. In order to support this focus, the chain utilizes a single employee or a few employees to do a large number and variety of jobs. The clerk that checks you in is also responsible for taking reservations, handling wake-up calls, giving directions to customers, and so on. While these process choices reduce cost, they also sacrifice much of the flexibility and quality that is prized by full-service hotels such as Four Seasons. For example, a Four Seasons hotel would have specific employees dedicated to check-in/checkout, wake-up calls and room service, directions and sightseeing (the concierge), and so on. These specialized employees provide a much higher level of service and quality, but also add significantly to the cost of each room.

TECHNOLOGY IN OPERATIONS MANAGEMENT

Electronic Check Processing

Banks have traditionally been heavy users of information technology to streamline and automate their back-office processes. After all, banking deals with a lot of information and numbers.

Both banks and customers benefit from electronic check processing. Many transactions have become paperless, with payments being exchanged electronically. This cuts the cost of physically processing checks dramatically. When customers do use physical checks, banks are increasingly processing electronic images rather than sending the physical checks through the mail. Taylor Vaugh, vice president of cash management at First Horizon National Corp. (a Memphis, Tennessee–based bank), estimates that adopting image processing of checks saves 0.75 to 3 cents per check. This may not sound substantial until it is multiplied by the 2 million checks the bank processes per day, resulting in a savings of between $15,000 and $60,000 per day.

First Horizon is typical of banks worldwide in seeking to save costs and to increase security. The Check Clearing for the Twenty-First Century Act (Check 21), which took effect on October 28, 2004, required paying banks to accept paper reproductions or "substitute" checks created from images of the original. This act was passed in response to the terrorist attacks of September 11, 2001, which brought the physical processing of checks to a halt because checks could not be processed between banks. Check 21 is aimed at preventing a recurrence of this physical breakdown. When combined with the potential cost savings from image processing, the forecast is for an eventual elimination of the 40 billion checks in circulation in the United States today. Over the past three to five years, overall paper check volumes have been decreasing at a rate of 3 percent per year.

Sources: A. Hawser, "Check 21 Pushes Paper Checks Closer to Oblivion," *Global Finance* 18, no. 10 (2004), 43–44; M. Kelly, "First Horizon Goes Paperless; Viewpointe Helps Tennessee Bank Pioneer Paperless Check Processing, Sharing," *eWeek* 22, no. 28 (July 18, 2005), 6.

Check sorting centers can process more than 1 million checks per day using high-speed processing equipment.

Technology Impacts

Technology has been a major driver of changes in process design throughout the twentieth century and will continue to have a large impact as we move into the twenty-first century. The foundations of mass production were laid in the early 1900s by men such as Henry Ford and Frederick Winslow Taylor based on new technologies such as standardized parts and machine tools, division of labor, and assembly line techniques. Office and service work has been similarly affected by improvements in transportation, office equipment (such as electric typewriters, photocopiers, and telephones), and construction techniques, including improved lighting and central air conditioning and heating. Among the numerous technologies affecting the business environment at the end of the twentieth century are electronic devices such as cellular phones, personal digital assistants, and computers; genetic advances in identifying genes and related therapies; and materials advances that provide improved raw materials.

The connection of millions of individual computers and users through the Internet has provided one of the largest process design shifts that business has experienced. The Internet allows companies to market products directly to consumers, thus cutting out middlemen completely. Alternatively, the Internet allows much improved communication, as businesses can track their key inputs and outputs more easily. When consumers order goods over the Internet, the business fulfilling that order does not require a physical person to actually answer the phone or greet the customer. While there is still a need for someone to fill the order (i.e., pick the goods or services requested and ship/deliver them to the consumer), this transaction can now be more specialized and buffered. In other words, a company such as Office Depot does not need to have a large number of operators standing by to take orders over the telephone. Instead, it can have a crew of e-mail operators. This crew can be smaller because the orders do not need to be filled instantaneously (i.e., if a telephone is busy, the customer may well hang up rather than waiting on hold). In addition, Internet transactions often have the benefit of self-sourcing, with some of the work of inputting data being shifted to consumers. Consider a bank that formerly had many tellers; now that consumers can enter their own transactions via ATM or the Internet, the bank can cut back greatly on its workforce.

DESIGNING PROCESSES

Once an organization has chosen a basic process type for a facility or a product or service, there are several techniques for designing the specific steps, technologies, and labor utilization for that process. The following section examines three techniques for designing processes: break-even analysis, reengineering, and bottleneck analysis. These techniques are commonly used to provide a broad analysis of processes at a fairly high organizational level.

Break-Even Analysis

Break-even analysis is a mathematical technique that allows a comparison of total costs for different processes. This technique takes the fixed costs of buying or developing a process or technology, adds the variable costs for producing each unit, and finds the break-even point at which the cost of two or more processes is equal. For example, consider a neighborhood bakery that can form cookies in one of three ways: (1) by hand using a cookie cutter, (2) with an automated cookie-forming machine (the CookiePro 1000) that costs $10,000, or (3) with another automated machine (the CookiePro 2000) that costs $15,000.

● **Break-even analysis** a mathematical technique that allows a comparison of total costs for different processes

Forming cookies by hand is time consuming, with one worker earning $12 per hour being able to form 120 cookies per hour. Thus, the per-transaction cost (based on the time taken to perform each transaction) is $0.10. If the bakery buys the CookiePro 1000, the same worker will be able to form 600 cookies per hour. The per-cookie cost is then $12/600 cookies, or $0.02 per cookie. The CookiePro 2000 can make 900 cookies per hour, with a per-cookie cost of $12/900 cookies, or $0.0133 per cookie. If the bakery produces 200,000 cookies per year, how long will it take to recoup the costs of the two choices of automated machine?

In contrast to basic break-even analysis, in which there is a single break-even point, there are multiple break-even points when three or more alternatives are compared. The break-even point is found by setting the cost equations for manual and automated forming (with both the CookiePro 1000 and the CookiePro 2000) of cookies equal to each other. The cost equation is equal to the fixed cost of the equipment plus the variable cost per unit times the number of units produced. Solving for the number of units produced provides the break-even quantity. The first step is to solve for the break-even cost between the manual cookie process and the CookiePro 1000.

Manual Cookie Forming   CookiePro 1000

$$\$0.10 * Q = \$10{,}000 + \$0.02 * Q$$

where Q = number of units produced.
Solve for Q:

$$\$0.08Q = \$10{,}000$$
$$Q = 125{,}000 \text{ cookies}$$

Given that the break-even point is 125,000 cookies, it will take 7.5 months to pay for the CookiePro 1000 [(125,000 cookies to break even/200,000 cookies per year) * 12 months].

The second step is to solve for the break-even point between the two automated alternatives (CookiePro 1000 and CookiePro 2000).

CookiePro 1000   CookiePro 2000

$$\$10{,}000 + \$0.02 * Q = \$15{,}000 + \$0.0133 * Q$$

where Q = number of units produced.
Solve for Q:

$$\$0.0066Q = \$5{,}000$$
$$Q = 750{,}000 \text{ cookies}$$

As illustrated in Figure 4.5, the manual process is best if fewer than 125,000 cookies will be made, the CookiePro 1000 is least expensive if between 125,000 and 750,000 cookies will be made, and the CookiePro 2000 is least expensive if more than 750,000 cookies will be made.

Reengineering

● **Reengineering** a technique that involves a shift from a functional perspective on the business to a process-oriented perspective

Reengineering involves a shift from a functional perspective on the business to a process-oriented perspective. Reengineering arose as an important business initiative in the early 1990s following the lead of consultants such as Michael Hammer and James Champy (with their best-selling book *Reengineering the Corporation: A Manifesto for Business Revolution*) and James Harrington and Thomas Davenport. The goal is to identify core processes that add value to the finished product or service and eliminate steps that are inefficient or non-value-adding. Many of these inefficiencies result from communications difficulties caused by the separation of functional departments into silos. A primary component of reengineering involves drawing flowcharts of processes "as is," or as they currently exist. Then a flowchart is developed to show the process as it "should be." This ideal process is often more efficient because it sheds repetitive tasks, non-value-adding tasks, and other artifacts that are the result of changes that have occurred over a long time span since the original process was put into place.

A general methodology for reengineering involves six steps. First, the core processes with the greatest potential for improving competitiveness must be identified. Second, the process reengineering team must become familiar with the current problems and practices of the processes being studied. Next, information

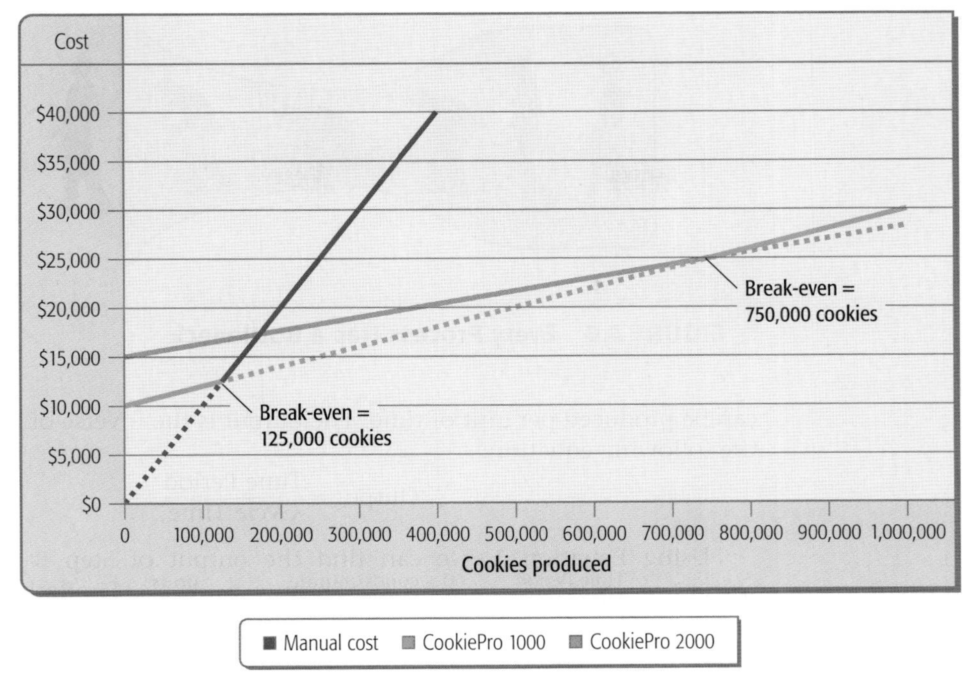

FIGURE 4.5 Break-Even Analysis: Cookie Dough Formation

should be gathered from customers in order to identify changes that must be made to improve these processes. The fourth step involves identifying enablers of change. Two primary enablers are information technology (IT), because of its ability to facilitate information exchange, and organizational enablers such as getting individuals from different areas of the company involved and committed to the project. The fifth step involves the review of proposed changes by the process reengineering team, customers, and personnel who will be involved with the redesign. The final step, implementing the new process, must be supported by top management and given appropriate financial resources.

Bottleneck Analysis

The objective of process design is to maximize the amount of output relative to the amount of input. This sounds like a simple objective, but in reality it is very complicated. The challenge comes from conflicting objectives, multiple inputs and outputs, and possible interactions among multiple processes. This section presents one method of analyzing processes based on the identification of **bottlenecks**, which are the steps with the slowest cycle time in a process. Every process has at least one bottleneck step that determines the overall productivity or output of that process, as illustrated by the people entering the bottle in Figure 4.6. While we will focus on determining the bottleneck for a given process, this is one element of a larger approach to improving operations. The theory of constraints was developed by Eliyahu Goldratt in his book *The Goal* and provides much more detail on bottleneck analysis.

- **Bottleneck** the step with the slowest cycle time in a given process; this is the step that limits the overall productivity for the process

In order to identify the bottleneck of a process, we start with some key terms. For a given process step, the **cycle time** is the time it takes to complete that step or action once. For example, if a printer has a cycle time of 10 seconds, then it can print 6 pages per minute (60 seconds per minute divided by 10 seconds per page); in other words, the printer can go through 6 cycles per minute, where each cycle is 10 seconds. The **output** of the process is the number of units that

- **Cycle time** the time it takes to complete a particular step or action once
- **Output** the number of units that can be produced per unit of time

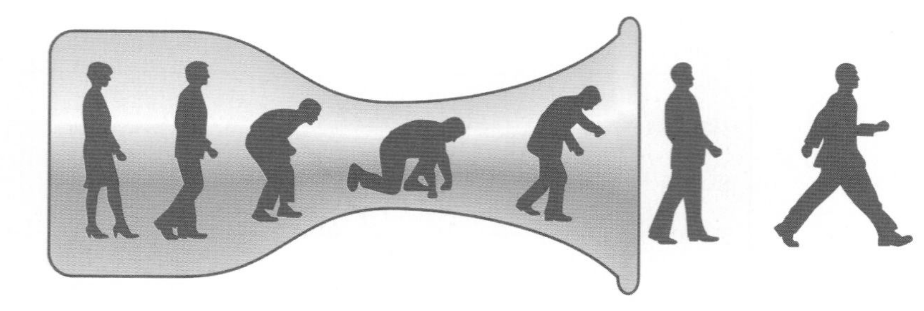

FIGURE 4.6 Every Process Has a Bottleneck

can be produced per unit of time. The output is the inverse of the cycle time, or the following equation:

$$\text{Output} = \frac{\text{Time Period}}{\text{Cycle Time}} \qquad \text{(Equation 1)}$$

Using Equation 1, we can find the output of Step B in Figure 4.7 as $\text{Output} = \frac{\text{Time Period}}{\text{Cycle Time}} = \frac{60 \text{ seconds/minute}}{10 \text{ seconds/unit}} = 6 \frac{\text{units}}{\text{minute}}$. Similarly, the output of Steps A and C can be calculated as 3 units per minute and 2 units per minute, respectively.

Note that for all the bottleneck analysis problems, we assume that the times given are deterministic—i.e., that they are known for certain, with no variability. This is not true in practice, but this assumption allows us to provide reasonably accurate predictions for output, cycle time, and utilization with fairly straightforward and simple analysis. In order to provide a more accurate and complete analysis, we need to incorporate stochastic times, where each step has a mean or average time and a variance or standard deviation associated with it. This type of analysis is somewhat more complicated and involves computer simulations, which will be discussed later in this chapter.

Defining and calculating cycle time and output for a single step is fairly straightforward, but when multiple steps are linked together, system output is somewhat harder to find. Returning to Figure 4.7, the output of each step calculated earlier assumes that there is always a supply of the input material to work on. In other words, if Step B needs one finished unit from Step A, there is *always* one available to work on. Unfortunately, this assumption is not true in practice. Let's assume that the process in Figure 4.7 is a paced process, in which all steps are linked together and the finished output from one step is passed to the next

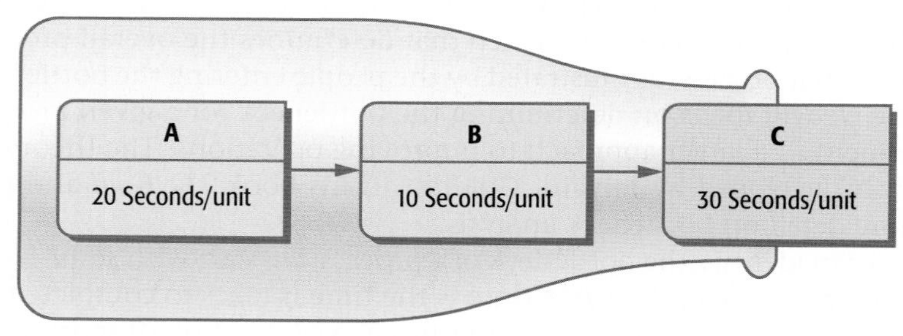

FIGURE 4.7 A Paced Assembly Process

step simultaneously. This can be compared to a line of people passing boxes of fruit from hand to hand in rhythm. In this case, the slowest (longest cycle time) of Steps A through C determines the speed of the entire system. Thus, Step C is the bottleneck, as it requires 30 seconds per cycle or has an output of 2 units per minute. This means that Steps A and B must both wait for Step C to finish its work. Another way of saying this is that Step C is blocking Steps A and B from achieving their full capacity. The output of the system is 2 units per minute (i.e., $\frac{\text{60 seconds/minute}}{\text{30 seconds/unit}}$).

To better illustrate the workings of the system in Figure 4.7, we introduce the concept of **utilization**, which is the percentage of available time that equipment, space, or labor is used and adding value. The utilization for Step A in Figure 4.7 is 66.6 percent (i.e., 20 seconds/30 seconds), while the utilization of Step B is 33.3 percent (i.e., 10 seconds/30 seconds). The utilization of the bottleneck step is always 100 percent (i.e., the utilization of Step C is 30 seconds/30 seconds).

● **Utilization** the percentage of available time that equipment, space, or labor is used and adding value

We use Equation 2 to calculate utilization:

$$U = \frac{\text{Cycle Time Step}}{\text{Cycle Time System}} * 100\% \qquad \text{(Equation 2)}$$

Thus, the output of the entire system in Figure 4.7 is 2 units per minute. This is the state of the system as is; if we wanted to increase output, how could that be done? By adding more resources or redesigning the process. Let's assume that there are currently three workers for the process in Figure 4.7 (one at Step A, one at Step B, and one at Step C); thus, the output per worker is 2/3 unit per minute. How can the output of this process be changed?

We will examine three typical constraints that are often encountered in process analysis:

1. Labor resources
2. Machine or equipment resources
3. Demand

Changing Labor Resources

The output or productivity can be changed in two fairly simple ways. First, we could assign only two workers to the entire process—one worker to Step C and one worker to do Steps A and B. This assignment is shown in Figure 4.8. If we do this, the process consists of two work stations: one with Steps A and B combined and 30 seconds (20 for Step A and 10 for Step B) of work per cycle, and one with Step C and 30 seconds of work per cycle. The system then has dual bottlenecks because Steps A/B and Step C have the same total time. The output for the system is thus 2 units per minute (i.e., $\frac{\text{60 seconds/minute}}{\text{30 seconds/unit}}$). This is the same output as

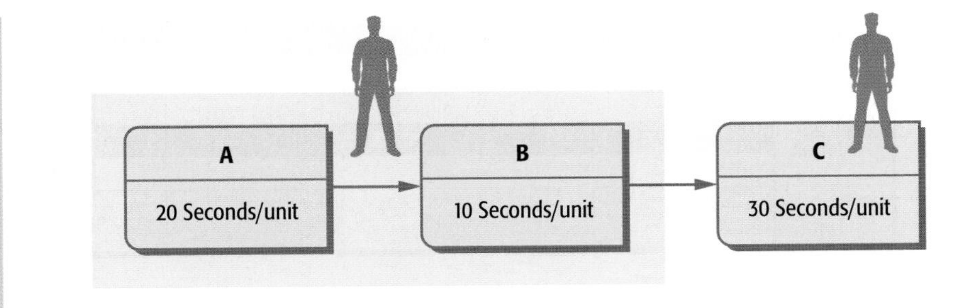

FIGURE 4.8 Process with Steps Combined

before, but with two workers rather than three. While output has stayed constant, the overall productivity (as measured by input/output) has increased from 2/3 unit per worker per minute to 1 unit per worker per minute.

The second way in which we can increase output or productivity for the process in Figure 4.7 is by adding a fourth worker to Step C. The cycle time for Step C would then be 15 seconds per unit (i.e., 30 seconds per unit/2 workers). Figure 4.9 shows the effects of adding a second worker to Step C. If each worker produces separately, then the average time between units will be 15 seconds. The bottom part of Figure 4.9 shows a Gantt chart for the time each worker will be finishing each unit. A **Gantt chart** provides a visual representation of schedules for the resources used in a particular process or project. The Gantt chart in Figure 4.9 illustrates the specific tasks that each worker is doing in each time period and also illustrates that while each worker takes 30 seconds for each unit that he or she works on, the overall cycle time for process C is now 15 seconds per unit because there are two workers at this step. Gantt charts can also be used to show the utilization of each resource, whether it is a worker or a piece of equipment.

● **Gantt chart** a visual representation of schedules for the resources used in a particular process or project.

Note that while Step C can produce 1 unit every 15 seconds *if* it has sufficient input, it is prevented from doing so because Step A can produce only 1 unit every 20 seconds. Step A is now the bottleneck for this process, and Steps B and C are said to be starving, which means that they are prevented from achieving 100 percent utilization because of a shortage of input materials. The output for the entire system is thus 3 units per minute (i.e., $\frac{60 \text{ seconds/minute}}{20 \text{ seconds/unit}}$). The utilization for Steps B and C is 50% ($U = \frac{\text{Cycle Time Step}}{\text{Cycle Time System}} * 100\% = \frac{10 \text{ seconds per unit}}{20 \text{ seconds per unit}} * 100\%$) and 75% ($U = \frac{\text{Cycle Time Step}}{\text{Cycle Time System}} * 100\% = \frac{15 \text{ seconds per unit}}{20 \text{ seconds per unit}} * 100\%$), respectively.

We can compare Figure 4.8 and Figure 4.9 to determine the best approach to changing labor resources. In Figure 4.8, total productivity was 1 unit per worker by combining Steps A and B with one worker. In contrast, adding a fourth worker

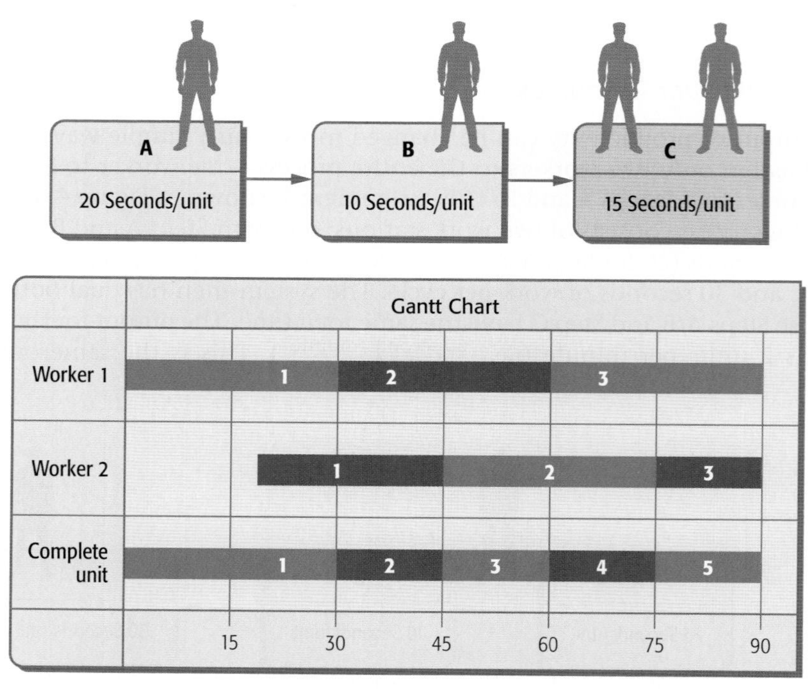

FIGURE 4.9 Process with Worker Added to Step C (top portion) and Gantt Chart (bottom portion)

to Step C in Figure 4.9 results in total productivity of ¾ units per worker per minute. Thus, in terms of overall productivity per worker, the approach taken in Figure 4.8 is best. Note that it would also be possible to duplicate the work in Figure 4.8 in order to get total output above the situation in Figure 4.9. In other words, two sets of work stations—4 workers total (2 doing Steps A and B and 2 doing Step C) would result in overall output of 4 units per minute.

NOTE: While each worker takes 30 seconds to complete 1 unit individually, on average the output of the 2 workers combined will be 1 unit every 15 seconds.

Machine and Equipment Resources

While people can be, and often are, the bottlenecks in a process, it is also possible and common that there is a capacity limitation on a machine or piece of equipment that forms a bottleneck. Figure 4.10 illustrates a pizza production process in which the equipment (oven) is the bottleneck. There are two workers, each with a cycle time of 3 minutes. It takes 12 minutes to bake one pizza. That is the **throughput time**, which is the time that an individual unit must spend in a given process or step. The cycle time for the oven, because it can hold 3 pizzas at a time, is 12 minutes per pizza/3 pizzas per cycle = 4 minutes per cycle. The cycle time is calculated for steps with capacity greater than 1 unit using Equation 3:

● **Throughput time** the time that an individual unit must spend in a given process or step

$$\text{CT} = \frac{T}{C} \qquad \text{(Equation 3)}$$

where CT = cycle time
T = throughput time
C = capacity

Thus, while each pizza has a throughput time of 12 minutes, the average cycle time is 4 minutes—the pizza shop can serve one customer every 4 minutes. The bottleneck in this case is the oven and its limited capacity.

Demand as a Constraint

In the sections on labor and equipment, we implicitly assumed that we can sell everything that we produce. While that assumption simplifies our calculations, it is not very realistic. Let's examine the effect of demand as a constraint. Suppose that if pizzas are priced at $10 each, there is enough demand that we average 1 order every 4 minutes for the example in Figure 4.10. This makes demand and equipment capacity perfectly matched—the oven limits the process to 1 pizza every 4 minutes, and that is exactly the amount of demand.

But what happens if we have an opportunity for $100 to upgrade the oven so that it has a capacity of 4 pizzas? Should we do it? Not if demand stays the

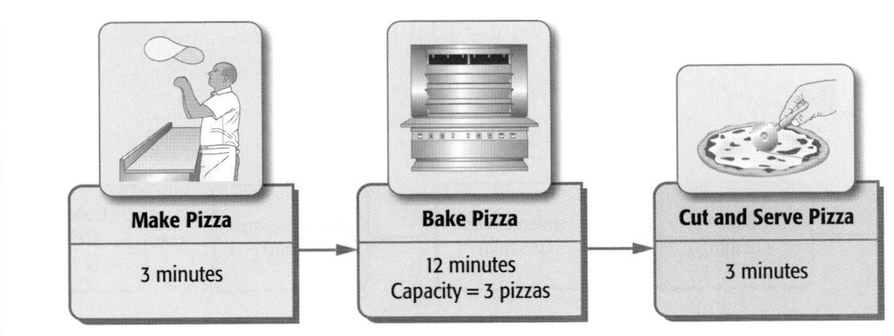

FIGURE 4.10 Pizza Baking with an Equipment Bottleneck

same. Upgrading the oven to 4 pizzas would allow it to have a cycle time of 3 minutes, but demand is for only 1 pizza every 4 minutes. Thus, while we can make more pizzas, we cannot sell them.

What if we try to influence demand? This is a job for marketing. Suppose that if we offer pizzas for $9 each, then demand increases to 1 pizza every 3 minutes. Now we can benefit from extra capacity at our oven. With the smaller oven, our output was 1 pizza every 4 minutes or 15 pizzas per hour (60 minutes per hour/4 minutes per pizza), for a revenue of $150 per hour (15 pizzas * $10 per hour). With the increase in demand and a larger oven, we can produce and sell 20 pizzas per hour (60 minutes per hour/3 minutes per pizza), for a revenue of $180 per hour (20 pizzas * $9 per hour). Thus, the extra $100 to upgrade the oven can be paid for in a little over 3 hours [$100/($180 per hour – $150 per hour) = 3.33 hours].

Simultaneous Labor, Machine, and Demand Constraints

All processes have a combination of labor, machine/equipment, and demand constraints. Thus, to really understand a process, we need to examine all three simultaneously, as shown for Mike's Sub Shack.

Solved Example

Mike's Sub Shack

Mike's Sub Shack makes toasted subs for carryout. He follows a fairly simple process (Figure 4.11) to make each sub. Answer the following questions about his process. Assume that the capacity of his oven is 3 subs at a time and that he starts with a single worker.

A. If customers arrive every 6 minutes, and there is only 1 sub per customer order, how many subs can Mike sell per 4-hour shift? How long does it take to fill each customer's order?

This means that the cycle time for demand is 6 minutes. Mike is the only worker; thus, he will have 6 minutes of labor per sub (2 minutes + 0.5 minute + 0.5 minute + 1 minute + 2 minutes). The cycle time for the oven, following equation 3, is $CT = \frac{T}{C} = \frac{\text{12 minutes per sub}}{\text{3 subs per cycle}} =$ 4.0 minutes. Thus, there is a combined bottleneck of demand and labor (both of which are 6 minutes per cycle). Mike can make 10 subs per hour ($\text{Output} = \frac{\text{Time Period}}{\text{Cycle Time}} = \frac{\text{60 minutes per hour}}{\text{6 minutes per sub}} = \text{10 subs per hour}$), and 4 hours * 10 subs per hour = 40 subs in a 4-hour shift. It takes 18 minutes for a customer to get his or her order (6 minutes labor + 12 minutes baking = throughput time = 18 minutes).

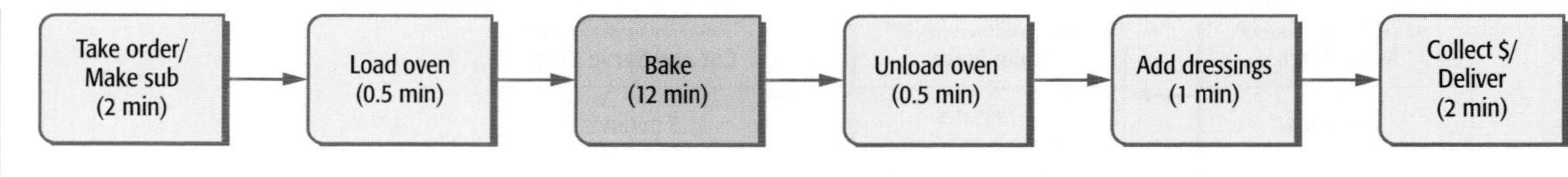

FIGURE 4.11 Steps in the Process at Mike's Sub Shack

B. What will the utilization of a single worker (Mike) be? What will the utilization of the oven be?

Because Mike is a bottleneck, his utilization will be 100 percent, or $U = \frac{\text{Cycle Time Step}}{\text{Cycle Time System}} * 100\% = \frac{\text{6 minutes per cycle}}{\text{6 minutes per cycle}}$. The utilization of the oven will be $U = \frac{\text{Cycle Time Step}}{\text{Cycle Time System}} * 100\% = \frac{\text{4 minutes per cycle}}{\text{6 minutes per cycle}} * 100\% = 66.7\%$.

C. If each sub is sold for $6 and the ingredients cost $2.50, what amount of profit (excluding the cost of labor) can Mike make per hour? What would the value of a second worker be? What will the utilization of the workers be if a second worker is hired? (Note: You will need to describe which jobs each worker will do.)

To determine profit, we multiply the profit per sub by the output:

$$(\$6 - \$2.50) * 10 \text{ subs per hour} = \$35 \text{ per hour}$$

To determine the value of a second worker, we look at all the bottlenecks. Adding a second worker makes the cycle time for labor 3 minutes (i.e., 6 minutes labor/2 workers). Demand is still the bottleneck because we can sell only 1 sub every 6 minutes. Thus, the utilization of each worker will be 50 percent. In effect, hiring a second worker will not increase the output, so it should not be done.

D. Evaluate the value of a reduction in the price of a sub to $5 if that will result in an average of 1 customer every 4 minutes. Assume that there are 2 workers from the end of Part C.

By offering incentives, we increase demand, thus changing the bottleneck—the new bottleneck is both the oven at 4 minutes per sub and demand at 1 customer every 4 minutes. Thus, our output can increase:

$$\text{Output} = \frac{\text{Time Period}}{\text{Cycle Time}} = \frac{\text{60 minutes per hour}}{\text{4 minutes per sub}} = 15 \text{ subs per hour}$$
$$\text{Profit} = 15 \text{ subs per hour} * (\$5 - \$2.50) = \$37.50$$

The increase from $35 to $37.50 is positive, but that is not much money for having added another worker (in Part C) and made a change in the sub price. If we wanted to continue to improve output, we might consider adding capacity to the oven to mitigate that as the bottleneck.

Parallel Processing

Up until now, we have worked only with serial processes that occur in a linear sequence. Figure 4.12 provides an example of a parallel process, where two operations on a product can occur simultaneously, with the results merged at a later point. For example, a car may have two teams of workers, one that works on the right or passenger side of the car, and one that works on the driver's side. These steps occur in parallel.

In Figure 4.12, the production at Steps A and B occurs in parallel. Then, Step C involves assembling the parts produced in the previous two steps. This operation is paced like those examined earlier, so that all parts move on a common cycle time—that of the slowest operation, which is A. Thus, the cycle time for this process is 30 seconds per unit and the output is Output $= \frac{\text{Time Period}}{\text{Cycle Time}} = \frac{\text{1 minute}}{\text{30 seconds per unit}} * \frac{\text{60 seconds}}{\text{1 hour}} * \frac{\text{60 minutes}}{\text{1 hour}} = 120$ units per hour. The utilization of the steps is as follows:

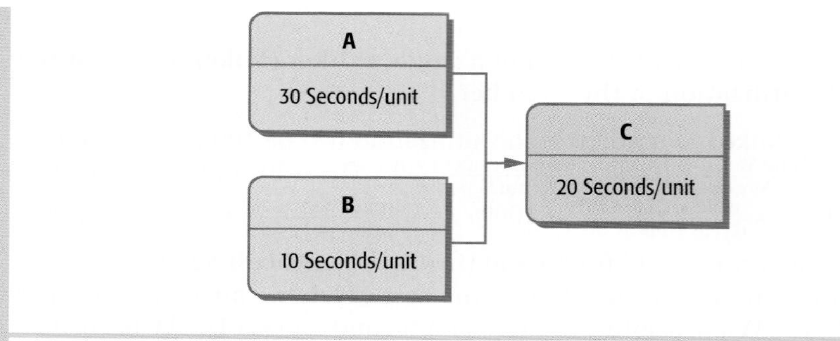

FIGURE 4.12 An Example of Parallel Processing

$$U_A = \frac{\text{Cycle Time Step}}{\text{Cycle Time System}} * 100\% = \frac{30 \text{ seconds}}{30 \text{ seconds}} * 100\% = 100\%$$

$$U_B = \frac{\text{Cycle Time Step}}{\text{Cycle Time System}} * 100\% = \frac{10 \text{ seconds}}{30 \text{ seconds}} * 100\% = 33.3\%$$

$$U_C = \frac{\text{Cycle Time Step}}{\text{Cycle Time System}} * 100\% = \frac{20 \text{ seconds}}{30 \text{ seconds}} * 100\% = 66.7\%$$

Thus, A is the bottleneck process and has a utilization of 100 percent.

Process Analysis Techniques

This section presents additional process analysis techniques. In contrast to the previous section on designing processes, this section presents three analysis techniques (flowcharting, simulation, and from-to charts) that are generally used to draw more micro, detail-oriented maps of very specific steps and to make detailed decisions.

Flowcharting

Flowcharting involves graphically portraying the key elements, steps, participants, and materials of a process. Flowcharting (also called process modeling, or value stream mapping) provides a means of quickly conveying the key elements of a process, or, as the saying goes, "a picture is worth a thousand words." Both current and future business processes can be diagrammed. This technique helps illustrate areas where improvements can be made and steps eliminated. In addition, the steps involved in documenting processes help develop a thorough understanding of those processes.

Modeling begins with high-level models that distill an organization's operations into no more than a dozen processes. The goal is to reveal the departments involved and allow people to (1) see the sequence of steps, (2) draw boundaries around the processes, (3) identify key players and functional groups within the bounded processes, (4) identify handoffs between subprocesses, and (5) identify supplier/customer interfaces. The International Benchmark Clearing House has categorized common business processes for all organizations, including

- Generate demand
- Fulfill demand
- Plan and manage the enterprise
- Develop products and services

- **Flowcharting** a technique that involves graphically portraying the key elements, steps, participants, and materials of a process
- **Service blueprint** a technique for describing and analyzing a service that incorporates the actions of both the customer and the server
- **Line of visibility** the point at which customers lose physical sight of the steps in a particular process; separates front-office operations that directly interact with customers from back-office operations that are more independent.
- **Process simulation** a technique that employs computer software to develop a visual model of a process that incorporates multiple work centers, inputs, and processing techniques as variables

High-level process modeling, however, remains too abstract unless it is supported by successive layers of detail. This detail breaks out high-level process models into finer degrees of specification, ultimately ending with a detailed workflow that documents the individual actions of the work force and information technology. This process is similar to examining a map of a country that you intend to visit, then examining a more detailed map of specific cities or places within that country, and finally examining a detailed street map of a particular neighborhood to help you walk to your destination.

A **service blueprint** is a technique for describing and analyzing a service that incorporates the actions of both the customer and the server. While it is similar to a flowchart, a service blueprint more explicitly recognizes that customers are an integral part of the process and seeks to identify interactions between customers and servers. This blueprint also shows the **line of visibility**, or the point at which customers lose physical sight of the steps in a particular process. It separates front-office operations that directly interact with customers from back-office operations that are more independent. This allows processes to be designed with more effective methods and techniques.

Figure 4.13 provides an example of a typical flowchart. Figure 4.14 gives an overview of commonly accepted flowcharting symbols. It is important to use identical symbols and language across different applications so that it is fairly easy for people in different areas of the organization to quickly review and understand the flowchart.

Prescription processing at a walk-in pharmacy (top), and prescription processing at a mail-order pharmacy (bottom).

Simulation

Process simulation employs computer software to develop a visual model of a process that incorporates multiple work centers, inputs, and processing techniques as variables. Process simulation provides a dynamic view of the process in action, while flowcharting provides a static or fixed view. Different scenarios can be evaluated without actually changing processes and disrupting business as usual. Where bottleneck analysis assumes that all times are deterministic or static, simulation incorporates the more realistic assumption that times for processes are stochastic, with a mean and a variation. Thus, simulation can provide a more accurate model of an actual operation—but this requires more complexity.

As computer power has increased over the last two decades, simulation programs have been developed that can model business processes in such detail that an entire organization, such as a factory or a restaurant, can be represented. While simulation has historically been used primarily in manufacturing, there is an increasing emphasis on simulations of service processes. For example, a computer

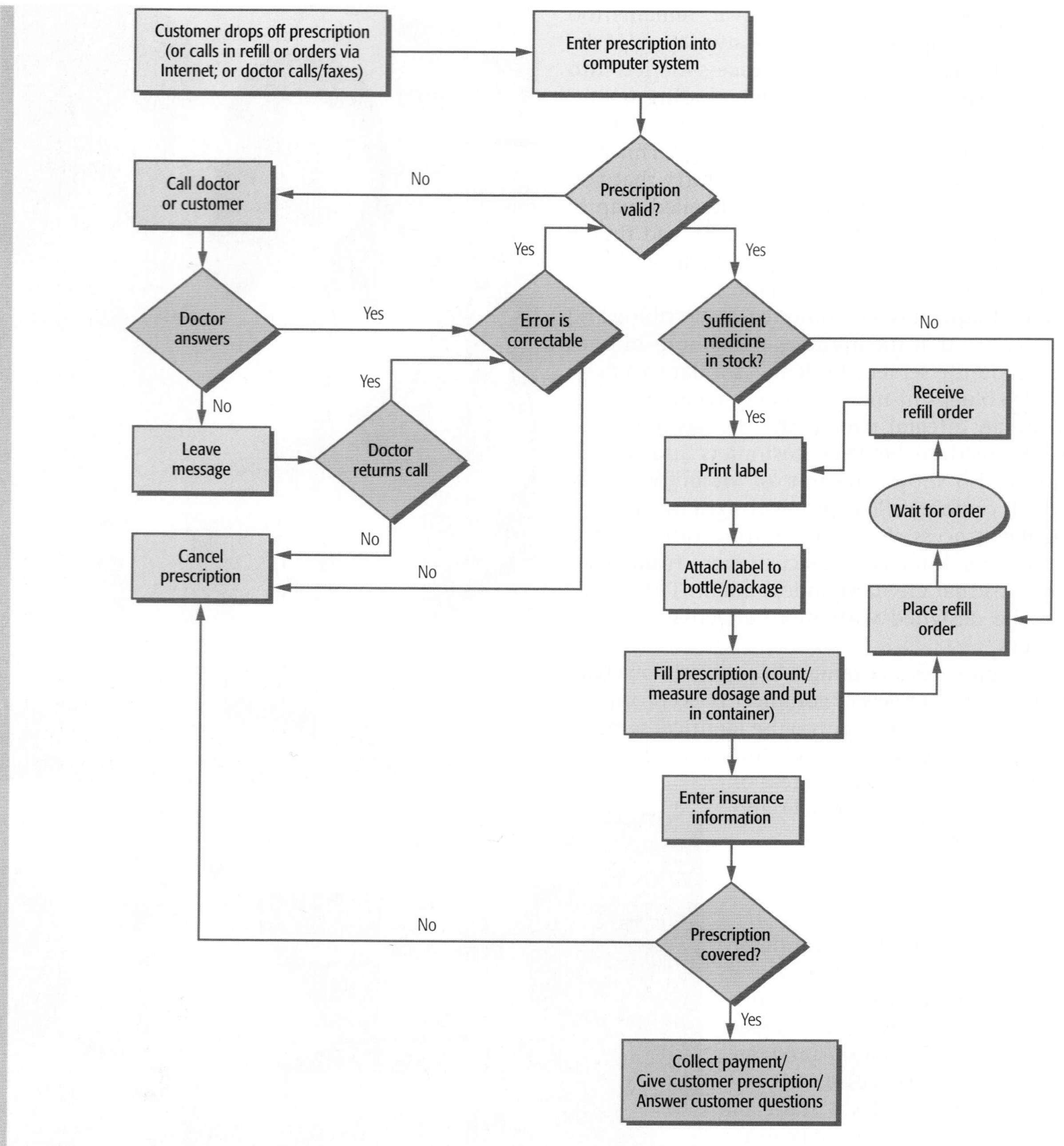

FIGURE 4.13 Flowchart for Filling a Prescription at a Walk-In Pharmacy

simulation could be developed to show the flow of customers through the checkout line at a grocery store. Variables that could be incorporated and studied in such a model might include the number of baggers (with a bagger assisting the cashier and specializing the work that each performs, customers should flow through the checkout line faster) or the time required to check each customer out (i.e., what is the effect of the person who forgets his or her checkbook or the effect of a price check?). There are numerous software programs that can be employed for simulation analysis.

BEST PRACTICES IN OPERATIONS MANAGEMENT

Filling Your Prescription

Have you ever watched the pharmacist fill a prescription while you were waiting? What steps occur when filling a prescription? How do these steps differ among different types of pharmacies?

A walk-in pharmacy such as those found at a Walgreens, a Rite-Aid, or a Wal-Mart has a process that is focused on satisfying customers who drop off their prescriptions. As a result, the process is largely a batch process, with each prescription following the same general steps, but with different specific tasks. As shown in the flowchart in Figure 4.13, there are a number of steps in which the pharmacist or assistant may need to break off from physically filling a prescription and contact the customer, the insurance company, or the doctor. Often, this introduces delays if any of the parties that need to be contacted are unavailable. Thus, the process of filling a prescription is filled with many potential interruptions. Walk-in pharmacies try to balance efficiency (number of prescriptions filled) with responsiveness (being able to fill a walk-in prescription quickly so that the customer can get his or her medicine quickly). The first photo (on page 127) in this section shows a pharmacist at a walk-in pharmacy putting medicine in a bottle.

In contrast to a walk-in pharmacy, a mail-order pharmacy such as Caremark or Medco Health Solutions fills prescriptions for long-term (90 days), recurrent health conditions. These pharmacies have less contact with customers (all contact is by mail, Internet, or phone); thus, they are able to manage interruptions in a way that results in greater efficiencies. In essence, the prescription process is broken into components that different individuals are focused on handling. Only prescriptions that have been through the necessary insurance, medical (i.e., doctor approval), and customer checks are released to the floor to be filled. The process of preparing the physical medicine is much more efficient than at a walk-in pharmacy. Another difference is that this process is very automated, with automatic prescription-filling machines to do much of the work. The second photo (also on page 127) shows prescription processing and the large amount of automated equipment that is typical at a mail-order pharmacy. With this type of operation, Caremark or Medco provides lower-cost prescriptions, but at a tradeoff—the customer must wait several days or weeks to get the prescription

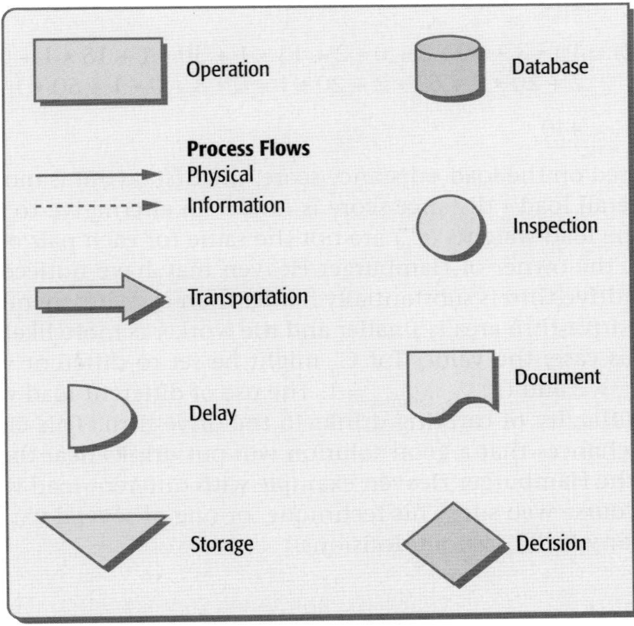

FIGURE 4.14 Common Flowcharting Symbols

From-To Charts

● **From-to charts** diagrams that show the number of trips or the amount of materials flowing between different departments or work centers

● **Load * distance score** a weighted calculation of the load times the distance covered

One of the most fundamental principles for managing and designing multistep, materials-oriented processes is to minimize the distance traveled by pieces, components, and finished products. While a variety of analysis techniques exist, the most elementary involves developing **from-to charts** that show the number of trips or the amount of materials flowing between different departments or work centers. The number of trips between departments/work centers is measured for each pair and shown in a chart like that in Table 4.2. These trips can be weighted according to their importance, difficulty, or some other criterion. For example, carrying drinks from the drink department to the drive-thru might receive a higher weight than carrying them to the counter because of the need to navigate other sources of interference.

When the trips in Table 4.2 are weighted equally, we can compare the two alternative layouts shown. This is done by computing the **load * distance score** by multiplying the number of trips in Table 4.2 by the distances covered. The distances in Table 4.2 are simple distances where adjoining cells are assigned a distance of 1 (e.g., the grill and the drive-thru in Layout 1), while cells that are not directly connected are given a distance of 2 or 3 (e.g., the grill and the drinks area are a distance of 3 in Layout 1). The load * distance score for Layout 1 is calculated as as

$$\mathrm{LD} = \sum_{i=1}^{N} \sum_{j=1}^{N} L_{ij}C_{ij}D_{ij} \qquad \text{(Equation 4)}$$

where L_{ij} represents the number of trips or loads moving between work centers (e.g., drinks and drive-thru for Hamburger Heaven) in a time period, C_{ij} represents the weight for that load, and D_{ij} represents the distances between departments. The distance (D_{ij}) is the only variable because it can be changed by different assignments of departments to locations. In situations where all loads are considered to have equal weight, C_{ij} is set equal to 1 (this is the case in this problem). For example, let's compare Layouts 1 and 2:

$$\begin{aligned}\text{LD (Layout 1)} &= 10 * 2 + 40 * 1 + 0 * 3 + 15 * 2 + 30 * 1 + 15 * 1 + 0 * 1 + 10 * \\ &\quad 2 + 20 * 1 + 60 * 2 + 20 * 1 + 0 * 2 + 0 * 1 + 50 * 2 + 10 * 3 \\ &= \underline{\underline{445}}\end{aligned}$$

$$\begin{aligned}\text{LD (Layout 2)} &= 10 * 3 + 40 * 2 + 0 * 2 + 15 * 1 + 30 * 1 + 15 * 1 + 0 * 1 + 10 * \\ &\quad 2 + 20 * 2 + 60 * 2 + 20 * 1 + 0 * 3 + 0 * 1 + 50 * 1 + 10 * 2 \\ &= \underline{\underline{440}}\end{aligned}$$

Thus, based on the load * distance score, the first layout is more efficient because the overall load * distance score is lower. An alternative to this method is used when the load weights (C_{ij}) are not the same for each pair of departments. For example, the owner of Hamburger Heaven may have noticed that carrying drinks to the drive-thru is substantially harder than carrying them to the counter (because the drive-thru area is smaller and the worker is more likely to have accidents). In this case, the values for C_{ij} might be set to different values, such as $C_{\text{Drinks, Drive-thru}} = 2$ and $C_{\text{Drinks, Counter}} = 1$. The use of different load weights reflects the greater difficulty of carrying drinks to the drive-thru. This change tends to increase the chances that a good solution will put drinks near the drive-thru. A solution for the Hamburger Heaven example with different load weights is available on the course web site. This technique, or one of several variations, can be applied to many facility layout decisions.

Please go to the course web site for an illustrated spreadsheet solving a problem with different load weights.

TABLE 4.2 From-To Chart for Hamburger Heaven

	Grill	Salad/ Sandwich Prep	Counter	Drinks	Order Assembly	Drive-Thru
Grill	—					
Salad/ Sandwich Prep	10	—				
Counter	40	15	—			
Drinks	0	0	60	—		
Order Assembly	15	10	20	0	—	
Drive-Thru	30	20	0	50	10	—

Alternative Layouts for Hamburger Heaven

Layout 1

Drive-thru	Salad/ Sandwich Prep	Drinks
Grill	Counter	Order Assembly

Revised Layout 2

Drive-thru	Drinks	Salad/ Sandwich Prep
Grill	Order Assembly	Counter

Distances Between Departments
[Note: distances in parentheses () are for layout 2]

	Grill	Salad/ Sandwich Prep	Counter	Drinks	Order Assembly	Drive-Thru
Grill	—					
Salad/ Sandwich Prep	2 (3)	—				
Counter	1 (2)	1 (1)	—			
Drinks	3 (2)	1 (1)	2 (2)	—		
Order Assembly	2 (1)	2 (2)	1 (1)	1 (1)	—	
Drive-Thru	1 (1)	1 (2)	2 (3)	2 (1)	3 (2)	—

PROCESS SELECTION—THE PROCESS SWAMP

The key to maximizing process value using process analysis and redesign techniques such as reengineering, flowcharting, simulation, and from-to charts is choosing processes to improve that will have the greatest impact. Business organizations have hundreds of processes, including things like purchasing, production planning, quality assessment, personnel recruiting, research and development, market research, and succession planning. Numerous examples of reengineering have been offered as both success and failure stories. While large operational improvements may seem impressive, the bottom-line profitability of the business may not improve. Numerous paradoxical outcomes have been cited, such as the insurance company that cuts claims processing time by 44 percent, yet still experiences a drop in profits. The difference between success and failure is often choosing the right process to improve. It is critical that the customer be considered in every decision because the end result must be an improvement in perceived value. For example, total quality management often simplifies processes by focusing on manufacturing-related or tangible output–related processes that can be objectively measured. Yet this approach ignores more intangible processes, such as product development or customer relations. Process management must be viewed as a holistic approach involving the improvement of all processes, but with priority being given to the ones that *matter most to consumers*. In the next two sections, we examine self-sourcing as a means of including customers as key elements in the product delivery process and outsourcing as a means of reducing the resource burden on the organization.

Self-Sourcing

● **Self-sourcing** a technique that includes customers in the process in a way that reduces the resource demands on the organization providing the product or service, while also providing the customer with improved service

Often, a process can be improved by getting customers to perform some of the key steps themselves. **Self-sourcing** includes customers in the process in a way that reduces the resource demands on the organization providing the product or service, while also providing the customer with improved service. Coffee shops where customers pour their own coffee from one of several selections and self-service gasoline are excellent examples of well-established self-sourcing practices. Allowing customers in coffee shops to pour their own coffee provides the customers with an increased level of choice and control of both ingredients and portions. From the restaurant's perspective, the self-serve coffee is easier to maintain because the restaurant employees do not have to pour every cup of coffee. Similarly, self-service gasoline results in a dramatic increase in productivity for gas stations because fewer employees are needed to process sales when the customers pump their own gas. Customers like this service because it is generally quicker and cheaper. However, companies must be aware that self-sourcing can lead to unforeseen changes in other components of the business. For example, coffee requires frequent rebrewing and cleaning, which may be hard to control with self-serve coffee because it is separated from the rest of the food preparation areas. Similarly, coffee shops require measures to control customer behavior so that the coffee is not harmed. Self-service gasoline also requires new procedures because customers have a tendency to forget to pay, forget to return the pump handle to the pump, or do many other things that can be costly or dangerous.

A critical advantage of the Internet is that it provides new ways to self-source that are beneficial to both consumers and companies. The sale of airplane, movie, sports, theater, or concert tickets through the Internet provides a good illustration of the benefits of self-sourcing for companies and customers. The sale of airplane tickets through the Internet allows customers to browse at their leisure, often finding information more quickly than they would have if they had telephoned the company directly, while also getting a better view of the various flight options. Web sites such as Travelocity allow consumers to compare prices for several airlines. From the airline's perspective, sales over the Internet allow customers to connect directly into the airline's computer system without the need to have a group of phone operators waiting for customers to call, at which point the operators must then read the same information to the customer. Clearly, it is to the airline's advantage to cut the operators out of the process if their main role is to simply relay information. Thus, Internet ticket sales can be very cost-effective while simultaneously offering customers more choice and better visibility. Most airlines sell a majority of their tickets online and in a paperless format, which is a substantial change from 2000, when most tickets were still sold via the phone and mailed to the customer. Similarly, the method of selling tickets for sporting events and other entertainment has changed substantially. Stubhub provides an interesting example of a marketplace that allows customers to resell tickets to other customers outside the company offering the original tickets.

Potential drawbacks to the use of the Internet are that it requires greater technical knowledge on the part of the company's employees, and that the Internet site itself must be designed in such a way that it is easy to understand and navigate. In addition, there are serious challenges regarding data entry errors, such as when a consumer accidentally chooses an unintended flight or destination. The best way to prevent these errors is to simplify the ordering process, but some procedures must be developed to handle the inevitable errors that result.

Outsourcing

Another means of improving a process is to separate the components of the process into those parts that the providing organization can do extremely well and other parts that are not core capabilities. Over the past decade, outsourcing of noncore production and service activities to external suppliers has become a common method of streamlining and improving processes. **Outsourcing** involves selecting suppliers with expertise in a particular area of business to produce and deliver a component part or service to another company. The use of outsourcing has increased for two primary reasons. First, the total quality management movement in the 1980s helped increase companies' awareness that it is difficult to be "world class" in multiple activities and that settling for second-best products produced "in-house" just to maintain the work within a single organization is not the best approach. Second, the rapid increase in the capabilities of information technologies and other communication devices has made managing multitier supply chains much easier. For example, first electronic data interchange (EDI) and now the Internet provide a quick and efficient method of communicating across organizational boundaries. Thus, many companies choose to focus on a single aspect of their business in which they are world class and then outsource many noncore activities. There are risks with outsourcing, including a loss of control, increased communication and coordination costs, and the challenges of working with different corporate cultures and national cultures.

● **Outsourcing** selecting suppliers with expertise in a particular area of business to produce and deliver a component part or service to another company

SUMMARY

1. Describe the service-process matrix for service organizations. Identify the key differences between and the advantages and disadvantages of each process type.

- The service-process matrix matches product characteristics with process characteristics for services and includes the service factory, service shop, mass service, and professional service as process types.

2. Describe the product-process matrix for manufacturing organizations. Identify the key differences between and the advantages and disadvantages of each process type.

- The product-process matrix matches product characteristics with process characteristics for manufactured products and includes project, job shop, batch, line flow, and continuous flow processes.
- In general, higher-volume processes have low per-unit costs, little flexibility, high capital investment, very specialized worker skills, and dedicated, single-purpose technology. In contrast, lower-volume processes have much higher flexibility, higher per-unit costs, lower capital investment, and both general worker skills and general-purpose equipment.

3. Explain the three physical types of layouts and describe the advantages and disadvantages of each type.

- Process layouts group together machines, equipment, or people with similar functions or goals. Process layouts are typically used for lower-volume, flexible processes such as job shop, batch, service shop, or professional service.
- Product layouts dedicate equipment and workers to specific products on a linear route. Product layouts are most often used for high-volume, relatively inflexible processes such as line, continuous flow, mass service, or service factory.
- Hybrid layouts attempt to combine the advantages of process and product layouts by grouping disparate machines into work centers or cells to work on products with similar shapes and processing requirements.

4. Characterize how strategic goals should be matched with appropriate process choices. Explain the effects of computerized technologies, including the Internet, on traditional product/process relationships.

- No single product or service must be made with a specific process type. Cookies can be made in a low-volume job shop or a high-volume line process; thus, the choice of process type must be carefully matched with strategy.
- Technological improvements offer a fundamental way to improve processes. Computerized technologies in particular provide customers with greater access, decrease costs for the organization offering the product or service, and help improve the tracking of and accounting for information.

5. Understand process analysis techniques, including break-even analysis, reengineering, flowcharting, from-to charts, and process simulation. Identify process bottlenecks in terms of human, equipment, or demand limitations.

- Each of these process analysis techniques can lead to improvements by comparing process alternatives and helping participants in the process to visualize and understand the process.
- Bottleneck analysis examines a process in terms of the cycle time, utilization, and capacity of discrete steps within an aggregate process. The goal is to identify the bottleneck step that is the limiting factor in increasing output. *Every* process has at least one bottleneck, which may be human labor, equipment capacity, or demand.

6. Describe the nature of the process swamp and the need to improve processes that matter to customers.

- Companies carry out hundreds or thousands of processes. It is critical to select processes to improve that most matter to customers; otherwise, improvements may be made that have no impact on end profits.

SOLVED PROBLEMS

Solved Problem 1

A manufacturer is considering adding a new plant to keep up with growth in demand. The location being considered will have fixed costs of \$25,000 per month and variable costs of \$25 per unit. The sales price per unit is \$45.

1. What volume is required per month to break even?

   The break-even is found by solving the equation

$$\begin{aligned} \$25{,}000 + \$25X &= \$45X \\ \$25{,}000 &= \$20X \\ X &= 1{,}250 \text{ units} \end{aligned}$$

2. What profit would be earned on 2,500 boxes?

$$\text{Profit} = 2{,}500 * \$45 - \$25{,}000 - \$25 * 2{,}500 = \$25{,}000$$

3. What volume is required to obtain a profit of \$100,000 per month?

$$\begin{aligned} \$100{,}000 &= X(\$45 - \$25) - \$25{,}000 \\ \$20X &= \$125{,}000 \\ X &= 6{,}250 \text{ units} \end{aligned}$$

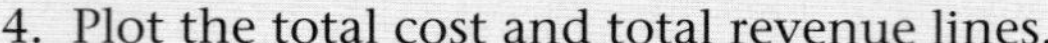

4. Plot the total cost and total revenue lines.

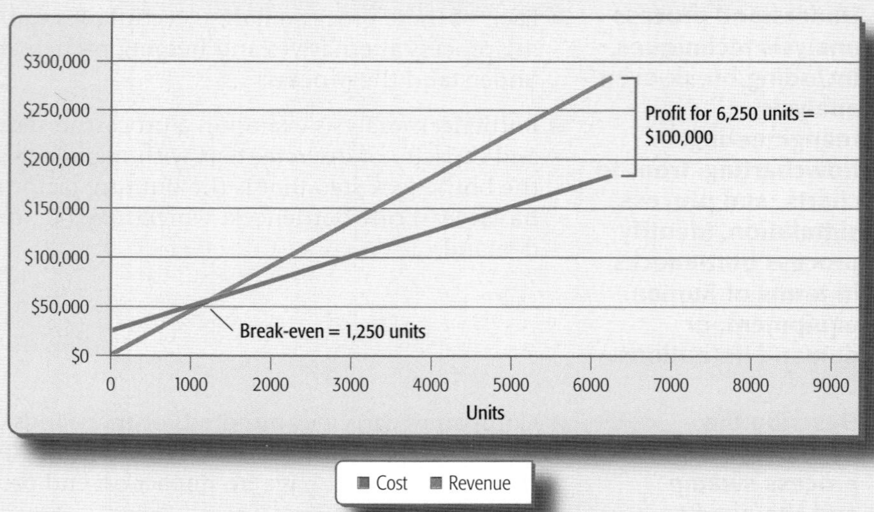

Solved Problem 2

A distribution center with six departments is being designed. Using the information in Table 4.3, assign departments to locations in order to minimize traffic flow through the distribution center.

TABLE 4.3 Available Locations

A	B	C
D	E	F

Trips Between Departments

	1	2	3	4	5	6
1	—	20	15	50	10	80
2		—	30	10	20	20
3			—	75	40	45
4				—	20	40
5					—	50
6						—

The goal is to make sure that the departments with large numbers of trips per day are adjacent to each other. The assignment of departments to location is done by starting with the assignment of department pairs with large numbers of trips to adjacent locations. The highlighted numbers in Table 4.3 show department pairs with large numbers of trips. We first assign departments 1 and 6 to the two middle locations (B and E) because they have 80 trips per day between them. Next, we place department 4 next to department 1 (location A) because there are 50 trips per day between them. Then we place department 3 next to department 6 (location D) because it has 45 trips between it and department 6, and departments 3 and 4 have 75 trips per day. Finally, we place departments 5 and 2 in locations C and F, respectively.

The proposed layout in Table 4.5 gets most of the large numbers in Table 4.3 to be adjacent as highlighted, using Euclidean distances as shown in Table 4.4.

TABLE 4.4 Distance Between Department Locations

	1	2	3	4	5	6
1	—	2	2	1	1	1
2		—	2	3	1	1
3			—	1	3	1
4				—	2	2
5					—	2
6						—

TABLE 4.5 Proposed Layout

A 4	**B** 1	**C** 5
D 3	**E** 6	**F** 2

This gives a load-distance score of

$$\begin{aligned}LD &= \sum_{i=1}^{N}\sum_{j=1}^{N} L_{ij}C_{ij}D_{ij}\\ &= 20*2+15*2+50*1+10*1+80*1+30*2+10*3+20*1+\\ &\quad 20*1+75*1+40*3+45*1+20*2+40*2+50*2\\ &= 800\end{aligned}$$

Solved Problem 3

A furniture manufacturing company produces tables using the process shown in Figure 4.15. All of the steps have one worker, except for the curing step (I), for a total of 6 workers. Assume that the entire system is paced (i.e., the entire system works at the pace of the slowest/bottleneck operation). Orders for new tables arrive every 10 minutes. The capacity at step I is 20 tables at a time.

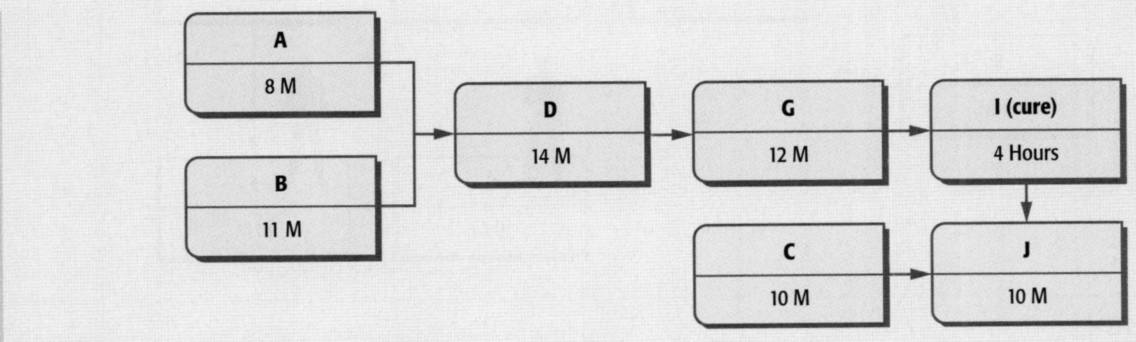

FIGURE 4.15

PART II Tools and Tactical Issues

1. What is the output in terms of products per hour?

The cycle time at step I is $CT = \frac{T}{C} = \frac{4 \text{ hours}}{20 \text{ units}} * \frac{60 \text{ minutes}}{1 \text{ hour}} = 12$ minutes per unit. Cycle time for demand is one table every 10 minutes. Thus, the bottleneck is step D (14 minutes per unit), and the output is

$$\text{Output} = \frac{\text{Time Period}}{\text{Cycle Time}} = \frac{60 \text{ minutes per hour}}{14 \text{ minutes per unit}} = 4.28 \text{ units per hour}$$

2. What does the capacity increase to if you can assign 2 additional workers (now 8 total)? Assume that workers are assigned to one (and only one) job and cannot rotate between multiple jobs. What is the utilization of the workers at stations D and G?

We assign the first worker to the bottleneck station (D). The new cycle time is then 14 minutes per unit/2 workers, or 7 minutes per unit. The next worker (#8) gets assigned to Step G, making the cycle time 6 minutes per unit (12 minutes per unit/2 workers). The diagram in Figure 4.16 shows the process after this step, with two workers at Steps D and G.

The new bottleneck is capacity at Step I, with a cycle time of 12 minutes per unit. This produces output of

$$\text{Output} = \frac{\text{Time Period}}{\text{Cycle Time}} = \frac{60 \text{ minutes per hour}}{12 \text{ minutes per unit}} = 5 \text{ units per hour}$$

3. What is the expected inventory of products that will accumulate at the curing station? Your calculation should be based on the process in Part 2.

Because the throughput time at I is 4 hours and the cycle time is 12 minutes, one unit will enter every 12 minutes. Each unit will spend 4 hours curing. Thus, the average inventory is

$$\text{Average inventory} = \frac{4 \text{ hours per unit}}{12 \text{ minutes per cycle}} * \frac{60 \text{ minutes}}{1 \text{ hour}} = 20 \text{ units}$$

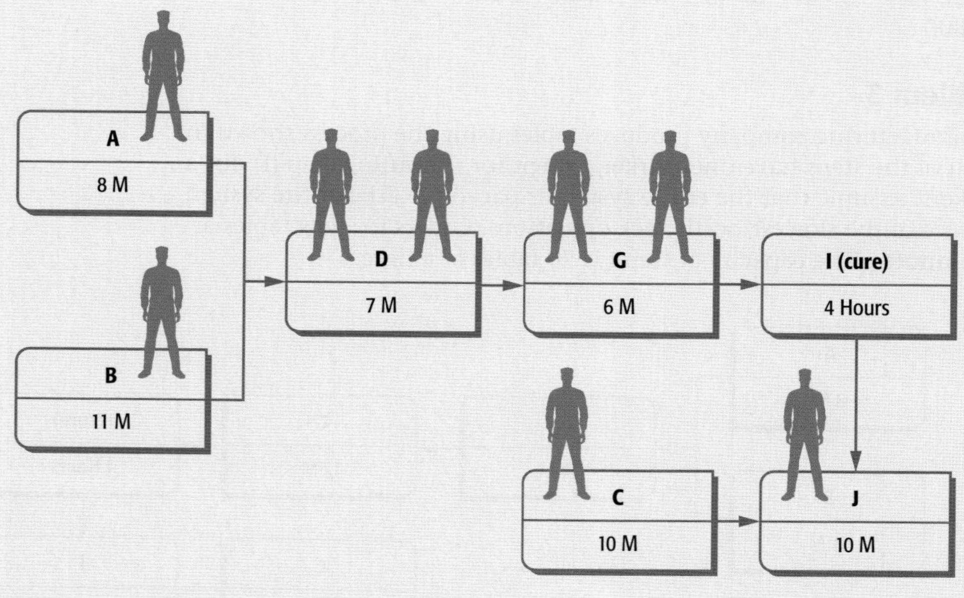

FIGURE 4.16

PROBLEMS

1. A department store is being planned for a new shopping mall. Using the information in Table 4.6, assign departments to locations in order to minimize traffic flow through the store.

2. Paulo's Pizza has a fairly simple process, as shown in Figure 4.17. Answer the following questions. Assume that the capacity of the oven is 3 pizzas at a time and that you start with a single worker.

   a. If orders for pizzas arrive every 10 minutes, how many pizzas can Paulo's sell per six-hour shift? How long will it take to fill a customer order?

   b. What will the utilization of the single worker be? What is the effect of variation in demand (i.e., orders do not arrive exactly 10 minutes apart, but instead average 10 minutes apart)?

   c. If a pizza sells for $16 and the ingredients cost $5, what amount of profit can Paulo's make per hour? What is the value of a second worker to help out Paulo? What will the utilization of the workers be? (Note: You need to describe which jobs each worker will do.)

   d. Evaluate the value of a reduction in the pizza price to $13 if that will result in an average of one order every 7 minutes.

3. Nine work centers must be located in a square building (3 × 3 layout). The locations of centers 1, 2, 3, and 4 are fixed as shown in Table 4.7 (on page 140). Assuming that transportation costs are $1 per load per meter, develop a suitable layout that minimizes transportation costs using the given information. Compute the total cost. Assume that distances are 10 meters for adjacent departments/locations (e.g., A and B), 20 meters for nonadjacent departments/locations (e.g., A and C or A and E), and 30 meters for departments in opposite corners (i.e., A and I or G and C).

4. The process depicted in Figure 4.18 is initially staffed with 5 workers. Each worker is assigned to one and only one step in the process. Step E does *not* require a human. The capacity of Step E is 4 units. Orders for 1 unit arrive every 6 minutes. Assume that the entire system is paced (i.e., the entire system works at the pace of the slowest/bottleneck operation).

   a. Determine the output in units per hour. Also, what is the utilization of Step C?

   b. If you can assign 2 additional workers (each worker is assigned to work exclusively at one

TABLE 4.6

A	B	C
D	E	F

Customer Trips

	Men's	Women's	Kids'	Sporting	Kitchen	Electronics
Men's	—	20	15	50	10	70
Women's		—	80	10	60	20
Kids'			—	25	40	15
Sporting				—	20	60
Kitchen					—	15
Electronics						—

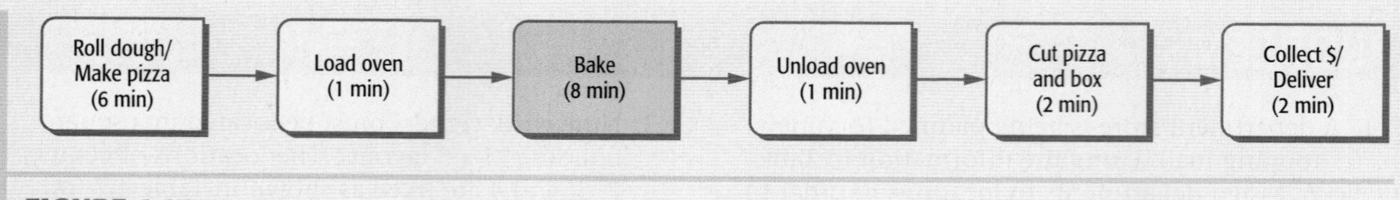

FIGURE 4.17

TABLE 4.7

A 1	**B**	**C** 2
D	**E**	**F**
G 3	**H**	**I** 4

	Loads per Day								
	1	**2**	**3**	**4**	**5**	**6**	**7**	**8**	**9**
1	—	20	40	60	70	10	30	100	300
2		—	30	50	90	20	400	150	
3			—	60	40	200	15	30	250
4				—	140	250	150	20	10
5					—	200	80	120	130
6						—	40	60	30
7							—	20	40
8								—	30
9									—

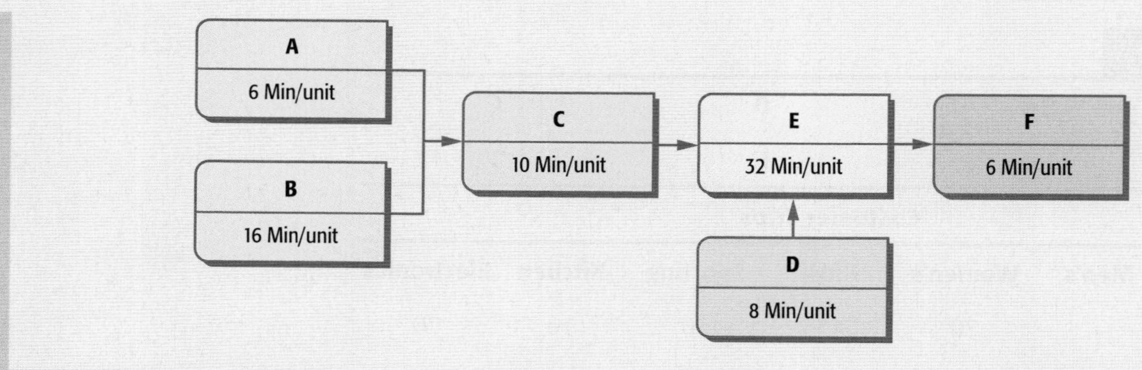

FIGURE 4.18

step), which two steps would be assigned an additional worker? Determine the output in units per hour. Also, what is the utilization of Step C?

c. What is the expected work-in-progress inventory at Step E?

d. If you can assign another worker (there is now a total of 8 workers), which step would be assigned an additional worker? Determine the output in units per hour. Will the process be able to produce and sell 50 units in an eight-hour shift? If the units have a gross profit margin (after subtracting materials but not labor) of $35 per unit, what will the gross profit per hour be? What will the revenue per worker be?

e. If you can expand Step E to a capacity of 8, how does this change the output, utilization, and gross profit?

f. If demand can be increased to 1 unit every 4 minutes by decreasing the price so that the gross profit is $30 per unit, should you do this? Assume that you have a ninth worker.

5. Joe's Machine Shop has identified the grinding station as its key bottleneck and has identified two options for expansion. The Grinder 1000 has fixed costs of $20,000 and $10 per unit variable costs. The Grinder 2000 has fixed costs of $40,000 and $8 per unit variable costs. Revenue per unit is projected to be $16.

a. Determine the break-even point for each alternative.

b. At what volume of output would the two alternatives yield the same profit?

c. If demand is 13,000 units, which option yields a higher profit? How much?

6. Consider the process in Figure 4.19.

a. If 1 worker is assigned to handle each step, for a total of 5 workers, what is the output in terms of products per hour?

b. What is the utilization of Step B?

c. What is the effect on output and utilization of hiring a sixth worker? To which step will this worker be assigned?

7. Tyworth Inc. is examining three alternative technologies with the fixed and variable costs given in Table 4.6. Plot the cost lines for these technologies and determine break-even quantities.

a. What is the lowest-cost technology if 10,000 units will be produced per year? What will the cost of production be for this quantity?

b. What is the lowest-cost technology if 20,000 units will be produced per year? What will the cost of production be for this quantity?

c. What is the lowest-cost technology if 50,000 units will be produced per year? What will the cost of production be for this quantity?

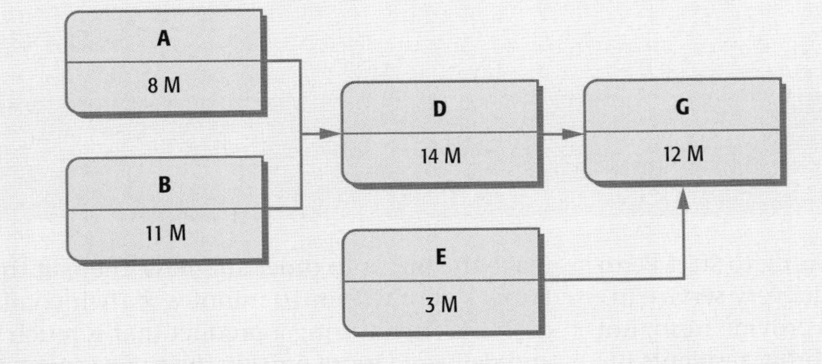

FIGURE 4.19

TABLE 4.8

Technology	Fixed Cost (annual)	Variable Cost
A	$2,000	$2 per unit
B	$8,000	$1.50 per unit
C	$16,000	$1.30 per unit

8. Consider the process in Figure 4.20.

   a. If 1 worker is assigned to handle each step, for a total of 4 workers, what is the output in terms of products per hour?

   b. What is the utilization of Step B?

9. A plastic cup manufacturer is considering adding a new plant to keep up with growth in demand. The location being considered will have fixed costs of $15,200 per month and variable costs of $10 per box of 1,000 cups produced. Cups are sold for a price of $15 per box of 1,000.

   a. What volume of cups is required per month to break even?

   b. What profit would be earned on 6,000 boxes?

   c. What volume is required to obtain a profit of $10,000 per month?

   d. Plot the total cost and total revenue lines.

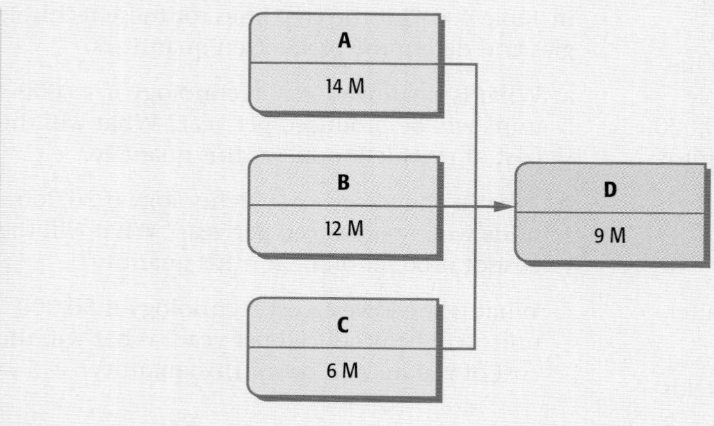

FIGURE 4.20

CASE STUDY

Penn & Pat's Pretty Hot Pizza Pronto

You and your roommate are preparing to start Penn & Pat's Pretty Hot Pizza Pronto delivery service in your apartment. The company will provide fresh, hot pizza with a short lead time to the other residents in your very large apartment complex. However, before you start, you need to conduct some preliminary analysis of the pizza-making process and determine your costs (and your profit!) and your capacity.

Business Concept

Your idea is to bake fresh pizzas to order and allow the customers to determine the toppings from a list of more than 15 different items; you will offer pizzas only in a "large" size to simplify the ordering and making process. The pizzas will be available for delivery only to other apartments in your very large building. You believe that this is a good market because the closest competitor is five miles away, making it very difficult for the people in your building to get a hot pizza delivered in a timely fashion. Your strategy is to make the pizzas to order and have them at the customer's door within 10 minutes of their coming out of the oven, ensuring a product that is much hotter and delivered more quickly than your competitor can deliver. In addition, both you and your roommate have worked in pizza places, so you feel you have the necessary pizza-making skills and know-how to be successful.

The Production Process

Making pizza is a relatively simple process: premade dough is flattened out, the customer-designated ingredients are put onto the flattened dough, the raw pizza is carefully loaded into the oven to ensure that it cooks evenly, the pizza cooks, it is taken out and quickly sliced and boxed, and finally the pizza is delivered to the customer's door. You already own the necessary capital equipment of an oven, three pizza trays, and enough containers to store all the offered ingredients. However, your countertop and oven are both very small and can accommodate only one large pizza at a time. Your landlord pays your electric bill, so you don't need to worry about the cost of running the oven. Therefore, your variable costs are simply the cost of the ingredients (estimated to average $5.50 per pizza), the $0.50 cost of the pizza box, and your time (you will have to estimate the value of your time). You both have pizza-making experience, and you have been able to practice in your apartment to streamline the process and have estimated the following times to be necessary to make pizzas.

Because your building has a very reliable computer network, it is possible for customers to send electronic messages directly to you when they would like a pizza—and the added benefit is that the customer is responsible for ensuring the accuracy of the order (selected ingredients and delivery location). Because the ordering process for you is virtually instantaneous, it doesn't need to be a consideration in your time and capacity analysis.

Once you have received an order, it takes approximately 2 minutes to flatten out the dough; you both have the exotic ability to do this by spinning and tossing the dough in the air, which you feel makes a lighter and crisper crust. Once the dough is flattened, it must be placed onto the pizza tray waiting on the counter, and you have to spend about 5 minutes, for an average pizza, putting on all of the ingredients. This includes the time needed to retrieve and replace the refrigerated items that are already prepared and stored in containers in the refrigerator. Once the pizza is "built," it must be placed in the oven to cook for roughly 8 minutes. Your oven is rather small and can barely hold one large pizza, so it takes about 1 minute to be sure it has been placed correctly so that it isn't touching the sides of the oven and will cook evenly. After it has cooked, you take it out of the oven (it is very hot, so you do this so quickly that the time doesn't figure into your calculations), and it takes about 1 minute to slice and pack the piping hot pizza. Finally, you can deliver the pizza to any other apartment in you large building in roughly 5 minutes, on average.

This is a simplification of the process, for illustrative purposes. For example, the time needed to preheat the oven, to prepare or slice the various ingredients and put them into containers, and to clean up are not included in this analysis.

KEY QUESTIONS TO ANSWER BEFORE LAUNCHING THE BUSINESS

Before launching Penn and Pat's Pretty Hot Pizza Pronto, you need to set prices and determine your capacity. Also, because night classes are pretty common, there will be some times when only one of you is able to work.

1. What is the shortest amount of time for a customer to receive a pizza if there are no other products in the queue?
2. How many orders could you start and deliver in one hour if only one of you is working? If both of you are working?
3. How much time would you need (beyond one hour) to make and deliver one more pizza if only one of you is working? If both of you are working?
4. If you sell the pizzas for $8.00 (including delivery), how much will you earn per pizza? How much will you earn per minute of work for each pizza? What are you earning per hour if only one of you is working? If both of you are working? How much would you like to sell a pizza for, and why?
5. How much time of each resource are you using if only one of you is available to work? If both of you are working?
6. What is your bottleneck?
7. What changes could you make, if any, to increase your capacity?

Source: Case written by Andrea Prud'homme, Michigan State University, January 2006.

CHAPTER 5

Forecasting

LEARNING OBJECTIVES

1. Explain the need for forecasting of independent demand products.
2. Describe the basic principles of forecasting.
3. Discuss the fundamental components of demand and types of forecasting methods.
4. Demonstrate and apply time-series analysis in forecasting.
5. Evaluate forecast accuracy and determine the best method.
6. Discuss the application of qualitative and causal methods for forecasting.
7. Describe forecasting across the broader supply chain.

Special K = Special Challenges

The market for processed cereals such as Raisin Bran, Cheerios, Rice Krispies, or Wheaties is very challenging to make a profit in. This is true for two reasons: First, there is a great deal of competition, and second, sales are growing slowly—typically 1 to 5 percent per year. From a production point of view, forecasting demand is relatively easy for the manufacturer (Kellogg's or General Mills) because of the low growth rate and the fairly long shelf life of the finished product. In contrast, there are a few "breakout" products or categories with quickly growing sales that are more of a challenge to forecast.

One such category killer is Kellogg's Special K cereal, which has become the company's number one brand, with annual sales of $500 million globally. Sales have skyrocketed since Kellogg's and its advertising agency, Leo Burnett Worldwide, developed the Special K Challenge diet plan in 2001. U.S. sales of Special K cereal were up 16 percent, to $286 million, for the year ending September 6, 2006, and sales of Special K bars were up 67 percent, to $96 million. To further capitalize on the popularity of this product, Kellogg's planned to roll out a line of protein waters and protein bars for the diet section. The company also planned to launch new Special K products, including a Special K Chocolatey Delight during diet season in January 2007 and Special K Personal Trainer watches.

While all of this sounds good from a marketing perspective, it comes with substantial challenges on the supply chain side. One primary challenge involves forecasting, which needs to be done in order to plan the number of production and distribution facilities to operate, as well as the size and location of such facilities. In addition, forecasting affects the scheduling of delivery trucks, labor, and marketing campaigns.

While the cereal had sold well, as had the snack bars, there was no guarantee that the add-on products would sell well. According to one retail buyer, "You never know with these things. It could be the flavor of the month and only click for a while, or it could be the next big hit. It's hard to know." Kellogg's certainly hopes for a big hit—without one, the chances for underutilized facilities are quite high.

Kellogg's cereal.

Figure 5.1 illustrates that while Kellogg's sales of medium-sugar cereals in the United States are decreasing, sales of cereal bars are growing. As a result, the forecasting challenges are different. For cereals, the decreasing sales make forecasts important for limiting overproduction of cereals. In contrast, cereal bars are increasing in sales, so forecasts are used more to prevent lost sales in a growing market category. New products or families of products such as Special K Chocolatey Delight do not have past demand on which to base forecasts. Therefore, qualitative methods that allow subjective input are more likely to be used than more quantitative methods. In sum, this underscores some of the challenges in forecasting sales for either an overall product category or a specific product within a category. ■

Source: S. Thompson, "Kellogg Has Megabrand Ambitions for Special K," *Advertising Age* 77, no. 45 (2006), p. 6.

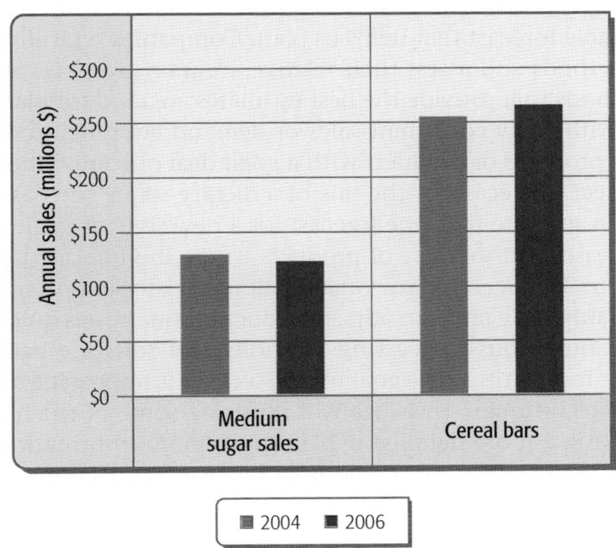

FIGURE 5.1 Kellogg's Sales of Medium-Sugar Cereal and Cereal Bars in the United States

Source: Breakfast Cereal, U.S. August, 2007 Supply Structure, Mintel International Group Limited

WHY WE NEED TO FORECAST

Forecasts are vitally important to organizations. They are used to plan facilities, production schedules, staffing allocation, capacity planning, and other such things. Many levels of a business or a supply chain employ forecasts for various types of planning. Let's consider house construction. At the first level of the supply chain, home builders use data on the national economy, the local economy, and recent home sales to develop a forecast for the number of homes they can sell in a given year. They then use this number to derive estimates for the amount of labor (number of employees) to hire, the number of lots or subdivisions to develop, and the timing of orders for building products, such as lumber, concrete, bricks, cabinets, and windows, that are used to complete a house. For example, the lead time to obtain a wide range of building supplies can increase from a few weeks to several months after a major natural disaster such as Hurricane Katrina (New Orleans and the Mississippi Gulf region, August 2005) or the Indian Ocean tsunami (December 26, 2004).

At the second level of the supply chain, retailers such as Lowe's and Home Depot must plan overall orders for each product, and also allocation of inventory to each store. Poor forecasts can lead to a significant excess or shortage of inventory. At the third level of the supply chain, manufacturers such as Anderson Windows, Merrillat Cabinets, and Brasscraft Plumbing must forecast demand for their products based on estimates of total home sales in a region and the company's market share. Masco Corporation, with annual sales in excess of $13 billion, announced a plan to cut 8,000 jobs in February 2007. This drastic move was attributable to lower sales at Lowe's and Home Depot as well as the slowdown in new home construction, which accounts for 40 percent of Masco's revenues. Finally, at the fourth level of the supply chain, suppliers of parts or raw materials like lumber to housing products companies like Masco must forecast demand for their products. At all levels, the accuracy and timeliness of forecasts is a critical component of decision making with respect to facility expansion/shrinkage, inventory allocation, labor allotment, and many other things.

Unfortunately, just like weather forecasts, business forecasts are incorrect more often than they're right. The goal is not to have a perfect forecast, but rather to have a reasonable forecast that helps us plan. Companies typically use a variety of forecasting methods and assess their relative accuracy over an extended time period. The methods that provide the best estimates are used for planning. Forecasts for products with fairly consistent sales or demand are much more reliable than those for new products or products with a great deal of competition. For example, we would expect a forecast for the sale of a dietary staple such as milk to be substantially more accurate than the forecast for a new style of clothing to be sold in the summer season. In the case of products where the forecast is typically off by more than 20 to 25 percent, many organizations seek to set up a responsive supply chain that is fairly agile and can adjust production quantities quickly.

There are numerous forecasting methods and software packages designed specifically for forecasting. The goal in this section is to provide a quick overview of forecasting techniques. Thus, we will illustrate some of the basic techniques. For those seeking a more detailed explanation, more information can be found in the references at the end of the book or by visiting this book's web site.

PRINCIPLES OF FORECASTING

Before we move to a detailed review of various forecasting models and approaches, it is useful to examine some basic principles of forecasting. These principles are not absolute laws, but they are true in the vast majority of cases. They provide a good foundation for understanding the benefits and limitations of forecasting.

Forecasts Are Wrong

Even the most sophisticated forecasting models, supported by the most advanced information technology and utilizing extensive historical data for a product's sales, will still be wrong far more often than they are right. It is close to impossible to predict anything *exactly*. The number of factors that affect the sales of any one product or item is simply too large and unknown to quantify exactly. The goal is, therefore, to get an estimate that is relatively close to actual demand.

Forecasts Get Worse the Farther into the Future They Go

In the short term, the factors that affect forecasts are fairly consistent and unlikely to change. Consider the demand for an electronics product such as a cell phone, camera, or MP3 player: For the next one to two months, demand should be fairly easy to predict, but as we go farther out into the future, predicting demand becomes harder because there is a greater likelihood of substantial change occurring, such as a competitor bringing a new product with better features to the market. The distance into the future for which a product can be forecasted with a reasonable degree of accuracy is related to its life cycle. Products with short life cycles, such as electronics products, often can be forecast only two to four months into the future, while products with longer life cycles, such as automobiles or furniture, can be forecast a year or more into the future.

Aggregated Forecasts for Product or Service Groups Tend to Be More Accurate

It is often easier to forecast for an aggregated group of similar products than to forecast for individual products separately. For example, sales of automobiles or cell phones for the entire world or for an individual company can be predicted with greater accuracy than sales of a particular model. This is true because individual products come in many different styles, sizes, and colors. The more options or choices that exist, the harder it is to forecast with any degree of accuracy. In clothing, one very popular color or style—say, pink is the "in" color—may sell in huge volumes, but the remaining colors and styles of the same product family will sell far less than predicted. In other words, the demands balance each other out. Of course, companies need to provide the final product, not some collection of the family of products. This is why paint companies long ago decided to ship white paint that could be mixed to a specific color with a small amount of colored mixing paint. The companies can predict total paint demand much better than the demand for each color—and carrying a small buffer amount of mixing paint is not very difficult or expensive.

Forecasts Are Not a Substitute for Derived Values

Given the degree of uncertainty and inaccuracy with forecasts, managers should use values derived from production plans where possible. For example, forecasting the amount of wood, screws, and bolts necessary to produce a certain number of tables is not very smart. Instead, given a forecast or production plan for a certain number of tables, the amount of wood, screws, and bolts should be derived. If each table requires 8 bolts, and we have forecasted or planned to produce 400 tables, it is best to derive that a total of 3,200 bolts (8 bolts * 400 tables) is required. The ability to use information about the required quantity of parts to produce an end item is one of the fundamental principles of dependent demand planning, which is the subject of Chapter 7.

COMPONENTS OF DEMAND AND FORECASTING METHODS

There are several categories of forecasting methods. These different methods are intended to address demand that differs in several ways across various products and services. Thus, we examine six basic components of demand.

Components of Demand

Demand for products or services consists of several components: average demand, trend, seasonal component, cyclical component, autocorrelation, and random variation. Figure 5.2 illustrates these demand components over a three-year period. In this case, the average demand appears to be around 120 units per month, and there is a trend for demand increasing by about 2½ units per month. There is also a seasonal increase in sales in the summer months (May to September). Such seasonal increases might be found for products such as ice cream or lawn mowers.

The random component of demand can be seen in the small hills and valleys of the curve. Random variation is caused by chance events—after all the other components of demand (average, trend, seasonal, cyclical, and autocorrelative) have been accounted for, the remainder is random variation, which is caused by chance.

Cyclical factors are similar to seasonal factors but have a much longer time period and are often harder to identify. For example, fashion runs in a cyclical pattern over a number of years or decades. Hot pink may be "in fashion" for a year or two, but then out of fashion for a number of years until a designer brings it to the forefront again. Cyclical factors for demand include things such as politics, economic conditions, war, and sociocultural influences. In many ways, cyclical factors are the hardest to predict because the timing of their pattern is

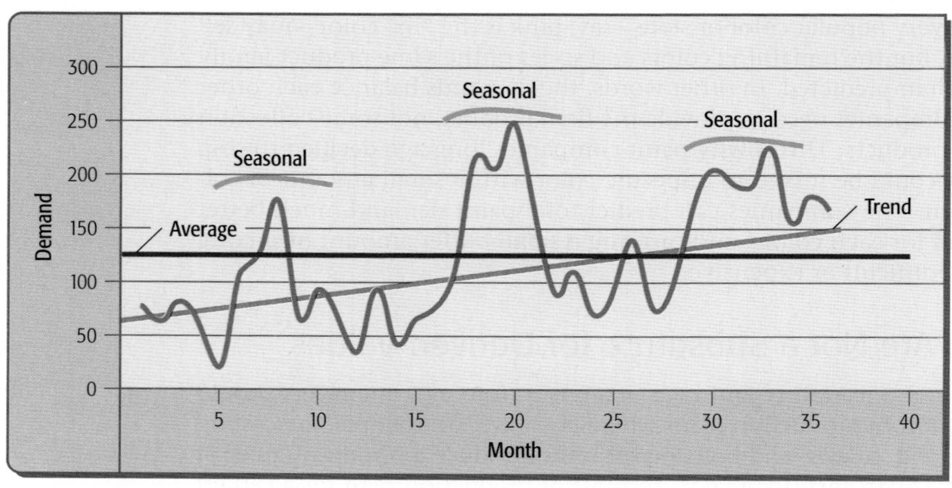

FIGURE 5.2 Components of Demand

unknown. Trends occur when demand is increasing or decreasing over time as a result of some factor such as word of mouth (or blogs), advertising, or changes in the population. Autocorrelation occurs when the value of one data point is highly correlated with the past values. For example, when waiting in a long line, the time for the fifteenth person in line is highly correlated with (and guaranteed to be longer than) the time for the tenth person in line.

Forecasting Methods

There are two basic types of forecasting: quantitative and qualitative. Quantitative techniques rely on existing data for demand and use mathematical formulas of varying complexity to accommodate different types of demand. There are two primary groups of quantitative methods. **Time-series analysis** utilizes past demand data to predict future demand by examining cyclical, trend, and seasonal influences. **Causal relationships** identify a connection between two factors, one that precedes and causes changes in the second or effect factor, such as the effect of advertising on sales. **Qualitative forecasting** is based on subjective factors, estimates, and opinions. Qualitative methods are important for new products or when past demand data are lacking.

In order to keep our discussion of forecasting brief, we focus on two major elements of forecasting: time-series analysis and measurement of errors.

- **Time-series analysis** a technique that utilizes past demand data to predict future demand by examining cyclical, trend, and seasonal influences
- **Causal relationships** a technique that identifies a connection between two factors, one that precedes and causes changes in the second or effect factor
- **Qualitative forecasting** a method of forecasting that is based on subjective factors, estimates, and opinions

TIME-SERIES ANALYSIS

Time-series analysis is based on historical data and the assumption that past patterns will continue in the future. The goal is to identify the underlying patterns of demand and develop a model to predict these patterns in the future. In this section, we will discuss five basic time-series techniques: naive forecasts, moving averages, exponential smoothing, trend-adjusted exponential smoothing, and seasonal patterns.

Naive Forecast

A **naive forecast** uses the demand for the current period as the forecast for the next period. Thus, if demand for Friday at a coffee shop is for 142 lattes, the forecast for Saturday is 142 lattes. If the actual demand for Saturday is 150 lattes, the forecast for Sunday will be 150 lattes. The naive forecast is very simple and low cost to use. It works best when demand, trend, and seasonal patterns are stable and there is relatively little random variation. The naive approach is the simplest of all the possible forecasting methods and works particularly well when there is autocorrelation.

- **Naive forecast** a method of forecasting that uses the demand for the current period as the forecast for the next period.

Estimating the Average

Every series of demand figures includes at least two of the six components of demand: an average and random variation. There may or may not be a trend, seasonal, cyclical, or autocorrelation component. Thus, we begin our discussion with the most basic case (after a naive forecast, which is a moving average with one period): a pattern with an average and random variation.

Figure 5.3 shows the number of daily customers at FoodCo Grocery over the past 12 days. A careful look at the figure indicates that there do not appear to be any trend, seasonal, or cyclical patterns. Thus, we will assume that the only components of demand are the average and random variation.

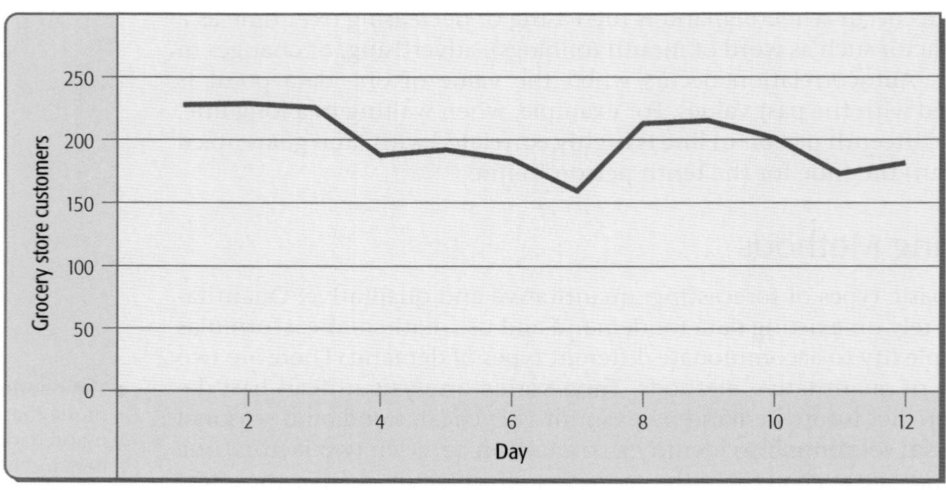

FIGURE 5.3 Daily Customers at FoodCo Grocery

Moving Averages

● **Moving average** a technique for estimating the average of a demand series and filtering out the effects of random variation

A **moving average** (MA) is a technique for estimating the average of a demand series and filtering out the effects of random variation. Developing a moving average involves computing the average of n previous periods of demand and then using this as the estimate for the next period of demand (or a period farther out in the future). The average is updated after every period to include the most recent demand data. The formula used to compute the forecast for period $t + 1$ is thus

$$F_{t+1} = \frac{\text{total of last } n \text{ periods of demand}}{n} = \frac{D_t + D_{t-1} + D_{t-2} + \cdots + D_{t-n+1}}{n} \quad \text{(Equation 1)}$$

where D_t = actual demand in period t
n = total number of periods in the average
F_{t+1} = forecast for period $t + 1$

Solved Example 1

Estimating Average Demand with the Moving-Average Method

1. Using the data shown in Figure 5.3 and Table 5.1, compute a four-day moving-average forecast for the number of customers on the fifth day.

TABLE 5.1 Daily Customers at FoodCo Grocery

Day	Customers
1	228
2	228
3	225
4	188

(continued)

The moving-average forecast at the end of day 4 for the number of customers on day 5 is

$$F_5 = \frac{D_1 + D_2 + D_3 + D_4}{n} = \frac{228 + 228 + 225 + 188}{4} = 217.25$$

Thus, at the end of day 4, we forecast that there will be 217 customers on day 5.

2. If the number of customers on day 5 turns out to be 193, compute the forecast for day 6.

$$F_6 = \frac{D_2 + D_3 + D_4 + D_5}{n} = \frac{228 + 225 + 188 + 193}{4} = 208.50$$

Thus, the forecast at the end of day 5 for customers on day 6 is 209 (the exact number of 208.50 can be rounded to the nearest integer for convenience). If we wish to forecast further into the future, we would apply this same number—i.e., the forecast for customers on days 7 through 12 would also be 209.

The moving-average technique can use as many periods of past demand as desired. Using more periods results in a more stable forecast, while using fewer periods results in a more responsive forecast. More periods should be used when demand changes relatively infrequently, while fewer periods should be used if the demand is volatile. Choosing between stability and responsiveness requires a tradeoff—it is impossible to get both in a single forecast.

Figure 5.4 shows the customer data from Figure 5.3 along with a two-day and a four-day moving-average forecast. Notice how the two-day MA jumps around more when demand changes—on day 10, the forecast is higher than for the four-day MA. This is because the two-day MA reacts more quickly to the increase in demand for days 8 and 9 relative to day 7. In contrast, the four-day MA is much smoother and more stable—it reacts more slowly. The advantage to this is that if

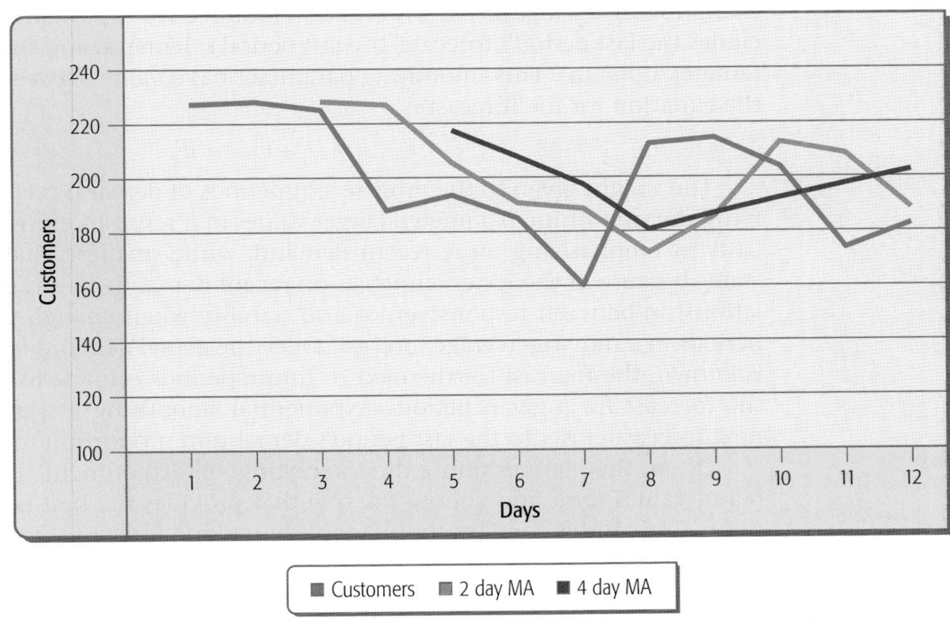

FIGURE 5.4 Comparison of Moving-Average Forecast with Two- and Four-Day Moving Average

demand is truly random, the longer MA is less likely to overreact. But if there turns out to be some type of trend, the shorter MA will react more quickly.

One of the limitations of the moving average is that it places equal weights on each time period. In contrast, weighted moving averages allow a higher or lower weight to be placed on specific periods.

Weighted Moving Average

● **Weighted moving average** a technique that allows periods to have different weights, with the total weight equaling 1.0 (one)

A **weighted moving average** is a technique that allows periods to have different weights, with the total weight equaling 1.0 (one). For example, a three-period weighted moving average might assign the most recent period a weight of 0.6, the second most recent period a weight of 0.25, and the third most recent period a weight of 0.15. Thus, the forecast for period $t + 1$ would be

$$F_{t+1} = 0.6D_t + 0.25D_{t-1} + 0.15D_{t-2}$$

The forecast for day 4 using the data in Figure 5.3 and Solved Example 1 would be

$$F_4 = 0.6D_3 + 0.25D_2 + 0.15D_1 = 0.6 * 225 + 0.25 * 228 + 0.15 * 228 = 226.2$$

The benefit of a weighted moving average is that it allows a greater emphasis on the most recent demand than on past demand. This has the effect of making the forecast more responsive to changes. In fact, seasonal and trend effects can be captured if high weights are used, but this method will still lag behind the trend. If the weights for a weighted moving average are equal, then the forecasts will be the same as for a moving average with the same number of periods.

The text web site includes a demonstration of how to use the SOLVER module within Microsoft Excel to find the best weights for a specific forecasting problem.

Exponential Smoothing

● **Exponential smoothing** a technique that calculates forecasts by giving more weight to recent demands than to earlier demands

Exponential smoothing calculates forecasts by giving more weight to recent demands than to earlier demands. This is one of the most frequently used methods because it is often easier to calculate than a weighted moving average and requires less data (the initial calculation for the first few forecasts is a bit more difficult, but after that exponential smoothing requires less data and less computation than moving averages). The information required for exponential smoothing includes the last period's forecast, the last period's demand, and the smoothing parameter alpha (α). This smoothing parameter has a value between 0 and 1.0, and the equation for the forecast is

$$F_{t+1} = \alpha D_t + (1 - \alpha)F_t \qquad \text{(Equation 2)}$$

The weight given to the most recent periods of demand is changed by modifying the smoothing parameter. Larger values of α result in more responsive forecasts by emphasizing more recent demand, while smaller values of α are more stable because of the lesser emphasis on recent demand. This is similar to the relationship between responsiveness and stability when changing the number of periods in a moving-average forecast. Once the actual demand for a given period is known, the forecast for the next or future periods is made using demand and the forecast for a given period—exponential smoothing works by moving the next forecast closer to the last period's demand in proportion to α.

Often, the planner doing the forecasting will experiment with a large number of values for α and choose the one that provides the best performance over time. This can be done by simultaneously making forecasts with numerous (often six to ten) values of α for several periods, then calculating measures of forecast error (to be covered later in this chapter) and choosing the value of α that provides the best or most accurate forecast.

To start, we need an initial forecast. This can be found by using the last period's demand or by taking a moving average. With either approach, the effect of the initial forecast will diminish over time because exponential smoothing gives increased weight to the most recent period of time. Thus, after four or five periods, the forecasts are primarily a function of the demand series and exponential smoothing, while the impact of the initial forecast is minimal. We illustrate as follows.

Solved Example 2

Forecasting with Exponential Smoothing

1. Using the data for customer arrivals to FoodCo Grocery from Figure 5.3 and Table 5.2, develop a forecast for the demand on day 4. Use $\alpha = 0.3$. Start your forecasting by using a moving average of the first two days as your forecast for day 3.

TABLE 5.2 Daily Customers at FoodCo Grocery

Day	Demand
1	228
2	228
3	225
4	188
5	193
6	185
7	160
8	213
9	215
10	203
11	175
12	184

The first step is to calculate a forecast for day 3 using the first two days of demand and a moving average:

$$F_3 = \frac{D_1 + D_2}{n} = \frac{228 + 228}{2} = 228$$

Next, we calculate the forecast for day 4:

$$F_4 = \alpha D_3 + (1 - \alpha)F_3 = 0.3 * 225 + (1 - 0.3) * 228 = 227.10$$

2. Calculate the forecast for days 5 through 13.

$$F_5 = \alpha D_4 + (1 - \alpha)F_4 = 0.3 * 188 + (1 - 0.3) * 227.10 = 215.37$$
$$F_6 = \alpha D_5 + (1 - \alpha)F_5 = 0.3 * 193 + (1 - 0.3) * 215.37 = 208.66$$
$$F_7 = \alpha D_6 + (1 - \alpha)F_6 = 0.3 * 185 + (1 - 0.3) * 208.66 = 201.56$$
$$F_8 = \alpha D_7 + (1 - \alpha)F_7 = 0.3 * 160 + (1 - 0.3) * 201.56 = 189.09$$
$$F_9 = \alpha D_8 + (1 - \alpha)F_8 = 0.3 * 213 + (1 - 0.3) * 189.09 = 196.27$$
$$F_{10} = \alpha D_9 + (1 - \alpha)F_9 = 0.3 * 215 + (1 - 0.3) * 196.27 = 201.89$$

(continued)

PART II Tools and Tactical Issues

$$F_{11} = \alpha D_{10} + (1 - \alpha)F_{10} = 0.3 * 203 + (1 - 0.3) * 201.89 = 202.22$$
$$F_{12} = \alpha D_{11} + (1 - \alpha)F_{11} = 0.3 * 175 + (1 - 0.3) * 202.22 = 194.05$$
$$F_{13} = \alpha D_{12} + (1 - \alpha)F_{12} = 0.3 * 184 + (1 - 0.3) * 194.05 = 191.04$$

Figure 5.5 illustrates the results from Solved Example 2 with two values of α. Notice how the forecasts with $\alpha = 0.5$ are more responsive than when $\alpha = 0.3$, but also tend to overshoot when there is a large fluctuation of demand from one day to another.

The spreadsheet for Solved Example 2 is available on the book web site. The spreadsheet allows the input of different values for α and shows the resulting forecast with measures of forecast error. The web site also includes a demonstration of how to use the SOLVER module within Microsoft Excel to find the best value of α.

Including a Trend

The methods discussed so far assume that there is no trend to the data. Weighted moving averages and exponential smoothing will adjust to a trend if high weights are given to more recent periods. However, either a weighted moving average or exponential smoothing will be biased when a trend is present because these methods are not specifically designed for this purpose. Consider situations where there is a trend: cell phones with a camera were a fast-growing trend in the period 2003–2005, with sales increasing very quickly; similarly, hybrid cars experienced a trend of greatly increased sales in the years after the Toyota Prius first appeared (the Prius was first introduced in Japan in 1997 and worldwide in 2001). Many companies find out to their dismay that trends go both directions—up and down. Filmmakers like Fuji and Kodak have been experiencing a long-term trend of declining film sales because of the phenomenal rise in sales of digital cameras.

Trend-adjusted exponential smoothing is a method for including a trend component in an exponentially smoothed forecast. The first step is to develop a current estimate of the trend component by comparing the average demand for the current period with the average demand for the previous period. Over a number of periods, this estimate is averaged to come up with a trend estimate. In other words, the estimates for both the average and the trend are smoothed us-

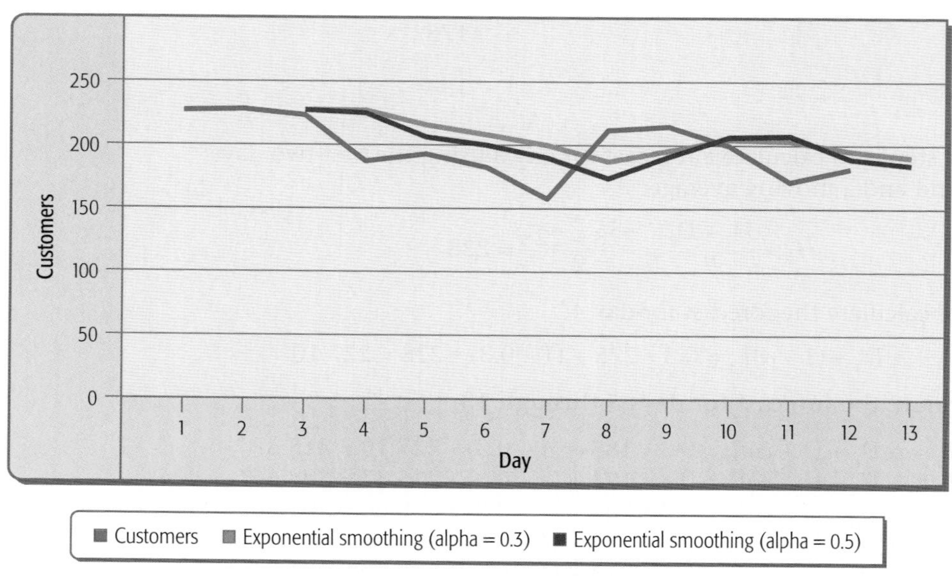

FIGURE 5.5 Illustration of Exponential Smoothing with $\alpha = 0.3$ and $\alpha = 0.5$

ing a smoothing factor α for the average and β for the trend. We calculate the average and trend for each period as follows:

$$A_t = \alpha D_t + (1 - \alpha)(A_{t-1} + T_{t-1}) \quad \text{(Equation 3)}$$

$$T_t = \beta(A_t - A_{t-1}) + (1 - \beta)T_{t-1} \quad \text{(Equation 4)}$$

$$F_{t+n} = A_t + nT_t \quad \text{(Equation 5)}$$

where A_t = exponentially smoothed average of the *series* in period t
T_t = exponentially smoothed average of the *trend* in period t
α = smoothing parameter for the *average* (value between 0 and 1)
β = smoothing parameter for the *trend* (value between 0 and 1)
D_t = demand in period t
F_{t+1} = forecast in period t for demand in period $t + 1$
n = number of periods in the future that the forecast is for

Equations 3 through 5 are used to come up with the forecast for the next period and to update the average and trend components of the forecast. We can also make forecasts for periods beyond the next period by multiplying the trend estimate T_t by the number of periods in the future we want to forecast and adding the results to the current average A_t.

As with exponential smoothing, we need to start with an estimate for the last period's average and the trend. We also need to pick values for α and β—often these are picked by experimenting with historical data and choosing the combination that gives the best forecasts overall.

Solved Example 3

Forecasting with Trend-Adjusted Exponential Smoothing

Axia Pharmaceuticals has a prescription drug for male pattern baldness that has experienced great success. Since being introduced six months ago, sales of this product, I'MNotBald, have grown over 50 percent. Last month's sales were 50,000 cases of I'MNotBald, and Axia's management estimates that the trend is increasing at 3,000 cases per month. This month's sales were 54,000 cases. In the following calculations, we will use $n = 1$ for all forecasts because forecasts are for the *next* period, except where noted.

1. Use $\alpha = 0.3$ and $\beta = 0.2$ to calculate a forecast for sales next month.

We start with $A_0 = 50{,}000$ and $T_0 = 3{,}000$; thus $F_1 = 50{,}000 + 3{,}000 = 53{,}000$.

$$A_1 = \alpha D_1 + (1 - \alpha)(A_0 + T_0) = 0.3 * 54{,}000 + (1 - 0.3)(50{,}000 + 3{,}000) = 53{,}300$$

$$T_1 = \beta(A_1 - A_0) + (1 - \beta)T_0 = 0.2 * (53{,}300 - 50{,}000) + (1 - 0.2) * 3{,}000 = 3{,}060$$

$$F_2 = A_1 + T_1 = 53{,}300 + 3{,}060 = 56{,}360$$

2. If sales in month 2 are actually 53,000, calculate the forecast for month 3.

$$A_2 = \alpha D_2 + (1 - \alpha)(A_1 + T_1) = 0.3 * 53{,}000 + (1 - 0.3)(53{,}300 + 3{,}060) = 55{,}352$$

$$T_2 = \beta(A_2 - A_1) + (1 - \beta)T_1 = 0.2 * (55{,}352 - 53{,}300) + (1 - 0.2) * 3{,}060 = 2{,}858.4$$

$$F_3 = A_2 + T_2 = 55{,}352 + 2{,}858.4 = 58{,}210.4$$

(continued)

3. If sales in month 3 are actually 60,500, calculate the forecast for month 4.

$$A_3 = \alpha D_3 + (1 - \alpha)(A_2 + T_2) = 0.3 * 60{,}500 + (1 - 0.3)(55{,}352 + 2{,}858.4) = 58{,}897.28$$

$$T_3 = \beta(A_3 - A_2) + (1 - \beta)T_2 = 0.2 * (58{,}897.28 - 55{,}352) + (1 - 0.2) * 2{,}858.4 = 2{,}995.78$$

$$F_4 = A_3 + T_3 = 58{,}897.28 + 2{,}995.78 = 61{,}893.06$$

4. Using the data in Table 5.3, develop forecasts for months 5 through 13.

The data that are "given" are highlighted in yellow, and the data that are calculated using equations 3 through 5 are highlighted in red. Note that forecasts are made for each period sequentially, and the process finishes with a forecast of 89,473.35 made in month 12 for sales in month 13.

TABLE 5.3 Demand and Forecasts with Trend-Adjusted Exponential Smoothing for I'MNotBald

Month	Demand	Forecast (*F*)	*A*	*T*
3	60.500	58,210.40	58,897.28	2,995.78
4	69,000	61,893.06	64,025.14	3,422.19
5	67,500	67,447.33	67,463.13	3,425.35
6	69,000	70,888.49	70,321.94	3,312.04
7	77,000	73,633.98	74,643.79	3,514.00
8	78,000	78,157.79	78,110.45	3,504.54
9	77,500	81,614.99	80,380.49	3,257.64
10	86,000	83,638.13	84,346.69	3,399.35
11	81,000	87,746.04	85,722.23	2,994.59
12	82,500	88,716.82	86,851.77	2,621.58
13		89,473.35		
14		92,094.93		
15		94,716.51		

5. Using the data in Table 5.3, develop forecasts for months 14 and 15.

There are forecasts for months 13, 14, and 15 in Table 5.3. Each of these forecasts is made at the end of month 12 by adding the exponentially smoothed average component ($A_{12} = 86{,}851.77$) and the trend component ($T_{12} = 2{,}621.58$) times the number of months in the future for that forecast. Thus, we calculate using Equation 5:

$$F_{t+n} = A_t + nT_t \text{ (for week 13, } n = 1)$$

$$F_{13} = A_{12} + 1 * T_{12} = 86{,}851.77 + 2{,}621.58 = 89{,}473.35$$

(continued)

For month 14, $n = 2$ because we are forecasting two months in the future from month 12:

$$F_{14} = A_{12} + 2 * T_{12} = 86{,}851.77 + 2 * 2{,}621.58 = 92{,}094.93$$

For month 15, $n = 3$ because we are forecasting three months in the future from month 12:

$$F_{15} = A_{12} + 3 * T_{12} = 86{,}851.77 + 3 * 2{,}621.58 = 94{,}716.51$$

Figure 5.6 shows a graph of the demand versus the forecast. Note that the forecasts for months 13 through 15 are made at the end of month 12.

The spreadsheet for Solved Example 3 is available on this book's web site. The spreadsheet allows the input of different values for α and β and shows the resulting forecast with measures of forecast error.

Including Seasonality

Many organizations sell products or services that have a seasonal demand. A seasonal demand is characterized by regular repetition of increases or decreases in demand as measured in time periods of less than a year (quarters, months, weeks, days, or hours). A season is the same as the time period. For example, a grocery store may have a seasonal pattern where demand is higher than average on Fridays, Saturdays, and Sundays and lower than average on other days of the week. Movie theaters tend to have a similar pattern of heavy demand on the weekends and lower demand on weekdays. In both cases, the seasonal pattern lasts a week, and the season is a day. A Starbucks has a shorter seasonal pattern of a day, with the season being an hour—demand is likely to be high in the morning, at lunchtime, and in the late afternoon and lower at other time periods. Finally, a manufacturer

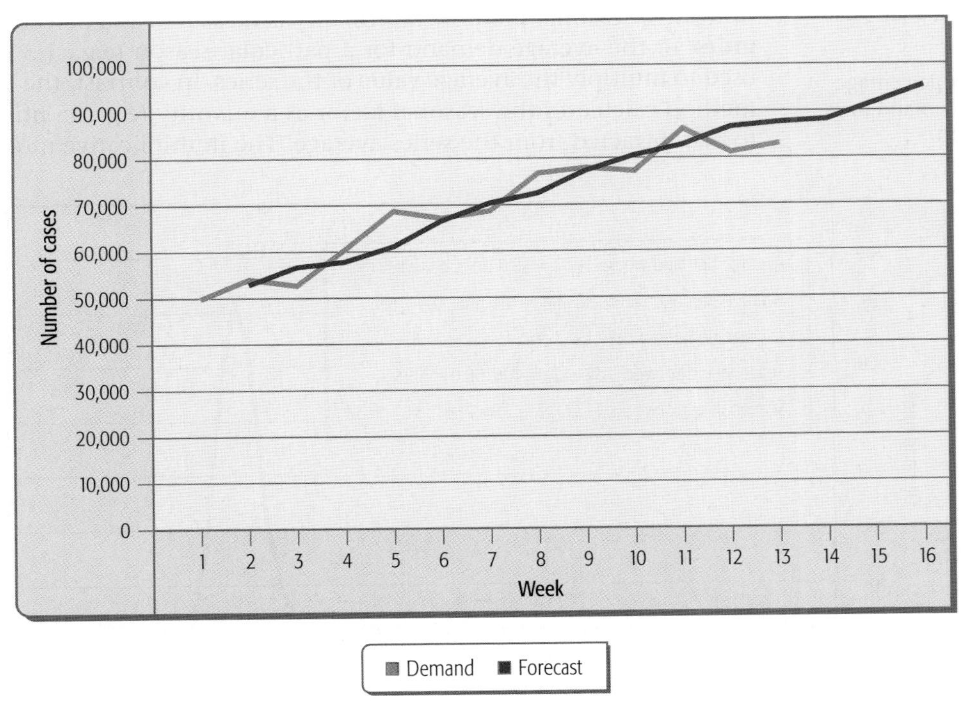

FIGURE 5.6 Graph of Demand and Trend-Adjusted Exponential Smoothing Forecast

of winter gloves has a seasonal pattern lasting a year, with the season being a month and the highest-demand period being October through February (at least in the northern hemisphere). Figure 5.7 illustrates data from the chainwide weekly sales for a regional grocery store for mousetraps (with week 0 corresponding to January 1–7). Can you think of other products that would have a similar pattern?

Figure 5.8 provides another illustration of a product or service that has a high seasonal component. Airline travel in the United States has substantially higher demand in the summer. Other peak periods occur around major holidays, such as Thanksgiving and Christmas. Figure 5.8 illustrates that air travel has a seasonal component that varies by month. There are also seasonal components that vary by week (e.g., Thanksgiving), day of the week (Sundays, Mondays, and Fridays tend to be busier than other days of the week), and time of the day. Forecasting at an aggregate level is often easier than forecasting at a more detailed level. In this case, forecasts for number of passengers on all airlines are easier than forecasts for specific airlines. The U.S. Bureau of Transportation Statistics offers a rich database of information on airline operations and demand.

There are several methods for estimating seasonal effects. One approach is to use one of the methods previously described, such as a moving average or exponential smoothing, but to limit the data to only those time periods in the same season. For example, the grocery store would use two sets of forecasting data, one for busy weekend days and one for slower weekdays. This approach is fairly simple to implement but has the disadvantage of discarding a lot of potentially useful information. Another approach is to use trend-adjusted exponential smoothing with a large weight on the trend component (i.e., a large value of β). This approach can work well, but it is likely to lag behind demand when the season starts and to overshoot demand when the season ends.

● **Multiplicative seasonal method** a forecasting method that calculates seasonal factors that are multiplied by an estimate of the average demand to develop a seasonal forecast

● **Seasonal index** percentage of the average demand for a particular season

There are several methods that analyze all the available past data and use a single model to forecast demand for all seasons. We focus on the **multiplicative seasonal method**, a method that calculates seasonal factors that are multiplied by an estimate of the average demand to develop a seasonal forecast. In the multiplicative seasonal method, seasonality is measured as a percentage or **seasonal index** of the average demand for a particular season (e.g., 1.3 or 2.2), which is used to multiply the average value of the series. In contrast, the additive seasonal method calculates the seasonal factor as a quantity (e.g., 45 units) that is added to or subtracted from the series average. The multiplicative model is used much

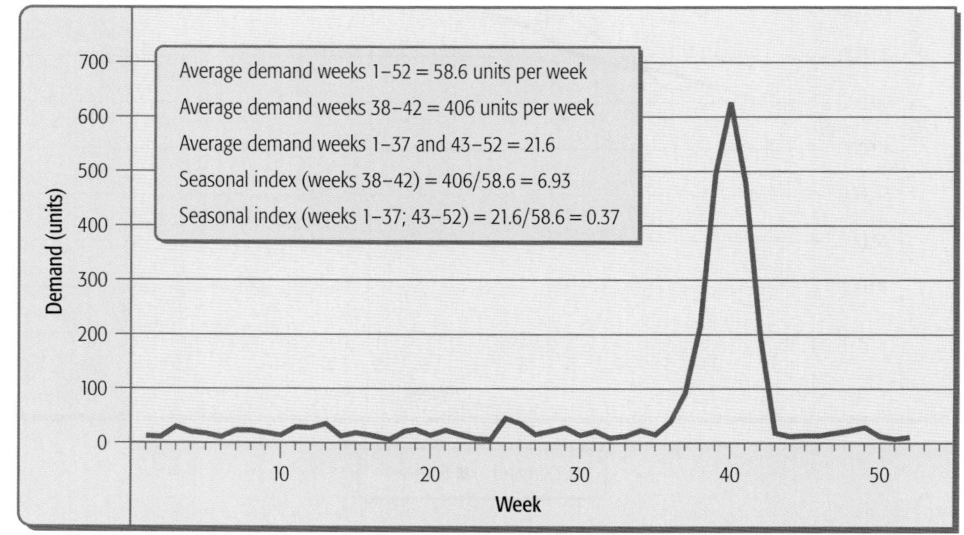

FIGURE 5.7 An Illustration of Demand for Mousetraps

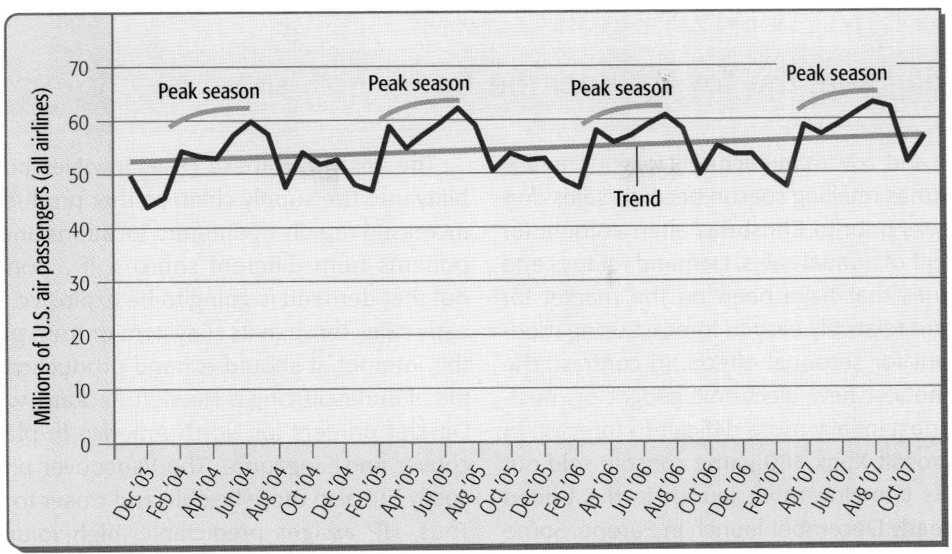

FIGURE 5.8 Airline Traffic for All U.S. Airlines, 2003–2007

Source: Data drawn from http://www.bts.gov/.

more widely by businesses because it tends to model actual demand more accurately. Figure 5.9 illustrates the differences between the performance of the additive and multiplicative seasonal methods, with the multiplicative method allowing for greater responsiveness or variety for seasonal patterns.

Figure 5.7 illustrates the use of seasonal indices for mousetraps by calculating the average demand during the peak period (weeks 38–42) and the lower demand period (weeks 1–37 and 43–52) and dividing each by the overall average

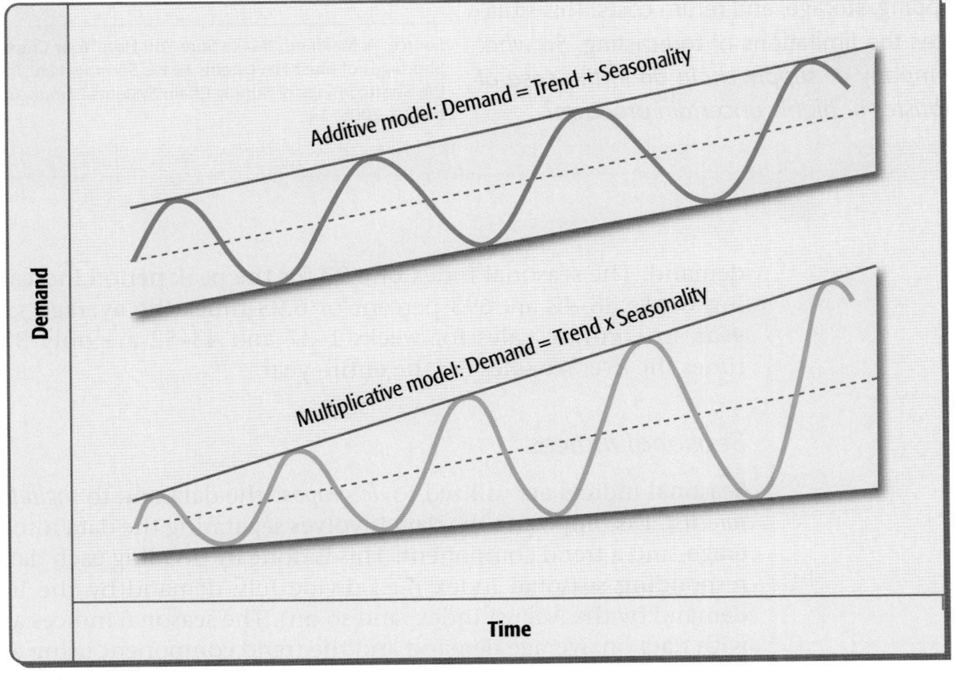

FIGURE 5.9 The Additive and Multiplicative Seasonal Methods versus a Linear Trend

BEST PRACTICES IN OPERATIONS MANAGEMENT

Making Sure the Toy Is Under the Tree

Both retailers and toy manufacturers eagerly anticipate the Christmas retailing season because sales during the six weeks prior to Christmas often account for 30 to 50 percent of annual sales. Demand for toys and electronic games that have been on the market for several years are relatively easy to forecast using models that account for seasonal effects. In contrast, the sales for the hottest new electronic gadget or must-have toy are substantially more difficult to forecast. In 2005, the Microsoft Xbox 360 game console sold out quickly after its late November launch in the United States and its early December launch in Europe. Some enterprising individuals who managed to obtain an Xbox 360 took advantage of its scarcity by selling it on eBay for as much as $1,000 compared to a retail price of $400. In 2004, the "in-demand" items were Robosapiens toys, iPods, and Sony Playstations—which were held up in a supertanker in the Suez Canal, forcing Sony to charter a Russian cargo plane to make deliveries. It seems that every year has one or more "must-have" toys for which manufacturers and retailers lose sales and profits because of shortages, and customers are disappointed. At the same time, there are also always piles of excess toys that could be termed "nobody wanted," which result in excess production, shipping, storage, and return costs. This situation illustrates the limitations of forecasting. *So what should a company or supply chain do in the case of these blockbuster or highly uncertain products?*

The answer in these cases involves building flexibility into the supply chain so that production can be increased rapidly in different locations and with components from different sources. If a company finds out that demand is going to be explosive, either from early sales through its IT system or from preorders via the Internet, it should expand production. An example of multisourcing is Hewlett-Packard, which makes Deskjet printers for North America in plants in Vancouver and Singapore. The Vancouver plant is more costly but also more flexible and closer to the market. Thus, HP assigns predictable, high-volume production to Singapore and uses the Vancouver plant to satisfy seasonal surges in demand. Another approach used by Jabil Circuit, a U.S. subcontractor of electronic manufacturing services, requires suppliers to be able to boost deliveries by 25 percent on one week's notice and by 400 percent with four weeks' notice. Finally, forecasting accuracy can be improved by pooling predictions of customer demand across a wide area rather than looking at it on a store-by-store basis. Wal-Mart is well known for its ability to aggregate data from thousands of stores and feed that information to suppliers in real time in order to increase forecast accuracy.

Source: A. Maitland, "Make Sure You Have Your Christmas Stock In: Shortages of Must-Have Items Leave Shoppers Frustrated and Expose the Shortcomings of Supply Chain Systems," *Financial Times*, December 19, 2005, 14.

demand. The seasonal index of 6.93 for the peak period indicates that sales during weeks 38–42 are 693 percent or 6.93 times the average sales for the entire year. In contrast, sales for weeks 1–37 and 43–52 are only 37 percent or 0.37 times the average sales for the entire year.

Seasonal Indices

Seasonal indices are utilized to *decompose* the data and to *include seasonality in the forecast.* Decomposing the data involves separating the data into a seasonal, an average, and a trend component. This is done by dividing each data point by its corresponding seasonal index (i.e., divide July demand by the July index, August demand by the August index, and so on). The seasonal indices are then combined with data on average demand and the trend component using a two-step process:

1. Develop trend estimates for the desired periods.

2 Add seasonality to the trend estimates by multiplying these trend estimates by the corresponding seasonal index.

Solved Example 4 illustrates this method.

Solved Example 4

Forecasting Ice Cream Sales Using Seasonality

An ice cream manufacturer wants to predict monthly demand for all flavors of its ice cream. The data consist of both trend and seasonal components. The forecast with trend component is calculated using the formula $F_t = 7{,}600 + 25t$. (This formula is based on previous demand and study of the trend for ice cream sales. Often trend values will be calculated based on past data and the use of a linear regression model to estimate the trend component.)

1. **Use the data in Table 5.4 to develop seasonal indices for each month.**
2. **Use this information to forecast demand for July and August of year 4.**

TABLE 5.4 Ice Cream Sales at Ecstasy Ice Cream

	Sales (Pints)		
	Year 1	**Year 2**	**Year 3**
January	5,000	5,200	5,300
Febuary	5,500	5,400	6,200
March	5,300	5,500	5,800
April	7,500	7,700	8,300
May	8,000	8,600	9,000
June	8,700	8,900	9,500
July	9,300	10,000	9,800
August	10,400	10,700	11,400
September	8,300	8,700	8,500
October	7,400	7,900	8,000
November	4,500	4,700	4,800
December	4,100	4,300	4,600
Average	7,000	7,300	7,600

SOLUTION

The first step is to calculate a seasonal index for each month. This is done for each month and each year. The second step is to take the average of the three seasonal indices over the three years. Note: A seasonal index can be calculated using a single seasonal pattern (in this case, one

(continued)

PART II Tools and Tactical Issues

year), but just as in other types of forecasts, the data are more reliable if they are based on multiple seasonal patterns (in this case, three years). The third step is to multiply the forecast by the seasonal index.

1. **We calculate the seasonal indices by dividing each month's demand by the average annual demand.**

$$\text{July, Year 1: } \frac{9{,}300}{7{,}000} = 1.33 \qquad \text{Year 2: } \frac{10{,}000}{7{,}300} = 1.37$$

$$\text{Year 3: } \frac{9{,}800}{7{,}600} = 1.29$$

$$\text{August, Year 1: } \frac{10{,}400}{7{,}000} = 1.49 \qquad \text{Year 2: } \frac{10{,}700}{7{,}300} = 1.47$$

$$\text{Year 3: } \frac{11{,}400}{7{,}600} = 1.50$$

The seasonal indices for the remaining months are shown in Table 5.5.

2. **The next step is to take the average of the seasonal indices for each month for the three years.**

$$\text{July: } \frac{1.33 + 1.37 + 1.29}{3} = 1.329$$

$$\text{August: } \frac{1.49 + 1.47 + 1.50}{3} = 1.484$$

The average index for each month is shown in Table 5.5.

3. **The last step is to take the average of the seasonal indices for each month for the three years.**
July: Trend forecast—July is the seventh month of year 4, so the trend is forecasted using the trend equation $F_t = 7{,}600 + 25t$.

$$F_t = 7{,}600 + 25t = 7{,}600 + 25 * 7 = 7{,}775$$

The final forecast is then the combination of the trend forecast and the seasonal index.

$$F_{\text{July}} = 7{,}775 * 1.329 = 10{,}335.33$$

August: Trend forecast—August is the eighth month of year 4, so the trend is forecasted using the trend equation $F_t = 7{,}600 + 25t$.

$$F_t = 7{,}600 + 25t = 7{,}600 + 25 * 8 = 7{,}800$$

The final forecast is then the combination of the trend forecast and the seasonal index.

$$F_{\text{August}} = 7{,}800 * 1.484 = 11{,}573.82$$

The complete results and calculations for all months are shown in Table 5.5.

Reducing Seasonality

While seasonal forecasts can be developed with a high degree of accuracy, the highly variable nature of demand for products with high seasonality often influences organizations to be more proactive in trying to reduce seasonality. Companies often try to extend the selling season through several methods. One method involves adver-

TABLE 5.5 Seasonal Forecasting of Ice Cream Sales

		Index				
	Year 1 Sales	**Year 1**	**Year 2**	**Year 3**	**Avg. Index**	**Forecast Year 4**
January	5,000 5,000/7,000	0.71	0.71	0.70	0.708 (7,600 + 1 * 25) * 0.708	5,398.46
Febuary	5,500 5,500/7,000	0.79	0.74	0.82	0.780 (7,600 + 2 * 25) * 0.780	5,970.14
March	5,300 5,300/7,000	0.76	0.75	0.76	0.758 (7,600 + 3 * 25) * 0.758	5, 816.95
April	7,500 7,500/7,000	1.07	1.05	1.09	1.073 (7,600 + 4 * 25) * 1.073	8,260.38
May	8,000 8,000/7,000	1.14	1.18	1.18	1.168 (7,600 + 5 * 25) * 1.168	9,025.76
June	8,700 8,700/7,000	1.24	1.22	1.25	1.237 (7,600 + 6 * 25) * 1.237	9,589.42
July	9,300 9,300/7,000	1.33	1.37	1.29	1.329 (7,600 + 7 * 25) * 1.329	10,335.33
August	10,400 10,400/7,000	1.49	1.47	1.50	1.484 (7,600 + 8 * 25) * 1.484	11,573.82
September	8,300 8,300/7,000	1.19	1.19	1.12	1.165 (7,600 + 9 * 25) * 1.165	9,118.51
October	7,400 7,400/7,000	1.06	1.08	1.05	1.064 (7,600 + 10 * 25) * 1.064	8,352.31
November	4,500 4,500/7,000	0.64	0.64	0.63	0.639 (7,600 + 11 * 25) * 0.639	5,035.46
December	4,100 4,100/7,000	0.59	0.59	0.61	0.593 (7,600 + 12 * 25) * 0.593	4,687.38
Average	7,000					

tising during slower-demand periods, such as advertising for sales of sodas and lemonade either in late winter/early spring or in late fall/early winter, when sales typically start to plummet. Another method involves discounting the product or service in periods of slower demand to increase sales. Yield management involves discounting the price of a product or service during a period of slow demand in order to achieve a more level overall pattern of demand. There are scores of examples of yield management, including matinee prices for movies or plays, airline discounts for off-peak travel, early bird specials for dinner, and twilight golf rates.

Figure 5.10 illustrates the fundamental idea behind reducing seasonality: providing incentives or advertising to shift demand from busy periods to slower periods in order to make the entire production schedule smoother and easier to manage. The photos on the next page illustrate the concept of complementary products. Demand for products such as ATVs and snowmobiles fluctuates substantially across the winter and summer seasons. Companies like Polaris balance fluctuations by making

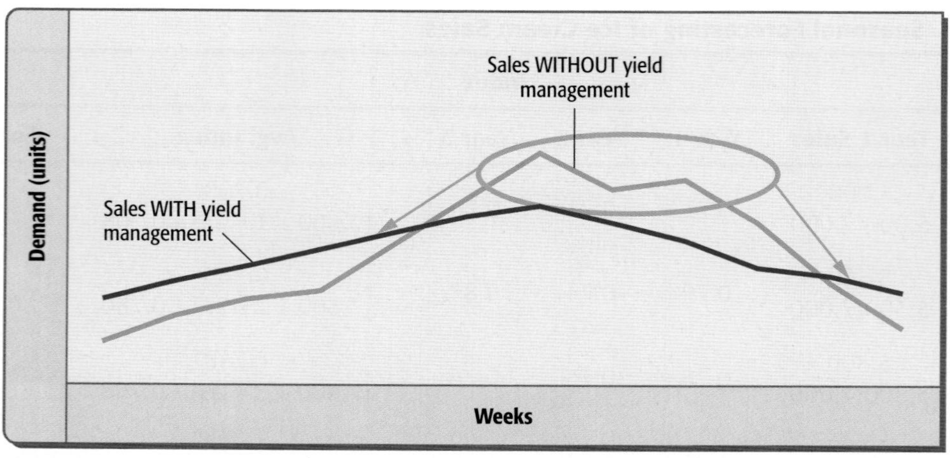

FIGURE 5.10 Illustration of Reducing Seasonality

Complementary seasonal products.

complementary products with seasonal cycles that counterbalance each other and share similar manufacturing methods.

MEASURING ERRORS AND SELECTING A TIME-SERIES METHOD

The best forecast is less wrong than the next best forecast. In other words, all forecasts are wrong to some extent, so how do we choose the "best" forecast? Generally, managers will examine a range of forecast types over a period of time and choose the one with the least amount of error.

Forecast error is the difference between the forecast and the actual demand for a given period. Forecast errors can be classified as either bias errors or random errors. Bias errors occur when the forecast is consistently over or under the actual demand. These errors often occur when a key demand component is neglected—for example, when an exponential smoothing model is used to forecast ice cream sales, which have a distinct seasonal component. Random errors result from unpredictable factors and do not exhibit a distinct pattern. Ideally, forecasters try to eliminate as much of both types of error as possible, but some error always remains.

Measures of Forecast Error

Calculating forecast error is fairly straightforward—it is simply the difference between actual demand and the forecast:

$$E_t = D_t - F_t \qquad \text{(Equation 6)}$$

where E_t = forecast error for period t
D_t = actual demand for period t
F_t = forecast for period t

Equation 6 provides a way to calculate a single forecast error, but we are most often interested in measuring forecast error over a long period of time. The **cumulative sum of forecast errors** (CFE) measures total forecast error:

$$\text{CFE} = \sum E_t \qquad \text{(Equation 7)}$$

Positive and negative errors tend to offset each other in CFE, unless there is a bias error. Thus, CFE is useful for finding a consistent bias. Dividing CFE by the number of periods (n) gives the mean forecast error $\bar{E}$. **Mean square error (MSE), standard deviation (σ), and mean absolute deviation (MAD)** all measure the dispersion of forecast errors.

$$\text{MSE} = \frac{\sum E_t^2}{n} \qquad \text{(Equation 8)}$$

$$\sigma = \sqrt{\frac{\sum (E_t - \bar{E})^2}{n-1}} \qquad \text{(Equation 9)}$$

$$\text{MAD} = \frac{\sum |E_t|}{n} \qquad \text{(Equation 10)}$$

If MSE, σ, or MAD is small, then the forecast is typically close to actual demand; thus, it is fairly accurate. Larger values indicate potentially large forecast errors. Each measure emphasizes errors slightly differently. MSE and σ tend to amplify large errors because the errors are squared, while MAD is often used because it is more intuitive—it provides an easy-to-interpret average of the amount by which forecasts are wrong.

● **Forecast error** the difference between the forecast and the actual demand for a given period

● **Cumulative sum of forecast errors** total forecast error over a long period of time

● **Mean square error (MSE), standard deviation (σ), and mean absolute deviation (MAD)** measures of the dispersion of forecast errors

PART II Tools and Tactical Issues

Solved Example 5

Quality Cabinets Evaluates Forecast Error

Table 5.6 provides demand for the past 6 weeks and the corresponding forecast for total cabinet sales at Quality Cabinets. Calculate the CFE, MSE, σ, and MAD for this set of forecasts.

TABLE 5.6 Quality Cabinets: Demand and Forecasts

Week	Demand	Forecast
1	200	190
2	220	198
3	190	210
4	245	195
5	225	217
6	210	235
7		218

Each of the measures of forecast error starts with a calculation of the error E_t from Equation 6; thus, we calculate the error for weeks 1 through 6:

$$E_1 = D_t - F_t = 200 - 190 = 10$$

(continued)

$$E_2 = 220 - 198 = 22$$
$$E_3 = 190 - 210 = -20$$
$$E_4 = 245 - 195 = 50$$
$$E_5 = 225 - 217 = 8$$
$$E_6 = 210 - 235 = -25$$

Next, we calculate cumulative forecast error (CFE), mean square error (MSE), standard deviation (σ), and mean absolute deviation (MAD) for each week:

$$\text{CFE} = \sum E_t = (E_1 + E_2 + E_3 + E_4 + E_5 + E_6) = 10 + 22 + (-20) + 50 + 8 + (-25) = 45$$

The mean forecast error is

$$\bar{E} = 45/6 = 7.5$$

$$\begin{aligned}\text{MSE} &= \frac{\sum E_t^2}{n}\\ &= \frac{(E_1^2 + E_2^2 + E_3^2 + E_4^2 + E_5^2 + E_6^2)}{6}\\ &= \frac{[10^2 + 22^2 + (-20)^2 + 50^2 + 8^2 + (-25)^2]}{6}\\ &= \frac{(100 + 484 + 400 + 2{,}500 + 64 + 625)}{6}\\ &= \frac{4{,}173}{6}\\ &= 695.5\end{aligned}$$

$$\begin{aligned}\sigma &= \sqrt{\frac{\sum (E_t - \bar{E})^2}{n-1}}\\ &= \sqrt{\frac{(E_1 - \bar{E})^2 + (E_2 - \bar{E})^2 + (E_3 - \bar{E})^2 + (E_4 - \bar{E})^2 + (E_5 - \bar{E})^2 + (E_6 - \bar{E})^2}{n-1}}\\ &= \sqrt{\frac{(10-7.5)^2 + (22-7.5)^2 + (-20-7.5)^2 + (50-7.5)^2 + (8-7.5)^2 + (-25-7.5)^2}{6-1}}\\ &= \sqrt{\frac{3{,}835.5}{6-1}}\\ &= 27.70\end{aligned}$$

$$\begin{aligned}\text{MAD} &= \frac{\sum |E_t|}{n}\\ &= \frac{|E_1| + |E_2| + |E_3| + |E_4| + |E_5| + |E_6|}{n}\\ &= \frac{|10| + |22| + |-20| + |50| + |8| + |-25|}{6}\\ &= 22.5\end{aligned}$$

Mean Absolute Percentage Error

Mean absolute percentage error a measure that reports error in proportion to the demand

Mean absolute percentage error (MAPE) is a measure that reports error in proportion to the demand. MAPE is useful because it presents errors as a percentage, which is often easier to understand. For example, with MAD or MSE, it is not possible to compare forecasts made for two different datasets, whereas MAPE can be compared because it uses a common measure, percentage of error.

$$\text{MAPE} = \frac{\sum \frac{|E_t|}{D}(100)}{n} \qquad \text{(Equation 11)}$$

Solved Example 6
Forecast Error Calculations

Table 5.7 shows the actual sales and forecasts made for each of the past 10 months for a specific type of wine. Calculate CFE, MSE, σ, MAD, and MAPE for this product and interpret.

TABLE 5.7 Wine Sales, Demand, Forecast, and Error Calculation

Month	Demand	Forecast	E_t	E_t^2	$\lvert E_t \rvert$	$\frac{\lvert E_t \rvert}{D}(100)$
1	225	228	−3	9	3	1.3%
2	188	227	−39	1,521	39	20.7%
3	193	215	−22	484	22	11.4%
4	185	209	−24	576	24	13.0%
5	160	202	−42	1,764	42	26.3%
6	213	189	24	576	24	11.3%
7	215	196	19	361	19	8.8%
8	203	202	1	1	1	0.5%
9	175	202	−27	729	27	15.4%
10	184	194	−10	100	10	5.4%
		Total	−123	6,121	211	114%

SOLUTION

Using the formulas given earlier, we calculate

$$\text{CFE} = \sum E_t = -123$$

$$\text{MSE} = \frac{\sum E_t^2}{n} = \frac{6{,}121}{10} = 612.1$$

$$\sigma = \sqrt{\frac{\sum (E_t - \bar{E})^2}{n-1}}$$

$$= \sqrt{\frac{\sum [E_t - (-12.3)]^2}{10-1}}$$

$$= \sqrt{\frac{[-3-(-12.3))^2 + (-39-(-12.3))^2 + \cdots + (-10-(-12.3)]^2}{9}}$$

$$= 22.63$$

$$\text{MAD} = \frac{\sum |E_t|}{n} = \frac{211}{10} = 21.1$$

(continued)

$$\text{MAPE} = \frac{\sum \frac{|E_t|}{D}(100)}{n} = \frac{114\%}{10} = 11.4\%$$

A CFE of –123 indicates that the forecast has a tendency to overestimate demand. MAD = 21.1 means that the average forecast error was 21.1 units in absolute value. The value for σ (22.63) indicates that the distribution of forecast errors has a standard deviation of 22.63 units. A MAPE of 11.4 percent indicates that the forecast error was 11.4 percent of demand.

While these numbers are generally acceptable, it may be possible to get better performance with a different forecasting technique. In particular, these data appear to have a trend component, so the forecaster might want to try using trend-adjusted exponential smoothing.

Solved Example 7

Using Measures of Forecast Error to Choose a Forecast Method

Table 5.8 provides the results of forecasting for a refrigerator manufacturer that is evaluating three different methods: a three-week moving average, exponential smoothing with $\alpha = 0.2$, and exponential

TABLE 5.8 Demand and Forecasts for a Refrigerator Manufacturer

Week	Demand	3-Week Moving Average	Exponential Smoothing ($\alpha = 0.2$)	Exponential Smoothing ($\alpha = 0.4$)
1	1,000.00			
2	1,080.00			
3	1,120.00	1,040.00	1,040.00	1,040.00
4	1,190.00	1,066.67	1,056.00	1,072.00
5	1,150.00	1,130.00	1,082.80	1,119.20
6	1,165.00	1,153.33	1,096.24	1,131.52
7	1,090.00	1,168.33	1,109.99	1,144.91
8	1,065.00	1,135.00	1,105.99	1,122.95
9	1,020.00	1,106.67	1,097.79	1, 099.77
10	1,070.00	1,058.33	1,082.24	1,067.86
11	990.00	1,051.67	1,079.79	1,068.72
12	1,000.00	1,026.67	1,061.83	1,037.23
13	950.00	1,020.00	1,049.46	1,022.34
14		980.00	1,029.57	993.40
	CFE	–146.67	–52.14	–116.49
	MSE	4,567.68	5,787.27	4,359.04
	MAD	58.18	68.37	58.67
	MAPE	5.44	6.36	5.46

(*continued*)

smoothing with $\alpha = 0.4$. Figure 5.11 shows the three forecasting methods plotted against actual demand. The values for CFE, MSE, MAD, and MAPE are calculated for the 11 weeks of forecast data supplied. Use these data to choose the best forecast method

This example is available on this book's web site with complete calculations for finding CFE, MSE, MAD, and MAPE.

As shown in Table 5.8, each of the three forecasting methods performs better than the others on at least one measure of forecast error. The moving-average method has the best score for MAD and MAPE, the exponential smoothing with $\alpha = 0.2$ has the best score for CFE, and the exponential smoothing with $\alpha = 0.4$ has the best score for MSE. This outcome is fairly typical because multiple forecasting methods often yield similar results. In this case, any of the three methods can be used with the expectation of achieving reasonable results. Note that in all three cases, the MAPE is in the range of 5 to 6 percent. The MAD and MSE give numbers that look very different—this is because the MSE uses the square of errors rather than the absolute value of errors, which gives greater weight to errors that are outliers.

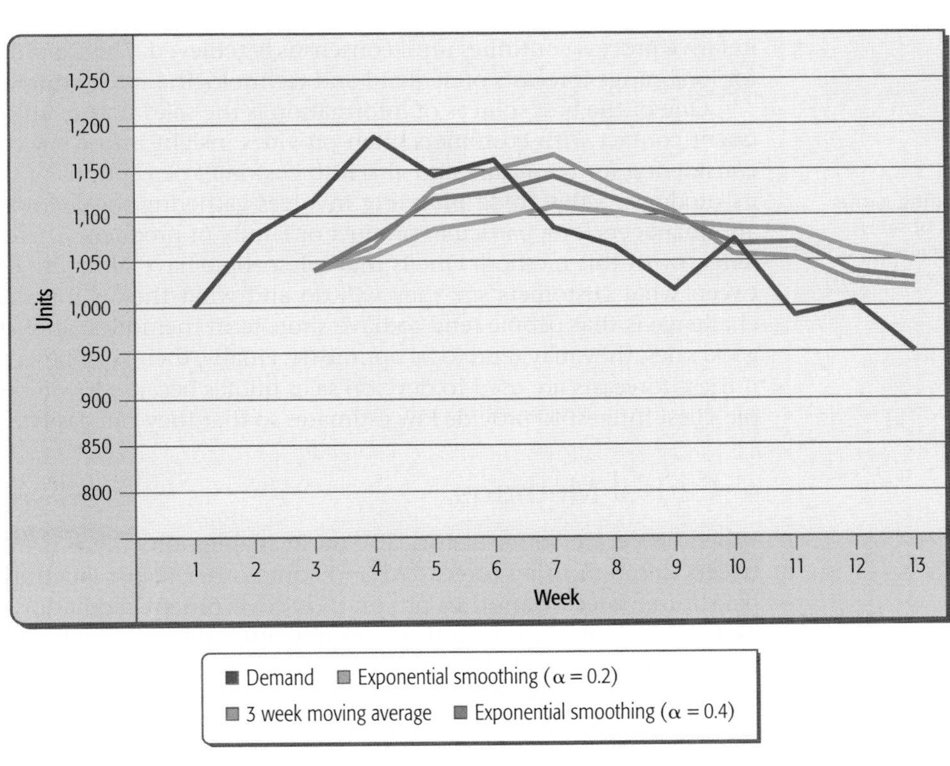

FIGURE 5.11 Comparison of Three Forecasting Methods

ADDITIONAL FORECASTING METHODS

While time-series analysis is one of the most common methods of forecasting, there are two additional methods that are important. Qualitative methods are commonly used when there is little quantitative data available and when subjective considerations are important. Causal methods are often used when there is a cause-and-effect relationship, such as the amount of advertising correlating to sales of a product.

Qualitative Methods

● **Market research** a systematic approach to measuring customer interest in a service or product through data-gathering surveys

● **Delphi method** a forecasting method that uses a team of experts to develop a consensus forecast

● **Sales force planning** gathering the opinions of salespeople and managers for a particular product or family of products

Often there are no previous sales data for a product and no other causal data that can be used for either a time-series forecast or a causal forecast. In this situation, there are several qualitative methods that can be applied. **Market research** uses a systematic approach to measure customer interest in a service or product through data-gathering surveys. There are several steps to market research, including designing a questionnaire, deciding how to administer it, selecting a representative sample of potential customers to contact, and analyzing the data gathered using statistical tools. Market research is widely used for new products, but it also has a high degree of uncertainty and must be interpreted with caution. More and more studies are being conducted via the Internet or other electronic media because of the ease of data collection, data entry, and the ability to present products in a variety of media.

The **Delphi method** uses a team of experts to develop a consensus forecast. A project manager sends a series of questions to the members of a group of outside experts, who often are anonymous and not known to one another. The project manager compiles a statistical summary of the responses and the supporting arguments. This report is sent to the same group for another round of responses in which the participants are asked to modify their responses based on the group response. This iterative process continues until consensus is achieved. The Delphi method is useful for long-range forecasts of demand and technological forecasting.

One of the best sources of information is the sales staff of an organization. Frequent contact with customers often provides insight into what customers may be considering for the future and also into customer perceptions of the company and its products. **Sales force planning** involves gathering the opinions of salespeople and managers for a particular product or family of products. There are several challenges with this method. One is that salespeople have difficulty differentiating between what customers say they will do and what they will actually do. Another challenge is that people tend to have short-term memories; after several periods of good sales, they may tend to be optimistic. Finally, there may be a conflict of interest if these forecasts are used to develop sales quotas because it will be in the salespeople's best interest to provide low estimates so that they can easily exceed them.

Causal Methods

When there are some historical data available, and there is a relationship between the item to be forecasted and some other factor (such as advertising expenditure, sales of another product, or government regulations), then a causal method is used. Causal methods employ mathematical techniques to relate one or more independent variables to the variable being forecast. While there are numerous causal methods that may be employed, we will focus on linear regression because it is one of the most commonly used.

Linear Regression

● **Linear regression** a statistical technique that expresses the forecast variable as a linear function of one or more independent variables

Linear regression is a statistical technique that expresses the forecast variable as a linear function of one or more independent variables. The forecast is the dependent variable (such as demand for Coca-Cola) because it is calculated based on the scores of the independent variables. The independent variables are factors that are assumed to cause the results observed in the past; they can include things such as advertising, temperature, or store promotions. Figure 5.12 illustrates a linear regression and its relationship to the raw data. This line is calculated to minimize the total of the squared deviations from the actual data.

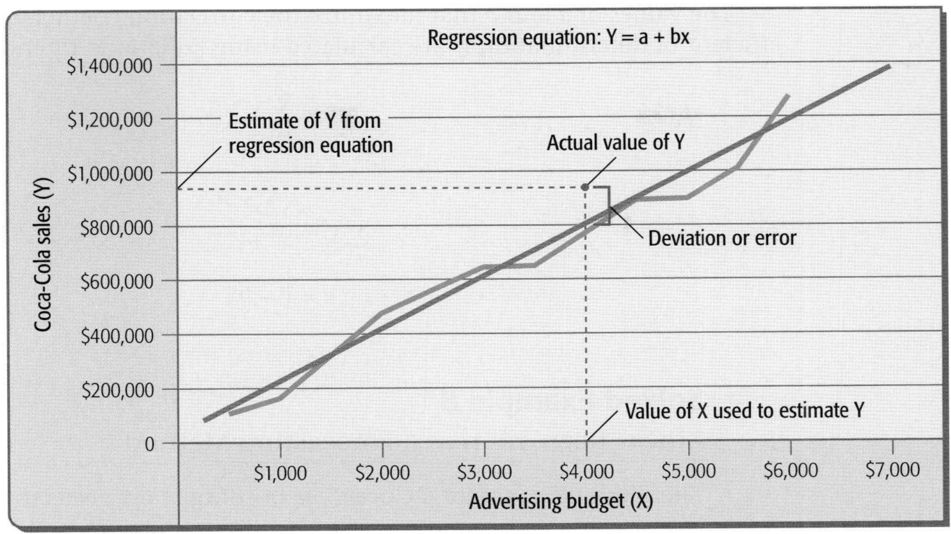

FIGURE 5.12 Linear Regression Line with Raw Data

Linear regression models can include multiple independent variables, with the theoretical relationship taking the form of a straight line. We examine the case with a single independent variable for ease of presentation and understanding.

$$Y = a + bX \qquad \text{(Equation 12)}$$

where Y = dependent variable or forecast
X = independent variable
a = Y-intercept of the line
b = slope of the line

Linear regression analysis uses straightforward formulas to find the values for a and b that minimize the sum of the squared deviations of the actual data points from the graphed line. For problems with more than a few observations, the computation of these values becomes complex; thus, computer programs such as Microsoft Excel are commonly used to compute a and b. Three measures are usually reported for a linear regression: the correlation coefficient, the coefficient of determination, and the standard error of the estimate.

The **correlation coefficient**, r, measures the strength and direction of the relationship between the independent variable X and the dependent variable Y. The value of r ranges between –1.0 and 1.0. A value of 1.0 indicates that changes in the direction of the independent variable (X) are always matched with changes in the same direction by the dependent variable (Y). In contrast, an r of –1.0 indicates that increases in X are always matched by decreases in Y. A zero (0.0) value of r indicates that there is no linear relationship between the variables. A better fit of the regression line to the points is indicated by values of r closer to ±1.0.

● **Correlation coefficient** a measure of the strength and direction of the relationship between the independent variable X and the dependent variable Y

The **coefficient of determination**, r^2, measures the amount of variation in the dependent variable that the regression line explains. The value of r^2 ranges from 0.0 to 1.0, with values close to 1.0 being better.

● **Coefficient of determination** a measure of the amount of variation in the dependent variable that the regression line explains

The **standard error of the estimate**, s_{yx}, measures the distance between the dependent variable and the regression line. While it is very similar to the standard deviation of the sample, it measures the error in the dependent variable, Y, relative to the regression line, rather than to the mean. Thus, s_{yx} is the standard deviation of the difference between the actual demand and the estimate from the regression equation. When conducting linear regression with multiple independent variables, the independent variable with the smallest value of s_{yx} should be selected.

● **Standard error of the estimate** a measure of the distance between the dependent variable and the regression line

The values of a and b that maximize the correlation coefficient r and the coefficient of determination r^2 are calculated using Equations 13 and 14.

$$b = \frac{\sum_{i=1}^{n} x_i y_i - \frac{\sum_{i=1}^{n} x_i \sum_{i=1}^{n} y_i}{n}}{\sum_{i=1}^{n} x_i^2 - \frac{(\sum_{i=1}^{n} x_i)^2}{n}} \qquad \text{(Equation 13)}$$

$$a = \bar{y} - b\bar{x} \qquad \text{(Equation 14)}$$

Solved Example 8

Linear Regression as a Forecasting Method

The plant manager for a Coca-Cola bottling plant needs to prepare forecasts for the amount of Coke Zero to produce. The sales for this product have been shown in the past to depend on multiple factors, including the weather, the advertising budget, and the actions of competitors. The best predictor in the past has been the advertising budget; thus, the data in Table 5.9 have been gathered.

TABLE 5.9 Advertising Expenditures and Sales for Coke Zero

Week	Advertising $	Coke Zero Sales
1	$5,000	$912,000
2	$5,500	$1,030,000
3	$6,000	$1,298,000
4	$3,500	$655,000
5	$4,000	$958,000
6	$3,000	$645,000
7	$1,000	$175,000
8	$2,000	$485,000
9	$4,500	$909,000

Use the data in Table 5.9 to develop a forecasting equation and to make a forecast for an advertising budget of $4,200 for the week.

SOLUTION

Table 5.10 gives the values for $\bar{y}$, $\bar{x}$, x^2, and xy.

We use Equations 13 and 14 to compute values for a and b:

(continued)

$$b = \frac{\sum_{i=1}^{n} x_i y_i - \frac{\sum_{i=1}^{n} x_i \sum_{i=1}^{n} y_i}{n}}{\sum_{i=1}^{n} x_i^2 - \frac{(\sum_{i=1}^{n} x_i)^2}{n}}$$

$$= \frac{31{,}308{,}000{,}000 - \frac{34{,}500 * 7{,}067{,}000}{9}}{153{,}750{,}000 - \frac{34{,}500^2}{9}}$$

$$= \$196.18$$

$$a = \bar{y} - b\bar{x} = \$785{,}222 - \$196.18 * \$3{,}833 = \$33{,}205.43$$

Putting these values into Equation 12, we get

$$Y = \$33{,}205.43 + \$196.18X$$

TABLE 5.10 Values Used for Linear Regression Calculation

Week	Advertising $ (x)	Coca-Cola Sales (y)	x^2	xy
1	$5,000	$912,000	25,000,000	4,560,000,000
2	$5,500	$1,030,000	30,250,000	5,665,000,000
3	$6,000	$1,298,000	36,000,000	7,788,000,000
4	$3,500	$655,000	12,250,000	2,292,500,000
5	$4,000	$958,000	16,000,000	3,832,000,000
6	$3,000	$645,000	9,000,000	1,935,000,000
7	$1,000	$175,000	1,000,000	175,000,000
8	$2,000	$485,000	4,000,000	970,000,000
9	$4,500	$909,000	20,250,000	4,090,500,000
Sum	$34,500	$7,067,000	153,750,000	31,308,000,000
Average	$3,833	$785,222		

ALTERNATIVE SOLUTION USING MICROSOFT EXCEL

Instead of performing the calculations by hand and entering them into Equations 13 and 14, we can also use Microsoft Excel to calculate the linear regression. This is done using the following formula in Excel:

=LINEST(*known_y's, known_x's, true, true)*

where known_y's is a column with all of the *y* values and known_x's is a column with all of the *x* values for the linear regression line to be developed.

This function returns the values in Table 5.11.

(continued)

TABLE 5.11 Output of LINEST Function in MS Excel for Data Given in Table 5.9

B = 196.18	a = 33,205.43
se_y = 19.25	se_x = 79,571.60
r^2 = 0.94	89,267.02
103.84	7.00
827,447,350,129.20	55,780,205,426.36

From the data given in Table 5.11, we can see that Excel gives matching *a* and *b* values and provides the value $r^2 = 0.94$ (this means that the regression equation explains 94 percent of the variation in the dependent variable, sales of Coke Zero), indicating that this regression line is a good fit.

Finally, using the equation $Y = \$33,205.43 + \$196.18X$, we can calculate the predicted sales for an advertising budget of $4,200:

$$Y = \$33,205.43 + \$196.18 * \$4,200 = \$857,154.43$$

The spreadsheet for calculating this regression is available on this book's web site. Several additional examples with solutions are also available.

BEST PRACTICES IN OPERATIONS MANAGEMENT

Statin Wars: Anticholesterol Drug Makers Estimate Sales

Sales of anticholesterol drugs such as Lipitor, Crestor, Zocor, and Vytorin exploded between 2000 and 2007, with the worldwide market estimated as $22 billion in 2007, up from $14 billion in 2001. While this is good for all the manufacturers and promoters of these drugs, there is intense jockeying for position within the broader market. In 2001, Lipitor (made by Pfizer) represented 40 percent of the market, had annual sales of over $6 billion, and was the best-selling drug in the world. At that time, AstraZeneca was in Phase III clinical trials of its drug Crestor (pharmaceutical drugs are required to go through a lengthy testing and approval process before being approved for sale; in the United States, this process is regulated by the Food and Drug Administration). Forecasts for Crestor, which had developed a reputation as a "super statin" with better cholesterol-lowering properties than Lipitor, were for worldwide sales of $4 billion. This forecast was made a full 15 months before the drug was to come to market. Forecasts predicted that the global market for worldwide sales of all statins would be $25 billion in 2006 and that Lipitor would have flatter growth as competing drugs came to market.

In 2006, Lipitor had sales of over $13 billion, while Crestor had sales of $1.5 billion. In short, Lipitor did better than expected, while Crestor did worse than expected. Good for Pfizer; bad for AstraZeneca. The forecasts for sales of Crestor and later of a similar drug called Vytorin (made by Schering-Plough Corp. and Merck & Co.) were based on several causal factors, each of which had to be estimated and given a weight. These factors included

- The size of the total statin market. The 2001 projection was that by 2006, there would be 37 million senior citizens in the United States, of whom 40 percent would be at risk of developing high cholesterol.
- Results from a physician panel. A majority of a panel of 42 physicians and expert cardiologists said that they were likely to prescribe Crestor for new patients.
- Number of pharmaceutical representatives. A projection for total sales of $1.8 billion for Vytorin was made in 2004 based in part on an

(continued)

BEST PRACTICES IN OPERATIONS MANAGEMENT

Statin Wars: Anticholesterol Drug Makers Estimate Sales (*continued*)

estimate of 3,770 pharmaceutical reps presenting the drug to five doctors per day.

- Advertising budget. Companies spend millions promoting individual drugs to potential customers. In 2006, the total advertising spending was $11.4 billion.

These factors all affect the sales of an individual drug. The challenge is determining the exact cause-and-effect relationship. Physicians routinely overstate their intention to prescribe a drug, while patients routinely overstate their intention to ask their physician about a new drug. According to Howard Ziment, CEO of the research firm Ziment, "No one has ever been able to properly adjust to this overstatement." Pharmaceutical firms, like many firms with innovative products, do their best to forecast, employing a variety of quantitative and qualitative methods. Recognizing the limitations of forecasting, however, many such firms also make efforts to make their supply chain responsive so that they can adapt to changes in demand as smoothly and cost-efficiently as possible.

Sources: J. Rubin, "The Statin Wars," *Medical Marketing and Media* 36, no. 7 (2001), 138–141; "Forecasting Company Predicts Anticholesterol Market Share for Vytorin," *Heart Disease Weekly* (September 5, 2004), 100; "New Research Technique Offers Improved Pharmaceutical Product Forecasting," *Drug Week* (June 4, 2004), 578; "America: And Now a Word from Our Pharmaceutical Manufacturer," *Marketing Week* (November 23, 2006), 36.

SUPPLY CHAIN FORECASTING

The mathematics forming the foundation for forecasting, particularly for time-series and causal models, have stayed largely the same for many years, albeit with small enhancements to very sophisticated models that can improve accuracy by a few tenths of a percentage point. The biggest gains over the last 10 years have come with the development of more powerful information technology that can capture and process enormous amounts of data and that can quickly connect numerous players within a supply chain at fairly low cost in terms of time and effort. Whereas 10 to 15 years ago, most forecasting was concentrated at fairly high levels of an organization, i.e., at the product or family level, now forecasts can be made for every store, distribution center, manufacturing location, and so on, with these forecasts being linked in real time so that a change in one is reflected by a change in another. We focus on two technologies/processes for sharing information across organizations. Then we examine ways in which companies strive to make the supply chain more responsive in order to minimize the challenges involved in forecasting.

Information Systems for Sharing Data Across the Supply Chain

There are numerous technologies for managing forecasting technologies. Selecting the "best" technology for a specific business or situation is a continuous challenge because IT, hardware, and techniques are always changing and there are numerous factors that affect the performance of any particular choice. Companies such as Wal-Mart, Dell, Cisco Systems, and Amazon are routinely cited as examples of companies that are proactive in developing and applying new technologies for forecasting purposes. We focus on two technologies that are of particular interest.

● **Radio frequency identification** a technology that utilizes an integrated circuit and a tag antenna printed on a tag to transmit and record information on a product

Radio frequency identification (RFID) utilizes an integrated circuit and a tag antenna printed on a tag to transmit and record information on a product. RFID addresses two of the key limitations of bar codes. First, while bar codes require a direct line of sight to be read and generally require human hands to physically scan the items, RFID can allow indirect reads and permit multiple items to be read simultaneously. The second major advantage of RFID is its ability to carry substantially more information than most bar codes, as well as to both read and write information on a tag. Thousands of companies are examining methods of reaping the benefits of this technology, including applications in preventing counterfeit drug sales, tracking the supply chain for meat products, and improved forecasting. The ability to capture more information on a product in a faster, cheaper manner offers companies a chance to exchange more information across the supply chain and improve overall forecasting accuracy. Leading organizations in the effort to develop RFID applications include Wal-Mart; the Metro Group, the world's fifth largest retailer; Tesco, the U.K.'s largest retailer; the U.S. Food and Drug Administration; and the U.S. Department of Defense.

● **Collaborative planning, forecasting, and replenishment (CPFR)** a group of business processes supported by information technology where supply chain members agree to shared business objectives and measures, develop joint sales and operational plans, and collaborate electronically to generate and revise forecasts and production plans

Collaborative planning, forecasting, and replenishment (CPFR) is a group of business processes supported by information technology where supply chain members agree to shared business objectives and measures, develop joint sales and operational plans, and collaborate electronically to generate and revise forecasts and production plans. The central feature of CPFR is the exchange of information across different members of the supply chain and the shared visibility of forecasts. CPFR was developed by Wal-Mart in the mid-1990s and has been developed into an industry standard sponsored by VICS (Voluntary Inter-Industry Commerce Standards). The industry standard defines the form that data should take when passed among different organizations so that it can be easily and correctly read directly into databases running on different technology platforms. One of the biggest benefits is that increased communication between partners allows changes in demand, promotions, or policies to be quickly incorporated into planning models. This minimizes the need for after-the-fact corrections. For example, when a retailer runs a weekly special on Kraft macaroni and cheese, this can be communicated ahead of time so that the inevitable spike in demand can be accounted for as the result of a promotion rather than as a random effect. Results from implementing CPFR across a range of companies include an increase in forecast accuracy of from 20 to 30 percent, sales revenue increases of 8 to 10 percent, and a reduction in lead time of 25 to 30 percent.[1]

TECHNOLOGY IN OPERATIONS MANAGEMENT

Wal-Mart's Application of RFID and CPFR: Sharing Data Across the Supply Chain to Maximize Forecast Accuracy

Wal-Mart is widely acknowledged as one of the best-managed retailers in the world—and the company's competitive advantage starts with its carefully refined supply chain. The company has pioneered and perfected numerous supply chain practices, one of which is the application of powerful information technology to forecasting. The company has inventory and sales systems integrated downstream from stores to its distribution centers, and upstream from its distribution centers to hundreds of suppliers. The volume of data that is managed is simply staggering. The IT system has 99.992 percent uptime for the processing of 20 million customers per day at more than 5,000 stores around the world. The system maintains inventory data on more than 693 million items, of which 335 million are reviewed for potential reordering each day. In addition, all credit card approvals are processed in less than one second, and all transac-

(continued)

[1] R. Ireland, "ABCs of Collaborative Planning, Forecasting and Replenishment," *Journal of Business Forecasting* 24, no. 2 (2005), 3–5.

TECHNOLOGY IN OPERATIONS MANAGEMENT

Wal-Mart's Application of RFID and CPFR: Sharing Data Across the Supply Chain to Maximize Forecast Accuracy (*continued*)

tion data are fed to a centralized data warehouse within 15 minutes of the actual transaction.

The speed of data collection and the quantity of data collected by Wal-Mart facilitates its forecasting. Linda Dillman, CP and CIO, did some analysis on stores along the North Carolina coast in the days preceding Hurricane Isabel in the fall of 2003. She expected to see a spike in sales of certain items, and indeed, sales of bottled water tripled from normal levels, while tarpaulin and manual can opener sales were up by 7 times, and spotlight sales jumped by a factor of 16. Some of the surprise items included Spam, which shot off store shelves at 7 times its normal volume, and Kellogg's Pop-Tarts, which tripled in sales. The ability to gather data quickly and analyze them for patterns such as these is tremendously helpful for future forecasting and inventory management, allowing Wal-Mart to make adjustments for stores in certain areas when similar natural disasters or events occur.

Information technology forms the foundation of Wal-Mart's ability to forecast better than its competitors. In particular, two technologies that are receiving extra attention are RFID and CPFR. Wal-Mart has been one of the leaders in adopting RFID, issuing a mandate that required its top 100 suppliers to start tagging all cases and pallets of merchandise by January 2005. While there has been a lot of controversy regarding the degree of success of these efforts and the cost associated with them, Wal-Mart publicly states that its efforts are conveying substantial benefits. As of February 2007, Wal-Mart said that 600 of its suppliers and 1,000 of its stores were RFID-enabled. Simon Langford, Wal-Mart's director of RFID and transportation systems, estimated that RFID cut the incidence of out-of-stock products by 30 percent and improved the efficiency of moving products from backrooms to store shelves by 60 percent. In addition, the use of RFID by suppliers leads to faster information transfer from Wal-Mart stores and distribution centers back to manufacturers, which leads to improved forecasting.

Wal-Mart's second major technology/tool is CPFR. The company maintains a data warehouse that has 7.5 terabytes of data on inventory, forecasts, demographics, markdowns, returns, and market baskets—the largest private database in the world. Each of its 693 million items has 65 weeks of data tabulated by item, store, and day. The data warehouse is accessible by Wal-Mart's buyers, merchandisers, and logistics and forecasting associates, and also by 3,500 of its vendors. Forecasting involves a close relationship between buyers and suppliers. To illustrate, the forecast starts with the data warehouse, where the retail link extracts relevant data—for example, Warner-Lambert product sales. Wal-Mart's buying agents use a spreadsheet or CPFR workbench to develop a preliminary forecast, which then appears on Warner-Lambert's CPFR server. Warner-Lambert's planners then can add comments and suggest changes to the Wal-Mart planners. After several iterations, a common forecast is agreed to and frozen for each product. This forecast is then used for production planning at Warner-Lambert using enterprise resource planning (ERP) applications and for inventory management at Wal-Mart.

Sources: M. L. Songini, "Wal-Mart Shifts RFID Plans," *Computerworld* 41 (February 26, 2007), 14; P. S. Foote and M. Krishnamurthy, "Forecasting Using Data Warehousing Model: Wal-Mart's Experience," *Journal of Business Forecasting Methods & Systems* 20, no. 3 (2001), 13–17; R. Ireland, "ABCs of Collaborative Planning, Forecasting and Replenishment," *Journal of Business Forecasting* 24, no. 2 (2005), 3–5.

Building a Responsive Organization/Supply Chain

Forecasting is always necessary for planning purposes, but when innovative products with relatively unpredictable demand are offered, accuracy tends to be greatly compromised. Products with a fairly short life cycle (three months to a year) and many variations often can command a premium contribution margin of 20 to 60 percent (as opposed to 5 to 20 percent for functional products). This is the driving factor behind the continual effort that many companies make to develop and introduce new products. The downside is that such innovative products also come with an average margin of forecast error of 40 to 100 percent, an average stockout rate of 10 to 40 percent, and an average end-of-season markdown rate of 10 to 25 percent. In contrast, more predictable, functional products have an average margin of forecast error of around 10 percent, an average stockout rate of 1 to 2 percent, and a near zero end-of season markdown rate.

When faced with an innovative product with unpredictable demand, a company should seek to make its supply chain more responsive. Dell was one of the first companies to develop such a supply chain in order to offer customized computers shipped to a customer's doorstep. The primary purpose of Dell's supply chain is to respond quickly to unpredictable demand in an effort to minimize stockouts, markdowns, and obsolete inventory. The techniques that Dell uses to make its supply chain more responsive include the following:

- *Deploy excess buffer capacity.* Extra capacity is expensive, but it allows the company to produce products quickly in response to changing sales patterns. For example, a manufacturing plant might reserve extra capacity to produce high-demand products that are at risk of stockouts.
- *Deploy buffer stocks of parts or finished goods.* Dell stocks extra inventory for the components of computers, including hard drives, memory chips, batteries, and other such elements, and then assembles them to a specific customer order.
- *Invest in lead-time reduction.* Dell ships computers via UPS or FedEx at a greater cost than using bulk shipping.
- *Select suppliers on the basis of speed, flexibility, and quality rather than cost.*
- *Employ a modular design.* Modular designs allow manufacturers to postpone product differentiation until late in the process. Another advantage of modular design is substitutability—if Dell is out of the 3-gigabyte memory chip that a customer wants, the customer will often be offered a 3.2-gigabyte chip for the same price.

Developing a responsive supply chain can alleviate the pressure on forecasters to "get it right." This is critical because innovative and new products come with a degree of uncertainty that makes accurate forecasting impossible. Other examples of responsive supply chains include Lands' End's custom pants, Cisco Systems, and Blue Nile (custom jewelry).[2]

[2] More information on responsive supply chains can be found in M. L. Fisher, "What Is the Right Supply Chain for Your Product?" *Harvard Business Review* (March–April 1997), 105–116; and R. Duray, P. T. Ward, G. W. Milligan, and W. L. Berry, "Approaches to Mass Customization: Configurations and Empirical Validation," *Journal of Operations Management* 18, no. 6 (2000), 605–625.

SUMMARY

1. Explain the need for forecasting of independent demand products

- Forecasts are vitally important for planning facilities, work force schedules, inventory, and other such elements. While every forecast is wrong to some extent, good forecasting helps an organization plan for the future.

2. Describe the basic principles of forecasting.

- There are four basic principles of forecasting that hold true in the vast majority of situations. Understanding these principles allows managers to set realistic expectations regarding their forecasting system and outcomes.
- Principle 1: Forecasts are wrong. While a forecast can help guide decision making, it is essentially an educated guess; thus, the goal should be to get a reasonably close estimate rather than an exact one.
- Principle 2: Forecasts get worse the farther into the future they go. Just as with the weather, it is easier to forecast for 30 minutes or 1 day from now than for a month or a year.
- Principle 3: Aggregated forecasts for product or service groups tend to be more accurate. Forecasting for a group or family of similar products, such as mountain bicycles, is generally more accurate than forecasting for a specific bicycle model.
- Principle 4: Forecasts are not a substitute for derived values. Dependent demand items, such as parts for a refrigerator, should not be forecast; they should be derived based on forecasts and plans for their parent items.

3. Discuss the fundamental components of demand and types of forecasting methods.

- The basic components of demand that forecasts assess include average demand, random variation, trend, seasonal component, cyclical component, and autocorrelation. Distinct types of forecasting techniques are available to address any combination of these components.
- Forecasting methods include several types: time-series analysis, qualitative methods, and causal analysis.

4. Demonstrate and apply time-series analysis in forecasting.

- Time-series methods include moving average, weighted moving average, exponential smoothing, trend-adjusted exponential smoothing, and inclusion of seasonality.
- Each type of time-series method can be modified to be either more responsive (by using fewer periods of data for a moving average or a larger α for exponential smoothing) or more stable.

5. Evaluate forecast accuracy and determine the best method.

- No forecast is 100 percent accurate. Forecast accuracy must be evaluated and multiple methods compared to find the best-performing method.
- Measures of forecast accuracy include cumulative sum of forecast errors (CFE), mean square error (MSE), standard deviation (σ), mean absolute deviation (MAD), and mean absolute percentage error (MAPE).

6. Discuss the application of qualitative and causal methods for forecasting.

- Qualitative methods are employed when no quantitative data are available. Commonly used methods include market research, the Delphi method, and sales force planning.
- Causal models utilize historical data to predict a relationship between an independent variable and the dependent variable (forecast). Linear regression is a common statistical method used to derive a linear function to develop a forecast.

7. Describe forecasting across the broader supply chain.

- Information systems and computers have allowed companies to share information across multiple levels of the supply chain in recent years and to increase the accuracy of forecasting at all levels. Two key technologies are RFID and CPFR.
- Responsive supply chains should be used for innovative products that have unpredictable demand. Methods for increasing responsiveness include deploying excess buffer capacity; deploying inventories of parts or finished goods; investing in lead-time reduction; selecting suppliers for speed, flexibility, and quality rather than cost; and developing modular designs to postpone product differentiation.

SOLVED PROBLEM 1

Moving Average and Exponential Smoothing

Given the data in Table 5.12, develop forecasts for months 4 through 8 using a moving average with $n = 2$ and exponential smoothing with $\alpha = 0.2$. For the exponential smoothing, use the average of the first two months' demand for the starting forecast for month 3.

TABLE 5.12 Demand Data for a Product

Month	Demand
1	100
2	90
3	85
4	108
5	97
6	105
7	109

SOLUTION

For the moving average, the forecast for months 4 through 8 is

$$F_4 = \frac{D_2 + D_3}{n} = \frac{90 + 85}{2} = 87.5$$

$$F_5 = \frac{D_3 + D_4}{n} = \frac{85 + 108}{2} = 96.5$$

$$F_6 = \frac{D_4 + D_5}{n} = \frac{108 + 97}{2} = 102.5$$

$$F_7 = \frac{D_5 + D_6}{n} = \frac{97 + 105}{2} = 101$$

$$F_8 = \frac{D_6 + D_7}{n} = \frac{105 + 109}{2} = 107$$

For the exponential smoothing, we start with $F_3 = 95$ and $\alpha = 0.2$.

$$F_4 = \alpha D_3 + (1 - \alpha)F_3 = 0.2 * 85 + (1 - 0.2) * 95 = 93.00$$
$$F_5 = \alpha D_4 + (1 - \alpha)F_4 = 0.2 * 108 + (1 - 0.2) * 93 = 96.00$$
$$F_6 = \alpha D_5 + (1 - \alpha)F_5 = 0.2 * 97 + (1 - 0.2) * 96 = 96.20$$

$$F_7 = \alpha D_6 + (1 - \alpha)F_6 = 0.2 * 105 + (1 - 0.2) * 96.2 = 97.96$$
$$F_8 = \alpha D_7 + (1 - \alpha)F_7 = 0.2 * 109 + (1 - 0.2) * 97.96 = 100.17$$

Table 5.13 shows the moving average and exponential smoothing forecasts side by side.

TABLE 5.13 Solution for Solved Problem 1

Month	Demand	Moving Average	Exponential Smoothing
1	100		
2	90		
3	85		
4	108	87.50	93.00
5	97	96.50	96.00
6	105	102.50	96.20
7	109	101.00	97.96
8		107.00	100.17

SOLVED PROBLEM 2

Exponential Smoothing with Trend

Custom Pants Inc. has been receiving more and more orders for its made-to-order pants. These pants are made in a factory in Guangzhou, China, and air-freighted to the end customer via FedEx. Jessica Monroe, the production planning manager for Custom Pants, wants to forecast sales for the coming six months. These data will be used both to plan production at the Guangzhou plant (additional employees will need to be hired and more space acquired) and to negotiate a new shipping agreement with FedEx. Use the data in Table 5.14 to develop a forecast using an exponential smoothing with trend model. Use $\alpha = 0.15$ and $\beta = 0.25$ for the smoothing parameters. Jessica estimates the trend at 12 additional pairs of pants per month. Develop a forecast for each of the next six months using the data in Table 5.14.

TABLE 5.14 Demand for Custom Pants Inc.

Month	Pairs of Pants
1	440
2	422
3	458
4	506
5	468
6	556

SOLUTION

Using Equations 3 through 5 and the given data,

$$\alpha = 0.15$$
$$\beta = 0.25$$
$$A_1 = 440$$
$$F_1 = 400$$
$$T_1 = 12$$

Our first forecast is for month 2:

$$F_{t+n} = A_t + nT_t \rightarrow F_2 = A_1 + 1T_1 = 440 + 12 = 452$$

We then calculate A_2 and T_2, followed by F_3:

$$A_2 = \alpha D_2 + (1 - \alpha)(A_1 + T_1) = 0.15 * 422 + (1 - 0.15)(440 + 12) = 447.50$$
$$T_2 = \beta(A_2 - A_1) + (1 - \beta)T_1 = 0.25 * (447.50 - 440) + (1 - 0.25) * 12 = 10.88$$
$$F_3 = A_2 + T_2 = 447.50 + 10.88 = 458.38$$

Repeating these calculations to get forecasts for months 4 through 7, we get

$$A_3 = \alpha D_3 + (1 - \alpha)(A_2 + T_2) = 0.15 * 458 + (1 - 0.15)(447.50 + 10.88) = 458.32$$
$$T_3 = \beta(A_3 - A_2) + (1 - \beta)T_2 = 0.25 * (458.32 - 447.50) + (1 - 0.25) * 10.88 = 10.86$$
$$F_4 = A_3 + T_3 = 458.32 + 10.86 = 469.18$$

$$A_4 = \alpha D_4 + (1 - \alpha)(A_3 + T_3) = 0.15 * 506 + (1 - 0.15)(458.32 + 10.86) = 474.70$$
$$T_4 = \beta(A_4 - A_3) + (1 - \beta)T_3 = 0.25 * (474.70 - 458.32) + (1 - 0.25) * 10.86 = 12.24$$
$$F_5 = A_4 + T_4 = 474.70 + 12.24 = 486.94$$

$$A_5 = \alpha D_5 + (1 - \alpha)(A_4 + T_4) = 0.15 * 468 + (1 - 0.15)(474.70 + 12.24) = 484.10$$
$$T_5 = \beta(A_5 - A_4) + (1 - \beta)T_4 = 0.25 * (484.10 - 474.70) + (1 - 0.25) * 12.24 = 11.53$$
$$F_6 = A_5 + T_5 = 484.10 + 11.53 = 495.63$$

$$A_6 = \alpha D_6 + (1 - \alpha)(A_5 + T_5) = 0.15 * 556 + (1 - 0.15)(484.10 + 11.53) = 504.69$$
$$T_6 = \beta(A_6 - A_5) + (1 - \beta)T_5 = 0.25 * (504.69 - 484.10) + (1 - 0.25) * 11.53 = 13.80$$
$$F_7 = A_6 + T_6 = 504.69 + 13.80 = 518.48$$

To calculate a forecast for month 8, we use $n = 2$ in equation 5:

$$F_8 = A_6 + 2 * T_6 = 504.69 + 2 * 13.80 = 532.28$$

Table 5.15 shows the values for *A*, *T*, and *F*, and Figure 5.13 shows a plot of actual demand versus forecast.

TABLE 5.15

Month	Pairs of Pants	*F*	*A*	*T*
1	440		440.00	12.00
2	422	452.00	447.50	10.88
3	458	458.38	458.32	10.86
4	506	469.18	474.70	12.24
5	468	486.94	484.10	11.53
6	556	495.63	504.69	13.80
7		518.48		
8		532.28		

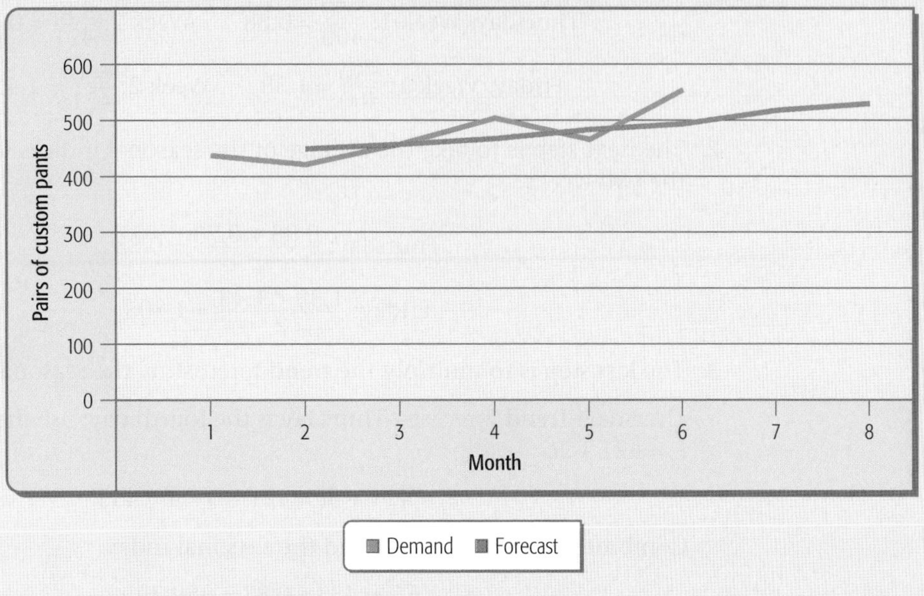

FIGURE 5.13 Graph of Demand versus Forecast

SOLVED PROBLEM 3

Seasonal Forecasting

7-Day Dry Cleaners is situated in a major city and is open seven days per week. The cleaner experiences a very seasonal demand, as it varies fairly regularly by day of the week. Use the data in Table 5.16 for the number of customers on each day for the last two weeks to forecast demand for Thursday and Friday of week 3. The data consist of both trend and seasonal components. The forecast with trend component is calculated using the formula $F_t = 421 + 3t$.

TABLE 5.16 Two Weeks of Customer Data for 7-Day Dry Cleaners

	Week 1	Week 2
Monday	500	490
Tuesday	440	400
Wednesday	400	410
Thursday	350	330
Friday	550	600
Saturday	320	400
Sunday	240	317
Total	2,800	2,947
Average	400	421

SOLUTION

1. Calculate the seasonal indices by dividing each day's demand by the average daily demand.

$$\text{Thursday, Week 1: } \frac{350}{400} = 0.88 \qquad \text{Week 2: } \frac{330}{421} = 0.78$$

$$\text{Friday, Week 1: } \frac{550}{400} = 1.38 \qquad \text{Week 2: } \frac{600}{421} = 1.43$$

2. The next step is to take the average of the seasonal indices for each day for the two weeks.

$$\text{Thursday: } \frac{0.88 + 0.78}{2} = 0.83$$

$$\text{Friday: } \frac{1.38 + 1.43}{2} = 1.405$$

3. The last step is to multiply the trend forecast by the seasonal index.

Thursday: Trend forecast—Thursday is the fourth day; use the trend equation $F_t = 421 + 3t$.

$$F_t = 421 + 3t = 421 + 3 * 4 = 433$$

Combine the trend forecast and the seasonal index.

$$F_{\text{Th}} = 433 * 0.83 = 359.39$$

Friday: Trend forecast—Friday is the fifth day.

$$F_t = 421 + 3t = 421 + 3 * 5 = 436$$
$$F_{\text{Fri}} = 436 * 1.405 = 612.58$$

Table 5.17 shows forecasts using this method for each day of week 3.

TABLE 5.17 Forecasts for 7-Day Dry Cleaners

	Week 1	Week 2	Forecast
Monday	500	490	511.75
Tuesday	440	400	437.70
Wednesday	400	410	424.38
Thursday	350	330	359.14
Friday	550	600	612.58
Saturday	320	400	384.15
Sunday	240	317	299.01
Total	2,800	2,947	
Average	400	421	

SOLVED PROBLEM 4

Comparing Forecast Methods Based on Forecast Error

Quantum Electronics employs two forecasting methods for its Gamestation 19 product: an exponential smoothing with $\alpha = 0.6$ and a trend-adjusted exponential smoothing with $\alpha = 0.25$ and $\beta = 0.10$. Calculate CFE, MSE, MAD, and MAPE for the data given in Table 5.18. Based on the scores for these forecast error measures, recommend which of the two forecasting methods should be employed.

TABLE 5.18 Forecast Data for Quantum Electronics

Month	Demand	Exponential Smoothing ($\alpha = 0.6$)	Forecast with Trend ($\alpha = 0.25, \beta = 0.10$)
0	500		
1	540	520.00	527.00
2	530	526.00	557.58
3	650	600.40	577.32
4	690	654.16	623.94
5	675	666.66	670.56
6	690	680.67	701.88
7	770	734.27	728.83
8	780	761.71	770.07
9	750	754.68	803.75
10	860	817.87	820.16
11	810	813.15	860.97
12	825	820.26	877.80

SOLUTION

1. Calculate the error E_t for each forecast method:

Exponential Smoothing	Forecast with Trend
$E_1 = D_t - F_t = 540 - 520.00 = 20.00$	$E_1 = D_t - F_t = 540 - 527.00 = 13.00$
$E_2 = 530 - 526.00 = 4.00$	$E_2 = 650 - 577.32 = 72.68$
⋮	⋮
$E_{11} = 810 - 813.15 = -3.15$	$E_{11} = 810 - 860.97 = -50.97$
$E_{12} = 825 - 820.26 = 4.74$	$E_{12} = 825 - 877.80 = -52.80$

2. Calculate the cumulative forecast error (CFE) and mean forecast error (MFE):

$$\text{CFE} = \sum E_t = (E_1 + E_2 + \cdots + E_{11} + E_{12})$$

$$\text{MFE} = \bar{E} = \frac{\text{CFE}}{n}$$

Exponential Smoothing	Forecast with Trend
CFE = 20.00 + 4.00 + ⋯ + (–3.15) + 4.74 = 220.17	CFE = 13.00 + (–27.58) + … + (–50.97) + (–52.8) = 50.14
$\bar{E} = \frac{220.17}{12} = 18.35$	$\bar{E} = \frac{50.14}{12} = 4.18$

3. Calculate the mean squared error (MSE).

$$\text{MSE} = \frac{\sum E_t^2}{n} = \frac{E_1^2 + E_2^2 + \cdots + E_{11}^2 + E_{12}^2}{12}$$

Exponential Smoothing	Forecast with Trend
$\frac{20^2 + 4^2 + \cdots + (-3.15)^2 + 4.74^2}{12}$ $= 7{,}757.84$	$\frac{13^2 + (-27.58)^2 + \ldots + (-50.97)^2 + (-52.8)^2}{12}$ $= 22{,}392.29$
$\text{MSE} = \frac{7{,}757.84}{12} = 646.49$	$\text{MSE} = \frac{22{,}392.29}{12} = 1{,}866.02$

4. Calculate the σ of error:

$$\sigma = \sqrt{\frac{\sum (E_t - \bar{E})^2}{n-1}} = \sqrt{\frac{(E_1 - \bar{E})^2 + (E_2 - \bar{E})^2 + \cdots + (E_{11} - \bar{E})^2 + (E_{12} - \bar{E})^2}{12-1}}$$

Exponential Smoothing

$$\sigma = \sqrt{\frac{(20 - 18.35)^2 + (4 - 18.35)^2 + \cdots + (-3.15 - 18.35)^2 + (4.74 - 18.35)^2}{12-1}}$$

$$\sigma = \sqrt{\frac{3{,}718.5}{12-1}} = 18.39$$

Forecast with Trend

$$\sigma = \sqrt{\frac{(13 - 4.18)^2 + (-27.58 - 4.18)^2 + \cdots + (-50.97 - 4.18)^2 + (-52.8 - 4.18)^2}{12-1}}$$

$$\sigma = \sqrt{\frac{24{,}592.17}{12-1}} = 47.28$$

5. Calculate the mean absolute deviation (MAD).

$$\text{MAD} = \frac{\sum |E_t|}{n} = \frac{|E_1| + |E_2| + \cdots + |E_{11}| + |E_{12}|}{12}$$

Exponential Smoothing	Forecast with Trend
$\frac{\|20\| + \|4\| + \cdots + \|-3.15\| + \|4.74\|}{12}$ $= 235.84$	$\frac{\|13\| + \|-27.58\| + \ldots + \|-50.97\| + \|-52.80\|}{12}$ $= 444.10$
$\text{MAD} = \frac{235.84}{12} = 19.65$	$\text{MAD} = \frac{444.10}{12} = 37.01$

6. Calculate the mean absolute percentage error (MAPE).

$$\text{MAPE} = \frac{\sum \frac{|E_t|}{D}(100)}{n} = \frac{\left(\frac{|E_1|}{D_1} + \frac{|E_2|}{D_2} + \cdots + \frac{|E_{11}|}{D_{11}} + \frac{|E_{12}|}{D_{12}}\right) * 100}{12}$$

Exponential Smoothing	Forecast with Trend
$$\frac{\left(\frac{20}{540}+\frac{4}{530}+\cdots+\frac{3.15}{810}+\frac{4.74}{825}\right)*100}{12}=$$	$$\frac{\left(\frac{13}{540}+\frac{27.58}{530}+\cdots+\frac{50.97}{810}+\frac{52.80}{825}\right)*100}{12}=$$
$$\text{MAPE}=\frac{33.34\%}{12}=2.78\%$$	$$\text{MAPE}=\frac{61.86\%}{12}=5.15\%$$

Tables 5.19 and 5.20 summarize the data for the two forecasting methods, and Table 5.21 compares the two methods.

TABLE 5.19 Exponential Smoothing Solution

Month	Demand	Forecast	Error	Error Squared	Absolute Error	Absolute Percentage Error
0	500					
1	540	520.00	20.00	400.00	20.00	3.70%
2	530	526.00	4.00	16.00	4.00	0.75%
3	650	600.40	49.60	2,460.16	49.60	7.63%
4	690	654.16	35.84	1,284.51	35.84	5.19%
5	675	666.66	8.34	69.49	8.34	1.23%
6	690	680.67	9.33	87.13	9.33	1.35%
7	770	734.27	35.73	1,276.90	35.73	4.64%
8	780	761.71	18.29	334.65	18.29	2.35%
9	750	754.68	–4.68	21.93	4.68	0.62%
10	860	817.87	42.13	1,774.68	42.13	4.90%
11	810	813.15	–3.15	9.92	3.15	0.39%
12	825	820.26	4.74	22.47	4.74	0.57%
	Totals		220.17	7,757.84	235.84	33.34%

TABLE 5.20 Forecast with Trend Solution

Month	Demand	Forecast	Error	Error Squared	Absolute Error	Absolute Percentage Error
0	500					
1	540	527.00	13.00	169.00	13.00	2.41%
2	530	557.58	–27.58	760.38	27.58	5.20%
3	650	577.32	72.68	5,282.84	72.68	11.18%
4	690	623.94	66.06	4,363.88	66.06	9.57%
5	675	670.56	4.44	19.72	4.44	0.66%
6	690	701.88	–11.88	141.25	11.88	1.72%
7	770	728.83	41.17	1,694.83	41.17	5.35%
8	780	770.07	9.93	98.58	9.93	1.27%
9	750	803.75	–53.75	2,888.94	53.75	7.17%
10	860	820.16	39.84	1,586.95	39.84	4.63%
11	810	860.97	–50.97	2,597.97	50.97	6.29%
12	825	877.80	–52.80	2,787.96	52.80	6.40%
	Totals		50.14	22,392.29	444.10	61.86%

TABLE 5.21 Comparison of Forecast Error

	Exponential Smoothing	Exponential Smoothing with Trend
CFE	220.17	50.14
MFE	18.35	4.18
MSE	646.49	1,866.02
σ	18.39	44.91
MAD	19.65	37.01
MAPE	2.78%	5.15%

The exponential smoothing forecast outperforms the exponential smoothing with trend on four out of six measures of forecast error; thus, this method should be employed to obtain the best forecast.

PROBLEMS

1. The original Spear cell phone has a negative trend in sales. The product's sales have decreased in each of the last eight months on the market. The forecast for month 2 was 1,850 ($F_2 = 1{,}850$) (see table at right), with $A_6 = 1{,}785$ and $T_6 = 65$. Using smoothing components $\alpha = 0.10$ and $\beta = 0.20$, develop forecasts for weeks 3 through 9.

Month	Demand
1	2,000
2	1,800
3	1,780
4	1,700
5	1,650
6	1,550
7	1,500
8	1,460

2. Given the data in Table 5.22, compute the error measurements indicated.

TABLE 5.22

Month	Demand	Weighted Moving Average (0.6, 0.3, 0.1)	Error	Squared Error	Absolute Error	Absolute Percentage Error
0	500					
1	530					
2	552					
3	653	540.20	112.80	12,723.84	112.80	17.27%
4	687	610.40	76.60	5,867.56	76.60	11.15%
5	680	663.30	16.70	278.89	16.70	2.46%
6	702	679.40	22.60	510.76	22.60	3.22%
7	768	693.90	74.10	5,490.81	74.10	9.65%
8	777	739.40	37.60	1,413.76	37.60	4.84%
9	741	766.80	–25.80	665.64	25.80	3.48%
10	856	754.50	101.50	10,302.25	101.50	11.86%
11	830	813.60	16.40	268.96	16.40	1.98%
12	822	828.90	–6.90	47.61	6.90	0.84%
Total	9,098	7,090.40	425.60	37,570.08	491.00	66.74%
CFE						
MFE						
MSE						
A						
MAD						
MAPE						

3. Tough Face, a manufacturer of rock-climbing gear, has been enjoying steady growth of its very reliable and colorful carabiner products. Using the sales history, calculate the trend-adjusted exponential in the table at the right smoothing forecast for the next three years. The growth trend appears to be 150 cases, $\alpha = 0.75$, and $\beta = 0.85$.

Year 1	250
Year 2	369
Year 3	507
Year 4	658
Year 5	903

4. Table 5.23 provides the demand and forecast for the television model G2000 at a major electronics retailer. Calculate the CFE, MSE, MAD, and MAPE.

TABLE 5.23 Demand and Forecasts for Television Model G2000

Month	Demand	Forecast	Error	Error Squared	Absolute Error	Absolute Percentage Error
1	50	57	–7	42.25	6.5	13.0%
2	60	54	6	36	6	10.0%
3	55	55	0	0	0	0.0%
4	45	58	–13	156.25	12.5	27.8%
5	70	50	20	400	20	28.6%
6	58	58	1	0.25	0.5	0.9%
7	64	64	0	0	0	0.0%
8	53	61	–8	64	8	15.1%
9	59	59	1	0.25	0.5	0.8%
10	62	56	6	36	6	9.7%
		Total	6	735	60	106%

5. A recently introduced product has a positive trend in sales. The product's sales have increased in each of its first eight weeks on the market. The forecast for week 6 was 1,325 (F_6 = 1,325) (see table at right), with A_6 = 1,283 and T_6 = 42. Using smoothing components α = 0.20 and β = 0.30, develop forecasts for weeks 7 and 8.

Week	Demand
1	1,000
2	1,050
3	1,125
4	1,150
5	1,250
6	1,300
7	1,310
8	1,400

6. Given the data in Table 5.24, compute the forecast error measurements indicated.

TABLE 5.24

Month	Demand	Exponential Smoothing (α = 0.4)	Error	Squared Error	Absolute Error	Absolute Percentage Error
1	530	515.00	15.00	225.00	15.00	2.83%
2	552	529.80	22.20	492.84	22.20	4.02%
3	653	579.08	73.92	5,464.17	73.92	11.32%
4	687	622.25	64.75	4,192.82	64.75	9.43%
5	680	645.35	34.65	1,200.71	34.65	5.10%
6	702	668.01	33.99	1,155.37	33.99	4.84%
7	768	708.01	59.99	3,599.33	59.99	7.81%
8	777	735.60	41.40	1,713.68	41.40	5.33%
9	741	737.76	3.24	10.48	3.24	0.44%
10	856	785.06	70.94	5,032.88	70.94	8.29%
11	830	803.03	26.97	727.15	26.97	3.25%
12	822	810.62	11.38	129.49	11.38	1.38%
Total	9,098	8,139.57	458.43	23,943.92	458.43	64.03%
CFE						
MFE						
MSE						
A						
MAD						
MAPE						

7. Egg sales are a major concern at MV Grocery. The following gives the demand for the past eight weeks (in dozens).

Week	Demand
1	250
2	200
3	220
4	190
5	230
6	240
7	260
8	230

a. Using a two-week moving average, develop forecasts for weeks 6 through 9.

b. Using a weighted moving average with weights of 0.40, 0.30, 0.20, and 0.10, develop forecasts for weeks 6 through 9

c. Using exponential smoothing with $\alpha = 0.4$ and a week 5 forecast of 210, find the forecast for week 6.

8. Chez Swanky restaurant has a seasonal demand pattern and has had a general increase (trend) in business since receiving a favorable review in the gourmet section of the local paper. Given the following number of tables served each evening, calculate the demand for next week. The growth trend has been estimated as $F_t = 35 + 5t$.

Week 1		Week 2		Week 3	
Thursday	20	Thursday	23	Thursday	27
Friday	25	Friday	29	Friday	33
Saturday	35	Saturday	41	Saturday	45
Sunday	15	Sunday	17	Sunday	20

9. A product has the following demand history for the past six months:

January	212
February	201
March	242
April	188
May	198
June	208

a. Using a four-month moving average, find the July forecast.

b. Using a weighted moving average with weights of 0.50, 0.30, and 0.20, find the July forecast.

c. Using exponential smoothing with $\alpha = 0.2$ and a June forecast of 196, find the July forecast.

10. Funsville Party Supply has the following sales history for its most popular product:

Week 1		Week 2		Week 3	
Monday	6	Monday	12	Monday	8
Tuesday	8	Tuesday	10	Tuesday	9
Wednesday	15	Wednesday	18	Wednesday	17
Thursday	23	Thursday	22	Thursday	25
Friday	35	Friday	39	Friday	42
Saturday	28	Saturday	26	Saturday	30
Sunday	10	Sunday	11	Sunday	9

a. Given the obvious seasonality, calculate the forecast for Thursday, Friday, and Saturday of week 4.

11. DFG Clocks has the following demand history for the past six months:

January	54
February	62
March	74
April	65
May	50
June	58

a. Using a three-month moving average, find the July forecast.

b. Using a weighted moving average with weights of 0.70, 0.20, and 0.10, find the July forecast.

c. Using exponential smoothing with $\alpha = 0.25$ and a June forecast of 56, find the July forecast.

12. Happy Feet Dance Studio has had the following number of people signing up for dance lessons over the past three years. Calculate the anticipated demand for lessons in March, April, and May of next year, given the seasonality of demand and a trend of $F_t = 100 + 15_t$.

Year 1		Year 2		Year 3	
January	20	January	28	January	40
February	106	February	115	February	122
March	50	March	62	March	77
April	100	April	110	April	123
May	107	May	122	May	135

CHAPTER 6

Independent Demand Inventory

LEARNING OBJECTIVES

1. List the reasons for and against having inventory.
2. Learn the basic types of inventory.
3. Apply the continuous review and periodic review systems. Describe other important inventory systems.

A Wal-Mart store.

The Wal-Mart Effect

Wal-Mart became the world's largest retailer in large part because of its excellent management of inventory. The company has annual sales of over $300 billion and operates more than 3,500 stores in the United States and more than 2,500 stores in 15 other countries, including Japan, Nicaragua, the United Kingdom, and Brazil. Wal-Mart employs more than 1.3 million people in the United States and an additional half million in other countries, and the company is the largest employer in both the United States and Mexico. The scale of Wal-Mart's operations and the number of inventory decisions made on a daily basis are astounding. With more than 6,000 stores and at least 10,000 stock-keeping units (SKUs) at each store, Wal-Mart manages at least 60 million individual stocking locations—which leads to at least a quarter of a million line-item orders per day.

The tremendous impact that Wal-Mart's inventory decisions have on its suppliers has been dubbed "the Wal-Mart Effect." When Wal-Mart announced a major effort to reduce its inventory costs by $6 billion in 2006, or 20 percent of its yearly total, suppliers took notice. Wal-Mart accounts for 10 to 30 percent of many suppliers' sales, including giants like Kellogg's, Procter & Gamble, and Sara Lee. Battery maker Spectrum Brands Inc. suffered a 28 percent drop in stock market value on April 6 after blaming Wal-Mart's inventory reductions. Wal-Mart accounts for 18 percent of Spectrum's total sales and 16 percent of Procter & Gamble's. The correction of Wal-Mart's inventory also affects shippers, with estimates of a $300 to $400 million reduction in freight revenue. Swift Transportation, J.B. Hunt Transport Services, and Knight Transportation all experienced drops in stock price as a result of Wal-Mart's inventory reductions. Both J.B. Hunt and Swift receive about 15 percent of their revenue from Wal-Mart.

Wal-Mart's inventory reduction reflects its strategy of cutting costs and improving margins by pruning the range of items offered in stores. Steps taken to reduce inventory include revising its distribution system to facilitate more frequent delivery to stores of fast-moving items such as toilet paper, light bulbs, and garbage bags. The company is also seeking to reduce store inventory that isn't on shelves, including backroom stock, stock on overhead shelves, and stock in off-site warehouses. The linkage between Wal-Mart's actions and those of its many suppliers provides an excellent illustration of the bullwhip effect, where the decisions of one part of the supply chain ripple through the entire system. ■

● **Inventory** the physical stock of any item or resources used in an organization

Inventory is the physical stock of any item or resources used in an organization. The policies and procedures that monitor levels of inventory and determine when to place an order make up the inventory management system.

The objective of an inventory system is to specify

1 When items should be ordered

2 What quantity of each item should be ordered

These two decisions need to be made both for manufacturing and for services. In manufacturing, types of inventory include raw materials, work in process, finished goods, component parts, and supplies. In services, inventory refers to tangible goods that are sold as part of the service and maintenance, repair, and operating (MRO) supplies that are necessary to keep the business running.

INVENTORY EQUILIBRIUM

Determining the proper amount of inventory for a particular item is similar to balancing a scale. It is important to assess the benefits of carrying larger amounts of inventory against the drawbacks and risks of carrying that inventory. Managers should carefully assess several factors that may tip the balance toward higher or lower amounts for a given product or part.

Reasons to Carry Inventory

All organizations (including companies that utilize lean production and companies like Google that sell "virtual" products) carry some inventory, for the following reasons.

1. Setup and Ordering Cost

Producing an item involves two steps: setting up the materials and resources necessary to produce the item and doing the actual processing or transformation of the item. Setup and ordering cost is the cost in time and/or money to prepare all necessary materials and resources for production. Processing cost is the cost in time and/or money to machine, assemble, or transform an item. As an example, if you want to change one light bulb in the chandelier in your foyer, the setup time (cost) might be 5 minutes—this is the time involved in getting out a ladder, finding a light bulb, and preparing any necessary tools. The processing time for actually changing the light bulb might then be 10 seconds. The time (cost) needed to change one light bulb is 5.16 minutes (5 minutes setup + 10 seconds processing). To change all 10 light bulbs in the chandelier would require a total of only 6.67 minutes (5 minutes setup plus 10 * 10 seconds processing). This is one of the reasons that maintenance people in office buildings often change all the light bulbs at once—the other is that it increases reliability in terms of when the lights work. In general, the higher the demand for a good or service, the greater the incentive to increase the order size to spread the order/setup cost over more units. Setup cost is generally used in manufacturing situations where physical steps need to be taken to prepare for an order. Ordering cost is used when purchasing items from a supplier or retailer because of the time or cost necessary to initiate the order and process it when it is received. When order sizes increase, average cycle inventory levels increase.

2. Customer Service and Variation in Demand

While demand can be predicted, it cannot be predicted with great accuracy. Average demand in a 7-Eleven (U.S.) or a Twenty Four Seven (India) convenience store for a bottle of milk might be 100 units per day; however, some days will have demand of 150, and some will have demand of 75. A store or other business often carries buffer inventory so that there is a higher customer service level—i.e., less chance that the store is out of stock.

3. Labor and Equipment Utilization

Organizations will often produce extra inventory in order to keep equipment and people occupied, believing that if the time is not used, it is lost. Larger orders also have the benefit of reducing the number of setups and increasing the proportion of time that is spent processing an order (i.e., adding value).

4. Transportation Cost

Transportation cost is closely linked to the size of the order. When large items or large quantities of smaller items are shipped, it is much more efficient to have an entire truckload (or railroad car or plane or some other vehicle) than to have a partial load. Internet retailers such as Amazon, Zappos, and Newegg all try to influence customers to have multiple items in their orders in order to reduce the per-unit cost of transportation. Transportation cost is similar to setup cost—larger orders tend to reduce the per-unit cost.

5. Costs of Materials/Quantity Discounts

Just as one company benefits from larger orders in terms of setup cost, labor and equipment utilization, and transportation, so do companies that supply goods to other companies. Thus, it is fairly common for companies to offer quantity discounts. For example, a company might offer a certain part at the price of $5.00 per unit, but offer a discounted price of $4.50 if a single individual or company buys 100 or more and a steeper discount to $4.00 if 500 or more are bought. This is done because of the savings resulting from larger orders—the selling company passes part of this savings on to the buying company as an incentive to increase the order size. In addition, many companies will carry extra inventory as a hedge against inflation.

Reasons to Reduce Inventory

1. Storage and Handling

The greater the amount of inventory carried, the more storage and handling is necessary. There is a cost associated with owning, renting, and maintaining extra space to hold extra inventory. In addition, having a large amount of extra inventory increases the chances of misplacing an item because it is less visible and less likely to stand out.

2. Interest and Opportunity Cost

Money tied up in inventory could be used for other purposes. It could be used to buy other resources, be invested in bonds or stocks, or be invested in some other way. Typically companies assign a cost of capital to this cost—anywhere between 3 and 30 percent per year. To illustrate, suppose there was a great deal on T-shirts and you bought 20, even though you can use only 10 per year. If the T-shirts cost $10 each, then 10 of the T-shirts are inventory that will not be used for an entire year, and you have $100 (10 * $10) tied up in inventory. This money could be used for other purposes—if you put this money in a bank, you might earn 4 percent interest; thus, it costs $4 to hold those T-shirts for one year.

3. Property Taxes and Insurance Premiums

Taxes are often assessed on inventory in proportion to the amount. Thus, a company holding $1 million of inventory will pay twice as much tax as a company holding $500,000 of inventory. As a result, there is an incentive to reduce inventory—particularly right before the tax bill is due. Television ads often show "inventory clearance" sales, which are designed to reduce inventory to reduce tax bills.

Similarly, insurance premiums on inventory are proportional to the amount. Thus, reducing the amount of inventory results in lower premiums because there is less inventory at risk if there is a fire or other disaster.

4. Shrinkage and Spoilage

Companies producing or marketing products whose styles change quickly or products that can go bad have a problem with obsolescence or spoilage. A store that carries 100 gallons of milk but sells only 30 gallons in a week risks the milk spoiling when it expires. Similarly, holding many units of Sony's Playstation 2 console may become problematic when the PS-3 comes out. Often an obsolete product such as this must be sold at a deep discount.

Shrinkage occurs when products are misplaced, stolen, or shoplifted. A customer might select a quart of ice cream, then decide 10 minutes later that he does not want it. If the customer just leaves the ice cream on a shelf that is not designed for ice cream, it will melt. Customers or employees may also take items without paying for them. Sometimes this can be done without conscious intent—i.e., a customer forgets that something is at the bottom of his or her grocery cart and thus does not pay for it. Other times it is done consciously—i.e., the customer or employee is stealing a product. Either way, the result is the same: more inventory gives more opportunity for spoilage or shrinkage to occur.

Figure 6.1 illustrates that the pressures to carry a large or small amount of inventory should be considered simultaneously and balanced as much as possible.

INVENTORY TYPES

There are several basic types of inventory: cycle, safety stock, anticipation, pipeline, work-in-process, and remanufactured/reconditioned. These are not necessarily physical or visible—you cannot look at a pile of screws and identify whether it is safety stock or cycle inventory. However, there are important conceptual differences between the types, and each serves a distinct purpose in the supply chain. Understanding these types is important for clearly grasping inventory theory and for identifying methods for reducing inventory and improving performance.

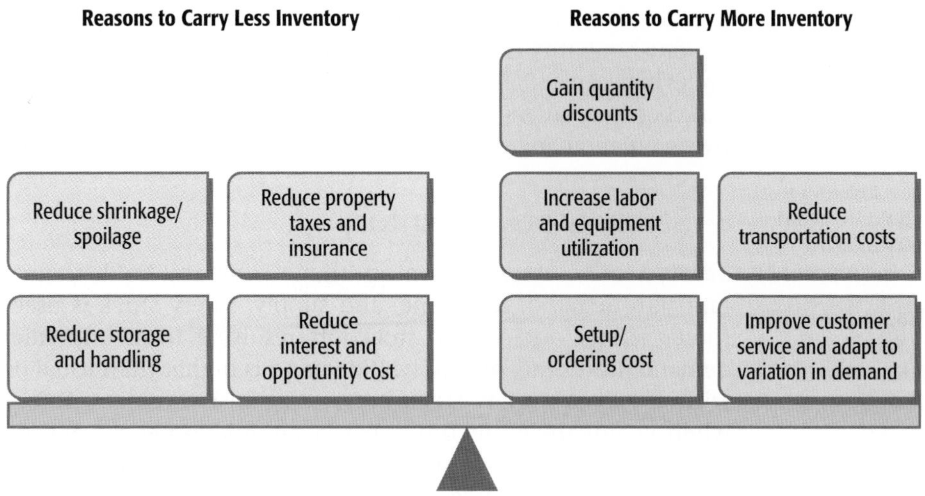

FIGURE 6.1 Pressures for Small/Large Inventory

Cycle Inventory

Cycle inventory varies in proportion to order quantity—larger orders result in higher cycle inventory, while smaller orders result in lower. The order quantity Q is proportional to the time between orders (cycle). The longer the time between orders, the higher the order quantity. The term *cycle inventory* comes from the nature of this type of inventory—at the beginning of an order, cycle inventory is at its maximum. As demand occurs, the inventory level drops until it is zero, at which point a new order is placed/received. The average cycle inventory is thus

● **Cycle inventory** a quantity of inventory that varies in proportion to order quantity

$$\text{Average Inventory} = \frac{Q + 0}{2} = \frac{Q}{2}$$

Figure 6.2 illustrates the concept of cycle inventory, assuming that the demand rate is constant and uniform. While demand is decidedly *not* constant and uniform

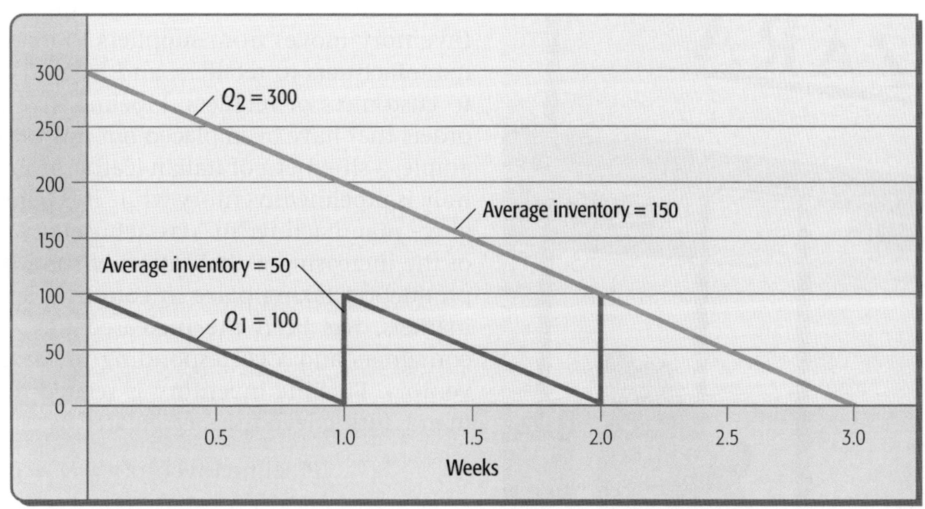

FIGURE 6.2 Cycle Inventory

The cycle time for a larger order ($Q = 300$) is longer than the cycle time for a smaller order ($Q = 100$). In this case, there will be three order cycles for the smaller order for every one cycle of the larger order.

in real life, the principle of cycle inventory still holds. Figure 6.2 shows that when the order quantity is 100 and average demand is 100 units per week, the inventory cycles between a high of 100 and a low of 0, with average inventory equal to 50. The time between orders is 1 week. If the order quantity is tripled, to 300, the time between orders changes to 3 weeks and the average inventory is 150.

- **Safety stock** excess inventory that a company holds to guard against uncertainty in demand, lead time, and supply
- **Anticipation inventory** inventory that is held for future use at a time when demand will exceed available capacity
- **Pipeline inventory** inventory that is in the process of moving from one location in the supply chain to another

Safety Stock Inventory

Safety stock is excess inventory that a company holds to guard against uncertainty in demand, lead time, and supply. Safety stock is used to improve customer service and reduce stockouts resulting from unpredictable changes in demand, lead time, or supply. If demand is higher than usual or a supplier is late with a delivery, safety stock protects against shortages. Safety stock is created when a company either orders before an order is needed or orders more than the expected demand. For example, if an order for 100 units was placed in Figure 6.2 on day 6 of week 1, there would be excess inventory because this inventory is not needed until the end of week 1—on day 7.

Anticipation Inventory

Anticipation inventory is inventory that is held for future use at a time when demand will exceed available capacity. Many businesses have very seasonal demand that is difficult to satisfy with manufacturing capacity on a timely basis. For example, a snowmobile company may sell 75 percent of its annual total of 36,000 snowmobiles during the months of November to February. Anticipation inventory would be created if the company produces 3,000 snowmobiles per month in order to keep production constant. Inventory would build up prior to November, then be used to meet the surge in demand. The photo here shows a Zara storefront. Zara is a European-based retailer that has developed a very responsive and quick supply chain to minimize the need for anticipation inventory.

Rather than use anticipation inventory, which can lead to excess supply of some products and shortages of others, Zara has been a leader in developing a responsive supply chain that can get orders for new products in as little as two weeks (versus an industry average of four to six months).

Pipeline Inventory

Pipeline inventory is inventory that is in the process of moving from one location in the supply chain to another. Inventory moves from suppliers to manufacturers, from manufacturers to retailers, and from distribution centers to customers or retailers. Pipeline inventory consists of orders that have been placed but not yet received. For example, a shipment of Italian leather from the producer in Italy is pipeline inventory while it is being shipped to the glove manufacturer in Massachusetts. One of the effects of the increasing globalization of the supply chain, with production taking place in countries far away from end markets, has been the increased use of large shipping containers and a corresponding increase in pipeline inventory. Pipeline inventory is related to the average demand during lead time, calculated as

$$\text{Pipeline Inventory} = \overline{D}_L = d * L$$

where d = demand per period
L = the lead time to move inventory between two points

Notice that pipeline inventory does *not* depend on the order quantity. Increasing the order quantity means that there will be more inventory during the lead time for *that order,* but because there are proportionately *fewer* orders, the average pipeline inventory is the same.

Inventory in transit.

Work-in-Process (WIP) Inventory

Work-in-process (WIP) inventory is inventory that is in the process of being transformed from one state to another. It cannot be sold to a customer because it is not yet finished. For example, 50 chairs that have been painted but are drying for two hours are work-in-process inventory. WIP is proportional to the order or production quantity. One of the central principles of lean production is reducing the production quantity so that there is less WIP, as we will see in greater detail in Chapter 12. WIP is necessary in most manufacturing, service, and supply chain contexts in order to cushion fluctuations in demand and variations in production time and to allow for fewer setups. In particular, WIP is often used so that one setup for a step or process can be used to make many units of the same item.

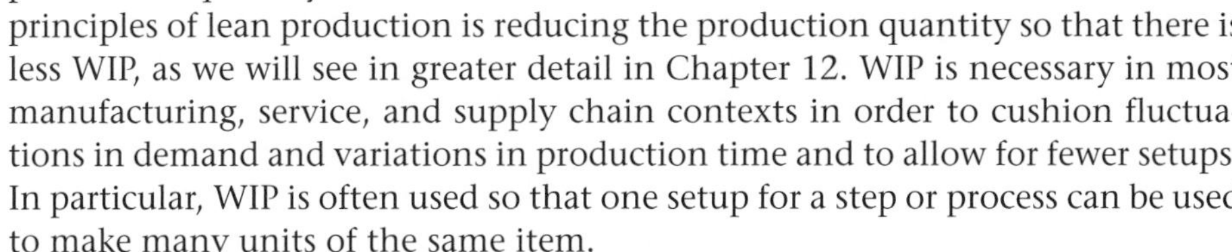

● **Work-in-process (WIP) inventory** inventory that is in the process of being transformed from one state to another

Remanufactured/Reconditioned Inventory

Remanufactured/reconditioned inventory consists of products that have been used by a customer and then reacquired by a company and either remanufactured or reconditioned for resale. Examples of products that fit this definition include printer cartridges, cell phones, computers, and parts for various industrial products and automobiles. The initial motivation for companies to reuse existing parts and products was concern for the environment and efforts to reduce the adverse impact of manufacturing. However, over time, many manufacturers have discovered that remanufacturing can reduce raw material acquisition costs and allow new customers to be targeted. Inventory policies for remanufactured/reconditioned inventory are substantially the same as those for first-generation products, with one exception: Manufacturers that rework products must acquire the products that will be reworked. Unfortunately, not all products that come back from customers are of good enough quality to be remanufactured at a reasonable cost. For example, a printer cartridge retailer such as Redeemplc (www.redeemplc.com) may need to buy 140 used cartridges to get 100 that are in good enough shape to remanufacture. Thus, there are inventory systems for determining how many used products to acquire. We do not cover those in detail, but believe that this is an important and growing area.

● **Remanufactured/reconditioned inventory** products that have been used by a customer and then reacquired by a company and either remanufactured or reconditioned for resale

Independent versus Dependent Demand

Independent demand is for items that are considered end items that go directly to a customer, and for which demand is influenced by market conditions and not related to inventory decisions for any other item. Independent demand must be forecast. Typical items with independent demand include things like books, food or other items in a retail store, cars, televisions, and computers. In contrast, **dependent demand** is demand for items that are used to make another item or are considered to be component parts. Dependent demand can be derived from the production decisions for the parent items. Items with dependent demand include the parts that are used to assemble a bicycle, the parts required for

● **Independent demand** demand for items that are considered end items that go directly to a customer, and for which demand is influenced by market conditions and not related to inventory decisions for any other item

● **Dependent demand** demand for items that are used to make another item or are considered to be component parts

a computer, and the ingredients in baking a cake. This chapter focuses on independent demand items, while Chapter 7 focuses on dependent demand items and the systems that are most commonly used to manage them.

INVENTORY SYSTEMS

An inventory system provides the structure and operating policies for maintaining and controlling goods to be stocked in inventory. The system is responsible for ordering, tracking, and receiving goods. The two essential policies for every item that a company stocks in inventory or uses in its processes are

1. How much or *what quantity* of an item to order?
2. *When* should an order for that item be placed?

In addition, the system must follow up to clarify miscommunication; for example, it must make sure that a supplier has received an order or check whether an order has been shipped. Figure 6.3 illustrates the fundamental concepts of inventory management. The water in the tank represents the inventory level for a certain part or product. Demand for that product reduces the inventory (water) level, as does the need to scrap or reject poor-quality parts or products that get damaged or stolen by customers. The inflow of new products is determined by the size and timing of orders. The reorder point line shows one technique for determining when to place a new order—when the inventory level drops to that point.

Two Types of Systems

There are two general types of inventory systems: continuous review systems (also called economic order quantity systems or Q-systems) and periodic review systems (also called fixed-period systems or P-systems).

● **Continuous review system** an inventory system that always orders the same quantity of items, but has differing periods of time between orders

● **Periodic review system** an inventory system that has a fixed time between orders but has different order quantities from order to order

The basic distinction between the two is that **continuous review systems** always order the same quantity of items, but may have differing periods of time between orders, while **periodic review systems** always have the same time between orders but may have different order quantities from order to order. Continuous review systems monitor inventory levels regularly and place an order as soon as a certain inventory level or reorder point is reached. Periodic review systems need to monitor inventory only periodically because at the end of the prescribed time period (a week, a month, or some other time increment), the order quantity is determined based on the difference between a target inventory level and the existing inventory level at the end of the time period.

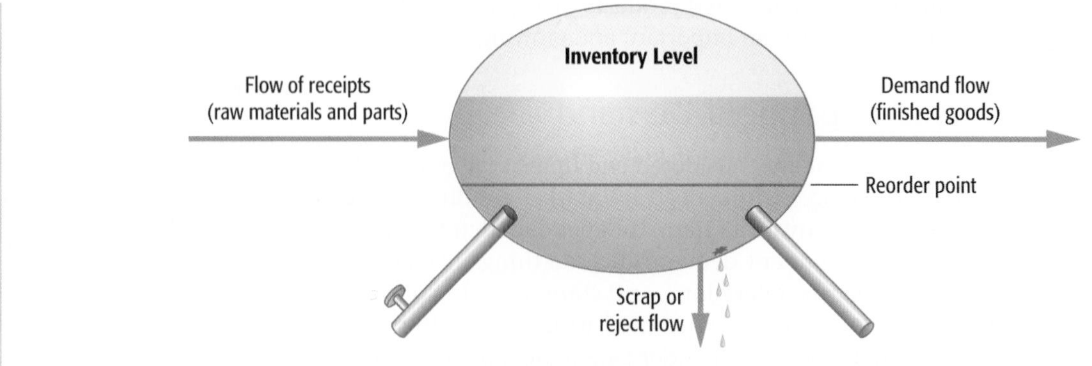

FIGURE 6.3 Inventory Management as a Water Tank

There are numerous variations of these two inventory systems that differ in relatively small ways, but all inventory systems can be neatly classified into one of the two categories. Each system has relative advantages and disadvantages, as outlined in Table 6.1.

Continuous Review Systems

These systems consist of two components: the order quantity Q and the reorder point R. Both are expressed in terms of units, such as number of pencils, number of packages of pencils, or number of cases of pencils. In some cases, the units can be for a volume, such as gallons of paint or pounds of sugar. When the inventory position drops to or below the quantity R (as a result of outgoing orders), then an order for a quantity Q is placed. **Inventory position** is defined as on-hand inventory plus outstanding orders, minus any backorder quantities (items promised to a customer but not yet delivered).

● **Inventory position** on-hand inventory plus outstanding orders, minus any backorder quantities (items promised to a customer but not yet delivered)

Setting the Order Quantity

The goal for the inventory system is to minimize total annual inventory cost:

Total Inventory Cost = Annual Ordering Cost + Annual Holding Cost

$$IC = \frac{D}{Q}S + \frac{Q}{2}H \qquad \text{(Equation 1)}$$

where IC = total annual cost
D = annual demand
Q = order quantity
S = setup or ordering cost
H = holding cost (often estimated as hC)

The annual ordering cost is calculated as $\frac{D}{Q}S$ (the cost to place an order). $\frac{D}{Q}$ is the number of times that orders will be placed in a given year. For example, an item with demand = 1,000 units per year and an order quantity of 100 will be ordered 10 times (1,000/100) per year. The setup/order cost S is the estimate of the cost of preparing for each order. For example, printing an order of books may require 30 minutes to set up the printing press with the correct paper, printing

TABLE 6.1 Differences Between Inventory Systems

	Q-system Continuous Review System	P-system Periodic Review System
Order quantity	Q = constant	Q = variable
Order timing	R (order when inventory position drops to or below the predetermined reorder point)	Order at the end of period P (can be daily, weekly, monthly, or some other time period)
Database update	Every time a withdrawal or addition is made	Only at end of period
Inventory size	Lower	Slightly higher because of the need to hold more safety stock

plates, ink, and other requirements. Thus, the setup cost might be estimated to be \$20 [½ hour (30 minutes) times \$40 per hour (the labor cost of the person preparing the printing press)].

The annual holding cost is the quantity $\frac{Q}{2}H$. $\frac{Q}{2}$ is the average inventory level (assuming that the inventory cycles between a high of Q units and a low of 0 units, as shown in Figure 6.2; the average is $\frac{Q}{2}$). H is the per-unit holding cost (which is typically estimated as a percentage of the purchased cost C of an item from the supplier, i.e., $H = hC$, where h = the carrying cost expressed as a percentage).

As shown in Figure 6.4, the total annual inventory cost is the sum of the cost of holding inventory ($\frac{Q}{2}H$) and the cost of ordering inventory ($\frac{D}{Q}S$). The resulting total cost curve is bowl-shaped; thus, the order quantity that minimizes total costs is in the middle of the bowl. As Figure 6.4 shows, the lowest possible cost is where the annual holding cost equals the annual ordering cost. Note that we do *not* include the cost to purchase an item (i.e., a unit costs \$2 or \$3 each); this is because we assume that we do not have any control over the price at which we purchase the goods. The only things that we can control are the size and timing of the order. When we can control the purchase price (for example, with quantity discounts of the type where orders of less than 50 are \$3 per unit and orders of 50 units or more are \$2.50), then there is a variation of this order point calculation (this situation will be covered in the section on quantity discounts, which adds the cost of purchased goods in Equation 1 to form Equation 5).

Figure 6.4 shows that smaller order quantities Q have low holding costs because holding costs increase in a linear fashion with increases in order quantity. However, the low holding cost is more than offset by a large order cost because small order quantities result in more frequent orders. In contrast, very large order quantities have a large holding cost and a small ordering cost because few orders will be placed each year. Table 6.2 (on page 206) shows an example with five different order quantities and the total annual cost assuming that D = 2,000 units per year, S = \$20 per order, and H = \$2 per unit per year. A small order quantity (Q = 50) results in very low holding costs (\$50), but very high ordering costs (\$800) because of the need to order frequently (40 orders per year). In contrast, a large

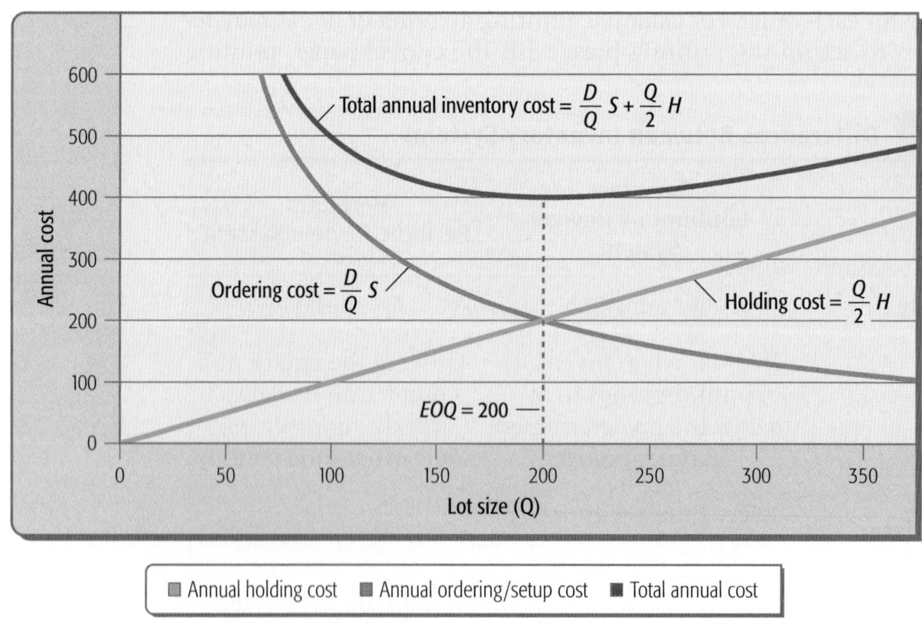

FIGURE 6.4 Annual Inventory Costs

order quantity ($Q = 500$) results in very large holding costs ($500) and relatively low ordering costs ($80). Both quantities lead to high total costs. The best order quantity is in the middle ($Q = 200$ results in the lowest total cost in Table 6.2).

Table 6.2 provides a good illustration of why the order quantity should be relatively in the middle, but finding an order quantity for every item in inventory using this method would be cumbersome. A much simpler way is to find the quantity that minimizes the total cost equation. This is done using calculus and taking the derivative of Equation 1 with respect to Q, setting this equation equal to zero, and solving for Q. The result is Equation 2 for calculating the economic order quantity (EOQ):

$$\text{EOQ} = \sqrt{\frac{2DS}{H}} \qquad \text{(Equation 2)}$$

The **economic order quantity** is the order quantity that minimizes the total annual cost of ordering and holding inventory for a particular item. Another approach to finding the economic order quantity builds off Figure 6.4, which shows that annual ordering costs are equal to annual holding costs. By setting these two costs equal to each other (i.e., $\frac{D}{Q}S = \frac{Q}{2}H$) and solving for Q, the result in Equation 2 is obtained. To illustrate the application of the EOQ to the example in Table 6.2:

● **Economic order quantity** the order quantity that minimizes the total annual cost of ordering and holding inventory for a particular item

$$\text{EOQ} = \sqrt{\frac{2 * 2{,}000 * \$20}{\$2}} = \sqrt{40{,}000} = 200$$

Solved Example 1

Setting an Optimal Order Quantity

Consider a store that buys a chocolate and caramel candy bar for $1 (the bar is then sold at retail for $1.50). Annual demand is 5,000 bars, the carrying rate is 20 percent, and the order cost is $10 per order. Currently the store orders the candy bar in quantities of 1,000 per order.

1. Calculate the annual inventory cost based on this policy.

The holding cost is calculated as $H = hC = 0.2 * \$1 = \$0.20$. The total annual cost is calculated using Equation 1:

$$\text{IC} = \frac{5{,}000}{1{,}000}\$10 + \frac{1{,}000}{2}\$0.20 = \$50 + \$100 = \$150$$

2. Calculate the economic order quantity for this item.

$$\text{EOQ} = \sqrt{\frac{2DS}{H}} = \sqrt{\frac{2 * 5{,}000 * \$10}{\$0.20}} = \sqrt{500{,}000} = 707.1$$

Obviously we cannot order 0.1 candy bar, so we would round this to 707. Also, it is common to round an order quantity to the nearest round number (such as 700) or a multiple of the number of items in a package. For example, if the candy bars are shipped in boxes of 36, we might round the order quantity to 720 (i.e., 20 boxes of 36 candy bars each).

3. Calculate the annual inventory cost if the EOQ is used.

$$\text{IC} = \frac{5{,}000}{707}\$10 + \frac{707}{2}\$0.20 = \$70.72 + \$70.70 = \$141.42$$

Thus, changing from the current order quantity of 1,000 to the EOQ = 707 would save $8.58 per year. An order quantity that is very

(continued)

close to the EOQ would result in a very small difference in total cost (if $Q = 720$ is used, then IC = \$141.44). Note that when the EOQ is used, holding and ordering costs are approximately equal.

Setting the Reorder Point with Certain Demand

● **Reorder point** the predetermined level that an inventory position must reach for an order to be placed

● **Lead time** the time between when an order is placed and when it is expected to arrive or be finished

In a continuous review system, the EOQ answers the question of how much to order. Now we turn to the question of when to order. To illustrate the concept, we assume that demand is certain, constant, and known. These assumptions are not realistic, but they help simplify the explanation. The **reorder point** (R) is the predetermined level that an inventory position must reach for an order to be placed. In Figure 6.5, R is exactly the amount of inventory that will be used during the lead time. **Lead time** (L) is the time between when an order is placed and when it is expected to arrive or be finished.

To illustrate, suppose that the lead time in Figure 6.5 is 2 weeks and the average demand is 10 clocks per week. Then the reorder point is set at 20, or 10 clocks per week * 2 weeks. If the EOQ in Figure 6.5 is 100, then an order of $Q = 100$ will be placed whenever the inventory position drops to or below the reorder point ($R = 20$). The reorder point is set so that there is just enough inventory to last until the order comes in, thus making the inventory cycle between a high of $Q = 100$ (immediately after an order is received) to a low of 0 (just before an order is received). Inventory position is calculated as

$$\text{IP} = \text{OH} + \text{SR} - \text{BO}$$

● **Scheduled receipt** an order that has been placed but not yet received

● **On-hand inventory** the amount of a unit that is physically available

● **backorder** an order that has been promised to a customer(s) but that is currently not in inventory.

A **scheduled receipt** (SR) is an order that has been placed but not yet received. **On-hand inventory** (OH) is the amount of a unit that is physically available. A **backorder** (BO) is an order that has been promised to a customer(s) but that is currently not in inventory. In retailing, this is often called a rain check—the customer is given a receipt for an item to be picked up after replacement inventory is received. Thus, in Figure 6.5, the dotted line shows the inventory position after an order of Q units is placed but before it is received. It is important to recognize the difference between inventory position and on-hand inventory. Inventory position includes both inventory that is in stock or on hand and order(s) that are in process but not yet received. In contrast, on-hand inventory consists only of units that are physically in place. This is done so that when on-

TABLE 6.2 Illustration of the Relationship Between Order Quantity and Holding, Ordering, and Total Cost

Order Quantity Q	Number of Orders per Year $\frac{D}{Q}$	Annual Order Cost $\frac{D}{Q}S$	Average Inventory $\frac{Q}{2}$	Annual Holding Cost $\frac{Q}{2}H$	Total Annual Inventory Cost $\frac{D}{Q}S + \frac{Q}{2}H$
50	40.00	\$800.00	25	\$50.00	\$850.00
100	20.00	\$400.00	50	\$100.00	\$500.00
200	10.00	\$200.00	100	\$200.00	\$400.00
300	6.67	\$133.33	150	\$300.00	\$433.33
500	4.00	\$80.00	250	\$500.00	\$580.00

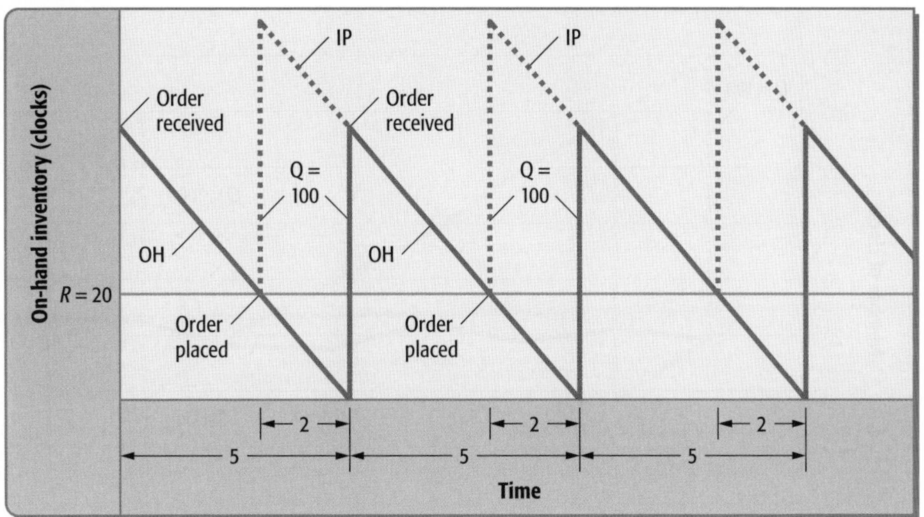

FIGURE 6.5 Cycle Inventory When Demand Is Certain

hand inventory is 19 clocks in Figure 6.5, the system knows that even though inventory = 19 < R = 20, no order should be placed because the inventory position is actually 19 + 100 (scheduled receipts).

Figure 6.5 also shows **time between orders** (TBO), defined as the length of time between the receipt of two successive orders. TBO is calculated as the quantity $\frac{Q}{\overline{D}_L}$. Thus, in Figure 6.5, with $Q = 100$ and $R = 20$, if $\overline{D}_L$ (average demand during lead time) = 10 units per week * 2 weeks = 20 units, then TBO = $\frac{D}{Q} = \frac{100}{20}$ = 5 weeks. TBO increases with increases in Q; thus, larger orders result in fewer exposures to possible stockouts.

● **Time between orders** the length of time between the receipt of two successive orders

Setting the Reorder Point with Uncertain Demand

Now we assume that demand and lead times are unpredictable. This is a much more realistic assumption because there is always variability and uncertainty in demand. For example, the store selling the clocks from Figure 6.5 may know that the average demand is 20 clocks per week and the average lead time is 1 week (note that this is different than in Figure 6.5). However, there is variability associated with these numbers—Figure 6.6 illustrates the demand, inventory position, and actual inventory using a reorder point of 20 with variable demand. If we had followed the reorder point system just derived, there probably would have been stockouts in weeks 2, 7 and 8. In weeks 7 and 8, this occurs because the actual inventory was 21 at the beginning of week 6, so no order was placed. Thus at the end of week 7, after demand of 24, the inventory position is –3 and an order of $Q = 100$ is placed. This order takes a week to arrive, thus the backlog reaches 29 units before the order of 100 arrives at the end of week 8 and brings the inventory position back to a positive 71. Because there is uncertainty in both demand and lead time, companies routinely increase the reorder point. *Safety stock* is extra inventory held to buffer against uncertainty in demand, lead time, and supply. For example, if we made the reorder point for clocks 25 instead of 20, the extra 5 units would be safety stock that would prevent a stockout from occurring in Figure 6.6.

Figure 6.7 shows how the continuous review system works when demand is uncertain and variable. The downward-sloping line for inventory indicates that demand fluctuates slightly from day to day. As a result, the time between orders is no longer constant and $TBO_1 \neq TBO_2 \neq TBO_3$. Because sales are unpredictable

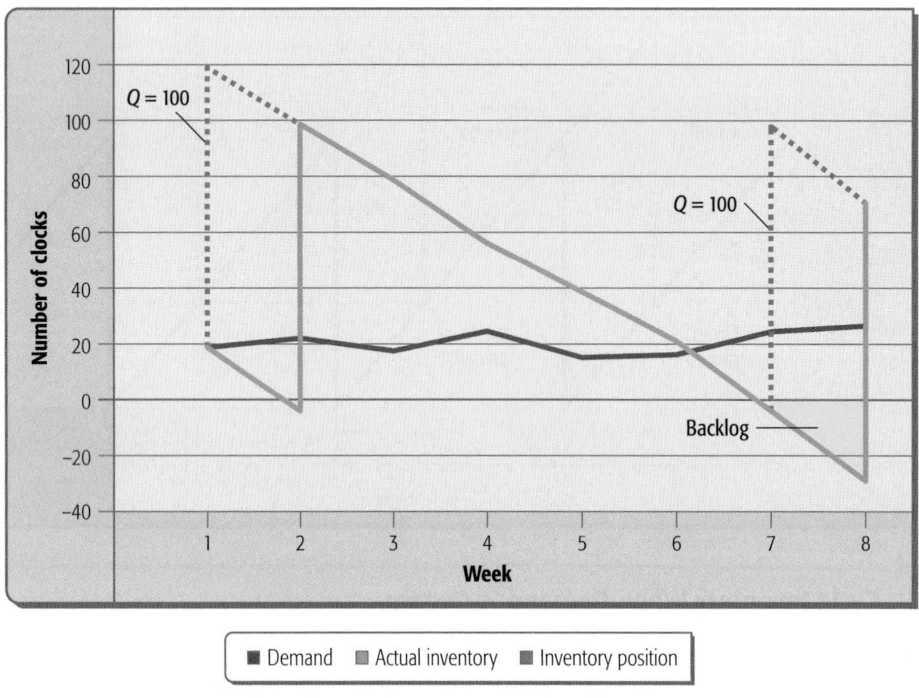

FIGURE 6.6 Demand, Orders, and Actual versus Calculated Inventory Position

and lead time is variable, the demand during lead time varies from order cycle to order cycle (i.e., $D_1 \neq D_2 \neq D_3$, where D_L refers to the demand during the lead time between when the order is placed and when it is received). For these reasons, safety stock is added to protect against stockouts. This is why R is larger in Figure 6.7 than in Figure 6.5.

The decision to be made is not just how much safety stock to carry, but also how to balance customer service and inventory holding costs. Carrying a very large amount of safety stock will minimize stockouts, thus facilitating high ser-

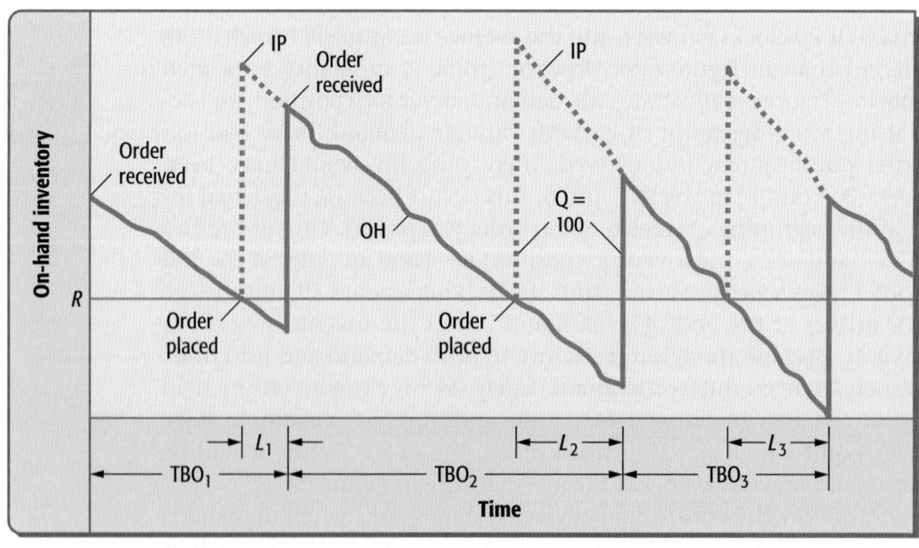

FIGURE 6.7 Reorder Point When Demand Is Uncertain

vice levels, but will be very expensive in terms of inventory cost. In contrast, carrying a low safety stock saves money in terms of inventory costs, but also results in poor customer service and frequent stockouts. Therefore, the inventory manager must decide on the appropriate **cycle-service level**—the probability of not running out of inventory in any one ordering cycle from when one order is received to when the next order is received.

● **Cycle-service level** the probability of not running out of inventory in any one ordering cycle from when one order is received to when the next order is received

Managers must decide how they want to balance the risk of stockouts against the cost of carrying extra inventory. In a drugstore, a medicine that is considered critical to satisfying customers may have a 95 percent cycle-service level, while a less critical item such as a bag of chips might have only an 80 percent cycle-service level. In the first case, this means that there is only a 5 percent (100 percent – 95 percent cycle-service level) chance of running out of stock during the protection interval. The **protection interval** is the time during which safety stock must protect against running out of stock. The risk of running out during the protection interval occurs only during the lead time because the system is vulnerable to stockout only when inventory $< R$, i.e., during the lead time. Thus, the stockout risk is less than or equal to 100 percent minus the cycle-service level. The overall stockout risk is typically less than this quantity because during a single order cycle, when there is no order in process (i.e., inventory $> R$), there is no chance (0 percent) of a stockout, and there is a 100 percent – cycle-service level chance of having a stockout during the lead time once an order has been placed (i.e., when inventory $< R$).

● **Protection interval** the time during which safety stock must protect against running out of stock

To determine a specific safety stock level, we must combine information on the demand during lead time and our choice of the appropriate cycle-service level. The safety stock is related to the variability in demand—when demand is fairly stable, little safety stock is needed. But when there is highly variable demand, then a larger amount of safety stock is required. This is shown in Figure 6.8, which illustrates two distributions of demand during lead time (low and high variability). Note that R needs to be substantially larger when the variability in demand is higher (i.e., $\sigma_L = 6$ versus $\sigma_L = 2$).

If the reorder point R is set to 20, the average demand during lead time, the cycle-service level will be 50 percent. Because R is the same as average demand during lead time, there is a 50 percent chance that demand will be less (thus, we will be overstocked) and a 50 percent chance that demand will be higher (we will be understocked). Figure 6.8 shows that in order to provide a cycle-service level of 90 percent, we need to carry safety stock sufficient to have 90 percent of the curve to the left of the orange lines and 10 percent of the curve to the right of the

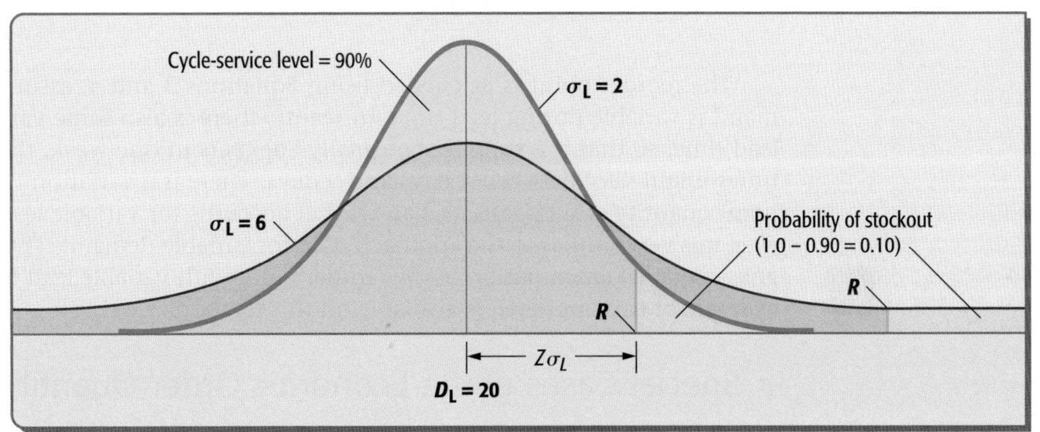

FIGURE 6.8 Finding Safety Stock with a Normal Probability Distribution with Low and High Variance

orange lines. We calculate the amount of safety stock using the standard deviation of demand during lead time and a quantity z, which is the number of standard deviations from the mean needed to achieve a given cycle-service level.

$$I_s = z\sigma_L \qquad \text{(Equation 3)}$$

$$R = \overline{D}_L + z\sigma_L \qquad \text{(Equation 4)}$$

where σ_L = the standard deviation of demand during lead time
I_s = the safety stock inventory
$\overline{D}_L$ = average demand during the lead time

Higher levels of z correspond to higher cycle-service levels. When $z = 0$, the cycle-service level is 50 percent. Let's see how to calculate the safety stock for a 90 percent cycle-service level.

Solved Example 2

Setting the Safety Stock and *R*

The clocks discussed earlier have demand during lead time that is normally distributed, with an average of 20 clocks per week and standard deviation $\sigma_L = 6$. What safety stock should be held to achieve a 90 percent cycle-service level? What should R be?

SOLUTION

We first must find z, the number of standard deviations to the right of average demand during lead time, such that 90 percent of the normal distribution curve will be to the left of that point. This is done by looking up the number 0.9000 in the normal distribution table (see the Appendix at the back of this book). The closest number in the table is 0.8997, which corresponds to 1.28 (1.2 in the row heading plus 0.08 in the column heading; adding these together gives 1.28). The next closest number is 0.9015, which corresponds to $z = 1.29$. Thus, we can interpolate and take the average of the two z's to get $z = 1.285$. Using this information, we can calculate

Safety stock = $z\sigma_L = 1.285 * 6 = 7.71$ or 8 (always round safety stock up to ensure at *least* the required cycle-service level)

Reorder point = $\overline{D}_L + z\sigma_L = 20 + 8 = 28$

The reorder point is calculated using Equations 3 and 4, assuming that demand is variable during lead time. In reality, there is also some variation in the lead time, so that if a supplier "normally" delivers in one week, the actual lead times might vary between 4 days and 9 days. There is a variation of the reorder point quantity and Equations 3 and 4 that accounts for variable lead time; however, it is very similar to the approach used for variable demand. Thus, we do not give a detailed examination of the reorder point with variable lead time here. An example of this approach is available on this textbook's web site.

Special Cases of the Economic Order Quantity

The economic order quantity is based on four basic assumptions:

1. Two relevant costs: ordering/setup (S) and holding (H)
2. Constant demand

3 Item independence

4 Certainty in demand, lead time, and supply

Each of these assumptions is required for the EOQ defined in Equation 2 to be feasible. A quick review of the assumptions suggests that they are likely to be violated in practice. Yet despite the fact that the assumptions are not "valid," the EOQ is one of the fundamental principles of inventory management. Some version of the EOQ is used in almost every company or organization dealing with inventory.

The EOQ works despite the fact that the assumptions are not strictly true for two reasons. First, it is relatively insensitive to errors because it involves a square root. Consider the EOQ from Solved Example 2, which was calculated to be $Q = 707$. If the annual demand for candy bars actually turned out to be 4,500 (instead of the 5,000 originally estimated in Solved Example 2), the new EOQ would be 671. Thus, while demand decreased from 5,000 to 4,500 (10 percent reduction), the EOQ based on this number decreased from 707 to 671 (5.1 percent reduction). In other words, the square root term in the EOQ dampens any changes in demand, setup cost, or holding cost, thus making the EOQ relatively insensitive to small errors in these quantities.

The second reason the EOQ works despite its slightly flawed assumptions is that adjustments for uncertainty are included in the overall inventory system. In a continuous review system, safety stock inventory is included in the reorder point in order to mitigate uncertainty in demand, lead time, and supply (assumption 4) and variability in demand (assumption 2). Periodic review systems also account for this uncertainty in determining the target inventory level, as will be shown later.

Assumption 3 states that items are independent. This means that sales or demand for a given item is not related to that for any other item. For the most part, this assumption is true, but there are some situations where some items have a relationship. One way in which some of the assumptions are addressed is through variations of the EOQ, which allow for different assumptions and for the assumptions given earlier to be relaxed. For clarity, we focus on the most common variation of the EOQ—the quantity discount model

EOQ with Quantity Discounts

Assumption 1 states that there are only two relevant costs for the EOQ: ordering/setup cost and holding cost. The logic underlying this assumption is that the annual total cost of ordering/setup and holding inventory can be controlled by varying the ordering quantity. As illustrated earlier, the EOQ determines the quantity that provides the lowest combined total for these costs. Part of assumption 1 is that the price that is paid for an item is not controlled by the purchaser—i.e., the supplier or retailer sets the purchase price; thus, it does not vary and is not a relevant factor when calculating the EOQ.

However, many companies offer discounted pricing for items that they sell. This is done to take advantage of economies of scale in production and the supply chain. For example, consider the purchase cost of latex gloves (such as those used in many fast-food restaurants when preparing food). The cost is discounted as follows to encourage larger orders:

- Cost per box of gloves, 1 to 124 boxes = \$5.00
- Cost per box of gloves, 125 to 499 boxes = \$4.00
- Cost per box of gloves, 500 or more boxes = \$3.00

The company producing the gloves offers these discounts because it gains economies of scale when it ships full cases or pallets, or even a truckload, to the fast-food company's distribution center rather than shipping a single box to you or a retailer. The glove producer also gains economies of scale in production by selling larger order quantities; these allow for fewer setups and higher equipment utilization.

The general approach that a purchaser can use in determining the order quantity that gives the lowest total cost is to calculate the EOQ for each possible price and check whether the quantity qualifies for that price. In some cases, the EOQ that is computed will be higher or lower than the range for that price. In addition, we also need to calculate the total cost at each price breakpoint. The following two-step procedure can be used:

1 Arrange the prices from lowest to highest. Starting with the lowest price, calculate the EOQ for each price until a feasible EOQ is found. A feasible price is one where the EOQ is within the given range for the price used to compute it.

2 If the first feasible EOQ is for the lowest price, this quantity is optimal and should be used. Otherwise, calculate the total annual cost for the first feasible EOQ and also calculate the total annual cost for each price breakpoint lower than the price associated with this feasible EOQ. The goal is to order just enough to qualify for the lower price. The optimal Q is the one with the lowest overall cost.

Figure 6.9 illustrates the solution to Solved Example 3. The EOQ values are computed from right to left, starting with the value for the lowest cost. The EOQ for $C = \$3$ is not feasible because $Q = 462$ does not qualify for the \$3 cost. One challenge with quantity discounts is that it is likely that a company will order more than it would if there were no discounts, as seen in Solved Example 3, where the order quantity was increased from EOQ = 400 to $Q = 500$ in order to take advantage of discounts. In some cases, the extra inventory will be substantial, and there is a risk of obsolescence and storage capacity issues. Thus, when working with quantity discounts, it is important to have a good sense of potential costs and the likelihood of obsolescence, as well as the limitations on available storage space.

Solved Example 3

Computing EOQ with Quantity Discounts

A manufacturer of latex gloves offers three different prices for its basic glove, depending on the quantity ordered. Use the data from a fast-food company that purchases these gloves to determine the quantity of gloves that should be ordered.

D = 16,000 boxes of gloves per year
S = \$5 to place each order
h = 25% of cost
C = cost per unit (box) of gloves
= \$5.00 for 1–99 boxes
= \$4.00 for 100–499 boxes
= \$3.00 for 500 or more boxes

SOLUTION

1. The first step is to solve for the EOQ from lowest cost to highest cost using Equation 2.

C = \$3.00

$$\text{EOQ} = \sqrt{\frac{2DS}{H}}$$

$$\sqrt{\frac{2 * 16{,}000 * \$5}{0.25 * \$3.00}}$$

EOQ = 461.9 rounded up to 462

This quantity is *not* feasible since Q = 462 would have a C = \$4

C = \$4.00

$$\sqrt{\frac{2 * 16{,}000 * \$5}{0.25 * \$4.00}}$$

EOQ = 400

Feasible

2. **The second step is to check the total annual cost for the feasible EOQ and for each price breakpoint with a lower cost. To compute total cost, the annual purchase cost of the gloves (*CQ*) is added to the ordering/setup and holding costs already included in Equation 1:**

$Q = 400$ $\qquad$ $Q = 500$ (lowest quantity to obtain $C = \$3.00$)

$$TC = \frac{D}{Q}S + \frac{Q}{2}H + CD \qquad \text{(Equation 5)}$$

$$TC_{400} = \frac{16{,}000}{400}\$5 + \frac{400}{2}0.25 * \$4 + \$4 * 16{,}000 = \$64{,}400.00$$

$$TC_{500} = \frac{16{,}000}{500}\$5 + \frac{500}{2}0.25 * \$3 + \$3 * 16{,}000 = \$48{,}347.50$$

The EOQ provides a total cost of \$64,400.00, while increasing the order quantity slightly leads to a much lower cost of \$48,347.50. The best order quantity is thus 500—just enough to qualify for the lower price. Figure 6.9 shows the cost curves for the different unit costs.

The spreadsheet used to generate this curve is available online at the textbook web site. Use this spreadsheet to experiment with different values of *C, D, H,* and *S.*

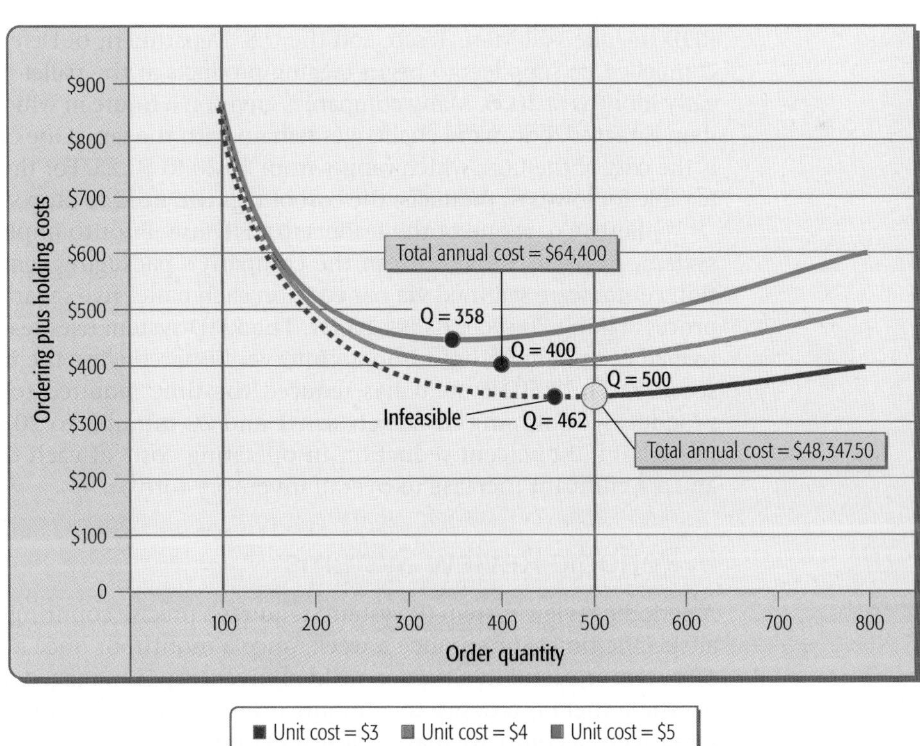

FIGURE 6.9 Quantity Discount Cost Curve

Each price/cost has a total cost curve (order plus holding cost) with a feasible range

Technological Applications

The biggest change in inventory management over the past 20 years is the ability of companies to use sophisticated software and hardware to track and monitor inventory very closely. Computer technology has facilitated much more precise tracking of inventory and has resulted in reductions in the total amount of inventory in both individual companies and entire supply chains. Three common technologies that companies employ for managing inventory are ERP, EDI, and RFID.

- **Enterprise resource planning (ERP)** a large, integrated information system that supports most enterprise processes and data storage needs across the entire organization
- **Radio frequency identification (RFID)** an automatic identification method that relies on storing and remotely retrieving data using devices such as RFID tags or transponders

Enterprise resource planning (ERP) provides a large, integrated information system that supports most enterprise processes and data storage needs across the entire organization. ERP systems combine most, if not all, of the information needs for a company in a single system, often replacing dozens of different systems used in different departments and applications. In many cases, ERP has led to dramatic reductions in inventory for firms such as Wal-Mart, Sony, Hunter Douglas, and Home Depot.

Radio frequency identification (RFID) is an automatic identification method that relies on storing and remotely retrieving data using devices such as RFID tags or transponders. An RFID tag is an object that can be attached to or incorporated into a product, animal, or person for the purpose of identification using radio waves. All RFID tags contain at least two parts. An *integrated circuit* stores and processes information, and translates a radio frequency signal. An *antenna* is employed for receiving and transmitting the signal. RFID has two primary advantages over bar codes. First, it does not require a line of sight for reading—i.e., it does not need a laser wanded over the tag. Second, RFID tags can be used to write data in addition to reading data. This allows information such as the production or expiration date of a product to be recorded on the tag.

Applications of RFID tags include blood identification, machine tool management, toll passes, and livestock monitoring. Companies leading in the adoption of RFID include Wal-Mart, Tesco, and the U.S. Department of Defense, each of which compelled its suppliers to begin tagging products at the pallet or case level in the early months of 2005. Many companies envision a future in which every product or item is tagged, but many challenges remain with the tags. One of the primary ones is the cost of the tags, which ranges from $0.20 to $0.25. For the use of RFID to be feasible for low-cost products, the cost of tags will need to drop substantially.

Gillette Co. is one of the leaders in RFID use. Prior to implementing its RFID system, products moving from the company's packaging center to its distribution center were scanned via bar code on each pallet five separate times, with the process taking 20 seconds per pallet. The RFID system uses readers in the tunnel to read each item without human intervention, reducing the time per pallet to 5 seconds. The RFID system has reduced the time required to pull and prepare products for shipping from between 1 and 20 minutes to 20 seconds. The end impact is a 20 percent reduction in operating costs at each distribution center and a significant increase in overall inventory turns.

Periodic Review Systems

A periodic review system (P-system) requires a precise counting of inventory only at specific times, often once a week, once a month, or once a quarter. This type of system is useful in situations where inventory is managed by an outside firm or where there is a desire to combine orders to save on transportation costs. Alternatively, a company may choose a periodic review system so that it can accurately predict when employees will be needed to count and verify inventory.

One situation in which a P-system is useful is when a manufacturer such as Pepsi or Kellogg's assigns drivers to various stores. The drivers' job is to visit each

TECHNOLOGY IN OPERATIONS MANAGEMENT

ERP Systems Manage Vital Health-Care Equipment

El Camino Hospital in Mountain View, California, utilizes an ERP system that has helped it achieve 99.8 percent product availability throughout the hospital. The system includes 64 supply stations that nurses use to check on and order products. Nurses access inventory that is stored in secure storage cabinets using a biometric fingerprint reader. The computer system shows a patient list, from which the patient's name is selected. Each item removed is catalogued with a "take" button, and the product's availability is updated, the central supply department and distributor are notified, and the patient's bill is updated for the charge. When products hit a predetermined reorder point, an electronic order is automatically generated.

The ERP system at El Camino has resulted in an inventory reduction of $750,000 combined with a reduction in purchasing staff to seven employees. When the supply of an item runs out, it is restocked within 45 minutes. The organization used to buy products in bulk, and products were handled several times before reaching their point of use. Now delivery is just-in-time, and El Camino is considering implementing the system in its operating rooms.

Similar results were achieved at the University of New Mexico Hospitals in Albuquerque. The ERP system resulted in a reduction of inventory from $900,000 to $360,000 with 30 inventory turns per year. Every day at 5 a.m., the ERP system creates an electronic purchase order notifying the hospital's distributor, McKesson Pharmaceuticals, which delivers supplies by 10 a.m. An add-on software program was used for computerized physician order entry and robotic filling of prescription drugs. The combination of the ERP system with a $900,000 prescription robot paid for itself within a year by reducing the number of pharmacists.

Source: L. A. Runy, "Supply Chain Management: Automation Improves Purchasing, Tracking, Storing and Distribution," *Hospitals & Health Networks* 4, no. 3 (2005), 26–30.

store on their route on a weekly basis and replace inventory such as sodas or snack products. In this case, the employee also performs a cycle count, which is a physical counting of inventory. It is important to understand that even in the twenty-first century with computerized inventory systems, we still must physically check how much inventory is actually available. This is true because customers often will misplace, shoplift, or eat inventory, or employees within the company may make data-entry mistakes. **Vendor-managed inventory (VMI)** occurs when vendors monitor sales at the retailer and replenish inventories when supplies are low. Suppliers track inventory by physically visiting the retail outlet and performing a cycle count, as in the case of Pepsi or Kellogg's, but also through electronic interchange of information using software systems such as ClearOrbit, Manhattan Associates, or SAP. **Electronic data interchange (EDI)** allows companies or units within a company to exchange orders, forecasts, and invoices electronically without human intervention to enter data into the receiving system. EDI is a critical component used to communicate orders, inventory status, and other data in a real-time manner. VMI uses frequent communication of inventory, stockouts, and planned promotions to reduce stockouts and excess inventory at both the retailer and the supplier. Wal-Mart was one of the leading pioneers of VMI in the mid-1990s, with hundreds or thousands of companies/partners utilizing the techniques today.

- **Vendor-managed inventory (VMI)** vendors monitor sales at the retailer and replenish inventories when supplies are low
- **Electronic data interchange (EDI)** a technology that allows companies or units within a company to exchange orders, forecasts, and invoices electronically without human intervention to enter data into the receiving system.

P-systems have a fixed time period, but the order quantity may vary substantially from period to period. This is because the system must adjust the amount ordered to compensate for variability in demand (unlike a continuous review

COMPANY ILLUSTRATION

Kellogg's Direct Store Delivery

Kellogg's has one of the best direct store delivery distribution (DSDD) systems in the world. Kellogg's bought Keebler (the maker of such brands as E.L. Fudge cookies and Cheez-It crackers) for $4.6 billion in March 2001—not for its cookies, but for its DSDD system. The company representatives deliver products directly to stores like Kroger, Target, Wal-Mart, and Safeway rather than delivering them in bulk to a distribution center owned by the retailer. While this approach is a bit more expensive for Kellogg's to run, it results in some large advantages. In particular, the reps are in charge of inventory at each store and can position the product so that it's visually appealing and catches the customer's eye. The reps have much more incentive to do this job well than the store's employees, who care only about selling all products—they don't much care whether what they sell is a Kellogg's or a Nabisco product. In addition, the reps gather competitive intelligence by observing how customers relate to competitors' products. The Kellogg's reps perform many functions, including product delivery, product restocking, cycle counting of inventory, billing, and competitive intelligence. Kellogg's is one of the leaders in this area, but many other companies, including Pepsi, Coca-Cola, Nabisco, and Sara Lee, have similar direct store delivery programs.

Source: Matthew Boyle, "The Man Who Fixed Kellogg," *Fortune*, September 6, 2004.

system, which adjusts the *timing* of orders). There is an increased risk of stockout relative to continuous review systems. This is because of the longer protection interval, which is the time period of the order cycle (P) plus the lead time to receive an order (L). Consider the situation where we are using $P = 1$ month, as in Figure 6.10. If we place an order of 100 on August 31, then the next time we can place an order is September 30 (one month later). Normally this will not be a major problem, but it is possible that on September 1 we sell 295 units of the item being ordered. If this results in a stockout, we will not be able to place another order for an entire month, and that order will not be received until one week after that. Thus, the protection interval for a P-system is the entire time $P + L$. Because this time period is much longer than the protection interval (L) for a continuous review system, we must carry substantially more safety stock in a P-system.

Early-era Kellogg's delivery.

Determining the Period and Order Quantity for a Periodic Review System

Often the period for a P-system is simply a convenient time period, such as a week or a month. For example, many retail stores (drugstores, grocery stores, or apparel stores) have weekly or monthly

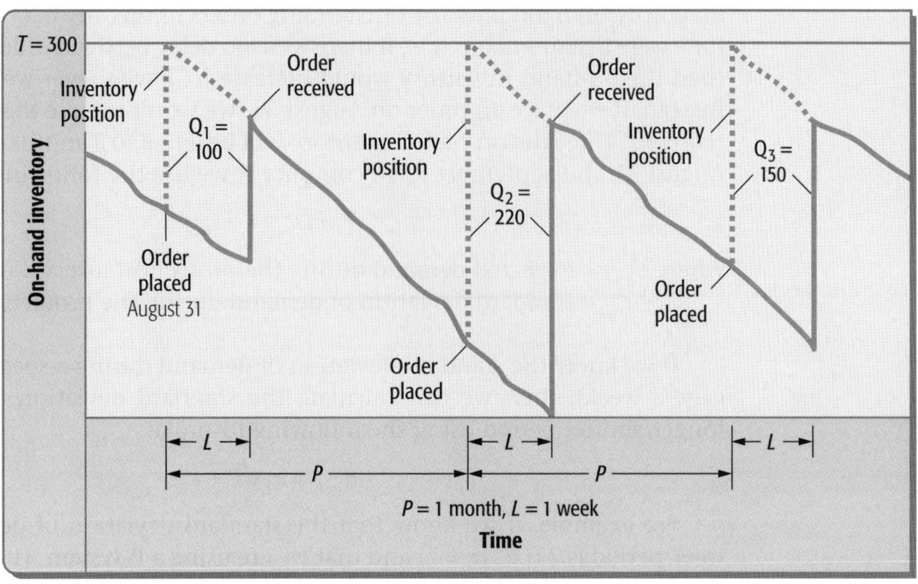

FIGURE 6.10 Periodic Review System

shipments from a central distribution center. Thus, a store can receive a shipment of any item it sells on its assigned day of the week or month (this policy is often used to balance the workload at the distribution center—20 percent of the stores served from that distribution center will be assigned to each day of the week, Monday through Friday). Alternatively, the period may be chosen to approximate the average time between orders (TBO), which would result in the continuous review system with an order quantity of the EOQ. This is done in order to try to balance ordering/setup costs with holding costs, while retaining the advantages of a periodic review system. This is done using Equation 6:

$$P = \frac{\text{EOQ}}{\overline{D}_t} \qquad \text{(Equation 6)}$$

where EOQ = economic order quantity for that item
$\overline{D}_t$ = average demand per period (usually weeks or months)

Solved Example 4
Setting the Order Period to Match the EOQ

If D = 2,000 units per year and EOQ = 200 units per order, what should the period be?

$P = \frac{\text{EOQ}}{\overline{D}_t} = \frac{200}{2{,}000 \text{ units per year}/52 \text{ weeks per year}}$ gives P = 5.2 weeks, which should be rounded to the nearest integer number of weeks, or P = 5 weeks.

● **Target inventory** the desired quantity of inventory that will cover expected demand during the protection interval plus enough safety stock to provide the desired cycle-service level

Once we have calculated or chosen the period P, we need to calculate the **target inventory** (T) level, which is the desired quantity of inventory that will cover expected demand during the protection interval plus enough safety stock to provide the desired cycle-service level. As shown in Figure 6.10, the target (T) is never actually reached; instead, we must track the inventory position, which equals actual inventory on hand plus any outstanding orders minus any backorders. If the lead time were instantaneous (i.e., if there were no delay between ordering and receipt), then the on-hand inventory would increase to T whenever we placed an order. Instead, if we place an order on August 31, we won't receive that order until September 7; thus, the on-hand inventory will be equal to T minus demand between August 31 and September 7. To compute T, we use the following equation:

$$T = \overline{D}_{P+L} + z\sigma_{P+L} \qquad \text{(Equation 7)}$$

where $\overline{D}_{P+L}$ = expected demand during the protection interval ($P + L$)
σ_{P+L} = standard deviation of demand during the protection interval

If we know the standard deviation of demand during a specified time period (say, a week), then we can calculate the standard deviation of demand for a longer/shorter period using the following formula:

$$\sigma_{P+L} = \sigma_t\sqrt{P + L} \qquad \text{(Equation 8)}$$

For example, if we know that the standard deviation of demand for a one-week period is 7 (i.e., $\sigma_t = 7$) and that we are using a P-system with $P = 3$ and $L = 1$, then we can calculate that the standard deviation for the protection interval is

$$\sigma_{P+L} = \sigma_t\sqrt{P + L} = 7\sqrt{3 + 1} = 7 * 2 = 14$$

Another way to think of this is that the standard deviation is larger for longer periods of time than for shorter periods of time. For example, a drought is a prolonged period of time with below-average rain. For a given location, the weekly rainfall might be 0.5 inch, with $\sigma_{1\text{ week}} = 0.1$, but over a 13-week time period, the standard deviation will be higher ($\sigma_{13\text{ weeks}} = 0.36 = 0.1\sqrt{13}$).

Once the target inventory level is set, then we order every P time periods, and we order the difference between the target inventory level and on-hand inventory, using the following equation:

$$Q = T - I \qquad \text{(Equation 9)}$$

where I = current inventory level, including any outstanding orders.

Solved Example 5

Determining *P* and *T* for Staplers

The demand for staplers at an office supply store is 1,092 per year, the holding cost is \$3 per stapler per year, and the setup cost is \$15 per order. Lead time is 1 week, and $\sigma_L = 5$. A cycle-service level of 85 percent is desired.

1. Determine the period (*P*) and the target inventory (*T*).

We first calculate the economic order quantity as

$$\text{EOQ} = \sqrt{\frac{2DS}{H}} = \sqrt{\frac{2 * 1{,}092 * \$15}{\$3}} = \sqrt{10{,}920} = 104.499$$

which we round down to 104.

Next, we calculate the period that best approximates this EOQ, using Equation 6.

$$P = \frac{\text{EOQ}}{D_t}$$

where $\overline{D}_t = \dfrac{1{,}092 \text{ staplers/year}}{52 \text{ weeks/year}} = 21$ staplers/week.

(*continued*)

$$P = \frac{104}{21} = 4.95 \text{ weeks}$$

which we round to the nearest integer, or 5 weeks.

Next, we determine the target inventory (T) level by first looking up the number of standard deviations of demand that corresponds to 85 percent. From the normal distribution table in the Appendix, we look for the value closest to 0.8500; there is a value of 0.8485 ($z = 1.03$) and a value of 0.8508 ($z = 1.04$), so we use $z = 1.035$ as a rough interpolation between the two values.

$$T = \overline{D}_{P+L} + z\sigma_{P+L} = 21 \text{ staplers/week} * (5 + 1) + 1.035 * 5 * \sqrt{5 + 1} = 126 + 12.68 = 138.68$$

which we round *up* to 139.

2. Compare the results with those for the Q-system.

The corresponding calculations to find Q and R for a continuous review system are

$$\text{EOQ} = \sqrt{\frac{2DS}{H}} = \sqrt{\frac{2 * 1{,}092 * \$15}{\$3}} = \sqrt{10{,}920} = 104.499$$

which we round down to 104.

$$\text{Reorder point} = \overline{D}_1 + z\sigma_L = 21 \text{ units/week} * 1 \text{ week} + 1.035 * 5 = 21 + 5.175 = 26.175$$

which we round up to 27.

Thus, we can compare the two systems as follows and see that while both provide an 85 percent cycle-service level, the P-system requires more safety stock (13 versus 6 units) because of its increased protection interval:

	Q-System (Continuous Review)	**P-System (Periodic Review)**
How much to order	$Q = 104$	$Q = T - I = 139 - I$
When to order	$I \leq R = 27$	Every $P = 5$ weeks
Protection interval	$L = 1$ week (lead time)	$P + L = 6$ weeks (period + lead time)
Safety stock	6 units	13 units

Other Types of Inventory Systems

Continuous review and periodic review systems define two ends of a spectrum of approaches for managing inventory. There are numerous variations on these two basic types of systems.

ABC Systems

ABC systems are an approach that recognizes that different items have different values and levels of importance. Thus, the goal is to divide all items held in inventory into groups that receive varying levels of attention. For example, a hospital has to track thousands of items ranging from specialized scalpels and equipment for heart, lung, and emergency surgery to Band-Aids, pens, pencils, and toilet paper. Clearly, it is a major crisis if a critical piece of equipment is missing in the middle of an open heart surgery. Thus, these types of "A" items are inventoried using a system that tracks them very closely. In contrast, less critical items such as pencils and toilet paper are classified as "C" items and tracked with a less exacting system.

- **ABC systems** inventory systems that utilize some measure of importance to classify inventory items and allocate control efforts accordingly
- **Bin system** a type of inventory system that uses either one or two bins to hold a quantity of the item being inventoried; an order is placed when one of two bins is empty or a line on a single bin is reached
- **Can order system** a type of inventory system that reviews the inventory position at fixed time intervals and places orders to bring the inventory up to an expected target level, but only if the inventory position is below a minimum quantity, similar to the reorder point in a continuous review system

ABC systems utilize some measure of importance to classify inventory items and allocate control efforts accordingly. ABC systems take advantage of what is commonly called the 80/20 rule, which holds that 20 percent of the items usually account for 80 percent of the value. The most common approach uses three levels, where category A contains the most important items, category B contains moderately important items, and category C contains the least important items, but many organizations use fewer or more categories. The most common classification measure is annual dollar value, but other measures include cost of a shortage, lead time, or risk of obsolescence. Typically, A items make up only 10 to 20 percent of the total number of items, yet account for 60 to 80 percent of *annual dollar value*. In contrast, C items account for 50 to 70 percent of the total *number* of items, yet account for only 10 to 20 percent of *annual dollar value*. A items receive the greatest attention, including frequent reviews of actual inventory levels, and may be accompanied by formal control systems for withdrawals.

An important point with ABC systems is that C items may well be of high importance, but because they account for relatively little annual inventory cost, it may be preferable to simply order them in large quantities and carry excess safety stock. This is one of the basic principles behind the bin system of inventory management described below.

Bin Systems

Many companies use a variation of the continuous review system. A **bin system** uses either one or two bins to hold a quantity of the item being inventoried; an order is placed when one of two bins is empty or when a line on a single bin is reached. A two-bin system holds items in a bin; when the bin is empty, a second bin filled with parts is pulled from the backroom or storage location, and an order is placed to replace the quantity in the empty bin. This system is common in hardware stores, where there are many small, inexpensive items such as nails, bolts, and screws that would be difficult to keep a precise count on. A one-bin system works in much the same way, except that only one bin is used and a line is drawn on that bin to indicate the order point.

A two-bin system at a hardware store.

Can Order Systems

These systems are a variation of the periodic review system. A **can order system** reviews the inventory position at fixed time intervals and places orders to bring the inventory up to an expected target level, but only if the inventory position is below a minimum quantity, similar to the

Solved Example 6
ABC Inventory

The annual dollar value of 10 items stocked by a doctor's office is shown in Table 6.3. The items are sorted by annual dollar values from lowest to highest. Two items (20 percent of the total) are classified as A items and account for 69.83 percent of total annual value, three items (30 percent of the total) are classified as B items and account for 23.88 percent of total annual value, and five items (50 percent of the total) are classified as C items and account for only 6.3 percent of annual value. The inventory systems to manage these items would be designed to maximize accuracy for the A items, including frequent cycle counting.

reorder point in a continuous review system. To illustrate, consider a system where the target is 200 and the minimum level is 100. The smallest order size will thus be 100 (target = 200 – minimum quantity = 100). If the order interval is complete, and it is time to place an order, an order will be placed if the inventory position is below 100, but no order will be placed if the inventory is 100 or higher. This system seeks to combine the benefits of a continuous and periodic review system and is particularly attractive if both review and order costs are high.

Base Stock Systems

A **base stock system** issues an order whenever a withdrawal is made from inventory. Items are replaced on a one-for-one basis. This system is often used for very expensive items, such as spare motors for manufacturing equipment or spare parts.

● **Base stock system** a type of inventory system that issues an order whenever a withdrawal is made from inventory

TABLE 6.3

Item	Annual Demand	Unit Cost	Annual Dollar Value	Percentage of Total Value	Cumulative Percentage of Total Value	Classification
A100	1,000	$800.00	$800,000.00	40.00%	40.00%	A
C100	500	$1,193.00	$596,500.00	29.83%	69.83%	A
D700	3,000	$65.50	$196,500.00	9.83%	79.65%	B
E350	2,000	$88.00	$176,000.00	8.80%	88.45%	B
E800	7,000	$15.00	$105,000.00	5.25%	93.70%	B
D400	8,000	$6.00	$48,000.00	2.40%	96.10%	C
A200	10,000	$3.50	$35,000.00	1.75%	97.85%	C
B200	4,000	$5.50	$22,000.00	1.10%	98.95%	C
B300	20,000	$0.90	$18,000.00	0.90%	99.85%	C
C300	2,000	$1.50	$3,000.00	0.15%	100.00%	C
		Total	$2,000,000.00			

An HVAC repairperson must stock a wide range of spare parts.

The Newsvendor Problem

The **newsvendor problem** determines how much inventory to order when handling perishable products or items that have a limited life span. Products that are handled with the newsvendor problem include perishable items (food, flowers, ice cream) and items with a limited life span (newspapers, T-shirts for a sporting event, wedding invitations, spare parts for specialized equipment). These items are considered to have a single period of demand, consisting of their life span. This is in contrast to other inventory models, which assume that products can be carried over from period to period. For example, a grocery store makes a decision to make a single purchase of pumpkins prior to Halloween. A shortage of pumpkins will result in lost sales, while an excess of pumpkins leads to waste because they must be thrown out as they rot.

The newsvendor problem focuses on two key costs: shortage and excess. The **shortage cost** is the lost profit from not being able to make a sale, plus any loss of customer goodwill. When a shortage or stockout occurs for an item used in production or a spare part for a critical machine, then the shortage cost is the actual cost of lost production. The following formula is used to express the shortage cost:

$$C_s = \text{Revenue per Unit} - \text{Cost per Unit} + \text{Loss of Customer Goodwill} \quad \text{(Equation 10)}$$

- **Newsvendor problem** a technique that determines how much inventory to order when handling perishable products or items that have a limited life span
- **Shortage cost** the lost profit from not being able to make a sale, plus any loss of customer goodwill
- **Excess cost** the difference between the purchase cost of an item and its salvage or discounted value

Excess cost is the difference between the purchase cost of an item and its salvage or discounted value. For example, consider a store that overstocks a certain type of pink swimsuit. The swimsuit is very unlikely to sell at the end of summer; thus, the store ends up selling the swimsuit for a large discount—say, 60 to 80 percent off the original price. Thus, the excess cost is calculated as

$$C_e = \text{Purchase Cost per Unit} - \text{Salvage Cost per Unit} \quad \text{(Equation 11)}$$

The objective of the newsvendor problem is to determine the order quantity Q_n that will balance shortage and excess costs. In general, if the shortage cost is less than the excess cost, the best Q_n will be less than expected demand. If the excess cost is less than the shortage cost, then Q_n will be larger than expected demand. Consider the situation with the pink swimsuits—pink might be the "hot" color for a given year, and thus a retail store needs to decide how many to buy by balancing the risks of running out against the risks of being stuck with an excess of pink swimsuits that can't be sold. Figure 6.11A shows that the order quantity will exceed expected demand when shortage costs exceed excess costs, while Figure 6.11B shows that the order quantity will be less than expected demand when excess costs exceed shortage costs

For a detailed tutorial on how to calculate Q_n, please go to the book web site.

Inventory Accuracy

The amount of inventory in the system (i.e., the computer) often differs from the amount of physical inventory that is on hand. This happens for a number of reasons: people enter quantities into the system incorrectly, inventory gets misplaced in the wrong location or stolen, or inventory gets damaged and the data on this do not get entered into the system. It is common for companies to have only 90 to 95 percent inventory accuracy. There are several common approaches

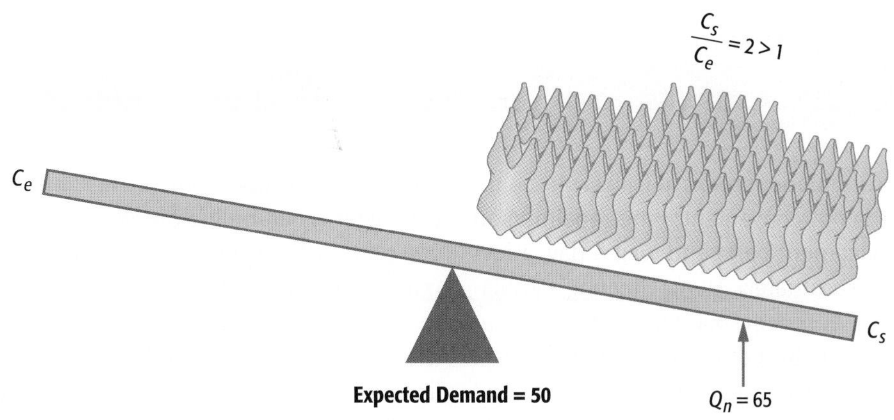

FIGURE 6.11A Newsvendor Problem for Pink Swimsuits: Shortage Costs Exceed Excess Costs

For this example, the purchased cost of swimsuits is \$20, the retail price is \$40, and the discounted sale price for any unsold swimsuits is \$10. Thus $C_s = \$40 - \$20 = \$20$ and $C_e = \$20 - \$10 = \$10$. The ratio of shortage to excess costs is thus $\frac{C_s}{C_e} = \frac{\$20}{\$10} = 2$. When this ratio exceeds 1, the order quantity Q_n is greater than expected demand.

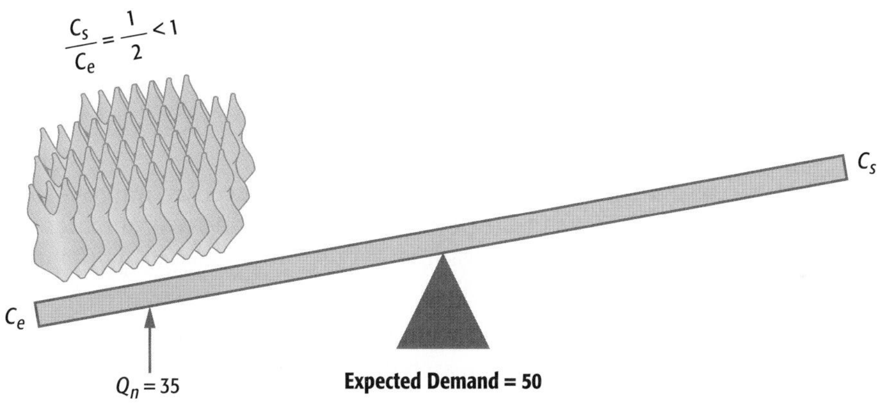

FIGURE 6.11B Newsvendor Problem for Pink Swimsuits: Excess Costs Exceed Shortage Costs

For this example, the purchased cost of swimsuits is \$30, the retail price is \$40, and the discounted sale price for any unsold swimsuits is \$10. Thus $C_s = \$40 - \$30 = \$10$ and $C_e = \$30 - \$10 = \$20$. The ratio of shortage to excess costs is thus $\frac{C_s}{C_e} = \frac{\$10}{\$20} = \frac{1}{2}$. When this ratio is less than 1, the order quantity Q_n is less than expected demand.

for minimizing the problem of inaccurate inventory. First, companies often assign specific employees to issue and receive orders and materials and to enter transaction data. Controlling the number of people who handle inventory or the associated transactions reduces the chance of errors substantially. A second approach is to place inventory in a locked and secured location. This is a practice that is common in both distribution centers and stores in urban or high-traffic areas, where high-value-to-weight items, such as alcohol or cigarettes, that are often stolen are placed in a separate, locked area. A third method involves **cycle counting**, which is a system in which employees physically count a percentage of the total number of items stocked in inventory and correct any errors that are found. Cycle counting is often combined with ABC inventory analysis, with the A items being counted most often, followed by B, and then C.

● **Cycle counting** a system in which employees physically count a percentage of the total number of items stocked in inventory and correct any errors that are found

COMPANY ILLUSTRATION

Preventing Stockouts from Turning Up the Heat on AC Repair

When your air conditioner breaks, it is likely to be on a hot day, so it is not convenient if the repairperson must order replacement parts and wait a day, a few days, or a week. Fortunately, HVAC (heating, ventilation, and air conditioning) repairpeople have a solution. Habegger Corp., based in Cincinnati, Ohio, is a distributor for Carrier/Payne in Ohio, Indiana, and Kentucky. Habegger has 23 branch offices and annual sales of $151 million. The company's inventory replenishment program helps HVAC contractors worry about their work rather than about maintaining an inventory system for the thousands of parts they deal with. Each individual person takes a daily inventory and reports his or her inventory needs to Habegger via an online ordering system, or a Habegger parts sales specialist calls on dealers to determine their inventory needs. The end result is trucks that are well stocked with over 90 percent of the most common items needed for the various repairs likely to be encountered. Any parts that are not immediately available on the truck are expedited.

Source: J. R. Hall, "Keep an Inventory of Parts for Truck Stock," *Air Conditioning, Heating & Refrigeration News* 228, no. 17 (2006), 22–23.

SUMMARY

1. List the reasons for and against having inventory.

- Inventory helps to lower setup/ordering costs, improve labor/equipment utilization, lower transportation costs, provide cost of material or quantity discounts, improve customer service, and provide a buffer against variability in demand/supply.
- Disadvantages of inventory include storage/handling costs, interest and opportunity cost, increased property taxes and insurance premiums, and shrinkage/spoilage.

2. Learn the basic types of inventory.

- Cycle inventory varies in proportion to order quantity.
- Safety stock is excess inventory that a company holds to guard against uncertainty in demand, lead time, and supply.
- Anticipation inventory is inventory that is held for future use at a time when demand will exceed available capacity.
- Pipeline inventory is inventory that is in the process of moving from one location to another in the supply chain. Work-in-process (WIP) inventory is inventory that is in the process of being transformed from one state to another.
- Remanufactured/reconditioned inventory consists of products that have been used by a customer and then reacquired and either remanufactured or reconditioned by a company for resale. This type of inventory is of increasing importance for reducing costs and adverse impacts on the environment.

3. Apply continuous review and periodic review systems. Describe other important inventory systems.

- The economic order quantity balances the costs of ordering/setting up with the costs of holding large amounts of inventory. The EOQ answers the question of *how much* to order.
- Continuous review systems place an order for quantity Q whenever the inventory level drops to or below the reorder point R. Periodic review systems place an order every P time periods for enough inventory to bring the inventory level up to a target T. Both continuous and periodic review systems answer the question about *when* to place an order.
- Other important inventory systems include ABC systems, for prioritizing the importance of items, and bin, can order, and base stock systems. The newsvendor problem determines how much inventory to order when handling perishable products or items that have a limited life span. It seeks to balance shortage and excess costs for either under- or overordering products.

SOLVED PROBLEM 1

Q-System: Continuous Review

Good Buy sells blank CDs for $5 per pack of 25. Annual demand is 1,200 packs, the carrying rate is 16 percent, and the order cost is $12 per order. Currently the store orders the CDs in quantities of 100 packs per order. The store is open 50 weeks out of the year, and the standard deviation of demand is 6 units per week. The distributor that services Good Buy has a lead time of 2 weeks.

1. Calculate the annual inventory cost based on this policy.

The holding cost is calculated as $H = hC = 0.16 * \$5 = \$0.80$. The total annual cost is calculated using Equation 1: $IC = \frac{1,200}{100}\$12 + \frac{100}{2}\$0.80 = \$144 + \$40 = \$184$.

2. Calculate the economic order quantity for this item.

$$EOQ = \sqrt{\frac{2DS}{H}} = \sqrt{\frac{2 * 1,200 * \$12}{\$0.80}} = \sqrt{36,000} = 189.74, \text{ rounded to } 190$$

It is common to round an order quantity to the nearest round number (such as 200) or a multiple of the number of items in a package.

3. Determine the reorder point (R) that provides a 96 percent cycle-service level.

We first need to determine the standard deviation of demand during lead time using Equation 8 (note that we set $P = 0$ because we are not using a periodic review system):

$$\sigma_2 = \sigma_t\sqrt{P + L} = 6\sqrt{0 + 2} = 8.49$$

Next, we find the z that provides a cycle-service level of 96 percent from the normal distribution table in the Appendix, $z = 1.75$, and we enter the numbers into Equation 4:

$$R = \overline{D}_L + z\sigma_L = 24 * 2 + 1.75 * 8.49 = 62.85$$

which is rounded up to 63.

SOLVED PROBLEM 2

Quantity Discounts

A purchasing manager for a manufacturer of cereal just received an updated price list from a supplier of packaging. The new prices are $19.25 per case of boxes for 3,000 or more cases, $19.50 per case for 2,000 to 2,999 cases, $19.75 per case for 1,000 to

1,999 cases, and \$20 per case for less than 1,000 cases. Ordering cost is \$60 per order, and holding cost is \$5.00 per case per year. The cereal manufacturer uses 9,000 cases of boxes per year. Find the order quantity that minimizes total cost.

D = 9,000 cases of boxes per year needed
S = \$60 to place each order
H = \$5.00 per case per year
C = cost per case of boxes
= \$20 for less than 1,000 cases per order
= \$19.75 for 1,000 to 1,999 cases
= \$19.50 for 2,000 to 2,999 cases
= \$19.25 for 3,000 or more cases

SOLUTION

1. The first step is to solve for the EOQ. Because the holding costs in this case are fixed at \$5.00, the EOQ solution is independent of the price paid per case.

$$\text{EOQ} = \sqrt{\frac{2DS}{H}} = \sqrt{\frac{2 * 9{,}000 * \$60}{\$5.00}} = \sqrt{216{,}000} = 465$$

2. The second step is to check the total annual cost for the feasible EOQ and for each price breakpoint with a lower cost. To compute total cost, the annual cost of the cases of boxes (*CD*) is added to the ordering/setup and holding costs using Equation 5:

$$\text{TC} = \frac{D}{Q}S + \frac{Q}{2}H + CD$$

At the EOQ, Q = 465 and C = \$20.

$$\text{TC} = \left(\frac{9{,}000}{465}\$60\right) + \left(\frac{465}{2}\$5.00\right) + (\$20 * 9{,}000) = \$182{,}323.79$$

First price break: Q = 1,000 (lowest quantity to obtain C = \$19.75).

$$\text{TC} = \left(\frac{9{,}000}{1{,}000}\$60\right) + \left(\frac{1{,}000}{2}\$5.00\right) + (\$19.75 * 9{,}000) = \$180{,}790.00$$

Next price break: Q = 2,000 (lowest quantity to obtain C = \$19.50).

$$\text{TC} = \left(\frac{9{,}000}{2{,}000}\$60\right) + \left(\frac{2{,}000}{2}\$5.00\right) + (\$19.50 * 9{,}000) = \$180{,}770.00$$

Next price break: Q = 3,000 (lowest quantity to obtain C = \$19.25).

$$\text{TC} = \left(\frac{9{,}000}{3{,}000}\$60\right) + \left(\frac{3{,}000}{2}\$5.00\right) + (\$19.25 * 9{,}000) = \$180{,}930.00$$

The EOQ provides a total cost of \$182,323.79 per year. However, in this case, increasing the order to 2,000 cases obtains the lower cost per unit of \$19.50, which results in a much lower total cost of \$180,770.00. Note that the lowest overall cost is for neither the EOQ quantity nor the lowest overall price of \$19.25 per unit. Ordering an additional 1,000 units (i.e., 3,000 instead of 2,000) increases the holding costs by \$2,500 but reduces the overall purchase cost by only \$2,250 (i.e., 9,000 units per year times \$0.25 savings).

SOLVED PROBLEM 3

P-System: Fixed Period

The demand for a given type of socks at a sporting goods store is 1,976 pair, the holding cost is $0.50 per pair of socks per year, and the setup cost is $20 per order. Lead time is 3 weeks, and $\sigma_1 = 4$. A cycle-service level of 88 percent is desired.

Determine the period (P) and the target inventory (T).

SOLUTION

We first calculate the economic order quantity as

$$\text{EOQ} = \sqrt{\frac{2DS}{H}} = \sqrt{\frac{2 * 1{,}976 * \$20}{\$0.50}} = \sqrt{158{,}080} = 397.59$$

which we round up to 398.

Next, we calculate the period that best approximates this EOQ, using Equation 6.

$$P = \frac{\text{EOQ}}{\overline{D}_t}$$

$$\text{where } \overline{D}_t = \frac{1{,}967 \text{ pairs of socks/year}}{52 \text{ weeks/year}} = 38 \text{ pair of socks/week}$$

$$P = \frac{398}{38} = 10.46 \text{ weeks}$$

which we round to the nearest integer, or 10 weeks.

Next, we determine the target inventory level, T, by first looking up the number of standard deviations of demand that corresponds to 88 percent. From the Appendix, we look for the value closest to 0.8800; there is a value of 0.8790 ($z = 1.17$) and a value of 0.8810 ($z = 1.18$), so we use $z = 1.175$ as a rough interpolation between the two values. We also use $\sigma_{P+L} = \sigma_{10+3} = \sigma_1\sqrt{P+L} = 4\sqrt{10+3} = 14.42$.

$$T = \overline{D}_{P+L} + z\sigma_{P+L} = 38 \text{ pair of socks/week} * (10 + 3) + 1.175 * 4 * \sqrt{10+3} = 494 + 16.95 = 510.95$$

which we round up to 511.

QUESTIONS

1. A watch repair shop buys batteries for a variety of products. The most frequent battery purchase is for a Y300, with demand of 3,000 per year. The order cost is $15 per order, and the holding cost is $0.50 per battery. Given the following price schedule, calculate the optimal order quantity.

Number of Batteries	Price
1–250	$6.00
250–499	$5.50
500–999	$5.00
1,000 or more	$4.75

2. Artists' Advantage sells painting supplies. The most basic brush for watercolors, the T100, sells 2,080 per year. The order cost is $30 per order, and the holding cost is $3.00 per box. The lead time for an order is 3 weeks, and the standard deviation of demand is 6 boxes per week.
   a. What is the optimal order quantity of brushes?
   b. What is the optimal number of orders per year?
   c. Compute the period that most closely matches this EOQ.
   d. What value of z should be used if A1 wishes to achieve a cycle-service level of 98 percent?
   e. Using the period from part c, compute the target inventory level T. How much safety stock of brushes does this provide? How does

PART II Tools and Tactical Issues

this compare to the safety stock if a continuous review system is used?

3. Office Express sells office suppliers to businesses on a membership basis—i.e., walk-in customers without a membership are not allowed. The company delivers supplies directly to the purchaser as long as a minimum purchase of $100 is made. In order to encourage bulk orders, Office Express offers the following discount schedule on purchase quantities of boxes of paper. Larry's Lumber has annual demand of 5,000 boxes of paper, a setup cost of $10 per order, and a holding cost of 22 percent of the purchase price. Calculate the optimal order quantity.

1–100 boxes	$5 per box
100–249 boxes	$4.75 per box
250–499 boxes	$4.50 per box
500 or more boxes	$4.25 per box

4. Arnie's Air Conditioners, Inc., manufactures a variety of heating and cooling equipment. The SuperCool model is one of the higher-demand items and is of particular interest because its manufactured cost is $600. Demand for the SuperCool is relatively constant, and demand data for the past 12 weeks is given here. The lead time to manufacture one order of SuperCool is 4 weeks. The holding cost percentage for Arnie's is 16 percent. The setup cost is $20 per order. The company operates 52 weeks per year.

$$\text{Average Demand} = 120 \text{ units/week}$$
$$\sigma_1 = 15 \text{ units/week}$$

a. Design a continuous review inventory management system for the SuperCool model and calculate the appropriate parameters to control two things: (1) *when* to order and (2) *how much* to order. Assume that Arnie's Air Conditioners wants to maintain an 86 percent cycle-service level.

b. What effect would increasing the cycle-service level to 94 percent have on customer service and inventory levels? Calculate the change in *numerical* terms, if appropriate.

c. What effect(s) would a decrease in the lead time from 4 weeks to 2 weeks have, assuming that the company maintains the 86 percent cycle-service level of part *a*?

5. Burgerama requires all employees who handle food to wear latex gloves for sanitary reasons. The annual demand for gloves is 250 boxes of 200 per year. The order cost is $11 per order, and the carrying cost is 25 percent per box per year of the purchase cost of $20 per box.

a. How many boxes of gloves should Burgerama order at one time?

b. What is the time between orders?

c. What would be the change in annual cost if Burgerama had storage space for only 15 boxes per order and thus was forced to use an order quantity of 15?

6. A1 Kitchens, Inc., installs kitchen cabinets, countertops, and floors. A1 uses 30,000 tubes of caulk per year (assume 50 weeks per year) in the installation process. The order cost is $24 per order, and the holding cost is $0.25 per tube of caulk. The lead time for an order is 1 week, and the standard deviation of demand is 25 tubes per week.

a. What is A1's optimal order quantity?

b. What is the optimal number of orders per year?

c. What is the reorder point if A1 desires a cycle-service level of 50 percent?

d. What value of z should be used if A1 wishes to achieve a cycle-service level of 94 percent?

e. What should the reorder point be?

7. Hottenstein, Giffith, and Hult, attorneys at law, do a great deal of printing. The firm uses a single type of printer with annual demand for print cartridges of 480 per year. The order cost is $15 per order, and the carrying cost is 20 percent per cartridge per year of the purchase cost of $35 per cartridge.

a. How many print cartridges should the firm order at one time?

b. What is the time between orders?

8. Smallville Bus System provides public transportation to the residents of Smallville. The maintenance department manages 1,000 buses and faces annual demand for 2,166 tires. The order cost is $50 per order, and the holding cost is $6 per tire. The lead time for an order is 2 weeks, and the standard deviation of demand is 7 tires per week.

a. What is the optimal order quantity of tires?

b. What is the optimal number of orders per year?

c. What is the reorder point if Smallville desires a cycle-service level of 50 percent?

d. What value of z should be used if Smallville wishes to achieve a cycle-service level of 92 percent?

e. What should the reorder point be? How much safety stock of tires does this provide?

9. The current order quantity for Electric Powerbars is 100 bars. The order cost is $10 per order, the holding cost is $0.25 per box per year, and the annual demand is 2,000 bars per year.

   a. Calculate the annual holding cost plus the annual ordering cost to get the total annual cost when using an order quantity of 100 bars.

   b. Calculate the EOQ and the total annual cost for this order quantity.

   c. How many orders per year are necessary when $Q = 100$? How many orders per year are necessary for the EOQ in part *b*?

   d. Graph the annual inventory cost (IC) using MS Excel. Show the holding cost, ordering cost, and total inventory cost as a function of order size Q.

10. An appliance manufacturer purchases the tub portion of washing machines from a supplier with these prices: less than 500, $20 each; 500–999, $19 each; 1,000–1,399, $18 each; 1,400–1,999, $17 each; and 2,000 or more, $16 each. Order costs are $30 per order, annual demand is 10,000 tubs, and holding costs are 30 percent of purchase cost. Determine the order quantity that will minimize total cost.

11. The current order quantity for Paul's Pasta Pinwheels is 200 boxes. The order cost is $4 per order, the holding cost is $0.40 per box per year, and the annual demand is 500 boxes per year.

    a. Calculate the annual holding cost plus the annual ordering cost to get the total annual cost when using an order quantity of 200 boxes.

    b. Calculate the EOQ and the total annual cost for this order quantity.

CASE STUDY

Dano's Drugstore

Margaret Dano opened her drugstore in 1951 on a busy street corner in a small suburb of Chicago. Originally, the store provided drugs and various other small items primarily to residents of the town. Over the course of decades, the store expanded as the suburbs of Chicago expanded. By 1996, the store had tripled from its original size, occupying 5,000 square feet of space. In the course of this expansion, the store increased its product range, so that in addition to the pharmacy, it offered other items such as snack food, dental care items, suntan lotion, and bug spray. The total breadth of the product line encompassed more than 10,000 items.

As the drugstore grew, managing inventory represented a significant challenge. Margaret has tried numerous systems over the past few years, but most of these have not been very successful. The average item has 75 days' worth of inventory, yet the fill rate of all customer orders is approximately 90 percent. Any item that is out of stock will be backordered (with a rain check provided) upon customer request. In approximately 50 percent of the cases where an item is out of stock, the customer simply buys the item from a competing drugstore. Margaret realizes that the current inventory methods are not working well. In addition, she realizes that her background as a pharmacist may not have properly prepared her for managing the inventory for thousands of items. Furthermore, Margaret would like to take a less active role in her business and spend her winters in Florida. Therefore, she has hired you as a consultant to evaluate and improve the inventory methods for Dano's.

Dano's Drugstore is currently affiliated with a major national drugstore chain that supplies all of the items that Dano's sells. Supplies are delivered weekly in a single shipment on Wednesday afternoon. Dano's must finalize its order by 9:00 a.m. Tuesday morning. The warehouse/service center that Dano's Drugstore orders from has close to a 100 percent fill rate; therefore, it is safe to assume that any orders placed on Tuesday morning will be delivered on Wednesday afternoon. Your initial assignment is to develop an inventory system for three items: (1) Tylenol aspirin caplets, (2) Milky Way candy bars, and (3) Raid rat poison. Demand data for the previous year for each of these three products is given in Exhibits 1 through 3.

The three products sell for $5.99 (Tylenol), $0.75 (Milky Way), and $9.99 (Raid). The profit margins on the three products are 30 percent, 40 percent, and 20 percent, respectively. The cost of placing any order, including stocking the order in the storeroom and on the store's display shelves, is estimated to be $3.

Dano's Drugstore has averaged a 15 percent annual return on assets over the past four years. Margaret has a revolving line of credit at the local bank that allows Dano's to borrow money at 10 percent. Currently, the drugstore has a loan in the amount of $145,000 outstanding. Annual rent for the store is $84,000, insurance is $24,000 per year, and maintenance expenses are approximately $20,000.

The current order policies for each of the three "test" units are as follows:

Tylenol Caplets	Milky Way	Raid Rat
$Q = 600$	$Q = 200$	Order 100 if inventory < 30
P = every 9 weeks	$R = 200$	If forecast > 50, order forecast number for next week

EXHIBIT 1 Tylenol Aspirin Caplets—Demand for Past Year

Week	Actual Demand	Week	Actual Demand	Week	Actual Demand	Week	Actual Demand
1	60	14	59	27	64	40	58
2	62	15	59	28	65	41	67
3	58	16	44	29	57	42	68
4	56	17	54	30	68	43	52
5	54	18	60	31	55	44	75
6	68	19	60	32	61	45	55
7	57	20	62	33	61	46	54
8	64	21	62	34	49	47	53
9	62	22	74	35	59	48	61
10	52	23	54	36	61	49	63
11	48	24	62	37	61	50	64
12	72	25	58	38	57	51	60
13	63	26	64	39	65	52	61

EXHIBIT 2 Milky Way Candy Bars—Demand for Past Year

Week	Actual Demand	Week	Actual Demand	Week	Actual Demand	Week	Actual Demand
1	150	14	162	27	141	40	145
2	120	15	184	28	159	41	171
3	165	16	151	29	139	42	153
4	121	17	137	30	136	43	147
5	131	18	157	31	168	44	146
6	185	19	128	32	152	45	161
7	144	20	190	33	129	46	153
8	165	21	150	34	152	47	132
9	133	22	150	35	152	48	148
10	157	23	99	36	115	49	159
11	168	24	105	37	160	50	146
12	152	25	174	38	162	51	167
13	145	26	170	39	165	52	163

(continued)

EXHIBIT 3 **Raid Rat Spray—Forecasted versus Actual Demand for Past Year**

Week	Fore-casted Demand	Actual Demand	Week	Fore-casted Demand	Actual Demand	Week	Fore-casted Demand	Actual Demand	Week	Fore-casted Demand	Actual Demand
1	14	10	14	33	12	27	33	17	40	500	630
2	10	12	15	12	18	28	17	22	41	630	480
3	12	25	16	18	15	29	22	30	42	480	200
4	25	18	17	15	8	30	30	19	43	200	21
5	18	16	18	8	22	31	19	22	44	21	15
6	16	9	19	22	25	32	22	11	45	15	18
7	9	22	20	25	14	33	11	17	46	18	17
8	22	24	21	14	21	34	17	25	47	17	22
9	24	17	22	21	17	35	25	19	48	22	26
10	17	14	23	17	8	36	19	44	49	26	33
11	14	27	24	8	7	37	44	95	50	33	15
12	27	28	25	7	44	38	95	220	51	15	14
13	28	33	26	44	33	39	220	500	52	14	17

QUESTIONS

1. What factors should be considered when developing inventory systems for the 10,000 items carried by Dano's? What are the key differences between items that would affect how their inventory is managed? For example, how should prescription drugs be handled differently from over-the-counter items? Or how do seasonal products differ from more stable products?

2. Develop an inventory system for Tylenol caplets and for Milky Way candy bars. Hint: You will need to choose an appropriate cycle-service level and an appropriate holding cost for each item.

3. Discuss the characteristics of Raid rat spray that might suggest that it should have a different type of inventory system. What factors should be considered in developing a system for Raid?

4. Compare the annual costs for your plan for Tylenol and Milky Way relative to the costs under the current plan. You may want to consider ordering, holding, and stockout costs.

CHAPTER 7

Dependent Demand Inventory

LEARNING OBJECTIVES

1. Contrast dependent and independent demand, and trace the development of material requirements planning (MRP).
2. Explain the inputs to an MRP system.
3. Compute single-level MRP records.
4. Compute multiple-level MRP records and explain the outputs generated.
5. Describe the evolution of MRP to enterprise resource planning (ERP) and identify ways in which ERP is utilized to integrate all the functions of an organization.
6. Explain how dependent demand is handled in service organizations and describe the use of technology.
7. Define three critical features for success with ERP.

Dependent Demand at Kellogg's

Kellogg's Company manufactures a wide variety of cereals, breakfast foods, and snacks. It employs dependent demand planning techniques, including material requirements planning. Every two months, a plan is developed for all production items in a given group of plants. For the morning foods division, Kellogg's develops a plan for three plants that produce Pop-Tarts. The plan shown in Figure 7.1 (for November–December 2006) indicates which products will be made in each week, as well as the number of days and shifts in each week (note that during the week of Christmas [12/25/06], the plants are shut down). The process of developing this plan is iterative and involves evaluating forecasted demand, available capacity, costs at the different plants, and a variety of other factors. Figure 7.1 indicates that the plan calls for 61,500 boxes of Hot Fudge Sundae Pop-Tarts and 54,000 boxes of Strawberry Pop-Tarts, along with other varieties, during the week of November 6.

Raw materials (top) and finished products (bottom) for Kellogg's Pop-Tarts.

Material requirements planning logic is then used to derive the ingredients and packaging required at each plant. Thus, Figure 7.2 shows the amount of packaging and raw ingredients needed at the Muncy plant for the week of December 11, 2006. For example, the 22-ounce box of chocolate chip Pop-Tarts requires over 2.1 million feet of liner (the plastic wrap around pairs of Pop-Tarts toaster pastries). Overall, the items to be produced at the Muncy plant will require over 21,000 pounds of chocolate chips and over 18,000 pounds of dehydrated strawberry flakes. Now that's a lot of chocolate and strawberry flakes!

Muncy P-T			313	TOT PROD							
11/6/2006											
		Days Scheduled Line 1:	**7**	**7**	**3**	**6**	**7**	**7**	**5**	**0**	**5**
		Shifts:	**21**	**21**	**7.5**	**17**	**21**	**21**	**13.5**	**0**	**15**
		Days Scheduled Line 3:	7	7	6	7	6	6	0	6	
		Shifts:	14	14	5	11.5	14	12	11	0	11.5
Item		**Descr**	**11/6/2006**	**11/13/2006**	**11/20/2006**	**11/27/2006**	**12/4/2006**	**12/11/2006**	**12/18/2006**	**12/25/2006**	**1/1/2007**
3800005966		PT CHOCOLATE CHIP 22 OZ.						53,400			
3800007482		PT CHOC CHIP 14.7 OZ.									
3800012334		PT 12CT REFRESHED 22OZ									
3800016323		HOT FUDGE SUNDAE PT 14.7OZ	61,500	12,500							
3800019721		POP-TARTS CHOC CHIP 72/2CT DIS						18,400			
3800022534		STRBRY MLKSHK PT 8CT 14.10 OZ									
3800029696		HOT FDG SUNDAE PT 12CT/22 OZ			13,200						
3800030004		PT BB 14.7 OZ.									
3800030104		PT BR SUG CINN 14 OZ.									57,500
3800030404		PT STRAW 14.7 OZ.	54,000						81,000		
3800030422		PT STRAWBERRY 22 OZ.									
3800030569		2CT HOT FUDGE SUNDAE POP-TART			14,850						
3800031004		PT FR BB 14.7 OZ.					118,500				
3800031022		PT FR BB 22 OZ.				40,800					
3800031032		POP-TARTS FRSTD BLUEBERRY 72/2				44,200					
3800031104		PT FR BRN SUG CINN 14 OZ.									37,500
3800031122		PT FR BRN SUG CINN 21 OZ.		4,800	4,800		57,600				
3800031122	0020	FR BS/CINN PT 21 OZ / TFA									
3800031122	0023	FR BS/CINN PT 21 OZ-XBOX LIVE	14,400	45,600							
3800031132		POP-TARTS FR BS CINN 72/2CT DI	15,600	54,600	5,200						
3800031132	0020	POP-TARTS FR BS CINN 72/2CT DI									
3800031204		PT APL CINN 14.7 OZ.									42,000
3800031304		PT FR CHOC FUDGE 14.7 OZ.		128,000	59,000						
3800031304	0020	PT US FR CHOC FUD / TFA									
3800031322		PT FR CHOC FUDGE 22 OZ. / TFA						17,000	60,750		
3800031322	0020	PT FR CHOC FUDGE 22 OZ. / TFA									
3800031332		POP-TARTS FRSTD CHOC FUDGE 72/						8,000			
3800031332	0020	PT FR CHOC FUDGE 72/2CT DSPLY									
3800031404		PT US FR GRAPE 8 CT									
3800031504		PT CHOC VAN CREAM 14.7 OZ.									
3800031604		PT FR RASPBERRY 14.7 OZ.									
3800031704		PT FR STRAWBERRY 14.7 OZ.					66,000	162,000	67,500		
3800031704	0023	FR STRAWBERRY PT 8CT/ 12TOYS CH									
3800031722		PT FR STRAWBERRY 22 OZ.					62,000				
3800031722	0020	PT FR STRAWBERRY 22 OZ. / TFA									
3800031732		POP-TARTS STRAWBERRY 72/2CT DI									
3800031732	0020	PT STRAWBERRY 72/2CT DISPLAY/									
3800031804		PT FR CHERRY 8 CT				153,000					
3800031822		PT 12CT FRSTD CHERRY 22 OZ	19,000								63,200
3800031822	0023	FR CHERRY PT 22 OZ/XBOX LIVE	35,000								
3800031832		POP-TARTS FRSTD CHERRY 72/2CT	35,200								19,600
3800032404		PT US WLD BERRY 8 CT	16,400								
3800032422		PT FR WILD BERRY 22.8 OZ.	17,200								
3800055104		LOW-FAT PT FR BRN SUG CINN 14									
3800055304		LOW-FAT PT FR CHOC FUDGE 14.7									
3800055704		LOW-FAT PT FR STRAWBERRY 14.7									
6410025659		Pop Tarts Chocolate Chip 400gm									
6410025659	0002	Pop Tarts Chocolate Chip TFA 4									

FIGURE 7.1 Production Plan for Kellogg's Pop-Tarts (November–December 2006)

Item		Descr	11/6/2006	11/13/2006	11/20/2006	11/27/2006	12/4/2006	12/11/2006	12/18/2006	12/25/2006	1/1/2007
6410025660		Pop Tarts Frosted Wildberry 40	7,500								
6410025660	0002	Pop Tarts Frosted Wildberry TF									
6410025661		Pop Tarts Frosted Choc/Fudge 4		15,000							
6410025661	0002	PopTarts Frosted Choc/Fudge TF									
6410025662		Pop Tarts Apple Cinnamon 400gm									
6410025662	0002	Pop Tarts Apple Cinnamon TFA 4									
6410025663		Pop Tarts Frosted Blueberry 40									
6410025663	0002	Pop Tarts Frosted Blueberry T									
6410025665		Pop Tarts Frosted Strawberry									
6410025665	0002	Pop Tarts Frosted Straw TFA 4									
6410025666		Pop Tarts Frosted Raspberry 40									
6410025666	0002	Pop Tarts Frosted Raspberry TF									
	Line 1										
	Line 3										
	Items highlighted in green indicate new items for a plant (> or < 6 months of running)										

FIGURE 7.1 Production Plan for Kellogg's Pop-Tarts (November–December 2006) (*continued*)

It is important to note that many of the ingredients are common to several products. For example, all Pop-Tarts toaster pastries require soft flour, corn syrup, and sugar; thus, more than 1 million pounds of soft flour, more than 396 thousand pounds of corn syrup, and more than 393 thousand pounds of sugar will be used in all five of the Pop-Tarts stock-keeping units (SKUs) to be produced at the Muncy plant that week. ■

HISTORY OF DEPENDENT DEMAND PLANNING

This chapter examines methods for dealing with dependent demand rather than independent demand. **Independent demand** is demand for items that are considered end items that go directly to a customer, and for which demand is influenced by market conditions and not related to inventory decisions for any other item. Items such as toothpaste, books, televisions, and refrigerators are independent demand items for which we must forecast the sales. **Dependent demand** is demand for items that are used to make another item or are considered to be parts of another item. For example, a refrigerator is an independent demand item, but the door, the motor, and each of the drawers that are required to produce it are dependent demand items. Similarly, a bicycle is an independent demand item, but the two wheels, the frame, and the seat required to produce one bicycle are dependent demand items.

- **Independent demand** demand for items that are considered end items that go directly to a customer, and for which demand is influenced by market conditions and not related to inventory decisions for any other item
- **Dependent demand** demand for items that are used to make another item or are considered to be parts of another item

The differences between independent and dependent demand allow for a specialized approach for dependent demand. **Material requirements planning (MRP)** is a computer-based system that develops plans for ordering and producing dependent demand items. MRP utilizes two basic principles: Requirements for dependent demand items are *derived* from the production schedule for their parents (the items that are assembled from component parts), and the production order is *offset* to account for the lead time.

- **Material requirements planning (MRP)** a computer-based system that develops plans for ordering and producing dependent demand items.

Up until about three decades ago, inventory and production planning was done using the techniques and systems for independent demand described in

Muncy P-T					
Item	**Descr**	**12/11/2006**	**Packaging needed for each SKU**	**Ingredients in pounds needed for all scheduled production**	
3800005966	PT CHOCOLATE CHIP 22 OZ.	53,400	Cartons = 650,412	Soft Flour	1,030,304.63
			Cases = 53,720.4	Corn Syrup	396,528.47
			Liner = 2,188,662.4 linear foot	Sugar	393,013.10
				Dextrose	388,091.04
3800019721	POP-TARTS CHOC CHIP 72/2CT DIS	18,400	Cartons = 224,112	Palm Oil	362,220.72
			Cases = 18,510.4	Fructose	328,925.55
			Liner = 1,351,296 imps.	Hard Flour	321,954.37
				Crackermeal	102,858.35
3800031322	PT FR CHOC FUDGE 22 OZ. / TFA	17,000	Cartons = 207,060	Whey	54,927.46
			Cases = 17,102	Wheat Starch	37,068.74
			Liner = 696,762 linear feet	Salt	27,159.54
				Choc Chips	21,091.50
3800031332	POP-TARTS FRSTD CHOC FUDGE 72/	8,000	Cartons = 97,440	Strawberry Flakes	18,399.19
			Cases = 8,048	Milk Choc Dry Stock	17,205.31
			Liner = 587,520 imps.	Dutched Cocoa	16,476.26
				Asst. Crunchlets	13,922.16
3800031704	PT FR STRAWBERRY 14.7 OZ.	162,000	Cartons = 1,973,150	Cane Juice Molasses	11,975.99
			Cases = 162,972	Natural Cocoa	10,761.36
			Liner = 4,426,488 linear feet	Corn Starch (bags)	6,732.00
				Corn Starch (bulk)	6,549.43
				Baking Soda	6,239.78
				Baking Powder	5,198.43
				Vitamin Premix	5,154.43
				Nonfat Dry Milk	4,432.49
				White Crunchlets	3,541.93
				Black Cocoa	3,219.03
				Art. Cookie Flavor	3,193.60
				Gelatin	3,045.37
				YT25 Caramel Color	3,028.41
				Sodium Alum. Phosphate	2,890.76
				Citric Acid	2,874.87
				Dimodan	2,257.54
				Vanilla 2x	2,078.25
				N&A Choc Flavor	2,064.64
				Egg Whites	1,938.68
				Paniplex	1,817.05
				Brown Lake Dispersion	1,505.71
				Xanthan Gum	1,052.54
				Lecithin	924.11
				Creamy Butter Flavor	908.52
				Panodan	721.31
				Caramel Color 2x	693.71
				Strawberry Shade	69.00

FIGURE 7.2 Material Requirements Plan for Muncy Pop-Tart Plant

Chapter 6. This was true despite the fact that dependent demand has some unique characteristics—in particular, it tends to be lumpy rather than even. This is true because retailers tend to order from upstream manufacturers in batches of larger quantities, whereas end customers tend to buy products in small quantities. In addition, with dependent demand, the time when an order will be required can be predicted based on an item's relationship with other products. Figure 7.3 shows demand for two products: a bicycle and a bicycle tire. Notice how the demand for the bicycle (an independent demand item because it is sold directly to end customers) is relatively even and smooth. In contrast, the demand for the bicycle tire (a dependent demand item because it is used to produce finished bicycles) is lumpy. The inventory systems from Chapter 6 will not work well in this situation.

MRP is a technique that has been employed since the 1940s and 1950s. The technique gained prominence in the mid-1970s with the development of more powerful computers, which have become irreplaceable operating tools in many companies. MRP really developed only when mainframe computers offered sufficient calculation power to perform the thousands of required calculations automatically. Leading pioneers of MRP include Joseph Orlicky, an engineer for IBM who first coded an MRP system for the JI Case company in Racine, Wisconsin; George W. Plossl, a widely read author and consultant; and Oliver Wight, the founder of Oliver Wight Associates, a leading application provider. Each of these three men worked closely with the American Production and Inventory and Control Society (APICS) and leading manufacturing businesses to develop the tools and techniques used for planning dependent demand via MRP. Today, you could manage a large company's inventory with a laptop (or even a cell phone) if it were properly set up; in 1975, this required a dedicated mainframe computer. The techniques in this chapter are relatively easy to understand in small examples, but they can become overwhelming without a firm grasp of basic principles

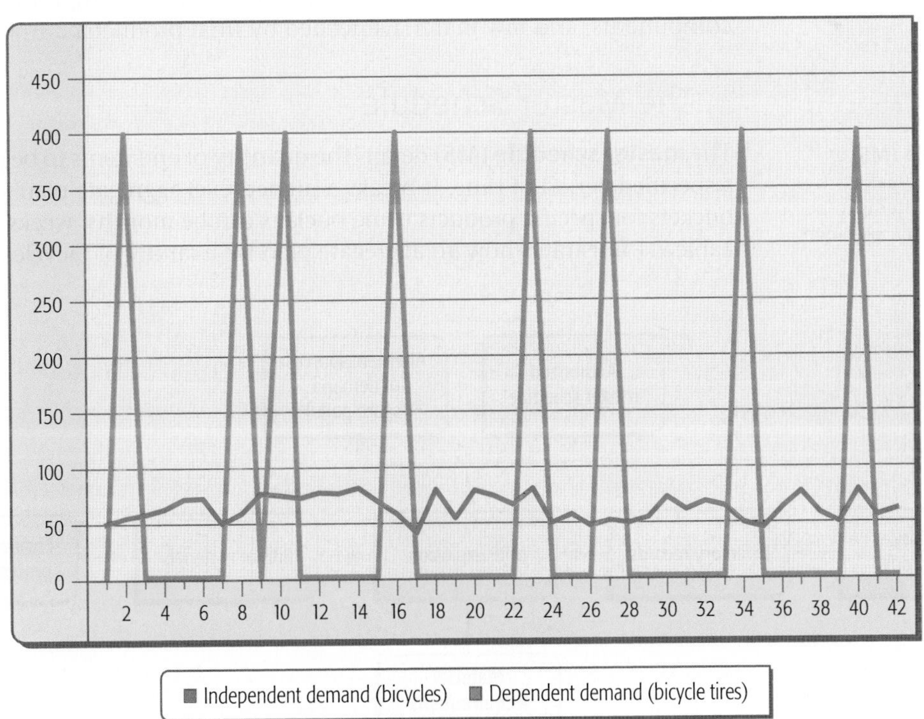

FIGURE 7.3 Demand Pattern for Independent versus Dependent Items

and a good computer system to perform the calculations. Developing a thorough understanding of the basic principles and techniques is thus more important than learning specific computer applications.

The use and application of MRP grew steadily through the 1970s and 1980s as the power of computer hardware and software increased. MRP gradually evolved into a broader system called manufacturing resource planning (MRP II), which links production planning and inventory with a company's financial and accounting systems. During the 1990s, MRP II evolved to become enterprise resource planning (ERP), which integrates all functional areas of a business.

This chapter examines the basic principles and techniques underlying MRP. This is done in four steps. We first examine the inputs and data that are needed to make MRP work. We then examine how to develop an inventory record for a single item. Next, we combine MRP records for all of the items that make up a product and show how to develop inventory records for multiple items that are linked together. Finally, we discuss the evolution of dependent demand planning systems (MRP, MRP II, and ERP) and how they are used in practice today. We conclude the chapter with a discussion of the use of these concepts for service-oriented businesses.

MRP INPUTS

● **Material requirements plan** a plan that specifies the timing and size of new production orders, adjustments to existing order quantities, and expediting or delay of late/early orders

An MRP system relies on three key inputs shown in Figure 7.4: a bill of materials database, a master schedule, and an inventory records database. The MRP system combines these inputs to develop a **material requirements plan** that specifies the timing and size of new production orders, adjustments to existing order quantities, and expediting or delay of late/early orders. The process of developing the material requirements plan is called MRP explosion; it is a technique for converting the requirements of final products into a material requirements plan that specifies the production/order quantities and timing for all subassemblies, components, and raw materials needed by final products.

The Master Schedule

● **Master schedule (MS)** a document that details the quantity of end items to be produced within a specified period of time

The **master schedule (MS)** details the quantity of end items to be produced within a specified period of time. It breaks a higher-level aggregate plan into smaller time buckets for specific products (time buckets can be months, weeks, days, or hours). Table 7.1 illustrates how an aggregate plan for a family of bicycles is broken into a

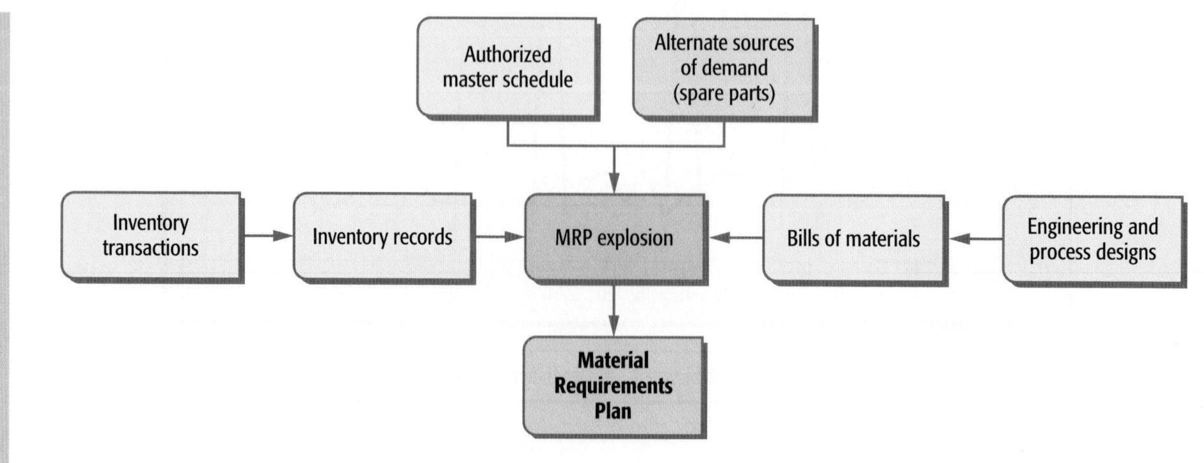

FIGURE 7.4 Material Requirements Plan Inputs

TABLE 7.1 Master Schedule for a Family of Bicycles

	February				March			
	Feb. 1	**Feb. 8**	**Feb. 15**	**Feb. 22**	**Mar. 1**	**Mar. 8**	**Mar. 15**	**Mar. 22**
Aggregate production plan for bicycle family	600				500			
Mountain bike	200		100			80		80
Road bike		50		100	100		100	
Tandem bike		75		75		70		70

master schedule for each of three different types of bicycles. The quantities shown refer to the time when the order must be released to the plant or supplier if the finished product is to be assembled in time to meet customer delivery promises. We will use this MS "start" quantity throughout the remainder of this chapter.

There are a number of objectives associated with developing a master schedule. The MS must balance the workload for a given company in terms of not only total capacity, but also capacity at each workstation and for each worker. The master schedule seeks to minimize total cost and provides a way of assessing the impact of new orders and providing delivery dates for accepted orders. The planned production quantities in the master schedule are intended to satisfy demand, which is estimated based on customer orders and forecasts. The MS is usually frozen or unchangeable in the near term (the next few days or weeks), slushy or slightly changeable in the middle term, and liquid or very changeable in the long term. The goal is to plan production but allow some flexibility to change orders as demand or customer requirements change.

For our purposes, we will treat the MS as a given—in other words, we will assume that it has already been developed to be used as input to our MRP. Techniques for developing the MS are very similar to those used for the MRP; we focus primarily on the MRP for the sake of simplicity and brevity. It is worth noting that while the quantities for production in the MS appear to be deterministic or certain, they are really estimates of stochastic or uncertain demand. The production quantities in the MS are based on forecasts, which are inevitably incorrect—when major adjustments are made to forecasts, the changes have a significant impact on the corresponding MRP records.

A tutorial and example of master scheduling used to develop an MS is available online at the textbook web site.

The master schedule in Table 7.1 illustrates several key aspects of master scheduling:

1. The sums of the quantities in the MS must equal those in the aggregate production plan. For example, 600 bikes will be produced in February for the aggregate schedule, which is the sum of the totals for mountain bikes (300–200 in the week of Feb. 1 and 100 in the week of Feb. 15), road bikes (150–50 in the week of Feb. 8 and 100 in the week of Feb. 22), and tandem bikes (150–75 in the week of Feb. 8 and 75 in the week of Feb. 22).

2. Aggregate production quantities should be planned efficiently over time in order to minimize setup, production, and inventory costs. The breakdown of types of bikes (i.e., mountain, road, and tandem) is based on historical

demand, marketing, and promotional considerations. The production planner should also select lot sizes for each bike type.

3 Capacity limitations must be considered before finalizing the MS, including labor and machine capacity, storage space, transportation equipment, and other such factors. The MS should be checked against the available resources and often must be changed in order to ensure that sufficient capacity is available.

The Bill of Materials

Bill of materials (BOM) a document that specifies all assemblies, subassemblies, parts, and raw materials that are required to produce one unit of the finished product

Every finished product has a **bill of materials (BOM)** that specifies all assemblies, subassemblies, parts, and raw materials that are required to produce one unit of the finished product.

A bill of materials is hierarchical in nature, with the finished product at the top and each lower level showing how many of each type of part or subassembly are needed to produce one unit of the parent item. Bills of material are often represented in visual form by a product structure tree. Figure 7.5 illustrates a partial BOM for a bicycle (some parts required to produce a bicycle have been omitted for clarity). The end product is 1 bicycle—this is the parent item. The parts (children) needed to produce one bicycle are shown at lower levels in Figure 7.5. Each finished bicycle requires 1 set of handlebars, 1 frame assembly, and 1 seat. In turn, 1 frame assembly requires 2 wheels and 1 frame. At the next level, 1 wheel is produced from 12 spokes and 1 tire rim, and 1 frame requires 5 feet of aluminum tubing and 1 gallon of paint. Note that the part quantities do not have to be in terms of specific parts but can be in different units—e.g., 1 gallon of paint is enough to cover 1 frame, and 5 feet of aluminum tubing can be bent and welded to form 1 frame.

Every part in a bill of materials is assigned a level. End items or finished products that are sold directly to an end customer are Level 0. These items are parents

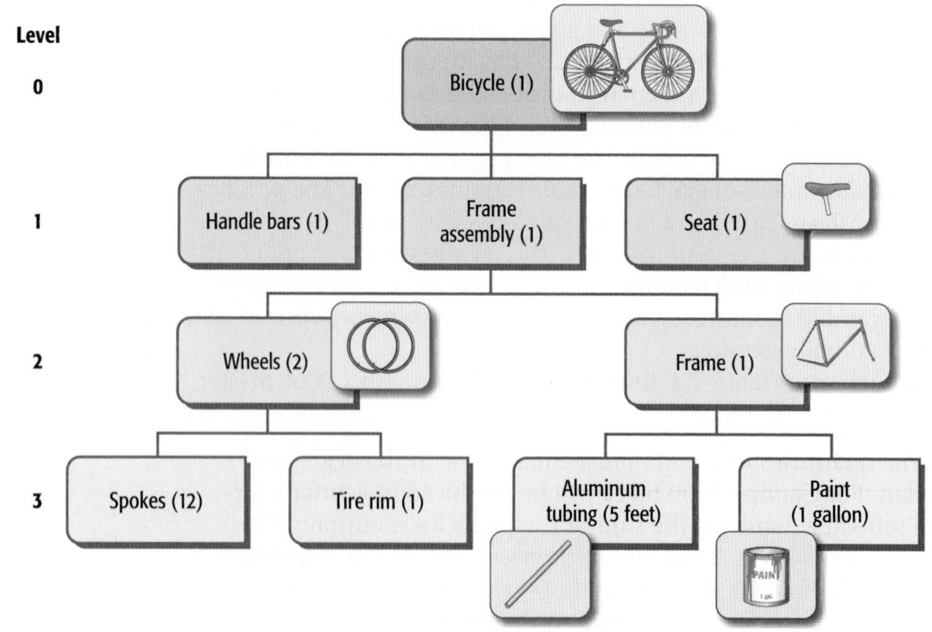

FIGURE 7.5 Partial Bill of Materials for a Bicycle

to lower-level parts, which are components of the higher-level part. Thus, in Figure 7.5, the handlebars, frame assembly, and seat are Level 1 parts that are components of a complete bicycle. The wheels and frame are Level 2 parts that are components of the frame assembly. The spokes and tire rim are Level 3 parts that are components of a wheel, while the aluminum tubing and paint are Level 3 components of the frame. Remember that the number of parts or amount of material required to produce 1 unit of the parent part is shown for each component part. Thus, to produce 5 bicycles, a total of 5 frame assemblies (1 frame assembly for each of 5 bicycles), 10 wheels (2 wheels per frame assembly times 5 frame assemblies), and 120 spokes (12 spokes per wheel times 10 wheels) are required (along with the appropriate numbers of the remaining parts in the BOM).

Figure 7.6 provides another example of a bill of materials for item A. This BOM also illustrates the concept of **common parts**, which are parts that are used in more than one place in a single product or in more than one product. For example, item G in Figure 7.6 might be a 2-inch screw that is used to hold two parts together. It is a common part—3 units of G are required for each unit of B, and 3 units of G are required for each unit of E. While part G appears at two levels (at Level 2 as a component of B and at Level 3 as a component of E), a part is typically assigned to the lowest level at which it appears in any BOM that a company produces. Thus, in Figure 7.6, part G is termed a Level 3 part. **Low-level coding** involves assigning a part to the lowest level at which it appears anywhere in the BOM. Another way to think of this is that a part is at one level lower than its lowest parent part (i.e., G has two parents [B = Level 1 and E = Level 2]); thus, G is a Level 3 part, which is one level lower than its lowest-level parent. In other words, the children can't come before the parents.

- **Common parts** parts that are used in more than one place in a single product or in more than one product
- **Low-level coding** involves assigning a part to the lowest level at which it appears anywhere in the BOM

Solved Example 1

Use the data presented in Figure 7.6 to

A. **Determine the quantities of parts B, C, D, E, F, and G required in order to complete one unit of A.**

B. **Determine the quantities of component parts B through G that would be required to produce 100 units of A.**

(continued)

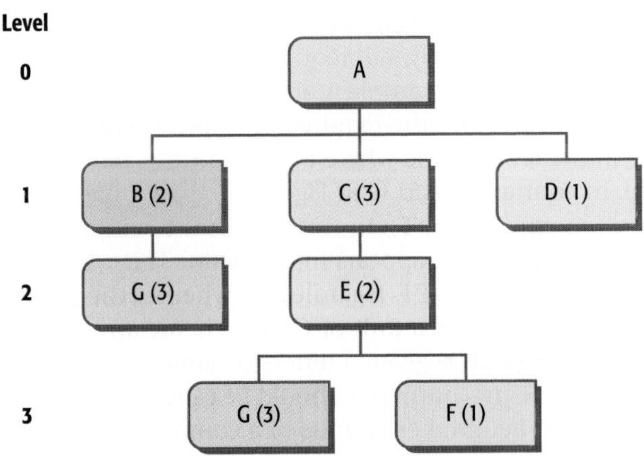

FIGURE 7.6 Product Structure Tree for Item A

Component		Level	Quantity to Produce 1 A	Quantity to Produce 100 A
B	2 Bs per A	1	2	200
C	3 Cs per A	1	3	300
D	1 D per A	1	1	100
E	2 Es per C × 3 Cs per A	2	6	600
G	3 Gs per B × 2 Bs per A + 3 Gs per E × 2 Es per C × 3 Cs per A	3	6 + 18 = 24	2,400
F	1 F per E × 2 Es per C × 3 Cs per A	3	6	600

Note that G appears in two places. The total requirements for G are 6 plus 18 equals 24 units of G to produce 1 unit of A. The last column shows that to produce 100 units of A, we need to multiply each quantity in the third column by 100. Thus, if 6 units of E are needed to produce 1 unit of A, then producing 100 units of A requires 6 * 100 = 600 units of G.

Determining the required quantities of parts and raw materials is usually not as straightforward as in Solved Example 1. For one thing, many finished products are made from hundreds, or even thousands, of parts, many of which appear multiple times in a single bill of materials. Think for a second—how many parts are there in a typical refrigerator, lawn tractor, or boat? These products can have 1,000 or more parts, and their BOM may consist of 20 or more levels. Second, the supply of parts is not 100 percent consistent—the people or suppliers in charge of producing a part or component may take longer than expected or deliver less than the expected number as a result of part defects. Third, timing of parts completion and delivery is critical. Consider Solved Example 1: It is not possible to produce 100 units of A if the inventory consists of 200 units of B and 300 units of C, but the 100 units of D are not available because of a delivery delay. *All* of the parts for a given parent item must be on hand in order to produce that item. Finally, some of the parts may already have some inventory on hand; thus, we must net out (i.e., subtract on-hand inventory from overall requirements) the requirements—if we have 50 units of item B in Solved Example 1 and we need 200, we should net out the on-hand inventory of 50 from the required 200 and should thus order 150 units.

Figure 7.7 shows an example where a part, in this case E, is buried within the BOM structure. In contrast to part G in Figure 7.6, part E has both parent items (D and C) and components (G and F). In this case, it is essential that item E have the same components anywhere it appears in the BOM. Thus, 1 unit of E is produced using 3 units of G and 1 unit of F, regardless of whether the unit of E will then be used to produce a unit of D or a unit of C. If there are any differences in components, then the part should be given a different name or part number—i.e., a part made up of 2 units of G and 1 unit of F should be called part H or something different from E. Note that the number of units of a common part such as E that are required for the parent items can differ; thus, Figure 7.7 indicates that 1 unit of E is required to produce 1 unit of D, while 2 units of E are required for each unit of C.

It is critical that the bill of materials is an accurate representation of the parts required to produce a product because errors at one level are magnified when they

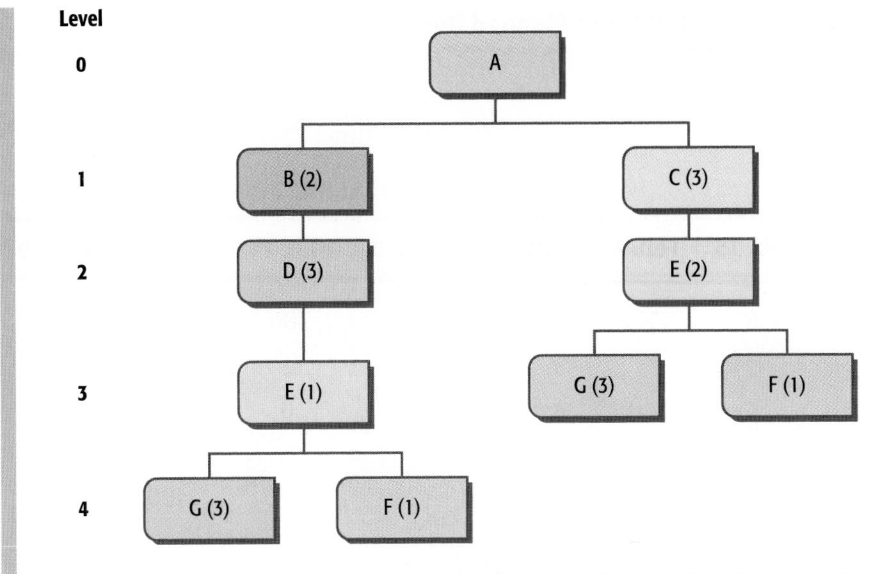

FIGURE 7.7 Bill of Materials with a Buried Component

are multiplied by parts requirements at lower levels. Although this seems fairly obvious, problems often occur when companies change the design of an item and forget to update the bill of materials in the inventory system or when someone mistakenly enters an incorrect quantity. While it may seem that paying close attention to a particular product should prevent errors, it is useful to realize that a company may be dealing with 100,000 or more parts, many of which are used in numerous different products. Thus, attention to detail and accuracy, combined with periodic updates and checks of BOMs, are essential if an MRP system is to work effectively.

Inventory Records

The third major input to an MRP system is an inventory record of transactions. An **inventory record** specifies order/lot size policy and lead time and records all transactions made for parts, assemblies, and components. An **inventory transaction** occurs when there is any change in the quantity of a specific part or material. Transactions include receipt of new orders, shipment of complete orders, scrapping of defective parts, release of new orders, adjustment of due dates for scheduled receipts, cancellation of orders, and confirmation of scrap losses and returns. The inventory record includes transactions both from manufacturing within an organization and from purchasing items from external suppliers. Recording inventory transactions accurately and promptly is a critical component of an effective MRP system.

- **inventory record** a document that specifies order/lot size policy and lead time and records all transactions made for parts, assemblies, and components
- **Inventory transaction** any change in the quantity of a specific part or material

MRP PROCESSING—CREATING AN INVENTORY RECORD FOR A SINGLE ITEM

As shown in Figure 7.4, the three inputs to an MRP system (the master schedule, the bill of materials, and the inventory records) are combined to come up with a material requirements plan. This is variously called either MRP explosion or MRP processing. We will describe MRP processing using the single item record for item B100 (a bicycle wheel) in Table 7.2. We first examine the development of an inventory record for a single item at a time. Later, we will examine how multiple component items that are used to produce a single parent product are developed and linked together.

TABLE 7.2 MRP Record for Bicycle Wheel Without Planned Receipts

Item:	B100					Lot size:	200		
Description:	Bicycle wheel					Lead time:	2 weeks		
Beg. inv.:	40					Safety stock:	15		
Week	**Feb. 1**	**Feb. 8**	**Feb. 15**	**Feb. 22**	**Mar. 1**	**Mar. 8**	**Mar. 15**	**Mar. 22**	**Mar. 29**
Gross requirements	0	124	0	176	100	70	100	70	0
Scheduled receipts	0	200	0	0	0	0	0	0	0
Planned OH inventory	40	116	116	–60	–160	–230	–330	–400	–400
Planned receipts									
Planned order release									

Developing Inventory Records for Single Items

● **Planning factors** three parameters—lot size, lead time, and safety stock—that are chosen by managers utilizing the MRP system

● **Lot size** the quantity of a part to be produced or ordered when additional inventory is required

● **Lead time** the time between when an order is placed and when it is expected to arrive or be finished

● **Safety stock** excess inventory that a company holds to guard against uncertainty in demand, lead time, and supply

Every MRP record includes three **planning factors**, lot size, lead time, and safety stock, which are parameters that are chosen by managers utilizing the MRP system. **Lot size** is the quantity of a part to be produced or ordered when additional inventory is required. As shown in Table 7.2, bicycle wheels are manufactured in quantities of 200 (alternatively, they could be bought from a supplier company in this quantity). The **lead time** is the time between when an order is placed and when it is expected to arrive or be finished. The lead time for the bicycle wheel in Table 7.2 is 2 weeks. Note that it probably does not take 2 weeks of actual production time to make 200 bicycle wheels, but the lead time is usually estimated to include slack time for items that must wait until resources or equipment is available, lead time for moving or shipping the items, and other sources of variance. **Safety stock** is excess inventory that a company holds to guard against uncertainty in demand, lead time, and supply. We will examine potential causes of errors in the MRP system later in the chapter. For now, it is important to understand that planning factors are managerial choices, meaning that someone must decide on the most appropriate lot size, lead time, and safety stock for a particular item.

Also included in every MRP record is a name for each item. In Table 7.2, the part number is B100 (companies usually assign a number or letter to each part for easy tracking). The description of the part is that this is a bicycle wheel.

The planning factors for an MRP record are fairly constant—they are entered into the system once and then may not be updated or changed for months or years. In contrast, one of the primary purposes of an MRP system is to update, calculate, and track several other pieces of information on a more frequent or daily basis. Table 7.2 will be used to illustrate this.

● **Time buckets** the periods of time into which an MRP record is divided

● **Planning horizon** the time period in the future that the MRP system plans for

Time buckets are the periods of time into which an MRP record is divided. The record in Table 7.2 has buckets of 1-week duration, but time buckets can also be a month, a day, an hour, or some other time period. The **planning horizon** is the time period in the future that we are planning for—for the record in Table 7.2, the planning horizon is 9 weeks.

Beginning inventory is the amount of inventory that was physically in stock at the end of the most recent time bucket. When looking at an MRP record as shown in Table 7.2, the time bucket for week 1 is assumed to be starting on a particular date—say, midnight on Monday, February 1. Thus, beginning inventory is the amount of inventory that was physically in stock at 11:59:59 p.m. on Sunday, January 31.

Gross requirements are the total number of units of a part or material derived from all parent production plans. The gross requirements also include any spare parts that may be sold as end products. For example, the bicycle wheels in Table 7.2 are both components of the bikes they go into and spare parts that may be sold to a bicycle repair shop. To simplify the illustration, we use a new set of gross requirements in Table 7.2 that is not linked to the master schedule in Table 7.1.

Scheduled receipts are orders that have been placed but not yet received or completed. For an item manufactured by the company, a scheduled receipt is an order that has been released (i.e., started) but is still waiting in line to be processed, is waiting for additional components, is in processing, or is waiting to be moved. For an item purchased from another company, a scheduled receipt indicates that the order has been released to the supplier but that the item may still be in process at the supplier, may be in transit from the supplier, or may not yet be registered as having been received within the purchasing company. Table 7.2 shows a scheduled receipt of 200 units in the week of February 8. This indicates that the order was released on January 24 (i.e., we are currently at February 1) and is expected to be received on February 8.

Projected on-hand inventory (abbreviated as projected OH inventory) is the estimated inventory that will be available after the gross requirements have been satisfied, plus any planned or scheduled receipts for that time bucket. The beginning inventory, shown as 40 units in Table 7.3, represents the on-hand inventory that was available at the time the MRP record was computed. Projected on-hand inventory is adjusted according to every inventory transaction, including scheduled and planned receipts. For now, we are dealing only with scheduled receipts. The entry for the first

- **Beginning inventory** the amount of inventory that was physically in stock at the end of the most recent time bucket
- **Gross requirements** the total number of units of a part or material derived from all parent production plans
- **Scheduled receipts** orders that have been placed but not yet received or completed
- **Projected on-hand inventory** the estimated inventory that will be available after the gross requirements have been satisfied, plus any planned or scheduled receipts for that time bucket

TABLE 7.3 Illustration of Projected On-Hand Inventory

Week	Starting Inventory	Scheduled Receipts	Gross Requirements	Projected On-Hand Inventory
February 1	40	+0	–0	= 40
February 8	40	+200	–124	= 116
February 15	116	+0	–0	= 116
February 22	116	+0	–176	= –60
March 1	–60	+0	–100	= –160
March 8	–160	+0	–70	= –230
March 15	–230	+0	–100	= –330
March 22	–330	+0	–70	= –400
March 29	–400	+0	–0	= –400

week (February 1) is the projection for the current week, while the entries for the remaining weeks are projections for the future. These entries are calculated as

(Projected On-Hand Inventory at End of Week $t + 1$) = (Projected On-Hand Inventory at End of Week t) + (Scheduled Receipts in Week $t + 1$) – (Gross Requirements in Week $t + 1$)

As shown in the example calculation in Table 7.3, inventory becomes negative in the week of February 22. This indicates a shortage or backorder. The goal of MRP is to avoid such shortages or backorders; thus, we add in planned receipts.

● **Planned receipts** future orders that have not yet been released but are planned in order to avoid a shortage or backlog of inventory

Planned receipts are future orders that have not yet been released but are planned in order to avoid a shortage or backlog of inventory. Planned receipts are calculated as follows:

1. Projected on-hand inventory is projected/calculated until a shortage appears. A shortage occurs when planned on-hand inventory is less than the required safety stock. A planned receipt corresponding to the lot size for that item is scheduled. The planned receipt is added to projected on-hand inventory and raises this quantity to at least the required safety stock.
2. Continue with the calculation of projected on-hand inventory until another shortage occurs (see Table 7.4). Add another planned receipt.

As highlighted in Table 7.4, the addition of a planned receipt of 200 units in the week of February 22 changes the projected OH inventory from a negative 60 (–60) if no receipt is planned (Table 7.3) to a positive 140. Continuing forward, no planned receipt is necessary in the week of March 1, but planned receipts are necessary for the weeks of March 8 and March 22.

● **Planned order release** when an order must be released in order to offset for the lead time so that the order will be received when planned

A **planned order release** indicates when an order must be released in order to offset the lead time so that the order will be received when planned. The release date is determined by subtracting the lead time from the date/time when a receipt is planned. Thus, in Table 7.4, the 200-unit planned receipt for the week of Febru-

TABLE 7.4 MRP Record for Bicycle Wheel with Planned Receipts

Item:	B100				Lot size:		200	
Description:	Bicycle wheel				Lead time:		2 weeks	
Beg. inv.:	40				Safety stock:		15	

Week	Feb. 1	Feb. 8	Feb. 15	Feb. 22	Mar. 1	Mar. 8	Mar. 15	Mar. 22	Mar. 29
Gross requirements	0	124	0	176	100	70	100	70	0
Scheduled receipts	0	200	0	0	0	0	0	0	0
Planned OH inventory	40	116	116	140	40	170	70	200	200
Planned receipts				200		200		200	
Planned order release		200		200		200			

Note: The planned receipt of 200 for March 22 is entered because without this, planned OH inventory would equal 0 and thus be less than the safety stock of 15.

ary 22 must be released two weeks prior to that, on February 8. The planned order release is the date when we will either release an order to our manufacturing plant to begin production or send the order to a supplier for shipment or delivery. Note the difference between a planned and a scheduled receipt: a planned receipt is not firmly committed to and can be changed relatively easily up until the time the order is released. As soon as an order is released, it becomes a scheduled order, which is much harder to change (i.e., increase or decrease the quantity or change the lead time) because it is out of the direct control of the MRP system.

An important part of MRP records involves the assumption made about when inventory flows occur. Most companies assume that all inventory flows occur at a uniform point in time—usually at the beginning, middle, or end of a time period. For example, in Table 7.4, we assume that the scheduled receipt of 200 units will be received at the beginning of the week of February 8 and that the planned receipt of 200 units will be received at the beginning of the week of February 22. In reality, the actual receipt of materials may occur at many points within a given week, but following the convention of using a single time makes the accounting much smoother. This is similar to the use of standard times for tracking time—for example, if the time is 9 p.m. in New York City on Eastern Standard Time, we know that the time is 8 p.m. in Chicago on Central Standard Time. If one measured by the sun, the difference in times would not be exactly one hour, but the convention on time zones simplifies life by making it fairly easy to compute times in different cities.

Determining Planning Factors

As discussed earlier, every MRP record includes three planning factors: lead time, lot size, and safety stock. These are called planning factors because the decisions managers make regarding these quantities have a large impact on how well the MRP system, and by extension the entire inventory system and supply chain (including external suppliers of parts and components), functions. Managers should carefully consider how these factors are set and should periodically reexamine how well they are working.

Lead Time

Lead time is an estimate of the time between releasing an order and receiving that order. Accuracy in lead times is very important because early or late orders can greatly affect other items and production schedules through excessive inventory holding costs or shortage, stockout, and expediting costs.

For purchased items, the lead time is the estimated time for the supplier to prepare or produce the order plus shipping time. For example, when ordering the bicycle wheel in Table 7.4, if this is a part that is bought from a supplier, the two-week lead time might consist of one week of production time at the supplier plus one week of shipping time. Lead times are usually assigned based on past history and discussion with the supplier; often the lead time is agreed to in a purchasing contract. It is important that lead times be tracked over time. If a supplier is consistently late or early, either the lead time should be changed or a discussion with the supplier on how to improve lead times should be conducted.

For items that are manufactured or produced within the company, the lead time must take into account a number of factors, including

- Setup time
- Processing time
- Materials handling time
- Waiting time

Every step that a part follows in the manufacturing process involves each of these times; thus, an estimate must be made for each. Typically, estimates for the first three (setup, processing, and materials handling time) are easier to make than an estimate for waiting time. This is because waiting time (i.e., time when an order is not being processed or moved) usually is highly variable. Waiting time tends to be different depending on whether a company uses a make-to-stock or make-to-order strategy, as well as the policy for releasing orders to the manufacturing floor. It is not uncommon for an order to spend 95 percent or more of its time waiting to be processed. For example, the bicycle wheels in Table 7.4 might require only 30 minutes of setup time, 400 minutes of processing time (200 wheels per order times 2 minutes per wheel), and 5 minutes of handling time, for a total time of 435 minutes. However, the 2-week lead time is based on the estimated amount of waiting time (assuming a 40-hour production week, the lead time is 2 weeks * 40 hours/week * 60 minutes/hour = 4,800 minutes, and the waiting time is 4,800 – 435 minutes = 4,365 minutes). In this example, the bicycle tires spend over 90.9 percent of the lead time waiting in a queue (i.e., 4,365 minutes/4,800 minutes).

Lot Size

The lot size rule determines the size of the order placed, and by extension the timing of orders. Every item must have a lot size rule assigned. Lot size rules are important because they determine the frequency of setups and the inventory holding costs for an item. We describe three types of lot size rules: fixed order quantity, periodic order quantity, and lot for lot.

● **Fixed order quantity (FOQ)** a lot size rule with a constant order size where the same quantity is ordered every time

Fixed Order Quantity **Fixed order quantity (FOQ)** lot sizes involve a constant order size, where the same quantity is ordered every time. Often the quantity is determined by equipment capacity, such as when a certain machine has a capacity limit. For example, if the bread-baking oven at a Subway restaurant has a capacity of 80 loaves (8 trays * 10 loaves per tray), then it makes sense to make the order quantity 80 in order to fully utilize the oven. Other reasons for choosing a certain FOQ are to mimic the EOQ (discussed in Chapter 6) or to make planning consistent. For purchased items, an FOQ may be chosen in order to receive a quantity discount, to minimize shipping costs, or to reach a minimum purchase quantity. For example, the lot size for buying screws is likely to be a multiple of the number of screws in one box; thus, if a box contains 500 screws, the FOQ will be a multiple such as 500, 1,000, or 1,500. Table 7.4 illustrates the FOQ rule. If an item's gross requirements within a given period are very large, then the order quantity becomes an integer multiple of the FOQ. This is shown in Table 7.5, which is identical to Table 7.4 except that the gross requirements in the week of March 8 and the corresponding planned receipt have changed. The planned order release is 400 (2 * 200) in the week of March 8.

● **Periodic order quantity (POQ)** a a lot size rule with a variable lot size designed to order exactly the amount required for a specified period of time

Periodic Order Quantity **Periodic order quantity (POQ)** lot sizes are variable and are designed to order exactly the amount required for a specified period of time. Specifically, the POQ is

POQ Lot Size to Arrive in Period t = (Gross Requirements for P Periods, Including Period t) – (Projected On-Hand Inventory at End of Period $t - 1$) + (Safety Stock)

or

$$Q_t = \sum_{t}^{t+p-1} GR_i - I_{t-1} + SS \qquad \text{(Equation 1)}$$

This is the amount that will exactly cover P periods of gross requirements and finish with exactly the amount of safety stock required. Table 7.6 shows the MRP record from Table 7.4 with the lot size rule changed to $P = 3$. This means that

TABLE 7.5 MRP Record for Bicycle Wheel with Fixed Order Quantity

Item:	B100	Lot size:	200
Description:	Bicycle wheel	Lead time:	2 weeks
Beg. inv.:	40	Safety stock:	15

Week	Feb. 1	Feb. 8	Feb. 15	Feb. 22	Mar. 1	Mar. 8	Mar. 15	Mar. 22	Mar. 29
Gross requirements	0	124	0	176	100	260	100	70	0
Scheduled receipts	0	200	0	0	0	0	0	0	0
Planned OH inventory	40	116	116	140	40	180	80	210	210
Planned receipts				200		400		200	
Planned order release		200		400		200			

when we need to place an order, we should order enough for three weeks' gross requirements. As in the previous example, the first planned receipt is due in the week of February 22; otherwise, planned on-hand inventory will be less than the required amount of safety stock. Thus, we plan a receipt of

$$POQ_{Feb22} = \text{(Gross Requirements for Weeks of Feb. 22, Mar. 1, and Mar. 8)} - \text{(Inventory at End of Feb. 15 Week)} + \text{(Safety Stock)}$$

$$= (176 + 100 + 70) - 116 + 15 = 245 \text{ units}$$

TABLE 7.6 MRP Record for Bicycle Wheel with $P = 3$ Lot Size

Item:	B100	Lot size:	$P = 3$
Description:	Bicycle wheel	Lead time:	2 weeks
Beg. inv.:	40	Safety stock:	15

Week	Feb. 1	Feb. 8	Feb. 15	Feb. 22	Mar. 1	Mar. 8	Mar. 15	Mar. 22	Mar. 29
Gross requirements	0	124	0	176	100	70	100	70	0
Scheduled receipts	0	200	0	0	0	0	0	0	0
Planned OH inventory	40	116	116	185	85	15	85	15	15
Planned receipts				245			170		
Planned order release		245			170				

The second planned receipt is for the week of March 15, for a quantity of (100 + 70 + 0) – 15 + 15 = 170 units.

It is important to note that a $P = 3$ lot size does not mean that you must order every 3 weeks; instead, it means that if you order, then you should order enough for 3 weeks. For example, if the gross requirements were 0 in the week of March 15 and were 100 in the week of March 29, then there would *not* be an order in the week of March 15, but there would be an order in the week of March 22. This situation is illustrated in Table 7.7.

Generally, periodic lot sizes are chosen to be a convenient time period—e.g., every two weeks, every three weeks, once a month, or some similar interval. Another method is to take the EOQ (see Chapter 6) and divide it by the average demand per period. In other words, express the lot size in terms of desired periods of supply rounded to the nearest integer.

● **Lot for lot (L4L)** a lot size rule that is a special case of the periodic order quantity with the period equal to 1

Lot for Lot (L4L) **Lot for lot (L4L)** lot sizes are a special case of the periodic order quantity with the period equal to 1. The primary objective is to minimize inventory levels by ordering only what is needed. The L4L lot size is calculated as

L4L Lot Size to Arrive in Period t = (Gross Requirements in Period t) – (Projected On-Hand Inventory at End of Period $t - 1$) + (Safety Stock)

or

$$Q_t = GR_t - I_{t-1} + SS \qquad \text{(Equation 2)}$$

Using a L4L order size means that the planned on-hand inventory should exactly equal the safety stock level at the end of each period.

Table 7.8 shows the results when a L4L rule is used for the bicycle wheel in Tables 7.4 and 7.5. The first order is still needed during the week of February 22, but that order quantity is calculated as

TABLE 7.7 Alternative MRP Record

Item:	B100				Lot size:		$P = 3$	
Description:	Bicycle wheel				Lead time:		2 weeks	
Beg. inv.:	40				Safety stock:		15	

Week	Feb. 1	Feb. 8	Feb. 15	Feb. 22	Mar. 1	Mar. 8	Mar. 15	Mar. 22	Mar. 29
Gross requirements	0	124	0	176	100	70	0	70	100
Scheduled receipts	0	200	0	0	0	0	0	0	0
Planned OH inventory	40	116	116	185	85	15	15	115	15
Planned receipts				245				170	
Planned order release		245				170			

TABLE 7.8 MRP Record with L4L order

Item:	B100	Lot size:	L4L
Description:	Bicycle wheel	Lead time:	2 weeks
Beg. inv.:	40	Safety stock:	15

Week	Feb. 1	Feb. 8	Feb. 15	Feb. 22	Mar. 1	Mar. 8	Mar. 15	Mar. 22	Mar. 29
Gross requirements	0	124	0	176	100	70	0	70	100
Scheduled receipts	0	200	0	0	0	0	0	0	0
Planned OH inventory	40	116	116	15	15	15	15	15	15
Planned receipts				75	100	70		70	100
Planned order release		75	100	70		70	100		

L4L Lot Size to Arrive in Period t = (Gross Requirements in Period t) – (Projected On-Hand Inventory at End of Period $t - 1$) + (Safety Stock)

$$L4L_{Feb22} = 176 - 116 + 15 = 75$$

Additional orders will be planned for receipt on March 1, March 8, March 22, and March 29.

Advantages/Disadvantages of Lot Size Rules The choice of lot size rule has a large impact on the efficacy of the MRP system. Lot size choice affects inventory and setup/order costs and also has an impact on capacity availability. To illustrate, let us examine the average on-hand inventory and the number of orders placed for each rule. Table 7.9 provides a summary of the average OH inventory during the weeks of February 22 to March 29 using three different rules for the same part.

TABLE 7.9 Comparison of Lot Size Rules

Lot Size Rule	Table with Original Data	Average OH Inventory	Number of Orders
FOQ = 200	7.4	(140 + 40 + 170 + 70 + 200 + 200)/6 = 136.67	3
POQ = 3	7.6	(185 + 85 + 15 + 85 + 15 + 15)/6 = 66.67	2
L4L	7.8	(15 + 15 + 15 + 15 + 15 + 15)/6 = 15	5

The L4L rule always has the lowest average inventory because of the ability to order exactly what is needed for a single period, but this comes at the cost of more frequent orders. Each rule has its advantages and disadvantages:

1. The FOQ rule has the highest average inventory because its fixed nature creates inventory remnants. For example, in Table 7.4, a planned receipt for 200 units is scheduled in the week of February 22, but this results in excess inventory or remnants of 140 – 15 (safety stock). In the worst case, if planned on-hand inventory was going to be 14 units without an order being placed for February 22, we would have to order 200 units, resulting in remnants of 199. FOQ lot sizes benefit from the predictability and ability to fit to a fixed unit of capacity, but generally increase inventory. The added inventory does lend some stability by protecting against unexpected scrap losses, late orders, inaccurate inventory records, and changing gross requirements.
2. The POQ rule reduces the amount of OH inventory by matching gross requirements with planned receipts. In Table 7.6, the planned OH inventory in the week of March 8 is 15 units, or exactly the safety stock desired—there are no remnants.
3. The L4L rule always minimizes inventory, but also requires more frequent setups/orders. This rule works well for expensive items and for items with low setup/ordering costs.

Both the POQ and L4L rules are prone to instability—if the gross requirements for a parent item change, then the lot size may change. This can lead to shortages of component items as such changes ripple through multiple levels of a BOM. This type of MRP uncertainty is a major problem and must be watched carefully.

Safety Stock

On first thought, it would seem that an MRP inventory system should not require safety stock. After all, computers don't make "mistakes." Unfortunately, this is not completely true; there are several reasons why some amount of safety stock is necessary. First, there may be bottlenecks or blockages that prevent orders from being completed on a timely basis. Second, quality problems often arise where an order will be only 95 percent filled. Third, humans may enter incorrect information into the system. Fourth, there is variability in demand, and the master schedule is made to match forecasts. When these forecasts are significantly off, the system may be short of some types of parts and have an excess of others. In short, just because the system is automated is no guarantee that it works perfectly. Holding extra safety stock to cover these unpredictable occurrences is one way in which managers can buffer against uncertainty.

● **MRP nervousness** a situation in MRP planning where a change at one part level ripples down to affect lower-level parts

Another cause of inventory shortages is **MRP nervousness** in items with multiple levels of component parts. A net change at one part level can ripple down to lower-level parts. This is one of the more challenging aspects of managing an MRP system, and it will be examined in more detail later in the chapter.

Managers have a variety of methods for managing uncertainty with regard to inventory amounts. A vital first step is to identify the activities that are most variable or limited in terms of capacity, then to monitor these activities closely for early signs of problems. Alternatively, additional safety stock can be carried; this is particularly useful for end items that have highly variable demand and for lower-level items that are inexpensive and low cost. A third approach involves using safety lead time, i.e., inflating the expected lead time in order to allow a margin for error. In all of these approaches, managers must balance the cost of carrying extra inventory against the protection provided.

MULTIPLE-LEVEL PROCESSING AND OUTPUT GENERATION

MRP systems provide a wealth of data, including reports, schedules, and notices, to help managers control the flow of inventory and ensure efficient and accurate operations. It is important to note that these systems are run by computers and process/generate a huge amount of data. The goal of these systems is to make the processing of data and information simple and easy for the humans who use the system. The best systems are designed to remove the need for extensive human involvement, but also to clearly highlight the points at which human involvement is necessary or beneficial. In this section, we show how the inventory records for the component parts that make up a single end item are developed and linked to each other. We also examine the data and outputs generated via an MRP system.

MRP Explosion

MRP explosion is the process of translating MRP inputs into a plan that specifies the required quantities and timing of all subassemblies, components, and raw materials required to produce parent items. An MRP record is generated for every item or part that a company works with. The gross requirements for an item are derived from three sources:

MRP explosion the process of translating MRP inputs into a plan that specifies required quantities and timing of all subassemblies, components, and raw materials required to produce parent items

- The MS for immediate parents that are end items
- The planned order releases for parents that are below the MS level
- Any other requirements, typically for spare parts

We will use the BOM from Figure 7.5 to illustrate MRP explosion. This BOM is repeated in Figure 7.8, with the items in blue denoting the parts for which we

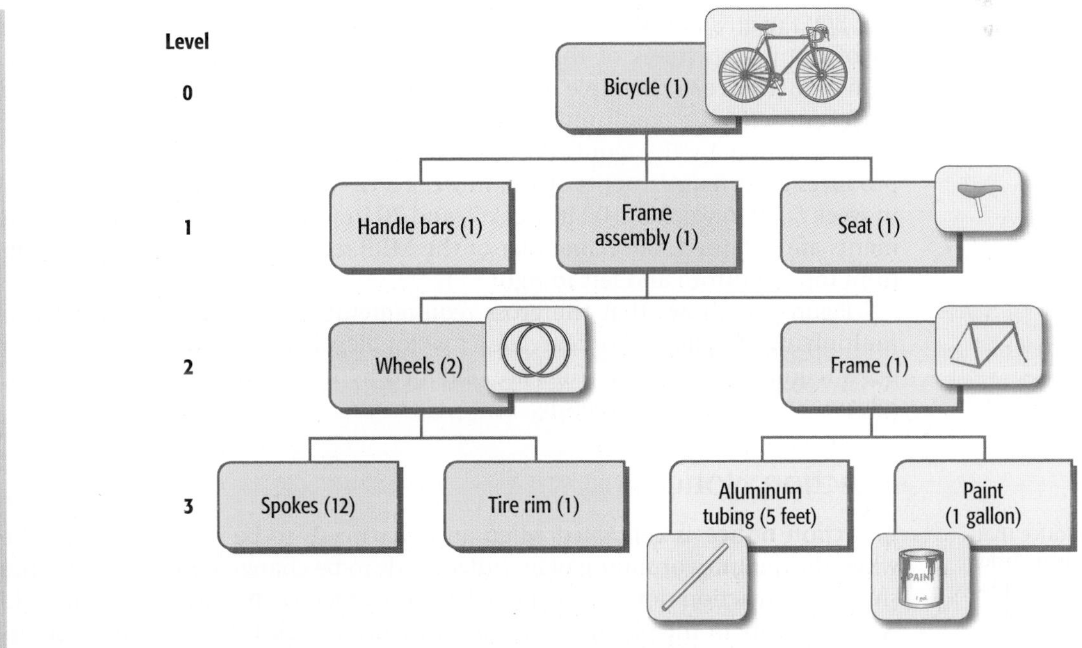

FIGURE 7.8 Bill of Materials for a Speedy Road Bicycle

will show MRP records (we exclude some parts in order to make the example easy to follow). For every bicycle produced, we need 1 set of handlebars, 1 frame assembly, and 1 seat. For every frame assembly, 2 wheels are required. In turn, 12 spokes and 1 tire rim are required for every wheel.

The questions we want to answer are:

- How many frame assemblies/wheels/spokes/tire rims do we need?
- When do we need them?

To answer these questions, we will explode the BOM by working from top to bottom. Figure 7.9 shows the end results. The first step is to derive the gross requirements for the highest-level items. In this BOM, the bicycle is the only Level 0 item, the frame assembly is a Level 1 item, wheels are a Level 2 item, and spokes and tire rim are both Level 3 items. We work from the highest level (Level 0) down to the lowest level (Level 3 in this case). The gross requirements for the frame assembly are derived by multiplying the master schedule for the Speedy Road Bicycle by 1. The quantity of 45 units in week 1 of the master schedule means that all of the parts necessary to produce 45 bicycles must be available at the beginning of that week. Although this is not shown in Figure 7.9, there is a lead time for assembling the bicycle from these parts, so the 45 bicycles will not be ready until sometime after the beginning of week 1 (we will see an example of lead times for master schedules later in this chapter). We obtain the gross requirements for the frame assembly by multiplying 1 * the master schedule quantities. Thus, 45 units of the frame assembly will be needed in week 1, 62 in week 3, 88 in week 5, 50 in week 6, 35 in week 7, 50 in week 8, and 35 in week 9. Once the gross requirements are obtained, the planning factors (lot size, lead time, and safety stock) and inventory records (beginning inventory and scheduled receipts) are used to calculate the completed MRP record for the frame assembly.

Following completion of the records for the frame assembly, all of the parent items for the bicycle wheel have been processed. In this case, the bicycle wheel is used in only one parent item, but we will see later that a single part can be used in many different products (e.g., multiple bike models) and in several places on one BOM (e.g., a bolt that is used in several places on a single bike). In this case, *all* of the parent items of that part must be processed before processing that item—we will see an example of this later. The gross requirements for the bicycle wheel are derived by multiplying the bottom row (planned order release) for the frame assembly by the required quantity—in this case, 2 wheels per frame. This produces gross requirements of 124 in week 2 (2 * 62), 176 in week 4 (2* 88), 100 in week 5, 70 in week 6, 100 in week 7, and 70 in week 8. Once the gross requirements are obtained, the remainder of the MRP record is completed by working from top to bottom and left to right.

Figure 7.8 shows that the gross requirements for spokes are calculated by multiplying the planned order release row for bicycle wheels by 12. Similarly, the gross requirements for tire rims are obtained by multiplying the planned order release row for bicycle wheels by 1.

Action Notices

● **Action notice** a notice that is generated when an order needs to be released or placed or when the quantity or timing of an order needs to be changed

An **action notice** is generated when an order needs to be released or placed or when the quantity or timing of an order needs to be changed. In Figure 7.9, there should be an action notice issued to release the order for 390 tire rims because this is the quantity in the planned order release row in week 1. Likewise, there should be an action notice to release the order for 2,500 spokes. As soon as these orders are released, the planned order release changes status (becomes 0) and a scheduled receipt in the same amount is recorded with the lead time added to the planned re-

Master Production Schedule – Speedy Road Bicycle

45	0	62	0	88	50	35	50	35

Item: A130 · Description: Frame assembly · Beginning inventory: 20 · Lot size: L4L · Lead time: 1 week · Safety stock: 20

1 frame assembly for each bicycle

Week	1	2	3	4	5	6	7	8	9
Gross requirements	45	0	62	0	88	50	35	50	35
Scheduled receipts	45								
Planned OH inventory	20	20	20	20	20	20	20	20	20
Planned receipts			62		88	50	35	50	35
Planned order release		62		88	50	35	50	35	

Item: B100 · Description: Bicycle wheel · Beginning inventory: 40 · Lot size: 200 · Lead time: 2 weeks · Safety stock: 15

2 wheels for each frame assembly = 2 x 62

Week	1	2	3	4	5	6	7	8	9
Gross requirements	0	124	0	176	100	70	100	70	0
Scheduled receipts	0	200	0	0	0	0	0	0	0
Planned OH inventory	40	116	116	140	40	170	70	200	200
Planned receipts				200		200		200	
Planned order release		200		200		200			

Item: z125 · Description: Spokes · Beginning inventory: 200 · Lot size: 2500 · Lead time: 3 weeks · Safety stock: 100

12 spokes for each wheel = 12 x 200

Week	1	2	3	4	5	6	7	8	9
Gross requirements		2400		2400		2400			
Scheduled receipts		2500							
Planned OH inventory	200	300	300	400	400	500			
Planned receipts				2500		2500			
Planned order release	2500		2500						

Item: D200 · Description: Tire rim · Beginning inventory: 220 · Lot size: P = 3 · Lead time: 3 weeks · Safety stock: 10

1 tire rim for each wheel

Week	1	2	3	4	5	6	7	8	9
Gross requirements		200		200		200			
Scheduled receipts									
Planned OH inventory	220	20	20	210	210	210	210	210	210
Planned receipts				390					
Planned order release	390								

FIGURE 7.9 Multiple-Level MRP for Parts in Blue in Figure 7.8

lease time. Action notices can be printed and mailed to a supplier or printed and placed in a queue within a manufacturing plant. Alternatively, action notices may involve sending an electronic order and calling it to the attention of the planner using the computer system. The vast majority of action notices are handled electronically in this manner, with little need for human intervention. For most transactions, the computer does the calculations and releases the order. Humans can access whatever information they need, but they do not need to actually push a button for the order to be released. In contrast, an action notice may occur if an item is late or early or if an incorrect quantity is ordered. Suppose that the

Horseradish production.

200 units of wheels scheduled to be received in week 2 were delayed and were not received until week 3. This would be a problem because then there would not be enough wheels available to produce the 62 frame assemblies that are scheduled to be started in week 2. In this case, an action notice would alert the planner to the problem. The planner might go to the work area where the bicycle wheels were being produced and determine that the delay was due to the order for wheels being tenth in line to be produced. The planner might then expedite the order by asking the employee at the work station to move the wheel order ahead in line (say, from tenth to fourth), thus getting the scheduled receipt back on time in week 2.

MRP as a Dynamic System

One of the most important things to understand about MRP is that it is a dynamic system—as orders are received, forecasts or the master schedule is updated, and so on; the MRP records are also changed. Typically MRP

BEST PRACTICES IN OPERATIONS MANAGEMENT

A Spicy Challenge for Horseradish Planning

On first thought, producing something like horseradish sauce shouldn't be that difficult. The annual consumption in the United States is 24 million pounds of horseradish roots to prepare 6 million gallons of horseradish sauce. Silver Spring Gardens, one of the leading manufacturers of horseradish, mustards, and other food products, faced some challenges. The company has two plants, one that makes horseradish sauce and mustard to order, and another that makes sauces, syrups, jams, and jellies. While the end products are different, the two plants share many of the same raw ingredients and suppliers/farmers. The production planners at each plant had to look at sales and inventory levels and prepare production orders manually. Production orders and requirements were exchanged between the two plants over the telephone, resulting in numerous miscommunications, mistakes, and inefficiencies.

In addition to standard production planning, the company needs to be able to track the ingredients from a specific batch of production backward to the source (i.e., a particular farm or shipment) and forward to the distribution center or retailer. When it must issue a recall of a product for health or safety reasons, the company is required by the Food and Drug Administration to be able to locate the shipped product within two hours. In addition, Controller Dan Kelm notes that "shelf life management was another important consideration. Because of the expiration date on our products, it is very important to properly rotate stock to get the oldest product out first."

The solution to these problems involved installing an MRP system, with additional components to track financial, sales, logistics, and plant maintenance data. The result was much more accurate and responsive inventory levels, as well as a substantial cost reduction. The MRP system helped make the entire production process less spicy!

Source: "Software Takes the Sting out of Horseradish Production," *Food Engineering* 75, no. 4 (2003): 78.

records are updated using one of two approaches. A **periodic update** involves collecting all new or updated information and processing it once a week or once a day. A **net change update** makes changes as soon as they occur. Twenty or thirty years ago, it was common to have periodic updates because a large amount of computer power was necessary to perform the thousands of calculations necessary for a company with hundreds of products and parts. Typically, the MRP system would be set to process updates late on a Friday or Saturday night. Today, your laptop computer is probably more powerful than a mainframe computer in 1980, so computing time is not a major issue. Some companies still use periodic updates because they provide greater stability, and it is easy to know when things are going to change. In contrast, net change updates are much more responsive to changes but may be disruptive in some cases.

● **Periodic update** an approach to updating that involves collecting all new or updated information and processing it once a week or once a day

● **Net change update** an approach to updating that makes changes as soon as they occur

Figure 7.10 provides an illustration of how updates work by updating the MRP records from Figure 7.9 after a week has gone by. In other words, Figure 7.9 was planned at the beginning of week 1, and it is now the beginning of week 2. The dark blue shading for week 1 of Figure 7.10 illustrates that this week is over. All of the planned order releases have been released; thus, the planned receipt of 2,500 Z125 spokes in week 4 has become a scheduled receipt for week 4, and the planned receipt of 390 D200 tire rims in week 4 has become a scheduled receipt for week 4. The only other change is the addition of a 100-unit order for the MS of the Speedy Road Bicycle in week 10 (shown in orange). This single change ripples down through all the lower-level parts as shaded in green and connected by the red arrows. Although this change does not appear to cause any problems (because it doesn't require a change to any already scheduled receipts—just to planned receipts that have not had their orders released yet), it may affect capacity; thus, we want to estimate its effect on capacity.

Figure 7.10 also illustrates the effects of MRP nervousness—one change at a high level ripples down to affect a number of lower-level parts. We changed the MS in week 10, but that one change resulted in a new planned order release for Z125 spokes in week 4. What would have happened if the MS quantity for 50 speedy road bicycles in week 6 had changed to 75? This would result in orders for items at the lowest levels (Z125 and D200) that are impossible to fill because their planned order release date was in the past. This is why MRP systems typically have a planning horizon that is as long as or longer than the longest lead time for all parts in the BOM.

Capacity Planning

While the steps underlying the processing of MRP records are logical and systematic, there is a major assumption that is critical to remember. The records developed *assume* that there is sufficient capacity available to produce the planned orders. This assumption is necessary to allow the development of inventory records, but it is often untrue. Individual machines or work centers will frequently have substantial capacity shortages and backlogs of work in process waiting to be completed. Consider the situation if there was a specific machine that was used to produce bicycle wheels and several other parts. If there was a capacity shortage such that several different orders were waiting in a queue at this machine, then the lead time for item B100 (bicycle wheels) in Figure 7.10 would probably increase above 2 weeks. This is one of the reasons that lead times for dependent demand items are typically padded with safety lead time (e.g., the production time to produce 200 bicycle wheels might be only 4 hours, but the lead time used is 2 weeks). When there are substantial problems with capacity, the MRP output must be adjusted.

The MRP system does not include capacity constraints when developing the production plan, instead assuming that whatever is needed can be produced.

Master Production Schedule – Speedy Road Bicycle

45	0	62	0	88	50	35	50	35	100

Item: A130 — Lot size: L4L
Description: Frame assembly — Lead time: 1 week
Beginning inventory: 20 — Safety stock: 20
1 frame assembly for each bicycle

Week	1	2	3	4	5	6	7	8	9	10
Gross requirements	45	0	62	0	88	50	35	50	35	100
Scheduled receipts	45									
Planned OH inventory	20	20	20	20	20	20	20	20	20	20
Planned receipts			62		88	50	35	50	35	100
Planned order release		62		88	50	35	50	35	100	

Item: B100 — Lot size: 200
Description: Bicycle wheel — Lead time: 2 weeks
Beginning inventory: 40 — Safety stock: 15
2 wheels for each frame assembly = 2 x 62

Week	1	2	3	4	5	6	7	8	9	10
Gross requirements	0	124	0	176	100	70	100	70	200	
Scheduled receipts	0	200	0	0	0	0	0	0	0	
Planned OH inventory	40	116	116	140	40	170	70	200	200	
Planned receipts				200		200		200	200	
Planned order release		200		200		200	200			

Item: z125 — Lot size: 2500
Description: Spokes — Lead time: 3 weeks
Beginning inventory: 200 — Safety stock: 100
12 spokes for each wheel = 12 x 200

Week	1	2	3	4	5	6	7	8	9	10
Gross requirements		2400		2400		2400	2400			
Scheduled receipts		2500		2500						
Planned OH inventory	200	300	300	400	400	500	600	600	600	600
Planned receipts						2500	2500			
Planned order release	2500		2500	2500						

Item: D200 — Lot size: P = 3
Description: Tire rim — Lead time: 2 weeks
Beginning inventory: 220 — Safety stock: 10
1 tire rim for each wheel

Week	1	2	3	4	5	6	7	8	9	10
Gross requirements		200		200		200	200			
Scheduled receipts				390						
Planned OH inventory	220	20	20	210	210	10	10	10	10	
Planned receipts							200			
Planned order release	390				200					

FIGURE 7.10 Illustration of a Rolling MRP Schedule
An update of Figure 7.9 one week later.

This can be a problem if a single machine, person, or resource becomes overloaded and falls behind. A critical role for managers is to evaluate the production plan developed by the MRP system and assess where capacity constraints might pose problems. Notice that we say *where* rather than *if*. With the increasing leanness of most production systems, most systems are operating increasingly close to 100 percent of capacity. This can save substantial amounts of money by fully utilizing resources, but also risks major problems if there are large backlogs and capacity imbalances. There are three approaches for managing capacity and ensuring that the MRP plan is feasible; for simplicity, we focus on the first, capacity requirements planning:

- Capacity requirements planning
- Finite capacity scheduling
- Input/output reports

Capacity requirements planning is the process of determining short-range capacity requirements. Short range generally refers to the next one to three months. Inputs include the planned order releases generated from the MRP system, workloads at each work center/piece of equipment in the manufacturing plant, routing information, and job setup/processing times. For each work center, the system generates a load report that shows required capacity and available capacity and highlights any underloads or overloads. If a work center has a substantial overload (underloads are also a problem, but generally are not as critical), then managers can take a number of steps to address the issue. The master schedule can be changed by moving order quantities forward or backward in time, by changing the size of orders, by changing the routing of parts, or by changing safety stock requirements. Changing production schedules can become very challenging because one change may have unintended consequences in another area of the plant.

● **Capacity requirements planning** the process of determining short-range capacity requirements based on a tentative MRP plan

The master schedule and the MRP plan are usually generated primarily by looking at what is needed to support sales, rather than what is possible. Once capacity requirements are estimated, the MRP plan often needs to be changed to address capacity limitations. Alternatively, management can add overtime or subcontracting in areas where there are capacity shortages. In short, capacity requirements planning often involves several iterations between the master schedule/MRP plan and the estimation of capacity loads. During each iteration, the master schedule and MRP plan are changed in order to decrease the amount and number of underloads and overloads. Once an MRP plan without major capacity problems is developed, then the first few periods of the MRP plan may be *frozen,* meaning that no changes can then be made to that portion of the schedule. Figure 7.11 presents an overview of the capacity planning process. Note that it is often necessary to go through several iterations of the MRP explosion/capacity planning cycle in order to arrive at a feasible schedule. Even then, this is a rough estimate, and there are likely to be some small capacity shortages and bottlenecks. Overall, this process works pretty well.

An important tool for capacity planning is the **load report**, which is a report for a department or work center that projects already scheduled and expected future capacity requirements against capacity availability. An example of a load report is shown in Table 7.10. The weekly capacity for each of the four grinding machines in department B is 80 hours per week (2 shifts * 40 hours per shift). The load report shows the *planned* hours of work, estimated from the MRP system for all future orders that will need to be routed through that grinding machine. The actual hours represent the existing queue of work that is already scheduled to be completed at the grinding machine (i.e., scheduled receipts). Combining these requirements provides the total hours for each of the four grinding machines. The load report highlights where demand will exceed available capacity. Based on this report, the manager for this department might (a) schedule some overtime for the weeks where there is insufficient capacity, (b) make a change to the MRP records to distribute demand more evenly, or (c) change the routing of some items.

● **Load report** a report for a department or work center that projects already scheduled and expected future capacity requirements against capacity availability

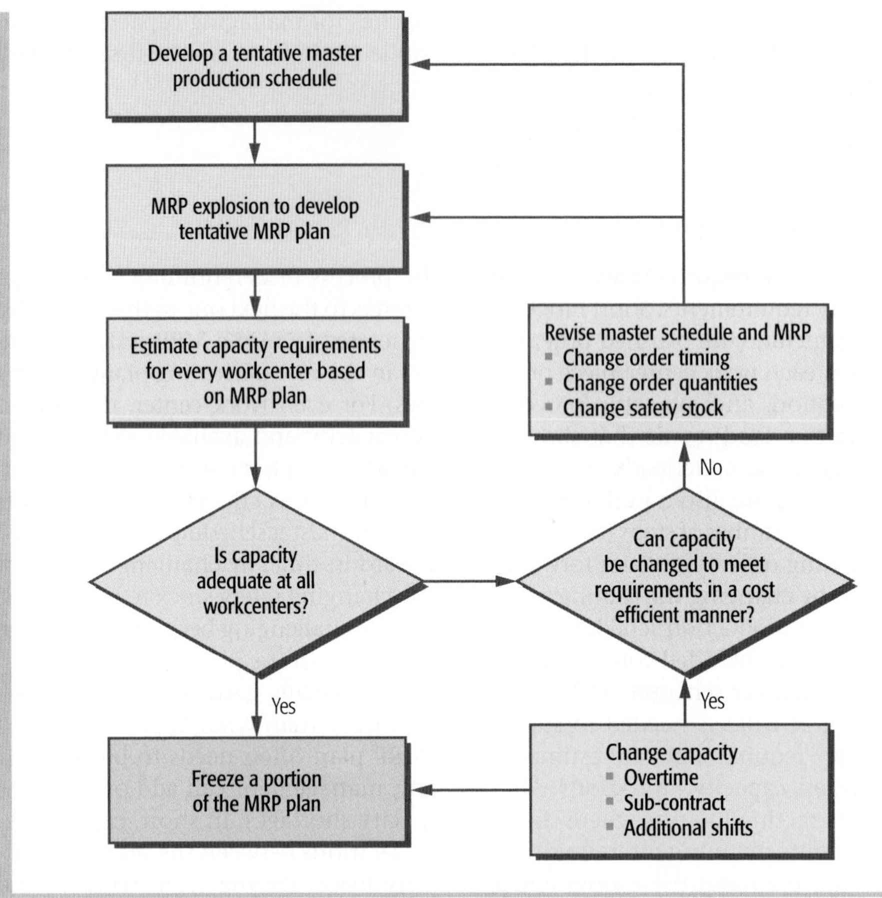

FIGURE 7.11 MRP with Capacity Planning Requirements

TABLE 7.10 Example of a Load Report

Date: Week 13 Department B, Grinder station Capacity: 80 hours/ week per machine		13	14	15	16
Machine 100	Planned hours	25	60	65	95
	Actual hours	50	30	10	0
	Total hours	75	90	75	95
Machine 200	Planned hours	60	30	40	70
	Actual hours	42	38	12	0
	Total hours	102	68	52	70
Machine 300	Planned hours	50	50	70	90
	Actual hours	30	20	25	0
	Total hours	80	70	95	90
Machine 400	Planned hours	60	50	35	75
	Actual hours	15	35	40	10
	Total hours	75	85	75	85

STRATEGIES FOR DEPENDENT DEMAND INVENTORY

The bulk of this chapter has been devoted to defining basic concepts and illustrating computational methods. It is important to develop an understanding and appreciation of several more strategic, less tactical issues. First, the early systems that allowed automatization of MRP in the 1970s have grown substantially in complexity and capability, so that the functions that form the core of a company's operations have been built into ERP systems. Second, while MRP started out as primarily a technique for manufacturing companies, the concepts and tools can and often are applied to service businesses. Finally, there are several important keys to making MRP work effectively. Each of these is examined here.

Evolution of MRP to Enterprise Resource Planning

While material requirements planning is limited in scope to physical products in a manufacturing environment, the basic techniques and tools have been expanded over time. **Manufacturing resource planning (MRP II)** is a system that links the basic MRP system to other company systems, including finance, accounting, purchasing, and logistics. The driver for MRP II was the increasing capabilities of computer hardware in the late 1970s and early 1980s. MRP II employed a common database and an integrated platform where sales, inventory, and purchasing transactions were updated in both inventory and accounting applications. This was a substantial improvement over the stand-alone systems that many companies possessed at the time. Two substantial problems with using separate stand-alone systems were the duplication of data entry (the same data often had to be entered multiple times into multiple systems) and errors in communication caused by mistakes when reentering data. MRP II provided an integrated system that reduced data entry and provided relatively quick access to data.

● **Manufacturing resource planning (MRP II)** a system that links the basic MRP system to other company systems, including finance, accounting, purchasing, and logistics

The primary limitation of MRP II was the manual linkage between operational activities and matching accounting transactions. For example, while the MRP II system tracked the movement of inbound and outbound inventory, as well as production from raw materials to finished goods and shipping/receiving transactions, it did not reflect the accounting implications of these transactions in the general ledger. Accounting transactions were typically summarized and applied to the general ledger at the end of the month. This led to a mismatch between operational and accounting data. To address this limitation, MRP II has in turn evolved into **enterprise resource planning (ERP)**, which provides a complete linkage of all functional areas of a business. ERP allows manufacturing to see new orders as soon as marketing or sales enters them into the system. In turn, sales can continuously track the status of an order. Sourcing has visibility into the materials that manufacturing needs, and distribution has data on when and where materials and orders need to be delivered. Accounting gets all financial data as soon as the relevant transaction occurs. In the early 1990s, several software companies offered packages that integrated substantially all areas of a business. The market position of the leading companies by 1999 was as follows:

● **Enterprise resource planning (ERP)** a system that provides a complete linkage of all functional areas of a business

- JD Edwards had more than 4,700 customers in over 100 countries. Note that in this case a customer is not an individual, but an entire business organization or business unit.
- Oracle had over 40,000 customers in the world and 16,000 in the United States.
- PeopleSoft was the software of choice for more than 50 percent of the human resources market.

- SAP was the world's largest interenterprise software company, employing more than 20,000 people in more than 50 countries.
- Baan had installed more than 2,800 systems at approximately 4,800 sites around the world.

By January 2005, mergers and acquisitions among this group of five had left the industry with two major players: Oracle and SAP.[1]

Service Resource Planning

Planning and control for manufacturing firms is focused primarily on tangible goods, whereas services generally require more of a mix of intangible and tangible goods. Yet the concept of dependent demand also applies to services where the demand for a service is based on the demand for a parent item.

Airlines plan for supporting items such as snacks, drinks, napkins, magazines, and fuel based on the master plan or flight schedule. Resources such as

TECHNOLOGY IN OPERATIONS MANAGEMENT

ERP—The Underpinnings of Under Armour's Success

When Kevin Plank founded Under Armour in 1996 with a single product—a T-shirt that provided compression and wicked perspiration off the skin—he had little need for an ERP system to manage production, distribution, and sales. Yet the marketplace embraced Under Armour's products for keeping athletes cool, dry, and light during practices, workouts, and games. Sales increased rapidly to $20 million in 2001, to $430 million in 2006, and to $606 million in 2007. Soon after the company went public with a very successful IPO in November 2005, supply chain executives recognized the need to invest in an ERP system to support its growing line of over 100 products in numerous sizes and colors, retail sales in numerous countries, and the increased compliance with federal regulations required for a publicly traded company.

The company chose SAP's Apparel and Footwear Solution and implemented the system within an eight-month time frame. More than 120 Under Armour employees were involved in the implementation, which occurred while the company was growing its business by 40 percent. The implementation has provided key benefits and capabilities that were previously lacking. Sales and customer service representatives now know not only inventory is on hand, but what inventory is "available to promise," or scheduled for production but not yet committed to a particular customer. This is important because while individual athletes are the ultimate end customers, Under Armour's direct customers are typically big-box retailers such as Sports Authority and Dick's Sporting Goods. These retailers place large orders for multiple SKUs in several sizes and colors, and getting a full rather than a partial order is a significant advantage to their supply chain operations. The system ensures that the correct sizes, colors, and styles are shipped, leading to satisfied customers and a substantial reduction in chargebacks and returned or unsalable inventory. Another key advantage of the system is the ability to collaborate with suppliers and retailers to forecast sales and develop new products to match consumer tastes. In short, the ERP system forms the underarmor for Under Armour's continued growth and prosperity.

Source: S. Kusterback, "Under Armour's Foundation for Future Growth," *Apparel* 48, no. 6 (February 2007), 12–15.

[1] An excellent review of the development of MRP II and ERP is provided by F. R. Jacobs and T. W. Weston, "Enterprise Resource Planning (ERP)—A Brief History," *Journal of Operations Management* 25, no. 2 (2007), 357–363.

gates, planes, and ground equipment are closely tied to the flight schedule, as are labor requirements for pilots, flight attendants, mechanics, and ground crews. The airline uses information on the timing and number of flights, as well as the number of passengers on each flight. A flight that is 90 percent full and traveling 1,500 miles will have a larger amount of snacks and drinks onboard than a flight that is only 70 percent full and traveling 600 miles.

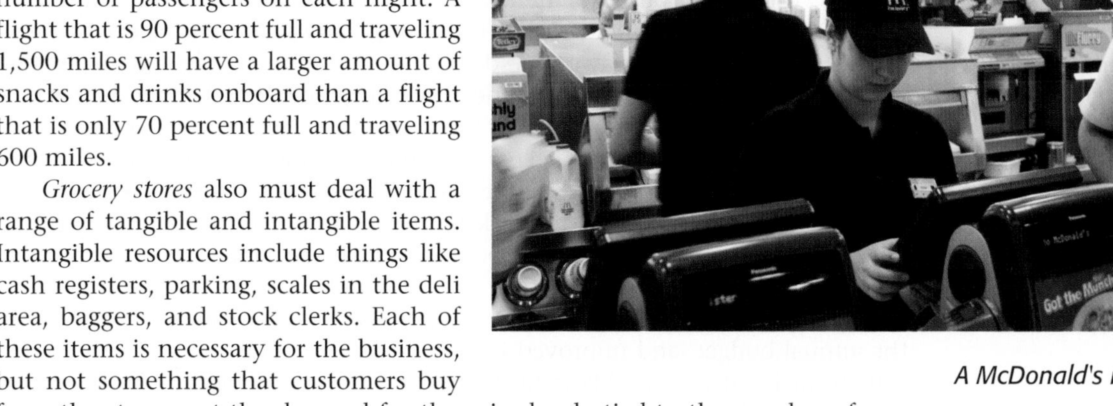

A McDonald's restaurant.

Grocery stores also must deal with a range of tangible and intangible items. Intangible resources include things like cash registers, parking, scales in the deli area, baggers, and stock clerks. Each of these items is necessary for the business, but not something that customers buy from the store—yet the demand for them is closely tied to the number of customers who shop in the store. Demand for groceries varies widely by day of the week and by time of the day. Stores in different neighborhoods have very different demand patterns, and resources need to be allocated accordingly. Labor costs are one of the major drivers for the use of self-checkout systems. Other materials that can be planned based on customer demand include **maintenance, repair, and operating supplies (MRO)**, which consist of items that a store or business requires to run the business. In grocery stores, this may include bags (paper or plastic?), cleaning supplies, disposable gloves for the delicatessen workers, lights,

● **Maintenance, repair, and operating supplies (MRO)** items that a store or business requires to run the business

COMPANY ILLUSTRATION

The Systems Behind McDonald's Success

McDonald's achieved much of its success based on its ability to help its franchisees plan and schedule their employees and materials. Labor is one of the primary costs of a fast-food restaurant. McDonald's worked closely with its franchisees in the 1950s and 1960s to develop a system for planning the number of workers required for a given day, a given time, and a given job. The guidelines take into account the size of the restaurant, the average and projected sales, and the availability of the restaurant's work force to develop a staffing plan for each week. The guidelines help the manager determine not only how many employees are needed at a given time, but also what specific jobs they should be doing. The planning systems also provide a form of MRP for taking forecasts of daily sales and translating them into a plan for the amount of hamburgers, French fries, napkins, wrapping materials, cleaning supplies, and all the other materials needed to keep the restaurant running smoothly. McDonald's was a pioneer in developing such guidelines, and today most fast-food companies that operate using a franchise system employ similar guidelines. Today the guidelines are programmed into a simple-to-use computer program that managers can operate from anywhere.[2]

[2] Labor planning systems for McDonald's have been widely examined in a number of sources. Basic overviews can be found in J. F. Love, *McDonald's: Behind the Arches,* Bantam, New York, 1995.

and other such expenses. Each of these items can also be tied to overall customer demand.

Restaurants typically use forecasts of customer demand to plan for both food items and nonfood items that are not sold to the customer. This includes tangible items like silverware (plastic or metal), napkins, tablecloths, cooking utensils, and dishwashers. Staffing levels, including those for chefs, waiters and waitresses, cashiers, valets, and busboys, are also highly dependent on demand forecasts. Often restaurants will offer specials for dining early (early bird specials) or on slow days (typically Monday or Tuesday). These are a form of **yield management**, which involves offering customers incentives to shape their demand patterns.

● **Yield management** a management technique that offers customers incentives to shape their demand patterns

Hospitals need to plan both labor (doctors, nurses, technicians, maintenance crew, receptionists, and cleaning crew) and materials (bedpans, needles, IV tubes, scalpels for surgery, and other such items). While tracking of drugs is clearly important, it is also important to track numerous nonmedical items. Quantities needed for many of these items can be planned based on forecasts of the number of admissions for a certain condition and the number of forecasted surgeries of a specific type. The cost of materials and supplies accounts for about 30 percent of the annual budget, and improved inventory techniques can result in a 20 percent annual cost savings. Many hospitals use a variation of basic ABC inventory analysis that classifies medicines as vital, essential, or desirable (VED).[3]

● **Customer relationship management** a system of planning and control activities and information systems that link an organization with its downstream customers

Customer relationship management (CRM) is a system of planning and control activities and information systems that link an organization with its downstream customers. In a broad sense, CRM is the services equivalent of MRP, helping to plan the activities of company personnel and resources in order to maximize customer satisfaction. CRM consists of three components that can be implemented independently of each other or in an integrated fashion. *Operational CRM* supports front-office business processes such as sales, marketing, and service. Software is used to document each interaction with a customer, and employees can retrieve this information whenever necessary. This allows customers to interact with different employees without having to repeat their story each time. Many call centers employ CRM to support their agents. *Collaborative CRM* supports direct interaction with customers using a variety of contact channels, including the Internet, e-mail, and automated phone. Often this type of CRM is employed to allow self-service by customers and to reduce cost. *Analytical CRM* facilitates the analysis of customer data to maximize marketing effectiveness; to support product and service design; and to improve customer acquisition, cross-selling, and retention.

Making MRP/ERP Work

Dependent demand planning and material requirements planning are critical components for numerous businesses, but especially for manufacturing businesses that work in a batch or job shop environment. The concepts of MRP are fairly simple, yet the application can be quite challenging because of the broad scope and breadth of the organization affected. Today's supply chains often call for applying these principles across multiple companies—such as when Dell passes its forecasts and higher-level records to its suppliers so that they can plan for the delivery of component parts to Dell's factories on a just-in-time basis. MRP and ERP can contribute greatly to an organization's success—or drag it down. Three key factors contribute to success. First, the hardware and software have to be carefully set up

[3] V. R. Thawani, A. V. Turankar, S. D. Sontakke, S. V. Pimpalkhute, G. N. Dakhale, K. S. Jaiswal, K. J. Gharpure, and S. D. Dharmadhikari, "Economic Analysis of Drug Expenditure in Government Medical College Hospital, Nagpur," *Indian Journal of Pharmacology* 36 (2004):15–17.

to fit with the organization's method of doing business. Often companies try to speed this process up and suffer serious problems. Second, the users of the system (employees) need to be thoroughly trained in the system, including allowing them some time to practice in a low-pressure situation. Finally, the input data need to be close to 100 percent accurate because MRP will magnify any inconsistencies.

Call center employees in action.

TECHNOLOGY IN OPERATIONS MANAGEMENT

Improving Contact at RxAmerica

An independent provider of prescription benefits, RxAmerica serves more than 6 million individuals through more than 55,000 pharmacies. The company faced a crisis during the fall of 2005 as many senior citizens grappled with the complications of a new prescription program from Medicare. RxAmerica realized that its single call center would not provide sufficient capacity to handle the expected surge in calls. The solution that executives devised was to employ outsourced call centers in various states throughout the United States. Yet the company still required a method "to deliver calls to multiple centers across the U.S. cost effectively," according to Eli Fillmore, manager of intelligent call routing.

To facilitate the routing of calls to centers, RxAmerica implemented UCN inContact, an on-demand suite of contact-handling applications. The software allows calls to be switched between locations–if a particular center has few available agents, Fillmore can lower the number of calls routed there and raise the number routed to other centers. The company's peak period was January 2006, when inContact was handling more than 40,000 calls per day. At times, RxAmerica was not able to "physically answer" all of the calls, but the CRM system allowed automatic addressing, greeting, and information on the status of the queue. It also presented an option for callers to leave a phone number and receive a call back. The CRM system also conducts automatic surveys linked to call frequency. Once a call service agent disconnects, the caller is linked to an automatic survey with 10 questions. The data are forwarded via e-mail within 10 seconds. According to Fillmore, "If it were ratings that were not too attractive for us and would merit some additional attention quickly for a customer retention effort or customer satisfaction effort, I can have a call back to that customer within 15 minutes."

The CRM system has saved RxAmerica in excess of $1 million in terms of reduction of hardware and personnel to support it. The system has also provided much more accurate and complete customer satisfaction data and an increased ability to respond to customer complaints. Finally, the system allows the work force to be scaled up or down to handle fluctuating call volumes.

Source: C. Bailor, "Call-Routing Headaches Take a Powder," *Customer Relationship Management* 10, no. 9 (2006), 24–32.

SUMMARY

1. Contrast dependent and independent demand, and trace the development of material requirements planning (MRP).

- Independent demand is the demand for any item that is sold to an end customer and not used as a part or input to another item.
- Dependent demand is the demand for any item that is used as a part or component in another item.
- The development of computer hardware and software beginning in the 1960s facilitated the use of planning systems for dependent demand that capitalized on the ability to derive demand requirements based on the demand for parent items and to account for planned lead times in the bill of materials.
- The capabilities and breadth of application of computerized inventory systems across the organization expanded as MRP evolved into MRP II in the 1980s, which in turn evolved into ERP in the 1990s.

2. Explain the inputs to an MRP system.

- A bill of materials database provides data on relationships between component parts and finished end items.
- A master schedule details the quantity of end items to be produced within a specified period of time.
- An inventory records database provides details on inventory levels and all transactions involving inventory.
- Requirements for each part or subassembly are derived from the demand for the parent items it goes into.
- Production of each part or subassembly is offset by the lead time necessary to produce it.
- MRP records are processed on a top-down basis, while physical production (assembly) occurs on a bottom-up basis.

3. Compute single-level MRP records.

- Planned on-hand inventory is calculated as (Projected On-Hand Inventory at End of Period $t + 1$) = (Projected On-Hand Inventory at End of Period t) + (Scheduled Receipts in Period $t + 1$) – (Gross Requirements in Period $t + 1$).
- A planned receipt is scheduled when planned on-hand inventory is equal to or less than safety stock.
- A planned order release is scheduled for L weeks (months, days) prior to the planned receipt, where L = lead time for that part.

4. Compute multiple-level MRP records and explain the outputs generated.

- The process involves computing the number of parts needed on a top-down basis, after all of an item's parent parts have already been processed.
- When multiple levels are involved, the system is prone to MRP nervousness, where changes at one level ripple down to other levels.

5. Describe the evolution of MRP to ERP and identify ways in which ERP is utilized to integrate all of the functions of an organization.	■ Developed originally for planning within a single company, MRP can now be applied across multiple organizations that produce components for a single end product. ■ This process requires accurate and timely information sharing to work effectively.
6. Explain how dependent demand is handled in service organizations and describe the use of technology.	■ Service organizations use computer software to plan for the scheduling of equipment, personnel, and facilities. The requirements are derived from forecasts of aggregate demand. Service organizations also use computer software to plan the inventory of MRO supplies and tangible goods that are used to run the business. ■ CRM allows organizations to link with customers to provide improved service and lower costs.
7. Define three critical features for success with ERP.	■ Hardware and software must be carefully matched with an organization's business model. ■ Users of electronic inventory systems must be extensively trained. ■ Input data accuracy for electronic inventory systems must be close to 100 percent.

SOLVED PROBLEM 1

Refer to the bill of materials for product C shown in Figure 7.12. If there is no inventory to start with, how many units of items E, G, and I must be ordered or purchased to produce 8 units of end item C?

SOLUTION

We start by determining the number of units of D required (notice that F is a component of D, so its requirements must be computed *after* those of D). Because 2 units of D are required for each unit of C, a total of 16 (8 * 2) units of D are required. Next, we compute the required units of G as 1 * 16 = 16 (1 unit of G for each unit of D). Next, we compute that 1 unit of F is required for unit of C and

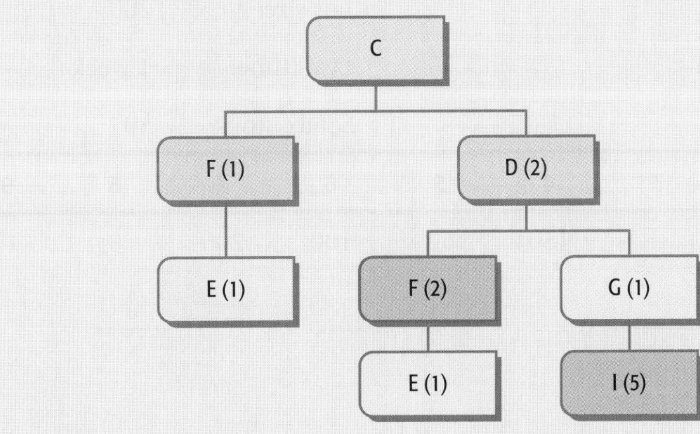

FIGURE 7.12

2 units of F are required for each unit of D. Thus, 40 units of F (2 F for each of 16 D plus 1 F for each of 8 C = 2 * 16 + 1 * 8) are needed. Next, because 1 unit of E is required for each unit of F, a total of 40 units of E are required (1 * 40). Finally, we compute that we need 5 * 16 = 80 units of I (5 units of I for each unit of G). *Thus, a total of 40 E, 16 G, and 80 I are required to produce 8 units of C.*

SOLVED PROBLEM 2

Using the data shown in the MRP record in Table 7.11, complete the record.

SOLUTION

We begin with the planned OH inventory in week 1 and work to the right and down. Projected OH inventory at the end of week 1 will equal

$$I_1 = \text{Beginning Inventory} + \text{SR}_1 - \text{GR}_1 = 200 + 0 - 150 = 50$$

Because this inventory is equal to or greater than the safety stock, we do *not* plan an order.

Projected OH inventory at the end of week 2 will be negative if we do *not* order:

$$I_2 = I_1 + SR_2 - GR_2 = 50 + 0 - 100 = -50$$

Therefore, we plan an order of $Q = 200$ to be received in week 2. The projected OH inventory is then

$$I_2 = I_1 + SR_2 - GR_2 + PR_2 = 50 + 0 - 100 + 200 = 150$$

In order to receive an order of 200 in week 2, we plan an order release of 200 in week 1, to account for the 1-week lead time. The remainder of the MRP record is calculated as follows:

$$I_3 = I_2 + SR_3 - GR_3 + PR_3 = 150 + 0 - 0 + 0 = 150$$
$$I_4 = I_3 + SR_4 - GR_4 + PR_4 = 150 + 0 - 150 + 200 = 200$$
$$I_5 = I_4 + SR_5 - GR_5 + PR_5 = 200 + 0 - 50 + 0 = 150$$
$$I_6 = I_5 + SR_6 - GR_6 + PR_6 = 150 + 0 - 100 + 0 = 50$$
$$I_7 = I_6 + SR_7 - GR_7 + PR_7 = 50 + 0 - 200 + 200 = 50$$
$$I_8 = I_7 + SR_8 - GR_8 + PR_8 = 50 + 0 - 0 + 0 = 50$$
$$I_9 = I_8 + SR_9 - GR_9 + PR_9 = 50 + 0 - 40 + 200 = 210$$

The answers are summarized in Table 7.12.

TABLE 7.11

Item: L100 — Lot size: 200

Lead time: 1 week

Beg. inv.: 200 — Safety stock: 50

Week	1	2	3	4	5	6	7	8	9
Gross requirements	150	100	0	150	50	100	200	0	40
Scheduled receipts									
Planned OH inventory									
Planned receipts									
Planned order release									

TABLE 7.12

Item: L100						Lot size:		200	
						Lead time:		1 week	
Beg. inv.: 200						Safety stock:		50	
Week	**1**	**2**	**3**	**4**	**5**	**6**	**7**	**8**	**9**
Gross requirements	150	100	0	150	50	100	200	0	40
Scheduled receipts									
Planned OH inventory	50	150	150	200	150	50	50	50	210
Planned receipts		200		200			200		200
Planned order release	200		200			200		200	

SOLVED PROBLEM 3

The master schedule for item A calls for 150 units in week 3, 100 units in week 4, 200 units in week 6, and 175 units in week 8. The bill of materials is shown in Figure 7.13, and the inventory record data are given in Table 7.13. Develop a material requirements plan for the next 8 weeks.

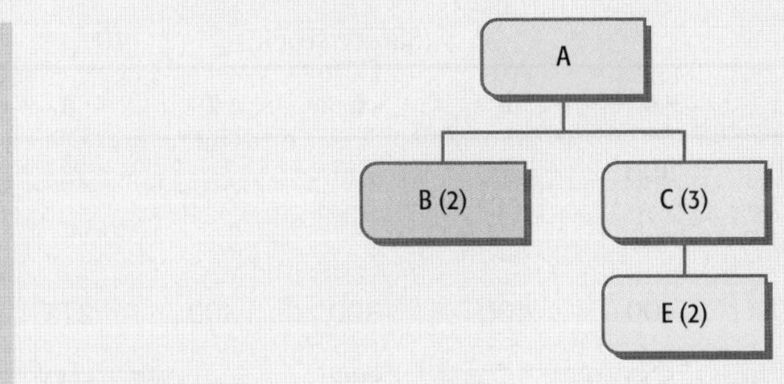

FIGURE 7.13

TABLE 7.13 Inventory Record Data

	B	**C**	**E**
Lot size	L4L	500	$P = 3$
Lead time	2 weeks	3 weeks	1 week
Scheduled receipts	None	500 (week 3)	1,000 (week 1)
Beginning inventory	100	150	200
Safety stock	20	40	100

SOLUTION

The first two items to be planned are B and C. Once C is completed, E can be planned. The MS for item A is multiplied by 2 to derive the gross requirements for B and multiplied by 3 to get the gross requirements for C. The gross requirements for E are calculated by multiplying the planned order releases of C by 2. Table 7.14 provides the completed MRP record.

TABLE 7.14

MS Item A			150	100		200		175

Item: B — Lot size: L4L
Lead time: 2 weeks
Beg. inv.: 100 — Safety stock: 20

Week	1	2	3	4	5	6	7	8
Gross requirements			300	200		400		350
Scheduled receipts								
Planned OH inventory	100	100	20	20	20	20	20	20
Planned receipts			220	200		400		350
Planned order release	220	200		400		350		

Item: C — Lot size: 500
Description: — Lead time: 3 weeks
Beg. inv.: 150 — Safety stock: 40

Week	1	2	3	4	5	6	7	8
Gross requirements			450	300		600		525
Scheduled receipts			500					
Planned OH inventory	150	150	200	400	400	300	300	275
Planned receipts				500		500		500
Planned order release	500		500		500			

Item: E — Lot size: $P = 3$
Description: — Lead time: 1 week
Beg. inv.: 200 — Safety stock: 100

Week	1	2	3	4	5	6	7	8
Gross requirements	1,000		1,000		1,000			
Scheduled receipts	1,000							
Planned OH inventory	200	200	1,100	1,100	100	100	100	100
Planned receipts			1,900					
Planned order release		1,900						

QUESTIONS

1. The partially completed MRP record in Table 7.15 provides gross requirements, scheduled receipts, lead time, and beginning on-hand inventory.
   a. Complete the record for a lot size of FOQ = 250 units.
   b. Complete the record for a lot size of $P = 2$.
   c. Complete the record for an L4L lot size.
   d. Which lot size rule results in the lowest average inventory?
   e. Which lot size rule results in the fewest/most orders?

TABLE 7.15

Item: A100 | Lot size:

Description: Pontiac Solstice hood | Lead time: 1 week

Beg. inv.: 250 | Safety stock: 20

Week	1	2	3	4	5	6	7	8	9
Gross requirements	200	150	300	100	150	200	250	0	200
Scheduled receipts									
Planned OH inventory									
Planned receipts									
Planned order release									

2. Develop MRP records for the items in Figure 7.14, Table 7.16, and Table 7.17. Forty units of D are required as spare parts in week 4, and 85 units of D are required in week 7.

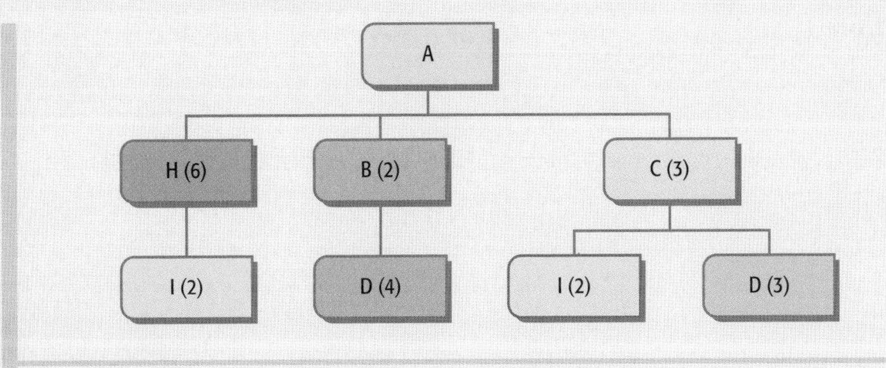

FIGURE 7.14

TABLE 7.16 MS Start

Product	1	2	3	4	5	6	7	8	9
A		130	90	80	60	100	70		50

TABLE 7.17 Planning Data

Data Category	B	C	D	H	I
Lot size rule	$P = 4$	450	L4L	1,000	$P = 2$
Lead time	1 week	1 week	1 week	2 weeks	2 weeks
Safety stock	15	30	10	45	75
Scheduled receipts	None	450 week 2	2,900 week 1	1,000 week 2	2,950 week 1
Beginning inventory	30	40	20	60	90

3. The partially completed MRP record in Table 7.18 provides gross requirements, scheduled receipts, lead time, and beginning on-hand inventory.
   a. Complete the record for a lot size of FOQ = 1,500 units.
   b. Complete the record for a lot size of $P = 3$.
   c. Complete the record for an L4L lot size.
   d. Which lot size rule results in the lowest average inventory?
   e. Which lot size rule results in the fewest/most orders?

TABLE 7.18

Item: F200 | Lot size:
Description: iPod ear buds | Lead time: 2 weeks
Beg. inv.: 200 | Safety stock: 10

Week	1	2	3	4	5	6	7	8	9
Gross requirements	1,000	1,100	750	900	1,200	0	400	0	1,300
Scheduled receipts	2,100								
Planned OH inventory									
Planned receipts									
Planned order release									

4. Develop MRP records for the items in Figure 7.15, Table 7.19, and Table 7.20. The lead time to complete item A is 2 weeks, and the lead time to complete item H is 1 week.

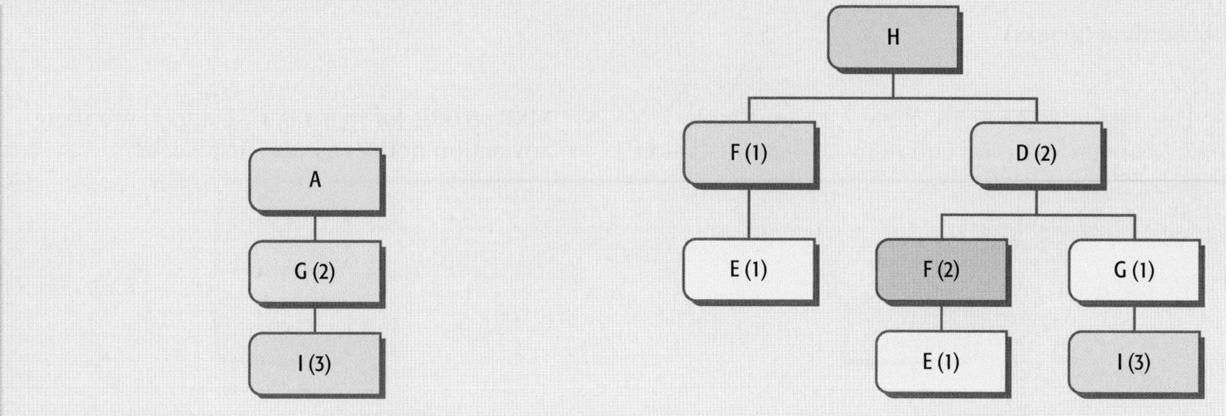

FIGURE 7.15

TABLE 7.19 MS Finish

Product	1	2	3	4	5	6	7	8	9
A				55	40		80		100
H				180	140	90		60	50

TABLE 7.20 Planning Data

Data Category	D	E	F	G	I
Lot size rule	$P = 2$	L4L	L4L	400	L4L
Lead time	2 weeks	1 week	1 week	2 weeks	2 weeks
Safety stock	15	25	20	35	0
Scheduled receipts	None	None	1,300 week 1	800 week 1	1,200 week 1
Beginning inventory	30	40	20	50	0

5. Product C is assembled from components D and E. Item D is made from item F and Item G. Item F is made from item J and item K. Item E is made from item H and item I. Item H is made from Item J. All parent items require 1 unit of their respective component items. The lead times for each item are listed in Table 7.21.

   a. What is the lead time required to respond to a customer order for product C, assuming that there are no existing inventories or scheduled receipts?

   b. What is the customer response time if items J and K are in stock (i.e., do not need to be ordered)?

   c. If you are allowed to keep either item G or item I in stock (along with items J and K from part b), which one would you choose?

TABLE 7.21

Item	C	D	E	F	G	H	I	J	K
Lead time (weeks)	3	5	6	5	1	1	3	1	3

6. The data in Figure 7.16, Table 7.22, and Table 7.23 are provided for end items A and H. Develop MRP records for items B, C, I, and E. Are there any action notices for the first week?

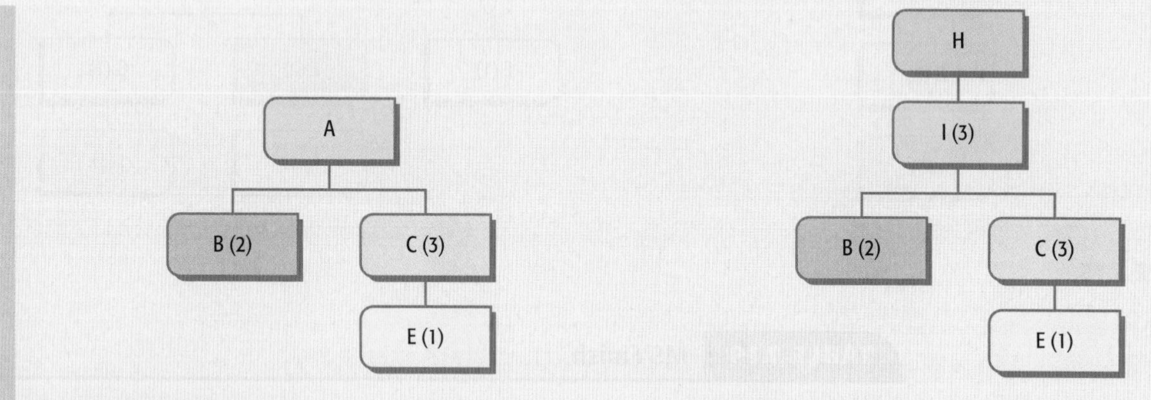

FIGURE 7.16

TABLE 7.22 MS Start

Product	1	2	3	4	5	6	7	8
A		25	10		40	50		70
H	90		20	30	15	45		

TABLE 7.23 Planning Data

Data Category	B	C	E	I
Lot size rule	300	*P* = 2	L4L	200
Lead time	1 week	2 weeks	2 weeks	1 week
Safety stock	25	10	10	45
Scheduled receipts	None	690 week 2	None	200 week 1
Beginning inventory	75	10	30	120

7. A table is made from one tabletop, four legs, and four hangers. Each of the legs is made from 4 feet of hickory wood and ¼ gallon of varnish. Each of the hangers is made from a brace and 4 bolts and 4 nuts. Draw the BOM for the table.

8. The partially completed MRP record in Table 7.24 provides gross requirements, scheduled receipts, lead time, and beginning on-hand inventory.
   a. Complete the record for a lot size of FOQ = 2,000 units.
   b. Complete the record for a lot size of $P = 4$.
   c. Complete the record for an L4L lot size.
   d. Which lot size rule results in the lowest average inventory?
   e. Which lot size rule results in the fewest/most orders?

TABLE 7.24

Item: F440						Lot size:			
Description: "Talk" key for cell phone						Lead time:	4 weeks		
Beg. inv.: 1,000						Safety stock:	150		
Week	**1**	**2**	**3**	**4**	**5**	**6**	**7**	**8**	**9**
Gross requirements	1,500	1,200	1,200	1,800		1,200	1,200	300	1,800
Scheduled receipts	5,000								
Planned OH inventory									
Planned receipts									
Planned order release									

9. For the bill of materials (BOM) in Figure 7.17:
   a. How many immediate parents does item B have? How many immediate parents does item E have?
   b. How many unique components does item A have at all levels?
   c. How many units of item F will be required to produce 10 units of item A?
   d. Based on the lead times provided, what should the planning horizon be (i.e., what is the longest lead time from top to bottom)?

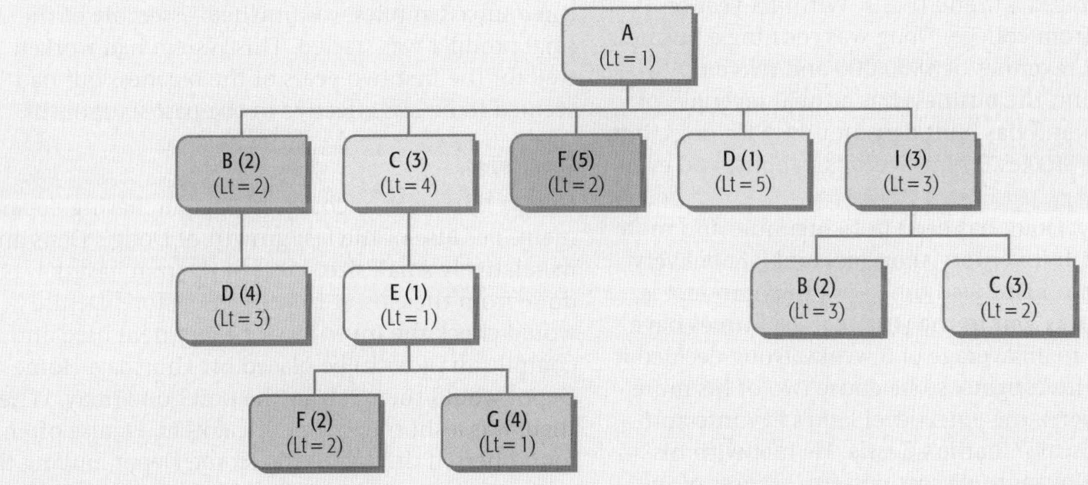

FIGURE 7.17

CASE STUDY

Doug's Dens

A custom-built doghouse.

Doug Johnson is a 25-year-old entrepreneur who started his own business while in college. He responded to an ad in the college newspaper seeking a student who was willing to build a doghouse for a family's Brittany spaniel. The job went well—he designed and built a doghouse that any dog would love. More importantly, the pet's owners were very impressed and referred Doug to several of their friends. Soon, Doug had more orders than he could keep up with, so he hired a friend of his. Within a year of graduating from college, Doug was running a business with annual revenues of $800,000 and two employees. At present, the business has annual revenues of $3.2 million and has built dens not only for dogs, but also for cats, snakes, lizards, gerbils, rabbits, and even one llama!

Recently, Doug has been noticing more and more problems with inventory shortages and late delivery times. The promised lead time for a final product is usually 3 weeks, but in the past year lead times have skyrocketed to an average of 8 weeks. Doug decided it was time to investigate, so he chose two of his more popular designs, the entry-level Fido's Favorite and the more upscale Charlie's Castle. He met with his various employees to discuss potential causes of inventory problems with these two products.

Marketing

Cathy Franks ran the marketing area of Doug's Dens. When Doug came to talk to her, she showed him the marketing plan and forecast for the following 12 months. The plans show the master schedule for the two items for the coming 12 months and are shown in Table 7.25. Cathy told Doug, "We generally are pretty accurate on yearly sales for each of these products, but there is more inaccuracy regarding when these sales occur. To level demand out, we will occasionally run specials and discount Charlie's Castle to spur more sales."

Production

The production department was supervised by Doug's best friend, Kevin Jones, who had studied entomology in college. All products were custom assembled for a particular customer order, typically in batches of one. There was a high degree of commonality in parts because roofs were made from one of five types of shingle, siding consisted of one of three types, and floors were one of four types. Dens were assembled from three main subassemblies: floor and foundation, frame, and roof. When a customer order was received, a production order was generated for each of the three subassemblies. Once each of the three subassemblies was finished, assembly of the final product was started. This system had worked well for the first two years of the business but had seemed to be less effective in the past six months.

Purchasing

Denise Mina was in charge of the purchasing department. Because of the fast growth of Doug's Dens and its relatively small size, most of the purchasing was done from the closest Home Depot store. Denise would check the inventory of every item used and compile an order to be placed on Thursday. Home Depot would then deliver the order on Friday. When there was a shortage of a critical item, Denise often found herself driving to the Home Depot, buying the necessary item, and carrying it back to work in the back of her pickup truck. Because Doug's did $1.5

million worth of business with Home Depot per year, it had negotiated a contract that provided the company with a 10 percent discount off the normal, walk-up price.

QUESTIONS

1. Is Doug's Dens a business that can effectively utilize MRP for planning its inventory? Why or why not?
2. Develop a material requirements plan for the next 8 weeks using the information in Table 7.25 and, on the next page, Table 7.26 and Figure 7.18.
3. Discuss how Doug should go about implementing MRP. What type of training should he provide? What kind of software and equipment? How long should he allow for the implementation?
4. A business consultant suggested that Doug's Dens build a master schedule at the subassembly level (i.e., for the floor, roof, and frame assemblies) rather than at the finished product level (i.e., Fido's Favorite and Charlie's Castle). The consultant said that this is the approach used by Dell (Doug idolizes Michael Dell as a role model). Discuss whether this approach makes sense and explain why or why not.

TABLE 7.25 Master Schedule

Month	Week	Fido's Favorite	Charlie's Castle
1	1	4	3
	2	5	3
	3	3	2
	4	3	5
2	5	4	4
	6	6	2
	7	3	2
	8	3	3
3		15	12
4		10	8
5		10	8
6		20	10
7		15	9
8		12	9
9		10	8
10		12	8
11		10	10
12		10	11

TABLE 7.26 Current Ordering Policy for Doug's Dens

Part/Subassembly	Order Quantity/Reorder Point
Corner brackets	$Q = 1{,}000$; $R = 500$
6-foot 2 × 4	$Q = 4{,}000$; $R = 1{,}000$
2-inch nails	$Q = 10{,}000$; $R = 1{,}000$

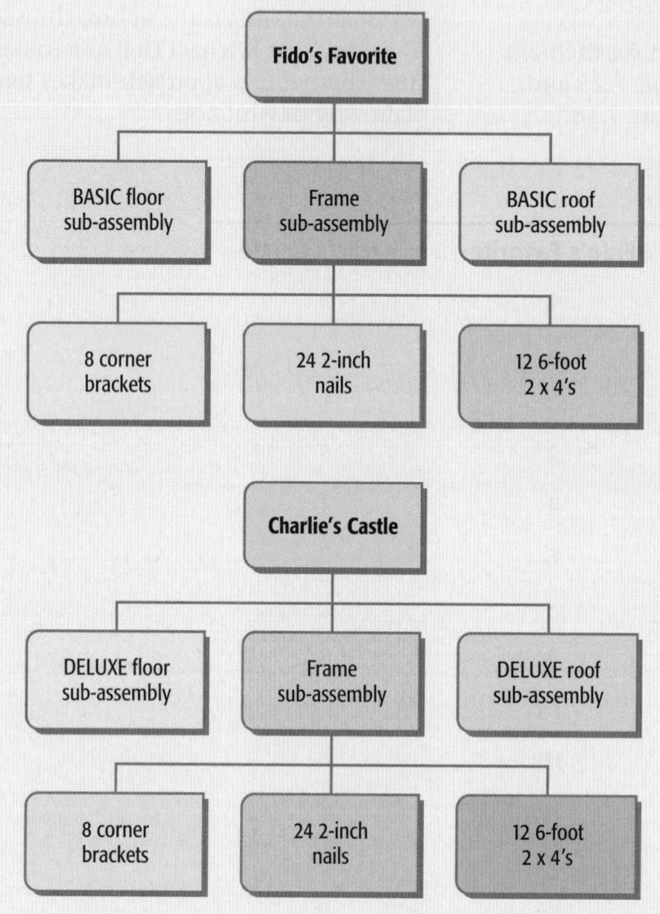

FIGURE 7.18 Partial BOM for Fido's Favorite and Charlie's Castle

CHAPTER 8

Project Management

LEARNING OBJECTIVES

1. Define the term *project,* list the steps involved in project management, and explain the role of the project manager.
2. Describe various project management tools and techniques, such as work breakdown structure, critical path method, program evaluation and review technique, cost and time tradeoff analysis, and resource management.
3. Understand how to execute projects successfully and how to avoid risks and failure.

Animated Movie Projects at Pixar

For Pixar, making a successful animated movie such as *Toy Story, Finding Nemo, Monsters Inc.,* or *Cars* requires an incredible set of artistic talents, the latest technology, and *world-class project management.* The rewards for success, such as winning prestigious Academy Awards and earning hundreds of millions of dollars in profits, are plentiful. At the same time, making a critically acclaimed animated movie is a very hard, expensive, time-consuming, and resource-intensive project. A number of tasks need to be completed in a specified time period and within a specified budget while ensuring that the goal and artistic vision of the project are met.

Woody and Buz Lightyear: characters from Pixar's animation movie Toy Story.

Pixar's animated movie projects typically go through four stages: (1) the *development stage,* or creation of the story line; (2) the *preproduction stage,* which includes troubleshooting the technical aspects; (3) the *production stage,* which means the making of the actual movie; and (4) the *postproduction stage,* which includes final editing and touch-up of the completed movie.

A movie project begins with the development of a master document that summarizes the main ideas of the story. The idea is first discussed among the members of Pixar's movie development team, taking into account its potential for commercial success, originality, technical considerations, resource requirements, and budget considerations, among other things. Often many versions of the supplementary ideas surrounding the core theme are developed during the early stages, to be confirmed later as the project evolves.

If the proposed idea survives the tough scrutiny of many different dimensions just described, it progresses to the next step in the development process: Hand-drawn comic-book versions of the story, known as storybooks, are created. The storybook serves as the blueprint of the movie for motion and dialogue sequences. Each storybook artist follows the movie script closely, including the intended mood and situation that the character is supposed to be in.

While the storybook is being finalized, the task of voice recording of dialogues is started. The early voice recordings for the movie characters are improvised and rerecorded by professional actors in many different versions over the next several weeks or months.

While the audio recording continues, the movie editorial process begins with the creation of a final sequence of storyboards that tell the complete story. At this stage, the movie editorial team fixes the length and other technical details (e.g., the color sequence, lighting, placement of characters, and so on) for each scene.

Now that the basic skeleton of the movie is complete, the members of the art department at Pixar use their creative imagination to start illustrating the movie characters and their environment for each scene. They also design the visual looks in terms of surfaces, colors, and lights. Using the art department's initial work, three-dimensional (3-D) drawings of the movie characters are created with specialized computer modeling programs. The 3-D images are developed along multiple fixed points of reference (known as "avars," or hinges) to create animation and the ability to move a character from one scene to the next scene (for example, Woody in *Toy Story* had 100 avars just on his face). The movie characters are then "dressed," and the sequence of scenes is created. These scenes are then linked together by Pixar's proprietary animation software. For example, the movie characters' movements and facial expressions change as the scene progresses.

After the basic animation is complete, a number of adjustments are made. For example, each movie character and complete screen within each scene is shaded appropriately to show the impact of the "digital" light present in the environment.

Finally, it is time to put everything together. The scenes, the sequences, the music, the audio recording, and the story line—everything needs to work in sync to create a perfect movie.

While the artistic components for each movie no doubt vary, it is not an exaggeration to state that Pixar has perfected the recipe (i.e., project management) for making successful animated movies. ■

The Palm Jumeirah Island: one of the world's largest planned communities (houses, condominiums, hotels, and resorts) constructed in the ocean.

The Great Wall of China, the Pyramids of Egypt, the sequencing of the human genome, the development of the

International Space Station, and the development of the Palm Jumeirah island in Dubai: These examples illustrate human accomplishments in many different fields. Yet they have something in common: They are all examples of extremely successful projects. This chapter is about understanding the necessary concepts and techniques for successful project management.

ELEMENTS OF PROJECT MANAGEMENT

This section describes the essential elements of project management. The term *project* is defined, and the steps involved in project management are listed and explained. This section also describes the role of a project manager.

What Is a Project?

A **project** can be defined as a set of interrelated activities necessary to achieve established goals using a specified amount of time, budget, and resources.

● **Project** a set of interrelated activities necessary to achieve established goals using a specified amount of time, budget, and resources

In simple terms, the *primary characteristics* of a project can be listed as

- A well-defined goal or objective
- Composed of a set of interrelated activities
- A specified beginning and ending time
- Specified resource and personnel requirements
- A specified budget
- Uniqueness (i.e., something that has not been done before)

In addition, *supplementary characteristics* for projects can be identified as the following:

- Projects typically include prespecified deliverables after completion.
- Because projects are defined to have specific objectives, they also have preestablished limits and exclusions.
- Projects generally have specific intermediate goals or performance milestones.
- Because a project contains some unique element, it also includes an element of risk.
- Project teams are generally made up of several individuals who come from different departments or functional areas or who have unique skills.
- Project team members often work on multiple projects at the same time—with each project having unique goals, deadlines, and requirements.

In today's global and multifunctional business environment, managing projects is no longer considered an exception. In fact, project management has become an essential part of the professional lives of employees working in business, not-for-profit, and government organizations.

Some examples of operations management projects include

- The development of new product and service offerings such as the Nintendo Wii, Sony Playstation, and Microsoft X-Box video-game systems.
- Quality improvement projects such as implementation of Six Sigma projects at a large service organization like American Express.

- The opening of a new production or customer service facility (e.g., the opening of a large software development facility in India by Google).
- Projects to comply with new government or industry regulations (e.g., renovation of Marriott Library at the University of Utah campus to comply with the latest earthquake regulations and standards).
- Preparation for ISO 9000 or ISO 14000 certifications. For example, because of increased emphasis on sustainability, a number of hotel chains around the world have initiated special projects to assess the environmental impact of their operations.
- New equipment installation at a production or health-care facility. For example, installation of the latest molecular imaging scanners at specialty-care hospitals (e.g., Huntsman Cancer Institute, Salt Lake City).
- Selection of suppliers for essential raw materials or components or selection of supply chain partners. For example, large manufacturing companies such as General Motors, Cargill, Kellogg, and others have to evaluate suppliers of the components and raw materials for each of their new product offerings.
- Implementation of new technology or software such as enterprise resource planning (ERP) systems. For example, the Kuali Foundation is undertaking a multiyear project to develop an open-source enterprise-wide financial reporting system for large academic institutions in the United States.[1]
- Community service activities undertaken by organizations. For example, many organizations undertake an annual "Christmas in April" community service project; this is a nationwide community service program that coordinates volunteers to help renovate and repair the homes of low-income, elderly, and/or disabled homeowners.

What Is Project Management?

● **Project management** the application of the knowledge, skills, tools, and techniques necessary to successfully complete a project

Project management can be defined as the application of the knowledge, skills, tools, and techniques necessary to successfully complete a project. Therefore, project management includes planning, directing, scheduling, and controlling resources (people, equipment, and material) to meet the technical, cost, and time constraints of the project.

The phrase *project management* was initially developed about fifty years ago (during the 1950s and early 1960s), when the size, scope, and duration of and the resources required for new government and commercial projects started becoming so large that these projects required more analysis and special attention. Over the next several decades, a number of project management tools were developed for application in different industries. Today, a variety of project management techniques, such as critical path method, uncertainty analysis, cost and time tradeoff analysis, and resource allocation techniques, are used globally by multibillion-dollar corporations, governments, and smaller organizations alike. A number of special software programs (e.g., Microsoft Project) have been developed to assist project managers in applying the techniques discussed in this chapter effectively.

According to the Project Management Institute (www.pmi.org), the body of knowledge of project management can be divided into five categories: initiation, planning, execution, control, and closure.

[1] www.kuali.org

Project Initiation

During the project initiation phase, a business problem or opportunity is identified, a solution is identified, and a project team is established. This process often involves selecting a project sponsor; setting the project scope, timeline, and budget; and appointing a project team and manager. The project manager is ultimately responsible for the successful execution of the project. Therefore, he or she is the main custodian of all information related to the project and controls the assignment of tasks to different team members. Because of their crucial role, the Project Management Institute recommends that project managers need to gain expertise in several different areas, including information integration, scope, time, cost, quality, human resources, communications, risk, and procurement.

Project Planning

Detailed planning begins during the second phase (project planning). This involves the creation of a number of planning documents such as those described here:

- The *project plan* outlines the activities, their interdependencies, and time estimates.
- The *resource plan* lists the labor, equipment, other resources, components, and raw materials required to complete the project activities. The quantities of different resources required during different project stages are estimated.
- The *financial plan* reports estimated costs and cash flow requirements at different project stages.
- *Quality plans* provide details on quality targets, control, and potential improvement measures.
- The *communications plan* often includes updates on project status relative to schedule, which needs to be communicated to key stakeholders.
- The *risk plan* provides an assessment of potential risks and uncertainties, and actions that might be necessary to overcome the challenges.

Project Execution

The project execution phase involves the actual completion of all activities that are part of the project. The project manager monitors the execution to ensure that each activity is completed on time using the allotted resources and budget. This phase also requires the project manager to start constructing the deliverables. The project deliverables can be sequenced in series so that neither the project team nor the recipient is overburdened by them.

Project Control

Project control means real-time assessment of the execution of a planned project. The real-time data (e.g., completion of activities, cost, and resource usage) are compared with the proposed plan, and corrective actions are taken as necessary. Therefore, project control requires time, cost, quality, resource, risk, and change management skills.

Project Closure

Finally, at the conclusion of all project activities and after submission of the required deliverables, a project is formally closed. Often organizations conduct a critical assessment of all project phases to identify the steps that went well and those that did not. Such an assessment allows the organization to learn from both successes and failures and to improve the execution of the next project.

The Project Manager

● **Project manager** the person responsible for delivering the goals of a project

All of the tasks and phases in a project that were defined earlier are the responsibility of the **project manager**. Therefore, a project manager himself or herself seldom participates directly in the activities that produce the end result; rather, he or she ensures that the different components of the project are executed properly.

A project manager is also the single point of contact for delivering the goals of a project to its customers. Therefore, the ability to adapt to the various project constraints quickly and effectively is essential in ensuring that the project is executed on time, within budget, and by using the resources provided.

● **Project time** the amount of time available to complete a project

● **Project cost** the budgeted amount available for the project

● **Project scope** the activities that must be completed to achieve a project's end goal

The project manager is responsible for successfully meeting three interrelated project constraints: *time, cost,* and *scope,* described in Figure 8.1. The **project time** constraint refers to the amount of time available to complete a project. The **project cost** constraint refers to the budgeted amount available for the project. The **project scope** constraint refers to what must be done to achieve a project's end goal. These three constraints are interrelated and are negatively correlated: For example, an increased scope typically means increased time and increased cost, a short time constraint could mean increased costs and reduced scope, and a limited budget could mean increased time and reduced scope.

PROJECT MANAGEMENT TOOLS AND TECHNIQUES

The discipline of project management has available a number of tools and procedures that enable the project team to organize its work to meet the constraints. In this section, we describe several commonly used project management techniques.

Work Breakdown Structure

● **Work breakdown structure** an approach that defines a project in terms of its sub-projects, tasks, and activities

The **work breakdown structure** (WBS) is the most fundamental technique for defining and organizing the total scope of a project. A large program (e.g., the development of a new video-game console by Sony) is divided into several loosely

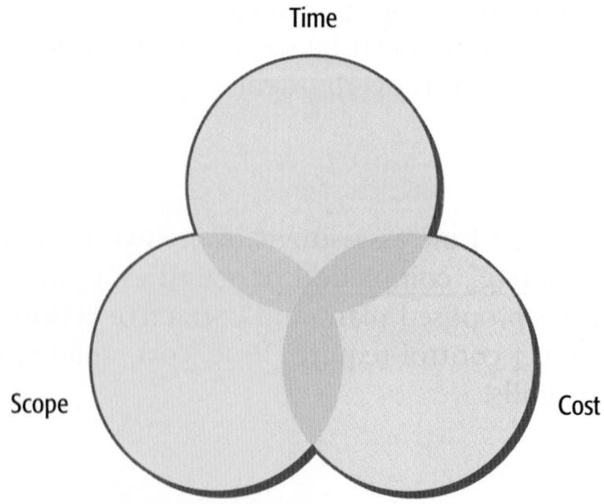

Time

Scope

Cost

FIGURE 8.1 Three Interrelated Constraints in Project Management

connected independent projects (e.g., the development of hardware and the development of software). Each project is then subdivided into its component subprojects (e.g., the development of the memory module and the development of the computer microprocessor), and then each subproject is divided into several tasks. These tasks are subdivided several times into component subtasks and finally to the smallest work package (or **activity**) that can be assigned to a single worker or a team. An example of a simple work breakdown structure is shown in Figure 8.2.

● **Activity** the smallest work package that can be assigned to a single worker or a team

Because the entire set of techniques described later in this chapter is based on project activities, it is essential that great care is taken to develop a realistic work breakdown structure.

Precedence Relationship and Time Estimates

A **precedence relationship analysis** is conducted to identify the sequence of activities defined by the work breakdown structure. Furthermore, great care is taken to estimate the approximate completion time for each activity. It will be demonstrated later in this chapter that the project schedule, cost, and resource requirements depend on the precedence relationships and time estimates for individual tasks.

● **Precedence relationship analysis** identification of the relationships and the sequence of activities within a project

Level	
0	Program
1	Project A — Project B
2	Task A.1 — Task A.2
3	Subtask A.1.1 — Subtask A.1.2
4	Work package A.1.1.1 — Work package A.1.1.2

FIGURE 8.2 Work Breakdown Structure

Solved Example 1

Sunny Beach Resort: Precedence Relationship and Activity Time Estimates

Sunny Beach Resort is a new all-inclusive vacation resort being planned by a large hotel company on the eastern coast of Florida. The parent company operates a chain of hotels that are for business travelers only and therefore has no experience developing a highly integrated facility such as a vacation resort close to a beach. Therefore, the senior management team has put together a small group of executives from several functional areas to identify the major project activities, their time estimates, and the interrelationships between activities necessary to successfully complete the Sunny Beach Resort project. The participants are to use their past experience and expertise when exploring this proposed project.

SOLUTION:

The results are presented in Table 8.1.

TABLE 8.1 Sunny Beach Resort: Activity Relationships and Time Estimates

Activity	Description	Immediate Predecessor	Time (weeks)
A	Select site	—	2
B	Select senior project staff	—	3
C	Select architect	B	2
D	Develop construction plan	A, C	4
E	Bring utilities to the site	A	2
F	Construct the buildings	D, E	16
G	Develop outdoor areas and landscape	F	8
H	Finish indoor areas and install necessary equipment	F	5
I	Select support personnel	B	3
J	Train support personnel	I	4
K	Get government approval for opening after final inspection	G, H, J	2

Gantt Chart

● **Gantt chart** a special type of horizontal bar chart used to display the schedule for an entire project

A **Gantt chart** (named after Henry Gantt, who originally developed the chart in the 1910s) is a special type of horizontal bar chart that displays the schedule for the entire project. It shows the beginning and end times for each activity and can also show the interrelationships between activities. A Gantt chart with different color codes can also be used to track performance while the project is in progress.

Figure 8.3 shows an example of a Gantt chart created prior to the beginning of a project. Figure 8.4 shows the status of the same project at the end of five

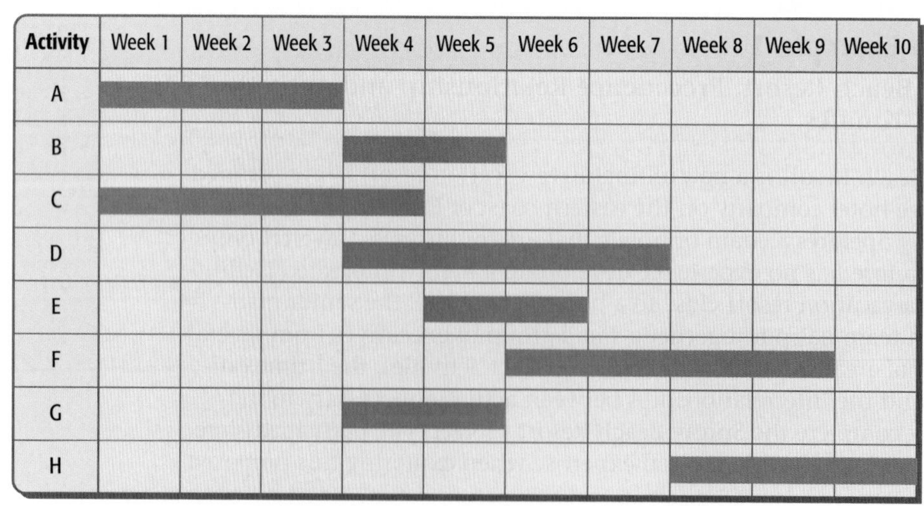

FIGURE 8.3 An Example of a Gantt Chart

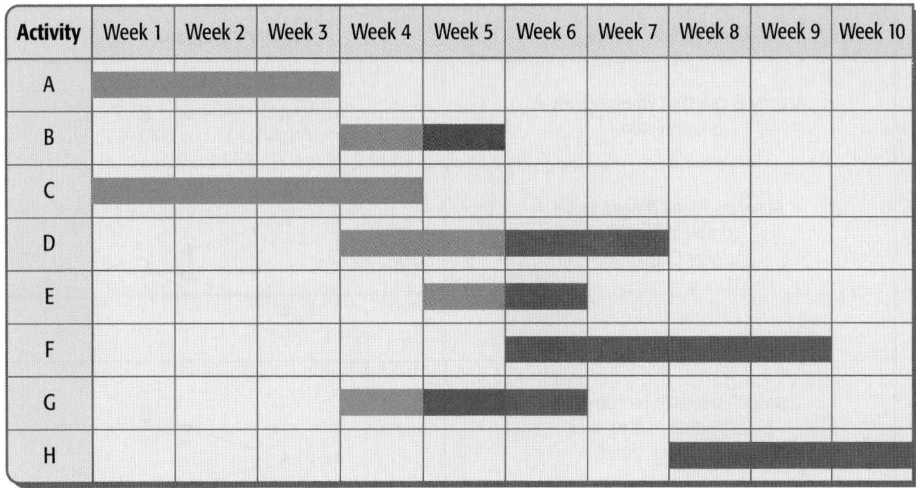

FIGURE 8.4 An Example of Project Planning: Gantt Chart While the Project Is in Progress

Note: This chart was created at the end of week 5.

weeks into execution. The green color means that the activity has been completed, the blue color means that the activity is in progress, and the red color means that the activity is behind schedule.

Network Diagram

A **network diagram** is used to show the precedence relationship among different activities. There are two conventions for building a network diagram. The **activity on node (AON) approach** shows each activity as a circle (or a node) and connects the activities with arrows. The direction of an arrow indicates the project direction. For example, if activity A precedes activity B, then the arrow will point from A to B. In practice, a second convention known as the **activity on arrow (AOA) convention** is also used. The AOA convention is opposite to AON: Each activity is represented by an arrow, and the nodes are used to show the beginning and end points. Examples of the AON and AOA conventions are given in Figure 8.5.

While both the AOA and the AON conventions are used in the industry, in this textbook, we will use only the AON convention for the sake of clarity and brevity. Following the logic of representing each activity on a node, a standard approach is used to draw the relationships between activities. Several examples are presented in Figure 8.6.

- **Network diagram** a diagram with arrows and nodes (circles) created to display a sequence of activities within a project
- **Activity on node (AON) approach** a network diagram that shows each activity as a circle (or a node) and connects the activities with arrows
- **Activity on arrow (AOA) convention** a network diagram in which each activity is represented by an arrow, and the nodes are used to show the beginning and end points

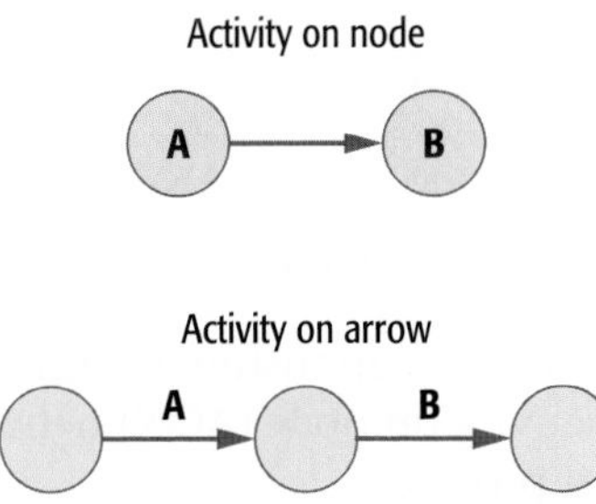

FIGURE 8.5 Activity on Node (AON) and Activity on Arrow (AOA) Conventions for Representing Network Diagrams

Activity Relationships	Network Diagram
Activity B can start when Activity A is completed.	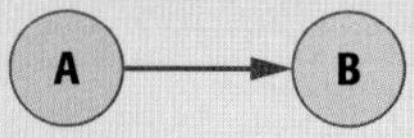 A → B
Activities A and B need to be completed before Activity C can start.	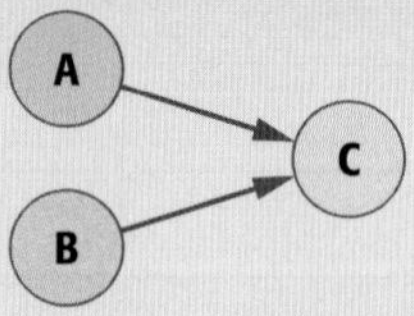 A → C; B → C
Activity A needs to be completed before either Activity B or Activity C can start.	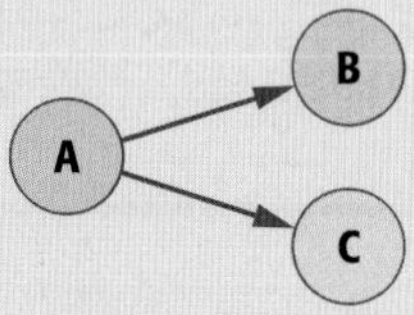 A → B; A → C
Activity C can start only when Activities A and B are completed, but Activity D can start as soon as Activity B is completed.	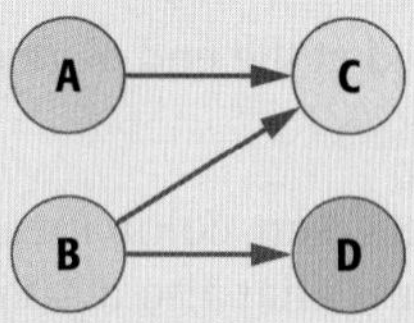 A → C; B → C; B → D
Activity C can start when Activty B is completed. Activity D can start when Activities A and C are completed. Activity E can start when Activity D is completed.	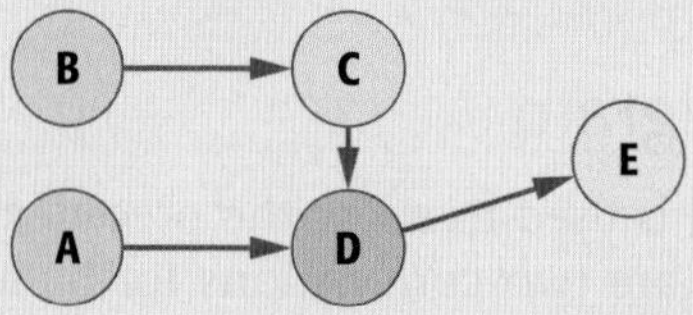 B → C; C → D; A → D; D → E
Activity C can start only when Activities A and B are completed. Activities D and E can only start when Activity C is completed.	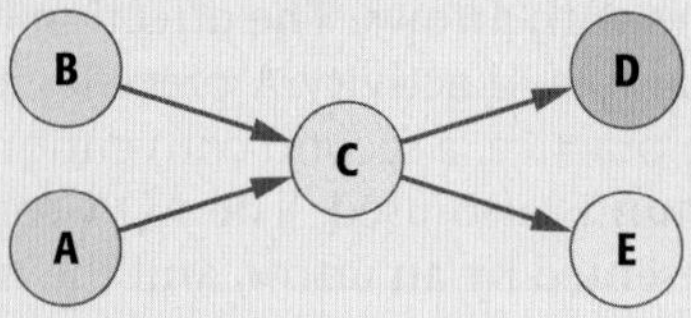 B → C; A → C; C → D; C → E

FIGURE 8.6 Activity on Node (AON) Network Diagram Examples

Solved Example 2

Sunny Beach Resort: Constructing a Network Diagram

Based on the precedence relationship information provided in Table 8.1, construct an activity on node (AON) network diagram for the Sunny Beach Resort project.

SOLUTION:

The results are presented in Figure 8.7.

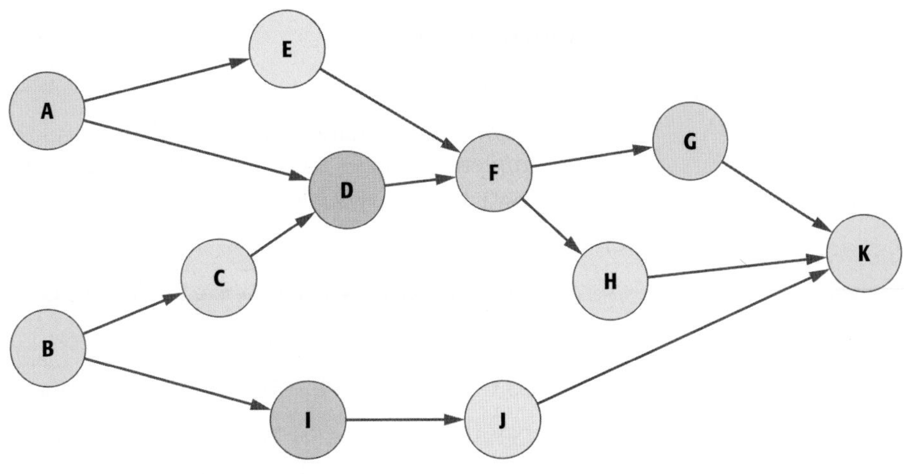

FIGURE 8.7 AON Network Diagram for Sunny Beach Resort Project

Critical Path Method (CPM)

The **critical path method** (CPM) is an algorithm for scheduling the activities within a project to achieve the fastest and most efficient execution of that project. The algorithm, originally developed by DuPont and Remington Rand Corporation in the 1950s, is an essential project management technique.

Using the information presented in the work breakdown structure and the precedence relationship and time estimates, the CPM algorithm estimates the time necessary to complete each part of the project. The path that takes the longest time to complete is known as the **critical path**. Because all paths within a project need to be completed before the project can be considered complete, the critical path (also known as the bottleneck path or the binding constraint) dictates the project's duration. The activities making up a critical path are known as **critical activities**. Any delay in the execution of a critical activity results in delaying the entire project.

● **Critical path method** an algorithm for scheduling activities within a project for the fastest and most efficient execution

● **Critical path** the path within a project that takes the longest time to complete

● **Critical activities** the project activities making up a critical path

PART II Tools and Tactical Issues

Solved Example 3
Sunny Beach Resort: Path Durations and Critical Activities

Based on the information provided in Table 8.1 and Figure 8.7, identify different project paths and their duration. Identify the critical path and critical activities.

SOLUTION:

The precedence diagram presented in Figure 8.7 shows the following seven paths:

Path 1: AEFGK

Path 2: AEFHK

Path 3: ADFGK

Path 4: ADFHK

Path 5: BCDFGK

(continued)

Path 6: BCDFHK

Path 7: BIJK

Table 8.1 shows the estimated time for each activity. Therefore, by adding the completion times for each activity, we can calculate the total time necessary to complete each path.

Completion time for

Path 1 (AEFGK) = 2 + 2 + 16 + 8 + 2 = 30 weeks

Path 2 (AEFHK) = 2 + 2 + 16 + 5 + 2 = 27 weeks

Path 3 (ADFGK) = 2 + 4 + 16 + 8 + 2 = 32 weeks

Path 4 (ADFHK) = 2 + 4 + 16 + 5 + 2 = 29 weeks

Path 5 (BCDFGK) = 3 + 2 + 4 + 16 + 8 + 2 = 35 weeks

Path 6 (BCDFHK) = 3 + 2 + 4 + 16 + 5 + 2 = 32 weeks

Path 7 (BIJK) = 3 + 3 + 4 + 2 = 12 weeks

Because path 5 is the longest, it is the critical path. Therefore, activities B, C, D, F, G, and K are critical activities. The paths and times are shown in Figure 8.8.

● **Slack** the amount of flexibility in scheduling an activity within a project

For a project that includes a small number of activities (such as Sunny Beach Resort), it may be possible to find the critical path by calculating the length of each path as demonstrated in Solved Example 3. However, this approach is ad hoc and does not provide much information about the noncritical activities. For example, we do not know how much **slack** (or flexibility) exists in scheduling the noncritical activities. Slack is the estimate of the maximum amount of time that a noncritical activity can be delayed without affecting the entire project schedule. Therefore, a systematic algorithm is used to calculate the critical path and identify slack for each activity. A systematic algorithm is also necessary to implement the CPM approach on a computer for very big projects because they contain a large number of paths and activities.

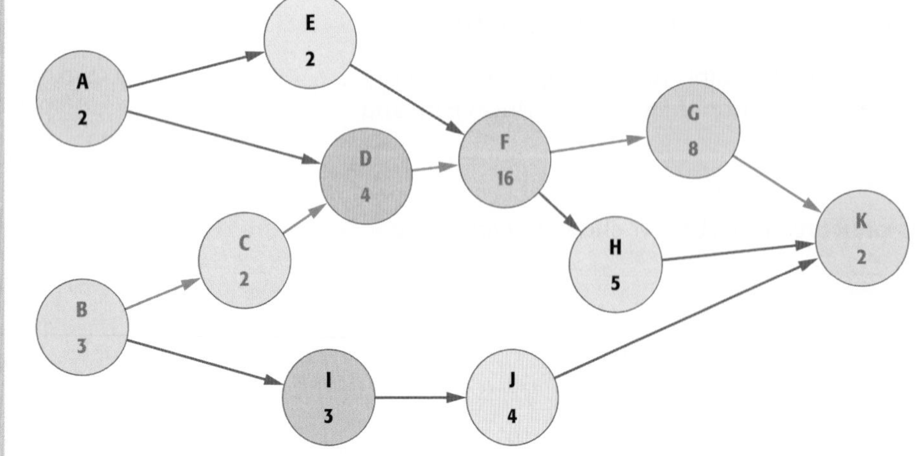

Path	Estimated Duration
AEFGK	30
AEFHK	27
ADFGK	32
ADFHK	29
BCDFGK	35
BCDFHK	32
BIJK	12

FIGURE 8.8 Sunny Beach Resort, Activity Paths, Estimated Completion Times, and Critical Path

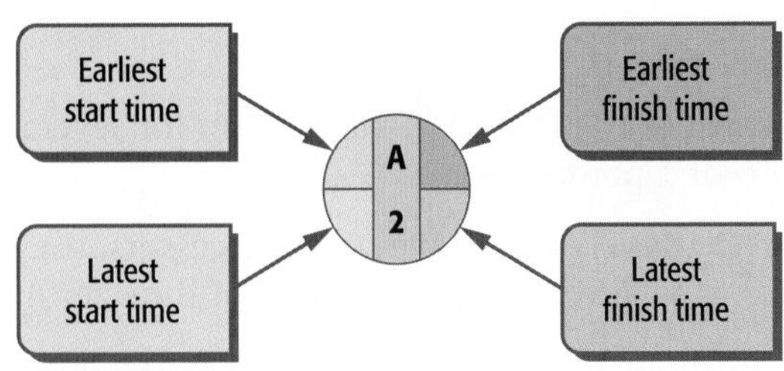

FIGURE 8.9 Convention for Displaying the Earliest and Latest Start and Finish Times

The algorithm for identifying the critical path and slack involves calculating the following four parameters for each activity:

Early start time (ES): the earliest time at which an activity can start, considering the beginning and ending times for each of the preceding activities.

Early finish time (EF): the sum of the early start time (ES) and the time required to complete the activity.

Late start time (LS): the latest time at which an activity can start, considering all the precedence relationships, without delaying the completion time for the project.

Late finish time (LF): the sum of the late start time and the time required to complete the activity.

The four parameters (ES, EF, LS, and LF) for each project activity are displayed according to the convention presented in Figure 8.9.

The implementation of the CPM algorithm begins by first identifying ES and EF for all activities. The procedure starts with the very first activity of a project, which has no predecessor. Once ES and EF for the first activity have been identified, the same procedure is repeated for the second activity, and so on. However, it is possible that the second and subsequent activities have many different precedence relationships with previously completed activities. Therefore, the calculation of ES and EF needs to be done very carefully so that none of the precedence relationships are ignored. Solved Example 4 demonstrates the calculation of ES and EF for Sunny Beach Resort.

PART II Tools and Tactical Issues

Solved Example 4

Sunny Beach Resort: Calculation of Early Start and Early Finish Times (Farward Pass)

Based on the information provided in Table 8.1 and Figure 8.8, calculate the early start (ES) and early finish (EF) times for the Sunny Beach Resort project.

SOLUTION:

First, a network diagram for the Sunny Beach Resort project is developed, using the convention described in Figure 8.9.

For the sake of clarity and consistency, let's assume that each time listed represents the end of the specified time period (e.g., 3 means the *end* of week 3, and so on).

(continued)

STEP 1

This step describes the ES and EF calculation for several activities that have either 0 or 1 predecessor.

- Because activities A and B have no predecessors, they can start as soon as the project is initiated (or at the end of time zero).
- The time estimate for activity A is 2 weeks; therefore, the earliest that it can finish is at the end of week 2.
- The time estimate for activity B is 3 weeks; therefore, the earliest that it can finish is at the end of week 3.
- Activity I depends only on the completion of activity B; therefore, it can start as soon as B is completed. Therefore, the earliest that activity I can start is at the end of week 3, and its earliest completion time will be at the end of week 6.
- Because activity I is the only predecessor of activity J, activity J can start at the end of week 6 at the earliest and finish at the end of week 10 at the earliest.
- Because activity C also has only one predecessor (activity B), it can start at the end of week 3 at the earliest and complete at the end of week 5 at the earliest.

Figure 8.10 displays these calculations.

STEP 2

During this step we will calculate the ES and EF for activities D and F, both of which have multiple predecessors.

- Activity D is preceded by activities A and C. Therefore, activity D can start only when both activities A and C are completed. The earliest that activity A can be completed is at the end of week 2, but the earliest that activity C can be completed is at the end of week 5. Therefore, ES for activity D is week 5, and EF is week 9.
- Activity F is preceded by activities D and E. The earliest that activity E can be completed is at the end of week 4, but the earliest that activity D can be completed is at the end of week 9. Therefore, ES for activity F is week 9, and EF is week 25.

Figure 8.11 displays these calculations.

STEP 3

During this step, we will calculate ES and EF for the remaining activities, G, H, and K.

- Activities G and H are both preceded by activity F. Therefore, ES for both G and H is week 25. Because of differences in their task durations, EF for G is week 33, and EF for H is week 30.
- The last activity, K, is preceded by three activities: G, H, and J. The EFs for these activities are weeks 33, 30, and 10, respectively. Therefore, ES for K is week 33, and EF is week 35.

Figure 8.12 displays these calculations.

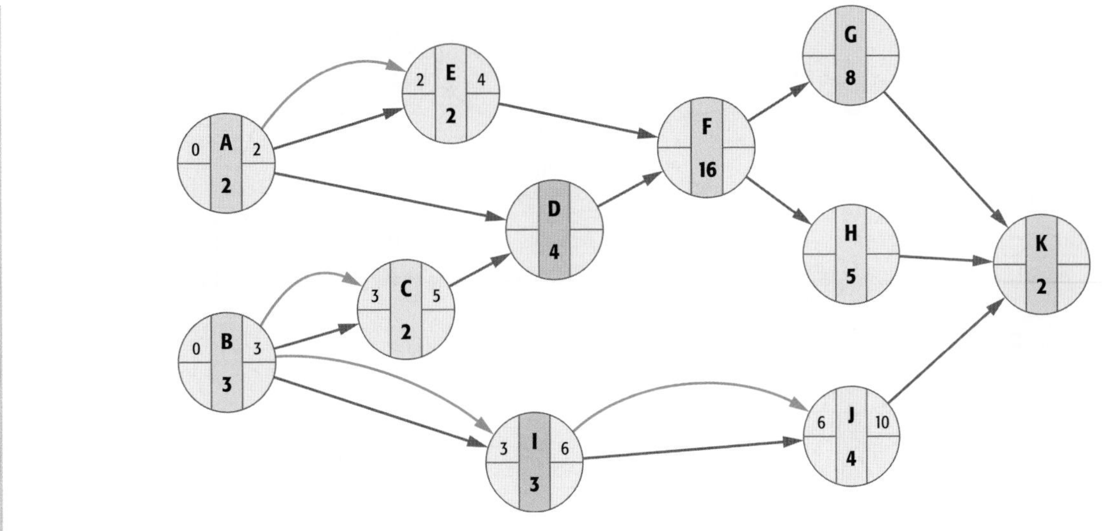

FIGURE 8.10 Calculation of Early Start and Finish Times—Step 1

The calculation of ES and EF for each activity provides the information about the earliest time a project can be completed (e.g., it will take 35 weeks to complete the Sunny Beach Resort project). However, the calculation of the late start time (LS) and late finish time (LF) is necessary to calculate slack and to identify the critical path.

The calculation of LS and LF starts from the very last activity in a project. The procedure begins by fixing LF for the last activity as equal to EF for the same activity, so that the project's latest completion time is the same as its earliest completion time. Working backward, then, LF and LS for each activity are identified. Solved Example 5 demonstrates the procedure for Sunny Beach Resort.

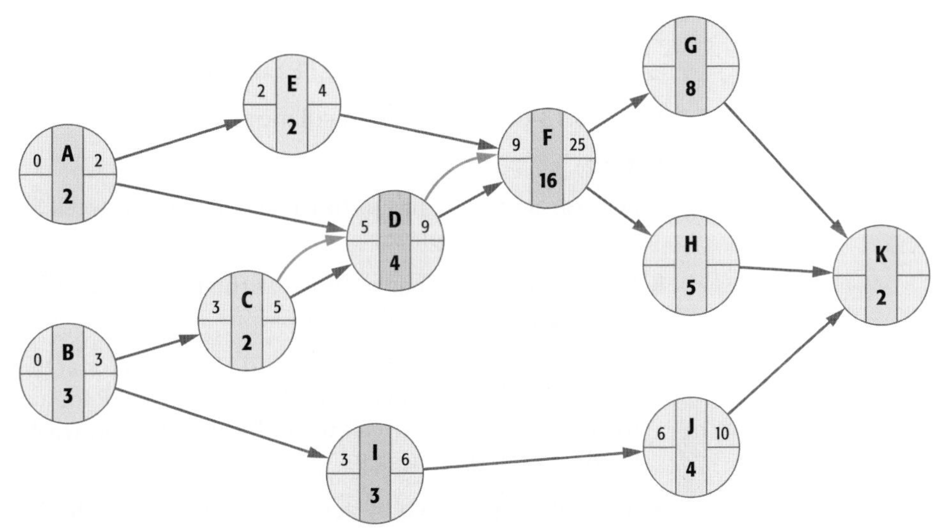

FIGURE 8.11 Calculation of Early Start and Finish Times—Step 2

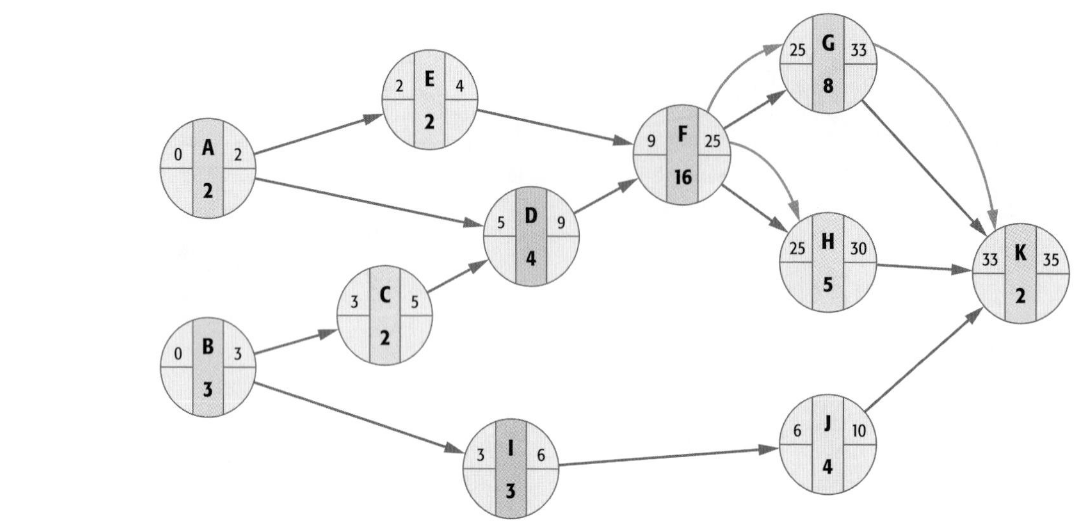

FIGURE 8.12 Calculation of Early Start and Finish Times—Step 3

Solved Example 5

Sunny Beach Resort: Calculation of Late Start and Late Finish Times (Backward Pass)

Based on the information provided in Table 8.1 and Figure 8.12, calculate the late start (LS) and late finish (LF) times for the Sunny Beach Resort project.

SOLUTION:

The calculation of LS and LF follows the calculation of ES and EF (see Figures 8.10 through 8.12).

STEP 1

- Because activity K can finish at the latest at week 35, it can begin at the latest at week 33.
- Activities G, H, and J are the predecessors of activity K. Because the LS for activity K is week 33, the LF for activities G, H, and J will be week 33.

Figure 8.13 displays these calculations.

STEP 2

- Because activity G has to finish at the latest at week 33, it must begin at the latest at week 25.
- Because activity H has to finish at the latest at week 33, it must begin at the latest at week 28.
- Activity F precedes activities G and H. The LS for activities G and H is weeks 25 and 28, respectively. Therefore, the LF for activity F must be week 25, or else activity G won't be able start on week 25. Hence, the LS for activity F is week 9.
- Activity F is preceded by activities D and E; therefore, their LF will be week 9. Therefore, the LS for activity E is week 7, and the LS for activity D is week 5.

(continued)

- Activity A precedes activities D and E. Because the LS for activities D and E is weeks 5 and 7, respectively, the LF for activity A is week 5. Therefore, the LS for activity A is week 3.
- Activity C precedes activity D; therefore, its LF is 5 and its LS is 3.
- Because the LF for activity J is 33, its LS is 29. Activity I precedes activity J; therefore, its LS and LF times are weeks 26 and 29, respectively.
- Activity B precedes activities C and I. The LS for activities C and I is weeks 3 and 26, respectively. Therefore, the LF for B will be week 3, and the LS will be week 0.

Figure 8.14 displays these calculations.

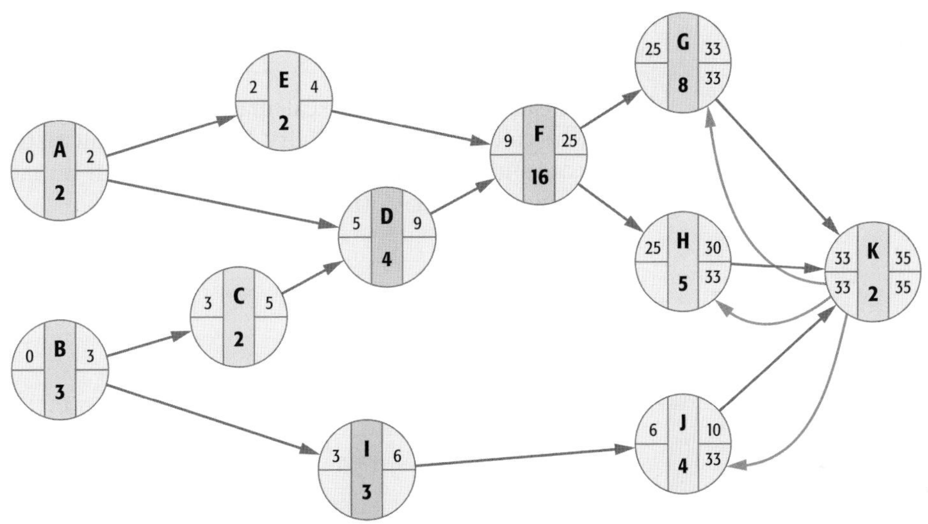

FIGURE 8.13 Calculation of Late Start and Late Finish Times—Step 1

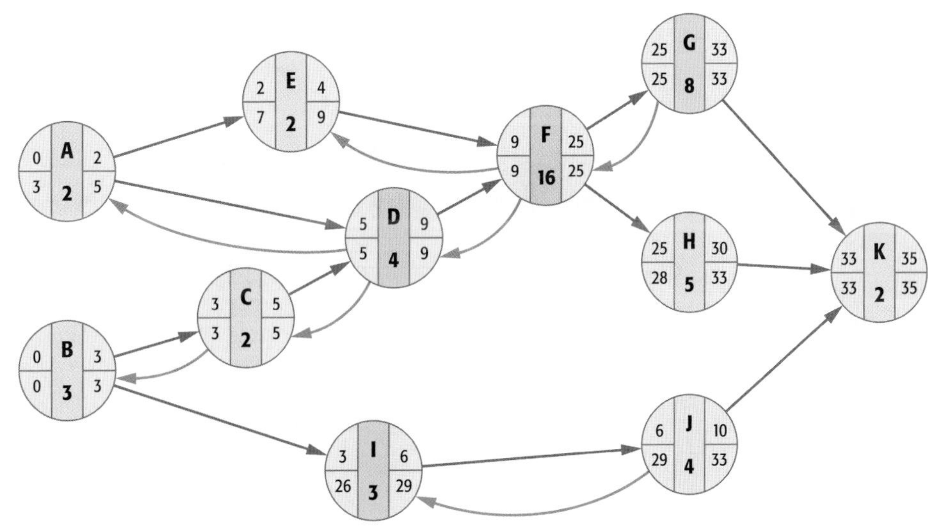

FIGURE 8.14 Calculation of Late Start and Late Finish Times—Step 2

The difference between the LS and the ES or the difference between the LF and the EF is known as slack because it represents the potential flexibility in starting an activity without affecting the project duration.

$$\text{Slack} = \text{LS} - \text{ES} = \text{LF} - \text{EF} \qquad \text{(Equation 1)}$$

The activities with zero slack are critical activities because there is no flexibility with regard to their beginning and ending schedule. Therefore, the project manager must ensure that critical activities do not get delayed. The noncritical activities, on the other hand, contain some slack and therefore can provide the necessary flexibility in scheduling the project. At the same time, if noncritical activities with very little slack are delayed extensively, then it may very well change the structure of the project and become critical.

Solved Example 6

Sunny Beach Resort: Calculation of Slack and Identification of Critical Path

Slack for each activity can be calculated using equation 1. Figure 8.15 shows the calculations for activity A. The slack calculations for all activities are shown in Figure 8.16. The critical path is made up of those activities with zero slack (marked in red).

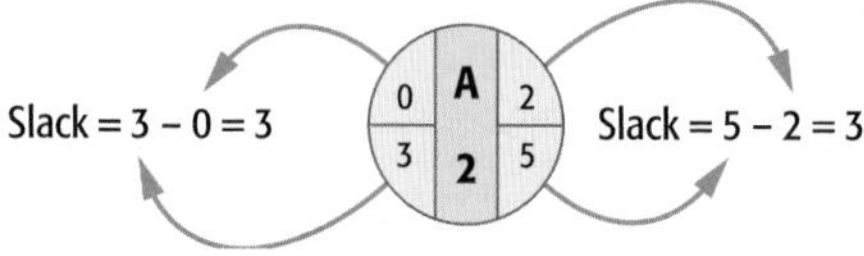

FIGURE 8.15 Calculation of Slack for Activity A

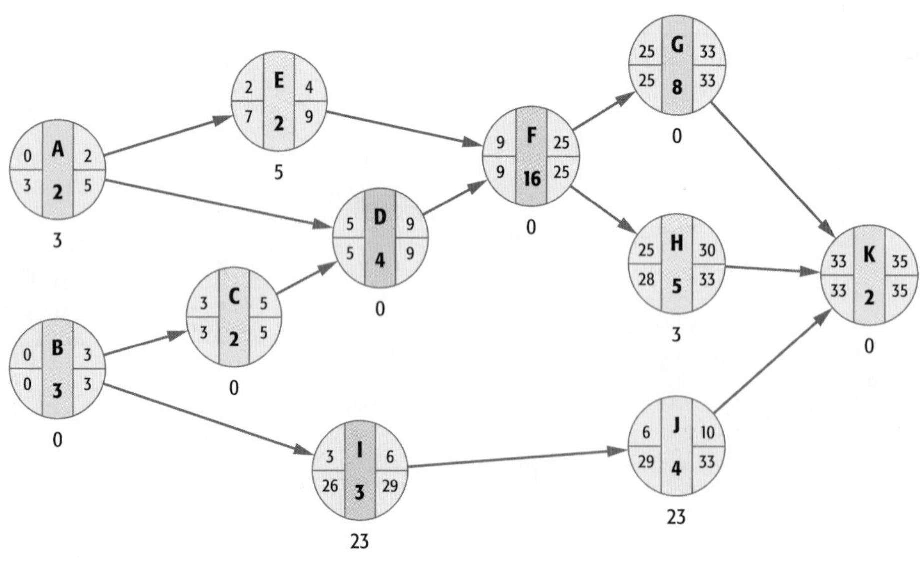

FIGURE 8.16 Identification of Critical Path Based on Slack Analysis

BEST PRACTICES IN OPERATIONS MANAGEMENT

The Project to Develop Affordable Blu-ray Video Players at Sony

The computing and electronics industry is known for constantly working on multiple projects leading to the development of new technology standards that can significantly enhance quality. While consumers often don't pay attention to technological developments until the final products are developed and released to the mass market, the projects often begin many years earlier and require significant cost and effort. In this feature, we will review the project undertaken to develop the Blu-ray player and disks that are increasingly used in video-game consoles and are also replacing DVD players.

The development was jump-started in February 2002, when nine companies (Hitachi Ltd., LG Electronics Inc., Matsushita Electric Industrial Co., Ltd., Pioneer Corporation, Royal Philips Electronics, Samsung Electronics Co. Ltd., Sharp Corporation, Sony Corporation, and Thomson Multimedia) jointly announced the establishment of the basic specifications for the next-generation large-capacity optical disk video-recording format called Blu-ray Disc. The Blu-ray Disc enables the recording, rewriting, and playback of up to 27 gigabytes (GB) of data on a single-sided single-layer 12-centimeter CD/DVD-size disk using a 405-nm blue-violet laser.

The Blu-ray founders then announced during a joint press conference in June 2002 that they had completed the next activity: the development of detailed specifications for the new standards. The aim of these disclosures was to give the manufacturers sufficient time to design and develop products based on the new format. The founders also started licensing the format to other manufacturers about a year after the original announcement (in February 2003).

The first commercial Blu-ray format video recorder was introduced by Sony in April–May 2003. The Blu-ray recorder was priced at close to $4,000 per piece. Sony also introduced the Blu-ray disks that can be used in the recorder for $30 each. Over the next year, a number of other manufacturers developed and introduced their own versions of Blu-ray disk recorders. Furthermore, movie producers such as the Walt Disney Company and Buena Vista Home Entertainment announced in December 2004 that they would also start releasing their titles in Blu-ray format.

Sony continued to develop Blu-ray technology. Some important milestones are listed here:

- In November 2005, Sony Pictures Home Entertainment (SPHE) announced that authoring had been completed on the first Blu-ray Disc to contain a full-length, high-definition feature film (*Charlie's Angels: Full Throttle*).
- In October 2006, Sony announced the arrival of the studio's first 50-GB dual-layer Blu-ray titles (*Black Hawk Down* and *Talladega Nights*).
- In November 2006, Sony announced that it now had six 50-GB Blu-ray Disc production lines up and running. The company started ramping up to produce up to 60,000 disks per day. In November, Sony also announced the launch of a new video-game console (Playstation 3, or PS3) that was based on Blu-ray technology. *(continued . . .)*

Launch of Blu-ray players.

BEST PRACTICES IN OPERATIONS MANAGEMENT

The Project to Develop Affordable Blu-ray Video Players at Sony (*continued*)

- Sony launched its next generation of Blu-ray video players, priced at approximately $1,000 per unit.
- In February 2007, Sony announced a reduction in the price of its next generation of Blu-ray player. This latest model is priced at $599.

The project to continue increasing the quality and affordability of the Blu-ray video player is still progressing, and we (as consumers) hope that by the time this textbook is ready to be shipped, Blu-ray players will be as affordable as a DVD player was in March 2007.

Cost and Time Tradeoff Analysis

The CPM method described earlier can be very helpful in identifying the most efficient schedule for executing a project. However, sometimes even the most efficient schedule is not sufficient for meeting customer needs. Under such circumstances, either the scope of the project needs to be changed or additional resources need to be assigned to speed up the project. For example, companies such as Sony that develop high-technology products have to constantly evaluate the cost of development and the completion time associated with each project. Similarly, large service companies such as American Express need to conduct cost and time tradeoff analysis associated with the development and launch of each of their new credit card or financial services offerings.

If the scope of the project is changed, then the project team can reevaluate the schedule based on the new guidelines using the critical path method described earlier. On the other hand, if additional resources are assigned to speed up the project schedule, a *cost and time tradeoff analysis* (also known as **crashing**) is conducted. Often a linear relationship between time reduction and additional cost is assumed (unless specified otherwise).

● **Crashing** a way to identify the lowest-cost approach for reducing the project duration

Each activity within the critical path is analyzed, and the additional resources are allocated to the activity for which the time can be reduced at the cheapest rate. This procedure is applied several times (one time unit at a time) to develop a time-cost tradeoff matrix or chart. Based on the available additional budget, the project manager can arrive at the optimum crashing decision.

Solved Example 7

Sunny Beach Resort: Cost and Time Tradeoff Analysis

Table 8.2 shows the estimated additional cost for crashing various activities that are part of the Sunny Beach Resort project. Assuming a linear relationship between the additional costs (referred to as *crash cost*) and the associated activity time reduction (normal time minus crash time), develop a cost and time tradeoff matrix. If an additional $40,000 can be spent, how soon can the project be completed?

SOLUTION

To conduct a cost and time tradeoff analysis, we need to first identify the critical path and duration for all project paths (see Figure 8.8).

(*continued*)

Because the critical path is made up of activities B, C, D, F, G, and K, the time required for any one of these activities can be reduced to speed up the project.

Among these critical activities, G is the cheapest to reduce ($2,000/week). Therefore, during the first step, G is reduced by 1 week. The same process is repeated twice more to reduce the project by another two weeks. However, two paths (BCDFGK and BCDFHK) now are of equal duration and are longest. Therefore, both paths need to be reduced to achieve a further reduction in project duration. Table 8.3 shows how project duration can be reduced to 23 weeks by allocating additional funds.

Figure 8.17 shows the plot of project time versus additional cost requirements. If an additional $40,000 is available, then the project can be completed in 26 weeks. Therefore this figure can be used to decide how much the project duration can be reduced if a certain amount of additional funds are available.

Program Evaluation and Review Technique (PERT)

The **program evaluation and review technique** was developed jointly by the U.S. Department of Defense and Booz Allen Hamilton during the development of the Polaris ballistic missile project in the late 1950s. PERT is a technique for addressing the impact of uncertainties in activity time estimates on the duration of the entire project duration. While it was orginally developed for a government project, PERT has found many applications in a variety of commercial projects across a wide range of industries.

● **Program evaluation and review technique** a technique for addressing the impact of uncertainties in activity time estimates on the duration of the entire project

TABLE 8.2 Sunny Beach Resort: Activity Relationships and Time Estimates

Activity	Description	Immediate Predecessor	Normal Time (weeks)	Crash Time (weeks)	Crash Cost	Crash Cost/Week
A	Select site	—	2	2	—	—
B	Select senior project staff	—	3	2	$5,000	$5,000
C	Select architect	B	2	1	$3,000	$3,000
D	Develop construction plan	A, C	4	2	$12,000	$6,000
E	Bring utilities to the site	A	2	2	—	—
F	Construct the buildings	D, E	16	12	$28,000	$7,000
G	Develop outdoor areas and landscape	F	8	4	$8,000	$2,000
H	Finish indoor areas and install necessary equipment	F	5	3	$6,000	$3,000
I	Select support personnel	B	3	2	$2,500	$2,500
J	Train support personnel	I	4	3	$3,500	$3,500
K	Get government approval for opening after final inspection	G, H, J	2	2	—	—

TABLE 8.3 Sunny Beach Resort: Crash Steps and Project Completion Time

PATH	AEFGK	AEFHK	ADFGK	ADFHK	BCDFGK	BCDFHK	BIJK
STEP 0	30	27	32	29	35	32	12
STEP 1	29	27	31	29	34	32	12
STEP 2	28	27	30	29	33	32	12
STEP 3	27	27	29	29	32	32	12
STEP 4	27	27	29	29	31	31	12
STEP 5	27	27	29	29	30	30	12
STEP 6	26	26	28	28	29	29	12
STEP 7	26	26	27	27	28	28	12
STEP 8	26	26	26	26	27	27	12
STEP 9	25	25	25	25	26	26	12
STEP 10	24	24	24	24	25	25	12
STEP 11	23	23	23	23	24	24	12
STEP 12	22	22	22	22	23	23	12

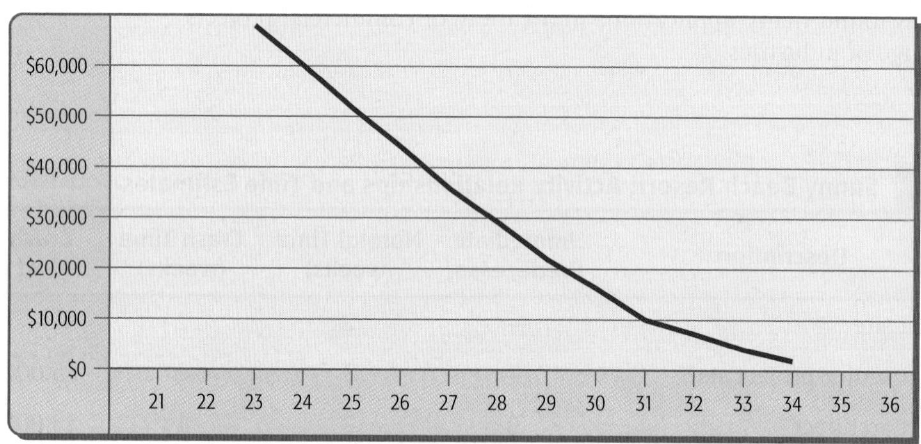

FIGURE 8.17 Additional Project Cost Versus Duration

PERT analysis is very similar to CPM analysis with respect to several concepts discussed earlier in this chapter (work breakdown structure, precedence relationships, and network diagram). However, because PERT attempts to address the uncertainties in a project schedule, four different estimates for activity times are developed.

Optimistic time (t_o): the minimum possible time required to complete an activity, assuming that everything proceeds better than is normally expected.

Pessimistic time (t_p): the maximum possible time required to complete an activity, assuming that everything proceeds at the slowest possible pace.

Most likely time (t_m): the best estimate of the time required to accomplish a task, assuming that everything proceeds normally.

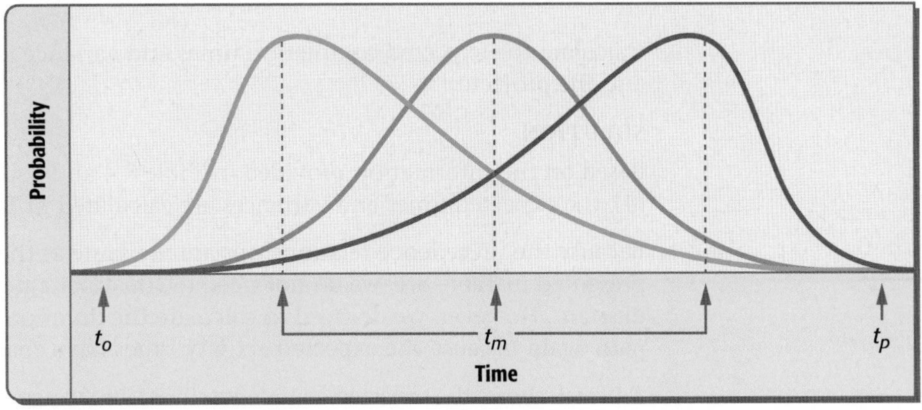

FIGURE 8.18 Potential Distributions of Activity Times

Expected time (t_e): the best estimate of the time required to accomplish an activity, considering the potential impact of t_o, t_m, and t_p.

Because by definition each project is unique, it is not possible to know the distribution of completion times associated with each project activity precisely (see Figure 8.18 for three potential distributions of activity times).

Therefore, an empirically derived equation is used to calculate the expected time (t_e) based on the other three activity time estimates.

$$\text{Expected Time for Project} = t_e = \frac{t_o + 4 * t_m + t_p}{6} \quad \text{(Equation 2)}$$

Furthermore, the variance in the estimated time for each activity can be calculated as

$$\text{Variance for an Activity} = \sigma^2 = \left(\frac{t_p - t_o}{6}\right)^2 \quad \text{(Equation 3)}$$

To conduct a PERT analysis, the expected time and variance for each activity is first calculated using equations (2) and (3). Then, as in CPM, the network diagram is constructed, and the critical path and activities are identified based on the time estimates. The variance of the critical path can be calculated as the sum of variances for the critical activities. Therefore

$$\text{Variance of Critical Path} = \sigma^2_{\text{critical\_path}} = \sum_{\text{all\_critical\_activities}} \left(\frac{t_p - t_o}{6}\right)^2 \quad \text{(Equation 4)}$$

$$\text{Standard Deviation for Critical Path} = \sigma_{\text{critical\_path}} = \sqrt{\sum_{\text{all\_critical activities}} \left(\frac{t_p - t_o}{6}\right)^2} \quad \text{(Equation 5)}$$

Solved Example 8

Sunny Beach Resort: PERT Analysis

Instead of using a single time estimate for each activity, three estimates were provided for the Sunny Beach Resort project. These estimates are summarized in Table 8.4.

(continued)

Calculate the expected completion times and variance for each activity and the project.

SOLUTION

Based on the information provided in Table 8.4 and equations (3) and (4), the expected times and variances are calculated in Table 8.5.

Because the precedence relationships are the same as the information presented in Table 8.1, we do not need to construct a new network diagram. However, we do need to calculate the duration of each project path again because the expected activity times have changed.

Table 8.6 shows the expected completion times and variances for each path.

The project is expected to complete in 36.3 weeks with a variance of 6.67.

The variance estimate for the critical path can be used to conduct many different statistical (or uncertainty) analyses related to the project completion times.

From statistics, we know that when several variables are added together, the resulting distribution starts to resemble a normal distribution. In our current context, therefore, the project completion time can be assumed to be represented by a normal distribution. The mean of this normal distribution will be the expected project completion time, and the variance will be same as the variance of the critical path. Therefore, using either the normal distribution table (in the Appendix) or the NORMDIST and NORMINV functions within Microsoft Excel, we can conduct various probability analyses. Several illustrations are presented in Solved Example 9.

TABLE 8.4 Sunny Beach Resort: Activity Relationships and Time Estimates

Activity	Description	Immediate Predecessor	Optimistic Time	Most Likely Time	Pessimistic Time
A	Select site	—	1	2	6
B	Select senior project staff	—	2	3	3
C	Select architect	B	1	2	4
D	Develop construction plan	A, C	3	4	6
E	Bring utilities to the site	A	2	2	4
F	Construct the buildings	D, E	12	16	25
G	Develop outdoor areas and landscape	F	4	8	10
H	Finish indoor areas and install necessary equipment	F	3	5	6
I	Select support personnel	B	2	3	4
J	Train support personnel	I	3	4	4
K	Get government approval for opening after final inspection	G, H, J	2	2	6

TABLE 8.5 Sunny Beach Resort: Expected Times and Variances

Activity	Description	Optimistic Time t_o	Most Likely Time t_m	Pessimistic Time t_p	Expected Time t_e	Variance σ^2
A	Select site	1	2	6	2.50	0.69
B	Select senior project staff	2	3	3	2.83	0.03
C	Select architect	1	2	4	2.17	0.25
D	Develop construction plan	3	4	6	4.17	0.25
E	Bring utilities to the site	2	2	4	2.33	0.11
F	Construct the buildings	12	16	25	16.83	4.69
G	Develop outdoor areas and landscape	4	8	10	7.67	1.00
H	Finish indoor areas and install necessary equipment	3	5	6	4.83	0.25
I	Select support personnel	2	3	4	3.00	0.11
J	Train support personnel	3	4	4	3.83	0.03
K	Get government approval for opening after final inspection	2	2	6	2.67	0.44

TABLE 8.6 Expected Path Times and Variances

PATH	Expected Time	Path Variance
AEFGK	32.0	6.94
AEFHK	29.2	6.19
ADFGK	33.8	7.08
ADFHK	31.0	6.33
BCDFGK	**36.3**	**6.67**
BCDFHK	33.5	5.92
BIJK	12.3	0.61

Solved Example 9

Sunny Beach Resort: Probability Calculations

Based on the information provided in Tables 8.5 and 8.6, calculate

1. **The probability that the project will be completed in 39 weeks or less**
2. **The probability that the project will be completed in between 33.5 and 38 weeks**
3. **With 95 percent probability, the date when the project can be expected to be completed**

(continued)

SOLUTION

1. **The probability can be calculated either by using the normal distribution table in the Appendix (also known as a z table) or by using software such as Microsoft Excel.**

   When using a normal distribution table, first a z value for the project completion time (39 weeks) is calculated using the following equation:

$$z - \text{value} = \frac{x - \mu}{\sigma} \qquad \text{(Equation 6)}$$

where x = the unknown variable
μ = mean (36.3 weeks)
σ = standard deviation = $\sqrt{\sigma^2} = \sqrt{6.67}$ = 2.58 weeks

Therefore,

$$z - \text{value} = \frac{39 - 36.3}{2.58} = 1.0465$$

Next, we can look at the z table (in the Appendix), which provides instructions on how to calculate the probability that the project will be completed in less than 1.0465 z value (which is equivalent to 39 weeks). The graphical representation of this calculation is presented in Figure 8.19.

The same calculation can be conducted in Microsoft Excel using the inbuilt function NORMDIST (screen shot included in Figure 8.20).

2. **The solution to this problem requires calculating z values for 33.5 and 38 weeks. Then we can find the probability that the project will be completed in 33.5 weeks or less, and the probability that the project will be completed in 38 weeks or less. The difference between the two numbers is the probability that the project will be completed in between 33.5 and 38 weeks.**

(continued)

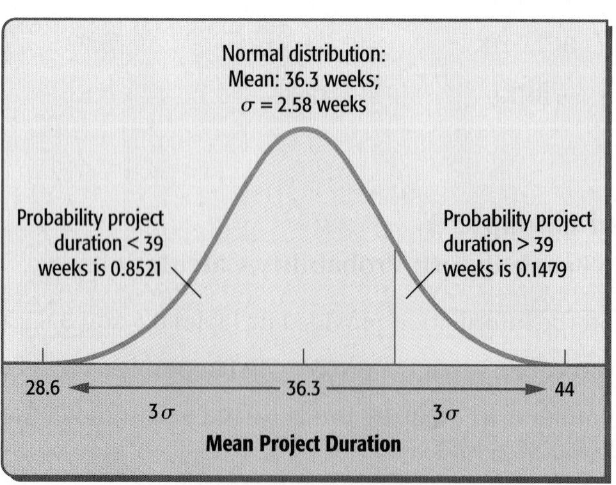

FIGURE 8.19 Probability of Completing the Project in 39 Weeks or Less

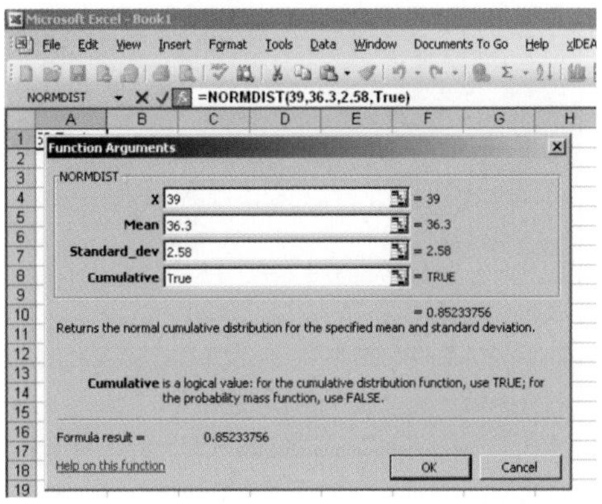

FIGURE 8.20 Using the NORMDIST Function in Microsoft Excel

z Value for 33.5 Weeks = –1.085

Probability That the Project Will Be Completed in 33.5 Weeks or Less = 0.139

z value for 38 weeks = 0.6589

Probability That the Project Will Be Completed in 38 Weeks or Less = 0.745

Therefore the probability that the project will be completed in between 33.5 and 38 weeks (see Figure 8.21) is

$$0.745 - 0.139 = 0.606 \text{ or } 60.6\%$$

3. **This question requires calculating the number of weeks necessary to complete the project with 95 percent probability. In other words, this problem asks us to do the calculations opposite to those in parts (1) and (2).**

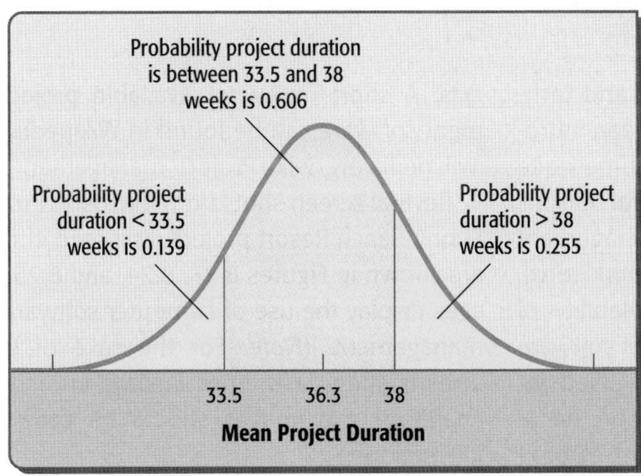

FIGURE 8.21 Probability of Completing the Project in Between 33.5 and 38 Weeks

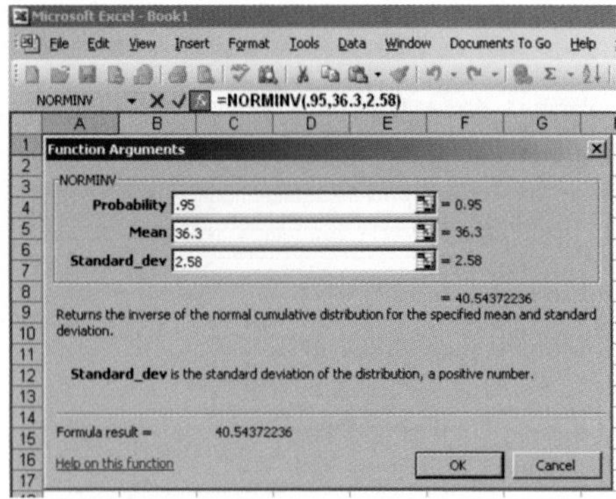

FIGURE 8.22 Using the NORMINV Function in Microsoft Excel

The given probability is 95 percent, or 0.95. Therefore, the first step is to find the z value corresponding to probability = 0.95.

From the Appendix, we can find that the z value is 1.645. Applying Equation (6), we can write

$$1.645 = \frac{x - 36.3}{2.58}$$

Therefore $x = 1.645 * 2.58 + 36.3 = 40.54$ weeks.

Thus, 40.54 weeks are needed to complete the project with 95 percent probability.

The same calculations can be conducted in Microsoft Excel using the function NORMINV. A sample screen shot is shown in Figure 8.22.

TECHNOLOGY IN OPERATIONS MANAGEMENT

Project Management Software

While a large number of concepts, tools, and techniques for project management have been introduced since the 1950s, their use has become quite widespread in recent years. There are several reasons for this increase in the use of project management techniques, such as a globally diverse work force, multiproject environments, and the availability of user-friendly software. Project management software such as Microsoft Project is now widely used for scheduling, resource allocation, collaboration, documentation, planning, and real-time control of projects. A short review of available project management software can be found in Wikipedia (http://en.wikipedia.org/wiki/Project_management_software).

Several screen shots from Microsoft Project for the Sunny Beach Resort project discussed in this chapter are shown in Figures 8.23, 8.24, and 8.25. These images display the use of computer software in project management. (*Note:* For the sake of brevity, the screens show task times in days instead of weeks. Therefore, the images should be considered only illustrations.)

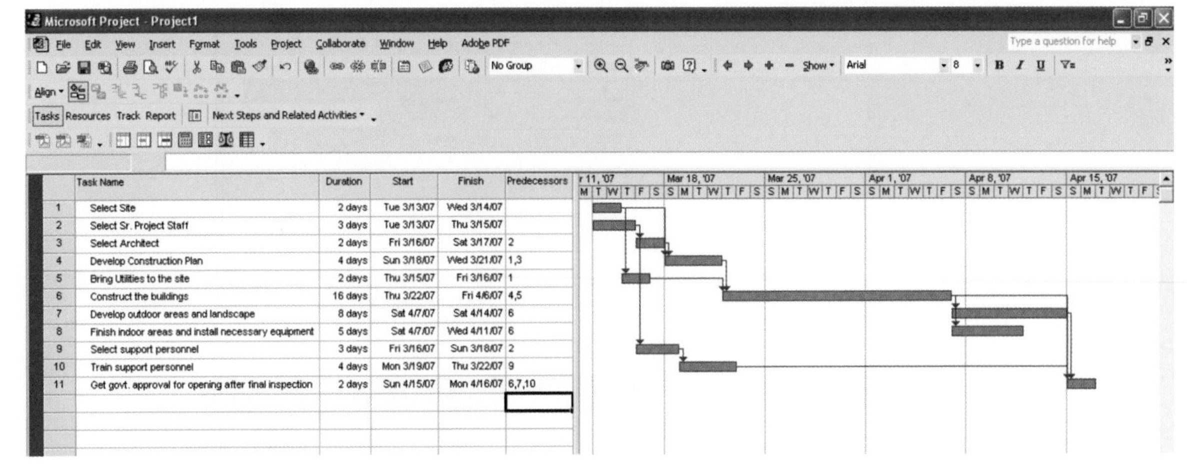

	Task Name	Duration	Start	Finish	Predecessors
1	Select Site	2 days	Tue 3/13/07	Wed 3/14/07	
2	Select Sr. Project Staff	3 days	Tue 3/13/07	Thu 3/15/07	
3	Select Architect	2 days	Fri 3/16/07	Sat 3/17/07	2
4	Develop Construction Plan	4 days	Sun 3/18/07	Wed 3/21/07	1,3
5	Bring Utilities to the site	2 days	Thu 3/15/07	Fri 3/16/07	1
6	Construct the buildings	16 days	Thu 3/22/07	Fri 4/6/07	4,5
7	Develop outdoor areas and landscape	8 days	Sat 4/7/07	Sat 4/14/07	6
8	Finish indoor areas and install necessary equipment	5 days	Sat 4/7/07	Wed 4/11/07	6
9	Select support personnel	3 days	Fri 3/16/07	Sun 3/18/07	2
10	Train support personnel	4 days	Mon 3/19/07	Thu 3/22/07	9
11	Get govt. approval for opening after final inspection	2 days	Sun 4/15/07	Mon 4/16/07	6,7,10

FIGURE 8.23 Gantt Chart for Sunny Beach Resort Created by Microsoft Project

Resource Management

The project management techniques described in this chapter assume that a project team has the necessary resources to complete each activity within the specified time and budget. However, in reality, this might not be the case. Therefore, a number of supplementary techniques are designed to allocate resources to different project activities effectively. Two commonly used resource management techniques are described here.

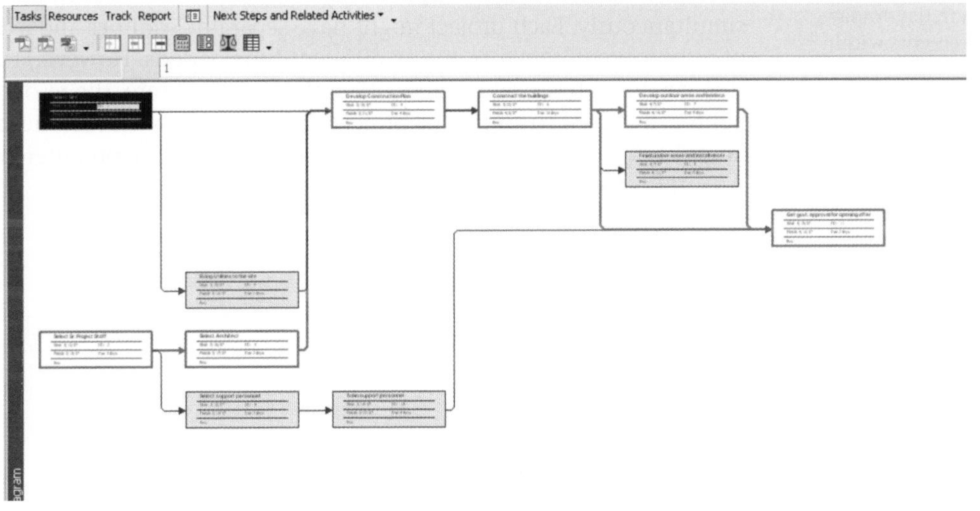

FIGURE 8.24 Critical Path for Sunny Beach Resort Calculated by Microsoft Project

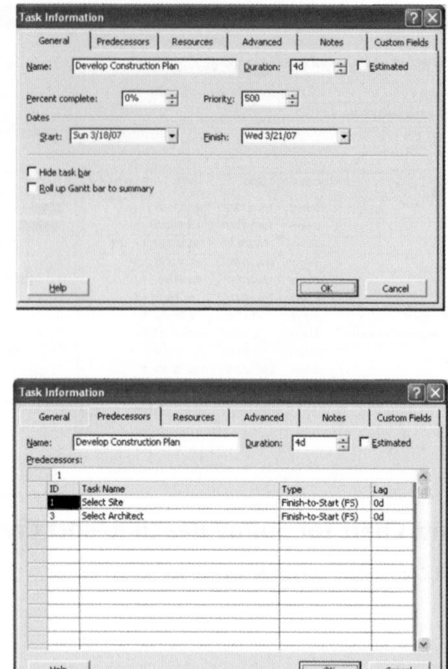

FIGURE 8.25 Some Options for Project Control Within Microsoft Project

● **Resource breakdown structure** a standardized list of personnel required to complete various activities in a project

● **Resource leveling** an approach to reduce the amount of fluctuations in day-to-day resource requirements within an organization

- A **resource breakdown structure** (RBS) is a standardized list of personnel required to complete various activities in a project. This technique is often used in combination with the work breakdown structure.
- **Resource leveling** is an approach to reduce the amount of fluctuations in day-to-day resource requirements within an organization. This approach is especially useful when employees in an organization work on multiple projects simultaneously. Each project might have separate deadlines and a different set of resource requirements during different time periods. However, the organization generally has a set number of employees. Therefore, the resource leveling approach is used to adjust the project schedule so that almost the same amount of personnel time is required every day to work on different projects. A sample example is presented in Figure 8.26.

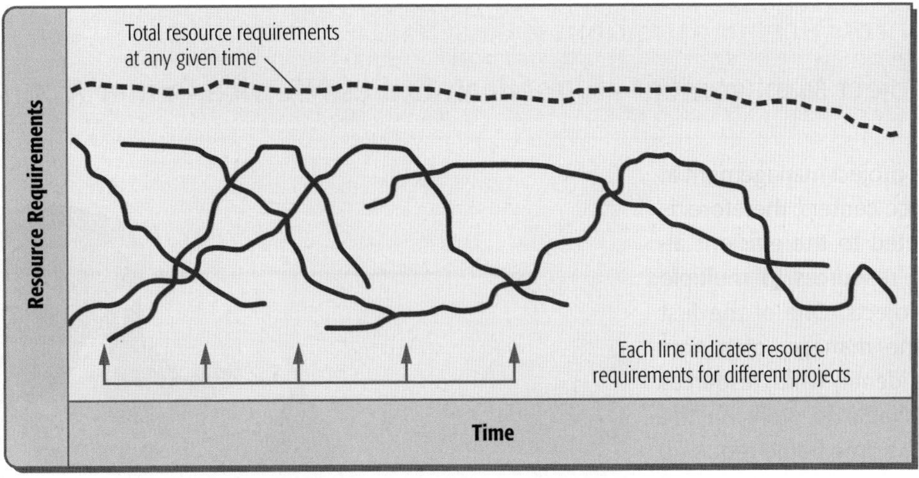

FIGURE 8.26 Resource Requirements in Multiproject Environments

BEST PRACTICES IN OPERATIONS MANAGEMENT

Project Management at American Express Service Center

When a customer dials one of the toll-free numbers listed on his or her American Express (AMEX) card, the call will be routed to one of the several service centers located around the globe. The managers and employess at American Express service centers located in various places in the United States (Salt Lake City, Utah; Phoenix, Arizona; Greensboro, North Carolina; and Plantation; Florida) and the rest of the world (e.g., the United Kingdom, India, and Australia) not only support customer phone calls but also engage in a number of other ongoing projects.

While some projects require the participation of employees from only one AMEX service center, a large number of project teams are dispersed globally. For instance, the launching of a new credit card might be initiated by corporate headquarters (New York), but the completed application forms from potential customers may be processed at one or more service centers located elsewhere. Each service center will need to ensure that the systems are ready for the new product, employees are trained on the features and benefits of the product so that they can answer questions, and procedures for processing applications are spelled out. Such a project would typically have a very tight time frame and fixed deadlines for completion of the various steps, would require multiple stakeholders across business units, and would need to be coordinated and prioritized accordingly. Six Sigma projects to address customer satisfaction issues are another example of projects that may require participation of employees from multiple locations and across business units.

It is very common for a typical manager and the members of his or her team to be participating in multiple projects, each with its own set of requirements, time schedules, and deadlines. The manager's role in each project might also vary—for some projects, he or she might be the project leader, whereas for other projects, he or she might be a subject matter expert with a narrower scope of responsibility. Very often, a new project may be introduced while others are in progress, necessitating reprioritizing and reallocation of funds and resources.

(continued)

BEST PRACTICES IN OPERATIONS MANAGEMENT

Project Management at American Express Service Center (*continued*)

Effective project management at AMEX service centers, therefore, is closely related to the efficient allocation of resources to multiple ongoing projects. One of the first tasks for the manager of a new project is to identify which resources will be available to work on the project in the time frame required. The project duration, in turn, will depend upon the availability of resources outside the manager's immediate team and often in other business units. Managing a project thus becomes more a question of getting buy-in and commitment from the leadership to dedicate resources to the project and juggling schedules to keep the project schedule from slipping. From the individual employees' standpoint, assignment to multiple projects implies that they have to effectively manage the time allocated to different activities. If an employee ends up spending more than the allotted time on one project, this may have undesirable implications for the execution of other projects—some involving employess and processes in a totally different part of the world. Project management at AMEX, therefore, is very closely linked with resource management.

Project resource management requires intense discussions among team members.

SUCCESS FACTORS IN PROJECT MANAGEMENT

It should be clear from the discussion provided in this chapter that project management requires a comprehensive set of skills and expertise. To understand how to be successful, we must start by discussing why projects fail.

Why Do Projects Fail?

Over the years, a number of scholars have studied the factors that affect the success or failure of a project. In a recent article, Dilts and Pence (2006) summarized the critical factors that were identified as causes for project failure (Table 8.7).

Based on a review of several large-scale consulting projects conducted in various countries around the world, Pinto and Kharbanda (1996) have identified 12 critical reasons why projects fail (Table 8.8). They conclude that some projects fail simply because projects are inherently risky. However, they also suggest that, by taking proper precautions and developing appropriate contingency plans, the chances of a project's failure can be reduced.

Project Risk Management

Even with careful planning, it is not possible to anticipate everything that can put a project's scope, schedule, or budget at risk. Therefore, a careful manager also develops plans for managing various risks associated with the project. The risks associated with projects can be divided into four broad categories (e.g., Gary, 2005):

- Financial resource risk, such as cash overruns, budget shortfalls, and cash flow problems
- Human resource risk, such as changes in project personnel
- Supply risk, such as suppliers not providing the required materials on time
- Quality risk, or the possibility that the quality of individual tasks gets compromised when trying to keep up with the project schedule

An appropriate project risk management plan includes a thorough assessment of all potential problems and the development of a contingency plan. The guideline provided here could be used to develop a project risk minimization plan.

The first step in any risk assessment plan involves developing a comprehensive list of all potential problems that might hinder the successful execution of a project. The identified problems can be classified according to the following criteria:

TABLE 8.7 Critical Factors in Project Failure

1	Change in initial project expectations
2	Change in the overall project importance to the organization
3	Change in the need for the project by the organization
4	Change in overall complexity
5	Change in overall time to completion
6	Change in user needs
7	Change in overall project resources (people, materials, funds)
8	Change in technical difficulties
9	Change in funding source
10	Change in regulatory problems
11	Internal politics within the organization
12	External politics to the organization
13	Change in commitment by project champion

Source: Reprinted from *Journal of Operations Management,* Vol. 24, Issue 4, Dilts, D.M. and K.R. Pence. "Impact of Role in the Decision to Fail: An Exploratory Study of Terminated Projects," p. 381, Copyright 2006, with permission from Elsevier.

TABLE 8.8 How to Successfully FAIL in a Project

1	Ignore the project environment (including stakeholders)
2	Push a new technology to market too quickly
3	Don't bother building a fallback option
4	When problems occur, shoot the one most visible
5	Let new ideas starve to death from inertia
6	Don't bother conducting feasibility studies
7	Never admit that a project is a failure
8	Overmanage project managers and their teams
9	Never, *never* conduct postfailure analysis
10	Never bother to understand project tradeoffs
11	Allow political expediency and infighting to dictate crucial project decisions
12	Make sure the project is run by a weak leader

Source: Reprinted from *Business Horizons,* 39, Pinto, J. K. and O. P. Kharbanda. "How to Fail in Project Management (Without Really Trying)," p. 46, Copyright 1996, with permission from Elsevier.

- *Severity:* What percentage of the project's scope will be affected by a problem?
- *Probability:* What are the chances that a specific problem will occur?
- *Timing:* At what point in the project is the specific problem likely to appear?
- *Dynamic risk:* As the project proceeds, will the probability of the problem occurrence increase, decrease, or stay constant?

Once the project risks have been categorized on these four dimensions, they can be mapped on a template for easy reference during the project execution phase (Table 8.9).

After the development of the project risk template, several additional analyses can be conducted with respect to each potential problem as described here:

- The project manager should attempt to quantify the impact of each potential problem on a common basis, such as time delays or cost overruns.
- Once the risks are presented on the same scale, a prioritization scheme can be developed to minimize the probability that a particular problem will occur.
- The project team should develop a contingency plan in case the identified problems do occur during the project execution.
- The project manager should also develop a potential upside for the project if the potential problem is avoided.
- Finally, different project team members should be assigned the responsibility for monitoring the signs of each potential problem. During project update meetings, each member should update his or her project colleagues regarding the status of the potential problems he or she is monitoring. This approach ensures that the probability of a problem's occurring will be minimized.

TABLE 8.9 Project Risk Map Template

Type of Risk	Severity (scale: 0–100), Based on Impact on Project Execution	Probability of Occurrence	Possible Time of Occurrence: 1st Quarter	2nd Quarter	3rd Quarter	4th Quarter	Probability of Occurrence w.r.t. with Time
Risk 1	20	80					Constant
Risk 2	60	40					Decreases
Risk 3	75	60					Increases
⋮							
Risk n	80	10					Constant

Why Do Projects Succeed?

Several things must go right for a project to be successful:

- Successful execution of a project requires a strong project leadership. The project manager must focus on meeting the three constraints: scope, time, and budget. A successful project means that all deliverables are completed on time, within budget, and at a level of quality that is acceptable to the project's sponsors and stakeholders.
- It is necessary to develop clear and measurable project goals. Projects with uncertain objectives fail more often than projects in which the goals are clearly defined and communicated to all stakeholders.
- For a project to be successful, the roles and responsibilities of each team member should be clearly defined. The project team must agree on the finished deliverables so that all effort is focused in the same direction. Therefore, vague descriptions of tasks and responsibilities should be avoided at all costs.
- The project execution strategy and implementation plan must be well defined and clear to all stakeholders. The single most important activity that an excellent project manager engages in is carefully planning all aspects of the project prior to and during execution.
- Business executives also believe that it is necessary for the project team members to have a sense of urgency about the execution of the project. Because projects are finite endeavors with limited time, money, and other resources available, they must be kept moving toward completion. Because most team members have lots of other priorities, it's up to the project manager to keep their attention focused on project deliverables and deadlines. Regular status checks, meetings, and reminders are essential.
- All project deliverables and all project activities must be visualized and communicated in detail to all team members and the stakeholders.

Andy Munns (University of Dundee, United Kingdom) has developed a simple checklist to assess the potential for a project's success. This checklist is given in Figure 8.27.

Because managers in most organizations work on multiple projects at all times, it is necessary to identify and prioritize projects so that each executed project has

Answer each of the questions yes or no. Score 2 points for each yes answer, and 0 for a no. The maximum score is 100; your potential for success will be a proportion based on your total score. Please note that this is only a potential; we cannot guarantee success, but if we score highly in all 10 areas, we increase our chances of being a success. Each area has a maximum score of 10; weak areas will have a lower score. If we are to be successful, we will need to target some resources to the areas with a lower score.

1. Clearly Defined Goals

- Is there a clear and written-down objective for the project?
- Are the main tasks structured?
- Has the scope of the project been agreed?
- Does the team know and agree with the goals?
- Are there clear milestones along the way?

2. Project Manager Ability

- Is the project manager skilled and experienced?
- Does the project manager have a plan and a budget?
- Does the project manager have technical knowledge in the area of the project?
- Does the project manager have leadership skills?
- Can the project manager motivate the team?

3. Team Member Skills

- Do we know what skills are required on this project?
- Does the team have all these skills?
- Is there a training program for team members?
- Is there a range of skills and experience on the project?
- Are people there because of what they bring to the project and not due to their position in the organization?

4. Top Management Support

- Is there support from top management for the project?
- Does the project have a champion in top management?
- Have adequate resources been allocated to the project?
- Does top management have a stake in the outcome of the project?
- Does the project fit with organization objectives?

5. Project Planning

- Is there a clear method for achieving the project?
- Has a plan for the project life been prepared from this method?
- Is there good short-term planning?
- Is progress measured against a plan?
- Is the plan adjusted to match progress?

6. Communication

- Are there clear channels of communication to all parties on the project?
- Can team members discuss issues openly?
- Can team members communicate their opinions on decisions?
- Do team members get feedback on performance?
- Do team members trust each other enough to communicate freely at all times?

7. User Involvement

- Do we know the end users of the project?
- Have the end users been involved in setting the project outcomes?
- Is it easy for end users to get involved in the project?
- Do the end users give feedback on progress?
- Do the end users have ownership of the solution?

(continued)

FIGURE 8.27 Assessing the Potential for Project Management Success

8. Commitment of Team

- Are team members behind the goals of the project?
- Do the team members own the project outcome?
- Are team members involved in decision making?
- Can team members make suggestions about improving and changing the project?
- Do team members go beyond their job description for the good of the project?

9. Control Systems

- Does the project have a control system?
- Do we check planned time and cost against actual duration and expenditure?
- Are checks carried out early enough to detect problems and correct them?
- Do we give feedback on progress to the team?
- Do we check that action on feedback is effective?

10. Risk Management

- Have key risks on the project been identified?
- Has the effect of each risk been measured?
- Have responses been decided for key risks?
- Have action plans been prepared for each response?
- Does the team have a plan for managing unexpected risks?

FIGURE 8.27 Assessing the Potential for Project Management Success (*continued*)

Source: Andy Munns, University of Dundee. Reprinted with permission from the author.

a higher chance of success. Therefore, Wheelwright and Clark (2003) suggest that companies should develop an aggregate project plan and decide which projects to pursue. They recommend an eight-step plan for identifying and prioritizing projects (Table 8.10).

TABLE 8.10 Guidelines for Developing an Aggregate Project Plan

Step 1	Define project types as either breakthrough, platform, derivative, R&D, or partnered projects
Step 2	Identify existing projects and classify by project type
Step 3	Estimate the average time and resources needed for each project type based on past experience
Step 4	Identify existing resource capacity
Step 5	Determine the desired mix of projects
Step 6	Estimate the number of projects that existing resources can support
Step 7	Decide which specific projects to purse
Step 8	Work to improve development capabilities

Source: Reprinted by permission of *Harvard Business Review*. From "Creating Project Plans to Focus Product Development," by Weelwright S. C. and K. Clark.

SUMMARY

1. Define the term *project,* list the steps involved in project management, and explain the role of the project manager

- Projects have finite beginning and ending dates, budgets, and resources.
- Every project includes some tasks and activities that have never been done before.
- A project has specific objectives and may include several deliverables and the meeting of many performance milestones.
- The project manager is responsible for providing leadership and for the successful execution of a project.

2. Describe various project management tools and techniques, such as work breakdown structure, critical path method, program evaluation and review technique, cost and time tradeoff analysis, and resource management.

- A project can be subdivided into its component subprojects and activities.
- Interrelationships between project activities need to be identified for effective scheduling. The precedence relationships between activities are used to identify different project paths.
- The task times and precedence relationships for project activities can be used to identify the critical path. The length of the critical path determines the duration of the project.
- Critical activities have zero slack and therefore cannot be delayed without delaying the entire project. Noncritical activities contain slack and therefore provide flexibility in scheduling. Additional resources are necessary to speed up the project completion time.
- PERT (program evaluation and review technique) is used to assess the impact of time-related uncertainties on the project schedule. Using PERT, probabilities for completing a project within specified time periods can be estimated.
- Most organizations have a relatively fixed number of managers, and therefore project management is also closely related to resource or capacity management.

3. Understand how to execute projects successfully and how to avoid risks and failure.

- Many factors contribute to the success or failure of a project. A project may fail if severe changes are made to project expectations, scope, and complexity or if additional constraints are added (e.g., a reduced resource commitment).
- Even with careful planning, it is not possible to anticipate everything that can put a project's scope, schedule, or budget at risk. The risks associated with projects can be divided into four broad categories: financial, human resource, supply, and quality risks.
- An appropriate project risk management plan includes a thorough assessment of all potential problems and the development of a contingency plan. A project risk assessment plan includes developing a comprehensive list of all potential problems that might hinder the successful execution of a project. The identified problems can be classified according to their severity, probability, timing, and whether the nature of the risk is dynamic.

SOLVED PROBLEM 1

The time estimates for the setup of a new production line at Ithaca Custom Manufacturing (ICM) Inc. are listed in Table 8.11.

TABLE 8.11 Activity Times and Immediate Predecessors

Activity	Time (hours)	Immediate Predecessor
A	4	—
B	3	A
C	5	A
D	2	A
E	3	B, C
F	4	C, D
G	1	E, F

1. Draw a network diagram for ICM Inc. using the AON convention.
2. Calculate the slack associated with each activity and identify the critical path.

SOLUTION

The network diagram, with early start, early finish, late start, and late finish times and slack, is shown in Figure 8.28.

Critical activities are ACFG.

The duration of the critical path for the project is 14 hours.

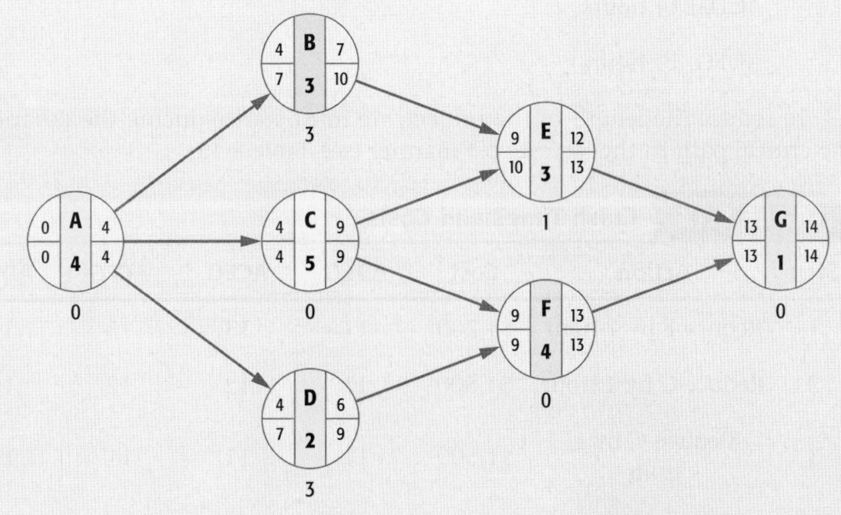

FIGURE 8.28 Network Diagram and Critical Path Calculations

SOLVED PROBLEM 2

The normal time, crash time, and cost estimates for the setup of a new production line at Ithaca Custom Manufacturing (ICM) Inc. are listed in Table 8.12.

TABLE 8.12 Activity Times and Immediate Predecessors

Activity	Normal Time (hours)	Crash Time (hours)	Crash Cost (per hour)	Immediate Predecessor
A	4	3	\$2,000	—
B	3	3	—	A
C	5	3	\$1,500	A
D	2	2	—	A
E	3	2	\$1,000	B, C
F	4	2	\$1,200	C, D
G	1	1	—	E, F

1. Based on the information provided in Table 8.12, develop a cost and time tradeoff table.
2. If an additional \$4,000 can be spent, what will be the new project duration?

SOLUTION

1. The project includes four paths:

   ABEG: 11 hours

   ACEG: 13 hours

   ACFG: 14 hours

   ADFG: 11 hours

To reduce the length of the project, we must start reducing the duration of the critical path in the lowest-cost manner (see Table 8.13).

TABLE 8.13 Crash Times and Costs

Step	Action	Cost	ABEG	ACEG	ACFG	ADFG
1	Reduce F by 1 hour	\$1,200	11	13	13	10
2	Reduce C by 1 hour	\$1,500	11	12	12	10
3	Reduce C by 1 hour	\$1,500	11	11	11	10
4	Reduce E by 1 hour and F by 1 hour	\$2,200	10	10	10	9

2. If an additional $4,000 were available, then the first two steps in Table 8.13 could be completed. Therefore, the new project duration would be 12 hours.

SOLVED PROBLEM 3

Table 8.14 shows the optimistic, most likely, and pessimistic time estimates for the setup of a new production line at Ithaca Custom Manufacturing (ICM) Inc.

TABLE 8.14 Activity, Immediate Predecessors, and Three Time Estimates

Activity	Optimistic Time	Most Likely Time	Pessimistic Time	Immediate Predecessor
A	3	3	5	—
B	3	4	5	A
C	4	5	7	A
D	2	2	4	A
E	1	2	2	B, C
F	2	3	6	C, D
G	1	1	4	E, F

1. Based on the information provided in Table 8.14, calculate the expected time and variance for each activity.
2. Develop an AON network diagram and calculate the project completion time and variance.
3. What is the probability that the project will be completed in 15 hours or less?

SOLUTION

1. The expected time and variance for each activity can be calculated by using Equations 2 and 3. The results are presented in Table 8.15.
2. Because the precedence diagram for this problem is the same as that of Solved Problem 1, we can calculate the duration of the four paths to identify the critical path.

   ABEG: 10.67 hours

   ACEG: 11.83 hours

   ACFG: 13.33 hours

   ADFG: 10.5 hours

   Therefore, the critical path is ACFG with the duration of 13.33 hours. The variance of the critical path is 0.11 + 0.25 + 0.44 + 0.25 = 1.05.

TABLE 8.15 Expected Time and Variance Calculations

Activity	Optimistic Time	Most Likely Time	Pessimistic Time	Expected Time	Variance
A	3	3	5	3.33	0.11
B	3	4	5	4.00	0.11
C	4	5	7	5.17	0.25
D	2	2	4	2.33	0.11
E	1	2	2	1.83	0.03
F	2	3	6	3.33	0.44
G	1	1	4	1.50	0.25

3. Using the NORMDIST function in Excel or the normal distribution table in the Appendix, we can find the probability that the project will be completed in 15 hours or less to be 0.9484.

PROBLEMS

1. Table 8.16 shows the activities, durations, and precedence relationships for a project.

TABLE 8.16 Activity Times and Immediate Predecessors

Activity	Duration (days)	Immediate Predecessor
P	3	None
Q	5	P
R	4	P
S	2	Q, R
T	6	S

a. Construct an activity on node (AON) network for this project.

b. Calculate the length of each project path and find how long it will take to complete the project.

c. Identify the project critical path and critical activities.

2. Table 8.17 shows the normal time, crash time, and crash costs for the project described in Table 8.16 (Problem 1).

TABLE 8.17 Activity Times and Immediate Predecessors

Activity	Normal Duration (days)	Crash Duration (days)	Crash Cost (per day)
P	3	2	$5,000
Q	5	3	$2,000
R	4	4	—
S	2	2	—
T	6	4	$1,500

a. Based on the information provided in Table 8.17, develop a cost and time tradeoff table.

b. If an additional $10,000 can be spent, what will be the new project duration?

3. Table 8.18 shows the activities, three estimates of project durations, and the precedence relationships for a project.

   a. Construct an activity on node (AON) network for this project.

   b. Calculate the expected time and standard deviation for each project activity.

   c. Calculate the length of each project path and identify the expected project completion time.

   d. Calculate the expected project completion time.

   e. Calculate the variance associated with the project completion time.

TABLE 8.18 Task Times and Three Time Estimates

Activity	Optimistic Time (days)	Most Likely Time (days)	Pessimistic Time (days)	Immediate Predecessor
A	3	4	5	None
B	7	8	9	A
C	6	6	6	B
D	5	5	5	A
E	2	3	3	C, D

CASE STUDY

Global Textbook Publishers

Rohan, an MBA fresh from the university, found an attractive position with a local publishing company in his town. Global Textbook Publishers (GTP), Inc., is a privately held company (originally named Global Technical Publishers) that was founded by the grandfather of the current president and CEO, Emily Morgan. For a period of over 40 years, GTP mostly printed instruction manuals that typically accompany electronic and household products, such as DVD players, camcorders, toaster ovens, and so on.

When Emily returned to take over the leadership of GTP after working as a consultant for many years, she decided to focus her attention on a totally different market—publishing of textbooks that are used in schools and colleges.

While the publication of instruction manuals still continues, Emily intends to phase out of this business as GTP develops more expertise in publishing college textbooks. Because none of the existing staff members at GTP is knowledgeable about the college textbook publishing process, Emily decided to hire the top-ranked graduating MBA student, Rohan, and assigned him to develop a project plan for publishing textbooks. She assigned Rohan to develop a plan for the efficient production of textbooks and strongly encouraged him (hinting that his success might mean a very rapid growth in his career prospects).

Armed with many tools he learned during the MBA program, Rohan was excited about the opportunity and was confident that he could find a perfect recipe for rapidly gearing up GTP for college textbook publishing. He started his research by searching for information at the local library, at the university library (where he still had access as a recent graduate), and on the Internet. Rohan also interviewed several textbook authors, including some of his past professors from the MBA program. He then talked to sales representatives from other publishing companies and attended a conference organized by the Association of American Publishers (http://www.publishers.org/).

After five months of intense research, he had more information about the textbook publishing process than he could have ever imagined. His one-line assessment was that the process is complicated and quite uncertain, and that the chances of success depend heavily on the project scope/quality, timeliness, and budget.

Rohan came up with a list of key activities that are necessary to complete a textbook. He identified the interrelationships between the activities and the optimistic, most likely, and pessimistic time estimates. He started the final phase of his analysis by putting the information about the activities in a table.

Based on the information provided in Table 8.19, calculate the estimated time to complete a textbook project.

TABLE 8.19 Precedence Relationships and Time Estimates for Global Textbook Publishers

Activity	Description	Immediate Predecessor	Optimistic Time (weeks)	Most Likely Time (weeks)	Pessimistic Time (weeks)
A	Identify the subject for the textbook	—	2	6	8
B	Conduct a market assessment	—	4	6	8
C	Submit the book proposal and get approval from senior management	A, B	1	2	2
D	Identify potential authors for the textbook	A	1	2	4
E	Initiate discussions with the shortlisted authors	C, D	1	4	8
F	Select the author team	E	2	2	4
G	Negotiate contract with the selected authors	F	1	2	2
H	Select technical support staff for web materials	C	1	1	1
I	Select the editorial team	C	1	2	2
J	Select an advisory board for authors	F	2	4	8
K	Authors complete 1st batch of chapters	G	12	16	24
L	Authors complete 2nd batch of chapters	K	12	16	24
M	Authors complete 3rd batch of chapters	L	12	16	24
O	Review 1st batch of chapters	K	3	3	4
P	Review 2nd batch of chapters	L	3	3	4
Q	Review 3rd batch of chapters	M	3	3	4
R	Authors complete the revised versions of each chapter	I, J, O, P, Q	12	16	16
S	Page proofs are completed	R	10	12	16
T	Authors cross-check page proofs for content	S	2	4	6
U	Editors cross-check page proofs for grammatical and other errors	S	4	4	6
V	Textbook production	T, U	12	18	20
W	Compilation of web materials	H	16	20	24
X	Textbook launched	V	2	2	2

CHAPTER 9

Optimization and Simulation Modeling

LEARNING OBJECTIVES

1. Formulate and solve linear programming problems.
2. Describe the use of computer simulation modeling in operations decision making.

Assortment of cereals produced by Kellogg's.

Linear Programming Helps Kellogg's Optimize Production, Inventory, and Distribution

As one of the largest producers of cereals in the world, Kellogg's needs to manage a highly complex production, inventory control, and distribution system. Like many large corporations, Kellogg's employs an enterprise resource planning (ERP) system to coordinate its raw material purchases, production, distribution, and demand. However, the many different varieties of products and brands, packaged in many different sizes and produced at several different plants, also require the use of an optimization approach known as linear programming.

Kellogg's operates five large production plants in the United States and Canada (Battle Creek, Michigan; Memphis, Tennessee; Omaha, Nebraska; Lancaster, Pennsylvania; and London, Ontario). It also operates seven distribution centers and more than fifteen co-packers that contract to produce or pack Kellogg's products. In the cereal business alone, Kellogg's coordinates the production of more than 80 products and more than 600 SKUs produced on roughly 90 production lines and 180 packaging lines and distributes these products from more than 25 locations. Clearly, this is a very complex process to run based only on intuition!

Perhaps the complexity of the system can be better understood by focusing on a single product, Kellogg's Variety Pak. This pack contains 10 small boxes of different types of cereals (e.g., Corn Flakes, Rice Krispies, and so on). Because not all Kellogg's plants produce each type of cereal, the finished goods from different locations are brought to a packing or distribution location in Battle Creek for the final assembly of the Variety Pak. To minimize costs, therefore, the company needs to account for price differentials in production, packaging, inventory, and transportation costs for each plant location.

Furthermore, this analysis must be conducted for multiple time horizons (several days and weeks) because the demand and supply fluctuate over time.

Even though Kellogg's optimization problem is complex, the innovative use of optimization techniques has allowed the company to develop a system that is estimated to save between $35 million and $40 million annually. A simplified version of linear programming formulation is described in this chapter. ■

Source: G. Brown, J. Keegan, B. Vigus, and K. Wood, "The Kellogg Company Optimizes Production, Inventory, and Distribution," *Interfaces,* November–December 2001.

This textbook discusses a number of important concepts for the effective management of manufacturing and service operations. While it is necessary for managers to understand the conceptual and theoretical foundations, their knowledge is incomplete without an understanding of the tools and techniques that will help them in various operational decision-making situations. Throughout the textbook, we have described a variety of decision-making tools, such as forecasting (Chapter 5), project management (Chapter 8), quality control and Six Sigma (Chapters 2 and 11), and inventory management (Chapters 6 and 7). In this chapter, we discuss two additional decision-making techniques that are widely used in various operations management contexts. These tools are fairly detailed and complex. They can be applied to solve complicated forecasting, project management, or inventory management/scheduling problems that have been presented in simpler forms throughout this text.

The decision-making techniques used in operations management are often considered to be part of a sister discipline known as operations research (OR) or management science (MS). The terms *operations research* and *management science* are used synonymously and interchangeably, and the discipline is sometimes called OR/MS. **Operations research or management science** techniques involve the use of interdisciplinary scientific methods like mathematical modeling, statistics, and algorithms to aid decision making for complex real-world problems that are concerned with coordination and execution of the operations within an organization. The goal of these techniques is to derive the best possible solution to a problem or to optimize the performance of the organization. In this chapter, we discuss two commonly used decision-making techniques and describe their applications to a variety of industries.

● **Operations research or management science** the use of interdisciplinary scientific methods such as mathematical modeling, statistics, and algorithms that aid decision making for complex real-world problems of coordination and execution of the operations in an organization

LINEAR PROGRAMMING

Linear programming is a widely used decision-making technique that involves the use of constrained optimization. The term **optimization** means arriving at a maximum or minimum point of a mathematical function. The term **constraints** refers to the necessary conditions that must be met when a mathematical function is being optimized.

In operations management, linear programming is used to solve a wide variety of problems, such as production planning, transportation planning, labor scheduling, revenue management, productivity assessment, capacity planning, and so on. **Linear programming** is a special formulation of an optimization problem in which all equations and inequalities are linear. While each application of linear programming can be unique, the formulation of each decision problem uses a very similar format. Therefore, this chapter will first describe the general formulation of linear programming, then describe several applications.

● **Optimization** arriving at a maximum or minimum point of a mathematical function

● **Constraints** the necessary conditions that must be met when a mathematical function is being optimized

● **Linear programming** a special formulation of an optimization problem in which all equations and inequalities are linear

● **Objective function** a mathematical formulation of the criterion by which all decisions should be evaluated

● **Decision variables** the parameters that can be changed by the decision makers to achieve a higher or lower value of the objective function

Formulation of a Linear Programming Problem

A linear programming problem can be considered to have five main components:

- **Objective function.** The objective function is a mathematical formulation of the criterion by which all decisions should be evaluated.
- **Decision variables.** Decision variables are the parameters that can be changed by the decision maker to achieve a higher or lower value of the objective function.
- **Constraints.** Constraints are restrictions placed on the decision scenario.
- **Linearity.** When formulating linear programming problems, all mathematical equations or inequalities are represented as straight lines.
- **Nonnegativity.** Finally, each decision variable within a linear programming formulation is assumed to take only nonnegative values, although this is not essential.

The linearity assumptions associated with linear programming formulation have allowed the development of very efficient algorithms to solve extremely complex problems. For example, the linear programming formulation of an airline's fleet scheduling problem might include more than one hundred thousand decision variables and an even larger number of constraints.

Because of the advances in computing and the derivation of efficient algorithms for solving linear programming problems, it is possible for managers simply to formulate the problems and then use computers to derive the results. Therefore, in this chapter, we spend the majority of the time discussing the formulation of a variety of linear programming problems rather than discussing solution algorithms.

As described in the opening vignette for this chapter, many organizations have to produce more than one product (e.g., different types of cereals for Kellogg) that might require similar resources (e.g., labor, equipment, raw materials, and components). However, most organizations have a limited amount of each type of resources available. Therefore, a product-mix problem often involves maximizing profits or revenue subject to several constraints. A simple product-mix problem is described in Solved Example 1.

Solved Example 1

Product-Mix Problem

Fashionable Bikes Inc. (FBI) has the hottest new product on the upscale toy market—high-quality boys' and girls' bikes in bright fashion colors. Because there is a seller's market for high-quality toys, FBI can sell bikes at the following profit margin: boys' bikes, $30; girls' bikes, $50. The marketing department recommends that at least 250 bikes of each type be produced per day. A boy's bike requires 4 labor-hours in the fabrication department and 1 labor-hour in the assembly department. A girl's bike requires 4 labor-hours in the fabrication department and 2 labor-hours in the assembly department. Currently FBI employs 200 workers in the fabrication department and 100 workers in the assembly department each shift. There are three 8-hour shifts per day (overtime is not permitted). Formulate this information as a profit-maximizing linear programming problem.

(continued)

SOLUTION

To formulate a linear programming solution to this problem, we must identify the decision variables and then identify the objective function and all the constraints. Furthermore, we must ensure that each equation or inequality within the formulation is linear.

Decision Variables. Based on the information provided in the problem, Fashionable Bikes Inc. can change two variables: the numbers of boys' and girls' bikes produced. Therefore, there are two decision variables:

Boys'_Bikes: Number of boys' bikes produced every day

Girls'_Bikes: Number of girls' bikes produced every day

Objective Function. While the problem statement does not specify the revenue or costs associated with the production of each type of bike, we do know the profit contribution for each type of bike: $30 for each boys' bike and $50 for each girls' bike. Therefore, the objective function (maximization of profit) can be written as

Maximize Profit = Maximize ($30 * Boys'_Bikes + $50 * Girls'_Bikes)

Constraints. The problem description discusses several conditions or constraints that must be satisfied. We describe each constraint here.

Marketing constraints. The problem states that the marketing department would like at least 250 of each type of bike to be produced every day. These constraints can be written as

Boys'_Bikes ≥ 250

Girls'_Bikes ≥ 250

Fabrication constraints. The problem states that both a boy's bike and a girl's bike require 4 labor-hours in the fabrication department. The problem further states that 200 workers per 8-hour shift are available in the fabrication department. Therefore, a total of 4,800 labor-hours (3 * 8 * 200) are available within the fabrication department. Hence, the fabrication constraint can be written in the following manner:

4 * Boys'_Bikes + 4 * Girls'_Bikes ≤ 4,800

Assembly constraint. The problem states that a boy's bike requires 1 hour in the assembly department and a girl's bike requires 2 hours in the assembly department. The assembly department employs 100 workers during each of its three 8-hour shifts. Therefore, there are 2,400 labor-hours (3 * 8 * 100) available in the assembly department. The assembly constraint can be written as

1 * Boys'_Bikes + 2 * Girls'_Bikes ≤ 2,400

While there is no additional information provided within the problem statement, the formulation of a linear programming problem also requires that the decision variables are nonnegative. Therefore, we must add two additional constraints:

Boys'_Bikes ≥ 0

Girls'_Bikes ≥ 0

Solution of a Linear Programming Problem by a Graphical Method

A simple linear programming problem (such as the one described in Solved Example 1) can be solved by using a graphical method. Because all the equations within a linear programming problem are either straight lines or inequalities, the constraints are first plotted to find the region that satisfies all conditions. Once that region is identified, the researcher evaluates the objective function at each corner of the feasible region. One of the corners contains the best or optimum solution. For the sake of quick illustration, the graphical solution to Solved Example 1 is presented in Solved Example 2.

Solved Example 2

Graphical Solution of the Product-Mix Problem

Solve the product-mix problem described in Solved Example 1 using a graphical method.

SOLUTION

Because there are only two decision variables in this problem, we can plot all the constraints on a graph and identify the feasible solution space.

Step 1. To solve the problem, we first plot all the constraints on a graph where the *x* axis represents Boys'_Bikes and the *y* axis represents Girls'_Bikes (Figure 9.1 on page 330).

Step 2. We plot the first constraint (Boys'_Bikes ≥ 250). This equation states that Boys'_Bikes should be at least 250.

We will first plot a line that represents Boys'_Bikes = 250. Next, we will identify the region that represents greater than 250. The plotted constraint is shown in Figure 9.2 (on page 330).

Step 3. We plot the next constraint, which states that at least 250 Girls'_Bikes should be produced. The shaded area in Figure 9.3 (on page 331) shows the region of the graph that satisfies the constraints listed in Steps 2 and 3.

Step 4. We plot the next constraint, fabrication, represented as

4 * Boys'_Bikes + 4 * Girls'_Bikes ≤ 4,800

To plot this constraint, again we must first plot the straight line:

4 * Boys'_Bikes + 4 * Girls'_Bikes = 4,800

To plot any straight line, we must identify two points that are on the line. The straight line can then be plotted by simply connecting the two points. An easy way to find two points that lie on a straight line are to set one of the decision variables equal to zero and solve for the second variable. We can follow this approach twice—once for Boys'_Bikes and then again for Girls'_Bikes—to get two points.

If Boys'_Bikes = 0, then

4 * Girls'_Bikes = 4,800

(*continued*)

Therefore,

Girls'_Bikes = 4,800/4 = 1,200

If Girls'_Bikes = 0, then

4 * Boys'_Bikes = 4,800

Therefore,

Boys'_Bikes = 4,800/4 = 1,200

Therefore, the two points on the straight line are (0, 1,200) and (1,200, 0). After identifying the points, we can connect them to find the straight line.

Once the straight line is plotted, the area that represents less than 4,800 is identified. To identify the less-than area easily, we can find the value of the equation for a specific value of Boys'_Bikes and Girls'_Bikes. If the resulting value satisfies the condition, then we know that this particular point is on the correct side.

For example, suppose we substitute zeros for both Boys'_Bikes and Girls'_Bikes in the above equation. The resulting calculation will show that $0 \leq 4,800$. Because this calculation satisfies the condition, we know that (0, 0) is on the correct side of the straight line representing less than 4,800. The shaded region in Figure 9.4 (on page 331) shows the area that satisfies all constraints.

Step 5. Using the same procedure as in Step 4, we can plot the assembly constraint and identify the region that satisfies all of the constraints. The resulting graph is shown in Figure 9.5 (on page 331).

Step 6. The shaded region in Figure 9.5 satisfies all of the constraints. Therefore, we know that any combination of Boys'_Bikes and Girls'_Bikes that falls within the shaded region is a possible solution. While there is an infinite number of combinations within the shaded region, we can simplify the problem by realizing that the best solution must be at one of the three corners. The reason for this observation is the fact that the objective function is a combination of two decision variables (30 * Boys'_Bikes + 50 * Girls'_Bikes); therefore, going away from the origin will mean higher profits. If we keep moving away from the origin, we will finally reach a corner point.

The shaded region has three corner points (A, B, and C), which were formed because of intersections of different straight lines (see Figure 9.6 on page 332). The coordinates of Points A, B, and C can be found by solving the two sets of equations simultaneously.

Corner Point A

Boys'_Bikes = 250

Girls'_Bikes = 250

Corner Point B

Boys'_Bikes = 250

Girls'_Bikes = 950 (by substituting Boys'_Bikes = 250)

(continued)

Corner Point C

Girls'_Bikes = 250

Boys'_Bikes = 950 (by substituting Girls'_Bikes = 250)

Step 7. During this step, we will evaluate the objective function at each of the three corner points. The point that provides the highest profit is the solution.

Profit at Point A: 30 * 250 + 50 * 250 = $20,000

Profit at Point B: 30 * 250 + 50 * 950 = $55,000

Profit at Point C: 30 * 950 + 50 * 250 = $41,000

The optimum solution is found at Point B. Therefore, the company should produce 250 boys' bikes and 950 girls' bikes.

FIGURE 9.1 Graphical Method: Step 1

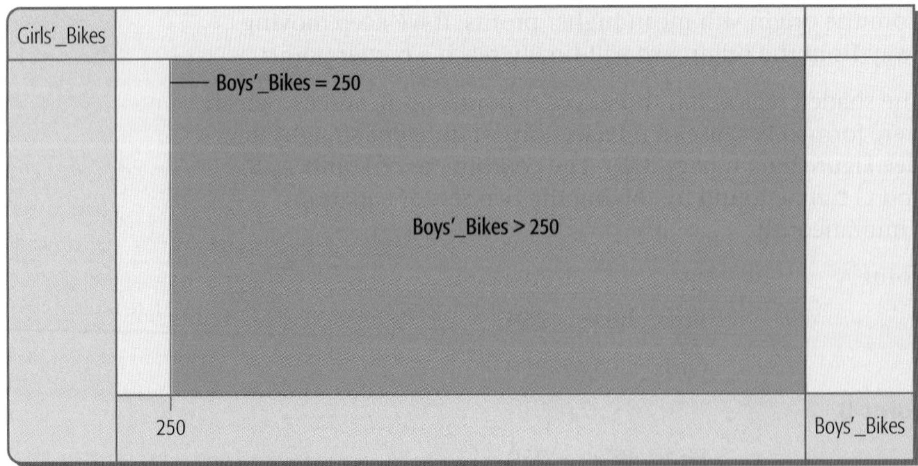

FIGURE 9.2 Graphical Method: Step 2

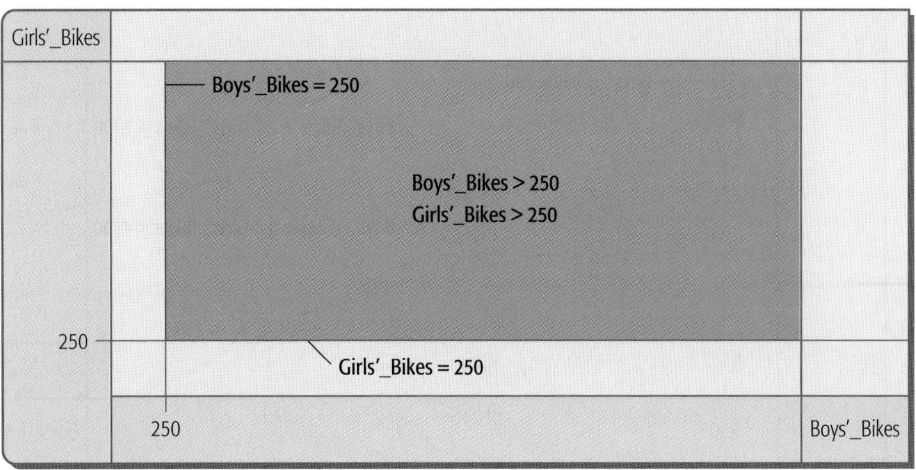

FIGURE 9.3 Graphical Method: Step 3

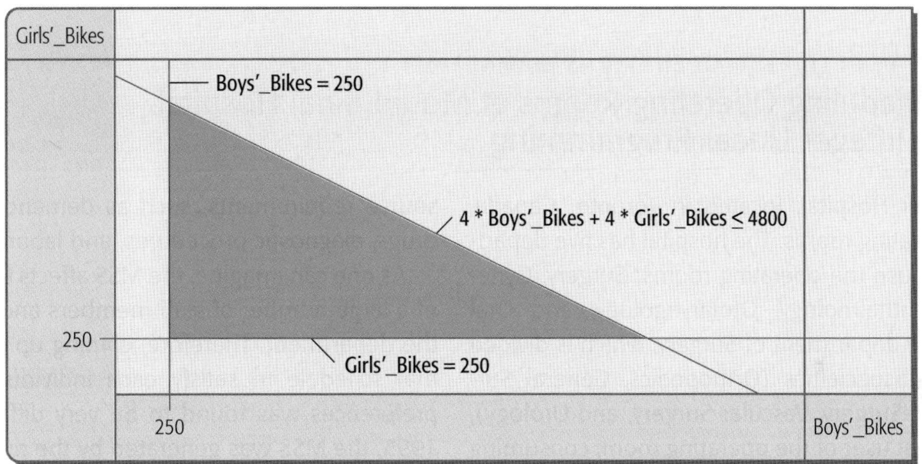

FIGURE 9.4 Graphical Method: Step 4

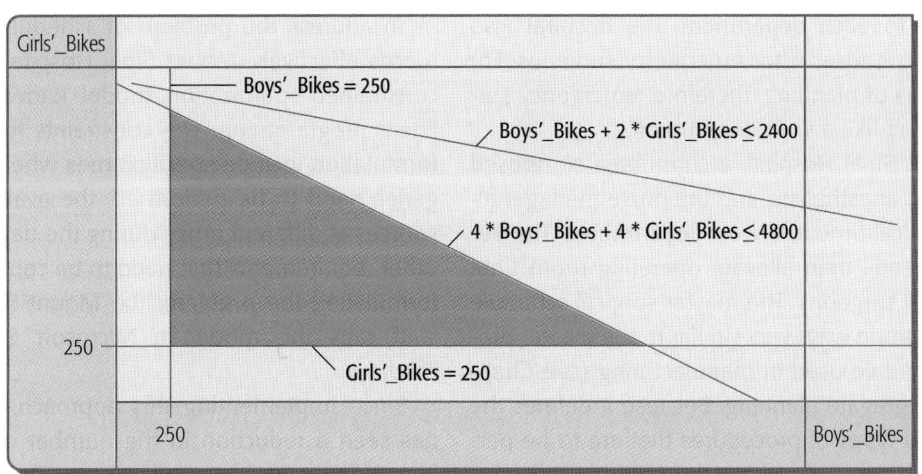

FIGURE 9.5 Graphical Method: Step 5

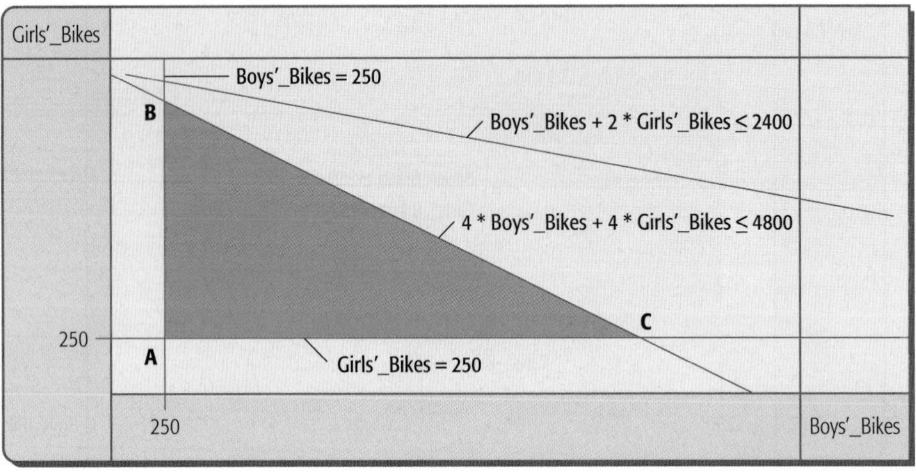

FIGURE 9.6 Graphical Method: Step 6

BEST PRACTICES IN OPERATIONS MANAGEMENT

Scheduling Operating Rooms at Mount Sinai Hospital by Integer Linear Programming

Mount Sinai Hospital, located in Toronto, Canada, has 14 operating rooms. The hospital has five departments that use the operating rooms: Surgery, Gynecology, Ophthalmology, Otolaryngology, and Oral Surgery. The department of Surgery, which is divided into five subspecialties (Orthopedics, General Surgery, Plastic Surgery, Vascular Surgery, and Urology), is the biggest user of the operating room, consuming 189 hours of surgical time per week (approximately 47.5 percent of the 397.5 hours available). The smallest department, Oral Surgery, consumes only 19.7 hours per week. In addition to allocating operating room time to each department, the hospital also likes to keep a reserve for emergency surgeries. For the purposes of planning, therefore, emergency surgery is treated like a sixth department.

At Mount Sinai Hospital, a committee composed of surgeons, anesthetists, and the nurse manager allocates surgical time to the six departments. The department heads then allocate operating room time to individual surgeons. The master surgical schedule (MSS) is in some ways very similar to the master production schedule used in manufacturing (see Chapter 7) for aggregate planning. Because it defines the number and types of procedures that are to be performed in the medium term, the MSS identifies resource requirements, such as demands for nurses, drugs, diagnostic procedures, and laboratory tests.

As one can imagine, the MSS affects the schedules of a large number of staff members and units within the department. Therefore, coming up with an optimal schedule to satisfy each individual's personal preferences was found to be very difficult. Prior to 1995, the MSS was generated by the nurse manager without using any decision-making models. Therefore, even after several rounds of negotiations, many individuals often were not satisfied with the operating room schedule that had been developed.

To address the problem of scheduling operating rooms effectively, Mount Sinai Hospital now uses a constrained-optimization model known as integer linear programming. The constraints for this model formulation include specific times when certain surgeries need to be performed, the availability of resources at different times during the day, and several other requirements that need to be considered. After formulating the problem, the Mount Sinai Hospital staff runs the model in Microsoft Excel's Solver module.

Since implementing this approach, the hospital has seen a reduction in the number of conflicts in scheduling operating room times. The clerical time

(continued)

BEST PRACTICES IN OPERATIONS MANAGEMENT

Scheduling Operating Rooms at Mount Sinai Hospital by Integer Linear Programming (*continued*)

required to produce the operating room schedule has decreased from several days to only two hours. Therefore, the hospital also enjoys an annual cost savings of $20,000. More importantly, the fast turnaround time for schedule development means that during each revision, many different scenarios can be evaluated quickly. This gives hospital administrators greater flexibility and an increased ability to explore more creative scheduling options. In the end, a better schedule means more effective care for Mount Sinai Hospital's patients.

Source: J. T. Blake and J. Donald, "Mount Sinai Hospital Uses Integer Programming to Allocate Operating Room Time," *Interfaces*, March–April 2002; http://www.mtsinai.on.ca/AboutUs/FastFacts.htm.

Solution of a Linear Programming Problem Using Microsoft Excel Solver

The graphical solution to a linear programming problem can be used when there are only two decision variables. However, in many actual applications, the number of variables and constraints can be very large. For example, the opening vignette described the use of linear programming for production planning at Kellogg, which requires solving for more than 80 products and more than 600 SKUs produced at roughly 90 production lines and 180 packaging lines. Scheduling and routing problems associated with airlines and large logistics companies can often require solving for thousands of decision variables. The development of sophisticated linear program solution algorithms and fast computing now allows users to apply software to solve even extremely large linear programming problems. While there are many software programs for solving linear programming problems available, we will describe the use of Solver Module, included within Microsoft Excel.

Solved Example 3

Solution of a Product-Mix Linear Programming Problem by Microsoft Excel Solver

Solve the problem presented in Solved Example 1 using Microsoft Excel.

SOLUTION

We will represent the two variables (Boys'_Bikes and Girls'_Bikes) by cells A1 and B1, the objective function (Profit) by cell D1, and the four constraints by cells C1 through C4.

Step 1 (Naming Cells)

1. **Click on cell A1.**
2. **Click on the name box at the left end of the formula bar.**
3. **Type "Boys'_Bikes."**
4. **Press Enter.**

(*continued*)

5. **Input the names of the other cells to be used in this problem in the same way.**
6. **In the name box for**

   B1, type "Girls'_Bikes."

   C1, type "Fabrication."

   C2, type "Assembly."

   C3, type "Market_Boys."

   C4, type "Market_Girls."

   D1, type "Profit."

Step 2 (Objective Function)

1. **Click on D1.**
2. **Enter the profit function in terms of variable names as**

   30 * Boys'_Bikes + 50 * Girls'_Bikes

Step 3 (Constraints)

1. **Click on C1; enter the left-hand side of Equation 2 as**

   4 * Boys'_Bikes + 4 * Girls'_Bikes
2. **Click on C2; enter the left-hand side of Equation 3 as**

   Boys'_Bikes + 2 * Girls'_Bikes
3. **Click on C3; enter the left-hand side of Equation 4 as**

   = Boys'_Bikes
4. **Click on C4; enter the left-hand side of Equation 5 as: = A1**

   = Girls'_Bikes

Step 4 (Solver Steps)

1. **Open Solver.**
2. **Set Target Cell represents the objective function. Make sure that this space is highlighted (completely black), and click on D1 to enter the objective function. This space should now contain $D$1. Alternatively, you can type "Profit" (the name of cell D1) directly in this space.**
3. **The sample problem requires maximization of the objective. Make sure that Max is highlighted (by a black circle).**
4. **Click on By Changing Cells. You need to input the location of the two decision variables (Boys'_Bikes and Girls'_Bikes) here. Therefore, highlight cells A1 and B1. The By Changing Cells space should now contain $A$1:$B$1. Alternatively, you can type "Boys'_Bikes, Girls'_Bikes" in this space.**
5. **Click on Add to begin adding constraints.**

(continued)

6. **Add constraint 1. Click Cell Reference. Click on cell C1. $C$1 should appear in Cell Reference (alternatively, type "Fabrication"). Make sure that Constraint shows the ≤ sign. If it does not, then click on the ↓ and select ≤. Enter 4800 in the right cell. Click on Add.**
7. **Add constraint 2. (This process is similar to instructions 5 and 6.)**
8. **Add constraint 3. Click Cell Reference. Click on cell C3. $C$3 should appear in Cell Reference (alternatively, type "Boys'_Bikes").** ***Make sure that Constraint shows the ≥ sign.*** **If it does not, then click on the ↓ and select ≥. Enter 250 in the right cell. Click on Add.**
9. **Add constraint 4. (This process is similar to instruction 8.) After adding the last constraint, click OK (instead of clicking Add). The Solver template will reappear (see Figure 9.7 on page 336).**
10. **Click on Options. A new template will open up. Click Assume Linear Models (a × will appear in the box). Click OK; the Solver template will reappear.**
11. **Click on Solve. The solver will return with the following values in the cells:**

    A1 = 250; B1 = 950; C1 = 4800; C2 = 2150; C3 = 250;
    C4 = 950; D1 = 55000

12. **Press Ctrl and click on Answer Report and Sensitivity Report. The reports will appear as separate sheets. The reports (Table 9.1 and Table 9.2) show that FBI should produce 250 boys' bikes and 950 girls' bikes per day (which result in an optimum profit of $55,000/day). Available labor-hours in the fabrication department and the minimum production requirement for boys' bikes are binding constraints. Therefore, each additional labor-hour in the fabrication department can add $12.50 to profit (see the shadow price column in Table 9.2). Similarly, each additional boys' bike produced per day will reduce profit by $20.**
13. **Print the two reports.**

The two reports include important information about the problem. The Answer Report shows that the company should produce 250 boys' bikes and 950 girls' bikes, which will generate a profit of $55,000. It also shows that two constraints (Fabrication and Market requirements for Boys'_Bikes) are binding. The other two constraints are nonbinding. The Sensitivity Report shows the ranges for each decision variable and the constraints for which the solution is valid. Furthermore, the Sensitivity Report shows the shadow price, which can be of immense use to managers. For example, the shadow price for the fabrication department is 12.5. This means that if an additional hour is available in the fabrication department, then the company will make an additional profit of $12.50. Thus, the sensitivity analysis helps a manager estimate the value of an additional resource—in this case the company should

(*continued*)

@ add capacity to the fabrication area if the cost of labor is less than $12.50 per hour. The interactive version of this problem can be found at this text's web site.

TABLE 9.1 Answer Report

Target Cell			
Cell	**Name**	**Original Value**	**Final Value**
$D$1	Profit	0	55,000

Adjustable Cells			
Cell	**Name**	**Original Value**	**Final Value**
$A$1	Boys_Bikes	0	250
$B$1	Girls_Bikes	0	950

Constraints					
Cell	**Name**	**Cell Value**	**Formula**	**Status**	**Slack**
$C$1	Fabrication	4,800	$C$1<=4,800	Binding	0
$C$2	Assembly	2,150	$C$2<=2,400	Not Binding	250
$C$3	Market_Boys	250	$C$3>=250	Binding	0
$C$4	Market_Girls	950	$C$4>=250	Not Binding	700

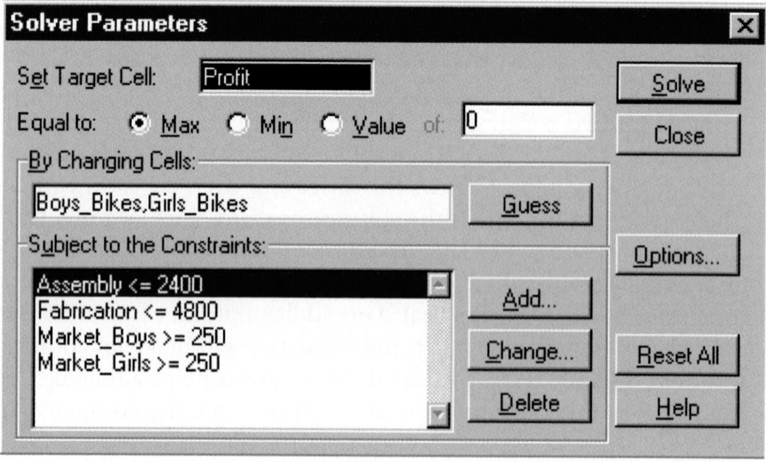

FIGURE 9.7 Complete Solver Template

TABLE 9.2 Sensitivity Report

Changing Cells						
Cell	**Name**	**Final Value**	**Reduced Cost**	**Objective Coefficient**	**Allowable Increase**	**Allowable Decrease**
$A$1	Boys_Bikes	250	0	30	20	1E + 30
$B$1	Girls_Bikes	950	0	50	1E + 30	20
Constraints						
Cell	**Name**	**Final Value**	**Shadow Price**	**Constraint R.H. Side**	**Allowable Increase**	**Allowable Decrease**
$C$1	Fabrication	4,800	12.5	4,800	500	2,800
$C$2	Assembly	2,150	0	2,400	1E + 30	250
$C$3	Market_Boys	250	–20	250	700	250
$C$4	Market_Girls	950	0	250	700	1E + 30

TECHNOLOGY IN OPERATIONS MANAGEMENT

PLATO Helps Athens Win Gold During 2004 Summer Olympic Games

If you think that it is difficult to win an Olympic gold medal, try organizing the events in which the athletes compete! During the 2004 Olympic Games in Athens, over the course of 16 days, more than 2,000 athletes participated in 300 events in 28 different sports across 36 venues located across the city. The events were watched by 3.6 million spectators in the stadiums, 22,000 journalists and broadcasters, and 2,500 members of the international committees. The Athens Olympics was the most watched sports event in human history up to that time.

The planning and execution of the Athens Olympic Games were facilitated by a budget of more than $8 billion, a work force of more than 130,000, and several years' worth of planning and coordination. The task in front of the Athens Olympic Games Organizing Committee (ATHOC) was straightforward, but it was a highly complex one with not much room for error. The committee had only one shot at getting the events right. Therefore, the organizing team developed PLATO, the Process Logistics Advanced Technical Optimization approach.

The organizing committee needed a holistic solution to the Olympic Games logistics program because of the interdependence of processes, athletes, staff, viewers, and venues. Therefore, the PLATO project was launched in 2001 to address a wide spectrum of interrelated problems. In the end, the PLATO project accomplished the following:

- It developed business process models for the various venues.
- It developed computer simulation models that enabled managers to conduct a variety of what-if analyses.
- It developed software that guided ATHOC personnel in using the business process and simulation models.

A special team of mathematical analysts worked with members of different functional areas to develop and validate the computer models. ATHOC used these models extensively in its planning process to design venue operations and to determine the resources required. In total, PLATO developed 25 venue-specific

(continued)

TECHNOLOGY IN OPERATIONS MANAGEMENT

PLATO Helps Athens Win Gold During 2004 Summer Olympic Games (*cont.*)

computer models, 6 noncompetition venue models, and 18 generic models that describe processes common to all venues for large-scale sports events such as ticketing, seat assignment, transportation, and management of food booths. The computer models were primarily based on three interrelated approaches known as business-process modeling, goal programming, and scenario modeling.

The development and use of PLATO produced many tangible and intangible benefits with far-reaching implications, as described in Table 9.3. The estimated direct benefits resulting from the use of the PLATO approach were close to $70 million. Don't you think PLATO deserves a gold medal?

Source: D. A. Beis, P. Loucopoulos, Y. Pyrgiotis, and K. G. Zografos, "PLATO Helps Athens Win Gold: Olympic Games Knowledge Modeling for Organizational Change and Resource Management," *Interfaces*, January–February 2006.

Olympic stadium, Athens.

Other Decision-Making Applications of Linear Programming in Operations Management

As described in several previous examples, linear programming and associated techniques (e.g., integer linear programming, nonlinear programming, dynamic programming, and goal programming) are used to solve a variety of decision-making problems in manufacturing and service businesses. While it is not possible to include an exhaustive list of all applications of linear programming, we describe two examples here. We have presented only the formulation of the problems; the Microsoft Excel Solver solutions can be obtained from this textbook's web site. Additional types of linear programming problems for decision-making scenarios (e.g., production planning and multifactor productivity analysis) are also available on this textbook's web site.

TABLE 9.3 Benefits of PLATO

Benefits	During Planning	During Games	Long Term
ATHOC benefits	—Savings from reducing planning and design effort —Savings from reducing construction work —Savings from optimizing the use of intrastructure resources —Savings from optimizing technological resources —Improved knowledge management for planning venue operations —Shift of the organizational culture toward quantitative and fact-based management	—Savings from reducing number of volunteers —Savings from streamlining crowd-support facilities	Not applicable
National benefits	Not applicable	—Positive reporting in international media on management of the games —Worldwide focus on Athens and Greece	—Increase in foreign investments —Increase in tourism —Increase in the competitiveness of Greece to undertake the organization of large-scale events —Human resource development in the area of management
International benefits	—Reduction of planning cost for other Olympic Games organizing committees —Improved knowledge management for other Olympic Games organizing committees	—Improved estimation of resources needed for future Olymic Games	—Contribution to the long-term sustainability of the character of the games —Establishment of academic programs for sport and large-scale event management

Source: Reprinted by permission, Beis, D. A., P. Loucopoulos, Y. Pyrgiotis, and K. G. Zografos. "PLATO Helps Athens Win Gold: Olympic Games Knowledge Modeling and Organizational Change and Resource Management," *Interfaces* 36 (1), Jan–Feb 2006, p. 38. Copyright © 2006, the Institute for Operations Research and Management Sciences (INFORMS), 7240 Parkway Drive, Suite 300, Hanover, MD 21067 USA.

Solved Example 4

Labor Scheduling Linear Programming Problem

A customer service center needs to schedule enough employees to meet the expected call volumes over the 24 hours of every day. Based on estimated demand, the minimum number of employees required during each three-hour time interval is given in Table 9.4.

The employees can begin their shifts at the starting time of any of these time periods. However, they have to work for exactly six hours. What is

(*continued*)

the minimum number of employees required to satisfy the requirements? Note that while we keep the problem "simple" by forcing employees to work six-hour shifts, the approach could easily be modified to allow for the choice of four-, five-, six-, seven-, eight-hour, or any length shift options.

TABLE 9.4 Labor Requirements for Different Time Periods

Time Period	Minimum Number of Customer Service Agents Needed
Midnight–3 a.m.	5
3 a.m.–6 a.m.	4
6 a.m.–9 a.m.	8
9 a.m.–noon	15
Noon–3 p.m.	20
3 p.m.–6 p.m.	12
6 p.m.–9 p.m.	16
9 p.m.–midnight	8

SOLUTION

Because the employees can begin their shifts at any of the starting times, there are eight possible overlapping shifts. Therefore, there are eight decision variables in this problem:

A = number of employees who start work at midnight and end work at 6 a.m.

B = number of employees who start work at 3 a.m. and end work at 9 a.m.

C = number of employees who start work at 6 a.m. and end work at noon

D = number of employees who start work at 9 a.m. and end work at 3 p.m.

E = number of employees who start work at noon and end work at 6 p.m.

F = number of employees who start work at 3 p.m. and end work at 9 p.m.

G = number of employees who start work at 6 p.m. and end work at midnight

H = number of employees who start work at 9 p.m. and end work at 3 a.m.

The objective of this problem is to find the minimum number of employees that will satisfy the requirements. Therefore, we can state the objective function as

$$\text{Minimize } (A + B + C + D + E + F + G + H)$$

The minimum staffing requirements for each time period must be met by the employees working each of the eight shifts. Therefore, the re-

(*continued*)

quirements for and availability of employees during each shift are as given in Table 9.5.

Table 9.5 shows the requirements for and availability of employees during each of the eight time periods. Therefore, we can formulate eight constraints stating that availability during each time period must at least be equal to the requirements.

Constraints

During midnight–3 a.m.	$A + H \geq 5$
During 3 a.m.–6 a.m.	$A + B \geq 4$
During 6 a.m.–9 a.m.	$B + C \geq 8$
During 9 a.m.–noon	$C + D \geq 15$
During noon–3 p.m.	$D + E \geq 20$
During 3 p.m.–6 p.m.	$E + F \geq 12$
During 6 p.m.–9 p.m.	$F + G \geq 16$
During 9 p.m.–midnight	$G + H \geq 8$

In addition, we must add constraints stating that the number of employees during any shift cannot be negative.

$$A, B, C, D, E, F, G, H \geq 0$$

Because the number of variables for this problem is greater than two, we can use Microsoft Excel Solver to solve the problem. The solution to the above problem is available at the text's web site.

TABLE 9.5 Shift Starting and Ending Times

Time Period	Requirements	Starting Midnight	Starting 3 a.m.	Starting 6 a.m.	Starting 9 a.m.	Starting Noon	Starting 3 p.m.	Starting 6 p.m.	Starting 9 p.m.
Midnight–3 a.m.	5	A							H
3 a.m.–6 a.m.	4	A	B						
6 a.m.–9 a.m.	8		B	C					
9 a.m.–noon	15			C	D				
Noon–3 p.m.	20				D	E			
3 p.m.–6 p.m.	12					E	F		
6 p.m.–9 p.m.	16						F	G	
9 p.m.–midnight	8							G	H

Solved Example 5

Transportation Problem

Fashion Forward Clothing (FFC) has production facilities in Rochester, Salt Lake City, and Phoenix. Production capabilities for these plants over the four-week planning period for children's clothing are listed in Table 9.6 in terms of number of shipments (each shipment is equivalent to the volume of clothing that can be shipped on one truck).

TABLE 9.6 Production Capacity

Plant Location	Production Capacity
Rochester	350
Salt Lake City	300
Phoenix	250

The firm distributes its clothes to retailers across the country through four regional distribution centers located in New York, Chicago, Los Angeles, and Omaha. The forecasts of demand for each of the distribution centers are given in Table 9.7.

TABLE 9.7 Forecasted Demand

Distribution Center	Demand
New York	200
Chicago	150
Los Angeles	225
Omaha	325

Management would like to determine how much of its production should be shipped from each plant to each distribution center. The cost for each unit shipped via each route is given in Table 9.8.

TABLE 9.8 Shipping Costs

Destination Origin	New York	Chicago	Los Angeles	Omaha
Rochester	$350	$150	$350	$200
Salt Lake City	$600	$275	$100	$150
Phoenix	$400	$325	$100	$175

SOLUTION

This problem requires us to consider shipping products from each of the three production facilities to each of the four distribution centers in the most cost-effective manner. Therefore, there are 12 potential routes

(*continued*)

(3 manufacturing facilities × 4 distribution centers). The decision variables are listed here:

RN = number of shipments from Rochester to New York

RC = number of shipments from Rochester to Chicago

RL = number of shipments from Rochester to Los Angeles

RO = number of shipments from Rochester to Omaha

SN = number of shipments from Salt Lake City to New York

SC = number of shipments from Salt Lake City to Chicago

SL = number of shipments from Salt Lake City to Los Angeles

SO = number of shipments from Salt Lake City to Omaha

PN = number of shipments from Phoenix to New York

PC = number of shipments from Phoenix to Chicago

PL = number of shipments from Phoenix to Los Angeles

PO = number of shipments from Phoenix to Omaha

The objective is to find the minimum-cost shipment plan. Therefore, the objective function can be written as the minimum of the total cost of shipment from each origin to each destination:

Minimize $350\,RN + 150\,RC + 350\,RL + 200\,RO + 600\,SN + 275\,SC + 100\,SL + 150\,SO + 400\,PN + 325\,PC + 100\,PL + 175\,PO$

Constraints. The constraints for this problem can be divided into two parts: production constraints and demand constraints. The production constraints state that the shipments from any production facility cannot exceed its capacity. The demand constraints state that shipments to any distribution center must be equal to at least its forecasted demand.

Production Capacity Constraints.

Rochester: $RN + RC + RL + RO \leq 350$

Salt Lake City $SN + SC + SL + SO \leq 300$

Phoenix $PN + PC + PL + PO \leq 250$

Demand Requirements Constraints.

New York $RN + SN + PN \geq 200$

Chicago $RC + SC + PC \geq 150$

Los Angeles $RL + SL + PL \geq 225$

Omaha $RO + SO + PO \geq 325$

Finally, we must add a set of constraints that state that all 12 variables are nonnegative.

$$RN, RC, RL, RO, SN, SC, SL, SO, PN, PC, PL, PO \geq 0$$

Because the number of variables for this problem is greater than two, we can use Microsoft Excel Solver to solve the problem. The solution to the above problem can be found at the text's web site.

@

BEST PRACTICES IN OPERATIONS MANAGEMENT

VOLCANO Saves $187 Million for UPS

In 1907 there was a great need in America for private messenger and delivery services. To help meet this need, an enterprising 19-year-old, James E. ("Jim") Casey, borrowed $100 from a friend and established the American Messenger Company in Seattle, Washington. In response to telephone calls received at the company's basement headquarters, messengers ran errands; delivered packages; and carried notes, baggage, and trays of food from restaurants. They made most deliveries on foot and used bicycles for longer trips.

In 1919 the company made its first expansion beyond Seattle to Oakland, California, and adopted its present name, United Parcel Service. Over time, UPS has become a leader in global supply chain management. Now UPS carries more than 13 million packages to more than 8 million customers in more than 200 countries daily. The company operates more than 300 aircraft and is currently the eleventh largest commercial airline in the world. The airline service is essential to UPS operations because it facilitates the expedited (next-day and same-day) delivery services for approximately 10 percent of the packages. The airline business is also extremely important for the company's financial success because it generates over $5 billion in annual revenue.

To ensure timely next-day service to its customers, UPS operates a large airline hub in Louisville, Kentucky, and six regional hubs in Columbia, South Carolina; Dallas, Texas; Hartford, Connecticut; Ontario, California; Philadelphia, Pennsylvania; and Rockford, Illinois. UPS airplanes fly more than 1,800 flight legs to approximately 100 airports daily. The airline needs to operate on a very strict time schedule to meet the deadlines established for package pickups and deliveries, typically between 6:00 p.m. and 8:00 a.m. After 8:00 a.m., the packages are transferred to UPS trucks, which deliver them to their final destinations.

The brief description of UPS operations given here illustrates the complexity of managing a very large logistics company. While the airline operations provide many benefits and a large amount of revenue to the company, they are also very expensive to operate. Inefficient use of expensive assets such as airplanes can very quickly wipe out all the revenue received from them. Therefore, UPS, along with a team of researchers from Massachusetts Institute of Technology (MIT), developed and implemented Volume, Location, and Aircraft Network Optimization (VOLCANO), an optimization-based planning system that is transforming the business processes within UPS. The VOLCANO system is an interactive transportation modeling and optimization approach.

(*continued*)

Air and ground transport are coordinated at UPS.

BEST PRACTICES IN OPERATIONS MANAGEMENT

VOLCANO Saves $187 Million for UPS (*continued*)

Prior to VOLCANO, it used to take planners up to nine months to develop a single transportation plan for UPS airline operations manually. Furthermore, such plans did not include any sensitivity analysis for important process parameters such as package volume. At the same time, the development of large-scale transportation optimization is far from easy. The modelers needed to consider costs, fleet assignment, and package flows that satisfied various constraints such as availability of aircraft, landing restrictions at airports, aircraft capability (speed, range, load capacity), and so on. After a series of trials and different model formulations, the first complete version of VOLCANO was ready for use in late 2000. Since that time, many enhancements to the initial system have been made, and VOLCANO is expected to save more than $189 million for UPS within the next decade. A simple interactive example of a transportation planning problem is available at the text's web site. @

Source: A. P. Armacost, C. Barnhart, K. Ware, and A. M. Wilson, "UPS Optimizes Its Air Network," *Interfaces,* January–February 2004.

SIMULATION MODELING

Computer simulation models are used in decision making because testing proposed new operating procedures in an actual operation is often expensive, complicated, and risky. In contrast, computer simulation models allow the user to try out different strategies or alternatives without actually implementing them in practice. This can reduce costs because changing real systems can be expensive. Models can also reduce consumer dissatisfaction because customers, in general, do not like to be part of "failed experiments." Once the value of a new idea has been verified through a carefully constructed simulation, that idea may be implemented with a great deal of confidence.

Another reason to build simulation models is that it can be difficult to predict outcomes in complex, real-world operating environments because of the effects of chance. Simulation models allow managers to evaluate multiple operations designs and perform what-if types of analyses. Such models can also be used to evaluate the effects of any changes in the operating or marketing strategies of hospitality firms (for example, the influence on customer arrival rates or service requests when specific marketing promotions are introduced). Similarly, factory managers can use computer simulation to determine the best way to control the flow of raw materials and to find the most effective way to schedule and deploy expensive resources. Simulation replaces the wasteful and often unreliable practice of testing managers' ideas through trial-and-error methods. As a general guideline, computer simulation is an appropriate tool for process analysis if

- The system has one or more interdependent, random variables.
- The system dynamics are extremely complex.
- The objective is to observe system behavior over a period of time.

Numerical Simulation

Numerical simulation involves simulating outcomes that are controlled by chance, but where the state of the system at specific times is not of interest. The focus in numerical simulations is the aggregate behavior, or outcomes, associated

● **Numerical simulation** simulating outcomes that are controlled by chance, but where the state of the system at specific times is not of interest

with managers' decisions. These types of simulations are often performed for financial modeling—for example, simulating the effects of particular decisions on a range of chance-controlled outcomes.

Numerical simulations can typically be performed in computer-spreadsheet software. For example, the function "=RAND()" in Excel will generate uniformly distributed pseudorandom numbers between 0 and 1. One can then use these random numbers to serve many other purposes. For example, let's say we wanted to simulate the size of parties arriving at a restaurant, where 40 percent of parties are singles and 60 percent are deuces. We would first generate a random number, which we call x_p, for party p. We would then use that number, and a translator function, to tell us the size of the next party, size p. In this case, our translator function would be

$$\text{Size}_p = \begin{cases} 1, \text{ if } x_p < 0.4 \\ 2, \text{ otherwise} \end{cases} \quad \text{(Equation 1)}$$

There are standard translation functions that can convert the uniformly distributed random numbers to random numbers from other probability distributions, such as normal or negative exponential. The random numbers generated can be used as parameters in any application (e.g., to generate arrivals distribution in the restaurant example just discussed), and the performance of the system can be evaluated.

Discrete-Event Simulation

Discrete-event simulation a type of simulation that is applicable when the state of a system over time is the major concern. The term *discrete event* describes the nature of such systems, where the system changes at discrete times when particular events occur

Discrete-event simulation is applicable when the state of a system over time is the major concern. The term *discrete event* describes the nature of such systems, where the system changes at discrete times when particular events occur. A simple example of a situation in which discrete-event simulation could be applied would be the check-in process at a hotel. The events that occur are guest arrival, service commencement, and service completion. Depending on the state of the system when the guest arrives, either service commences immediately or the customer joins a queue. Building a simulation model of the check-in process allows the user to evaluate a number of system characteristics, including the effects of new technologies, different staffing levels, and a flexible checkout time. Discrete-event simulation has three major uses: for validating the results of other models, for modeling alternative process designs, and for creating management decision-making games.

- *Validating other models.* Computer simulation is a valuable tool for validating other decision models. Simulation enables the user to evaluate theories under a variety of chance-controlled environments. If the theories perform well in the simulated environments, it increases the confidence that they will also perform well in practice. Again, we want to implement only theories or ideas that have a strong likelihood of actually performing well.
- *Process design.* Discrete-event simulation is useful for evaluating alternative process designs. Examples of processes for which simulation would be useful are restaurant back-of-house operations and queuing policies at theme parks, ski resorts, and so on. It is uncertainty about customer arrival times, customer service times, and—in the case of theme parks and ski resorts—the services selected by customers that makes simulation an appropriate and highly effective investigative tool. Similarly, a production manager in a factory can use simulation to determine many process parameters, such as the optimum number of machines at each station, the layout and flow of materials, and the deployment of labor resources.
- *Management decision-making games.* Computer simulation can form the backbone of management decision-making games. Again, the key feature of ap-

propriate decision-making environments is that chance plays an important role. Such decision-making games often feature a widely used technique known as "game-theory" to simulate the collective behavior of many decision makers within one organization or across different companies.

TECHNOLOGY IN OPERATIONS MANAGEMENT

Simulation of the Mix of Tables for a Restaurant

Professor Gary Thompson of the School of Hotel Administration at Cornell University has developed an interactive tool for simulation and optimization of the mix of tables in a restaurant. This interactive simulation-based tool, known as Tablemix (see http://www.hotelschool.cornell.edu/research/chr/pubs/tools/tooldetails.html?repid=14044), allows one to investigate how different table mixes perform in a restaurant, given information about the restaurant's customer mix.

Tablemix inputs include the number of days to simulate, the limit on the number of waiting parties, and the rule used in assigning waiting parties to available tables (e.g., are they assigned to the party waiting the longest or to the largest waiting party?). Inputs for each party size are the probability of that size party, the mean and standard deviation of dining time, the distribution of dining times (normal or lognormal), the maximum wait tolerated, and the estimated monetary value of the party. Tablemix also requires information on the number of parties expected to arrive, by 15-minute periods, during a peak window of a user-defined duration. If you are simulating a specific restaurant layout, Tablemix requires you to specify the position of each table and identify which tables can be combined with other tables (to seat larger parties).

Tablemix can be run in a visual mode, in which case it shows the status of the restaurant—that is, which tables are occupied, how many seats are occupied at each table, which tables have been combined into a larger table, and the number and size of parties waiting for tables (color-coded by the length of time they have been waiting).

Figure 9.8 (on page 349) presents a screen capture of the visual simulator in action (in this case, at the simulated time of 9:28 p.m.). The main portion of the screen shows the tables. Blue circles indicate unoccupied seats, green circles indicate occupied seats, and purple circles indicate tables that are "on hold," awaiting the departure of the party so that the table can be combined with an adjacent table to seat a large party. The third table from the left in the bottom row is actually two four-seaters that have been combined to seat a party of five. Those tables will be separated once the party has finished dining. At the top right of the screen shot is a visual display of the waiting parties. Parties that have been waiting the longest appear at the top of the screen. As of 9:28 p.m., there are eight parties waiting for tables: one party each of 9, 8, and 7 people; two parties of 5 people; and three parties of 2 people. Finally, the visual mode also reports the number of parties and customers who have been served and lost during the current dining period. As of 9:23 p.m., for example, 141 parties of two have been served, and 594 total customers have been served.

Tablemix outputs fall into three categories: resource use, customer service, and aggregate measures. Tablemix presents the utilization of each resource (i.e., each size of table and seats), by 15-minute time periods, in both tabular and graphic formats. Customer service measures, which are provided for each party size, include the number of customers served and lost, the expected value of customers served and lost, and the average and maximum waits. Aggregate performance measures are seat use, number of customers served per available seat, revenue per available seat hour, total number of customers served and lost, total expected value of customers served and lost, and the average customer waiting time.

Tablemix can be used to evaluate the performance of a specified mix of tables, or it can be used to find the best mix of tables given a specified limit on the number of seats.

Figure 9.9 (on page 350) shows the utilization of seats and tables for a specific midscale restaurant, using its existing table mix. Figure 9.9 also shows

(continued)

TECHNOLOGY IN OPERATIONS MANAGEMENT

Simulation of the Mix of Tables for a Restaurant (*continued*)

table use under the ideal mix of tables. Seat use is similar in the two graphs, peaking during the 6:00–8:00 p.m. time period in the range of 61 to 63 percent for the existing table mix and in the range of 61 to 65 percent for the ideal mix. However, the key story is told by the table utilization.

As Figure 9.9 shows, the current mix of tables is close to maximum capacity, averaging about 95 percent utilization for the four-tops for the 6:00–8:00 p.m. period and hitting 90 percent utilization of the six-tops during the same period. By contrast, the ideal mix of tables yields table use of under 75 percent during the peak 6:00–8:00 p.m. period. The net effect of optimizing the mix of tables is that the effective capacity of the restaurant is increased. The enhanced capacity can enable the restaurant to process about 40 percent more customers during the peak dining period. Of course, the restaurant still needs to determine the number of staff (waiters, cooks, buspeople, etc.), the amount and type of kitchen space, and other operating decisions. Luckily, simulation can also help with these decisions.

Source: G. M. Thompson and R. Verma, "Computer Simulation in Hospitality Teaching, Practice, and Research," *Cornell Quarterly*, April 2003.

Building Simulation Models

Simulation models are generally constructed using spreadsheets, simulation-modeling tools, or general-purpose computer languages.

Spreadsheet-Based Models

As noted earlier, numerical simulation models can generally be developed in spreadsheets. Modelers with knowledge of Excel's programming language, VBA (Visual Basic for Applications), can build sophisticated discrete-event simulation models (such as the Tablemix model mentioned in the box.) The advantages of building simulation models in spreadsheets are that knowledge of spreadsheets is widespread and that the cost of spreadsheet software is relatively low. The disadvantages, which apply mainly to complex discrete-event models, include the amount of programming knowledge needed, the time required to develop complex models, and the relatively slow speed at which the simulation model executes.

Simulation-Modeling Tools

Simulation has been used both in commercial applications and in classrooms for the past two to three decades. During the DOS and mainframe computing era, programming languages (for example, FORTRAN, C, and C++) were used to develop simulation models. Although sophisticated and detailed, those programs had either limited or no ability to display the models graphically. Additionally, programming even a simple model required at least several hours (and often months) of development time.

More recent simulation programs, on the other hand, are relatively easy to use, display information graphically, and do not require knowledge of a programming language. They do, however, require an understanding of simulation-modeling concepts, logic, and statistics. A number of graphics- and animation-based simulation programs that attempt to reduce model-development time have been developed. XCELL® is an excellent example of one of the first widely used graphics-based

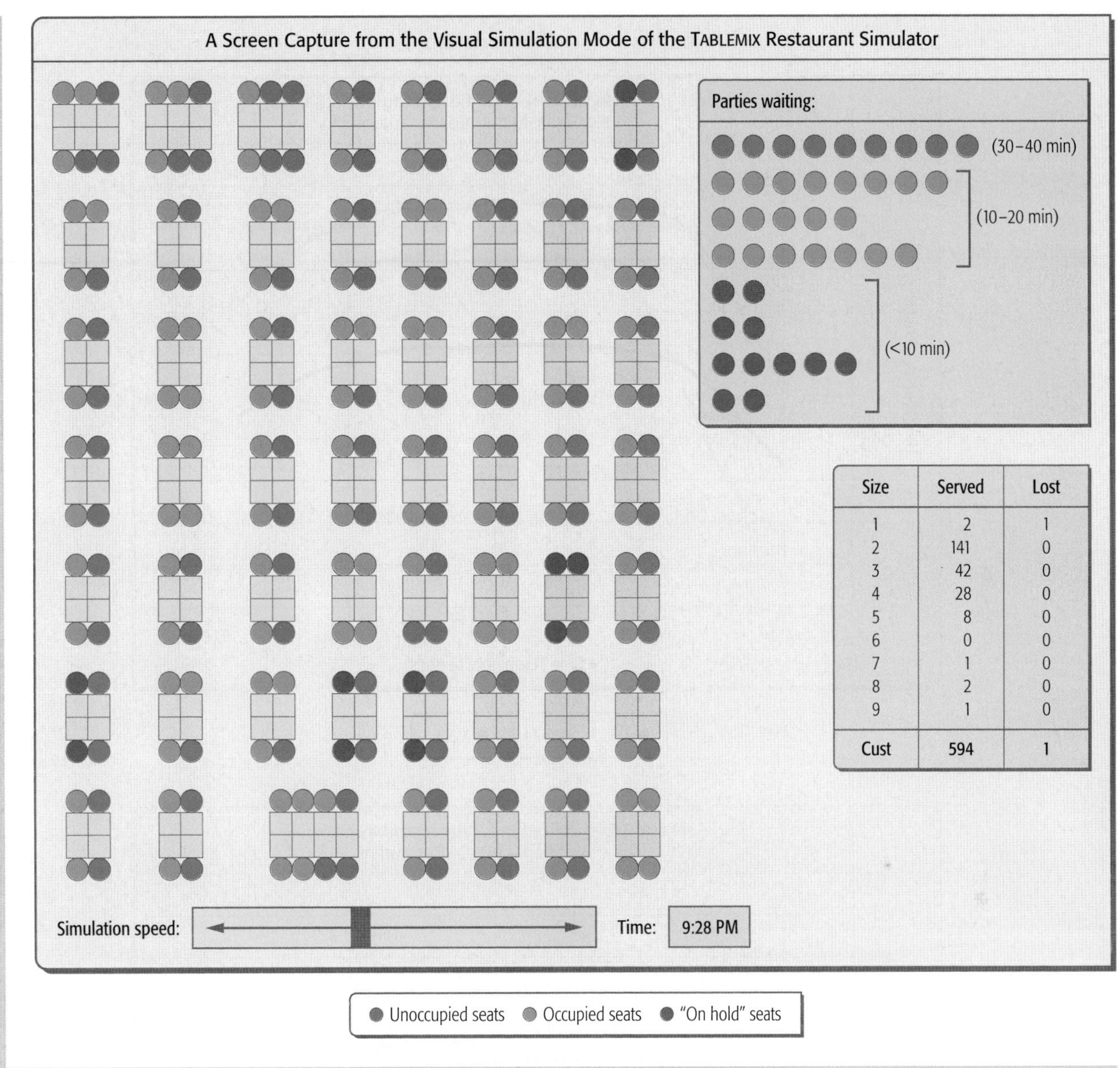

Size	Served	Lost
1	2	1
2	141	0
3	42	0
4	28	0
5	8	0
6	0	0
7	1	0
8	2	0
9	1	0
Cust	594	1

FIGURE 9.8 Example from Tablemix Simulator

Source: Thompson, G. M. and R. Verma. "Computer Simulation in Hospitality Teaching, Practice, and Reseach," *Cornell Hotel and Restaurant Administration Quarterly,* April 2003. Copyright © 2003 by Sage Publications. Reprinted with permission.

simulation-modeling programs. Currently, there are a number of animation-based simulation-modeling tools available in the market.[1] The authors of this textbook have used ServiceModel® and Promodel® extensively in teaching, research, and consulting applications over the past several years.

ServiceModel allows users to design virtually any service process and evaluate its performance visually over time. Users can decide the layout of the service process to be simulated, the customer arrival rate (including market segments), the number and schedule of service providers, capacity, resources, and other service attributes. Based on the requirements and the model assumptions, the user can redesign various alternatives and run the model for several hours, days, or months of "real" time in minutes of simulation time. In addition, ServiceModel

[1] For reviews and comparisons of various commercially available simulation tools, see http://lionhrtpub.com/orms/surveys/Simulation/Simulation.html.

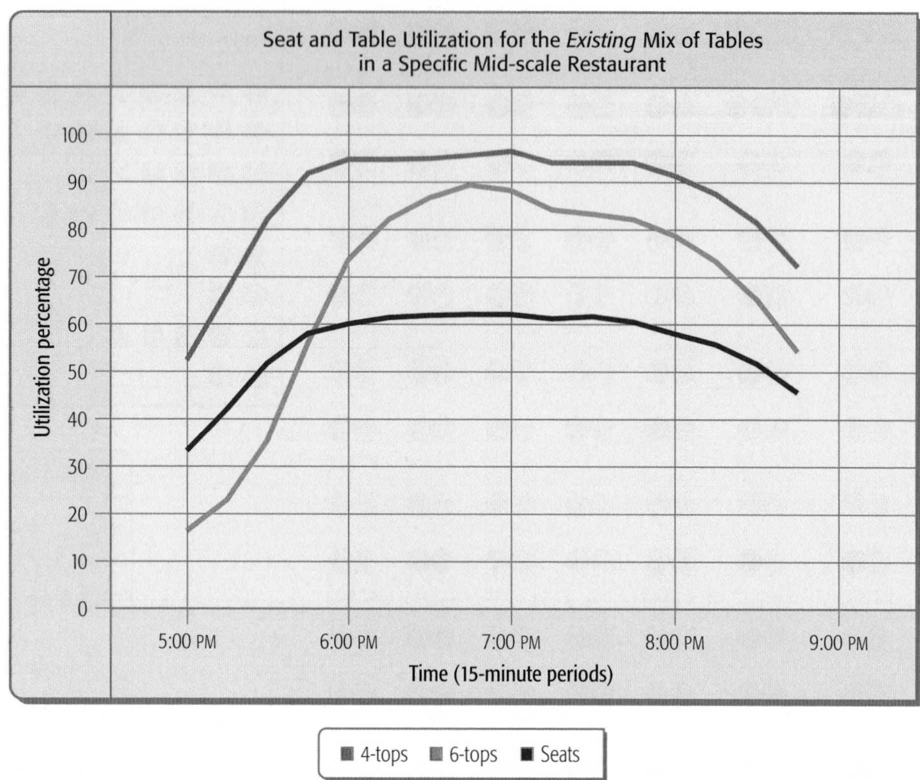

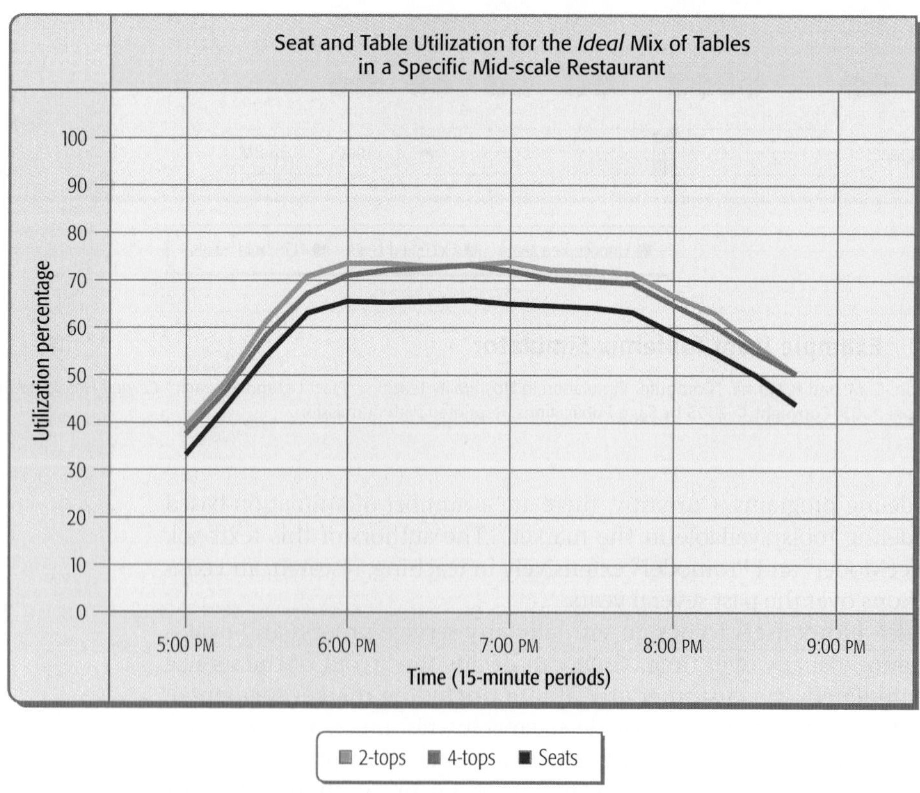

FIGURE 9.9 Example Results from Tablemix Simulator

Source: Thompson, G. M. and R. Verma. "Computer Simulation in Hospitality Teaching, Practice, and Research," *Cornell Hotel and Restaurant Administration Quarterly,* April 2003.

comes with an optimization and experimental design program, SimRunner, that can be used to test whether changes in certain input parameters influence selected output measures. SimRunner can conduct full or fractional factorial experiments with multiple attributes with user-defined objective functions. The optimized regression models can estimate both the main effects and the interaction effects among input variables on the objective functions. The estimated equations can be easily incorporated into spreadsheet-based decision-support systems for use in day-to-day management and decision making. In fact, the most recent version of ServiceModel is compatible with Microsoft's ActiveX control protocols, which allow users to control various functionalities of the simulation via Microsoft Excel macros. An illustration of ServiceModel for a banking application is presented in the following box.

TECHNOLOGY IN OPERATIONS MANAGEMENT

Computer Simulation of Check Processing Operations

One of the largest commercial banks in the United States asked one of the authors of this text to develop a simulation model of the upgrade and redesign plan for its check processing operations at its central check processing facility in Chicago. The objective of the project was to assess whether it was worthwhile to spend more than $1 million for new equipment for check processing operations.

The check processing facility processed approximately three million checks during each 24-hour cycle. The monetary amount on each check varied from a few dollars to several million and on average amounted to a total of over $3.0 billion daily. Therefore, the efficiency of this central check processing operation was of utmost importance to the corporation. In addition, it was essential that the check processing operation complete its daily work in a timely manner so that customer accounts could be posted and online balance information updated for branch operations. An overview of the check processing operation analyzed in this study is shown in Figure 9.10 (on page 352).

The reject repair and balancing process is used to manually process any check that the automatic sorter is not able to read. The reject repair process that was used at the time was very labor-intensive, and its replacement by an automated process based on high-speed image technology connected to a series of computer workstations was under discussion. We developed animated simulation models to understand the old and new reject repair processes. The simulation models provided valuable insights about the check processing operation. For example, the models were able to identify bottlenecks, waiting times, and productivity data for various operating scenarios.

It is generally not possible to include all features of a real system in any simulation model. It is also important to realize that a model is only an abstraction of reality. Therefore, models should include all essential and relevant elements of the real system and leave the nonessential elements out. Using these guidelines, and based on real process data, we modeled the current and new check reject repair processes.

In order to develop realistic models, we first collected actual process data for several days to estimate various model parameters and input distributions. The mainframe computer tracked batch sizes and arrival and departure times at various check processing stations. Therefore, the task of identifying input parameters was reduced to going through several pages of mainframe computer output and recording relevant information for each job. Based on the identified input parameters and process logic, two models were developed using ServiceModel. Figures 9.11 and 9.12 (on pages 353 and 354, respectively) show screen prints of the models. Tables 9.9 and 9.10 (on page 353) show summarized results for both the current and the new processes.

This study demonstrates the value of animated simulation in the design and improvement of complex service processes. Data collection, model development, and analysis for the simulation exercise described here were completed within one month. This application of simulation occurred in the late 1990s. Since that time, banks have largely moved to electronic

(*continued*)

TECHNOLOGY IN OPERATIONS MANAGEMENT

Computer Simulation of Check Processing Operations (*continued*)

checking, where images of checks are scanned and the checks are destroyed rather than returned to customers. Electronic images of checks are now available online. This approach saves the bank quite a bit of labor and money. Simulation can be used to model the effects of such new technology.

The advantages of simulation-modeling tools include the ability to create complex discrete-event models without knowledge of programming and the speed at which models can be created by experienced modelers. The speed with which simulation models can be constructed with these tools makes the tools suited to rapid prototyping of process designs. The disadvantages of simulation-modeling tools include a slow speed of execution and the cost of the software, which can be in the tens of thousands of dollars per copy.

Simulation, like any quantitative-decision aid, is dependent on accurate data. If a simulation model has incorrect or inaccurate parameters, then the results of that model will be incorrect. Certainly the old adage "garbage in, garbage out" applies to simulation. To overcome this liability, it is important to validate a simulation model. One can use a variety of means to do that. First, the model can be used to simulate an existing system. The behavior of the model should match that of the existing system. Second, one can ask experts in the area about the type of behavior they would expect the system to exhibit under certain situations, and this can then be compared to the simulation model's outputs under those circumstances. Such experts are thus giving the simulation model a sort of "reality check."

Another potential drawback of simulation relates to its ease of use. Because simulation models are relatively easy to create, simulation is often overused. In other words, simulation may be used when other tools, such as mathematical programming (linear programming is an example of mathematical programming), might be more appropriate. This limitation can be overcome by ensuring that the modelers have a broad knowledge of different decision aids and know which tools are most useful for which types of situations. The point here is that if the only thing one knows is simulation, then everything tends to look like a simulation problem. However, when used correctly, simulation is a useful tool for operations managers.

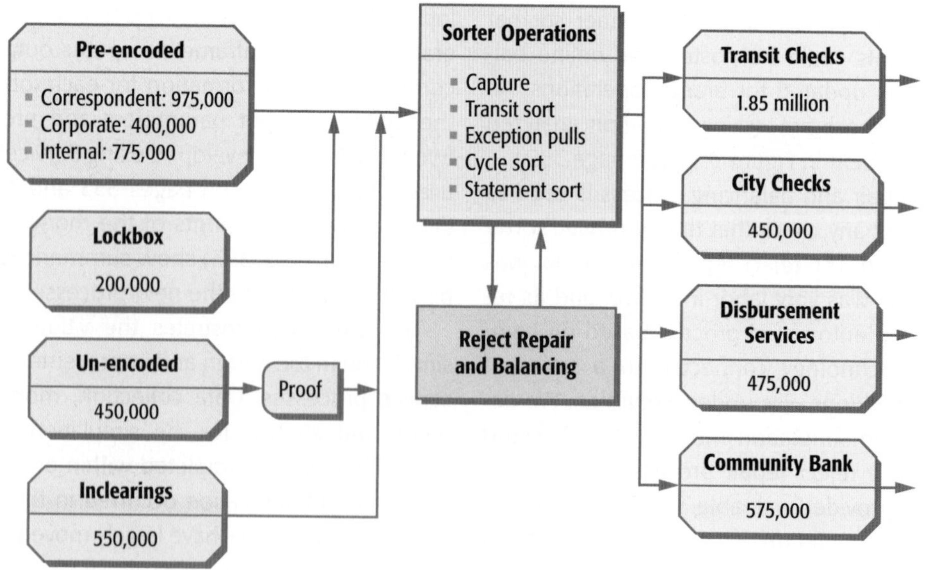

FIGURE 9.10 Check Processing Workflow Schematic

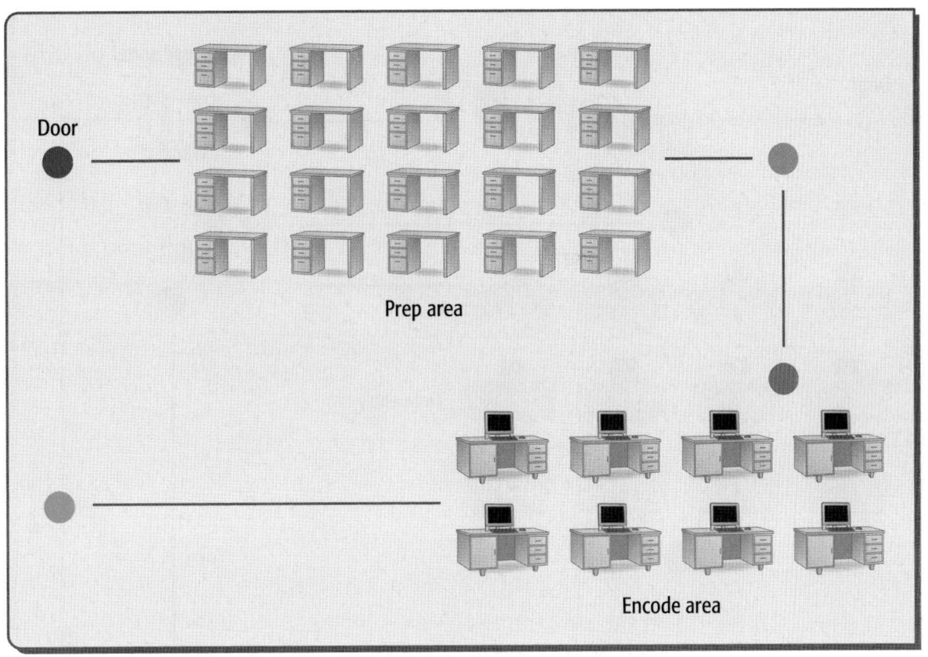

FIGURE 9.11 Old Check Reject Repair Process Simulation Model

TABLE 9.9 Summarized Simulation Results for the Current Process

Location	Average Processing Time	Utilization
Prep	122.95 minutes	99.58%
Encode	0.01 minute	4.14%

TABLE 9.10 Summarized Simulation Results for the New Process

Location	Average Processing Time	Utilization
Prep	9.68 minutes	50.67%
Image capture	0.022 minute	21.51%
Data entry	0.03 minute	0.19%

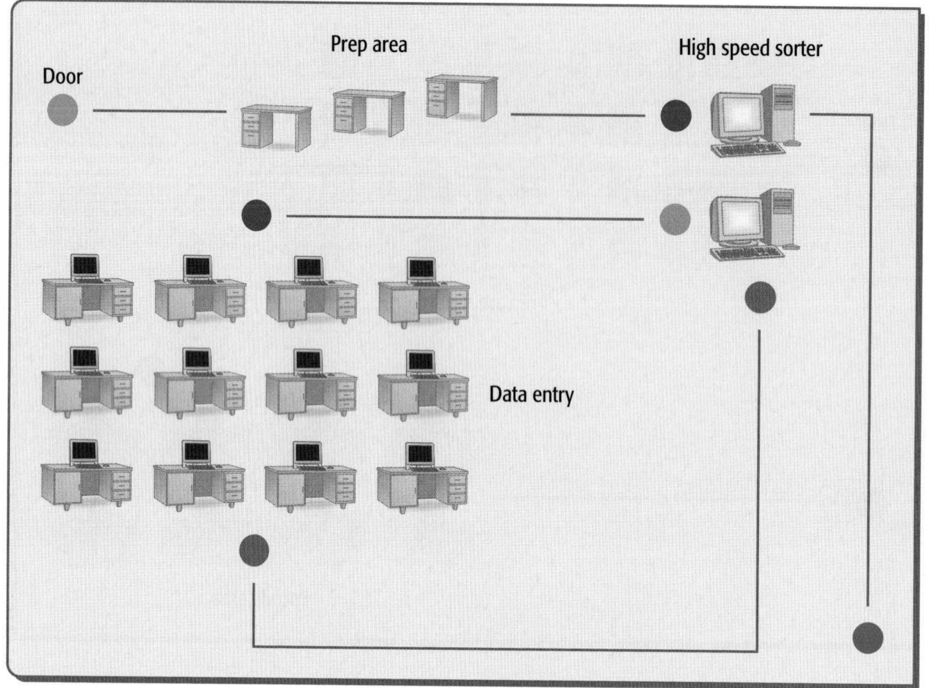

FIGURE 9.12 New Check Reject Repair Process Simulation Model

SUMMARY

1. Formulate and solve linear programming problems.

- Linear programming is a special formulation of an optimization problem in which all equations and inequalities are linear. It is used to solve a wide variety of operations problems, such as production planning, transportation planning, labor scheduling, revenue management, productivity assessment, capacity planning, and so on.
- Linear programming formulation requires the identification of decision variables, the objective, and constraints. All information must be represented by straight lines or inequalities.
- Linear programming problems with two decision variables can be solved by a graphical method. If the number of variables is higher than two, then computer-based algorithms (such as Solver Module of Microsoft Excel) can be used.

2. Describe the use of computer simulation modeling in operations decision making.

- Computer simulation models are used in decision making because testing proposed new operating procedures in an actual operation is often expensive, complicated, and risky. Simulation models allow managers to evaluate multiple operations designs and perform what-if types of analyses.
- Numerical simulation involves simulating outcomes that are controlled by chance, but where the state of the system at specific times is not of interest.
- Discrete-event simulation is applicable when the state of a system over time is the major concern.
- Simulation models are generally constructed using spreadsheets, simulation-modeling tools, or general-purpose computer languages.
- Animated computer simulation programs such as ServiceModel allow the users to create models and evaluate them relatively quickly without actually changing the real operations system.

SOLVED PROBLEM 1

Setting Up a Linear Programming Problem

A financial services company processes applications for home mortgages and commercial loans for its clients. Both types of applications are first reviewed by the screening department. It takes this department 30 minutes to review each home mortgage application and 80 minutes to review each commercial loan application. After the screening, a credit check is performed, which takes 2 hours for each type of application. Finally, the applications are sent to a loan officer for a final evaluation. It takes a loan officer 1.5 hours to review a mortgage application and 2.5 hours to review a commercial loan application. The company also wants to ensure that it processes at least 50 loans and 50 mortgages each week.

The company currently employs 10 staff members in the screening department, 20 staff members in the credit check department, and 15 loan officers. Each employee receives the same salary and works 40 hours per week. The company receives $250 for processing each home mortgage application and $400 for processing each commercial loan application.

Based on the information provided and assuming unlimited demand, set up a profit-maximizing linear programming formulation.

SOLUTION

Decision Variables.

Mortgages: Number of home mortgage applications processed every week

Loans: Number of commercial loans processed every week.

Objective.

Maximize profit.

Objective Function.

$$\$250 * \text{Mortgages} + \$400 * \text{Loans}$$

Constraints.

Screening Department Constraint The screening department takes 30 minutes for each mortgage application and 80 minutes for each loan application. It has 10 staff members, each working 40 hours per week. Therefore, the screening department has 40 * 60 * 10 = 24,000 minutes of available capacity. The time allocated to processing mortgages and loans cannot exceed the available capacity.

Therefore,

$$30 * \text{mortgages} + 80 * \text{loans} \leq 24{,}000$$

Credit Check Constraint The credit check department takes 120 minutes for each application. It employs 20 staff members and therefore has 48,000 minutes (20 * 40 * 60) of capacity.

Therefore,

$$120 * \text{mortgages} + 120 * \text{loans} \leq 48{,}000$$

Loan Officer Constraint Similar to the other two departments, the requirements and capacity for the loan officer can be set in the following manner:

$$90 * \text{mortgages} + 150 * \text{loans} \leq 36{,}000$$

Furthermore, we should add constraints to ensure that at least 50 mortgages and 50 loans are processed each week.

$$\text{Mortgages} \geq 50$$
$$\text{Loans} \geq 50$$

SOLVED PROBLEM 2

Graphical Solution to a Linear Programming Problem

Solve the linear programming formulation presented in Solved Problem 1 using the graphical method. Identify the optimum number of mortgages and loans.

SOLUTION

The following equations represent the linear programming formulation of Solved Problem 1:

Objective Function.

$$\$250 * \text{Mortgages} + \$400 * \text{Loans}$$

Constraints.

$$30 * \text{Mortgages} + 80 * \text{Loans} \leq 24{,}000 \text{ (screening)}$$

$$120 * \text{Mortgages} + 120 * \text{Loans} \leq 48{,}000 \text{ (credit check)}$$

$$90 * \text{Mortgages} + 150 * \text{Loans} \leq 36{,}000 \text{ (loan officer)}$$

$$\text{Mortgages} \geq 50 \text{ (minimum processing)}$$

$$\text{Loans} \geq 50 \text{ (minimum processing)}$$

We will first plot each of the five constraints on a graph and identify the region that satisfies all the constraints.

Plotting the Screening Constraint To identify two points on the straight line representing the boundary of the screening constraint, each variable is set to zero, and the value of the other variable is calculated.

If mortgages = 0, then

$$80 * \text{Loans} = 24{,}000$$

Therefore,

$$\text{Loans} = 24{,}000/80 = 300$$

If loans = 0, then

$$30 * \text{Mortgages} = 24{,}000$$

Therefore

$$\text{Mortgages} = 24{,}000/30 = 800$$

Therefore, the following two points appear on the straight line: (0, 300) and (800, 0).

The graph in Figure 9.13 (on page 358) shows the plot of the screening constraint. The shaded region represents the region that satisfies the constraint.

Plotting the Credit Check Constraint As with the screening constraint, we must first find two points on the straight line representing the boundary of the credit check constraint. The two points on the straight line are (0, 400) and (400, 0). The shaded area in Figure 9.14 (on page 358) shows the region that satisfies both the screening and the credit check constraints.

Plotting the Loan Officer Constraint The two points on the straight line are (0, 240) and (400, 0). The shaded area in Figure 9.15 (on page 359) shows the region that satisfies all three constraints.

Plotting the Minimum Processing Constraints Finally, we can plot the two minimum processing constraints. The shaded area in Figure 9.16 (on page 359) shows the feasible solution region that satisfies all five constraints.

Identifying Corner Points The feasible solution region is bounded by three corner points: A, B, and C.

We need to find the coordinates of the three corner points and evaluate the objective function at each location to find the optimum solution.

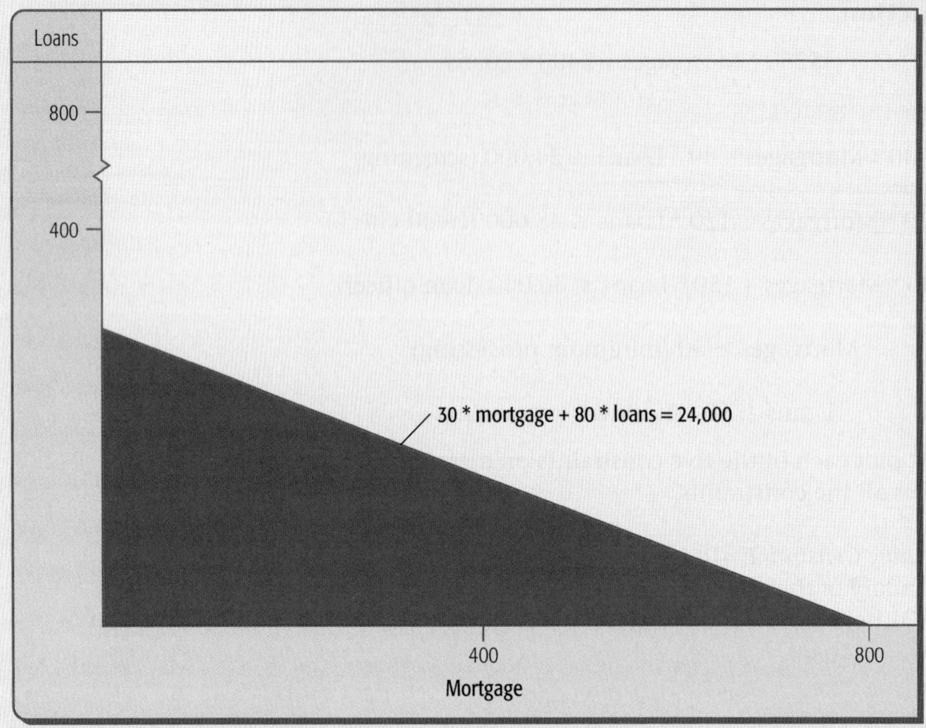

FIGURE 9.13

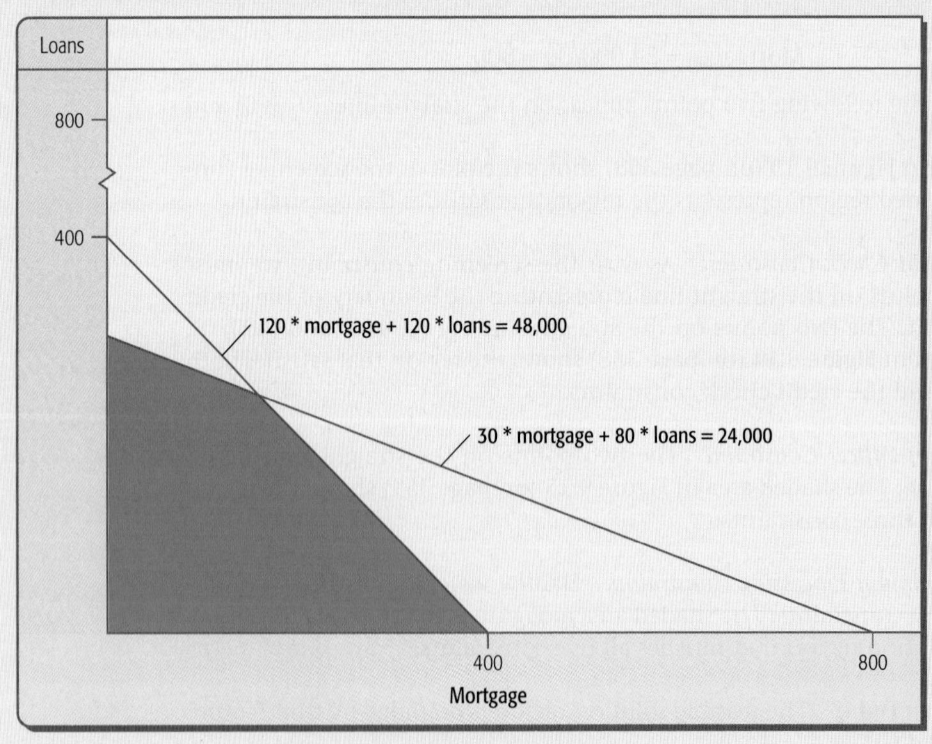

FIGURE 9.14

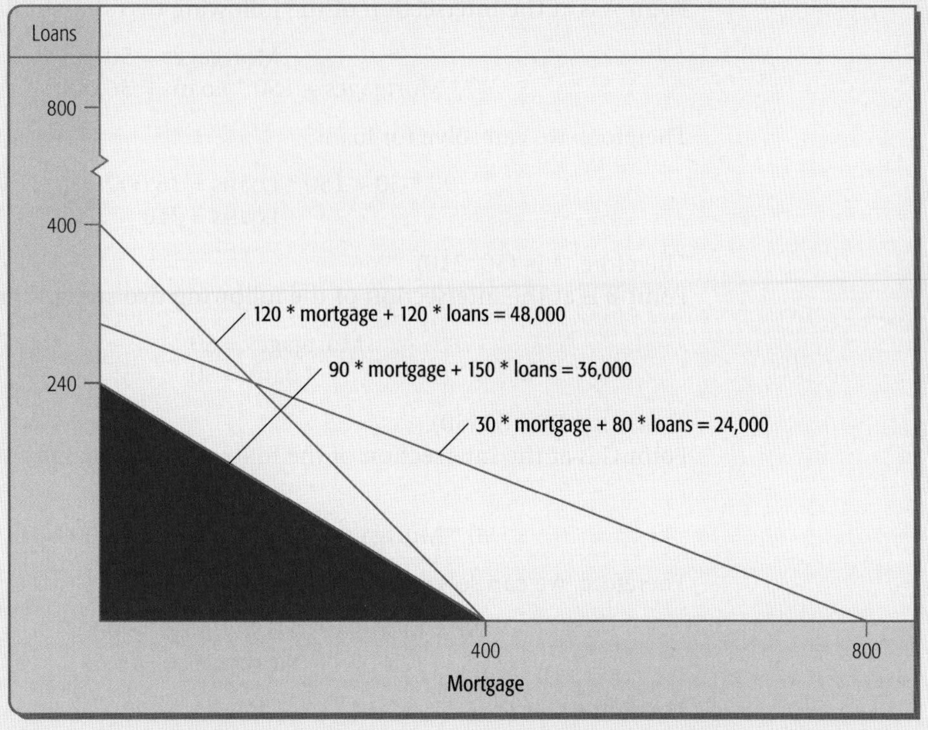

FIGURE 9.15

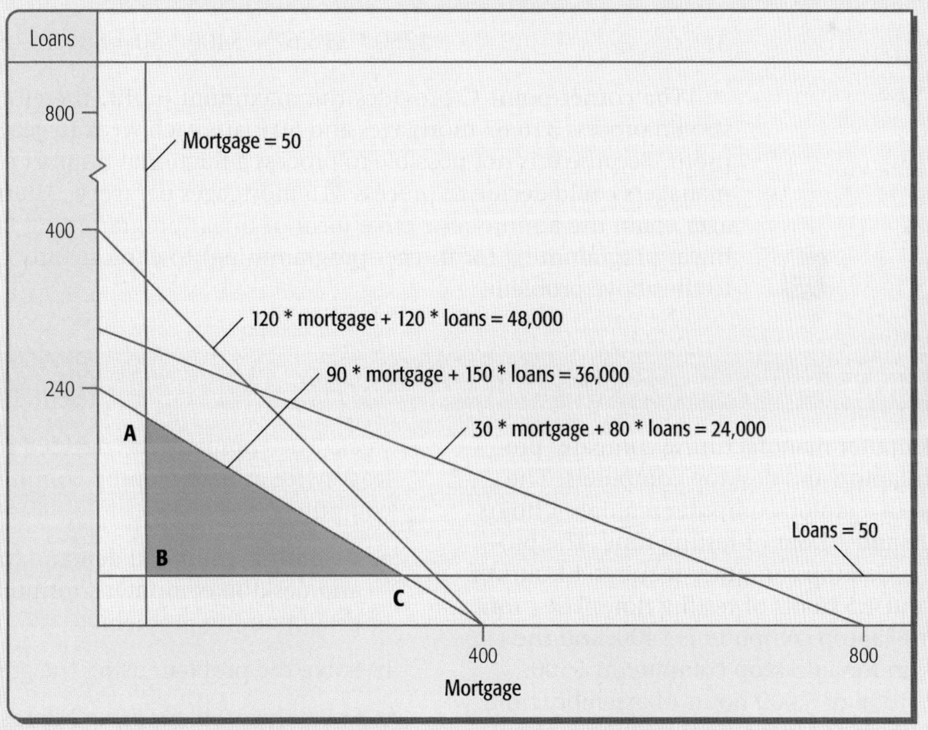

FIGURE 9.16

Point A is at the intersection of the following two straight lines:

$$\text{Mortgages} = 50$$
$$90 * \text{Mortgages} + 150 * \text{Loans} = 36{,}000$$

Therefore, we can solve for loans:

$$90 * 50 + 150 * \text{Loans} = 36{,}000$$
$$\text{Loans} = 210$$

Therefore, A is (50, 210).
Point B is at the intersection of the following two straight lines:

$$\text{Mortgages} = 50$$
$$\text{Loans} = 50$$

Therefore, B is (50, 50).
Point C is at the intersection of the following two straight lines:

$$\text{Loans} = 50$$
$$90 * \text{Mortgages} + 150 * \text{Loans} = 36{,}000$$

Therefore, we can solve for mortgages:

$$90 * \text{Mortgages} + 150 * 50 = 36{,}000$$
$$\text{Mortgages} = 316.67$$

Therefore, C is (316.67, 50).

Evaluating the Objective Function at Corner Points The values of the objective function at the corner points are

At A: $\$250 * 50 + \$400 * 210 = \$96{,}500$

At B: $\$250 * 50 + \$400 * 50 = \$32{,}500$

At C: $\$250 * 316.67 + \$400 * 50 = \$99{,}167.50$

The corner point C provides the maximum profit; therefore, the company should process 316.67 mortgages and 50 loans each week to generate $99,167.50 profit. Because it is not possible to process a fractional number of mortgages, the managers could decide to process 316 mortgages per week. Alternately, the manager could use a more restrictive form of linear programming known as integer linear programming (or integer programming) to explore only integer solutions to the above problem.

PROBLEMS

1. A small computer manufacturing company produces both laptop and desktop computers. The production of a laptop computer requires 4 hours of assembly and 1 hour of testing time. The production of a desktop computer requires 4 hours of assembly and 1.5 hours of testing time. The profit margin for a laptop computer is $400, and the profit margin for a desktop computer is $500. There are a total of 5,000 hours of assembly time and 1,000 hours of testing time available every week. The company has decided to produce at least twice as many laptop computers as desktop computers.

   a. Assuming unlimited demand for both laptop and desktop computers, formulate a linear programming problem.

   b. Solve the problem using the graphical method.

   c. Solve the problem using Microsoft Excel Solver.

2. A customer service center needs to schedule enough employees to meet the expected call volumes during the 24 hours of every day. Based on estimated demand, the minimum number of required employees during each four-hour time interval is given in Table 9.11.

TABLE 9.11 Time Period and Labor Requirements

Time Period	Minimum Number of Customer Service Agents Needed
Midnight–4 a.m.	8
4 a.m.–8 a.m.	6
8 a.m.–noon	12
Noon–4 p.m.	15
4 p.m.–8 p.m.	9
8 p.m.–midnight	5

The employees can begin their shifts at the beginning of any time period. However, they have to work for 8 hours. What is the minimum number of employees needed to satisfy the requirements?

3. Mounting Biking Specialists makes two types of bicycles: mountain bikes and road bikes. A mountain bike sells for $350, and a road bike sells for $250. The marketing department recommends that at least 500 bikes of each type be produced each day. A mountain bike requires 3 labor-hours in the fabrication department and 2 labor-hours in the assembly department. A road bike requires 2 labor-hours in the fabrication department and 2 labor-hours in the assembly department. Each bike needs 1 hour in the quality-testing department. There are a total of 4,000, 3,000 and 1,000 hours available in the fabrication, assembly, and testing departments, respectively. Formulate this information as a revenue-maximizing linear programming problem.

4. Quality Food Manufacturers (QFM) has production facilities in Lansing, Dallas, and Seattle. Production capabilities for these plants over the four-week planning period for children's clothing are listed in Table 9.12 in terms of number of shipments (each shipment is equivalent to the volume of clothing that can be shipped on one truck).

TABLE 9.12 Production Capacity

Plant Location	Production Capacity
Lansing	370
Dallas	430
Seattle	500

The firm distributes its clothes to retailers across the country through four regional distribution centers located in Ithaca, Miami, Atlanta, and Corpus Christi. The forecasts of demand for each of the distribution centers are given in Table 9.13.

TABLE 9.13 Forecasted Demand

Distribution Center	Demand
Ithaca	450
Miami	250
Atlanta	200
Corpus Christi	400

Management would like to determine how much of its production should be shipped from each plant to each distribution center. The cost for each unit shipped via each route is given in Table 9.14.

TABLE 9.14 Shipping Costs

Destination Origin	Ithaca	Miami	Atlanta	Corpus Christi
Lansing	$250	$175	$450	$300
Dallas	$400	$275	$200	$250
Seattle	$300	$325	$300	$375

CASE STUDY

Multiperiod Production Planning at Zeta

Zeta is a producer of a variety of microprocessors and memory chips that are used in products such as automobiles, computers, digital cameras, and so on. Although the microprocessors for each application are unique, they can be broadly placed into three classes: low grade (LG), medium grade (MG), and high grade (HG). Because of long supplier lead times, Zeta plans its production based on a six-month rolling horizon. Table 9.15 shows the expected demand for each of the three types of microprocessors for the next six months.

The company can produce only up to 7,500 units per month (in any combination of LG, MG, and HG). Because the designs of the microprocessors evolve constantly, the chips need to be sold during the month in which they are produced.

The production cost for each LG is currently \$10, and it is expected to go up to \$12 starting Month 4. The production cost for MG is currently \$15, and it is expected to go up by \$1 every month for the next three months and then stay at the same level. The production cost for HG is \$20, and it is expected to stay constant. Currently, the selling price per unit for LG, MG, and HG is \$50, \$75, and \$100, respectively.

Based on the information provided, develop a linear programming model for Zeta's production planning. Solve the problem using the Linear Programming module within Excel Solver, and develop a production plan for Zeta for the next six months.

TABLE 9.15 Expected Demand

Month	LG	MG	HG
1	50,000	25,000	15,000
2	45,000	20,000	18,000
3	35,000	35,000	20,000
4	40,000	30,000	22,000
5	46,000	28,000	21,000
6	60,000	32,000	20,000

Capacity Planning

LEARNING OBJECTIVES

1. Describe methods of measuring capacity, planning capacity, and calculating capacity utilization. Explain the impact of economies of scale, diseconomies of scale, and experience curves on capacity.
2. Explain differences in capacity strategy in terms of the timing and sizing of expansion options.
3. Describe the benefits of a capacity cushion and the strategic reasons to increase or decrease the cushion.
4. Understand how to evaluate capacity alternatives.
5. Discuss how to plan capacity expansions to address gaps between demand and supply.
6. Explain the importance of special factors for managing service capacity.

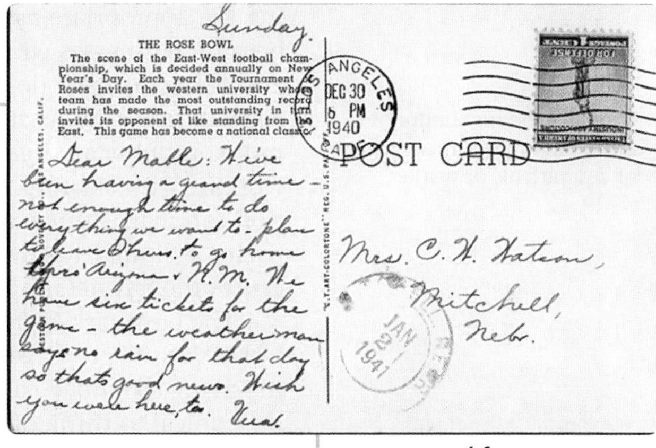

A postcard from Pasadena, CA.

Postmarked Gone

What do the cities of Bridgeport, Connecticut; Newark, New Jersey; and Pasadena, California, have in common? They are all cities that have recently had their postmarks removed by the U.S. Postal Service. In December 2006, the USPS closed mail processing centers in each of these cities, plus nine others, in an effort to shrink its capacity to better fit demand. Each of these communities now has the postmark of a neighboring community where its mail is processed.

Why the change? Because while total mail volume, including packages and bulk mail, has grown, the amount of first-class mail is decreasing—from 103.7 billion pieces in 2001 to 98.1 billion in 2005. More and more people are corresponding by e-mail and the Internet, and thus, there is less mail correspondence; even those dreaded bills and the checks to pay them are increasingly being handled by online banking. The result? According to USPS spokesman Gerry McKiernan, "In certain geographic areas of the country, single-piece first-class mail has declined to such a rate that it doesn't take a full shift of employees and machines to process." Thus, the USPS is consolidating postal workers into fewer processing centers; in turn, there are fewer postmarks.

While this is a perfectly rational response to match capacity with shrinking demand, it can hurt those cities' civic pride. For example, Pasadena, home to the granddaddy

SOURCE: Melanie Eversley, "De-Prioritized: 12 U.S. Cities Lose Postmarks," *USA Today,* December 27, 2005, p. 3A.

of all bowl games, the Rose Bowl, no longer feels the sense of pride that accompanied having its own postmark. Similarly, *St. Petersburg Times* columnist Sue Carlton wrote of the indignity of having local mail postmarked as from Tampa: "It's not enough that St. Petersburg, an actual city in its own right, has to put up with local sports franchises named the Tampa Bay Devil Rays and the Tampa Bay Buccaneers. Now the Postal Service is considering taking away the St. Petersburg postmark on first-class mail." ■

CAPACITY MANAGEMENT AND ITS RELATIONSHIP TO VALUE

● **Capacity** the maximum output of an organization, piece of equipment, or worker

Capacity management is a critical component of long-term decision making because it is a fundamental part of all facility investment decisions, which are difficult to change or reverse. Organizations must have excess capacity to handle demand uncertainty—the greater the variation and uncertainty of demand, the greater the amount of extra or cushion capacity needed. On a macro level, choosing the appropriate amount of capacity for an entire supply chain is important because businesses with too much capacity are wasting resources on equipment and personnel that do not earn a return, while businesses with a capacity shortage will lose sales as customers find alternative suppliers. **Capacity** is the maximum output of an organization, piece of equipment, or worker. On a micro level, working with existing facilities and equipment to maximize and equalize utilization can make a huge difference in the profitability of a business. In general, capacity is similar to inventory in that too much of it is expensive, yet too little causes the business to lose sales.

The postmark example illustrates one of the basic challenges of capacity: It is just as possible to have excess capacity as it is to have a shortage. There are costs to having too much capacity, just as there are costs to not having enough. While it is typical to think of expanding capacity, particularly in growing industries or businesses, it is important to realize that shrinking capacity, particularly in established industries, is also critically important.

Capacity Measures

While there are aspects of capacity planning that must be customized for a specific industry and business, there are also several key concepts that generally apply to a wide variety of organizations. There is a high degree of commonality regarding measures of capacity, economies of scale, experience curves, and diseconomies of scale. Each of these concepts is fundamental to successful capacity planning in most organizations and will be described in detail in the following sections.

Capacity measures must be tailored to fit specific situations. Restaurants measure capacity in terms of the number of diners or meals that can be served during a day or during a specific mealtime. An amusement park assesses the number of patrons that can visit the park per day or that can be accommodated on a particular ride. A delivery company measures the number of packages that can be delivered per day. A manufacturing company may count the number of units (computers, phones, chairs, etc.) made per day or measure its capacity in terms of the number of machine hours available. While each of these methods of

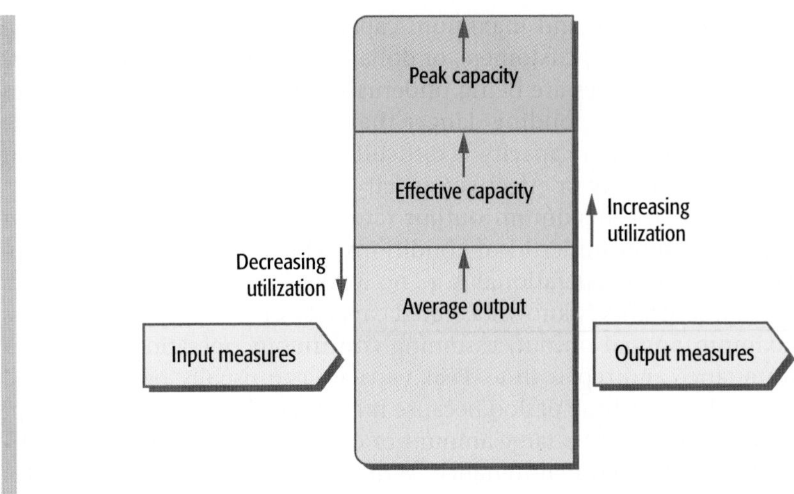

FIGURE 10.1 Illustration of Utilization as Related to Average Output and Capacity

assessing capacity is specific to its application, capacity measures can be grouped broadly as either output or input measures. Figure 10.1 illustrates the basic relationships. Utilization is the ratio of average output to either effective or peak capacity. Utilization increases or decreases as average output is increased or peak or effective capacity is changed. Capacity can be measured using either input or output measures.

Output measures assess the units coming out of a process or facility as finished goods or services. Line flow processes typically use very specific measures. A candy manufacturer such as Nestlé might measure capacity in terms of the total number of candy bars that can be produced in a year. The total capacity might be 150,000,000 candy bars per year. Nestlé can measure capacity in this manner because, while the company makes a number of different types of candy bars, they are fairly similar in terms of production resources. Businesses that have a wider product range and a greater degree of customization typically have a more challenging time measuring capacity. For example, a fast-food restaurant typically offers 40 to 50 different products and cannot realistically measure capacity individually for each. Thus, capacity might be tracked in terms of total sales (e.g., $4,400 per day), number of customers (1,400 per day), or transactions per group of products (e.g., 1,100 sandwiches per day, 800 orders of fries, and 900 drinks). Output measures are commonly employed to assess processes or businesses that offer relatively few fairly standardized products or services.

● **Output measures** measures of the units coming out of a process or facility as finished goods or services

Input measures assess the resources that are put into a supply chain or process. They tend to fit processes or businesses that have a high degree of customization. For example, capacity in a copy shop would probably be measured in terms of total machine hours or the number of machines available. A neighborhood bakery might measure the number of baking hours or machines available, or simply measure the pounds of product.

● **Input measures** measures that assess the resources that are put into a supply chain or process

Utilization is defined as the percentage of the available time that equipment, space, or labor is used and adding value. Utilization is a fundamental measure of capacity and is typically expressed as a percentage:

● **Utilization** the percentage of the available time that equipment, space, or labor is used and adding value

$$U = \frac{O}{M_c} \qquad \text{(Equation 1)}$$

where O = average output
M_c = maximum capacity

The average output rate and maximum capacity must be measured in the same units—e.g., time, units, customers, or dollars. Low utilization rates suggest that equipment or employees are being underused, while high utilization rates suggest overuse and a corresponding danger that demand will exceed available capacity. Defining maximum capacity is difficult; however, it can be defined in terms of either peak capacity or effective capacity.

● **Peak capacity** the maximum output rate that a process or facility can achieve in the short term under ideal conditions

Peak capacity is the maximum output rate that a process or facility can achieve in the short term under ideal conditions. This assumes that all equipment and workers are fully operational (e.g., no workers are sick) and do not take breaks. For equipment, this is known as rated capacity or an engineering assessment of maximum annual output, assuming continuous operation except for normal maintenance and repair time. Peak capacity can usually be maintained for only a relatively short time period because it assumes that the business is operating at its maximum, with a large amount of overtime, extra shifts, overstaffing, and possibly postponed maintenance. While this level of output is helpful for meeting peak periods of demand, it is also similar to driving an automobile at 100 miles an hour for weeks at a time—sooner or later, the car is bound to break down or crash. Organizations that make heavy use of overtime or extra shifts often find that the cost premiums (i.e., overtime pay or shift differentials) outweigh the benefits. Furthermore, quality and productivity usually suffer as overworked employees and equipment reach their effective limits.

● **Effective capacity** the maximum output that a company or process can economically sustain under normal circumstances for an extended time period

Effective capacity is the maximum output that a company or process can economically sustain under normal circumstances for an extended time period. For example, accounting firms typically expect accountants to work long hours during the period between March 1 and April 15, when individual IRS tax forms are due. The peak capacity for this period might be 60 hours per week per accountant. This might translate to 30 clients per week if each client takes 2 hours. However, the accounting firm could not possibly operate at this level all year because the accountants would burn out, make a much higher proportion of mistakes, and generally not be very effective. Thus, the effective capacity at an accounting firm is more likely to be 40 hours per week per accountant.

FedEx provides a good illustration of the difference between peak and effective capacity. The average daily volume of packages delivered throughout the year is 6 million per day in the FedEx Express and FedEx Ground networks. During the Christmas holiday season of 2007, FedEx projected that December 17, 2007, would be its busiest single day ever, with more than 11.3 million packages moving through the system. Thus, peak capacity is more than 60 percent higher than effective capacity.

Capacity Factors

There are several factors that affect the estimation of capacity. These include economies of scale, experience curves, and diseconomies of scale. Each of these is discussed in the following sections, along with their impact on capacity estimation.

Economies of Scale

● **Economies of scale** positive effects that result when large volumes of a product or service are produced together, allowing the producer to spread the fixed costs associated with preparing that product or service over all the units

Economies of scale result when large volumes of a product or service are produced together, allowing the producer to spread the fixed costs associated with preparing that product or service over all the units. Consider an everyday example: grilled cheese sandwiches. If you make yourself one grilled cheese sandwich, then it might take you 4 minutes to set up for production by gathering the required materials, such as cheese, bread, butter, a frying pan, a knife, and a plate; waiting for the stove to heat up, and then putting the materials away and cleaning up after finishing the sandwich. The actual time that it takes you to make the sandwich would probably be about 6 minutes, including the time required to spread butter on the bread and place cheese on it plus the time required to cook the sandwich. Thus, the time or cost associated with the sandwich is 10 minutes (if a worker producing the sandwich was paid $12 hour, the production cost would be $2). However, if you were making sandwiches for the entire family (say, 6 people), the 6 sandwiches would take the same 4 minutes of setup time with 36 minutes of production time (6 sandwiches * 6 minutes per sandwich), for a total of 40 minutes. The time per sandwich is then 6.67 minutes (40 minutes/6 sandwiches), with a resulting cost of $1.33 per sandwich. Often processes will be designed with a degree of capacity that will allow parallel processing. For example, restaurants usually have large cooking grills so that the cooks can make numerous grilled cheese sandwiches at the same time, while taking advantages of economies of scale in preparing the sandwiches.

Economies of scale result from the ability to spread setup costs, the ability to obtain quantity purchase discounts, the ability to spread construction costs, and various process advantages. Many raw materials and supplies can be purchased in large volumes less expensively than in smaller orders. Large grocery store chains such as Winn Dixie, Big Bear, and Kroger can buy products more cheaply than independent grocers because manufacturers can deliver bulk quantities to only a few locations. In contrast, independent grocers do not have the same leverage, which is one of the reasons that there is an organization called the Independent Grocers of America (IGA)—this association allows small grocers to pool their resources and achieve some economies of scale in their distribution and purchasing operations. Typically, companies offer their customers quantity discounts not out of the goodness of their hearts, but because they themselves reap some benefits. Consider Sam's Club, the warehouse-style selling arm of Wal-Mart. Because Sam's sells in bulk, it does not have to break up boxes or containers of smaller products (e.g., customers might buy a box of 24 bottles of Tylenol), does not need to have as appealing displays (displays are designed for efficiency instead), and can schedule shipments by the truckload rather than with multiple items per truck.

Experience Curves

Experience curves (also called learning curves) display the relationship between total direct labor per unit and the cumulative quantity of product or service produced. For products or services for which tasks are repetitive, experience curves show the relationship between productivity and experience. Typically, the more times a task has been done, the faster the task can be completed. This phenomenon occurs because of individual worker learning, improved tools and procedures, and better work methods. A typical experience curve is shown in Figure 10.2, which shows that the time per unit decreases fairly rapidly for the first 200 units. The rate of decrease is much less rapid after the two-hundredth unit, so we identify this point on the curve as the standard time. Capacity should be calculated using this standard time rather than a time from the initial production or learning part of the curve. Figure 10.2 illustrates the importance of recognizing learning effects—if the fiftieth unit takes 0.24 hour and the two-hundredth unit takes 0.20 hour, it is important to use the standard time from that unit (shown in blue) in future calculations. Figure 10.2 is not meant to illustrate the calculation of learning curves (which can be highly detailed), but rather to point out that all products or services go through a period of learning. The most important thing is to estimate the capacity required for a product once it has reached its standard time.

● **Experience curves** graphs that display the relationship between total direct labor per unit and the cumulative quantity of product or service produced

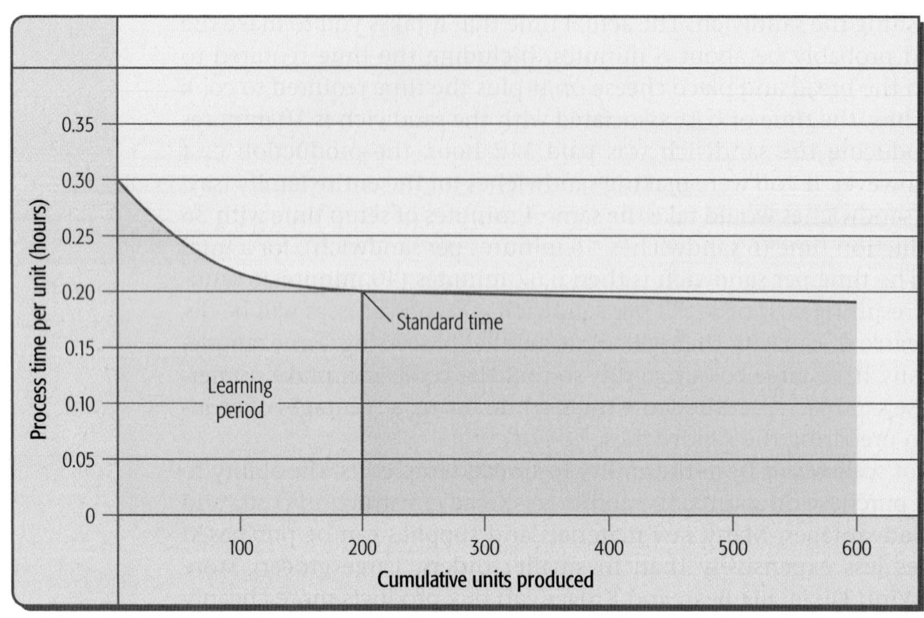

FIGURE 10.2 An Example of a Learning Curve

Diseconomies of Scale

● **Diseconomies of scale** inefficiencies that occur when an organization has grown so large that the cost of managing and tracking its activities outweighs the benefits associated with size

Diseconomies of scale occur when an organization has grown so large that the cost of managing and tracking its activities outweighs the benefits associated with size. Increasing size can bring greater complexity, inefficiencies resulting from the need to manage a complex system, and a loss of focus. In a manufacturing company, benefits in processing time and speed can be outweighed by increases in transportation cost. This commonly occurs when low-cost products are outsourced to a plant in another country. Organizations that suffer from bureaucracy, with decisions being passed up and down a chain of command, experience large diseconomies of scale. Many small, quickly growing organizations with fewer than 100 employees experience significant drops in their growth rate and profitability when they pass the 100-employee threshold. The smaller company could operate quite well on an informal basis because it was fairly likely that all the employees knew one another and had frequent interactions. However, as companies grow, it is no longer possible for all employees to know everyone else, and communication often becomes more complicated and more formal. The bureaucratization or standardization of communication allows an organization to control its processes more tightly because no one individual can manage so many people efficiently, but this bureaucracy comes at the expense of efficiency.

CAPACITY STRATEGIES

● **Capacity strategy** a term that refers to several aspects of capacity management, including the timing of expansion (or contraction), the sizing of facilities, and the linkage with marketing/business plans

While much of capacity management involves understanding how to calculate capacity usage at individual machines, work centers or facilities, there is also a strong need for an organization to determine a strategic approach to capacity. In essence, the idea is to determine whether a company would prefer to have a large amount of excess capacity or to try to manage capacity to be as close to demand as possible. **Capacity strategy** refers to several aspects of capacity management, including the timing of expansion (or contraction), the sizing of facilities, and the linkage with marketing/business plans. While there are an infinite number of specific approaches, we can describe two general strategies that represent the ends of a continuum. One tool that is commonly used regardless of strategy is **subcontracting/outsourcing**, which involves contracting with another company to provide products during a period of excess demand.

● **Subcontracting/outsourcing** contracting with another company to provide products during a period of excess demand.

Wait and See

A **wait-and-see strategy** typically involves postponing firm commitments to build expensive new facilities until demand has already exceeded capacity. Facility expansion typically occurs in a series of small steps that lag behind demand, as shown in Figure 10.3. Organizations utilizing this strategy generally employ short-term tactics such as overtime, postponement of sales, subcontracting, and temporary workers to compensate for any differences between supply and demand. The primary advantage of this approach is that it allows the organization to postpone making large, difficult-to-reverse investments in new facilities and capacity. However, the firm risks losing business if the marketplace expands faster than projected. This approach can also compromise quality and flexibility because it involves working at higher utilization levels.

● **Wait-and-see strategy** postponing firm commitments to build expensive new facilities until demand has already exceeded capacity

A wait-and-see strategy typically fits best in industries with fairly slow growth where facilities are very expensive. In this situation, the risk of overexpanding and being saddled with facilities that are underutilized far outweighs the risk of losing market share. Another factor to consider when choosing a capacity strategy is the speed of technological change. In an industry where technology changes quickly, it generally is not a good idea to expand too quickly for fear of overinvesting in a technology that quickly becomes obsolete.

BEST PRACTICES IN OPERATIONS MANAGEMENT

Capacity at American Express

What are the capacity concerns that American Express must manage? They are numerous. Customer statements must be processed and sent out—either by mail or electronically—once per month. This is one area of capacity where the company can simplify its processing by scheduling customer payment dates in such a way that "demand," or payments requiring processing, is evenly distributed throughout the month. To do this, the company would schedule 1 out of 30 customers for each date of the month; i.e., 3.33 percent of the customers would have their bills due on the first of the month, 3.33 percent would have their bills due on the second, and so on, until 3.33 percent would have their payments due on the thirtieth of the month. This arrangement leads to a fairly predictable workload for both mailing out the bills and processing the payments when they come in.

In contrast, managing capacity for individual transactions is substantially more challenging. There are large fluctuations by time of day, day of the week, month, and season of the year. American Express cannot spread these transactions out in an even way. Furthermore, any time there is a long queue or delay, there is a risk that the customer may balk and cancel the transaction. Because American Express must provide a high level of service and does not want customers or merchants processing a transaction to face lengthy wait times, the company is forced to carry a large capacity cushion. The computers, phone and Internet lines, and other equipment that is required to post transactions across the world have substantially more capacity than the average demand.

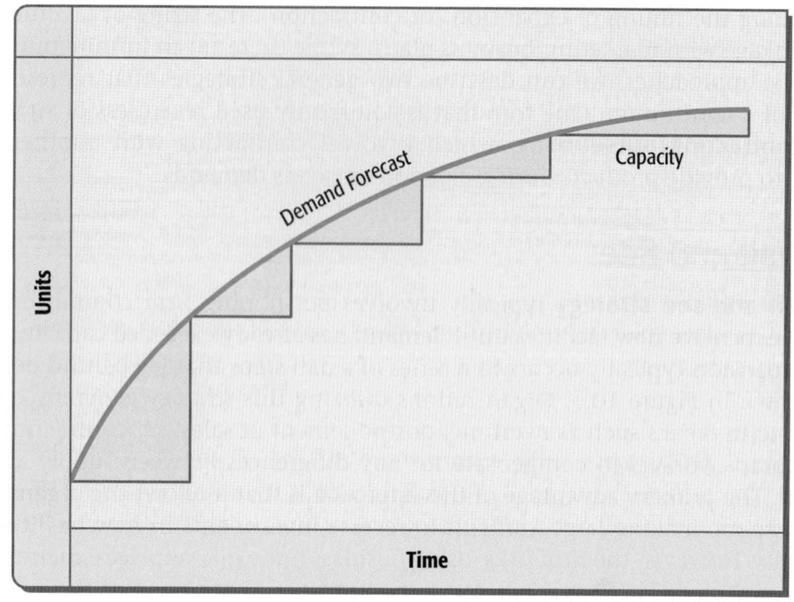

FIGURE 10.3 Wait-and-See Capacity Strategy

● **Aggressive expansion** a strategy in which capacity is added in large leaps, with the expectation that demand will eventually catch up

Aggressive Expansion

An alternative strategy involves the **aggressive expansion** of facilities, with capacity being built to exceed projected demand in the short term. Capacity is added in large leaps, with the expectation that demand will eventually catch up. Figure 10.4 illustrates a typical aggressive expansion strategy.

An aggressive expansion strategy is most advantageous in a growing market, where excess capacity allows an organization to capture market share through first mover advantages. If an organization maintains acceptable quality and the market grows to match the available capacity, such a first mover advantage can be very difficult to overcome. This strategy helps preempt competition because customers typically are reluctant to switch from a market share leader as long as reasonable service levels are provided. In addition, an aggressive strategy offers the ability to capitalize on economies of scale because facilities will be built in larger volumes than in a wait-and-see strategy. For example, the fixed costs (building permits, zoning changes, legal fees, architectural drawings, and other such requirements) are proportionately less for a 300,000-square-foot facility than for a 40,000-square-foot facility. It is important to remember that there are some significant risks associated with aggressive expansion. The largest is that actual demand will not match projections. There is also a risk of technological obsolescence, with a facility that is state-of-the-art when it is built being eclipsed by a competitor's newer, more up-to-date facility.

Starbucks followed an aggressive expansion strategy in building 16,000 stores throughout the United States and internationally in 44 countries in the period from 1995 to 2007. As the market has become saturated, growth has slowed. During the summer of 2008, Starbucks announced the closing of more than 600 stores across the United States.

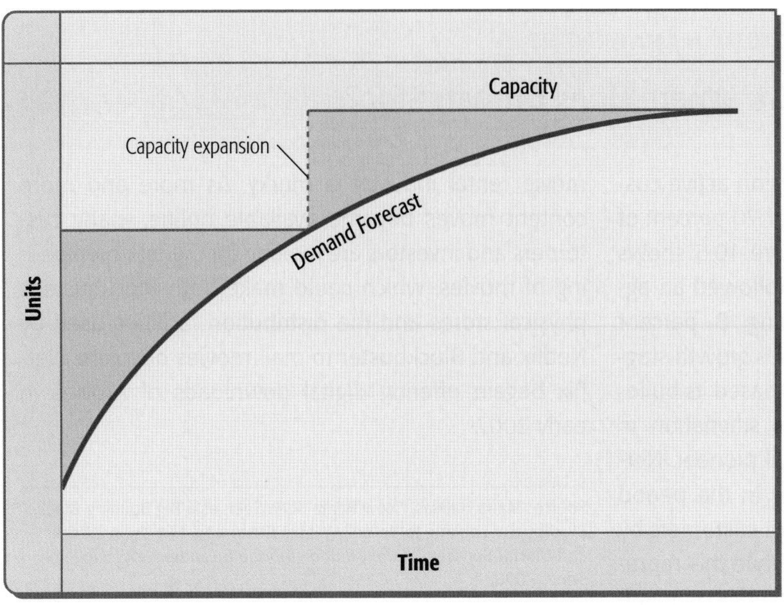

FIGURE 10.4 An Aggressive Capacity Strategy

An aggressive strategy fits well in situations where a company is in a growing industry, is a market share leader, or wants to maintain a high quality of service. Excess capacity helps ensure that a company will be able to be flexible and meet customer demand. In contrast, organizations that compete primarily on the basis of low cost are more likely to follow a wait-and-see strategy.

CAPACITY CUSHION

A central component of capacity strategy is the recognition that it is impossible to exactly match capacity to demand; thus, most companies maintain a capacity cushion of some size. A **capacity cushion** is the difference between average utilization and 100 percent capacity. If the expected demand for widgets is $280 million per year for Plastic Co., and the manufacturing plant is designed to handle $350 million per year, the capacity cushion is 20 percent. As shown in Figure 10.6, the capacity cushion is calculated as the percentage of capacity that is unused on average.

● **Capacity cushion** the difference between average utilization and 100 percent capacity

When making fixed investments in facilities and equipment, the capacity cushion is determined based on a number of strategic objectives and factors. Once a company has built facilities, it is almost always in that company's best interest to sell as much of its product or service as possible. In other words, the decision regarding the size of facilities (and the resulting capacity cushion) and the decision regarding the best way to utilize this capacity are separate. The concept of yield or revenue management as a method for maximizing the utilization of capacity once it has been built or installed is described later in this chapter.

The size of the capacity cushion that a company wishes to have varies greatly based on a number of factors. First, organizations that compete based on low cost will generally choose to have fairly small capacity cushions. In comparison, organizations that compete based on quality or flexibility will generally employ larger cushions. The reasoning is fairly simple: A larger cushion allows the company more

BEST PRACTICES IN OPERATIONS MANAGEMENT

Blockbuster and Netflix: Where Does Growth Stop?

Blockbuster Inc. has more than 32 million active customers and stores within 10 minutes of 70 percent of the U.S. population. The graph in Figure 10.5 shows that from 1996 to 2002, Blockbuster followed an aggressive expansion strategy (averaging 8 percent growth in stores per year), but then sales growth stagnated and the company drastically decreased its building of new stores. The cause of this stagnation in growth? Netflix, the online rent-by-mail pioneer. Netflix grew even faster than Blockbuster in the period from 2000 to 2006, reaching 5.6 million customers by the end of the third quarter of 2006. While this represents one-sixth of Blockbuster's total, Netflix's capitalization is $1.9 billion versus Blockbuster's $755 million. The photograph shows a Netflix shipping center.

In an effort to regain its edge, in November 2006, Blockbuster announced a new program, Total Access, that allows customers to rent videos online and return them to their local store—an offering that Netflix, with no physical stores, could not offer. Blockbuster's goal was to have 2 million online customers by the end of 2007, up from 1.5 million at the time of the announcement.

While investors and customers greeted Blockbuster's Total Access plan with enthusiasm, the future of both Blockbuster and the entire movie rental industry is murky. As more and more content moves become available online, many customers and investors are looking for digital downloading of movies, which could make both Blockbuster's physical stores and the distribution facilities used by Netflix and Blockbuster to mail movies obsolete. Netflix begain offering digital downloads of movies in early 2007.

Source: Maria Halkias, "New Rental Idea Seen as a Big Building Block, Blockbuster Looking to Retool, Will Let Customers Mix Online, Brick-and-Mortar Services," *Knight Ridder Tribune Business News,* November 2, 2006.

A worker filling orders at a Netflix distribution center.

room to change orders and/or fix any problems that occur. For example, when a printer breaks down when you are printing a report for a meeting that is two days away, it is not a big problem because of your time cushion. However, when the printer breaks and your meeting is in five minutes, this is a *big* problem. Another way to provide a cushion is to have more than one printer. Other factors that affect the optimal size of a capacity cushion include (1) variability of demand, (2) availability of alternative suppliers, (3) availability of alternative products, (4) how soon forecasts become available, and (5) the profitability of the product or service being

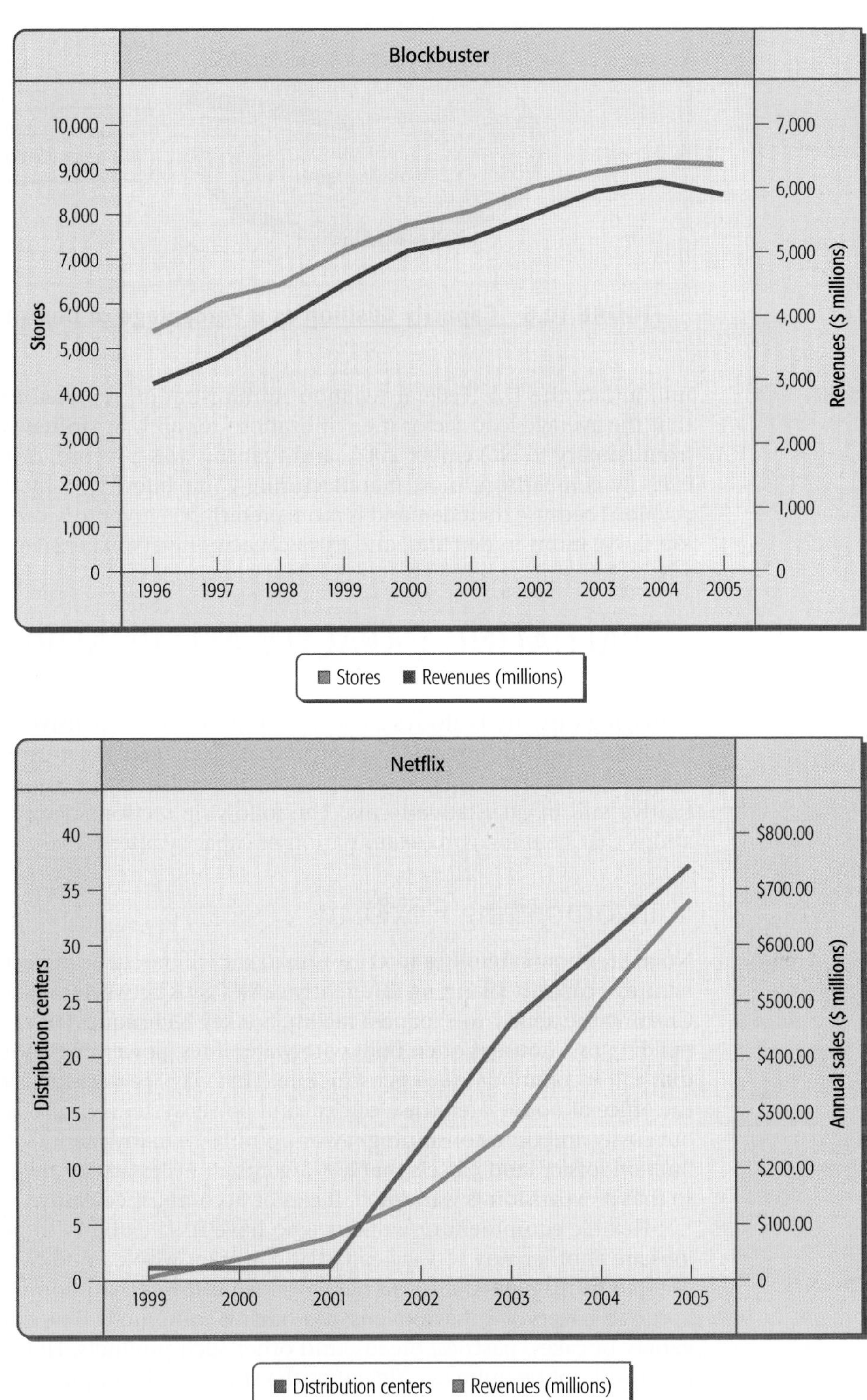

FIGURE 10.5 Blockbuster and Netflix: Store, Customer, and Revenue Growth

sold. For example, airlines and hotels typically have fairly large cushions because their demand is extremely variable with respect to time of day, day of the week, and time of year. To illustrate, while it may *feel* as if every flight is almost 100 percent

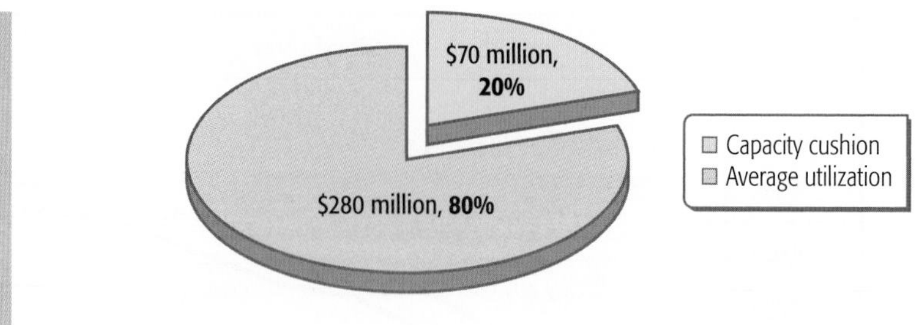

FIGURE 10.6 Capacity Cushion as a Percentage of Design Capacity

full, in fact the U.S. Federal Aviation Administration reported in February 2008 that the average load factor (i.e., utilization) for all U.S. airlines was 80.3 percent from January to November 2007, and that this was a record, or the highest load ever. By comparison, most manufacturing companies typically have fairly small cushions because their demand is more predictable, inventory can be used to cushion fluctuations in demand, and extra capacity is very expensive.

EVALUATING CAPACITY ALTERNATIVES

Managing capacity is always a concern: Too much is expensive to maintain, and too little results in lost sales opportunities. Managers must carefully examine a range of alternatives for every process element in their operations, both in quantitative and in qualitative terms. The following sections describe key considerations that help focus an examination of capacity alternatives.

Incorporating Flexibility

No matter how carefully a forecast is made, it will rarely be perfect. The long-term nature of capacity planning inherently causes gaps between capacity and demand. Creating the ability to expand a facility is a key technique. For example, an office building or a house is often built with water lines, power lines, and waste disposal that will accommodate a larger structure. That way, if a decision is made to expand the office or house later, the electrical and power systems can be added onto without costly and time-consuming rework. Similarly, many manufacturing plants are built on lots or land parcels that are larger than necessary for the original building so that if expansion is warranted, it can be accomplished easily.

Flexible equipment or workers who have the flexibility to perform multiple jobs are another way to vary capacity. A worker who can do two jobs instead of one can be reassigned if his or her workload is lower than normal. A local neighborhood bakery will have ovens and baking equipment that can handle a wide variety of cakes, pastries, breads, and other such products. However, this equipment will not be quite as efficient as the specialized equipment designed to produce only a single type of bread for Wonder, Turano, or Pillsbury, which make bread in huge volumes at a central manufacturing plant.

Accounting for Life-Cycle Stage

Life-cycle stage and capacity are tightly linked. In the introduction phase of any product or service, there is a high degree of uncertainty regarding demand; thus, companies should be careful when making large or inflexible investments in capacity. Often companies will sacrifice some degree of efficiency to have a higher degree of flexibility at this stage in the life cycle. Many companies will use outsourcing at this stage in order to provide flexible capacity.

The growth phase of the product life cycle is characterized by rapid increases in sales. The challenge for companies is that not all products or services make it to the growth stage, and also that while industry sales or sales of the general product category may increase rapidly, the company's market share may not increase proportionally. While this is an exciting stage for a company, there needs to be some caution about overshooting capacity—many companies have found themselves in trouble after investing in too much capacity early in the growth phase. The risks of investing in too much capacity include the chance that demand will not continue growing at projected rates, that competitors will capture the lion's share of the market, and that a new product will push aside the current leader. As retailers began selling via the Internet, there were numerous companies, such as Webvan and eToys, that optimistically built large facilities in the expectation that fast-growing demand would soon fill them up. Unfortunately for these companies, both of which soon went bankrupt in the period 1999–2001, Internet retailing did not grow as fast as they had predicted, and other competitors captured greater market share.

The maturity phase of the life cycle is characterized by relatively stable demand. Many times organizations will look for ways to increase the utilization of their current capacity or get more production out of the same amount of equipment or resources. Competition during this stage tends to be well established and focused on cutting costs, so companies are most likely to increase the efficiency and utilization of existing equipment.

The final decline phase for a product or service is challenging for many organizations. As demand falls off, organizations face decisions about staying in a market and trying to maintain falling sales or taking the alternative, which is to sell off or reduce existing capacity in preparation for selling other products or services. Flexible equipment or workers are very useful in this stage, as in the introduction and growth stages, as some declining products can still be quite profitable, but the organization needs to start to look for ways to shift to new products in the future. The example of the U.S. Postal Service and first-class mail at the beginning of the chapter is one of a company in the late maturity or decline stage. Similarly, the automobile industry is in the maturity stage—it is not growing quickly, and if a new power source such as hybrid or hydrogen-powered vehicles takes off, the existing auto companies will be challenged to change their production facilities over to the new technology.

Looking at the Big Picture

When evaluating capacity alternatives, it is important to consider capacity as part of an interrelated system in addition to individual steps in a process. Consider all the capacity decisions that must be made for a restaurant. A decision to have seating capacity for 100 people must be evaluated along with capacity decisions for the kitchen, bar, restrooms, waiting area, and even parking lot. More than one restaurant has suffered from problems with insufficient parking.

The goal is to provide a system that is reasonably well balanced. Try to avoid bottleneck operations that limit the flow of goods or services. A **bottleneck** is the step with the slowest cycle time in a given process. This is the limiting step that limits productivity for the process. Figure 10.7(a) shows three operations at an Internet bookseller: pick the order, wrap the order, and ship the order. Wrapping represents a bottleneck because only 7,500 orders per hour can be wrapped; thus, only 7,500 complete orders can be processed. The order picking operation is said to be *blocked* because the next operation (wrapping) cannot keep pace. In contrast, the shipping operation is *starved* because it could handle more orders than

● **bottleneck** the step with the slowest cycle time in a given process. This is the limiting step that limits productivity for the process.

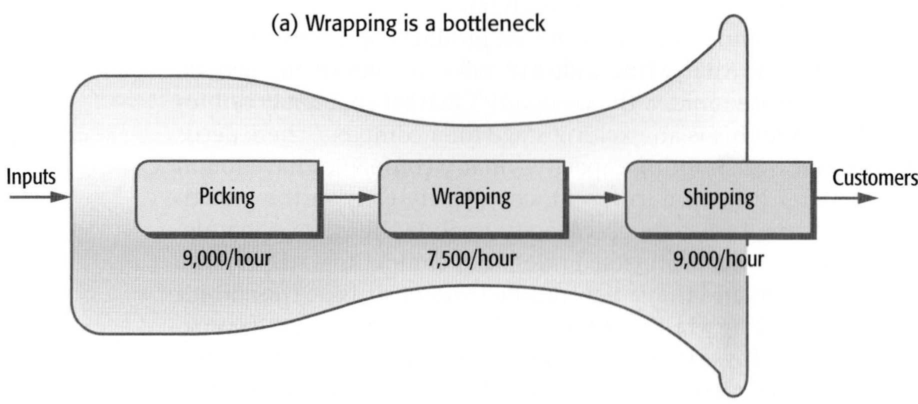

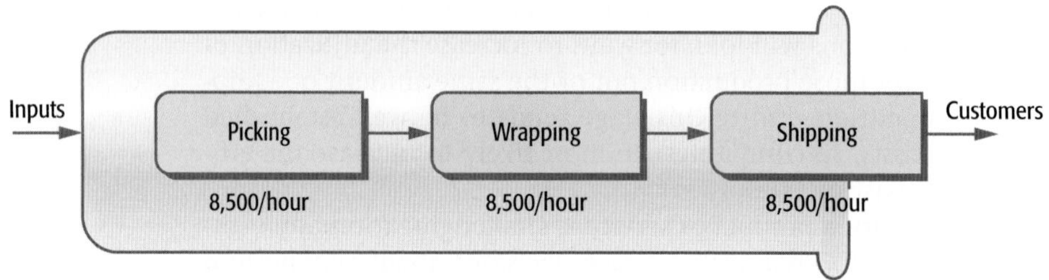

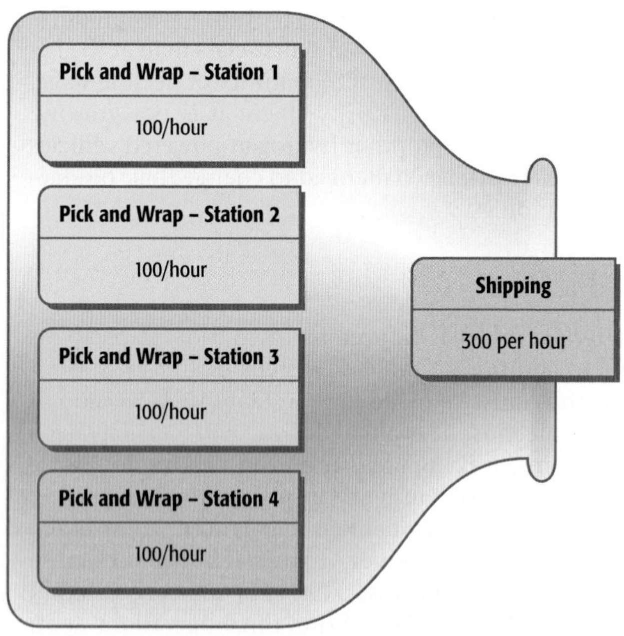

FIGURE 10.7 Capacity Bottlenecks at an Internet Bookseller

wrapping is capable of providing. If the bookseller can reassign employees and resources across the three operations to equalize output, as shown in Figure 10.7(b), then a total of 8,500 orders per hour can be processed.

Figure 10.7(c) presents another illustration. Here, the Internet bookseller has four individual stations used for picking and wrapping orders, each of which may involve one or more employees. The aggregate or total capacity for picking and wrapping is thus 4 * 100, or 400 items/orders per hour. In this case, shipping is the bottleneck because it can handle only 300 orders per hour. This imbalance can be rectified by adding capacity to the shipping station, or by removing one of the pick/wrap stations.

The examples in Figure 10.7 illustrate the importance of looking at the big picture and balancing capacity across multiple steps or operations. A general rule of thumb is that there is always a bottleneck somewhere—in the best case, such as Figure 10.7(b), all steps are equal, and thus all are simultaneously bottlenecks. Nevertheless, it is important that an organization be aware of where and which bottlenecks exist. More discussion of how to identify and modify bottlenecks is provided in Chapter 4, "Process Design and Analysis."

Dealing with Capacity Increments

Capacity increases often come in large increments rather than small ones, which makes it challenging to match capacity and demand. Consider an airline where the average demand for a given flight is 85 passengers, and the plane assigned to that flight holds 100 passengers. This is a fairly good fit, but if demand increases to an average of 116 passengers as a result of a marketing campaign, then the airline must allocate an entire new airplane to this route. This results in a drop in average utilization from 85 percent to 58 percent. Many times equipment capacities come in large increments such as this. Companies must carefully manage this type of investment in capacity. One technique is to use yield or revenue management to alter demand so that it fits better with the available capacity. This technique will be discussed later in this chapter.

Smoothing Out Capacity Requirements

Variations in demand create major challenges for companies managing capacity. One fundamental approach for firms that manufacture or deal with tangible products is to utilize inventory, buying or making large amounts in anticipation of future demand. For example, a manufacturer of snow shovels might produce more than the number of snow shovels (see Figure 10.8) expected to be sold during the slow months (i.e., spring and summer) in order to stockpile shovels for high-demand periods. This has the advantage of keeping production capacity relatively constant, but it is a reactive strategy that is vulnerable if forecasts are not accurate. Figure 10.8 illustrates the stockpiling of inventory during the months of April through October 2009 in anticipation of forecasted demand. This excess inventory is then used up during the months of November 2009 to March 2010, when the forecast exceeds the production level—this is a period of inventory drawdown.

Abnormal weather can send demand skyrocketing or crashing; for example, the winter of 2006–2007 was abnormally warm from November through the first couple of weeks of January. This caused problems for manufacturers of winter items such as snow shovels, coats, gloves, and snowmobiles, as well as for operators of ski resorts. Production systems that are subject to weather fluctuations tend to alternate between periods of underutilization and periods of overutilization. Increasing capacity helps a company deal with peak periods but can add

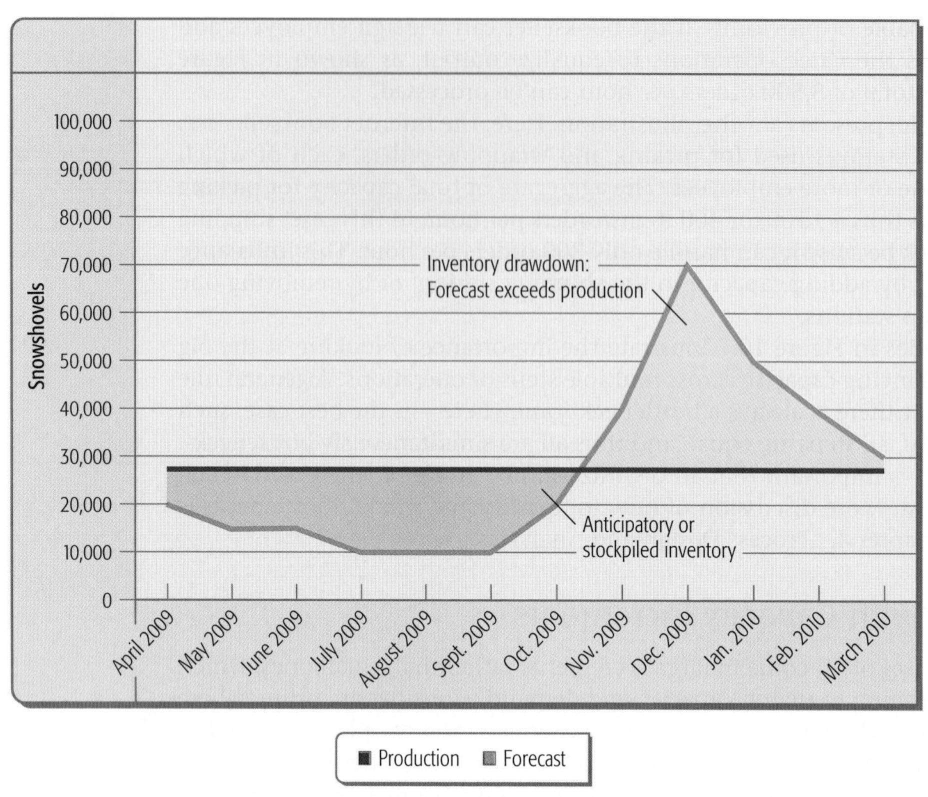

FIGURE 10.8 Stockpiling Inventory of Snow Shovels to Meet Anticipated Demand

substantially to costs during slower periods. Two techniques that help facilitate capacity management are yield/revenue management, which seeks to proactively price products or services in order to shape and smooth demand, and complementary products, a technique that seeks to use similar products with different demand patterns to create one relatively stable aggregate pattern of demand.

Yield/Revenue Management

Some fluctuations in demand are predictable because they are seasonal, weekly, hourly, or generally follow some pattern. For example, restaurants tend to have predictable peak periods around breakfast, lunch, and dinner. Movie theaters tend to be busiest on weekends and for night shows. Call centers tend to have peak periods on Mondays because customers want to get their problems solved at the first opportunity after a business has been closed for the weekend. Yield/revenue management is a technique that is used to shape demand to make it more smooth and predictable. Movie theaters offer matinees at lower prices to draw more customers during the slower afternoon hours. Similarly, restaurants offer early bird specials to get customers to dine before peak periods.

● **Yield/revenue management** allocating a perishable product (such as airline seats, restaurant tables, or parking spaces) to the right kind of customer so as to maximize revenue rather than simply maximizing utilization

Yield/revenue management involves allocating a perishable product (such as airline seats, restaurant tables, or parking spaces) to the right kind of customer so as to maximize revenue rather than simply maximizing utilization. There are numerous planning techniques associated with yield management that are primarily associated with managing service-sector businesses. Consider the reservation system at a resort hotel such as the Hyatt Regency Grand Cayman Resort & Villas. While the manager would ideally like to book all the rooms at the highest rate possible ($375 per night for a Sea View room during the peak season of January), this is rarely possible because during periods of lesser demand, this policy is likely to result in a glut of empty rooms. Instead, the basic premise of yield management involves pricing rooms to stimulate demand during periods of lesser demand. For example, the same Sea View room can be booked for "only" $210 during the slow season of July. The main goal is to maximize revenue rather than focus exclusively on utilization. The Hyatt Regency Grand Cayman makes more money by selling fewer rooms (80 percent) during its peak season for a higher price ($375 per night) rather than selling more rooms (98 percent) at a lesser rate of $280 per night. In addition, the lower price of $210 per night during the nonpeak season should have the effect of attracting some customers who otherwise might not come. Thus, revenue is likely to be higher if the utilization can be increased from 40 percent to 80 percent during the nonpeak period by reducing the price.

The example in the next "Best Practices" box illustrates projected demand for the Grand Luxor Hotel using standard pricing with a single room rate and using adjusted pricing with incentives to shape demand. This example shows how a company may be able to utilize yield management to simultaneously increase revenue and smooth demand.

Yield management techniques are appropriate when an organization meets most of the following criteria: relatively fixed capacity, demand that can be segmented into clearly distinct categories, products that are perishable and are sold in advance, and demand that fluctuates substantially. The two most visible industries in which yield management is applied effectively are hotels and airlines. Both industries have relatively fixed capacity (adding airplanes or hotel rooms is expensive); demand can be differentiated into distinct categories, such as business or leisure; and products (airline seats and hotel rooms) are certainly perishable and are most often sold well in advance of their use. Because it is very difficult to change capacity in the short term, the focus is on utilizing capacity in the best or most profitable way possible.

Exercise
The Use of Yield Management

Can you describe ways in which yield management is used at specific companies in the following industries?

1. **Golf courses**
2. **Parking lots**
3. **Hotels**
4. **Airlines**
5. **Movie theaters**
6. **Apartment rentals**
7. **Highway tolls**
8. **Restaurants**
9. **Public transportation**

Can you think of other examples of businesses or industries that use yield management?

BEST PRACTICES IN OPERATIONS MANAGEMENT

Grand Luxor Hotel Applies Yield Management to Smooth Demand and Increase Revenue

The Grand Luxor Hotel is a major hotel in a large city in India that primarily serves business customers. As Table 10.1 shows, demand is very high on Monday through Thursday nights, but low on Friday through Sunday nights. By changing prices from a standard price of $200 per room per night to a two-tier price of $220 per night on Monday through Thursday and $160 on Friday through Sunday, the hotel can increase revenue while also smoothing demand. The smoother demand, as shown in Figure 10.9, makes operations and staffing at the hotel more efficient, and the extra revenue should translate into higher profits. Note that the hotel was 100 percent utilized on Monday and Wednesday nights prior to the new pricing scheme. By charging a higher price, the Grand Luxor may lose a few customers but actually increase revenue. Note that the overall demand changes very slightly, from 1,090 room nights to 1,105 with the adjusted pricing.

TABLE 10.1 Demand and Revenue for Grand Luxor Hotel for a Forecasted Week with Standard Versus Adjusted Prices

	Demand with Standard Prices	Room Price	Revenue
Monday	200	$200.00	$40,000.00
Tuesday	184	$200.00	$36,800.00
Wednesday	200	$200.00	$40,000.00
Thursday	196	$200.00	$39,200.00
Friday	120	$200.00	$24,000.00
Saturday	80	$200.00	$16,000.00
Sunday	110	$200.00	$22,000.00
Total	1,090		$218,000.00
	Demand with Adjusted Prices	**Room Price**	**Revenue**
Monday	182	$220.00	$40,040.00
Tuesday	168	$220.00	$36,960.00
Wednesday	183	$220.00	$40,260.00
Thursday	179	$220.00	$39,380.00
Friday	147	$160.00	$23,520.00
Saturday	120	$160.00	$19,200.00
Sunday	126	$160.00	$20,160.00
Total	1,105		$219,520.00

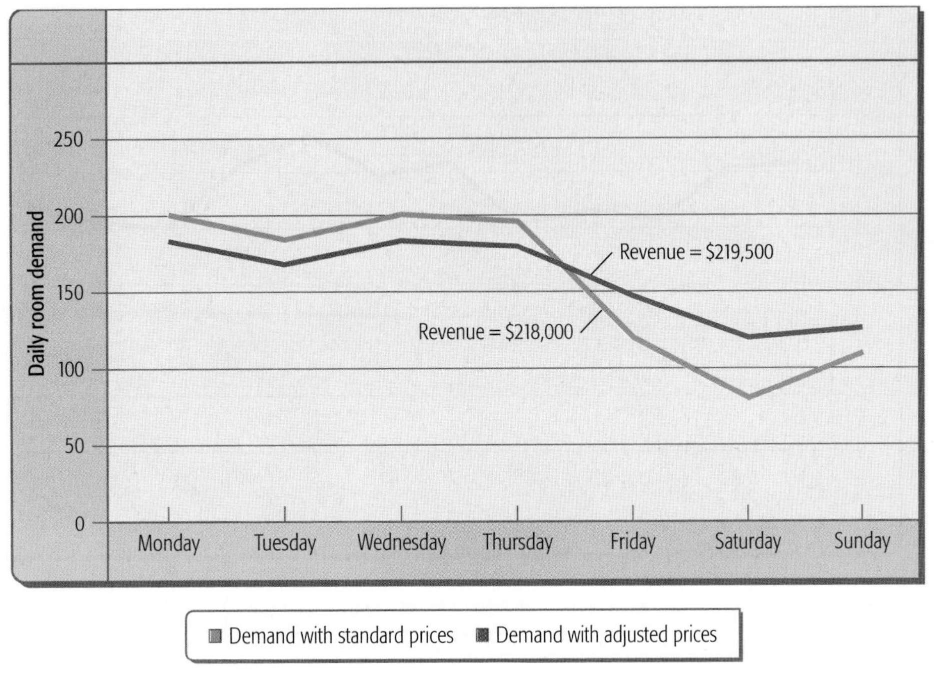

FIGURE 10.9 Demand and Revenue for Grand Luxor

Services in particular have benefited from the power of new technologies that allow them to plan and utilize capacity more effectively. Electronic mail and the Internet allow much simpler communication and booking of orders. Most of the major airlines have utilized electronic mail to take yield management to a new extreme. Customers of Delta Airlines can sign up for an electronic club that e-mails them on Wednesday with a listing of "super saver" flights for the coming weekend. These flights are chosen each week based on Delta's analysis of the available seats—any routes on which the total bookings for the weekend are less than some cutoff (say, 40 percent) are steeply discounted for that weekend. This allows the airlines to sell off seats on nearly empty flights (that would have to fly anyway) at a low cost and pull in extra revenue. The electronic exchange of information and the ability to quickly analyze the demand for various routes is combined to offer this new form of yield management. This is the essential principle under which discount airfare specialist Priceline.com operates.

Complementary Products

Another technique that firms often use is offering complementary products. These must be products that balance out seasonal patterns, where the peak period for one product occurs during the slow period for another, and vice versa. Figure 10.10 shows two products that help balance demand—Product A is one that has very high demand during the summer months in the northern hemisphere, while Product B has high demand during the winter months. Taken together, the aggregate demand for both products is much more even than the demand for either product separately. The other way in which products should be complementary is in terms of production requirements. For example, Products A and B would fit well in the same facility if they were lawn mowers and snow blowers because similar equipment is needed to make power machines of these types. Matching swimsuits with snow blowers would require different production tools; thus, swimsuits are more likely to be matched with coat production. Another tool for managing

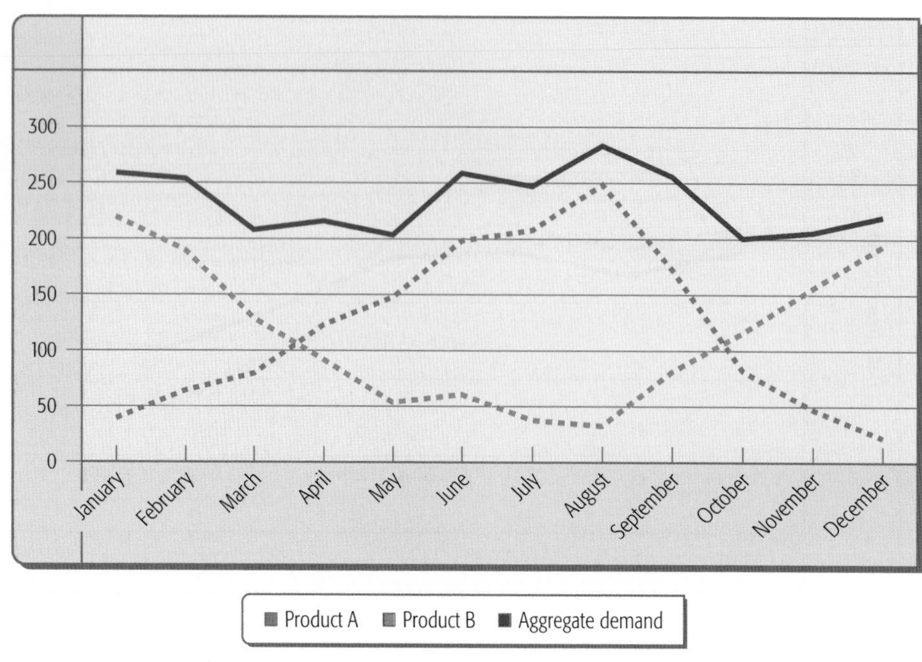

FIGURE 10.10 Complementary Products Help Balance Demand

uneven demand is subcontracting. A company with a very high demand during a certain period or time of year might subcontract some of its production to another company with a shortage of demand. For example, a bicycle manufacturer might work with a manufacturer of snow blowers to subcontract for each other during each company's off-peak periods.

SYSTEMATIC CAPACITY PLANNING

While every case is unique, there is a general sequence of steps that is usually followed when planning capacity. Capacity planning is typically reviewed on a yearly basis or at any time when there is a substantial change in market forces or demand or when the organization is faced with a dramatic shortage or excess of capacity. It is assumed that the organization starts off with an accurate assessment of its existing capacity. Capacity planning involves both decisions to expand or contract capacity and decisions on how best to utilize the existing capacity.

This chapter focuses on a more general treatment of capacity within both manufacturing and services. Chapter 7 provides more detail on capacity planning in a manufacturing setting and describes concepts including the following:

- *Master schedules,* a medium-term planning tool that sets the number of end items or products (and by extension has capacity implications) within a specified time period, usually 3 to 12 months.
- *Capacity requirements planning,* the process of determining short-range (usually 1 to 6 months) capacity requirements.

- *Load reports,* reports for a department or work center that measure already scheduled and expected future capacity requirements against capacity availability.

Our current focus is on long-range planning of capacity for the next one to five years. The following steps are typically followed to assess future capacity needs:

1. Estimate future capacity requirements.
2. Identify gaps between existing capacity and projected requirements.
3. Develop alternative strategies for addressing these gaps.
4. Choose the most appropriate alternative, based on both qualitative and quantitative assessment.

Step 1. Estimating Requirements

The foundation of capacity planning is forecasting capacity requirements for both the short and the long term. Companies often forecast demand for three general time periods: the short term (less than a year), the medium term (one to three years), and the long term (three to ten years). The farther into the future an organization projects, the less certain the forecast. Factors that need to be considered when estimating capacity requirements include competitors' actions, demand trends, technological trends (i.e., is technology that is state-of-the-art today likely to become obsolete), and strategic goals. Unfortunately, it is difficult to combine all these factors into one single capacity forecast.

The end goal for this step is to develop a single quantitative prediction of demand that can be compared to the measure of capacity. As a result, capacity at high levels is often planned using aggregate measures of capacity. These aggregate measures are then broken down into ever more detailed measures of various components of the overall system during successive iterations of the four-step capacity-planning procedure. For example, suppose a restaurant company is considering adding a new restaurant location. The first step is to estimate demand for the entire restaurant in order to make a decision regarding how large a restaurant to build. However, once the initial decision on restaurant size (number of tables) has been made, numerous other decisions must be made, such as how large a kitchen to build, how many parking spaces to have, how many toilets to provide, and how many small/medium/large tables to have. It is important to match all of these individual decisions carefully so that few bottlenecks or shortages develop.

Equation 2 provides the formula for determining the number of machines or resources needed.

$$M = \frac{Dp}{N(1 - C/100)} \qquad \text{(Equation 2)}$$

where M = the number of machines or resources required to provide the necessary capacity, including the capacity cushion C
D = forecasted demand (number of units or customers) for each time period
p = processing time (time per unit or customer)
N = processing hours per year for each piece of equipment
C = desired capacity cushion

Solved Example 1

Number of Checkouts at a Store

Consider a grocery store that averages 300 customers per day. The store is open for 8 hours, and each customer takes an average of 4 minutes to check out. How many cash registers should the store have if it wishes to have a 20 percent capacity cushion?

The denominator of Equation 2 gives the amount of capacity provided by one cash register. Using $N = 8$ hours, because the store is open 8 hours and so the cash register will be open 8 hours, the denominator of Equation 2 is 384 minutes: $N * (1 - C/100) = 8 \text{ hours} * 60 \text{ minutes/hour} * (1 - 20/100)$. The numerator is the amount of time required for production, or 1,200 minutes: $Dp = 300 \text{ customers/day} * 4 \text{ minutes/customer}$. The solution to Equation 2 is then

$$M = \frac{Dp}{N(1 - C/100)} = \frac{300 \text{ customers per day} * 4 \text{ minutes per customer}}{8 \text{ hours per day} * 60 \text{ minutes per hour } (1 - 20/100)}$$
$$= 3.125$$

which is rounded to 4 cash registers.

The store needs to have 4 cash registers in order to maintain at least a 20 percent capacity cushion.

This type of analysis can be applied to a variety of situations at an aggregate level. For example, estimates could be made regarding the requirements for a restaurant, a grocery store, a manufacturer of clothing, or a doctor's office. While the general steps are the same, each situation calls for specialized measures of demand and capacity. In the situation in Solved Example 1, the grocery store needs to ensure that it has four checkouts installed for the coming year. However, analysis also needs to be done at a more detailed level to determine patterns of demand, such as identifying the busiest times of the day or week. For example, while the grocery store in Solved Example 1 may have four cash registers, during slow periods (for example 10 a.m. on a Wednesday), the store manager may choose to have only two of the registers open because of low projected demand. The grocery store also needs to look at capacity in many different areas—the number of checkouts, the number of cashiers, the number of parking spaces, and so on. Thus, it is important to realize that estimating capacity requirements is an iterative procedure that generally works from the top down, starting with an aggregate demand/capacity estimate, then refining the estimate to include greater levels of detail regarding specific machines, work centers, or people over successive iterations.

● **Setup time** the time associated with changing the machine settings, equipment being used, or personnel from making one product to making another

When multiple products or services are provided by a single location, there is a loss in production time or capacity associated with the need to change from one product to the next. **Setup time** is the time associated with changing the machine settings, the equipment being used, or personnel from making one product to making another. Consider a commercial printer; setup time occurs every time a different job is produced because of the need to change the printing plates from printing page 1 of a corporate report to printing page 25 of a magazine. When the print shop has color jobs, the setup time is even longer because color printing is typically done with multiple plates (i.e., there is a plate for printing black, one for printing yellow, one for printing cyan, and so on); thus, there are many more setups. The number of setups for a particular product can be found by dividing annual demand (D) by the lot size for that product (Q = number of units per lot). By adding setup time to Equation 2, we develop a more specialized Equation 3 that incorporates both processing and setup time:

$$M = \frac{\sum_{i=1}^{n}\left(D_i p_i + \frac{D_i}{Q_i} s_i\right)}{N(1 - C/100)} \qquad \text{(Equation 3)}$$

where M = the number of machines or resources required to provide the necessary capacity, including the capacity cushion C

D_i = forecasted demand (number of units or customers) for each time period for product i

p_i = processing time (time per unit or customer) for product i

s_i = setup time for product i

Q_i = order quantity for product i

N = processing hours per year for each piece of equipment

C = desired capacity cushion

Solved Example 2

Bob's Baked Goods

Bob's Baked Goods is a small specialty supplier to a national coffeehouse chain. Bob's produces four types of baked items (biscotti, croissants, muffins, and cookies). Bob's operates 250 days per year with a single 8-hour shift. Because orders can vary significantly from month to month, Bob wishes to maintain a 25 percent capacity cushion. Capacity is controlled by the number of production lines within the bakery (a line consists of mixing equipment, rolling and cutting equipment, an oven, and packaging equipment). Based on the information provided in Table 10.2, determine the number of production lines that Bob's should have.

TABLE 10.2

	Biscotti	Croissants	Muffins	Cookies
Annual demand (D)	500,000	400,000	300,000	300,000
Processing time (p = minutes per unit)	0.2	0.4	0.3	0.1
Average lot size (Q = units per order)	6,000	2,000	2,000	5,000
Setup time (S = minutes per order)	10	15	30	5

(*continued*)

SOLUTION

$$M = \frac{\sum_{i=1}^{n}\left(D_i p_i + \frac{D_i}{Q_i} s_i\right)}{N(1 - C/100)}$$

$$M = \frac{(300{,}000 * 0.3 + \frac{300{,}000}{2{,}000} * 30) + (300{,}000 * 0.1 + \frac{300{,}000}{5{,}000} * 5)}{250 \text{ days per year} * 8 \text{ hours per day} * 60 \text{ minutes per hour}\,(1 - 25/100)} + \frac{(500{,}000 * 0.2 + \frac{500{,}000}{6{,}000} * 10) + (400{,}000 * 0.4 + \frac{400{,}000}{2{,}000} * 15)}{250 \text{ days per year} * 8 \text{ hours per day} * 60 \text{ minutes per hour}\,(1 - 25/100)}$$

$$M = \frac{(90{,}000 + 4{,}500) + (30{,}000 + 300) + (100{,}000 + 833.33) + (160{,}000 + 3{,}000)}{90{,}000 \text{ minutes}}$$

$$M = \frac{388{,}633.33}{90{,}000} = 4.32 \rightarrow 5 \text{ production lines}$$

Answers are usually rounded up to the nearest integer in order to provide a capacity cushion of *at least* the requested amount. Alternatively, a manager might make a different choice and use only four machines. This would result in a cost savings, but would have a lower capacity cushion and a higher risk of running out of capacity if demand is higher or production takes longer.

Step 2. Identifying Gaps

● **Capacity gap** a difference (either a surplus or a shortage) between projected demand and current capacity

The second step is to identify capacity gaps by comparing requirements with existing capacity. A **capacity gap** is a difference (either a surplus or a shortage) between projected demand and current capacity. When identifying gaps, it is very important to consider the implications and biases associated with the choice of capacity measures. Grocery stores offer an excellent example of the need to choose appropriate measures of capacity carefully. A manager of a grocery store must manage capacity in terms of available cash registers, available employees in various departments (deli, meats, flowers, and so on), and size of the store. The goal is to have enough capacity to just meet demand at the busiest part of the day without having long waiting lines.

TECHNOLOGY IN OPERATIONS MANAGEMENT

Self-Checkout at Home Depot: Reducing Costs While Improving Service

Figure 10.11 (on page 388) shows the projected demand for a given day for a Home Depot store. Notice that the number of customers at different hours of the day varies substantially. Home improvement stores such as Home Depot or Lowe's also see great variation by day of the week. The particular store profiled in Figure 10.11 estimates that one checkout cashier can handle 25 customers per hour. The store has a slight cushion during most of the day in which the number of projected customers is less than the number of customers the checkout cashiers can handle (from 8 a.m. to 4 p.m. and after 7 p.m.). The store has a slight capacity shortage at 5 and 6 p.m. and is very tight on capacity at 8 p.m.

To address the capacity shortage, the Home Depot can assign extra cashiers (e.g., it might have six cashiers from 5 p.m. to 8 p.m.).

Alternatively, Home Depot is one of a growing

(*continued*)

TECHNOLOGY IN OPERATIONS MANAGEMENT

Self-Checkout at Home Depot (*continued*)

number of retailers offering a self-checkout option. The estimated value of self-checkout transactions in the United States is expected to rise from $475 billion in 2006 to $1.2 trillion in 2009. Home Depot reports that about one-third of its transactions occur at self-checkouts, and about 50 percent of grocery stores now offer the machines. Consumer opinions on the efficacy of this technology are decidedly mixed. Many people see self-checkout as a faster alternative that allows them more control and frees them from having to talk to store employees. Others think that they are doing the store's work for it or are intimidated when the technology does not work or they don't understand how to use it. One common problem is for the scanner to think that you have placed the wrong item(s) in the shopping bag. One of the main reasons for this error is that store checkouts weigh each item after scanning it. If the item does not weigh what the computer expects it to weigh, an error occurs. This can happen because the customer put the wrong item in the bag, the customer accidentally hit or leaned on the counter, or the store has an incorrect weight for the item recorded in its database. Many times the error is due to inaccurate information in the store's database, which can be very frustrating for customers. Some stores, such as Safeway grocery, do not use self-checkout technology for these reasons and for fear of alienating customers or compromising their service level. Yet the trend is clearly toward more and more usage of this technology. Many stores seem to have concluded that the technology's benefits in terms of improved capacity management and lower costs outweigh any risk of decreased service levels.

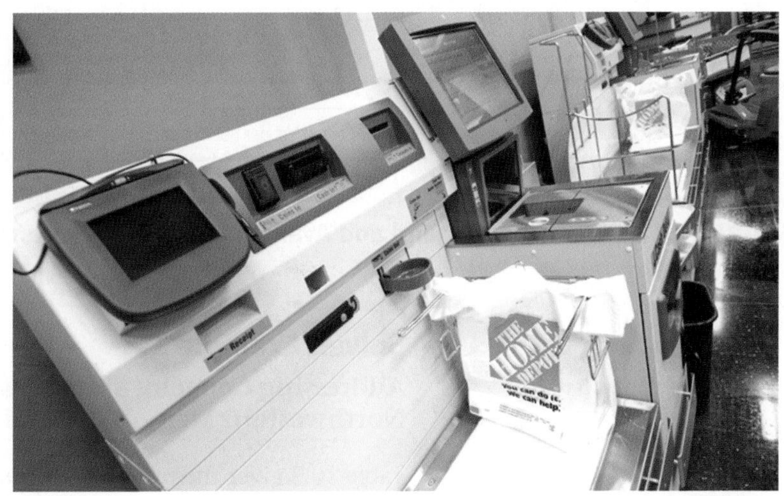

A self checkout machine for use at a Home Depot store.

Step 3. Developing Alternatives

Once capacity gaps are identified, the next step is to develop alternative methods of addressing them. One option is to do nothing; this works only if the organization has excess capacity. If the organization has a significant capacity gap (either too little or too much), then plans for adding or deleting capacity should be made. While we present a very aggregate-level, simplified example for ease of comprehension, the process of developing alternatives and analyzing them can be quite complex. Operations and supply chain managers have a wide range of decision-analysis tools available, most of which are embedded in application-specific software. These tools are very valuable and are reviewed in Chapter 9, "Optimization and Simulation Modeling."

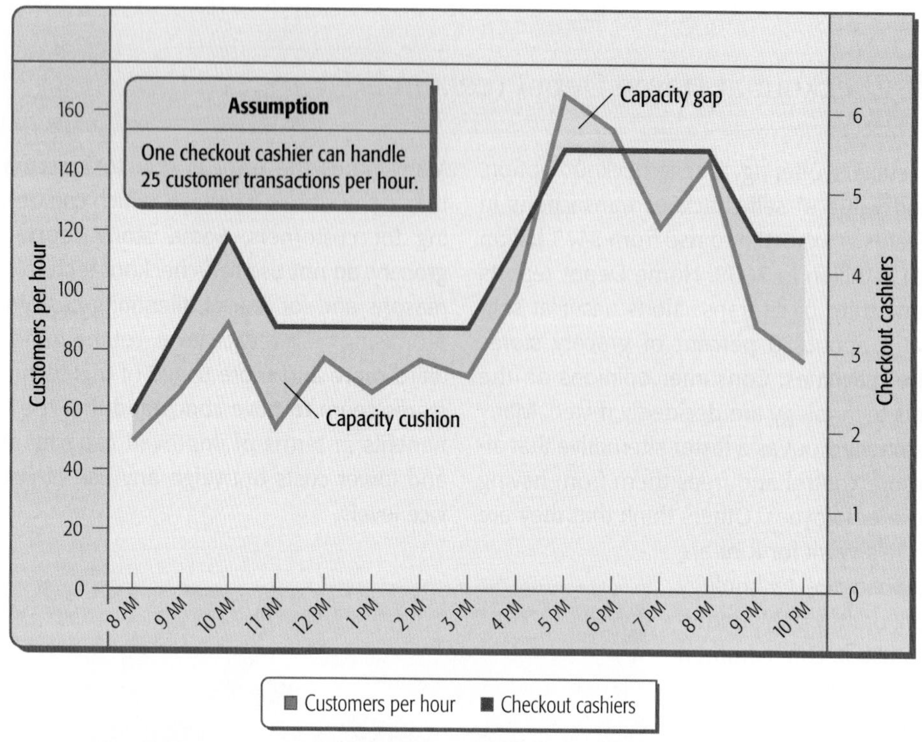

FIGURE 10.11 Predicted Demand and Available Capacity at a Home Depot

Solved Example 3

Addressing Capacity Shortages at Northwestern Memorial Hospital

Table 10.3 gives the projected annual demand in terms of patients seen at Northwestern Memorial Hospital. The hospital is open 365 days per year, 40 percent of patient visits require an overnight stay, and the average length of stay is 3 days with a standard deviation of ½ day. Of course, there is variability associated with the average stay, and so we choose to maintain a 10 percent cushion. The hospital currently has 125 guest rooms for patients. Calculate the capacity and capacity gaps for the next three years.

SOLUTION

We first calculate the demand for rooms. In year 1, the hospital requires 30,000 patients * 40% (of patients requiring overnight stay) * 3 days (average stay) = 36,000 room nights. A room night is 1 room demanded for 1 night. Given that the hospital operates 365 days per year, there is a requirement for 36,000/365 = 98.63 rooms. *But* this assumes that the hospital operates at 100 percent utilization. Because the hospital wants to maintain a 10 percent cushion, we calculate the number of rooms required as 98.63/(1 – 10/100) = 109.59. Table 10.4 gives the calculated values for years 2 through 4. This analysis shows that the hospital will have a shortage in years 3 and 4 of 14 rooms (139 – 125) and 22 rooms (147 – 125), respectively. The hospital should probably begin planning an expansion to meet demand in years 3 and 4.

(*continued*)

TABLE 10.3

	Projected Number of Patients
Year 1	30,000
Year 2	34,000
Year 3	38,000
Year 4	40,000
Patients requiring overnight stay	40%
Average length of stay	3 days
Desired capacity cushion	10%

TABLE 10.4

	Anual Patients	Patients Requiring Room	Rooms per Day	Rooms with 10% Cushion
Year 1	30,000	30,000 * 0.4 = 12,000	12,000 * 3 days/room/ 365 days per year = 98.63	98.63/(1 – 0.1) = 109.59
Year 2	34,000	13,600	111.78	124.20
Year 3	38,000	15,200	124.93	138.81
Year 4	40,000	16,000	131.51	146.12

Once a decision has been made to build patient rooms, there are still many other associated decisions. Should the rooms be built simultaneously or in steps? When should they be built? What should the mix of rooms be—i.e., how many standard versus deluxe rooms or how many private versus double rooms?

A hospital patient.

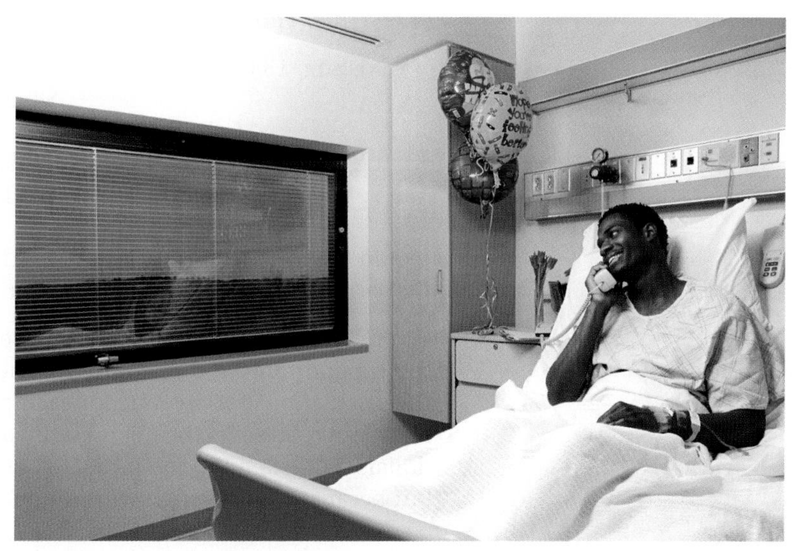

Step 4. Choosing Alternatives

The final step in capacity planning involves analyzing the various alternatives and identifying the best choice. Managers must be aware of both qualitative and quantitative factors that affect this decision. Many businesses have a tendency to put a greater weight on more objective, quantitative factors such as the financial costs of expansion, cash flows, capacity measures, and other "hard" numbers. However, it is important to remember that there are many subjective factors that cannot be measured as precisely or included in a single cash flow calculation. Often these subjective factors are neglected, resulting in major problems.

Qualitative Factors

These factors are fairly subjective in nature and difficult to measure or assess quantitatively. One of the primary things that managers must consider is how capacity expansion plans fit with the overall operations strategy of the business. Other factors that must be considered include the business climate, uncertainties regarding demand, the actions of competitors, and technological change. While it is often difficult to capture or assess these factors accurately in a quantitative manner, one technique is to make best-case, expected, and worst-case projections. By conducting what-if analysis in this fashion, the implications of each alternative can be weighed.

Quantitative Factors

Businesses tend to base many of their decisions on quantitative factors, such as the fixed and variable costs of adding or removing capacity, estimates of potential added revenues, and estimates of total market share and competitors' responses. Such quantitative factors can be analyzed in a straightforward manner to come up with a single assessment of an alternative's value. Typically, businesses employ the concept of net present value to calculate the potential value of each option. The **net present value** of an alternative is the financial impact of that alternative in present-day dollars.

● **Net present value** the financial impact of an alternative in present-day dollars

Consider Hawk Hollow Golf Course, which is weighing adding 9 or 18 holes to its existing 18-hole layout. On an average day at the peak of summer, it has a capacity of 240 golfers playing 18-hole rounds. This falls to 180 in the spring and fall, when the days are shorter; thus, the average number of rounds available throughout the year is 200 per day. Because of the variation in capacity resulting from the length of the day, Hawk Hollow tracks demand as a percentage of available rounds used. Figure 10.12 shows the demand for each day of the week, averaged over the course of the year, while Table 10.5 shows capacity utilization and cost figures for two alternative expansion options. It is clear that weekends (Friday through Sunday) are the crunch period. Jim Brown, the owner, is concerned that Hawk Hollow is losing sales because people cannot book their preferred tee times.

Hawk Hollow charges $25 for a round of 18 holes; thus, revenue can be calculated by multiplying the average demand by $25. Hawk Hollow averages 20 weeks per year of "good" golfing weather, so we use that as the number of weeks of revenue. Thus, total revenue for each option can be calculated as

Existing: 134.85 rounds/day * 7 days/week * 20 weeks/year * $25/round = $472,000/year

Add 9 holes: 186 rounds/day * 7 days/week * 20 weeks/year * $25/round = $651,000/year

Add 18 holes: 236 rounds/day * 7 days/week * 20 weeks/year * $25/round = $826,000/year

To choose the best alternative, we need to calculate the net present value of the expenditures and revenues for each option. Table 10.6 (on page 392) shows the calculations for revenue for each option on a yearly basis. The number in parentheses represents the net present value of a projected revenue stream in today's dollars. For example, the projected net profit for option 1 in year 1 is $139,000, but because that revenue will not be received until a year from now, it is worth

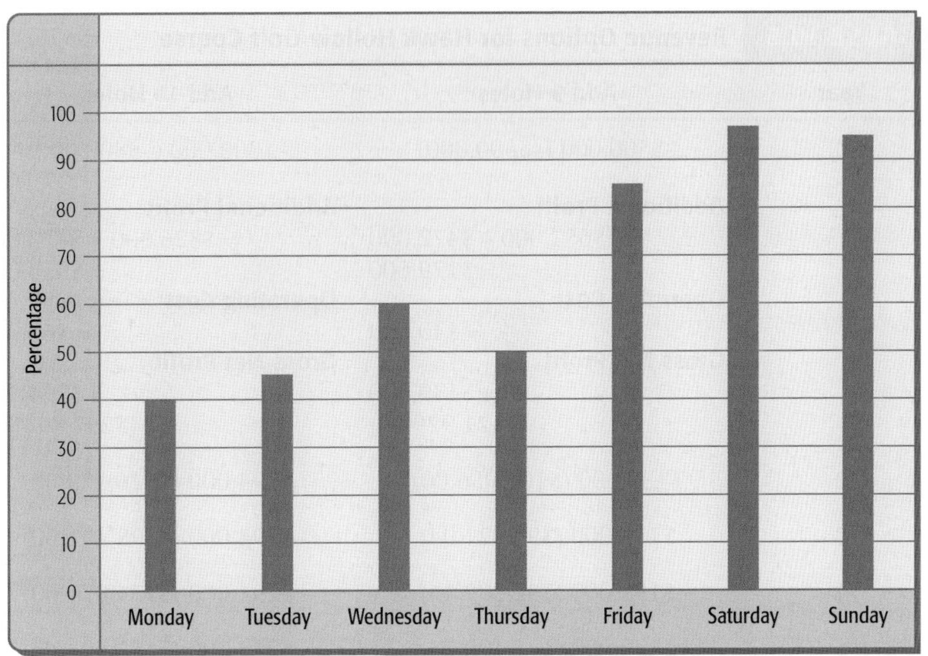

FIGURE 10.12 Daily Demand at Hawk Hollow Golf Course as a Percentage of Available Capacity

only $121,929.80, assuming a 14 percent discount rate. The assumption here is that any revenues we receive now could be invested and earn a return of 14 percent per year; thus, funds received in the future are worth proportionately less. The formula used to calculate the value of future revenue is

$$P = \frac{F}{(1 + r)^n} \qquad \text{(Equation 4)}$$

where F = the future value of an investment at the end of n periods
r = the yearly interest rate
n = the number of years for which the interest compounds
P = the present value of F

These calculations show that adding 9 holes to make the course a 27-hole facility produces $195,000 in increased cash flow, but the net present value of the cash flows is actually negative (–$22,801.70); thus, it does not look like a good investment. In contrast, adding 18 holes brings a net present value of $209,325.80, so this is a good investment for expanding Hawk Hollow.

TABLE 10.5 Capacity Expansion Alternatives for Hawk Hollow Golf Course

	Existing	Add 9 Holes	Add 18 Holes
Capacity	200 rounds per day	300 rounds per day	400 rounds per day
Demand projection	134.85 rounds per day	186 rounds per day	236 rounds per day
Capacity utilization	67.4%	62.0%	59.0%
Cost of adding capacity	NA	$500,000	$800,000
Yearly operating cost	NA	$40,000	$60,000

TABLE 10.6 Revenue Options for Hawk Hollow Golf Course

Year	Add 9 Holes	Add 18 Holes
0	–\$500,000 (–\$500,000)	–\$800,000 (–\$800,000)
1	**Additional Profit** = \$651,000 – \$472,000 = \$179,000 **Operating Cost** = \$40,000 **Gross Net Profit** = \$139,000 (\$121,929.80)	**Additional Profit** = \$826,000 – \$472,000 = \$354,000 **Operating Cost** = \$60,000 **Gross Net Profit** = \$294,000 (\$257,894.70)
2	\$139,000 (\$106,956.00)	\$294,000 (\$226,223.50)
3	\$139,000 (\$93,821.04)	\$294,000 (\$198,441.60)
4	\$139,000 (\$82,299.16)	\$294,000 (\$174,071.60)
5	\$139,000 (\$72,192.24)	\$294,000 (\$152,694.40)
Total	\$195,000 (–\$22,801.70)	\$670,000 (\$209,325.80)

NOTE: Values in parentheses in Table 10.6 represent the net present value of the funds in year 0.

SERVICE CAPACITY

This chapter has presented numerous service examples along with manufacturing examples. While capacity planning for services shares many similarities with planning for manufacturing, there are also some key differences. One major difference is that services generally cannot make use of inventory to cushion against fluctuations in demand. The service being offered is time- and place-dependent; in addition, services are subject to highly volatile demand, and utilization is highly correlated with service quality. The unique characteristics of services offer some challenges, but also some opportunities, as illustrated earlier in the discussion of yield management and illustrated with the example on the Grand Luxor Hotel, where revenue was increased and demand made more even by adjusting the pricing scheme.

Time

Services cannot be inventoried for later use; thus, capacity must be available when the customer wants the service—if it is not, a potential sale may be lost or a customer left unsatisfied. For example, if the waiting line in a fast-food restaurant gets too long, customers become more likely to balk and leave. This is particularly true for drive-up service, where it is fairly easy to drive down the street to a less busy restaurant. Similarly, a movie theater may have 40 percent of its seats available for a 7:30 p.m. show but be fully sold out for the 10 p.m. show. The seats from the early show are "lost" and cannot be used to cover the higher demand for the later show. Some customers are likely to leave the later show even before the show is completely sold out if they cannot get good seats or if groups of people cannot get seats together. For these reasons, service businesses commonly use some type of yield management to attempt to influence demand so that it is smoother and more predictable.

Location

Services must be near the customer because the customer is usually involved in the service. In contrast, most manufacturing occurs at a distance, and the final product is then shipped to various retail locations that are closer to the customer. Stores that sell physical products must be close to their customers. Similarly, a seat at a movie theater for a certain show is of no use to the customer if it is at a different theater from the one where he or she is.

Volatility of Demand

Services experience greater demand volatility for multiple reasons. First, services cannot be stored; thus, capacity must be equal to or larger than demand at all times (unless the company is willing to risk losing some customers). Second, customers interact with the delivery system more for services than for manufactured products. These customers will have different needs and different levels of experience with the process or service and may require different numbers or types of transactions. These factors lead to greater variability in the processing time per customer and thus contribute to greater variability in the minimum level of capacity needed. Consider how many times you have been in line behind someone who had a very complicated transaction at a bank, a store, a theater, a restaurant, or some other service provider, and you ended up waiting a long time in line. The final reason that services have greater volatility is that service demand is dependent on customer behavior. College towns live and die by when students are in school—during term breaks, parking is much more available and lines are substantially shorter. Restaurants tend to be extremely busy during certain periods—breakfast, lunch, and dinner—and relatively slow during off periods. Airlines have peak travel periods around the holidays or to popular destinations. Trips to a skiing location are difficult to book during prime skiing season. Because of the higher volatility of demand, service businesses often plan capacity in smaller increments (15 minutes to an hour) rather than the one-week planning horizon common in manufacturing.

Capacity Utilization and Service Quality

As service utilization increases, costs will decrease, but so will service quality. Figure 10.13 shows the relationship between the rate of service utilization and service quality. The *y* axis is the arrival rate in terms of customers per hour, and the *x* axis is the processing rate at which customers can be served. If arrivals come faster than they can be processed, there will be long lines and poor service quality—i.e., the zone of nonservice. Figure 10.13 shows that the best operating point is at around 70 percent of maximum capacity—this is the boundary between the zone of service and the critical zone The goal is to keep employees busy, but to allow enough time for them to serve customers and keep some capacity cushion so as not to create inappropriate delays and inconveniences. In the critical zone, customers are processed through the system, but service quality declines. This occurs not because the average customer takes more time than is available, but because a single customer with a difficult or lengthy transaction may clog up the system and create a backlog. In addition, arrival times and processing times are stochastic (they are not certain, and they have variability), and thus several customers may arrive in a short period, resulting in long lines. Above the critical zone, customers arrive faster than they can be processed; thus, a line continuously builds up, and customers will not get served.

The optimal utilization rate is very situation-dependent. An emergency room in a hospital will generally be less utilized and have more cushion than a private practice doctor's office. This is true because of the life-and-death nature of many

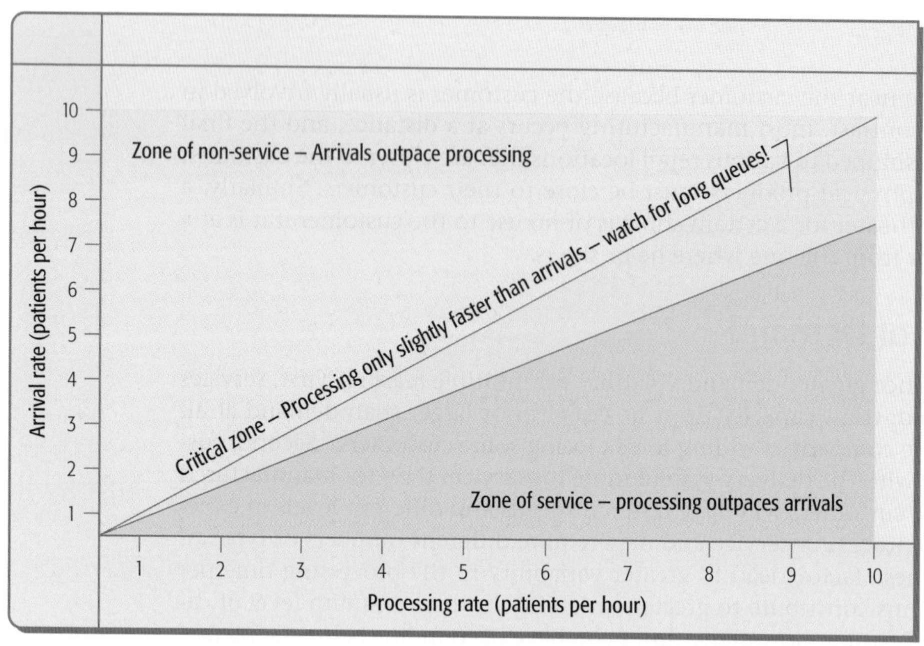

FIGURE 10.13 Relationship Between Service Utilization and Service Quality

emergency room visits; the main goal is to ensure adequate capacity to treat all critically ill patients. In contrast, a private practice physician's office is designed to maximize capacity utilization. This can be done because the patients visiting are less likely to be critical in terms of need to be treated immediately. A physician's office also typically utilizes appointments to provide an even, relatively predictable flow of patients. There is also greater consistency of patient treatment times, allowing the capacity utilization to be much higher. Low utilization rates are desirable when there is a large amount of uncertainty of demand and the consequences of long lines or delays are substantial. In addition to hospital emergency rooms, fire departments, police stations, and lifeguards all have relatively lower utilizations.

When demand is relatively predictable and the consequences of long lines or delays are lower, then higher utilization will be maintained. Mail-order distribution facilities for companies like Amazon, Caremark, Zappos, or Land's End maintain high utilization rates because customer contact is minimal and delays of a few hours or days can be easily tolerated. The backroom operations of many financial services companies, such as the processing area for bill payments at American Express, typically operate at close to 100 percent utilization.

There is a third group of service businesses that seeks to have nearly 100 percent utilization. Restaurants want to be fully utilized, not just for the revenue effects, but also because there is a psychological impact: Customers believe the restaurant is better because so many people want to eat there. In addition, most restaurants make a substantial portion of their profits from selling customers drinks while they wait in the bar for their table to become available. Similarly, sporting events, stage performances, and bars all seek close to 100 percent utilization because being seen as the "hot ticket" generates great publicity and atmosphere for the organization. Sports teams like sellouts not only because of the extra revenue, but also because they create an exciting atmosphere, boost the performance of the team, and tend to increase future ticket sales. Unlike customers of many other businesses, a fan who can't get a ticket often will not be too upset and will simply go to a ticket scalper or an online ticket exchange such as eBay or StubHub to purchase a ticket at higher than face value.

WRAP-UP

Managing capacity is one of the fundamental challenges of business operations. Having excess capacity leads to excess costs, while having capacity shortages leads to poor customer service and lost sales. It is important to realize that it is impossible to get exactly the "right" amount of capacity because variations in demand will always lead to fluctuations in utilization. A company's decision on the size of its capacity cushion is a strategic decision—a higher cushion is important in industries or businesses that have large variations in demand and/or high costs of poor service or lost sales. Lower cushions can be maintained when demand is more constant and/or the cost of poor service or lost sales is lower.

Businesses must consider their capacity strategy carefully and can take either an aggressive approach or a more conservative wait-and-see approach to growth (decline). Approaches to maximizing the utility of existing capacity include incorporating flexibility; accounting for life-cycle stage; looking at the big, system-wide picture; dealing with capacity increments; and smoothing out capacity requirements. Two techniques for balancing capacity requirements include yield management, which seeks to use marketing incentives to smooth the demand curve, and complementary products, which help offset peaks in demand to make an aggregate demand curve that is more predictable and constant.

Systematic capacity planning is a four-step process consisting of (1) estimating future capacity requirements, (2) identifying capacity gaps, (3) developing alternative strategies for addressing gaps, and (4) choosing appropriate alternatives. This approach to planning capacity is a general-purpose tool that is used by most companies. Finally, services offer some unique capacity challenges that require special tools and techniques.

SUMMARY

1. Describe methods of measuring capacity, planning capacity, and calculating capacity utilization. Explain the impact of economies of scale, diseconomies of scale, and experience curves on capacity.

- Capacity measures are divided into output measures and input measures. Output measures are generally more applicable to high-volume processes, whereas input measures are more applicable to processes with a high degree of customization.
- Utilization is the percentage of the available time that equipment, space, or labor is used. Utilization is a fundamental measure of capacity.
- Peak capacity is the maximum output rate for the short term, whereas effective capacity is the output rate that can be maintained for extended periods of time.
- Economies of scale result when large volumes of a product or service are produced together. Economies of scale result in an increase in effective capacity because more time is spent in processing rather than setup for operations.
- Diseconomies of scale occur when an organization or process grows so large that the costs of managing and tracking its activities outweigh the benefits associated with size. When confronted with diseconomies of scale, organizations are better off with multiple smaller facilities or processes than with fewer large facilities.
- An experience curve relates improvements in production/service time to the total quantity produced.

2. Explain differences in capacity strategy in terms of the timing and sizing of expansion options.

- An aggressive expansion strategy is preferred when an industry or market is growing quickly, whereas a wait-and-see strategy is preferred when the industry or market is stagnant or is growing or shrinking slowly.
- The risks of losing sales if capacity is insufficient must be weighed against the risk of having excess capacity.

3. Describe the benefits of a capacity cushion and the strategic reasons to increase or decrease the cushion.

- The choice of capacity cushion is linked to the importance of customer service; generally, organizations that focus primarily on low cost will have low capacity cushions, whereas those that focus on high quality or flexibility will maintain higher cushions.
- The timing and size of expansion options need to be carefully evaluated through a four-step iterative process that links with the organization's operations strategy.

4. Understand how to evaluate capacity alternatives.

- Evaluation of capacity alternatives must account for the stage in the life cycle of the product or products a firm provides. Companies with many products that are early in the life cycle generally should plan more aggressive expansion than those with more products that are in later life-cycle stages.
- In evaluating capacity alternatives, companies must look at the big picture for the entire facility or set of facilities. Identifying where bottlenecks exist is of critical importance.

- Capacity expansion is often limited by the increments available, so planning must proceed accordingly.
- Proactively taking steps to smooth out demand through the use of either yield management or complementary products can greatly simplify capacity management.
    (a) Yield management seeks to maximize revenue by charging different prices for perishable products during different time periods. The goal is to either increase demand during slack periods or shift demand from busy periods to make the aggregate demand pattern more stable.

    (b) Yield management typically involves offering lower prices during slack periods, such as movie matinees, early bird specials at restaurants, or unlimited calls during nonpeak periods for cellular phones.

    (c) Yield management seeks to maximize capacity usage once the organization has committed to a particular level of capacity.

5. Discuss how to plan capacity expansions to address gaps between demand and supply.

- Capacity planning consists of four general steps. These steps provide an approach to capacity planning that should be implemented on an annual basis or whenever the organization or process is faced with either a substantial change in market forces or demand or a dramatic shortage or excess of capacity.
    (a) Estimate future capacity requirements.

    (b) Identify gaps between existing capacity and projected requirements.

    (c) Develop alternative strategies for addressing these gaps.

    (d) Choose the most appropriate alternative, based on both qualitative and quantitative assessment.

6. Explain the importance of special factors for managing service capacity.

- Service capacity cannot be inventoried for future use; thus, yield management to reshape the demand curve is a vital tool.
- Location is critical because the customer is typically a participant in the process. Services thus place a premium on the desirability of a location from the customer's perspective.
- Services have much more volatile demand than manufactured products; thus, capacity planning must look at peak periods rather than the average.
- There is a strong relationship between capacity utilization and service quality. Service organizations should carefully monitor whether they are in the critical zone (above 70 percent utilization) or in the zone of nonservice (over 100 percent utilization). Customer service drops dramatically as utilization approaches 100 percent.

SOLVED PROBLEM 1

Staffing a Physician's Office

Meridian Pediatrics is a medical clinic focused on patients from 0 to 15 years of age. The average patient visit requires 10 minutes of front-office staff time to process paperwork, bills, and checkout. The average visit also requires 20 minutes of physician time. The office sees an average of 80 patients per day. The office operates for 6 hours per day (the physicians spend another 1 to 2 hours per day completing paperwork and making rounds at the hospital) and seeks to maintain a 10 percent capacity cushion. Calculate the number of staff members and physicians needed.

SOLUTION

Staff:

$$M = \frac{Dp}{N(1 - C/100)} = \frac{\text{80 patients per day} * \text{10 minutes per patient}}{\text{6 hours per day} * \text{60 minutes per hour } (1 - 10/100)}$$

$$= \frac{\text{800 minutes per day}}{\text{324 minutes per day}} = 2.47 \rightarrow \text{rounded up to 3 staff members}$$

Physicians:

$$M = \frac{Dp}{N(1 - C/100)} = \frac{\text{80 patients per day} * \text{20 minutes per patient}}{\text{6 hours per day} * \text{60 minutes per hour } (1 - 10/100)}$$

$$= \frac{\text{1,600 minutes per day}}{\text{324 minutes per day}} = 4.94 \rightarrow \text{rounded up to 5 physicans}$$

SOLVED PROBLEM 2

A small manufacturing plant makes three basic products, with the quantities, processing time, setup time, and lot sizes given in Table 10.7. The plant manager wishes to maintain a 10 percent capacity cushion, and each of the products uses the same type of machine. The machine is available for 14 hours a day for 250 days per year. Determine how many machines the plant should have.

TABLE 10.7 Shipping Costs

	Product 1	Product 2	Product 3
Annual demand (*D*)	100,000	80,000	40,000
Processing time (*p* = minutes per unit)	3	4	6
Average lot size (*Q* = units per order)	20,000	5,000	2,000
Setup time (*S* = minutes per order)	10	20	30

SOLUTION

$$M = \frac{\sum_{i=1}^{n}\left(D_i p_i + \frac{D_i}{Q_i} s_i\right)}{N(1 - C/100)}$$

$$M = \frac{(100{,}000 * 3.0 + \frac{100{,}000}{20{,}000} * 10) + (80{,}000 * 4.0 + \frac{80{,}000}{5{,}000} * 20) + (40{,}000 * 6.0 + \frac{40{,}000}{2{,}000} * 30)}{250 \text{ days per year} * 14 \text{ hours per day} * 60 \text{ minutes per hour } (1 - 10/100)}$$

$$M = \frac{(300{,}000 + 50) + (320{,}000 + 320) + (240{,}000 + 600)}{189{,}000 \text{ minutes}}$$

$$M = \frac{860{,}970}{189{,}000} = 4.56 \rightarrow 5 \text{ machines}$$

Answers are usually rounded up to the nearest integer.

SOLVED PROBLEM 3

Demand for an average week for a parking garage is given in Table 10.8. Assume that the garage is open 6 days per week and wishes to maintain a capacity cushion of 5 percent. Assume that each customer uses an average of 1.1 parking spots because of bad parking and some oversize vehicles. Calculate the utilization for each day and identify any capacity gaps if the garage currently has 190 spots.

TABLE 10.8

	9 a.m. to 1 p.m.	9 a.m. to 5 p.m.	1 p.m. to 5 p.m.
Monday	100	75	90
Tuesday	85	80	75
Wednesday	85	75	90
Thursday	90	60	95
Friday	80	50	110
Saturday	95	50	70

SOLUTION

We calculate the demand for two time periods, 9 a.m. to 1 p.m. and 1 p.m. to 5 p.m., because Table 10.8 shows that there are three separate groups of customers: those who park all day, those who park for the morning, and those who park for the afternoon. As Table 10.9 shows, we add the first two columns to obtain the number of spots demanded from 9 a.m. to 1 p.m. and add the second two columns to obtain the number of spots demanded from 1 p.m. to 5 p.m.

TABLE 10.9

	9 a.m. to 1 p.m.	1 p.m. to 5 p.m.
Monday	175 = 100 + 75	165 = 75 + 90
Tuesday	165 = 85 + 80	155 = 80 + 75
Wednesday	160 = 85 + 75	165 = 75 + 90
Thursday	150 = 90 + 60	155 = 60 + 95
Friday	130 = 80 + 50	160 = 50 + 110
Saturday	145 = 95 + 50	120 = 50 + 70

Next, we multiply the results in Table 10.9 by 1.1 to obtain the total number of spots required (because people need an average of 1.1 spots). We then divide each number by the 185 spots available. The results are given in Table 10.10.

TABLE 10.10

	9 a.m. to 1 p.m.	1 p.m. to 5 p.m.	Utilization 9 a.m. to 1 p.m.	Utilization 1 p.m. to 5 p.m.
Monday	192.5 = 175 * 1.1	181.5 = 165 * 1.1	104.05% = 192.5/185	98.11% = 181.5/185
Tuesday	181.5	170.5	98.11%	92.16%
Wednesday	176	181.5	95.14%	98.11%
Thursday	165	170.5	89.19%	92.16%
Friday	143	176	77.30%	95.14%
Saturday	159.5	132	86.22%	71.35%

The highlighted cells in Table 10.10 show where there is higher utilization than the planned 95 percent rate (with a 5 percent cushion). Note that the only period where utilization is actually over 100 percent is Mondays from 9 a.m. to 1 p.m. The rest of the time periods are under 100 percent utilization. Thus, the owners could choose to keep the garage the current size, with the risk of losing a few customers. Alternately, the owners of the garage may still want to consider expansion because they are not able to maintain the desired capacity cushion.

PROBLEMS

1. A hospital emergency room averages 50 patients per shift. A shift is 8 hours long, and the average patient requires 20 minutes in the exam room.
   a. How many exam rooms should the hospital have if it wishes to maintain a 30 percent capacity cushion?
   b. Discuss whether you think a 30 percent capacity cushion is appropriate for a hospital emergency room. What factors would you consider when setting this cushion?
2. A fast-food restaurant averages 150 customers per hour. The average processing time per customer is 90 seconds.
   a. Determine how many cash registers the restaurant should have if it wishes to maintain a 10 percent capacity cushion.
   b. Discuss whether you think a 10 percent capacity cushion is appropriate for a fast-food restaurant. What factors would you consider when setting this cushion?
3. A university has demand for 10,000 classroom seats per day (one student in one class is a classroom seat). All classrooms have 50 seats, and the day is considered to be 10 hours long for scheduling purposes. Each class takes 1 hour. Determine the number of classrooms required if the university seeks to maintain a 20 percent capacity cushion.
4. MondoCycle manufactures three different types of bikes: the Tiny Tike, the Adult Aero, and the Mountain Monger. Given the production schedule in Table 10.11, including setup and processing times and lot sizes, calculate the required capacity for this year's production. Note that the times are given for individual production lines, so capacity calculations should be in terms of the number of lines necessary. Assume that MondoCycle operates two shifts, each with 2,000 hours per year, and wishes to maintain a 15 percent capacity cushion.

TABLE 10.11

	Tiny Tike	Adult Aero	Mountain Monger
Annual demand	12,000	18,000	19,000
Processing time (minutes)	6.0	12.0	10.0
Average lot size	120	450	200
Setup time (minutes)	50	40	70

5. A local bakery, Main Street Bakery, produces and sells to a national grocery chain five varieties of pastry: Muffin Tops, Doughnut Slices, Cookies, Cream Puffs, and Fritters. Assuming that Main Street operates a single shift for 1,800 hours per year, calculate the required capacity. The processing time per unit, setup time per lot, annual demand, and lot size are given in Table 10.12. Assume that the times given are for a production cell of four workers each, so the required capacity should be in terms of the number of production cells needed. Main Street would like to maintain a 10 percent capacity cushion.
6. Two machines (a grinding machine and a rolling machine) are required to make each of five products with the processing time, average lot size, and setup time given in Table 10.13. Each machine is notorious for breaking down frequently; thus, the company wants to maintain a 30 percent capacity cushion. Each machine is available for 12 hours per day, 260 days per year. Determine how many machines of each type are required.

TABLE 10.12

	Muffin Tops	Doughnut Slices	Cookies	Cream Puffs	Fritters
Annual demand	400,000	500,000	1,000,000	220,000	160,000
Processing time (minutes)	0.1	0.1	0.06	0.2	0.15
Average lot size	400	300	1,000	200	300
Setup time (minutes)	20	10	5	20	15

TABLE 10.13

	Product A	Product B	Product C	Product D	Product E
Annual demand	20,000	30,000	24,000	10,000	20,000
Average lot size	500	1,000	3,000	800	2,000
Grinding machine					
Processing time (minutes)	4	7	11	9	5
Setup time (minutes)	100	240	400	150	90
Rolling machine					
Processing time (minutes)	1	0.5	2	3	1.5
Setup time (minutes)	40	70	100	50	45

7. Determine the utilization for each of these situations:
   a. A gas station has three pumps with an effective capacity to serve 20 customers per hour. Average demand is 45 customers per hour.
   b. An appliance repairperson services 6 appliances per day but has an effective capacity of 7 appliances per day.
8. Demand for the next four years for a new hotel that has just been constructed is given in Table 10.14. Assume that the hotel is open 365 days per year and wishes to maintain a capacity cushion of 15 percent. Calculate the required capacity for each year and identify any capacity gaps if the hotel currently has 110 rooms.

TABLE 10.14

	Room Nights Demanded
Year 1	30,000
Year 2	33,000
Year 3	37,000
Year 4	40,000

9. Demand for a doctor's office is given in Table 10.15. The doctor's office has 3 exam rooms and operates 9 hours per day. The doctor's office seeks to maintain a 10 percent capacity cushion. Calculate the required capacity and identify any capacity gaps.

TABLE 10.15

	Low Patient Time (15 minutes per visit)	Medium Patient Time (30 minutes per visit)	High Patient Time (45 minutes per visit)
Number of daily patients	30	25	15

10. Table 10.16 shows projected demand for Jumbo Jets airline for a flight between Paris and Berlin on a given day. The Airbus plane used in this route has a capacity of 150 passengers.

    a. The standard price is $200 per seat regardless of the flight time. Calculate the total demand for the day, the average utilization, and the revenue for this pricing scheme.

    b. Assuming that Jumbo Jets changes its pricing for the flights to the scheme shown in the fourth column of Table 10.16, calculate the total demand for the day, the average utilization, and the revenue for this adjusted pricing scheme.

11. Table 10.17 shows projected demand for a peak summer weekend day at Timber Ridge Golf Course. Golfers prefer to play in the middle of the day, rather than very early or very late. Compare the effects of a standard pricing scheme of $50 per round with those of the adjusted pricing given in Table 10.17.

    a. The standard price is $50 per round regardless of the tee time. Calculate the total demand for the day and the revenue for this pricing scheme.

    b. Assuming Timber Ridge changes its pricing for the rounds to the scheme shown in the fourth column of Table 10.17, calculate the total demand for the day and the revenue for this adjusted pricing scheme.

TABLE 10.16

Flight Time	Demand (Seats) for Standard Pricing	Demand for Adjusted Pricing	Adjusted Price
6:00 a.m.	95	110	$200.00
8:00 a.m.	148	142	$300.00
10:00 a.m.	132	130	$250.00
12:00 p.m.	102	114	$200.00
3:00 p.m.	134	128	$250.00
6:00 p.m.	144	137	$300.00

TABLE 10.17

Tee Time	Demand (Rounds) for Standard Pricing	Demand for Adjusted Pricing	Adjusted Price
Early Riser (before 8 a.m.)	6	10	$35.00
Regular (8 a.m.–3 p.m.)	30	20	$60.00
Early Twilight (3 p.m.–5 p.m.)	8	9	$50.00
Twilight (after 5 p.m.)	7	14	$45.00

CASE STUDY

Carl's Sandwiches

Carl Fredrickson started a sandwich shop immediately upon graduation from college. The shop serves wraps with a twist: Carl's lets customers choose from one of 7 main ingredients (either meat or vegetarian offerings); any of 10 different toppings; one of 5 wrap types; and then the pièce de résistance, 30 different types of sauce ranging from sweet to semi-hot to melt-your-tongue-off hot. The total number of sandwich combinations is over 10,000 end sandwiches.

The shop did well from the first day it was open because customers loved Carl's sauces—many customers came in just for his special pepper chocolate sauce, which was spicy with just a hint of sweetness. The shop was primarily run by Carl and one of his best friends in the first year of operation. Sales for the first year were $150,000; sales for the second year were $280,000. Carl has been planning an expansion for the coming year. Table 10.18 shows the projected sales for this year (year 0) and the following seven years. He has two expansion options. He can lease a new facility in which to locate the shop, a 2,000-square-foot space that could be expanded by 2,000 square feet in steps of 1,000. Alternatively, he can lease a 2,000-square-foot space with no option to expand, but then open another restaurant location in another part of town.

Carl has been quoted a price of $350,000 to open a 2,000-square-foot facility. Each expansion of that facility to add a 1,000-square-foot addition will cost an additional $100,000. The alternative approach, opening a single 2,000-square-foot facility and then opening new facilities as needed, requires an investment of $300,000 for each 2,000-square-foot facility. Carl's operating costs for labor, utilities, equipment, and other expenses are 40 percent of his sales. The maximum capacity of a single 2,000-square-foot facility is $400,000 per year, so Carl must open a new facility or expand the existing facility when sales hit this number. Any new restaurant or expansion has a lead time of one year from the time Carl approves the idea to the time when the facility is up and running.

TABLE 10.18 Restaurant Expansion Options for Carl's

Year	Projected Sales
Year 0	$280,000
Year 1	$350,000
Year 2	$420,000
Year 3	$490,000
Year 4	$550,000
Year 5	$600,000
Year 6	$645,000
Year 7	$695,000

QUESTIONS

1. As a general strategy, would you recommend that Carl take an aggressive approach to capacity expansion or more of a wait-and-see approach?
2. Should Carl go with the option for one facility that can be expanded as needed, or should he plan to open one fixed-size restaurant and add new restaurants incrementally as needed? With either approach, when should Carl make expansion decisions?
3. What are the risks of your recommended capacity expansion strategy? How can Carl mitigate and minimize his risks?
4. Calculate the projected net present value of your proposed capacity expansion strategy.

CHAPTER 11

Quality Improvement Methods

LEARNING OBJECTIVES

1. Describe three sources for quality improvement ideas: customer feedback, benchmarking, and employee feedback.
2. Describe qualitative quality improvement tools, including brainstorming, affinity diagrams, interrelationship diagrams, tree diagrams, process decision program charts, flowcharts, cause-and-effect diagrams, failure modes and effects analysis, and mistake-proofing.
3. Describe quantitative quality improvement tools, including inspection and sampling, check sheets, Pareto analysis, histograms, scatter diagrams, process capability analysis, run charts, and statistical process control charts.

Two Scoops of Raisins in a Box of Kellogg's Raisin Bran

Kellogg's Raisin Bran, first introduced in 1942, is still a popular breakfast cereal in the United States. This cereal is known for its nutritional content, including a large amount of dietary fiber from whole grains in combination with just the right amount of raisins.

Cereal production is a highly automated process. The ingredients pass through a series of machines that automatically perform the necessary production steps, such as cleaning, toasting, baking, mixing, and finally packing the right amount of product in each package. So how does a company such as Kellogg's ensure that each box of Raisin Bran cereal contains exactly "two scoops" of raisins? For that matter, what is a "scoop"?

The answer is the careful use of quality management techniques such as establishing conformance standards, sampling, and statistical process control. These methods and a range of other process improvement methods (such as cause-and-effect diagrams, flowcharts, and the design of experiments) are used in the production of all types of cereals, other food and beverage products, and a wide range of other manufactured products.

Sampling and testing of cereal batches.

For Raisin Bran, first a conformance standard is established, and this standard defines the measure marketed as a "scoop." The scoop could be defined as a fixed number, volume, or weight of raisins per box. Alternatively, a range of values for number, volume, or weight that broadly defines the scoop could be established. To ensure that each box indeed contains the required amount of raisins, the ingredients and the finished products are sampled throughout the production process. At each stage, randomly sampled products are checked to ensure that they contain the exact amount of specified ingredients, such as raisins. Statistical quality control charts are used to determine whether the variations observed from one cereal box to the next are random or have a specific cause. Finally, quality assurance inspectors periodically open random samples of the packed boxes that are ready to be shipped to ensure that each shipment indeed includes "two scoops of raisins in each box of Raisin Bran." ■

This chapter discusses many different tools that are commonly used in quality management. Some of the techniques described in this chapter help companies to identify quality problems; others assist in determining the root causes of problems. Finally, the statistical methods described are used to systematically analyze the data collected at different steps in the production process for quality control and improvement.

A good quality improvement system consists of a series of steps that are systematically implemented throughout the organization. For example, an organization can use Deming's *Plan-Do-Check-Act* cycle (Chapter 2, Figure 2.5) or Six Sigma's *DMAIC* methodology (Chapter 2, Figure 2.16) as a guideline when initiating a quality improvement program.

When embarking on quality improvement, the organization must first clearly identify the goals and objectives of the program. Once the charter of the improvement program is established, it is necessary to identify the needs and preferences of the customers, users, or recipients of the processes that produce products and services. The third important step in any quality improvement process involves understanding the current state of affairs at the organization, such as understanding what is being done presently and whether the results are good.

Once the current environment is understood, the organization can start identifying the gaps between its present and preferred situations and identify opportunities for improvement. Such an analysis also involves understanding the constraints (e.g., resource limits, budget, technology inadequacy, or supply uncertainty) that might prevent the organization from achieving its quality goals. Understanding the organizational constraints naturally leads to identifying changes that will overcome the barriers and make it possible to achieve higher quality.

The steps outlined here set the stage for implementing quality improvement efforts. Therefore, the next task is to actually implement the plan and then periodically evaluate the performance. If the implemented plan shows the expected improvement in quality, then the next step is to ensure that the plan can be standardized for the future. However, if the plan does not show the expected improvement, then some of the earlier assumptions need to be reevaluated. Finally, at the conclusion of each quality improvement effort, it is time to celebrate and, more importantly, recap and summarize what was learned from the exercise for future reference. The expanded framework just described is presented in Figure 11.1 in easy-to-understand and commonsense language.

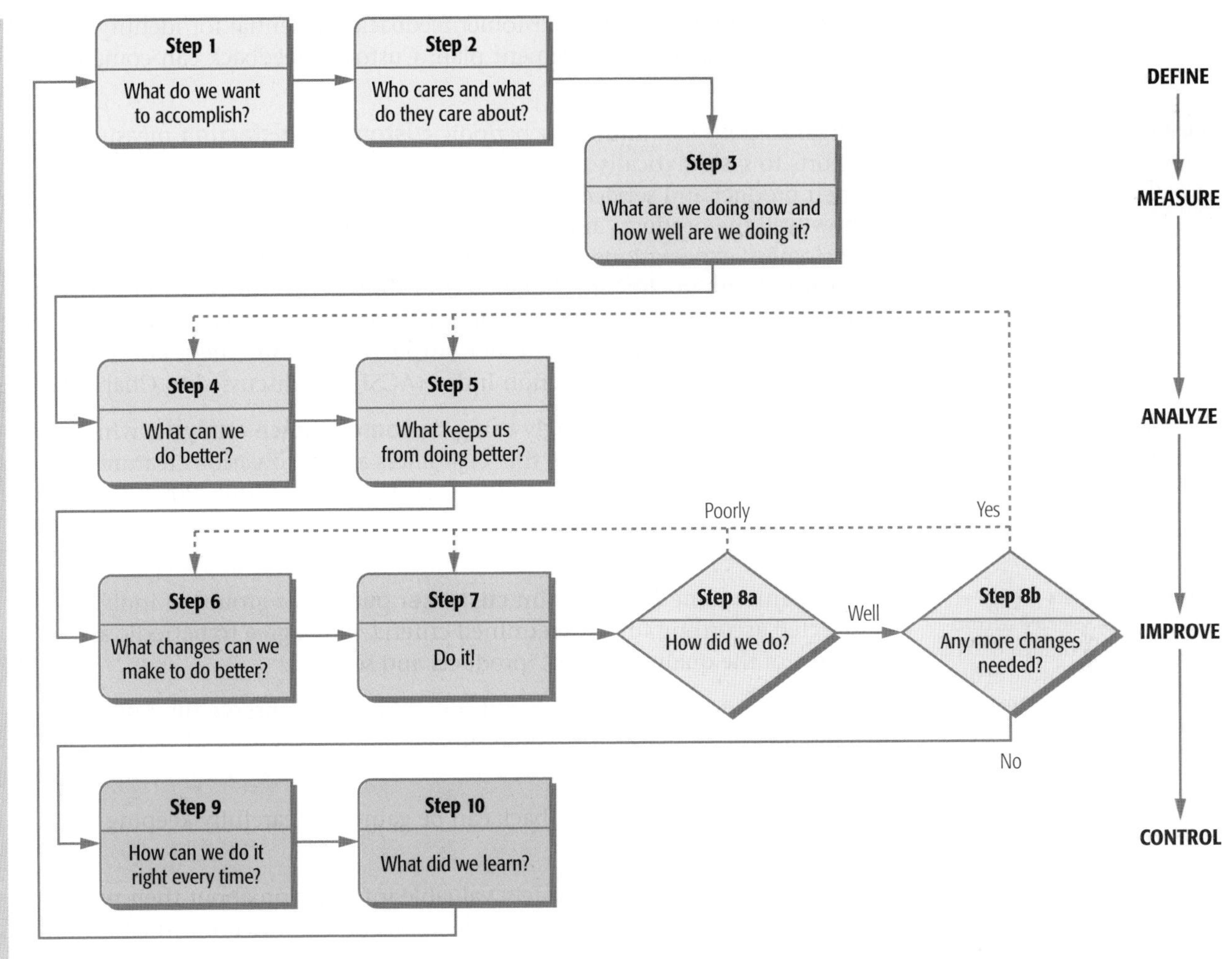

FIGURE 11.1 A Framework for the Quality Improvement Process

Source: "A Framework for the Quality Improvement Process," adapted with permission from *Quality Toolbox,* 2nd edition, ASQ Quality Press, © 2004 American Society for Quality.

In this chapter, we will discuss three aspects of a quality improvement plan: First, we will review sources of quality improvement ideas; second, we will learn a number of qualitative techniques; and third, we will discuss a variety of quantitative quality improvement tools.

SOURCES OF QUALITY IMPROVEMENT IDEAS

The initial part of any quality improvement plan is to identify the ideas for improvement (Steps 1 and 2 in Figure 11.1). Quality improvement ideas can come from many different sources, such as customers, employees, and other organizations.

Customer Feedback

The teachings of gurus, total quality management (TQM), the Malcolm Baldrige National Quality Award (MBNQA), Six Sigma, and all other quality improvement frameworks discussed in Chapter 2 are based on customers' definitions of product or service quality. Therefore, customer feedback is essential for identifying or developing any quality improvement plan. Customer feedback can come in many different formats:

- **Customer satisfaction** a measurement of how well the products and services that a firm supplies meet or exceed its customers' expectations

- Organizations can undertake periodic **customer satisfaction** measurement efforts to systematically collect customer feedback on different aspects of their product and service offerings. Customer satisfaction measures can assess how well the products and services that a firm supplies meet or exceed its customers' expectations, and also track how customers' perceptions of an organization's quality are changing over time as the organization initiates and continues with any improvement efforts. For example, a widely used and standardized approach to customer satisfaction measurement known as the American Customer Satisfaction Index (ACSI) was discussed in Chapter 2.

- **Customer choice analysis** an approach for quantifying the relative importance that customers assign to the various features and components of products and services

- Organizations are increasingly using **customer choice analysis**, which measures the relative importance that customers assign to various features and components when choosing products and services (Verma, 2007). The results of a customer choice study are used to identify the potential areas for quality improvement.

- **Customer panels** groups of individuals, selected according to predetermined criteria, who agree to provide periodic assessments of the quality of firms' products and services

- Companies sometimes appoint **customer panels**, or groups of individuals, selected according to predetermined criteria, who agree to periodic assessments of the quality of firms' products and services.
- Companies sometimes also recruit individuals and observe their use of a product or service in its natural surroundings to identify ideas for improvement.
- Very valuable customer feedback can be gained by carefully keeping track of customer complaints.
- Organizations can get extremely valuable information about their product and service offerings by monitoring various unstructured information sources such as Internet newsgroups and **blogs**, or web sites where individuals write commentary about a specific product, issue, or topic.

- **Blog** a web site where an individual writes a commentary about a specific product, issue, or topic

Benchmarking

- **Benchmarking** a structured process for comparing the business practices of an organization to the *best practices* that can be identified in other organizations (partner firms, competitors, or suppliers) or other divisions within a company

Benchmarking is a structured process for comparing the business practices of an organization to the *best practices* that can be identified in other organizations (partner firms, competitors, or suppliers) or other divisions within a company. A benchmark can be used as a reference point for identifying ideas for improvement and tracking performance, both of which significantly affect key stakeholders such as customers, employees, stockholders, and the community.

While the idea of learning from best practices is not new, the Xerox Corporation is credited with developing a structured approach to benchmarking. Today, benchmarking is a widely accepted approach for quality and performance improvement and is practiced in manufacturing, service, not-for-profit, and government organizations. For example, in an effort to reduce on-ground time at the airline terminals, Southwest Airlines, it is said, benchmarked crews that change tires and service cars within a few seconds during the Indy 500 races.

Benchmarking can also identify the drivers of best practices, such as an organization's culture, employee skills, recognition systems, and training programs. Benchmarking across companies therefore requires an unusual amount of cooperation among all participants. The companies sharing information do so openly and exchange information, data, and results with one another, with the objective of learning from one another and collectively improving everyone's quality.

Of course, the proprietary aspects of businesses are not shared in any benchmarking exercise.

Benchmarking can also be done internally within a company. A large company with multiple divisions and locations often has to perform the same business operations in multiple units. For example, American Express customer service centers located in different parts of the world keep track of standard performance measures (e.g., customer waiting time on the phone) within their divisions. They then compare the data periodically to identify best practices and learn from one another. Table 11.1 describes typical benchmarking steps.

TECHNOLOGY IN OPERATIONS MANAGEMENT

American Express Shares Benchmarked Quality Reports with Its Travel Service Clients

When consumers think of American Express, they most likely picture it as a financial services company that issues traveler's checks and credit cards. However, American Express also operates one of the world's largest travel agencies (recording $15.5 billion in worldwide travel sales in 2002). The clients of American Express's Corporate Services group (which includes travel services) include more than 70 percent of the Fortune 500 companies along with a large number of midsized companies. A majority of these companies use American Express's Interactive eFulfillment Center to make their travel reservations.

American Express Corporate Travels eFulfillment Center, established in 2001 in Miami Lakes, Florida, is a centralized service center that executes interactive client transactions and also provides 24-hours-a-day, 7-days-a-week telephone access to experienced travel counselors. American Express also operates eFulfillment Centers in Phoenix; Montreal; Sophia-Antipolis, France; and Stockholm, Sweden.

Starting in 2003, American Express started offering, free of charge to customers of its Interactive Travel eFulfillment Center, a new series of benchmarked reports designed to further streamline the online travel booking process. In the eFulfillment Center, American Express has created a sophisticated back-office process that fully automates the quality control and data-gathering processes that companies need in order to manage travel.

These unique interactive benchmarking reports help companies save money by reducing the number of reservations that require special handling or follow-up calls on the back end. The reports also help travel managers identify patterns of unnecessary use of text requests and telephone calls. Armed with these reports, corporate travel managers can analyze patterns of behavior and address them by sending messages to travelers or travel arrangers who make frequent special requests or by developing training sessions for groups of travelers. The reports streamline and speed the process, save money for both American Express and its clients, and, in the process, enhance the quality of the corporate travel services. This example clearly illustrates the important role that information technology is playing in quality management.

The review of benchmarking reports can provide valuable insights.

TABLE 11.1 Benchmarking Steps

1	Identify a clearly defined practice or process to benchmark. Note: This issue should be critical to the company, and the approach should have support from top management.
2	Organize a motivated, cross-functional team to undertake the benchmarking efforts.
3	Identify partner organizations that may have best practices. The partner organizations should have similar processes, but need not be from the same industry.
4	Collect data from the partner organizations. The data can be collected in many forms, including surveys, interviews, or actual observations.
5	Collect data from own company or division (in the case of internal benchmarking).
6	Systematically compare the data and determine the performance gaps between the organizations or divisions.
7	Determine which differences between the practices are potentially causing the performance gap.
8	Based on the comparison results, develop goals and action plans.
9	Implement action plans and review them periodically.

Employee Feedback

Employees in any organization are an excellent source of ideas for quality and process improvement. The employees know all the nuances of the production system firsthand, whether it is manufacturing goods or delivering services. For example, researchers have shown that by incorporating employee quality efforts in the production process (and also by taking care of employees), higher value is provided to the customers, which results in higher customer satisfaction, and creates greater loyalty and repeat business, and provides revenue growth and enhanced profitability for the company.

Feedback from employees on quality improvement plans can be compiled in many different ways. Some companies use a regular and formal system of collecting feedback from their employees, whereas others use informal and ad hoc approaches. One approach that is used extensively in Japanese companies is known as a quality circle. A **quality circle** is a small volunteer group of employees responsible for similar or related work functions that meets regularly to identify, analyze, and solve quality and production problems related to its work. A quality circle is a relatively autonomous unit within an organization and is usually led by a supervisor or a senior worker within a work unit. Employees who participate in quality circles usually receive training in formal quality improvement methods, described later in this chapter.

● **Quality circle** a small volunteer group of employees responsible for similar or related work functions that meets regularly to identify, analyze, and solve quality and production problems related to its work

Although they are most commonly found in manufacturing environments, quality circles are applicable to a wide variety of business situations and problems. For example, in recent years, the use of quality circles has spread to both manufacturing and service companies in different parts of the world. Xerox and United Airlines are two large companies in the United States that have used quality circles to identify approaches for eliminating waste within their operations.

They claim to have saved several millions of dollars by implementing suggestions derived from quality circles.

After the identification of quality improvement ideas, specific tools and techniques are used to prioritize, analyze, and address these issues systematically. These tools and techniques can be classified into two categories: qualitative and quantitative.

QUALITATIVE QUALITY IMPROVEMENT TOOLS

This section discusses several qualitative process improvement techniques that are used to understand and characterize the existing quality problems. Many of the techniques described here are used in combination with one another, and there is no specific order in which they should be implemented. The specific needs of the organization determine which techniques are most appropriate for analyzing a given quality problem or improvement idea.

Brainstorming

Brainstorming is a systematic method for generating a large number of creative problem-solving ideas in a relatively short amount of time based on input from many different individuals. Many different versions of the generic brainstorming technique described in this chapter (such as round-robin brainstorming, wildest-idea brainstorming, nominal group technique, and so on) are used in practice.

● **Brainstorming** a systematic method for generating a large number of creative problem-solving ideas in a relatively short amount of time based on input from many different individuals

Brainstorming is typically used in situations where a company needs to consider a broad range of solutions or options before coming to a conclusion. In addition, brainstorming is also an excellent approach for arriving at a solution based on the collective wisdom of a group of individuals. For example, Sony spent more than five years developing its new video-game console, Playstation 3. The product development team spent tens of hours brainstorming and trying to improve the quality of the next-generation game console based on feedback from employees in different functional areas within the firm and based on customer feedback about early designs and prototypes.

When brainstorming, the participants are advised on some basic rules, such as no criticism or early evaluation or dissection of proposed ideas. The participants are most strongly advised not to dismiss any proposed idea as stupid or irrelevant. In fact, they are encouraged to present the wildest ideas they can imagine. The only criterion for proposing an idea is that it should attempt to solve the problem that is being discussed or analyzed.

A combination of face-to-face and technology-mediated brainstorming.

After the initial discussion, there is usually a few minutes of silence so that participants can gather their thoughts about the problem and the potential solutions without any distractions. Finally, the participants are invited to present their ideas about the proposed solutions to the group, which then discusses, builds on, and refines those ideas and derives one or more solutions that can be implemented.

Solved Example 1

Brainstorming to Improve the Quality of a Pizza Restaurant and Delivery Service

Cheap N Fast Pizza is a chain of pizza restaurants located close to several regional universities. Its customer base primarily consists of students living in dormitories on campus or in apartments near the campus. The company deliveries pizza to its customers and also operates seven small sit-down restaurants in university towns. In an effort to improve the quality of its product and service offerings, the CEO, Kelly Heller, invited her store managers, pizza chefs, marketing managers, a few delivery personnel, and some of the company's most frequent customers to brainstorm and identify areas for improvement.

After several intensive discussion sessions, a large number of quality improvement ideas were suggested. Some of the frequently mentioned suggestions are given in Table 11.2.

TABLE 11.2 Quality Improvement Ideas

- Pizza taste needs improvement.
- There should be more than one choice for pizza crust.
- The number of available gourmet toppings should be increased.
- Use organic ingredients whenever possible.
- Offer price discounts for frequent customers.
- Offer price discounts during low-rush hours or for large orders.
- Décor, cleanliness, and upkeep of the restaurants need enhancement.
- Speed of service needs to be increased.
- Preferences and other information about frequent guests should be saved on restaurant computers so that subsequent transactions can be faster.
- There should be online ordering for delivery and takeout orders.
- In addition to its current product offerings (pizza, drinks, a few selected appetizers), the chain should consider offering sandwiches and pasta-based entrees.
- The size of the restaurants should be increased to seat large groups.
- Better thermal bags should be used so that pizza is delivered hot.

Affinity Diagram

● **Affinity diagram** a visual tool for organizing generated ideas into natural groups based on the collective wisdom of the participants

During brainstorming sessions, a large number of ideas are generated, but often in an unstructured format (see Solved Example 1). An **affinity diagram** is a visual tool for organizing these ideas into natural groups based on the collective wisdom of the participants.

To develop an affinity diagram, each viable idea generated during the brainstorming session is listed on a separate sticky note or card. The cards are randomly spread on a large work surface or wall so that they are visible to everyone. The entire team gathers around the notes and moves them into logical subgroups. Because all members of the team are moving the notes on the work surface simultaneously, the procedure appears chaotic in the beginning, but it slowly converges toward consensus groupings. Once the movement of cards stops (or once consensus is reached), the participants discuss the groups and try to identify the common themes within each group.

Solved Example 2

Affinity Diagram for Pizza Restaurant and Delivery Service Brainstorming

Based on the information presented in Solved Example 1, develop an affinity diagram for Cheap N Fast Pizza.

A sample solution is presented in Figure 11.2.

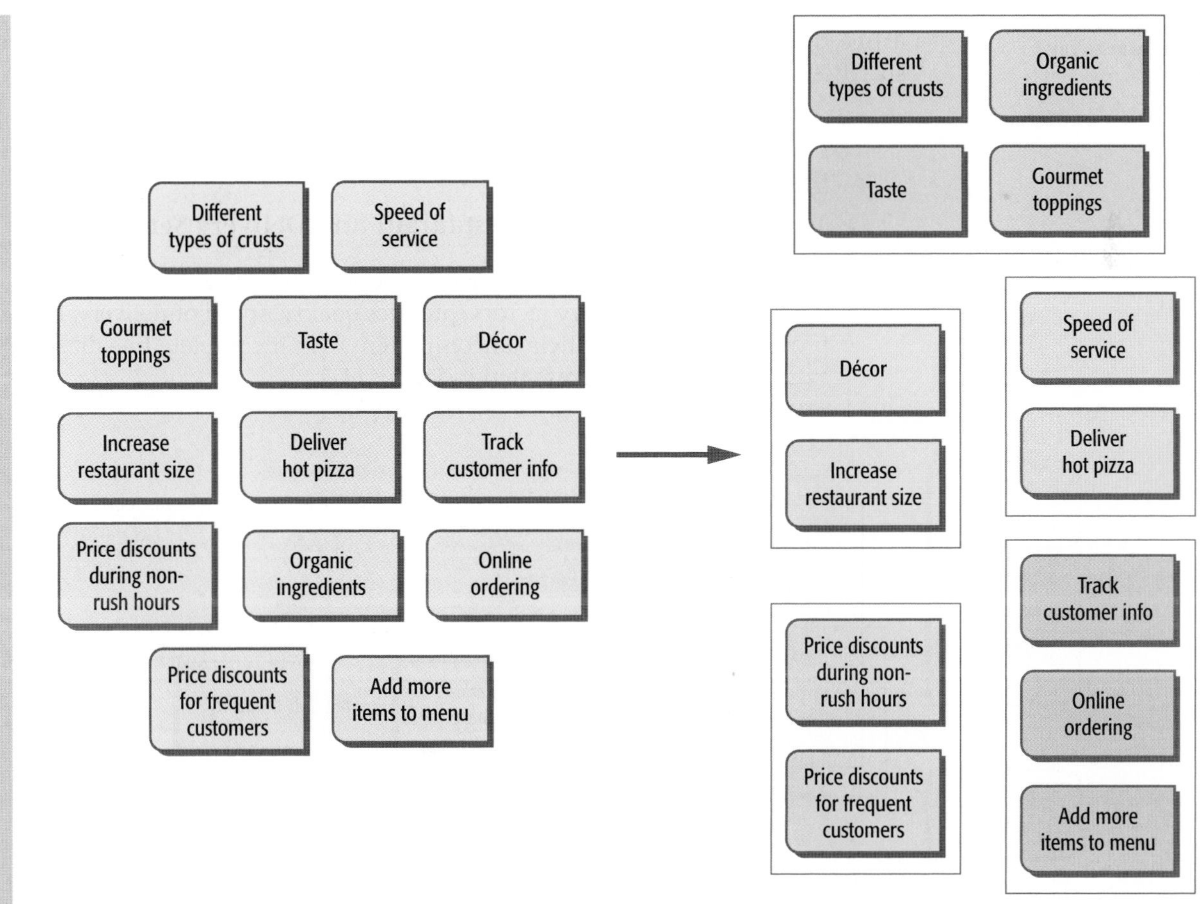

FIGURE 11.2 Affinity Diagram

Interrelationship Diagram

● **Interrelationship diagram** a diagram that shows the connections and natural relationships between different ideas or constructs identified for quality improvement

An **interrelationship diagram** shows the connections and natural relationships between different ideas or constructs identified for quality improvement. Often used in combination with brainstorming and an affinity diagram, the interrelationship diagram is based on the knowledge and expertise of the quality improvement team in identifying critical linkages across different concepts.

Solved Example 3

Interrelationship Diagram for Follow-up Brainstorming Session for Pizza Restaurant and Delivery Service

Kelly Heller convened a second brainstorming session to further understand the drivers of profitability. The team identified several broad constructs that affect one another (either positively or negatively) and presented the results to Kelly in the form of Figure 11.3.

Tree Diagram

● **Tree diagram** a diagram used to describe how one idea branches into two or more subideas, each of which branches into further subideas, and so on

A **tree diagram**, also known as a systematic diagram, a tree analysis, an analytical tree, or a hierarchy diagram, is used to describe how one idea branches into two or more subideas, each of which branches into further subideas, and so on. This procedure is used to break broad categories into finer details. Developing a tree diagram helps organizations move their analysis from general ideas to specifics.

Solved Example 4

Tree Diagram for Pizza Restaurant and Delivery Service

Kelly Heller and her team further developed a tree diagram to break down the three primary factors (product quality, speed of delivery, and product variety) into their subcomponents. An incomplete tree diagram from their session is presented in Figure 11.4.

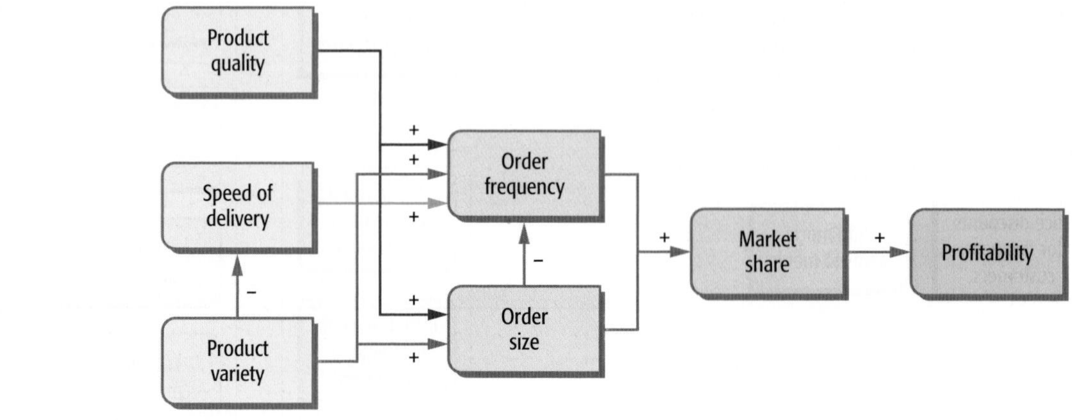

FIGURE 11.3 Interrelationship Diagram

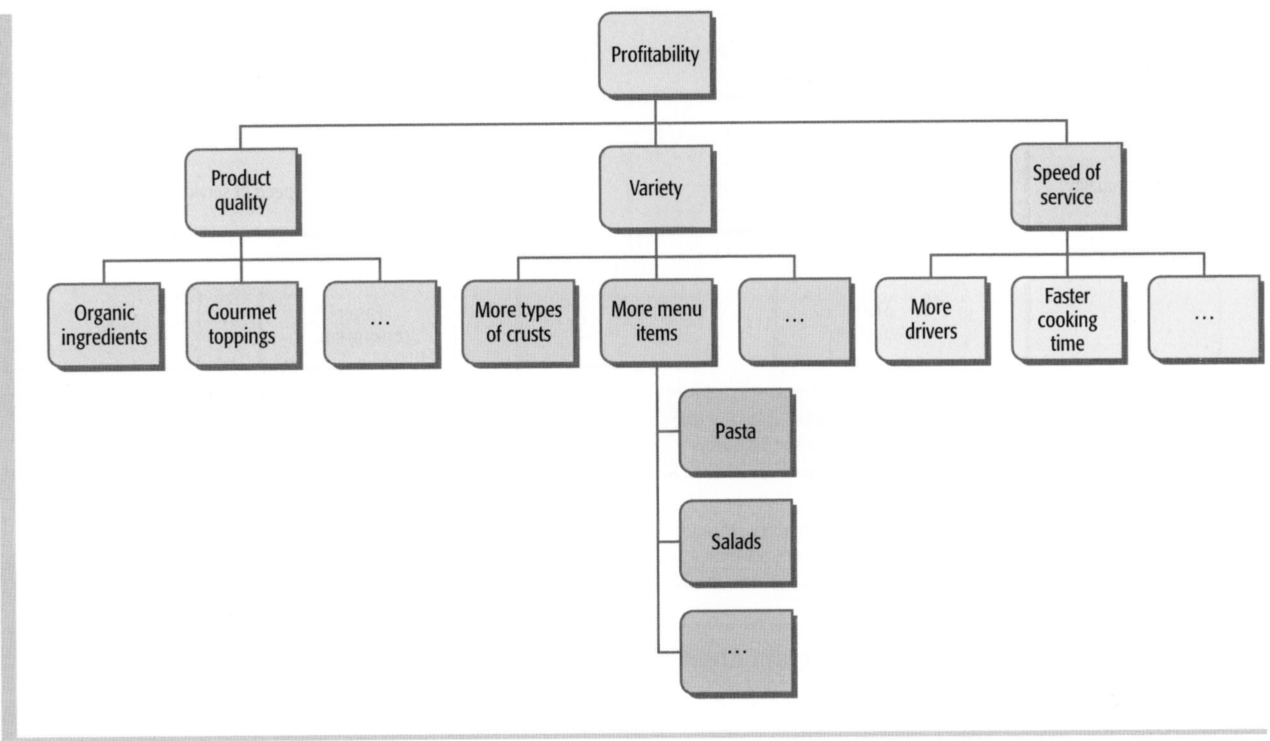

FIGURE 11.4 Tree Diagram

Process Decision Program Chart (PDPC)

A **process decision program chart** (PDPC) is used to systematically identify initiatives that might potentially go wrong in a quality improvement plan that is under consideration. The PDPC is used to develop countermeasures that could prevent or offset those potential problems. This approach is especially useful when the cost of failure is high. To construct a PDPC, a tree diagram of the proposed plan is first developed. Next, all potential problems are identified, and potential countermeasures are brainstormed.

● **Process decision program chart** a chart used to systematically identify initiatives that might potentially go wrong in a quality improvement plan that is under consideration

Solved Example 5

PDPC for Pizza Restaurant and Delivery Service

A partial PDPC for Cheap N Fast Pizza is presented in Figure 11.5.

Flowchart

A **flowchart** is a pictorial representation of the separate steps of a process in a sequential manner. Flowcharting is a very general tool that has a variety of uses in operations management. Chapter 4, "Process Design and Analysis," provides a detailed description of flowcharting.

● **Flowchart** a pictorial representation of the separate steps of a process in a sequential manner

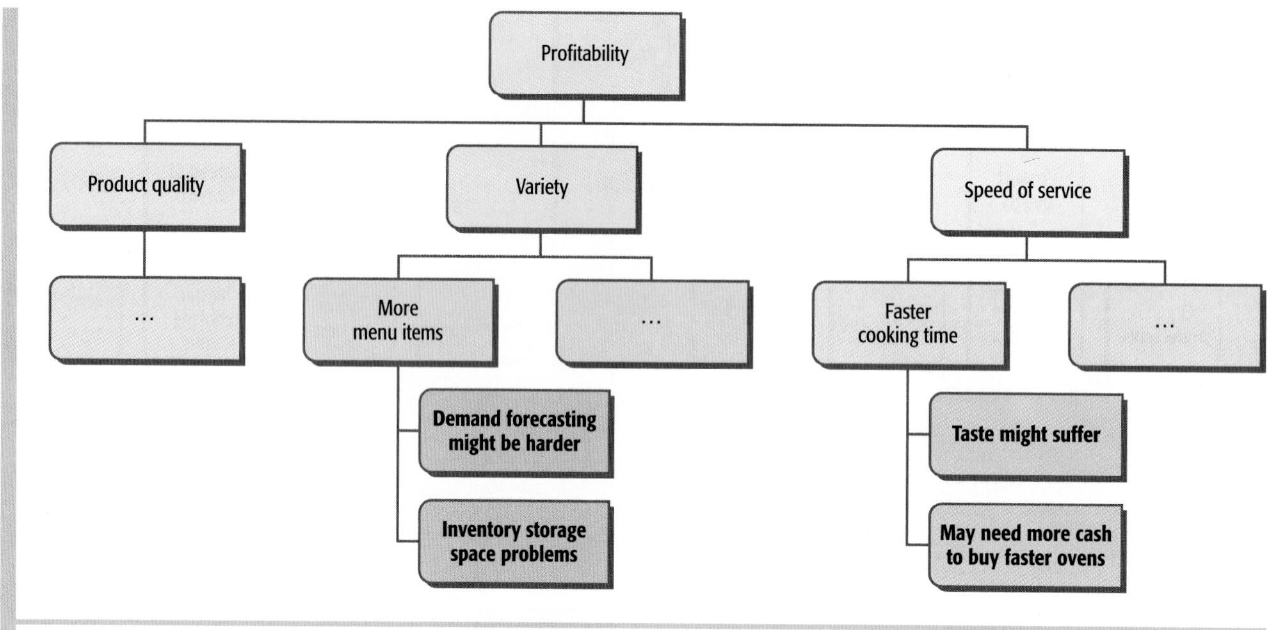

FIGURE 11.5 Process Decision Program Chart

Cause-and-Effect, Fishbone, or Ishikawa Diagram

● **Cause-and-effect diagram** a diagram used to illustrate the potential reasons for an outcome (usually a quality problem)

A **cause-and-effect diagram** (also known as a fishbone or Ishikawa diagram) is used to illustrate the potential reasons for an outcome (usually a quality problem). It is used to structure and explore potential reasons for any undesirable outcome (see Figure 11.6 for an example). Like many other quality improvement techniques, the cause-and-effect diagram was developed initially for manufacturing operations, but it has also been found useful in the service, government, education, and healthcare sectors.

Solved Example 6

Cause-and-Effect Diagram

Construct a cause-and-effect diagram for a late pizza delivered to the customer.

SOLUTION

The cause-and-effect diagram is shown in Figure 11.6.

Failure Modes and Effects Analysis (FMEA)

● **Failure modes and effects analysis** a systematic approach for identifying all possible failures in a design, a manufacturing process, or a service process

Failure modes and effects analysis (FMEA) is a systematic approach for identifying all possible failures in a design, a manufacturing process, or a service process. "Failure modes" means the ways in which something might fail. A failure is any type of error or defect, especially one that affects the customer, and it can be either potential or actual. Failures are prioritized according to how serious their consequences are, how frequently they occur, and how easily they can be detected. "Effects analysis" refers to studying the consequences of those failures. The purpose of FMEA is to take action to eliminate or reduce failures, starting with the highest-priority ones.

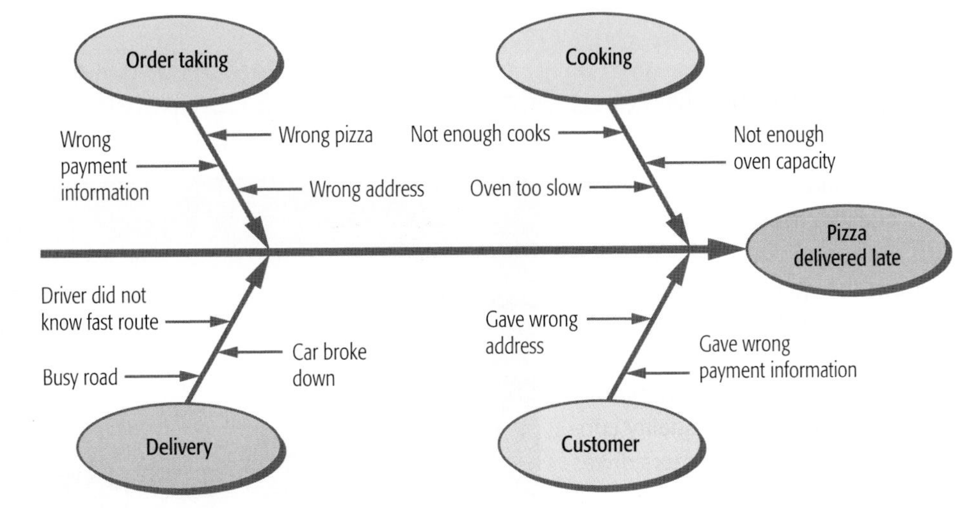

FIGURE 11.6 Cause-and-Effect Diagram

Mistake-proofing, Fail-safing, or Poka-Yoke

Mistake-proofing, fail-safing, or poka-yoke (its Japanese name, pronounced PO-ka yo-KAY) refers to the use of any automatic device or method that either makes it impossible for an error to occur or makes the error immediately obvious once it has occurred. This technique is used when the process steps have already been identified, but human errors can potentially cause mistakes that can have expensive or dangerous consequences. Professor John Grout has compiled many examples of poka-yoke on his web site (http://csob.berry.edu/faculty/jgrout/pokayoke.shtml). The size of the nozzle at a gasoline station is a simple yet elegant example of poka-yoke. The nozzle size of the gasoline pump is slightly different from the nozzle size of the diesel pump. This difference ensures that the owner of an automobile with a gasoline engine will not pump diesel into its engine by mistake. The featured example of Sony computer batteries in the "Best Practices" box shows that the costs of undetected mistakes can be quite extensive.

● **Mistake-proofing** the use of any automatic device or method that either makes it impossible for an error to occur or makes the error immediately obvious once it has occurred

BEST PRACTICES IN OPERATIONS MANAGEMENT

Recovering from Quality Mistakes: Sony Batteries in Dell Computers

Sony and Dell are both successful and well-respected companies, and their electronic products are widely used around the world. Yet even leading companies are not immune to very costly quality problems.

Sony's rechargeable lithium-ion batteries are used in many of Dell's laptop computers. During 2006, a handful of customers reported that the batteries were overheating, catching fire, and even exploding—including one much-publicized case at a conference in Japan that was captured on film and passed around over the Internet. On August 14, 2006, Dell announced that it would replace 4.1 million lithium-ion batteries made by Sony in laptop computers sold between 2004 and July 2006. The net cost of this recall was expected to be around $400 million.

While it was unfortunate that this quality problem occurred, both Dell and Sony took proactive steps to limit the damage to their consumers and themselves caused by potentially faulty batteries. They immediately recalled and replaced the lithium-ion batteries in more than 4 million laptop computers. While the news of the problem spread around the world, primarily through the Internet, Sony and Dell said that only six incidents of overheating of laptop computers

(*continued*)

BEST PRACTICES IN OPERATIONS MANAGEMENT

Recovering from Quality Mistakes: Sony Batteries in Dell Computers (*continued*)

had been reported. Compared with other companies facing product quality crises (e.g., Firestone's faulty tires in 2000), Dell and Sony quickly took initiatives to recover from the quality mistake, resulting in virtually no damage to their reputation and goodwill.

During the production process, a Sony battery goes through a number of very careful quality control checks. For example, a team of engineers drives a large metal nail through a battery cell to see if it explodes. In another trial, laboratory technicians bake the batteries in an oven to simulate the effects of leaving a digital device in a closed car on a sweltering day. On production runs, random batches of batteries are tested for temperature, efficiency, energy density, and output.

But even the rigorous processes that go into making sophisticated rechargeable lithium-ion batteries were apparently not enough. The quest for quality is a never-ending game.

A laptop computer's battery goes through extensive quality checks and testing.

QUANTITATIVE QUALITY IMPROVEMENT TOOLS

The previous section of this chapter discussed many nonstatistical techniques for quality and process improvement. This section describes quantitative (or numerical), data-driven approaches that are commonly used in quality and process improvement efforts.

Inspection and Sampling

Ideally, each and every product manufactured by a factory and each service delivered to the customer should be inspected to ensure that it meets or exceeds the established guidelines. However, inspecting every single item produced by the organization is often not possible because of cost and resource constraints. For example, in Chapter 2, we discussed quality *assurance costs,* which include the salaries of quality inspectors, costs of purchasing and using the necessary tools and equipment for quality checks, costs of conducting customer surveys for post-sale quality assessment, and so on. Therefore, companies use a combination of sampling and inspection techniques to collect and analyze data from a few selected outputs and then attempt to generalize to the entire production batch.

Sampling is the statistical practice of selecting a few observations intended to generate inferences about a population of interest. The specific sampling technique used is derived from probability theory, combined with the knowledge of best practices and cost and resource constraints.

● **Sampling** the statistical practice of selecting a few observations intended to generate inferences about a population of interest

The first step in any sampling plan is to clearly define the *population of interest.* Successful sampling requires a well-defined population of concern. For example, a company might be interested in understanding the needs of its most loyal or frequent customers. In this case, the population of interest will be all customers who purchase a predefined number or monetary value of products or who use the products or services offered by the company a prespecified minimum number of times.

By definition, a sample should represent the population of interest. Therefore, a sampling framework should ensure that the data collected are an appropriate representation of the population. For example, if a university wants to estimate the average height of its students, then it should not sample only the students enrolled in the basketball program. Clearly, this framework will result in a *biased sample* that most likely won't be representative of the entire student body on campus.

In many applications, a *simple random sampling* framework is selected. With this approach, each member of the population is equally likely to be selected as a sample (e.g., any box of cereal manufactured by Kellogg). In other applications, a *stratified sampling* framework is used. This approach is appropriate when the population of interest is believed to be made up of many distinct subgroups or strata (e.g., customers of American Express Blue, Green, Platinum, and Centurion credit cards). When using stratified sampling plans, care must be taken to ensure that the relative sample size for each stratum is an accurate representation of the population. Another commonly used sampling technique is known as *quota sampling.* This approach is used to collect a prespecified number of observations from each subgroup. It is appropriate when it is necessary to collect enough data to be able to make statistical inferences about certain subgroups that are underrepresented within the population. For example, a company might want to oversample responses from customers who rate its services as poor to proactively identify causes of customer dissatisfaction.

Along with the selection of a sampling framework, great care must be taken to ensure that the *sample size* is appropriate for making informed generalizations about the population of interest. A less than appropriate sample size can lead to a higher probability of the two types of errors commonly associated with any statistical analysis.

Type I Error

Statistically, a **Type I error, alpha error, or false positive** is the mistake of rejecting a hypothesis that should not have been rejected. Examples of Type I error include concluding that a batch of Raisin Bran does not contain the necessary amount of raisins, based on the results of a sample, when the batch actually does contain the necessary amount; concluding that a blood sample is HIV positive when it is not; and concluding that a product is defective when it is not.

● **Type I error, alpha error, or false positive** the mistake of rejecting a hypothesis that should have been accepted

Because a Type I error can lead a manufacturer or a service provider to reject a perfectly good product unnecessarily, this type of error is also known as *producers' risk* in quality management terminology. Statistically, Type I errors can be shown as the shaded area at the two tails of the normal distribution curve in Figure 11.7.

Type II Error

● **Type II error, beta error, or false negative** the mistake of failing to reject the hypothesis that everything within a population meets established standards when in reality the population does not conform to specifications

A **Type II error, beta error, or false negative** is the mistake of failing to reject the hypothesis that everything within a population meets established standards when in reality the population does not conform to specifications. For example, it is possible that an entire batch of Raisin Bran contains less than the necessary amount of raisins. However, if a few cereal boxes randomly sampled, by chance, contain enough raisins to meet the specifications, the manufacturer may conclude that the entire production batch meets established quality standards. Therefore, it might ship the entire batch of cereal boxes to the distribution centers to be sold to customers. Similarly, a blood test that concludes that a patient is free from HIV when he or she is actually HIV positive is another example of Type II error. In both these cases, the customers have to bear the consequences of lower quality. Therefore, a Type II error is also known as *consumers' risk*. Statistically, Type II errors can be shown as the shaded area in Figure 11.8.

Check Sheet

● **Check sheet** a structured, prepared form for collecting and analyzing sampled observations

A **check sheet** is a structured, prepared form for collecting and analyzing sampled observations. This is a generic tool that can be adapted for a wide variety of purposes. Prior to using sampling, inspection, or any other quantitative technique described in this section, the check sheet is used to compile the raw data collected from the population of interest. For example, the pizza delivery company described in the Solved Examples earlier in the chapter can use a check sheet to keep track of the number of wrong or late deliveries every day of the week or every hour of the day. An example of a check sheet is presented in Figure 11.9.

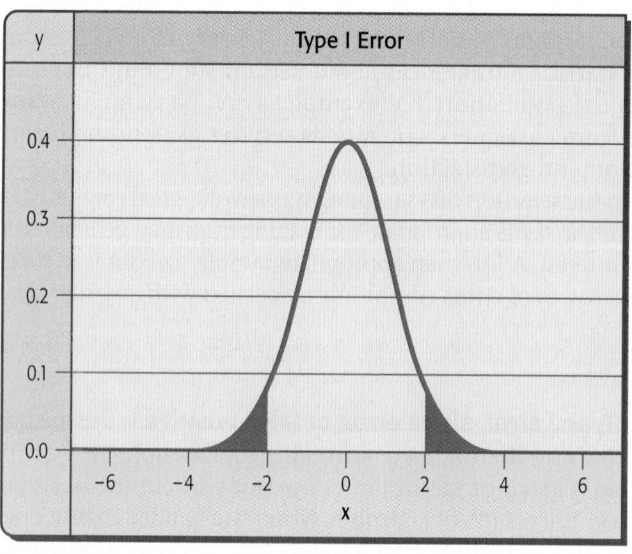

FIGURE 11.7 Type I Error

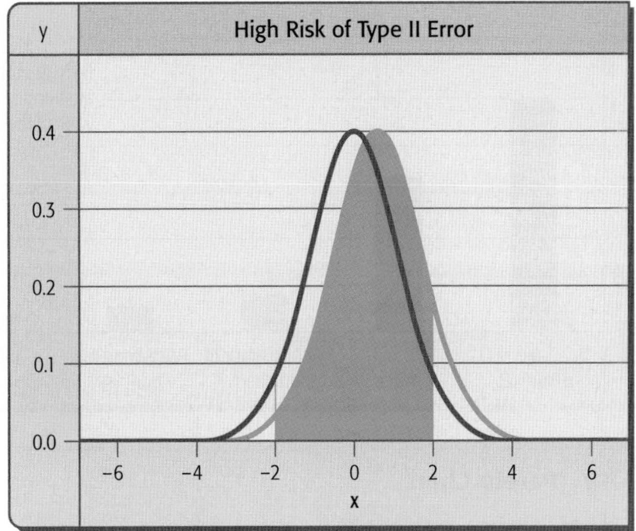

FIGURE 11.8 Type II Error

Pareto Analysis and Bar Charts

Pareto analysis is a statistical technique for identifying and categorizing data based on frequency and percentage of occurrences. This approach is named after the Italian economist Vilfredo Pareto, who first identified the concept that 80 percent of problems are often produced by 20 percent of the causes in many different applications. To conduct a Pareto analysis, a bar chart is constructed and arranged with the longest bar on the left and the shortest bar on the right (Figure 11.10). The example for the pizza delivery company presented in Figure 11.10 shows that the majority of the dissatisfied customers report only two problems, late deliveries and wrong orders.

● **Pareto analysis** a statistical technique for identifying and categorizing data based on frequency and percentage of occurrences

Histogram

A **histogram** is a type of graph used to show how often different values in a set of data occur. A histogram is the graph that is most commonly used to show frequency distributions of data collection on a continuous scale. It is used to summarize a large number of observations in a few data categories. An example of a histogram is presented in Figure 11.11. It shows the frequency distribution of delivery times to customers in 10-minute increments. The example shows that the majority of customers received deliveries within 40 to 60 minutes.

● **Histogram** a type of graph used to show how often different values in a set of data occur

	Monday	Tuesday	Wednesday	Thursday	Friday
Problem type 1	////	///	///	//	///
Problem type 2	/	///	//	/	/
Problem type 3	//		///	/	

FIGURE 11.9 Check Sheet

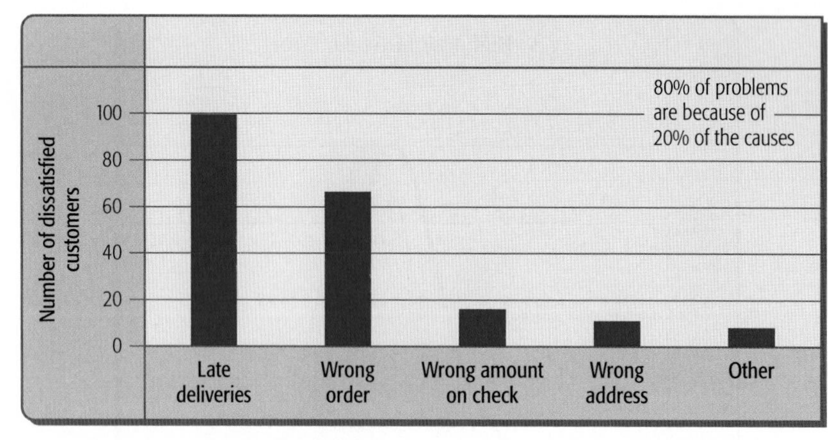

FIGURE 11.10 Pareto Chart

Scatter Diagram

Scatter diagram a graph of pairs of numerical data, with one variable on each axis, used to look for a relationship between the variables and identify potential correlations between them

A **scatter diagram**, which is a graph of pairs of numerical data, with one variable on each axis, is used to look for a relationship between the variables and identify potential correlations (see Figure 11.12). If the variables are correlated, the points will fall along a line or a curve. For example, Figure 11.12 shows that the delivery time and number of drivers are inversely related. When one variable increases, then the other variable goes down. The scatter diagram is an exploratory technique that looks for only the potential relationship between two variables; it cannot be used to infer that one variable causes the other. However, if a scatter diagram shows negligible correlation, then the analyst can be assured that neither of the two variables is affecting the other.

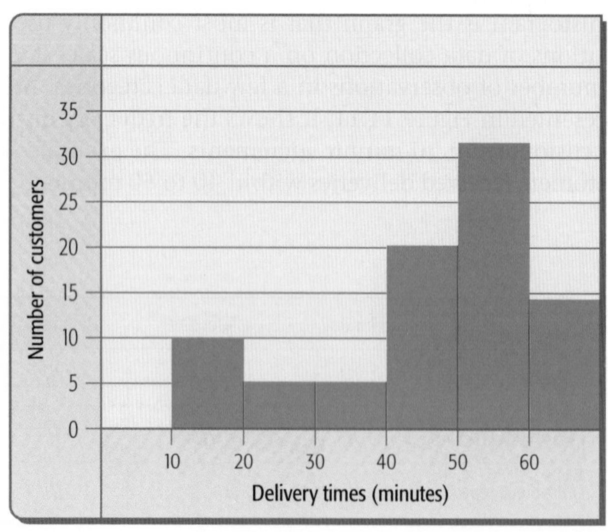

FIGURE 11.11 Histogram

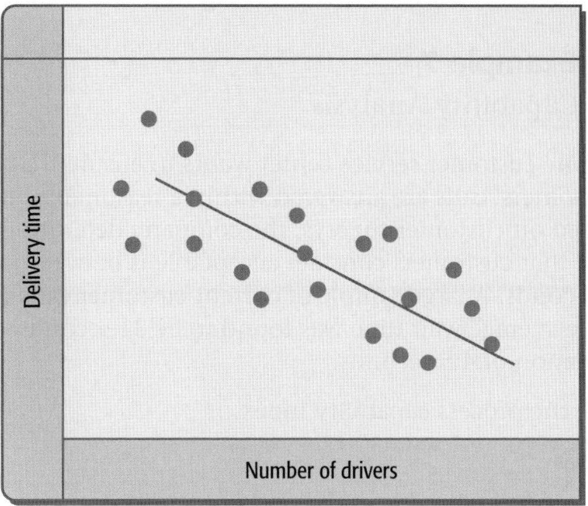

FIGURE 11.12 Scatter Diagram

Process Capability Analysis

A **process capability analysis** is a method used to compare the statistical variations present within a system with any predefined existing range. Quality managers are often required to compare the output of their processes with established criteria (e.g., on-time performance of an airplane, fuel efficiency of an automobile, delivery time for pizza, and so on).

● **Process capability analysis** a method used to compare the statistical variations present within a system with any predefined existing range

The process capability analysis is a ratio of the acceptable range of output with respect to the natural (or random) variations present within the production system. A **capable process** is one for which a prespecified percentage of measurements fall inside the specification limits.

● **Capable process** a process for which a prespecified percentage of measurements fall inside the specification limits

The process capability index is the minimum of the ratio of the distance from the mean to the upper tolerance limit (UTL) and the distance from the mean to the lower tolerance limit (LTL) with respect to three standard deviations (UTL and LTL were also defined in Chapter 2).

It is calculated in two steps.

Step 1: Calculate the process capability index for the upper and lower tolerance limits:

$$\text{Process Capability Index for UTL: } C_{pk\_UTL} = \frac{UTL - \mu}{3\sigma} \qquad \text{(Equation 1)}$$

$$\text{Process Capability Index for LTL: } C_{pk\_LTL} = \frac{\mu - LTL}{3\sigma} \qquad \text{(Equation 2)}$$

Step 2: Calculate the minimum of these two calculations.

$$\text{Process Capability Index: } C_{pk} = \min\{C_{pk\_UTL}, C_{pk\_LTL}\} \qquad \text{(Equation 3)}$$

A C_{pk} of 1 therefore means that the variations present are exactly equal to three standard deviations. A $C_{pk} \geq 1$ means that the process is capable of meeting the defined tolerances, i.e., a greater percentage of observations are within the tolerances than specified. A $C_{pk} < 1$ means the process is not capable of meeting the defined tolerances.

While companies have traditionally used C_{pk}, when many processes are not exactly centered, or when the impacts of not meeting quality specifications for the LTL and UTL are different, then it is better to track both C_{pk_LTL} and C_{pk_UTL} instead of C_{pk}.

Solved Example 7
Process Capability Analysis

A telephone customer service center wants to ensure that the majority of its customers' calls are answered within a reasonable amount of wait time. Based on customer surveys, the company determined that the wait time that customers consider acceptable is between 10 seconds and 45 seconds. A large sample of current customer calls was monitored. The average wait time was found to be 31 seconds with a standard deviation of 4.5 seconds.

Calculate the process capability index.

SOLUTION

Upper Tolerance Limit (UTL): 45 seconds

Lower Tolerance Limit (LTL): 10 seconds

Mean (μ): 31 seconds

Standard deviation (σ): 4.5 seconds

$$C_{pk\_UTL} = \frac{45 - 31}{3 * 4.5} = \frac{14}{13.5} = 1.037$$

$$C_{pk\_LTL} = \frac{31 - 10}{3 * 4.5} = \frac{21}{1.53} = 1.556$$

$$C_{pk} = \min\{1.037, 1.556\} = 1.037$$

The C_{pk} calculations show that the customer service center is meeting the lower specification with a higher "sigma level" (LTL) than that for the upper specification (UTL). The prespecification of 3σ in Equations 1–3 means that the process must be capable of delivering 99.7 or more good products (3 standard deviations above and below the mean for a normal curve includes 99.7% of the observations). Because C_{pk} is greater than 1, the customer service center answers more than 99.7% of the calls it receives within 10 to 45 seconds. Thus, the process is capable of meeting these tolerances.

Run Chart

● **Run chart** a simple graph used to display changes in observed data over a period of time

A **run chart** is a simple graph used to display changes in observed data over a period of time. Run charts are used to plot changes in critical performance data (e.g., pizza delivery time) as a function of time. Run charts can also be used to illustrate long-term changes or stability in the performance. An example of a run chart for the pizza delivery time in the earlier Solved Examples is shown in Figure 11.13. This chart shows that delivery times are increasing over time; hence there may be some type of quality problem.

Statistical Process Control Charts

● **Statistical process control chart** a specific type of run chart calculated with well-defined statistical properties

A **statistical process control chart** (SPC) is essentially a specific type of run chart calculated with well-defined statistical properties. The statistical process control chart was invented by Walter A. Shewhart while he was working for Bell Labs in the 1920s (therefore, the control charts are also known as Shewhart charts).

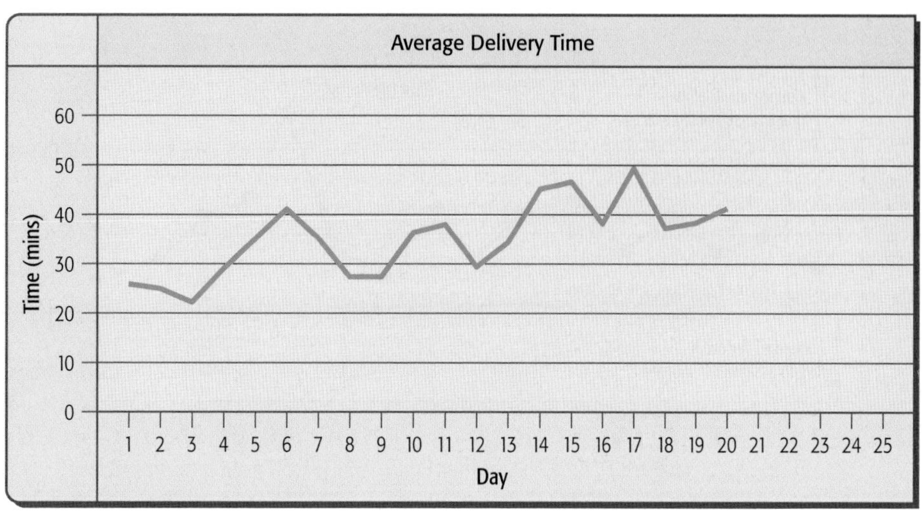

FIGURE 11.13 Run Chart

Shewhart's SPC innovation later came to the attention of W. Edwards Deming. Deming worked at the U.S. Department of Agriculture and eventually became an advisor to the Japanese government and industry leaders after the end of the Second World War. Deming strongly believed in the extraordinary insights gained from tracking the causes of the variations present within a production system by using SPC. He encouraged Japanese managers to implement SPC methodology for all critical operations that might affect the quality of the manufactured product. Today, SPC is an essential tool for operational analyses in a large number of manufacturing, service, healthcare, education, government, and not-for-profit organizations around the world.

Natural and Special-Cause Variations

Control charts can very effectively determine whether the variations present within a production system are **natural (or random) variations** or **special-cause or assignable variations** that need to be explored further. As the names suggest, natural variations occur at random, but there is a specific reason for an assignable-cause variation. For example, when calling a telephone customer service center, a customer might have to wait on hold before talking to a service representative. The slight variations in waiting time from one customer to another are most likely the result of the naturally occurring randomness of the process (e.g., variations in daily demand, variations in the time customers stay on the phone talking to the service representative, and so on).

- **Natural (or random) variations** variations observed in a process that appear to be random
- **Special-cause or assignable variation** a variation observed in a process that has a specific reason

It is also possible that at some point in time, the waiting time starts getting longer because of nonrandom causes. For example, if a low-quality product is introduced, then many customers will call the telephone service center to complain about it. Such an increase in phone call volume will result in a longer waiting time for each customer as a result of the special/assignable cause (launch of a lower-quality product).

An example of an SPC chart and associated natural and special-cause variations is presented in Figure 11.14. Because the control chart is a graph used to evaluate how a process changes over time, data are plotted in time order. A control chart always has a central line for the average, an upper line for the **upper control limit** (UCL), and a lower line for the **lower control limit** (LCL). The UCL and LCL lines are determined from historical data based on standard deviation calculations. The

- **Upper control limit** a line drawn at a prespecified distance (based on standard deviation units) above the mean value; the line represents the division between in-control and out-of-control processes.
- **Lower control limit** a line similar to the upper control limit, but drawn at a prespecified distance below the mean value

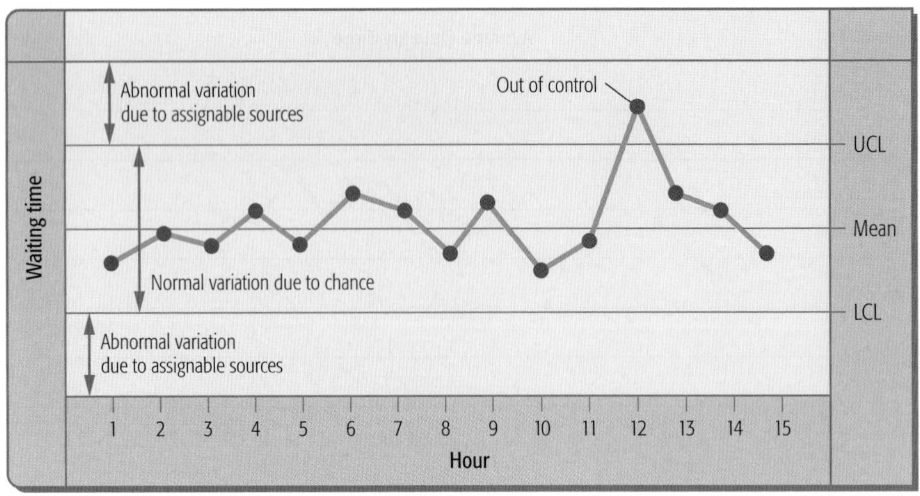

FIGURE 11.14 Statistical Process Control Chart

data points that fall between the two control limits are the result of random variations present in the process. However, if a data point falls outside the control limit, maybe the result of an assignable or special-cause variation, the process is said to appear to be *out of control*. Hour 12 in Figure 11.14 is outside the control limits and represents a situation where the operator or owner of the process would investigate and look for an assignable/special cause. If the operator finds an assignable cause such as a broken or improperly set machine, this would be corrected. However, the operator might investigate and find no special/assignable cause. The sample in this case would be a random variation, in which case a type 1, alpha, or false positive error has occurred. The construction of an SPC chart and its interpretation can be easily applied to a wide range of industries.

When constructing an SPC chart, we need to remember that any analysis conducted using a sample of data always has the potential of making *Type I* and *Type II* errors. The two errors are opposite to each other; therefore, setting the control limits (UCL and LCL) far from the mean will reduce Type I errors but potentially increase Type II errors. If the control limits are set too close to the mean, the probability of Type II errors decreases, but there will be a much higher probability of Type I errors.

Historically, the upper and lower control limits have been set at three standard deviations from the mean value, which represents a good balance between the two types of potential errors. Mathematically, the calculation of UCL and LCL can be represented as

$$\text{UCL} = \text{Mean} + 3 * \text{Standard Deviation} \qquad \text{(Equation 4)}$$

$$\text{LCL} = \text{Mean} - 3 * \text{Standard Deviation} \qquad \text{(Equation 5)}$$

The Central Limit Theorem

● **Central limit theorem** a theorem stating that the shape of the distribution of averages for samples follows a normal distribution even if the original distribution was very different

The theoretical foundation for developing control charts comes from the **central limit theorem** in statistics. In simple terms, this theorem states that the shape of the distribution of averages for samples follows a normal distribution even if the original distribution was very different. For example, an organization might not know the shape of the distribution of waiting times for customers calling its telephone service center. However, if several customers are sampled every hour, and their average waiting times are calculated and plotted, then the plot will resemble a normal distribution. Furthermore, as the sample size increases, the distribution of averages becomes closer to the normal distribution. An example of the central limit theorem is shown in Figure 11.15.

Control Chart for Variables

Many process data are measured on a continuous scale. Examples include waiting time, the weight of each cereal box, the fuel efficiency of an automobile measured in miles per gallon, and other such data. In SPC terminology, this type of data is known as **variable data**. The most commonly used SPC charts for variables are the **$\bar{x}$ chart** and the *R chart*. The $\bar{x}$ and *R* charts are used in combination because they track two different properties of a variable.

- **Variable data** process data measured on a continuous scale
- **$\bar{x}$ chart** a chart that shows how the process average changes over time

The $\bar{x}$ chart shows how the averages of a process change over time. For example, this type of chart can be used to track the changes in average customer waiting time when calling a telephone service center. It is used to track whether the long-term average of a process is changing over time because of special-cause variations.

The ***R* chart** (or range chart) is used to track the *range of variations* present within each sample of data collected. For example, it can be used to track the difference between the longest and shortest wait times observed every hour in a telephone service center.

- ***R* chart** a chart that shows how the range of variations within a process change over time

Control Chart for Attributes

Sometimes the characteristic of a process can best be measured by **attribute data** An attribute can be counted in different categories but cannot be measured on a continuous scale. For example, the organization might be interested in keeping track of the percentage of customers who call the telephone service center who are dissatisfied (instead of waiting time, which is measured as a continuous variable). Therefore, each customer will first have to be counted in either the satisfied or the dissatisfied category before an SPC chart can be developed. The primary reason companies employ attribute charts is that data collection is fairly easy because the data is in two catagories (bivariate). In other words, all that needs to be recorded is a simple yes or no: Is the customer satisified? Is the cellphone power on? Does the car stop? The disadvantage of attribute data is that it sacrifices the specific detail that variable data offers. For example,

- **Attribute data** the type of process data that cannot be measured on a continuous scale; the data are instead counted

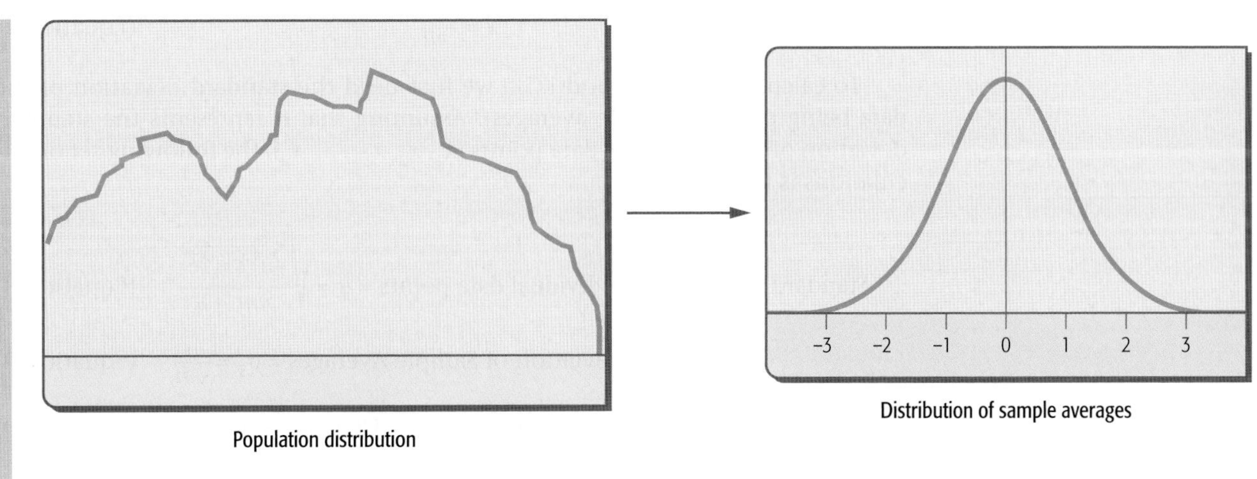

FIGURE 11.15 Central Limit Theorem

measuring how quickly (in feet or meters) a car stops provides much more precise data than simply observing whether it stops, but collecting this data takes more effort.

● ***p* chart** a chart that tracks the changes in percentages of a specified attribute over a period of time

The most commonly used SPC chart for attributes is known as a ***p* chart**. The *p* chart tracks the changes in percentages of a specified attribute over a period of time.

While many other special types of SPC charts are used for specific applications, we will discuss only the $\bar{x}$, *R*, and *p* charts in this chapter.

Constructing SPC Charts

The construction of a statistical process control chart begins with the identification of a variable or attribute of interest and the selection of appropriate control charts ($\bar{x}$ and *R* charts or a *p* chart, for example). Next, the appropriate sample size is selected to balance the probability of Type I and Type II errors with respect to the cost and effort associated with collecting the sample data. The sampling time frame (days, hours, minutes, or some other measure) is decided, and data are collected. Next, the UCL and LCL are calculated, and the data are plotted.

$\bar{x}$ Chart Let's assume that n represents the sample size and $x_1, x_2, x_3, \ldots, x_n$ represent the individual data collected within each sample. Let's also assume that m represents the number of times the sample data were collected (for example, if a telephone service center sampled 5 customers every hour for 20 hours to create a control chart for the waiting time, then $n = 5$ and $m = 20$).

We do not know the distribution of individual data points $(x_1, x_2, x_3, \ldots, x_n)$. However, we do know that the sample averages are normally distributed because of the central limit theorem. Therefore, the next step is to calculate sample averages for every time period:

$$\bar{x} = \frac{\sum_{i=1}^{n} x_i}{n} \qquad \text{(Equation 6)}$$

This calculation is repeated for every data collection time period (m times).

To calculate the upper and lower control limits for control charts, we need the mean and standard deviation of the data to be plotted. Because we're plotting sample averages ($\bar{x}$), the mean is the average of the sample averages.

$$\bar{\bar{x}} = \frac{\sum_{i=1}^{m} \bar{x}_i}{m} \qquad \text{(Equation 7)}$$

To calculate the UCL and LCL, we first need the standard deviation of the data being plotted (sample averages). Assuming that σ represents the standard deviation of the individual data points $(x_1, x_2, x_3, \ldots, x_n)$, the following set of calculations is needed:

$$\text{Standard deviation of individual data points} = \sigma = \sqrt{\frac{\sum_{i}^{nm}(xi - \bar{\bar{x}})^2}{nm - 1}} \qquad \text{(Equation 8)}$$

$$\text{Standard Deviation of Sample Averages} = \sigma_{\bar{x}} = \frac{\sigma}{\sqrt{n}} \qquad \text{(Equation 9)}$$

$$\text{Upper Control Limit (UCL)} = \text{UCL}_{\bar{x}} = \bar{\bar{x}} + 3 * \sigma_{\bar{x}} \qquad \text{(Equation 10)}$$

$$\text{Lower Control Limit (LCL)} = \text{LCL}_{\bar{x}} = \bar{\bar{x}} - 3 * \sigma_{\bar{x}} \qquad \text{(Equation 11)}$$

Solved Example 8
Constructing an $\bar{x}$ Chart

Table 11.3 shows the waiting time (in seconds) for a random sample of 5 customers calling a telephone service center during each hour. The sample data were collected for 10 hours. Construct an $\bar{x}$ chart.

SOLUTION

$$\text{Sample Size } (n) = 5$$

$$\text{Number of Samples } (m) = 10$$

Calculation of sample averages:

$$\text{Sample average for 8:00 a.m.} = \bar{x}_{8\text{ a.m.}} = \frac{45 + 60 + 55 + 49 + 63}{5} = 54.4$$

Similarly, sample averages for the other nine time periods can be calculated as

$\bar{x}_{9\text{ a.m.}} = 40.0$ $\bar{x}_{10\text{ a.m.}} = 46.0$ $\bar{x}_{11\text{ a.m.}} = 40.8$

$\bar{x}_{12\text{ p.m.}} = 41.8$ $\bar{x}_{1\text{ p.m.}} = 28.2$ $\bar{x}_{2\text{ p.m.}} = 33.6$

$\bar{x}_{3\text{ p.m.}} = 43.0$ $\bar{x}_{4\text{ p.m.}} = 35.6$ $\bar{x}_{5\text{ p.m.}} = 35.4$

Next, we can calculate the mean of the sample averages:

$$\bar{\bar{x}} = \frac{54.4 + 40 + 46 + 40 + \cdots + 35.4}{10} = 39.9$$

The standard deviation (σ) can be calculated by applying Equation 8 in the following manner:

$$\sigma = \sqrt{\frac{\sum(45 - 39.9)^2 + (60 - 39.9)^2 + \cdots + (40 - 39.9)^2}{5 * 10 - 1}} = 12.04$$

Note: While the calculation for standard deviation looks complicated, it can be done easily using a spreadsheet program such as Microsoft Excel. An example of this can be found on this textbook's web site.

@

Next we can calculate the standard deviation of sample averages ($\sigma_{\bar{x}}$), UCL, and LCL:

$$\sigma_{\bar{x}} = \frac{12.04}{\sqrt{5}} = 5.38$$

$$UCL_{\bar{x}} = 39.9 + 3 * 5.38 = 56.04$$

$$LCL_{\bar{x}} = 39.9 - 3 * 5.38 = 23.76$$

The resulting $\bar{x}$ chart is presented in Figure 11.16.

R Chart or Range Chart Like an $\bar{x}$ chart, an R chart requires calculating the data to be plotted (i.e., the ranges), including the overall mean of the data plotted (i.e., the average range), the UCL, and the LCL.

The range for each sample is calculated in the following manner:

$$R = \max(x_1, x_2, \ldots, x_n) - \min(x_1, x_2, \ldots, x_n) \quad \text{(Equation 12)}$$

TABLE 11.3 Waiting Time Samples

Sample #	Hour	Observation 1	Observation 2	Observation 3	Observation 4	Observation 5
1	8:00 a.m.	45	60	55	49	63
2	9:00 a.m.	31	37	44	37	51
3	10:00 a.m.	43	47	56	41	43
4	11:00 a.m.	37	61	31	28	47
5	12:00 p.m.	65	52	28	27	37
6	1:00 p.m.	29	20	27	34	31
7	2:00 p.m.	15	36	52	38	27
8	3:00 p.m.	62	40	45	39	29
9	4:00 p.m.	55	29	36	27	31
10	5:00 p.m.	42	37	39	19	40

This calculation is repeated *m* times (for each time period in which sample data are collected). Next, we calculate the average of all ranges (similar to calculating the averages of all $\overline{x}$).

$$\overline{R} = \frac{\sum_{i=1}^{m} R_i}{m} \qquad \text{(Equation 13)}$$

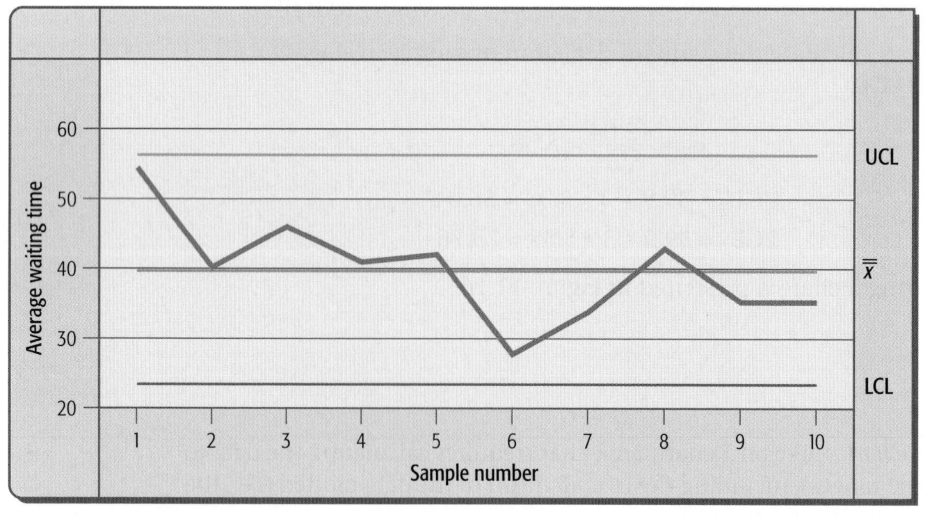

FIGURE 11.16 $\overline{x}$ Chart

This chart shows that the process *appears* to be in control. However, it is still possible that there is actually a quality problem and the samples chosen happened to still be within limits. This would be an example of a type 2 or beta error.

The equation used to calculate the standard deviation of ranges is quite complex; therefore, a simple table is used instead to calculate UCL and LCL directly in the following manner:

$$UCL_R = D_4\overline{R} \qquad \text{(Equation 14)}$$

$$LCL_R = D_3\overline{R} \qquad \text{(Equation 15)}$$

The parameters D_3 and D_4, equivalent to three-standard-deviation control limits, are provided in Table 11.4.

TABLE 11.4 Parameters for Computing Control Limits for *R* Charts

Sample Size	D_3	D_4
2	0	3.268
3	0	2.574
4	0	2.282
5	0	2.115
6	0	2.004
7	0.076	1.924
8	0.136	1.864
9	0.184	1.816
10	0.223	1.777

Source: *Quality Control of Materials* (Philadelphia: American Society for Testing Materials, 1951).

Solved Example 9
Constructing an *R* Chart

Construct an *R* chart for the data provided in Solved Example 8.

SOLUTION

First we need to calculate the range for each data collection period:

$$R_{8\text{ a.m.}} = \max(45, 60, 55, 49, 63) - \min(45, 60, 55, 49, 63) = 63 - 45 = 18$$

Similarly, we can find the ranges for the other time periods in the following manner:

$R_{9\text{ a.m.}} = 20$	$R_{10\text{ a.m.}} = 15$	$R_{11\text{ a.m.}} = 33$
$R_{12\text{ p.m.}} = 38$	$R_{1\text{ p.m.}} = 14$	$R_{2\text{ p.m.}} = 37$
$R_{3\text{ p.m.}} = 33$	$R_{4\text{ p.m.}} = 28$	$R_{5\text{ p.m.}} = 23$

Next, we calculate the average range using equation 13:

$$\overline{R} = \frac{18 + 20 + 15 + \cdots + 23}{10} = 25.9$$

(*continued*)

Next, D_3 and D_4 from Table 11.4 are needed to calculate the UCL and LCL. Because the sample size is 5,

$$D_3 = 0 \text{ (from Table 11.4, second column, fifth row)}$$

$$D_4 = 2.115 \text{ (from Table 11.4, third column, fifth row)}$$

$$\text{LCL} = 0 * 25.9 = 0$$

$$\text{UCL} = 2.115 * 25.9 = 54.78$$

The resulting R chart is presented in Figure 11.17.

Usually the R and $\bar{x}$ charts are interpreted together. This is done because it is possible to have a sample with one very high observation and one very low observation—for example, a customer who waits for 200 seconds paired with four customers who wait for zero seconds. The average for this sample would be 40 seconds, but the range would be 200. The high value for R would lead us to look for an assignable cause based on the R chart. This is an example of not letting one observation cancel out another—in other words, two wrongs do not make a right.

p Chart In constructing a p chart, first data are collected for various categories for the attribute of interest (e.g., the number of dissatisfied customers). Next, the data are converted into fractional form for each time period (e.g., the fraction of dissatisfied customers every day). As with $\bar{x}$ and R charts, plotting p charts also requires first calculating the overall average mean, standard deviation, and upper and lower control limits.

If p represents the fraction, the data were collected for m time periods, and the sample size was n, then

$$\text{Average fraction} = \bar{p} = \frac{\sum_{i=1}^{m} p_i}{m} \qquad \text{(Equation 16)}$$

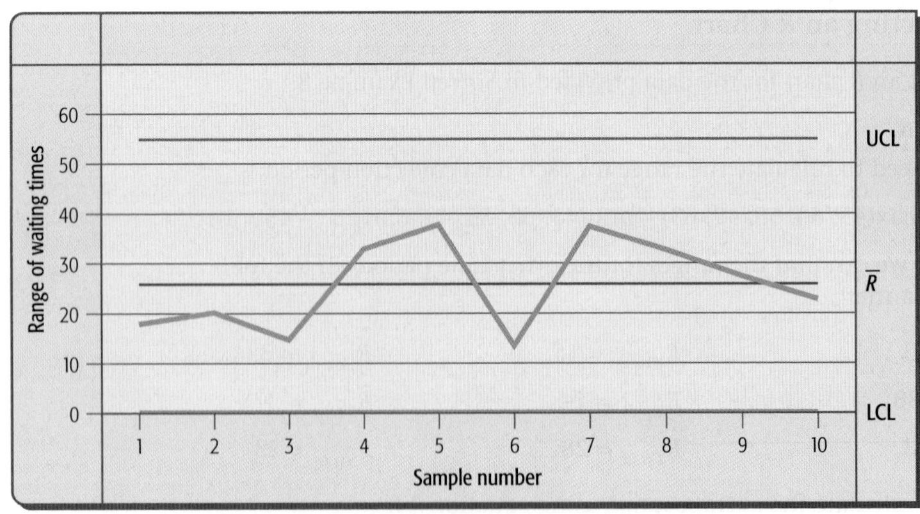

FIGURE 11.17 *R* Chart

The *R* chart indicates that the process *appears* to be in control. At the same time, it is also possible that this could be a type 2 or beta error.

$$\text{Standard Deviation for Average Fraction} = \sigma_{\bar{p}} = \sqrt{\frac{\bar{p} * (1 - \bar{p})}{n}} \quad \text{(Equation 17)}$$

$$\text{Upper Control Limit} = UCL_p = \bar{p} + z * \sigma_{\bar{p}} \quad \text{(Equation 18)}$$

$$\text{Lower Control Limit} = LCL_p = \bar{p} - z * \sigma_{\bar{p}} \quad \text{(Equation 19)}$$

The parameter z in equations 18 and 19 represents the standard normal distribution. A value of 3 is commonly used for z, which represents the 99.7% area within the normal distribution curve.

Solved Example 10

Constructing a *p* Chart

Samples of 25 customers were randomly selected every day to assess customer satisfaction with a telephone customer service center. The customers who complained about the service were classified as "dissatisfied." Table 11.5 shows the numbers of satisfied and dissatisfied customers and the fraction of dissatisfied customers for the last 12 days. Based on this information, construct a *p* chart.

TABLE 11.5 Data for *p* Chart

Sample #	Sample Size	Number of Satisfied Customers	Number of Dissatisfied Customers	Fraction of Dissatisfied Customers
1	25	24	1	0.04
2	25	23	2	0.08
3	25	25	0	0.00
4	25	22	3	0.12
5	25	24	1	0.04
6	25	25	0	0.00
7	25	21	4	0.16
8	25	24	1	0.04
9	25	20	5	0.20
10	25	25	0	0.00
11	25	23	2	0.08
12	25	22	3	0.12

SOLUTION

Sample Size (n) = 25

Number of Samples (m) = 12

(*continued*)

$$\text{Average Fraction} = \bar{p} = \frac{0.04 + 0.08 + \cdots + 0.12}{12} = 0.07$$

$$\text{Standard Deviation} = \sigma_{\bar{p}} = \sqrt{\frac{0.07 * (1 - 0.07)}{25}} = 0.051$$

$$\text{Upper Control Limit} = UCL_p = 0.07 + 3 * 0.051 = 0.223$$

$$\text{Lower Control Limit} = LCL_p = 0.07 - 3 * 0.051 = -0.083$$

Because the fraction of dissatisfied customers cannot be lower than zero, the LCL is adjusted to 0.0.

The resulting p chart is presented in Figure 11.18.

● **Out-of-control process** a process in which one or more points in an SPC chart fall outside the control limits; out-of-control patterns can also be identified when process data exhibit certain specific trends even when all points fall within the control limits

Out-of-Control Process The purpose of an SPC chart is to determine whether *natural* or *special-cause* variations are present in the observed process. If one of the plotted data points falls outside the established control limits (either UCL or LCL), the process contains special-cause variations. Such a process is called an **out-of-control process.** In practice, several additional rules can be used for early detection of out-of-control patterns. Some of the commonly used rules are listed in Table 11.6.

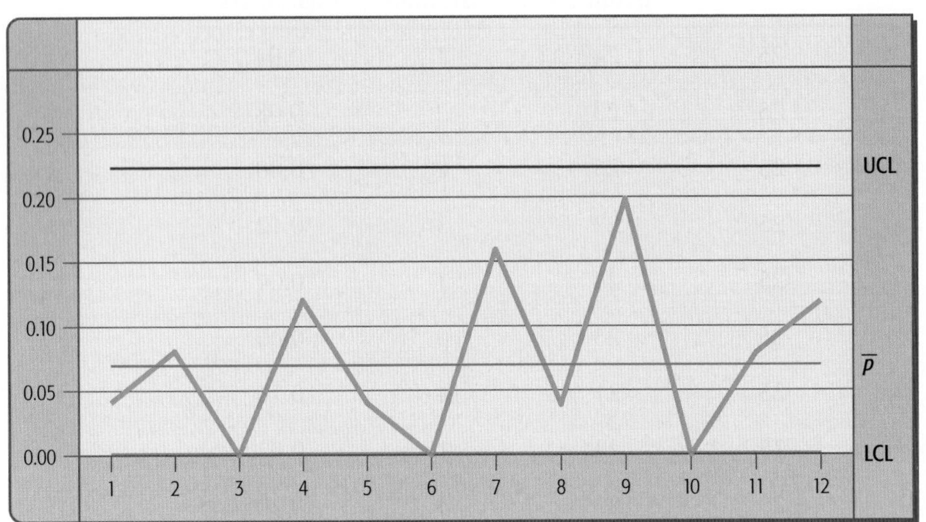

FIGURE 11.18 ***p* Chart**

This chart indicates that the process appears to be in control. Thus, we would let it operate normally without looking for a special/assignable cause. As always, it is important to remember that this could be a type 2 or beta error.

TABLE 11.6 Some Commonly Used Out-of-Control Rules

- A single point outside the control limits
- Two out of three successive points on the same side of the center line and farther than 2 standard deviations from the overall mean
- Four out of five successive points on the same side of the center line and farther than 1 standard deviation from the overall mean
- A run of nine data points in a row that are on the same side of the center line
- Six (or more) points in a row that are continually increasing (or decreasing)
- Fourteen (or more) points in a row that alternate in direction, increasing then decreasing
- Fifteen points in a row that are all within 1 standard deviation of the mean on either side of the mean
- Eight points in a row where none is within 1 standard deviation of the mean and the points are in both directions from the mean
- Obvious consistent or persistent patterns that suggest that there is something unusual about the data

SUMMARY

1. Describe three sources for quality improvement ideas: customer feedback, benchmarking, and employee feedback.

- Identifying the root causes of quality problems begins by collecting feedback from many different sources, such as customers and employees, and by benchmarking other organizations.
- Ideas for quality improvement from customers can be collected in a variety of formats and from a variety of sources, such as customer satisfaction surveys, customer choice analysis, and blogs.
- Benchmarking is used for comparing the business practices of an organization to the best practices that can be identified in other organizations (partner firms, competitors, or suppliers) or other divisions within a company.
- Feedback from employees about quality improvement plans can be compiled in many different ways. Some companies use a regular and formal system of collecting feedback from their employees, whereas others use informal and ad hoc approaches. One approach that is used extensively in Japanese companies is known as quality circles. A quality circle is made up of a small group of employees who are responsible for similar or related work functions.

2. Describe qualitative quality improvement tools, including brainstorming, affinity diagrams, interrelationship diagrams, tree diagrams, process decision program charts, flowcharts, cause-and-effect diagrams, failure modes and effects analysis, and mistake-proofing.

- Companies use a variety of qualitative quality improvement techniques in combination with one another, and there is no specific order in which they should be implemented. The specific needs of the organization determine which techniques are most appropriate for analyzing a given quality problem or improvement idea.
- Brainstorming is a systematic method for generating a large number of creative problem-solving ideas in a relatively short amount of time based on input from many different individuals.
- The affinity diagram is used as a visual tool for organizing the ideas generated during brainstorming into natural groups based on the collective wisdom of the participants.
- Often used in combination with brainstorming and affinity diagrams, an interrelationship diagram is used to show the connections and natural relationships among different ideas or constructs identified for quality improvement.
- A tree diagram is used to describe how one idea branches into two or more subideas, each of which branches into further subideas, and so on.
- The process decision program chart is used to systematically identify initiatives that might potentially go wrong in a quality improvement plan that is under consideration.
- A flowchart is used to visually represent the separate steps of a process in a sequential manner.
- A cause-and-effect diagram is used to illustrate the potential reasons for a quality problem.
- Failure modes and effects analysis (FMEA) is a systematic approach for identifying all possible failures in a design, a manufacturing process, or a service process.
- Mistake-proofing or poka-yoke refers to the use of any automatic device or method that either makes it impossible for an error to occur or makes the error immediately obvious once it has occurred.

3. Describe quantitative quality improvement tools, including inspection and sampling, check sheets, Pareto analysis, histograms, scatter diagrams, process capability analysis, run charts, and statistical process control charts.

- Implementing a successful quality improvement program requires systematic data sampling, data collection, and analysis.
- Because sample data are used to assess the quality of a larger population, the possibility of Type I and Type II errors exists and should not be ignored during analysis.
- The process capability index can be used to assess how well a process meets established standards.
- Statistical process control charts are used to assess whether the variations present in a process are natural or special-cause variations.
- $\bar{x}$ and R charts are commonly used in combination for process data that are measured on a continuous scale.
- p charts are commonly used for data that are counted in categories or for attributes.

SOLVED PROBLEM 1

Table 11.7 shows the actual temperature (in degrees Fahrenheit) of 6 cups of coffee bought from a gourmet coffee shop on each of the last 10 days. Plot $\bar{x}$ and R charts and find out if the process is in control. Federal health regulations require that coffee temperatures be between 160 and 180 degrees Fahrenheit. Based on these standards, calculate process capabilities indices. Briefly explain the results.

TABLE 11.7 Data for Constructing $\bar{x}$ and R charts

Day	Cup 1	Cup 2	Cup 3	Cup 4	Cup 5	Cup 6
1	160	173	171	159	164	171
2	165	156	167	165	159	168
3	169	162	168	157	173	173
4	155	164	168	155	159	159
5	159	165	169	162	169	174
6	163	166	167	165	164	173
7	155	167	162	163	166	169
8	172	163	166	168	172	168
9	174	165	169	167	180	172
10	171	162	169	164	179	172

SOLUTION

Constructing $\bar{x}$ and R charts:

Sample Size (n) = 6
Number of Samples (m) = 10

PART II Tools and Tactical Issues

Equations 6 and 12 can be used to calculate $\bar{x}$ and R for every day. Next, we can use Equations 7 and 13 to calculate $\bar{\bar{x}}$ and $\bar{R}$. The results are presented in Table 11.8.

TABLE 11.8 Calculation of $\bar{x}$ and R

Sample	$\bar{x}$	R
1	166.33	14
2	163.33	12
3	167.00	16
4	160.00	13
5	166.33	15
6	166.33	10
7	163.67	14
8	168.17	9
9	171.17	15
10	169.50	17
	$\bar{\bar{x}}$	$\bar{R}$
	166.18	13.50

Next, we can use Equations 8 and 9 to calculate σ and $\sigma_{\bar{x}}$:

$$\sigma = 5.71$$
$$\sigma_{\bar{x}} = 2.33$$

Equations 10 and 11 can be used to calculate UCL and LCL for the $\bar{x}$ chart:

$$UCL_{\bar{x}} = 166.18 + 3 * 2.33 = 173.17$$
$$LCL_{\bar{x}} = 166.18 - 3 * 2.33 = 159.19$$

Equations 14 and 15 and Table 11.4 are used to calculate UCL and LCL for the R chart. Because the sample size (n) is 6, D_3 and D_4 are found to be 0.0 and 2.004 from Table 11.4:

$$UCL_R = 2.004 * 13.5 = 27.054$$
$$LCL_R = 0 * 13.5 = 0$$

Based on these calculations, the $\bar{x}$ and R charts are plotted in Figure 11.19.

Both the $\bar{x}$ and the R charts show that all the data points are well within the control limits. Therefore, we conclude that the process is in control and that only natural random variations are present.

Process capability analysis: First we need to identify the upper and lower tolerance limits. The federal health standards must be met and therefore should be used as the upper and lower tolerance limits.

Upper Tolerance Limit (UTL) = 180
Lower Tolerance Limit (LTL) = 160

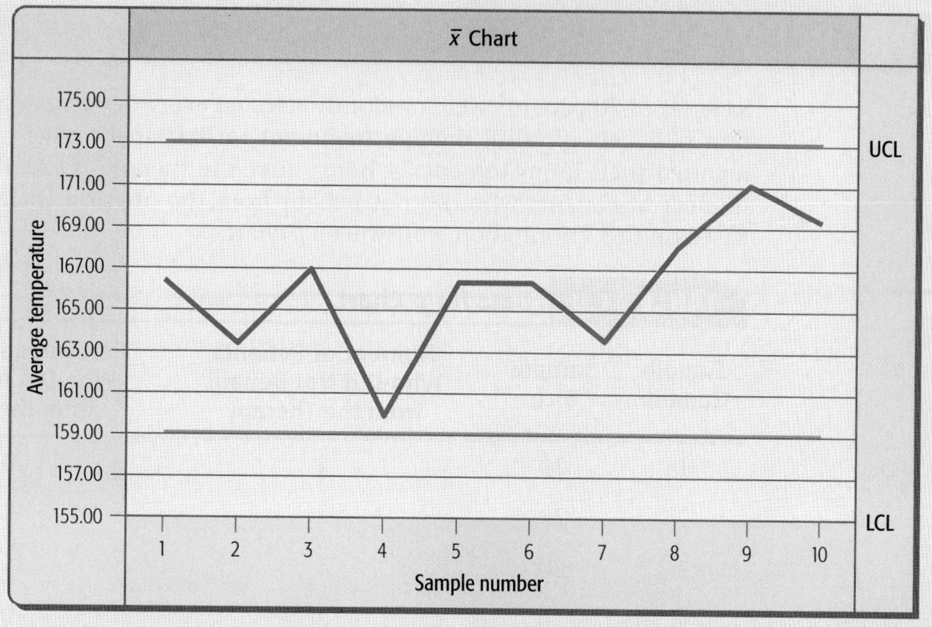

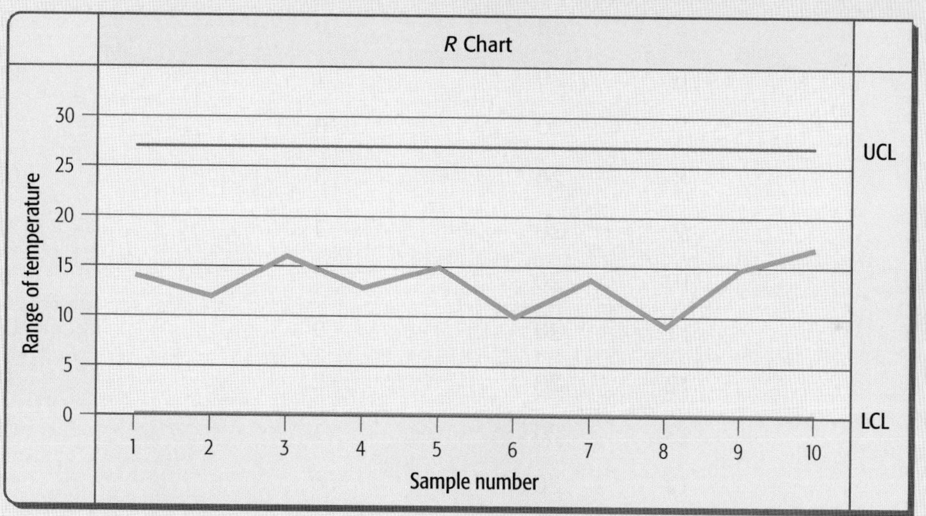

FIGURE 11.19 $\bar{x}$ **and *R* charts**

Next, we need to calculate the mean and standard deviation of the data provided. We have already calculated these two numbers when we plotted the $\bar{x}$ and *R* charts.

$$\text{Mean Temperature } (\bar{\bar{x}}) = 166.18$$
$$\text{Standard Deviation } (\sigma) = 5.71$$

We can calculate C_{pk_LTL}, C_{pk_UTL}, and C_{pk} using Equations 1, 2, and 3.

$$C_{pk\_LTL} = \frac{180 - 166.18}{3 * 5.71} = 0.808$$

$$C_{pk\_UTL} = \frac{166.18 - 160}{3 * 5.71} = 0.361$$

$$C_{pk} = \min(C_{pk\_LTL} \text{ and } C_{pk\_UTL}) = 0.361$$

Because the process capability index is significantly lower than 1.0, we can conclude that the process does a very poor job of meeting federal health standards.

SOLVED PROBLEM 2

Samples of 20 patients were randomly selected every day to assess the effectiveness of a new physical therapy treatment for back-pain relief. The customers reported their improvement 24 hours after the therapy. Table 11.9 shows the number of patients who did not benefit from the physical therapy treatment. Based on this information, construct a p chart.

TABLE 11.9 Data for *p* Chart

Sample Number	Sample Size	Number of Patients Who Did Not Benefit from the Therapy	Percentage of Patients Who Did Not Benefit from the Therapy
1	20	4	0.2
2	20	3	0.15
3	20	5	0.25
4	20	2	0.1
5	20	6	0.3
6	20	1	0.05
7	20	0	0
8	20	3	0.15
9	20	4	0.2
10	20	2	0.1
11	20	9	0.45
12	20	2	0.1
13	20	1	0.05
14	20	0	0
15	20	3	0.15

SOLUTION

$$\text{Sample Size } (n) = 20$$

$$\text{Number of Samples } (m) = 15$$

$$\text{Average Fraction} = \bar{p} = \frac{0.2 + 0.15 + \cdots + 0.15}{15} = 0.15$$

$$\text{Standard Deviation} = \sigma_{\bar{p}} = \sqrt{\frac{0.15 * (1 - 0.15)}{20}} = 0.08$$

$$\text{Upper Control Limit} = \text{UCL}_p = 0.15 + 3 * 0.08 = 0.39$$

$$\text{Lower Control Limit} = \text{LCL}_p = 0.15 - 3 * 0.08 = -0.09$$

Because the fraction of patients cannot be lower than zero, the LCL is adjusted to 0.0.

The resulting p chart is presented in Figure 11.20. Because one point falls outside the upper control limit, we can conclude that the process is out of control.

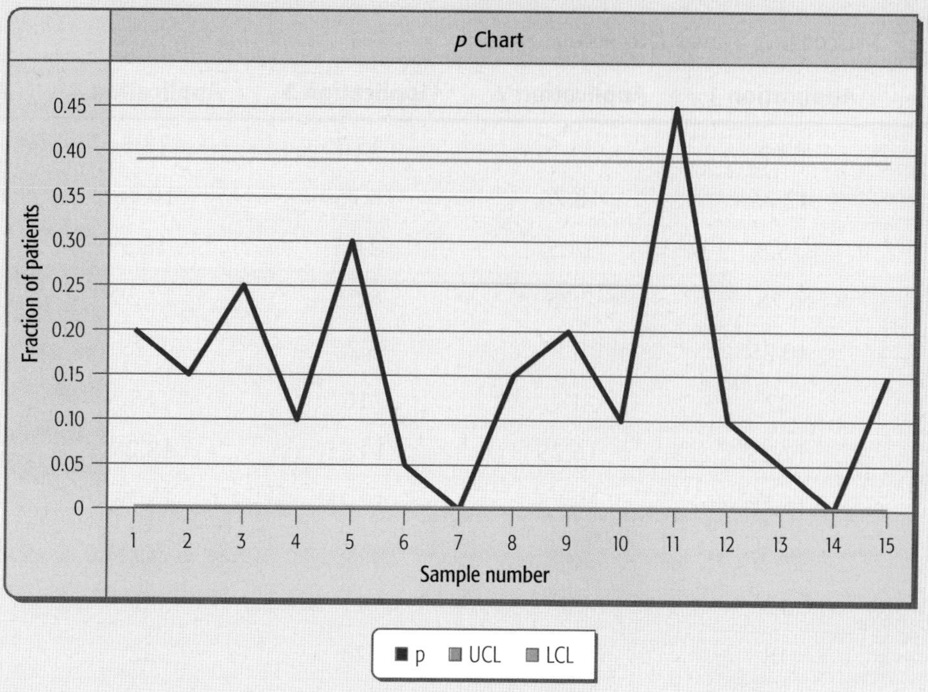

FIGURE 11.20 ***p* Chart**

PROBLEMS

1. The Ultra-Cool Ice Cream Company wants to ensure that all its products are prepared with precision to produce a consistent taste. Periodically, a sample of ice cream is removed from the processing area and tested for fat content. The company would like to have the fat content be between 35 and 40 percent of the total weight.

   Based on data collected for the last several days, the company found that the average fat content for its ice cream is 36 percent with a standard deviation of 2.5.

   Based on the information provided, calculate the current process capability index.

2. Table 11.10 shows the processing times (in hours) for samples of five home mortgage applications submitted at a financial services company each day for the last 15 days. The company guarantees to its customers that it will process all applications within a 24-hour time period. Based on these standards, calculate process capability indices. Also plot $\bar{x}$ and R charts and find out if the process is in control. Briefly explain the results.

3. To ensure the quality of microprocessor chips manufactured by Sigma Electronics, the quality control department samples 100 chips produced each day. These chips are subjected to extreme operating conditions for several hours. At the end of the test, the numbers of failed chips are reported. Table 11.11 shows the results for the last 20 test runs. Plot a p chart and report if the production process is in control.

TABLE 11.10 Processing Times (Hours)

Day	Application 1	Application 2	Application 3	Application 4	Application 5
1	14.5	11.5	15.5	13.5	9.5
2	12.75	12.75	8.75	10.75	13.75
3	15.5	17.5	21.5	18.5	14.5
4	6.25	7.25	8.25	12.25	9.25
5	10.25	10.25	6.25	9.25	12.25
6	22	18	16	15	16
7	17.25	16.25	14.25	18.25	17.25
8	15.75	12.75	12.75	15.75	12.75
9	9.5	7.5	3.5	2.5	0.5
10	12	9	11	8	12
11	18	21	23	22	19
12	11.5	11.5	10.5	9.5	13.5
13	22	23	19	18	15
14	21.75	24.75	24.75	26.75	29.75
15	12	9	10	11	10

TABLE 11.11 Number of Failed Microprocessor Chips

Sample Number	Number of Failed Microprocessor Chips
1	3
2	0
3	2
4	1
5	4
6	9
7	2
8	5
9	4
10	6
11	0
12	3
13	5
14	2
15	4

CASE STUDY

Southtown Medical Center

Dave Cash is the new CFO at Southtown Medical Center (SMC). Southtown provides dermatology services to an average of 90 patients each day. Dave's approach to management includes spending a day with each staff member in his department to understand that person's duties. After two days with the two billing clerks, he realized that nearly 50 percent of their typical day is consumed by reworking payment denials from insurance companies resulting from billing errors and resubmitting the charges to the insurance company. The rest of their day is spent handling patient telephone calls regarding their accounts. Dave noted that a large number of patient calls are from irate customers asking for an explanation of why the services provided by SMC were denied by their insurance payer. The remaining patient calls are requests for balances due or for explanations of outstanding charges on their accounts. Dave is quickly coming to the conclusion that thousands of dollars in insurance payments are being denied or delayed each week because of erroneous bills. He believes that in some cases, the insurance payment is never recovered, and either the patient or SMC is stuck with the bill. He is also very unhappy that a significant amount of his staff time is consumed with reworking billing errors. Something has to be done about this situation, and he is determined to investigate and find a remedy.

Federal laws require that "clean," or correct, electronically submitted bills be processed by the insurance company within 10 working days. Whether the bill is paid in full, partially paid, or denied, the reason for the action is stated on the explanation of benefits (EOB) from the insurance company. EOBs are mailed to both the patient and the provider of services, in this case, SMC.

Dave begins asking questions of everyone involved in SMC's billing process. Figure 11.21 shows flowcharts of the billing process. When a patient checks in to see a physician, a form is generated with the patient's demographic and insurance information. This form, known as an evaluation form, is placed on top of the patient's medical chart. When the medical visit is completed, the physician notes the patient's diagnosis and any procedures that are performed. The nursing staff then assigns a four- or five-digit International Classification of Diseases (ICD) code to the diagnosis and a five-digit Current Procedural Terminology (CPT) code to the procedure(s) performed. ICD and CPT are universal coding systems used by service providers and payers to describe, in detail, the procedure performed and the diagnosis that necessitated the procedure. The CPT code determines the fee, and it may be modified and additional charges added for more extensive procedures. The ICD code must support the need for the procedure, or the bill will be denied by the payer. An incorrect or missing digit in either code can result in a lower payment or complete denial of the bill.

The evaluation form is then given to the receptionist, who enters the codes into the patient's account on the computer system. The computer system does not have the capability to check the accuracy of the codes; it simply accepts whatever is entered. Bills are electronically submitted overnight to the appropriate insurance carrier. The process appears to be fast, yet it is not very effective because of the lack of quality checks in the process. Dave knows that he needs to dig further to determine exactly where breakdowns occur in the system.

Next, Dave meets with some of the nursing staff to learn their process for assigning ICD and CPT codes. One of the nurses explains that the members of the nursing staff are not really trained to assign ICD and CPT codes; they receive only one hour of formal instruction at the beginning of every year when the new codes are issued. The rest of their coding training comes from the more senior nurses in the department. She also fills him in on a secret: The nurses resent having to do the coding and sometimes just assign any code to get the paperwork out of their hands. Dave is astounded. The most important source of SMC revenue is being handled by inadequately trained staff members who resent the responsibility.

Dave goes back to his office to mull over this situation and determine his next step. He knows that he cannot justify hiring coding specialists at an additional cost unless he can first prove the existence of the problem with facts and numbers. He will also have to prove that coding specialists are necessary to correct the problem. Dave knows from previous experience that coding specialists can increase revenue by 10 to 20 percent on an ongoing basis by optimizing reimbursement through correct application of coding rules. Dave decides to call in Karen Coder, a coding consultant he has worked with previously, to conduct an initial study. She starts by sampling 20 bills each day over a 20-day period and comparing the billing information to the information in the medical chart. Figure 11.22 (on page 445) shows the results of this study. The revelations from this study are startling, and Karen and Dave immediately develop a plan to study all of the bills over a 20-day period and determine the number of incorrect bills for each doctor's office. Table 11.12 (on page 446) shows the results of this study.

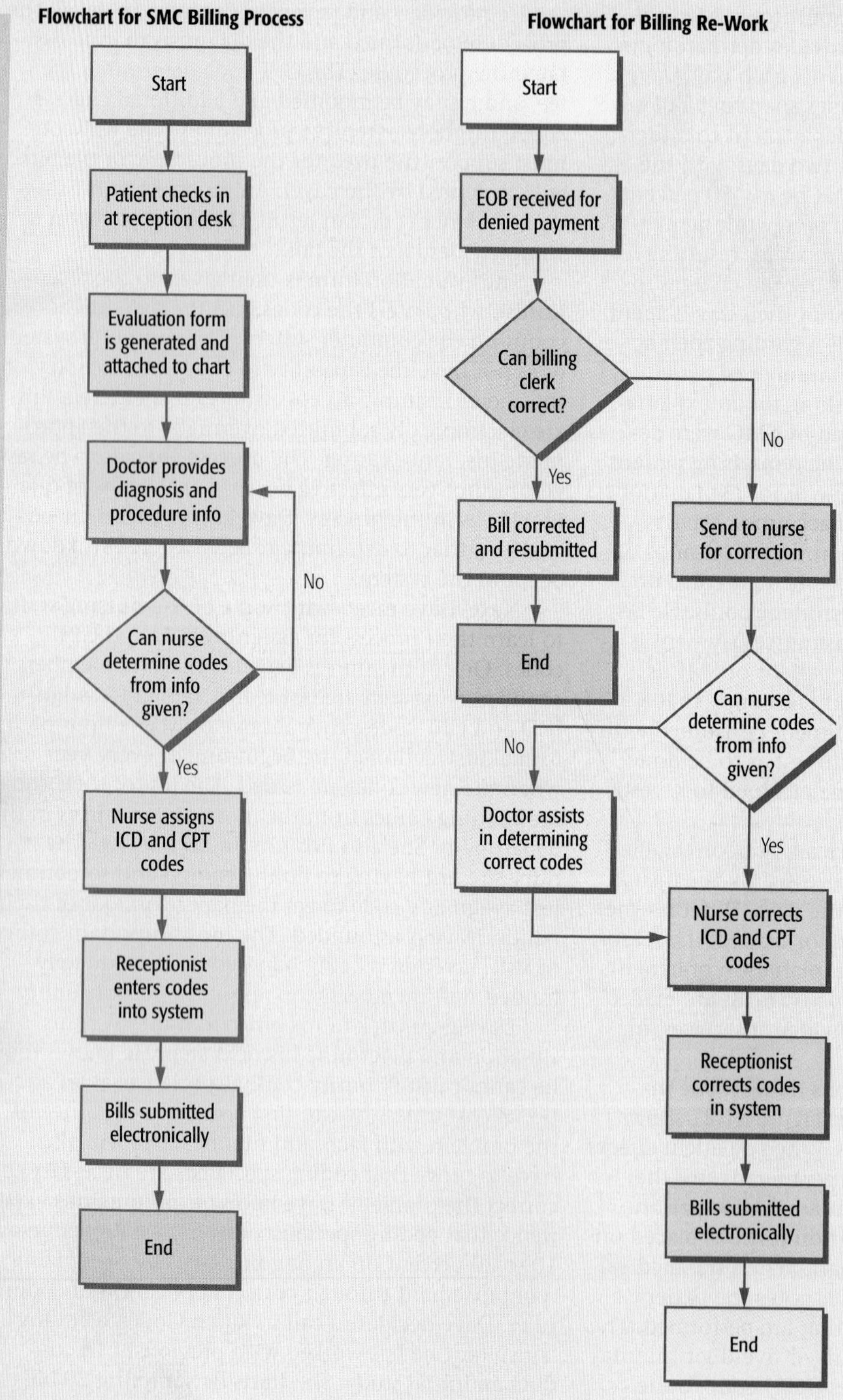

FIGURE 11.21

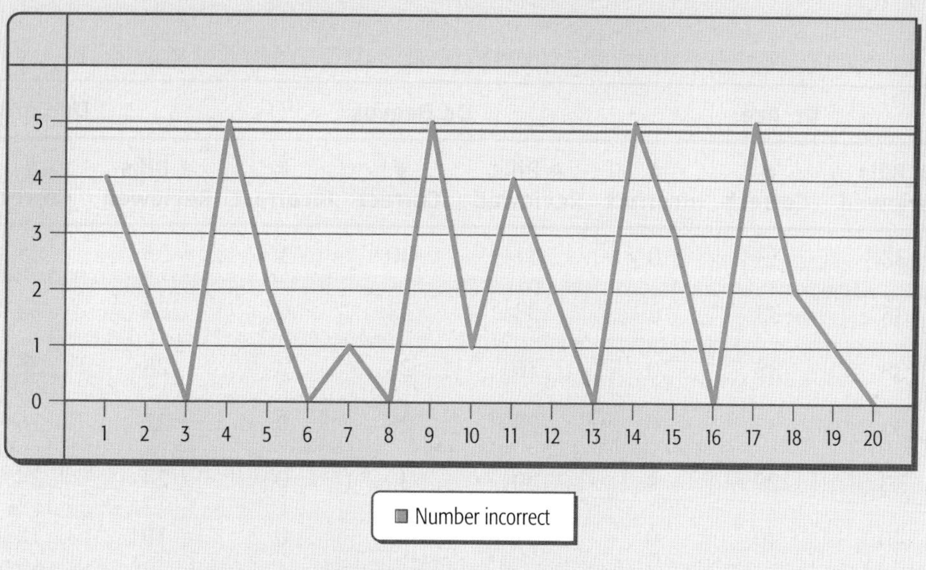

FIGURE 11.22

QUESTIONS

1. Analyze the data in Figure 11.22 and, using the appropriate control chart, determine whether the system is in control.
2. Using the data in Table 11.12, develop appropriate control charts to determine whether the coding process is under control for each doctor.
3. Suggest recommendations to reduce billing errors.

Table 11.12

	Dr. Ace			Dr. Beevus			Dr. Carry		
Day	**# Bills Reviewed**	**# Correct**	**# Incorrect**	**# Bills Reviewed**	**# Correct**	**# Incorrect**	**# Bills Reviewed**	**# Correct**	**# Incorrect**
1	33	33	0	31	30	1	25	25	0
2	35	33	2	33	33	0	24	24	0
3	38	38	0	30	28	2	28	26	2
4	35	35	0	28	28	0	22	16	6
5	33	29	4	30	30	0	24	24	0
6	40	40	0	31	31	0	19	12	7
7	37	37	0	29	28	1	24	20	4
8	41	39	2	30	29	1	23	17	6
9	34	34	0	32	30	2	23	19	4
10	32	31	1	30	29	1	25	25	0
11	36	36	0	28	28	0	24	24	0
12	35	35	0	30	30	0	16	10	6
13	40	38	2	24	24	0	26	21	5
14	38	38	0	33	32	1	25	25	0
15	36	36	0	34	33	1	24	24	0
16	38	38	0	30	30	0	26	26	0
17	34	32	2	29	28	1	24	18	6
18	35	35	0	28	28	0	28	28	0
19	36	35	1	30	30	0	25	25	0
20	34	34	0	30	29	1	25	23	2
Sum	720	706	14	600	588	12	480	432	48
Average	36	35.3	0.7	30	29.4	0.6	23.9	21.4	2.5
Error Rate			1.9			2.0			10.0

CHAPTER 12

Lean Enterprise

LEARNING OBJECTIVES

1. Describe the concepts of lean production and lean thinking.
2. Explain the different kinds of waste present in a production system.
3. Describe the components of a lean production system.
4. Discuss new advances related to lean thinking.

Lean thinking allows Toyota to quickly introduce high-quality cars.

Toyota and Lean Thinking

Toyota sold more than 2.3 million vehicles in the first three months of 2008. The growth of Toyota from an unknown manufacturer of cheap, low-quality automobiles to the world's largest producer is a fascinating and inspiring story of an innovative production system. While many factors have contributed to Toyota's success, the overarching reason for its phenomenal performance over the years has to do with a production philosophy known as the *Toyota Production System* or as *lean production.* Figures 12.1 and 12.2 show a schematic diagram and a simplified summary of the Toyota Production System, respectively. The following news report, adapted from BBC News, illustrates the uniqueness of the Toyota Production System.

On the assembly line at Toyota's giant plant, Laura Wilshire is not happy.

There is something wrong with a seatbelt fitting on the Camry she is working on. Laura pulls a cord which stops the production line. Her action prompts five fellow workers to crowd round. They soon see why the seatbelt is not screwed in properly and fix the problem. "I don't like to let something like that go," she says. "That's really important for people who buy our cars."

Workers at the Toyota plant in Georgetown, Kentucky, pull the cord 2,000 times a week—and their care is what makes Toyota one of the most reliable, and most desired, brands in the U.S. Pulling the cord (known as andan) is part of Toyota's "lean" production system, which means that it has been able to produce cars much more cheaply, and to a higher quality, than its U.S. rivals.

Toyota pioneered the "just-in-time" manufacturing system, in which suppliers send parts daily—or several times a day—and are notified electronically when the assembly line is running out. More than 400 trucks a day come in and out of Toyota's Georgetown plant, with a separate logistics company organizing the shipments from Toyota's

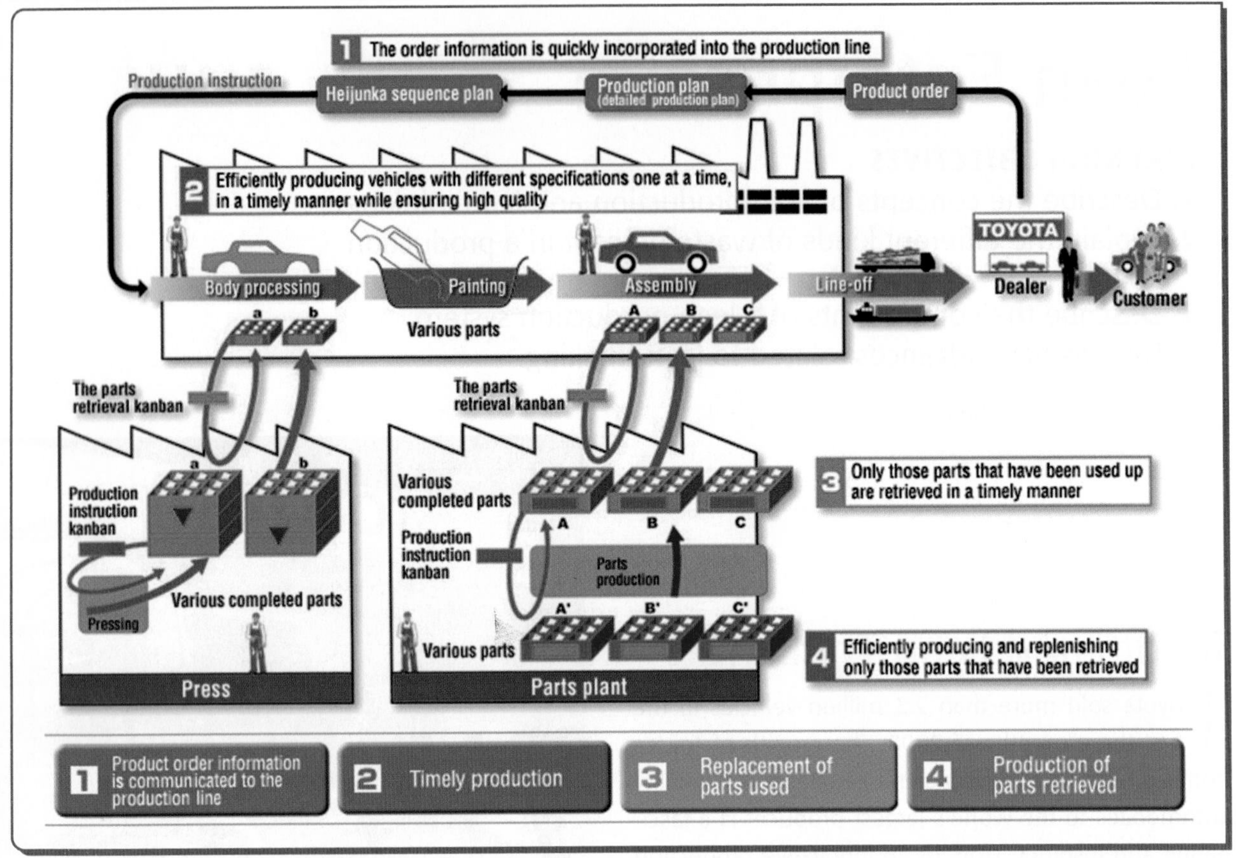

FIGURE 12.1 A Schematic Diagram of the Toyota Production System

Source (for this figure and Figure 12.5 on page 460):

300 suppliers—most located in neighboring states within half a day's drive of the plant. Toyota aims to build long-term relationships with its suppliers, many of whom it has taken a stake in, and says it now produces 80% of its parts within North America.

Toyota's North American president, Jim Press, says the key to their success is that they are customer-focused—and that requires quick reactions when consumer tastes change. "I think being nimble is really important. As the market grows and shifts so quickly, you have got to be able to respond and anticipate where things are going," he says.

Toyota can now develop a new model in 18 months, compared to the three years it takes GM. Toyota also has a close relationship with the dealers who sell its cars.

The production run is adjusted at the Georgetown plant, and extra Saturday working is added only when computerized orders from the dealer network show it is needed.

Toyota's president, Katsuaki Watanabe, recently said in a newspaper interview that he didn't care if Toyota became the biggest car company or not. "What is important is to be number one in quality."[1] ■

Adapted from Toyota's web site: http://www.toyota.co.jp/en/vision/production_system/just.html

[1] Source: BBC News Online, February 2007, http://news.bbc.co.uk/2/hi/business/6346315.stm. Copyright © 2008 BBC News Online. Adapted with permission.

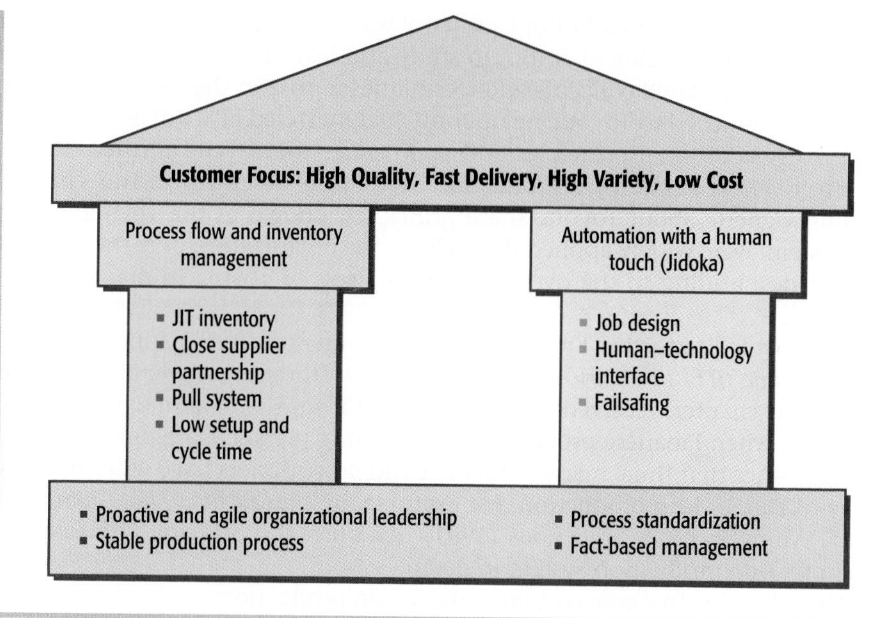

FIGURE 12.2 The House of Toyota Production System

LEAN PRODUCTION AND LEAN THINKING

This chapter provides an overview of an effective system for managing a business enterprise known as lean production. We will discuss the principle of lean production, the characteristics of a lean enterprise, and the tools and techniques for implementing the lean concepts in manufacturing and service organizations.

What Is Lean Production?

The concept of **lean production** is derived from the assembly line manufacturing methodology developed by Toyota to manufacture automobiles efficiently. The basic idea of the Toyota Production System (TPS) is to produce the kind of units needed, at the time needed, and in the quantities needed, so that unnecessary intermediate and finished product inventories can be eliminated. While definitions vary, the following definition represents the distillation of numerous scholarly sources "a sociotechnical production system whose main objective is to eliminate waste by concurrently reducing or minimizing supplier, customer, and internal variability."

● **Lean production** a sociotechnical production system whose main objective is to eliminate waste by concurrently reducing or minimizing supplier, customer, and internal variability

While the concepts of lean production were originally developed for manufacturing automobiles, the same principles and techniques can be applied to companies operating in other industries. In other words, lean thinking is more than a set of techniques and approaches; it is a mindset for all employees and managers that focuses on waste elimination and variability reduction in all business processes. Furthermore, the vast majority of lean production concepts can be easily applied in service-sector applications as well. In this chapter, we will discuss many different examples of lean production from a variety of industries, such as manufacturing, retail, health care, and financial services.

Lean Thinking

Scholars credit Henry Ford with developing the original principles behind lean thinking as the *Ford Production System* (FPS) during the early part of the twentieth century. When the Toyota Motor Company was established in 1937, it sent one of its lead engineers, Taiichi Ohno, to study and learn the Ford Production System and the associated concepts and techniques for use in the Japanese context. After Ohno returned to Toyota, he not only had mastered FPS, but also had identified many additional principles and approaches that would further enhance the effectiveness of the Ford Production System. As described in this chapter's opening vignette about Toyota, these principles, known as the Toyota Production System, were widely applied throughout the organization over the next several decades, leading to the overwhelming success of Toyota in markets across the world.

The Toyota Production System and Japanese manufacturing approaches such as *just-in-time (JIT) inventory, kanban,* and *kaizen* (these concepts are explained later in this chapter) received increased interest from U.S. manufacturers during the 1970s, when Japanese products started gaining market share during the U.S. oil crisis. Since that time, many academics and practitioners have written articles and books about lean production. For example, in *The Machine That Changed the World,* Womack, Jones, and Roos (1991) described the principles and components of a lean production system in detail.

They describe five core components of lean production:

Lean principle 1: The value in a production system should be defined from the customers' point of view for each product family.

Lean principle 2: Each production step should be evaluated in terms of its contribution to value creation. Those actions that do not add value should be eliminated.

Lean principle 3: The value-creating sequence of steps should be organized in a tight and integrated sequence to develop a smooth flow toward the customer.

Lean principle 4: Instead of organizing production to push finished products to the customers, products pulled by the customers should be the driver for planning, organizing, and scheduling upstream production activities.

Lean principle 5: All members of the organization should pursue perfection through continuous improvement.

During the last few years, several studies have been conducted to explore various aspects of a lean production system. Figure 12.3 shows a model that describes the essential components of a lean production system. It explains that a

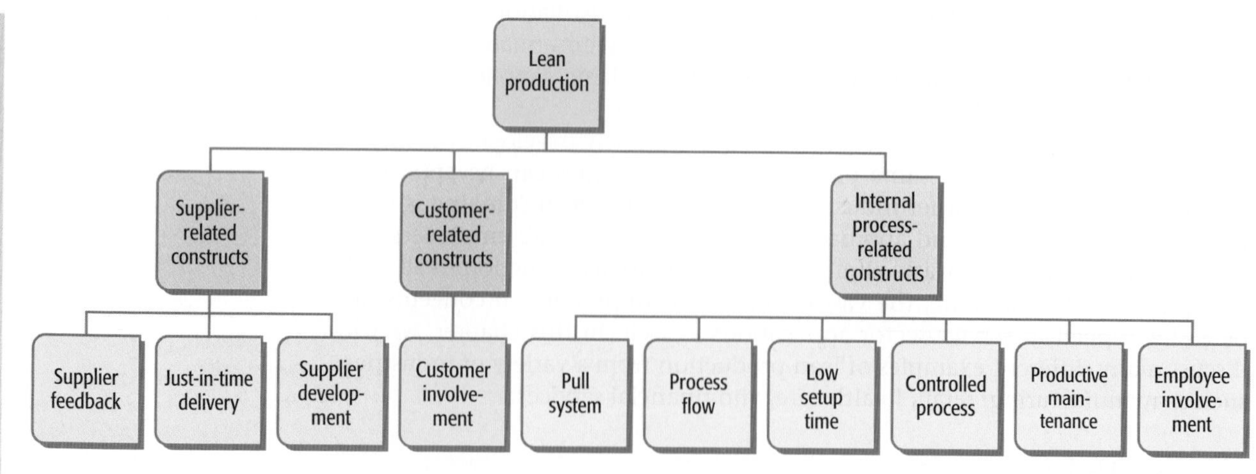

FIGURE 12.3 Components of a Lean Production System According to Shah and Ward (2007)

lean production system is made up of three types of constructs that are related to customers, suppliers, and internal processes. Each construct comprises several underlying concepts, such as a just-in-time inventory management system, customer involvement, and various aspects of production processes. These concepts are described and explained throughout this chapter.

Womack and Jones (1994) published a follow-up book titled *Lean Thinking* that included a detailed description of the underlying principles behind the approach. In recent years, the concept of lean production has been successfully applied to a wide range of industries in both the manufacturing and service sectors, such as health care and retailing. Therefore, this chapter describes the components of a lean production system in general terms, without focusing on one specific industry, with specific industry examples being provided in features.

BEST PRACTICES IN OPERATIONS MANAGEMENT

Lean Health Care at the Hospital for Sick Children (SickKids)

SickKids is an example of the successful application of lean thinking in service operations.

The Hospital for Sick Children (SickKids) is affiliated with the University of Toronto and is Canada's most research-intensive hospital and the largest center in the country dedicated to improving children's health. As innovators in child health, SickKids improves the health of children by integrating care, research, and teaching.

SickKids' staff includes professionals from all disciplines of health care and research. The hospital provides the best in complex and specialized care by creating scientific and clinical advances; sharing knowledge and expertise; and championing the development of an accessible, comprehensive, and sustainable child health system. For example, the hospital annually treats 300,000 patients, handles 50,000 emergency cases, and manages 12,000 operating room cases every year.

The Hospital for Sick Children has applied lean production principles to improve the efficiency of several of its units, such as its cytogenetics analysis laboratory. Cytogenetics is the study of the structure of human chromosomes with the aim of generating information regarding an individual's phenotype based on his or her DNA samples.

To begin the implementation of lean principles, an employee group was established, and the demand on the laboratory (numbers and types of referral) for each type of data (e.g., blood or tissue sample) was identified. Then every activity that is applied to a sample (both in the laboratory and administratively), from the moment it is received until the moment the final report is issued, was mapped. The mapping process also identified the points at which a sample sits and waits for the next step in the process. After the process steps were mapped, processing times were added to the framework to identify how long each step takes and how much time is "wasted" when the

(continued)

BEST PRACTICES IN OPERATIONS MANAGEMENT

Lean Health Care at the Hospital for Sick Children (SickKids) (*continued*)

sample is sitting between steps. Finally, the team identified the number of people required to complete each step. All the steps carried out in the laboratory were represented in the Current State Map.

Based on the Current State Map, the employee group identified the areas of the process that could be changed to improve workflow and reduce waste. They came up with several basic ideas, or kaizens (meaning "change for the better"), for improvements that could be made, and they recorded these ideas on a Future State Map.

These kaizens were then ranked so that the first ones acted on were the ones that were expected to have the greatest impact, ensuring that the biggest improvements would be made rapidly. For each kaizen, a working group was set up to develop a practical solution to the challenge. This group included people who worked in that particular area, and overall every member of the staff was involved in some way. While the program was still being implemented, the hospital was already benefiting from the application of lean thinking.

WASTE ELIMINATION

A lean production system is made up of several loosely connected sets of principles (see **http://www.lean.org** for additional details). The primary guiding principle behind lean thinking is the idea of value from the customers' point of view. If the customers do not find a product or a service offering valuable, they will not be willing to pay for it.

Therefore, within the lean thinking framework, all production activities must be carefully evaluated to ensure that they indeed provide value to the customers. This principle also means that all activities that do not add value should be eliminated or minimized.

According to the Toyota Production System, the types of waste in a production system can be categorized into three broad groups:

- **Muda** a Japanese term for production activities that are wasteful and do not add value to the goods or services

- **Muda**. Muda is a Japanese term for production activities that are wasteful and do not add value to the goods or services. "Value" in this context is defined from the customers' point of view. If an activity adds value, then the customer should be willing to pay for it.

- **Mura** waste associated with the unevenness of the processes

- **Mura**. The second type of waste present in a production system is that associated with the unevenness of the processes. Later in this chapter we describe the just-in-time (JIT) inventory management system, which is used to reduce the uncertainty and unevenness in the production processes.

- **Muri** the waste resulting from overburden or unreasonableness

- **Muri**. The waste resulting from overburden or unreasonableness is referred to as muri. This type of waste can be reduced by better standardization of the production processes.

These three general types of waste are observed in many different forms within manufacturing and service systems. Another breakdown of major types of waste is given in Figure 12.4.

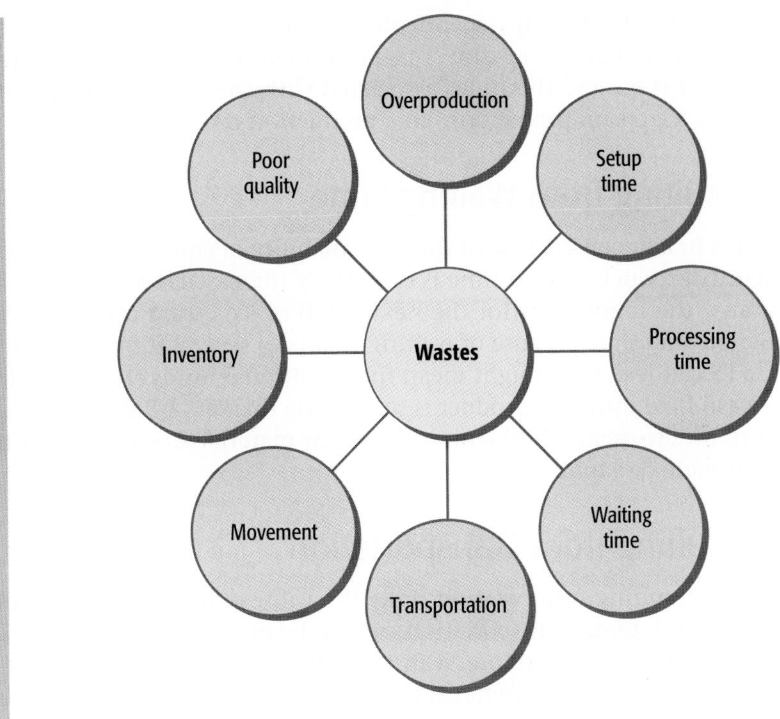

FIGURE 12.4 Wastes in a Production System

Waste Resulting from Overproduction

Organizations often schedule the production of products to maximize the use of production capacity. For example, an ice-cream manufacturer might decide to produce 1,000 gallons of a specific flavor (e.g., chocolate) to maximize the utilization of the capacity (i.e., the mixer) and minimize the impact of setup times. However, if the customer demand is only 800 gallons, then the quantity that is overproduced (200 gallons) will be wasted. Therefore, proponents of a lean system believe it is better to produce products in smaller quantities that are closer to market demand than to overproduce.

Waste Resulting from Setup Time

Setup times are essential components of any production process. However, during setup, the production process is not generating any output, as resources such as employees, raw materials, and components are idle. For example, the ice-cream manufacturer must set up the mixer with the ingredients for each flavor before starting the mixing process. Therefore, setup time is a necessary activity, but also one that generates waste. Employees' time is wasted while the mixer is being loaded with ice-cream ingredients. Therefore, in a lean production system, considerable effort is undertaken to reduce the setup time associated with various production process steps.

Waste Occurring During Processing Time

The total time required to produce a product is known as the processing time. Because the price of a product is usually based on its market value and not on the processing time, any nonessential time required in production is a waste. For example, the price of a quart of ice cream is based on its value as perceived by the customers and may not be directly dependent on the length of the mixing time. In a lean production system, extra care is taken to identify approaches that reduce the number of steps and the times associated with them (e.g., a reduction in mixing time for ice-cream production) in a production process.

Waste Resulting from Waiting Time

If a product waits in a queue because of the unavailability of equipment or other resources, then its production lead time is essentially increased. For example, if the mixer is busy, the ingredients for the next batch of ice cream must wait. A longer production lead time because of waiting results in several forms of waste. For example, a longer lead time might mean that additional funds are needed to maintain the cash flow until the product is sold in the market. A longer waiting time also contributes to quality problems because raw materials and components may become obsolete or expire.

Waste Resulting from Transportation

As with the waste resulting from waiting time, the value of a product does not increase because of its internal transportation among the production facility, warehouses, and retail locations. Therefore, lean thinking requires that the production facilities (such as factories, warehouses, and supplier facilities) be located as close to each other as possible. The opening vignette for this chapter describes how more than 300 suppliers are located in close proximity to Toyota's factory in Georgetown to minimize the waste resulting from transportation.

Waste Resulting from Movement

Unnecessary movement of raw materials and components within a production facility because of poor layout, work, and process design does not add value to the product. Therefore, within a lean facility, the layout (such as a U-shaped layout in many product assembly lines) is designed to minimize the waste resulting from movement.

Waste Resulting from Inventory

A certain minimum amount of inventory is necessary to ensure the smooth running of a production process. However, any additional inventory that is present in a production facility only adds waste because of extra storage and handling requirements. Furthermore, additional inventory also increases the production lead time and decreases a firm's ability to react quickly to any changes in the demand characteristics from the marketplace. Later in this chapter, we will describe the just-in-time (JIT) approach to inventory management, which minimizes the waste resulting from inventory.

Waste Resulting from Poor Quality

Any product or component that is not produced according to specifications needs to be scrapped and is wasted. Furthermore, the resources used to create the poor-quality product are also wasted. Therefore, quality and continuous improvement, known as **kaizen** in the Toyota Production System's terminology, are essential components of the lean thinking approach. Kaizen aims to eliminate waste by identifying and eliminating or minimizing the activities that add cost but do not add value or quality. Earlier in this chapter, we described an example of kaizen for the Hospital for Sick Children (SickKids).

● **Kaizen** eliminating waste by identifying and eliminating or minimizing the activities that add cost but do not add value or quality

Reducing the impact of the various types of production waste listed here requires careful systems thinking and a strong commitment to continuous improvement (refer to Chapters 2 and 11 for a description of the continuous improvement philosophy). It requires the long-term commitment and cooperation of all members of the organization to identify wastes, to troubleshoot, and finally to identify approaches for reducing all wastes.

COMPONENTS OF LEAN PRODUCTION SYSTEMS

A lean production system is made up of several interrelated elements. The main characteristics of lean systems are described here.

Pull Production System

Lean production is based on the pull system of process flow. A **pull system** is a production system that uses customer demand as the primary driver for production planning instead of pushing products to the marketplace to maximize the use of production resources. Ordering a sandwich at the quick-service restaurant Subway is an excellent example of a pull system. The sandwich assembly begins with each individual customer selecting the bread, meat, vegetables, cheese, and other ingredients. The customer follows the assembly of the custom sandwich in the aisle as it is created. Pull production approaches are also used by pizza home delivery companies such as Pizza Hut and Domino's. While these restaurants keep the necessary ingredients on site, they start the production of a pizza of a specific size with a specific type of crust, cheese, and toppings after receiving customer orders.

● **Pull system** a production system that uses customer demand as the primary driver for production planning

Examples of the pull production system can be seen in many different industries. For example, retailer Wal-Mart has cut its costs by sending point-of-sale (POS) data to all its vendors and replenishing store supplies twice a week, without goods ever sitting in inventory. Therefore, additional goods to be shelved at Wal-Mart stores are pulled from suppliers only if customer demand warrants it. Many products that are ordered directly from manufacturers (e.g., Dell computers) are also produced after the customer places an order at the company's web site. Because each computer can be configured in many different combinations (e.g., with different CPU speeds, amounts of memory, media, screen size, and so on), Dell simply advertises the components that are available in its inventory and produces only what the customer orders. This close connection between customer demand and pull production allows Dell to operate under very lean conditions.

● **Push system** a production system that focuses on maximizing the use of production capacity and therefore is based on estimated customer demand

A doughnut production line is an example of the push production system.

Push Production System

The **push system**, on the other hand, focuses on maximizing the use of production capacity and therefore is based on estimated customer demand. The push system allows companies to produce in large volume, thereby reducing the cost of production per unit. Doughnut production by Dunkin' Donuts is an example of push production. Based on past data and estimated demand, the store decides how many doughnuts of each specific type (glazed, cream-filled, chocolate-coated, and so on) can be sold during the next few hours. The store then decides on total production quantity and the product mix. An individual customer walking into the store sees the types of doughnuts that are available and places an order based on the available variety. Many products sold in supermarkets (such as milk, bread, vegetables, fruits, and meats) are also produced according to the push system.

The pull production approach has many advantages over push production when the demand is relatively stable. For example, this approach allows the producer to change product design quickly in response to changing market needs (see the feature example of Zara). At the same time, a pull production system may not be the most appropriate solution for all situations. For example, products that require extremely long setup times, seasonal products, or products with widely fluctuating demand might require push production instead.

Therefore, the choice between the push and pull production methods depends on each firm's unique situation. Producers that have highly repetitive processes, well-defined workflows, and standard products tend to use a pull method. Producers with processes that involve long lead times and for which reasonably accurate forecasts of demand are available, a variety of products that require common processes, and customers who will not wait long for the product tend to use a push method.

BEST PRACTICES IN OPERATIONS MANAGEMENT

Fast Fashion and Lean Thinking at Zara

Zara offers the latest trends in high-fashion clothing for men, women, and children. Zara's stores are located in the main commercial areas of cities across Europe, America, and Asia (more than 1,000 stores in 64 countries). Over the last several years, Zara has been extremely successful in leaping ahead of its competition. One of the main reasons for Zara's success has been its ability to take a design from drawing board to store in just two weeks. The secret behind Zara's success: lean thinking applied to the retail environment.

Fast-fashion clothing from Zara.

With an in-house design team based in La Coruña, Spain, and a tightly controlled factory and distribution network, the company introduces new items every week, which keeps customers coming back again and again to check out the latest styles. Even though at least half of Zara's factories are in Europe, where wages are many times higher than in Asia and Africa, Zara is still very profitable because of its use of pull production when other competitors are using push production.

(continued)

BEST PRACTICES IN OPERATIONS MANAGEMENT

Fast Fashion and Lean Thinking at Zara (*continued*)

The fast-response approach also helps Zara reduce its exposure to fashion fads that don't last long. Zara's fast pace means that some popular items appear and disappear within a week, creating an image of scarcity that many shoppers find irresistible. Therefore, Zara's products are virtually never on sale. Zara also ignores the traditional seasonal market calendar, and its retail store managers—not corporate executives—determine each store's product mix.

Zara's lean thinking strategy means that it can ignore many of the constraints of traditional push manufacturing and react quickly to changing market needs. For example, a typical retailer launches products according to seasonal cycles, and clothes are manufactured months in advance. Therefore, these retailers don't have the ability to react quickly to any new fashion trend.

Source: Adapted from Rachel Tiplady, "Zara: Taking the Lead in Fast-Fashion," *BusinessWeek*, April 4, 2006, http://www.businessweek.com/globalbiz/content/apr2006/gb20060404_167078.htm?chan=innovation_branding_brand+profiles

Small Batch Sizes

Lean production systems use batch sizes that are as small as possible. A **batch** is a quantity of products that are produced together. Small batches have the advantage of reducing the average level of inventory relative to that provided by large batches. Furthermore, small batches pass through the system faster than large batches, as explained in the feature about Zara. Small batches also allow for relatively early detection of any quality problems. If any defective items are discovered, large batches cause longer delays because the entire batch must be examined to find all of the products that have quality problems. Small batches also help achieve a uniform workload on the system. Large batches consume large chunks of capacity at work stations and, therefore, complicate scheduling. Small batches can be moved around more effectively, enabling schedulers to utilize capacities efficiently.

● **Batch** a quantity of products that are produced together

Short Setup Times

Although small lots are beneficial to operations, they have the disadvantage of increasing the number of setups. A **setup** is the set of activities needed to change or readjust a process between successive batches of products. Typically, a setup takes the same amount of time regardless of the batch size.

● **Setup** the set of activities needed to change or readjust a process between successive batches of products

Traditionally, producers selected the batch size that provided the most economical solution. An equation similar to the EOQ inventory model (see Chapters 6 for additional details) was typically used to find the optimum batch size.

Equation 1 shows a simplified form of the equation for the sake of illustration. If we assume that demand for a product is D, setup time is s, and processing time is h (alternatively, both s and h can be represented in cost units instead of time units), then the most economical batch size can be found in the following manner:

$$\text{Most Economical Batch Size} = \sqrt{\frac{2 * D * s}{h}} \qquad \text{(Equation 1)}$$

In other words, the most economical batch size is proportional to the square root of the setup time. Hence, a larger batch size is more economical than a smaller batch size if the setup times are long.

Robots and the SMED approach reduce setup time in automobile assembly.

While Equation 1 is useful, it considers the impact of setup time for only one process or piece of equipment. A larger batch will always result in higher inventory storage and handling costs throughout the production process, leading to several other types of waste and inefficiency. Therefore, in a lean organization, the focus is shifted from finding the optimum production batch size to troubleshooting and finding ways for reducing setup times. If setup times are decreased, then the most economical batch size will automatically be reduced.

Toyota and several other Japanese manufacturers spend considerable amounts of effort trying to identify approaches for reducing setup times. They developed the term **single-minute exchange of dies** (SMED) to highlight the usefulness of faster setup times. This approach allowed automobile manufacturers to reduce the setup time for changing dies from several hours to just a few minutes. The reduction in setup time resulted in huge reductions in the amount of in-process inventory, leading to significant cost reductions.

Although SMED originated in a manufacturing setting, the same principles of reducing non-value-added setup and changeover time apply for any good-producing or service-providing process.

Solved Example 1

Xeyon Computers uses the same assembly line to produce high-end laptop and desktop computers. The setup time for initiating production of either type of computer is currently 20 minutes. After setup, one laptop can be assembled every 6 minutes, and one desktop computer can be assembled every 4 minutes. The daily demand for laptop computers is 250, and the daily demand for desktop computers is 200.

QUESTION 1

What is the optimum or most economical production batch size for each type of computer?

SOLUTION

For desktop computers:

Demand: 200

Setup time: 20 minutes

Processing time: 4 minutes

$$\text{Most Economical Batch Size} = \sqrt{\frac{2 * D * s}{h}} = \sqrt{\frac{2 * 200 * 20}{4}} = 44.7$$

For laptop computers:

Demand: 250

(continued)

Setup time: 20 minutes

Processing time: 6 minutes

$$\text{Most Economical Batch Size} = \sqrt{\frac{2 * D * s}{h}} = \sqrt{\frac{2 * 250 * 20}{6}} = 40.8$$

Therefore, desktop computers should be manufactured in batches of 45, and laptop computers should be manufactured in batches of 41 (round to the closest integer).

QUESTION 2

Xeyon Computers wants to reduce the production batch sizes to get the benefits of lean production. Calculate how much the setup times for desktop and laptop computers should be reduced if the production batch sizes are to be reduced to 10. Also, calculate the setup time for a batch size of 1.

SOLUTION

$$\text{Most Economical Batch Size} = \sqrt{\frac{2 * D * s}{h}}$$

This equation can be rearranged to solve for the setup time in the following manner:

$$(\text{Most Economical Batch Size})^2 = \frac{2 * D * s}{h} \quad \text{(see Equation 1)}$$

Therefore,

$$s = \frac{h * (\text{Most Economical Batch Size})^2}{2 * D} \quad \text{(Equation 2)}$$

Equation 2 can be used to calculate the necessary setup times for the most economical production batch sizes.

For desktop computers, assuming the batch size to be 10,

$$s = \frac{h * (\text{Most Economical Batch Size})^2}{2 * D} = \frac{4 * 10 * 10}{2 * 200} = 1 \text{ minute}$$

Assuming the batch size to be 1,

$$s = \frac{4 * 1 * 1}{2 * 200} = 0.01 \text{ minute or } 0.6 \text{ second}$$

Clearly, the changeover time of 0.6 seconds is extremely low and therefore not possible to achieve for any realitic production process.

For laptop computers, assuming the batch size to be 10,

$$s = \frac{6 * 10 * 10}{2 * 250} = 1.2 \text{ minutes}$$

Assuming the batch size to be 1,

$$s = \frac{6 * 1 * 1}{2 * 250} = 0.012 \text{ minute or } 0.72 \text{ second}$$

Similar to calculations for desktop computers, the changeover time of 0.72 seconds is extremely low and therefore not possible to achieve for any realitic production process.

Just-In-Time Inventory

● **Just-in-time** an inventory management system designed to make the "right amount of inventory available at the right time" at all times

The **just-in-time** (JIT) inventory management approach was developed by Toyota. After returning from studying Ford's Production System, Taiichi Ohno realized that many production problems could be effectively solved by reducing inventory levels. The JIT inventory approach is based on the pull production system described earlier in this chapter. The objective of JIT is to make the "right amount of inventory available at the right time" at all times. Now JIT is widely used in a number of companies, such as Harley-Davidson and Hewlett-Packard, in addition to Toyota.

Kanban

● **Kanban** a word that means "card" or "visible record" in Japanese and refers to the cards used to control the flow of production through a factory

An automated assembly line needs uniform production planning.

In the Toyota Production System, the method for implementing JIT is known as a **kanban system**. *Kanban* means "card" or "visible record" in Japanese and refers to the cards used to control the flow of production through a factory. The kanban system has also been called the "supermarket method" because the original idea behind it was borrowed from supermarkets. Supermarkets and mass merchandising stores use product control cards on which product-related information, such as the product name, product code, and storage location, is entered.

In the most basic kanban system, a card is attached to each container of raw materials, components, or work-in-process inventory (Figure 12.5). The container holds a prespecified quantity of items. When the user of the parts empties a container, the card is removed from the container and put on a receiving post. The empty container is then taken to the storage area, and the card signals the need to produce another container of the part. When the container has been refilled, the card is put back on the container, which is then returned to a storage area. The cycle begins again when the user of the parts retrieves the container with the card attached.

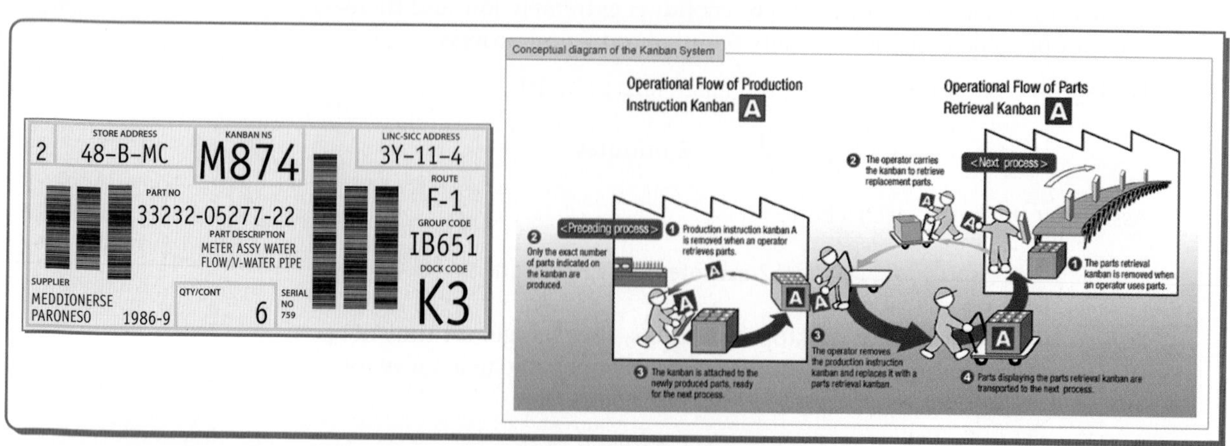

FIGURE 12.5 Example of a Kanban Card and Kanban System

Uniform Production Planning

A lean production system tends to work better when production conditions are stable. Because high fluctuation in demand requires either higher inventory or the ability to change the production capacity and schedule rapidly, great care is taken to stabilize the production load in a lean system.

In most production processes, additional efficiencies can be gained by analyzing work methods and documenting the improvements and by standardizing. In manufacturing operations, the standardization of components across multiple products, called **part commonality or modularity**, increases repeatability. An approach known as group technology is used to identify commonalities among components. Part commonality allows the company to quickly change from production of one product to production of another, thereby reducing the lead time and inventory requirements. Along with standardization of components, the lean production approach also advocates standardization of work functions. These efforts tend to increase productivity because, with increased repetition, workers learn to do their tasks more efficiently. Standardizing components and work methods helps a firm achieve the high-productivity, low-inventory objectives of a lean system. For example, several computer models produced by Dell or cars produced by Toyota share many common components.

● **Part commonality or modularity** standardization of components across multiple products

Takt Time

Takt time is defined as the maximum cycle time allowed for producing a product in order to meet demand. The term *takt time* is derived from the German word *Taktzeit,* which translates to "clock cycle." Product flow is expected to move at a pace that is less than or equal to the takt time. In a lean manufacturing environment, the pace time is set equal to the takt time.

● **Takt time** the maximum cycle time allowed for producing a product in order to meet demand

Takt time is defined as

$$T = \frac{T_a}{T_d} \qquad \text{(Equation 3)}$$

where T = takt time

T_a = net time available to work (excluding breaks, maintenance time, and so on)

T_d = total demand

Solved Example 2

Employees of Xeyon Computers work one 8-hour shift every day. They take 30 minutes for a lunch break and two additional breaks of 15 minutes each. Assuming the total demand to be 200 products, calculate the takt time.

SOLUTION

Net Available Time to Work = (8 hours × 60 minutes) – 30 – 15 – 15 = 420 minutes

Total Demand = 200

Therefore,

T = 420/200 = 2.1 minutes or 2 minutes and 6 seconds

This means that if each production step takes a maximum of 2 minutes and 6 seconds, then the facility can meet the demand of 200 units during each shift.

Continuous Improvement or Kaizen

● **Kaizen** a Japanese term that means "continuous improvement"

● **Quality at the source** a practice in which each employee is responsible for the quality of his or her work; therefore, each person acts as his or her own quality inspector

● **Jidoka** an approach for automated quality monitoring of equipment guided by a human touch

Kaizen is a Japanese term that means "continuous improvement." It originates from the words *Kai,* which means "continuous" and *zen,* which means "improvement." As mentioned earlier, producing goods and services based on customer expectations is an important characteristic of lean systems. The basic idea is to build quality into the production process rather than inspect finished goods for quality defects. One way to achieve this goal is by adhering to a practice called **quality at the source**, which means that each employee acts as his or her own quality inspector. The objective is to prevent a defective unit from leaving a work station and moving to the next process.

Another approach, known as **jidoka** in the Toyota Production System, is used to effectively prevent quality problems from occurring repetitively in a production process. If a defective part or equipment malfunction is discovered, the machine concerned automatically stops, and operators stop work and correct the problem. Therefore, jidoka can be defined as "automation with a human touch." The word *jidoka* traces its roots to the automatic loom invented by Sakichi Toyoda, founder of the Toyota Group. The automatic loom is a machine that spins thread for cloth and weaves textiles automatically. In the past, back-strap looms, ground looms, and high-warp looms were used to weave cloth manually. In 1896, Sakichi Toyoda invented Japan's first self-powered loom, called the Toyoda Power Loom. Subsequently, he incorporated numerous revolutionary inventions into his looms, including the weft-breakage automatic stopping device, which automatically stopped the loom when a thread breakage was detected; the warp supply device; and the automatic shuttle changer. Then, in 1924, Sakichi invented the world's first automatic loom, called the Type-G Toyoda Automatic Loom (with nonstop shuttle-change motion), which could change shuttles without stopping operation. Because the loom stopped when a problem arose, no defective products were produced. This meant that a single operator could be put in charge of numerous looms, resulting in a tremendous improvement in productivity.[2]

At Toyota, the term *jido* is applied to a machine with a built-in device for making judgments, although the regular Japanese term *jido* ("automation") simply refers to a machine that moves on its own. Jidoka is "automation with a human touch," as opposed to a machine that simply moves under the monitoring and supervision of an operator.

Close Supplier Relationships

Because lean systems operate with low levels of capacity slack and inventory, firms need to have close relationships with their suppliers. Supplies must be shipped frequently, have short lead times, arrive on schedule, and be of high quality. It is common for a supplier to deliver small quantities of goods to the production facility several times every day.

To ensure an uninterrupted supply of raw materials and components, therefore, lean producers need to develop long-term relationships with their suppliers. This means that lean producers cannot use price alone as the criterion for supplier selection. They need to consider suppliers as partners and co–value creators in their supply chain.

Therefore, in a lean production system, the number of suppliers is considerably lower than that used by nonlean producers. Furthermore, the suppliers are often located very close to the production facility to minimize transportation waste and to enable them to deliver raw materials and components at frequent intervals. While this approach puts a lot of pressure on suppliers to deliver high-

[2] Source: http://www.toyota.co.jp.

quality components on time, they also enjoy the benefits of long-term relationships with their lean producer customers. The producers often give suppliers access to their information systems so that the suppliers can also plan their production in advance. In addition, lean producers include their suppliers in the early phases of product development to avoid problems after production begins (this concept is also known as **concurrent engineering**. They also work with their suppliers' vendors, trying to achieve synchronized inventory flows throughout the entire supply chain. The close cooperation between companies and their suppliers can result in a win-win situation for everyone.

● **Concurrent engineering** a process in which multiple units/departments within an organization/supply chain are committed to working interactively to conceive, approve, develop, and implement new product development programs that meet predetermined objectives

BEST PRACTICES IN OPERATIONS MANAGEMENT

JIT II at Bose Corporation

Bose Corporation was founded in 1964 by Dr. Amar G. Bose, then professor of electrical engineering at the Massachusetts Institute of Technology. As an MIT grad student in the 1950s, Dr. Bose decided to purchase a new stereo system. He was disappointed to find that speakers with impressive technical specifications failed to reproduce the realism of a live performance. Over the years, Dr. Bose and his colleagues have developed a number of innovative and highest-quality speaker systems for use in music systems for homes, businesses, and automobiles.

Faced with a mandate to freeze hiring in the early 1990s but still needing help, Lance Dixon, then director of purchasing and logistics for Bose Corp., came up with an innovative idea that not only reduced the negative effects of the hiring freeze but also provided numerous other benefits. The solution: Arrange for representatives of suppliers to work on-site at Bose on a full-time or almost full-time basis. This concept has become known as JIT II, a term that signifies an extension of the JIT concept. The supplier representatives, called "inplants," place orders to their own companies, relieving the customer's buyers of this task. Many also become involved at a deeper level, such as participating in new product development projects, manufacturing planning, and other such activities.

The concept came along at the right time. In the early 1990s, more and more companies were beginning to understand the value of developing closer relationships with key suppliers. Since that time, the popularity of JIT II and other similar programs has expanded. Customers embraced the benefits of having resident experts available on a full-time basis, rather than having to place calls to suppliers to get answers or solutions, or having to wait for supplier reps to show up for their appointed visits. Suppliers embraced the concept as well, relishing the opportunity to become embedded in their customers' facilities, thus effectively gaining a customer for a long time. JIT II can offer benefits to both buyers and suppliers because it provides the organizational structure needed to improve coordination of suppliers by integrating the logistics, production, and purchasing processes. Several large corporations—including IBM, Intel, Honeywell, Roadway Express, Ingersoll-Rand, and Westinghouse—have implemented JIT II in their supply chains. Broadly speaking, JIT II can be considered an excellent example of vendor-managed inventory and a long-term customer-supplier partnership.

JIT II allows Bose and its suppliers to improve coordination and to develop high-quality new products.

Multifunctional Work Force

Workers in a lean production system are trained to perform more than one task. A benefit of flexibility is the ability to shift workers among work stations as necessary. This flexibility also allows the worker to perform the functions of other employees who are on vacation or out sick. At the same time, this operating environment requires more training for the workers. Because workers are responsible for ensuring quality at their own tasks, workers in a multifunctional work force require a higher skill level than workers in a nonlean environment possess. The workers, however, generally enjoy working in a multifunctional and team-based environment because it adds more variety to the job, which is more interesting than doing a repetitive task again and again.

Five S

Workers cannot be efficient if their workplaces are messy and disorganized. A great deal of time can be wasted looking for the right tool or moving around piles of materials that are scattered about. Within the lean production system, firms can use "five S" principles to create a more organized work environment (Table 12.1). The five S's are derived from Japanese terms: *seiri* (sort), *seiton* (straighten), *seiso* (shine), *seiketsu* (standardize), and *shitsuke* (sustain).

Visual Controls

● **Visual controls/andon** visual indicators that are placed in plain sight of all employees so that everyone can quickly and easily understand the status and performance of the work system

Visual controls/andon are indicators that are placed in plain sight of all employees so that everyone can quickly and easily understand the status and performance of the work system. They are also known as *andon,* from the Japanese term where the concept first originated. Many firms have cords that operators can pull to tell supervisors and other workers that a problem has occurred.

TABLE 12.1 Definitions of Five S

Five S Term	Definition
1. Sort	Separate needed from unneeded items and discard the unneeded.
2. Straighten	Neatly arrange what is left, with a place for everything and everything in its place. Organize the work area so that it is easy to find what is needed.
3. Shine	Clean and wash the work area and make it shine.
4. Standardize	Establish schedules and methods for performing the cleaning and sorting. Formalize the cleanliness that results from regularly carrying out the first three S practices so that perpetual cleanliness and a state of readiness are maintained.
5. Sustain	Create the discipline to perform the first four S practices, so that everyone understands, obeys, and practices the rules when in the plant. Implement mechanisms to sustain the gains by involving people and recognizing them via a performance measurement system.

Preventive Maintenance

Because lean production systems have little slack or buffer inventory between the work stations, any unplanned downtime can be very disruptive. Therefore, a requirement for lean operating systems is that all equipment and processes operate reliably. Unplanned downtime is far worse than planned downtime and scheduled maintenance. Preventive maintenance can reduce the frequency and duration of machine downtime. Maintenance is done on a schedule that balances the cost of the preventive maintenance program against the risks and costs of machine failure. Another tactic is to make workers responsible for routine maintenance of their own equipment and to develop employees' pride in keeping their machines in top condition.

Example of an andon.

Value Stream Mapping

The value stream mapping (VSM) method is a visualization tool developed as part of the Toyota Production System that has now become an essential component of a lean production system. VSM can serve as a starting point to help management, engineers, production associates, schedulers, suppliers, and customers recognize waste and identify its causes. Hence, while value stream mapping is primarily a communication technique, it is also used as a strategic planning tool.

The value stream mapping method visually maps the flow of materials and information from the time products come in the back door as raw material, through all production process steps, and until they move off the loading dock as finished products. The map shows both the current state and guidelines for arriving at a future desired state that is to be achieved by using lean production techniques. A number of icons and symbols are used to construct a value stream map. Some commonly used symbols are summarized in Figure 12.6. The value stream mapping approach can also be thought of as a specialized approach to flowcharting, which was described earlier in Chapter 4.

NEW ADVANCES IN LEAN PRODUCTION

Although most of the tools and approaches for lean enterprise that we described earlier are quite simple, information technology is becoming increasingly important in creating lean operating systems.

Technology in Lean Production

New forms of automated reasoning, learning, and control are now being used in production facilities. These include *expert systems* that use a set of "intelligent rules" to make logical decisions to solve a specific problem or control an operation or machine; advanced search algorithms to solve complex optimization

	VSM Process Symbols
 Customer/Supplier	This icon represents the supplier when it is in the upper left, the usual starting point for material flow. It represents the customer when it is placed in the upper right, the usual end point for material flow.
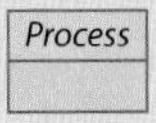 Process Dedicated Process	This icon represents a process, operation, machine, or department through which material flows. Typically, to avoid unwieldy mapping of every single processing step, it represents one department with a continuous, internal fixed flow path.
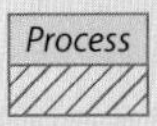 Process Shared Process	This is a process operation, department, or work center that other value stream families share.
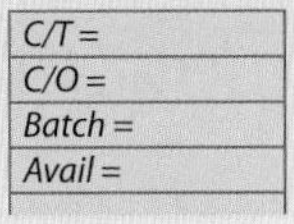 C/T = C/O = Batch = Avail = Data Box	This icon goes under other icons that have significant information/data required for analyzing and observing the system.
 Workcell	This symbol indicates that mulitple processes are integrated in a manufacturing work cell.

	VSM Material Symbols
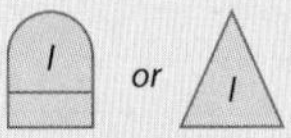 I or I Inventory	These icons show inventory between two processes. When mapping the current state, the amount of inventory can be approximated by a quick count, and that amount is noted beneath the triangle. If there is more than one inventory accumulation, use an icon for each. These icons also represent storage for raw materials and finished goods.
 Shipments	This icon represents movement of raw materials from suppliers to the receiving dock(s) of the factory. Or, it represents the movement of finished goods from the shipping dock(s) of the factory to the customers.
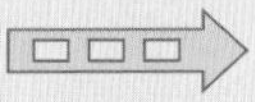 Push Arrow	This icon represents the "pushing" of material from one process to the next process. Pushing means that a process produces something regardless of the immediate needs of the downstream process.
 Supermarket	This is an inventory "supermarket." As in a supermarket, a small inventory is available and one or more downstream customers come to the supermarket to pick out what they need. The upstream work center then replenishes stocks as required.
 Material Pull	Supermarkets connect to downstream processes with this "pull" icon, which indicates physical removal.
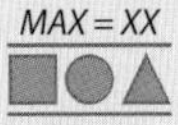 MAX = XX FIFO Lane	First-in-first-out inventory. Use this icon when processes are connected with a FIFO system that limits input.
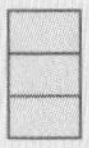 Safety Stock	This icon represents an inventory "hedge" (or safety stock) against problems such as downtime to protect the system against sudden fluctuations in customer orders or system failures.

FIGURE 12.6 Commonly Used Value Stream Mapping Symbols

Source: "Commonly Used Value Stream Mapping Symbols," VSM Icons referenced from the *Strategos Guide to Value Stream Mapping*; author, Q. Lee, publisher www.enna.com.

 **External Shipment**	Shipments from suppliers or to customers using external transport.

	VSM Information Symbols
Production Control **Production Control**	This box represents a central production scheduling or control department, person, or operation.
Daily **Manual Info**	A straight, thin arrow shows the general flow of information from memos, reports, or conversation.
Monthly **Electronic Info**	This wiggle arrow represents an electronic flow, such as electronic data interchange (EDI), the Internet, intranets, LANs (local area networks), and WANs (wide area networks).
P **Production Kanban**	This icon triggers the production of a predefined number of parts. It signals a supplying process to provide parts to a downstream process.
W **Withdrawal Kanban**	This icon represents a card or device that instructs a material handler to transfer parts from a supermarket to the receiving process. The material handler (or operator) goes to the supermarket and withdraws the necessary items.
S **Signal Kanban**	This icon is used whenever the on-hand inventory level in the supermarket between two processes drops to a trigger or minimum point. When a triangle kanban arrives at a supplying process, it signals a changeover and production of a predetermined batch size of the part noted on the kanban. It is also referred to as a "one-per-batch" kanban.
Kanban Post	A location where kanban signals reside for pickup. Often used with two-card systems to exchange withdrawal and production kanbans.
Sequenced Pull	This icon represents a pull system that gives instructions to subassembly processes to produce a predetermined type and quantity of product, typically one unit, without using a supermarket.
XOXO **Load Leveling**	This icon is a tool to batch kanbans in order to level the production volume and mix over a period of time.
MRP/ERP	Scheduling using MRP/ERP or other centralized systems.
Go See	Gathering of information through visual means.
Verbal Information	This icon represents verbal or personal information flow.

FIGURE 12.6 Commonly Used Value Stream Mapping Symbols (*continued*)

	VSM General Symbols
Kaizen Burst	This icon is used to highlight improvement needs and to plan kaizen workshops at specific processes that are critical to achieving the future state map of the value stream.
Operator	This icon represents an operator. It shows the number of operators required to process the VSM family at a particular work station.
Other Information Other	Other useful or potentially useful information.
VA VA NVA NVA NVA Timeline	The timeline shows value-added times (cycle times) and non-value-added times (wait times). Use this to calculate lead time and total cycle time.

FIGURE 12.6 Commonly Used Value Stream Mapping Symbols (*continued*)

problems; and "intelligent agents" that perform such tasks as machine scheduling, material transfer, and Web auction bidding. For example, Sony TiMMS has developed a series of software tools for the production of printed circuit boards. These software tools can be used to implement a variety of lean production principles. For example, the software keeps track of real-time data, optimizes production planning, and also keeps track of inventory as it moves through the production facility.

Use of radio frequency identification (RFID) is also becoming a more common way to manage lean inventory systems. As explained in Chapters 5 and 6, RFID is a data collection method that utilizes low-power radio waves to send and receive data between tags and readers. Using RFID, organizations can better track their inventory, thereby reducing the need to carry excess quantities. Although RFID technology is still in the experimental phase, experts believe that it has the potential to revolutionize the supply chain for products and further enhance the benefits of lean production practices.

Lean Production and Six Sigma = Lean Six Sigma

● **Lean Six Sigma** a management approach that combines the key components of both lean production and Six Sigma concepts

In numerous firms, lean production principles are linked with Six Sigma (see Chapter 2 for additional details about Six Sigma) because of that methodology's emphasis on the reduction of process variation (or of increasing its converse smoothness). The term **Lean Six Sigma** is used to describe the management approach that combines the key components of both lean production and Six Sigma concepts. It does so by focusing on improving process flow and speed and also improving quality by combining the concept of Six Sigma with the principles of lean production. The Lean Six Sigma approach utilizes five different "laws" in order to make the process successful. The five laws are

1. *The law of the market.* Customer needs define quality and are the highest priority for improvement.
2. *The law of flexibility.* The speed of any process is proportional to its flexibility.

3 *The law of focus.* Data show that 20 percent of the activities in a process cause 80 percent of the problems and delay. (This law is also known as the Pareto principle.)

4 *The law of velocity.* The speed of any process is inversely related to the amount of work or things in the process.

5 *The law of complexity and cost.* The complexity of a service or product offering generally adds more costs and work-in-process inventory than either poor quality (low sigma) or slow speed process problems.

Proponents of Lean Six Sigma cite many benefits, including reductions in cycle (processing) times, improvements in space utilization, increases in process throughput, smooth workloads, reductions in work-in-process and finished goods inventories, improvements in communication and information sharing in the value chain, improvements in quality and customer service, and reductions in working capital required to run the business Becoming lean requires a focus on details, discipline, persistence, and hard work to achieve results.

The concepts presented in this chapter provide a broad overview of the lean enterprise approach. These concepts are increasingly being applied to a wide range of manufacturing, service, and nonprofit organizations around the world. This approach is also being extended by combining with other frameworks such as Six Sigma. It is possible that the lean enterprise concepts may not be applicable to all organizations. However, the organizations that have been able to successfully apply these concepts have seen significant improvement in their operational performances.

SUMMARY

1. Describe the concepts of lean production and lean thinking.

- Lean thinking is an approach for eliminating or minimizing waste and variability within a production system.
- The principles of lean thinking are derived from the Toyota Production System and can be applied to a wide range of manufacturing and service organizations.
- Lean production is based on five guiding principles: customer focus, value creation, smooth production flows, pull production system, and organizationwide commitment.

2. Explain the different kinds of waste present in a production system.

- The wastes present in any production system can be classified into three broad categories: non-value-added activities (muda), unevenness of processes (mura), and overburden (muri).
- There are many different types of waste present in a typical production system, including wastes related to waiting time, setup and processing times, quality, and transportation.
- The lean production approach emphasizes the need for minimizing each type of waste present in a production system.

3. Describe the components of a lean production system.

- Lean production is configured as a pull system, which means that production is based on actual customer demand rather than forecasts. Therefore, lean production systems have relatively lower work-in-process inventory.
- Lean production systems also strive to achieve smaller batch sizes and shorter setup times to reduce work-in-process inventory further.
- A just-in-time (JIT) inventory system is used to deliver the right amount of inventory at the right time during the production process.
- A number of tools and techniques, such as kanbans, are used to implement JIT.
- Uniform production planning is facilitated by the calculation of takt time.
- Continuous improvement or kaizen, closer supplier relationships, and a multifunctional work force are essential for the success of a lean production system.
- A number of tools and techniques, such as five S, preventive maintenance, visual controls, and value stream mapping, are used during the implementation of a lean production system.

4. Discuss new advances related to lean thinking.

- New technology such as radio frequency identification (RFID) is making the implementation of a lean production system easier and more effective.
- A number of organizations have combined the key elements of a lean production system and Six Sigma and developed a more comprehensive framework known as Lean Six Sigma.

SOLVED PROBLEM 1

After specializing in pathology and laboratory medicine, Dr. Divya Sinha, a recent graduate of Cornell Weill Medical College in New York, moved back to her hometown in upstate New York. She decided to open a small laboratory that could conduct various advanced analyses for blood samples exclusively for the Weill Medical Center. Table 12.2 shows the setup time, processing times, and average number of tests ordered for each of the five types of tests conducted by Dr. Sinha's laboratory.

TABLE 12.2

Test Type	Setup Time (minutes)	Processing Time per Sample (minutes)	Approximate Daily Demand
Test A	30	10	25
Test B	10	10	50
Test C	60	20	20
Test D	20	5	100
Test E	45	10	75

QUESTION 1

Based on this information, calculate the optimum production (or testing) batch size for each type of test.

SOLUTION

Using Equation 1, the most economical batch size for each type of test can be found in the following manner:

$$\text{Most Economical Batch Size} = \sqrt{\frac{2 * D * s}{h}}$$

For Test A:

$$\text{Most Economical Batch Size} = \sqrt{\frac{2 * 25 * 30}{10}} = 12.24$$

which would be rounded to the nearest integer, or 12.

For Test B:

$$\text{Most Economical Batch Size} = \sqrt{\frac{2 * 50 * 10}{20}} = 10$$

For Test C:

$$\text{Most Economical Batch Size} = \sqrt{\frac{2 * 20 * 60}{20}} = 10.95$$

which would be rounded to the nearest integer, or 11.

For Test D:

$$\text{Most Economical Batch Size} = \sqrt{\frac{2 * 100 * 20}{5}} = 28.28$$

which would be rounded to the nearest integer, or 28.

For Test E:

$$\text{Most Economical Batch Size} = \sqrt{\frac{2 * 75 * 45}{10}} = 25.98$$

which would be rounded to the nearest integer, or 26.

QUESTION 2

If possible, Dr. Sinha would like to keep the batch size for each type of test constant at 5. Calculate how much the setup time for each test should be reduced to ensure that a batch size of 5 is the most economical.

SOLUTION

Equation 2 can be used to calculate the setup time corresponding to a demand, processing time, and production batch size in the following manner:

$$s = \frac{h * (\text{Most Economical Batch Size})^2}{2 * D}$$

Therefore, for Test A:

$$s = \frac{10 * 5^2}{2 * 25} = 5 \text{ minutes}$$

For Test B:

$$s = \frac{10 * 5^2}{2 * 50} = 2.5 \text{ minutes}$$

For Test C:

$$s = \frac{20 * 5^2}{2 * 20} = 12.5 \text{ minutes}$$

For Test D:

$$s = \frac{5 * 5^2}{2 * 100} = 0.625 \text{ minute}$$

For Test E:

$$s = \frac{10 * 5^2}{2 * 75} = 1.67 \text{ minutes}$$

SOLVED PROBLEM 2

Employees of Global Financial Associates process home mortgage applications during their 8-hour shift every day. They take 45 minutes for a lunch break and two additional breaks of 15 minutes each. Assuming the total demand to be 250 applications for each shift, calculate the takt time.

SOLUTION

$$\text{Net Available Time to Work} = (8 \text{ hours} \times 60 \text{ minutes}) - 45 - 15 - 15 = 405 \text{ minutes}$$

$$\text{Total Demand} = 250$$

Therefore,

$$T = 405/250 = 1.62 \text{ minutes or 1 minute and 37.2 seconds}$$

This means that if each production step takes a maximum of 1 minute and 37.2 seconds, the facility can meet the demand of processing 250 applications during each shift.

PROBLEMS

1. Components R We (CRW) is a small job shop facility that does contract manufacturing of components for a large automobile company located nearby. The following table gives the setup time, processing time, and approximate daily demand for each of the four components that CRW produces. Based on the information provided in Table 12.3, identify the optimum production batch size for each component for CRW.

TABLE 12.3

Component	Setup Time (minutes)	Processing Time per Component (minutes)	Approximate Daily Demand
Alpha	15	2	100
Beta	25	4	150
Gamma	60	1	75
Delta	45	3	200

2. For ease of production planning, CRW would like to keep the batch size for each type of component constant at 20. Calculate how much the setup time for each component should be reduced or increased to ensure that batch sizes of 20 are the most economical.

3. Employees of an online customer service center answer questions asked by e-mail by the company's customers. Each employee works an 8-hour shift that includes a 30-minute lunch break and two additional 15-minute breaks. The management has set a standard that each employee should be able to answer at least 400 e-mails during each shift. Calculate the takt time based on the information provided.

4. Because of new market promotions and sales growth, the online customer service center described in Problem 3 has started getting approximately 50,000 e-mails every day. The service center currently has 100 employees. The e-mails can be classified in two categories: routine inquiries and custom requests. Employees can answer the routine inquiries by picking prespecified answers from the database. This process takes only 30 seconds. The custom requests, on the other hand, require drafting specific responses and take approximately 2.5 minutes.

   a. Calculate the takt time for both routine and custom inquiries.

   b. Assuming that 75 percent of all requests are routine, calculate the overall takt time for the customer service center.

5. Provide examples of each of the eight types of waste described in this chapter for the following service operations:

   a. A supermarket

   b. A campus cafeteria

   c. A library

   d. A dentist's office

CASE STUDY

Tasty, Healthy and "Lean" Food Service for Olympic Champions

Laura, a new graduate from Cornell Unversity's School of Hotel Administration, could not believe her good luck. She was recently offered a new entry-level position as an operations analyst at ARAMARK, one of the most admired U.S. companies, according to *Fortune* magazine (ARAMARK is a leader in professional services, providing award-winning food services, facilities management, and uniform and career apparel to health care institutions, universities and school districts, stadiums and arenas, and businesses around the world).

The reason for Laura's excitement was also because of the unique opportunity she was getting in her first assignment: she was going to Beijing during the 2008 Olympics to work for ARAMARK food services.

Over the years, ARAMARK has provided food services to many large-scale events, including the last 13 Olympic Games. For example, during the 2004 Athens Olympics, ARAMARK worked with its partner, the Daskalantonakis Group (the leading Greek hospitality and tourism group), to provide meals for the largest Olympic Village in history. The Olympic Village in Athens hosted Summer Olympic and Paralympic Games participants, coaches, officials and Games personnel. ARAMARK and the Daskalantonakis Group served more than two million meals to participants, coaches, and officials throughout the 60-day duration of both the Olympic and Paralympic Games.

Some of the other large-scale food service events managed by ARAMARK included serving over 340,000 motor fans who attended one of the biggest events in Spain last year: the Spanish Formula 1 Grand Prix in Barcelona. More than 1,100 ARAMARK employees served attendees more than 9,000 fruit dishes, 120,000 sandwiches, 40,000 hot dogs, and 40,000 cups of coffee during the three-day event. Some specialty gourmet dishes were also served, such as barbequed lamb steak, pumpkin and orange soup, and sole rolls with shrimp cream.

While preparing for her job interview, Laura had become aware of the large scale of ARAMARK's food service engagements. However, nothing had prepared Laura for the scale of the Beijing 2008 Olympics food service operations; Laura and all the other new employees had received a pre-event memo from their new boss, which stated that the ARAMARK team would be responsible for serving 3.5 million meals during the event (or 10,000 people per hour) that would not only pack a punch for peak performance but had to have the smells and tastes of home. The food service operations would have a staff of nearly 7,000—including some 230 chefs from 10 countries—to feed almost 65,000 athletes, coaches, officials, and members of the media throughout the Olympics. The memo further stated that ARAMARK's biggest challenge would be to ensure that the food arrived at the right time, at the right temperature, and in the right quantities. In addition, dining during the Olympics would also be a social experience. Therefore, ARAMARK had to ensure that the athletes and visiting dignitaries got the highest quality service for a great experience. The memo also included a table (see Table 12.4), which listed some of the key inventories that needed to be managed to ensure that the food service operation was successful.

After going through the memo and the attached table, Laura wondered if she should still feel lucky or she should start panicking. Her job was to support the assistant director in effectively managing inventory for the food service operations. She wondered if she could apply the concepts she learned about lean enterprise in her final semester operations management class to this first "real-world" job.

QUESTIONS

1. What are the unique aspects of inventory management in large-scale food services such as ARAMARK's Olympic Games operations?
2. What lean production concepts can Laura apply in the above context? What challenges will she face?
3. What are the limits to applying lean principles in large food service operations such as ARAMARK's Olympic Games operations?

TABLE 12.4

Inventory for 2008 Beijing Olympics Food Service Operations

To serve a "world menu" of more than 800 recipes throughout the Games requires:

- 93,000 pounds of seafood
- 130 tons of meat
- 38,000 pounds of pasta (dry)
- 134,000 pounds of rice (about 20 million half-cup servings when cooked)
- 743,000 (or 232 tons) potatoes
- 800,000 (or 44 tons) eggs
- 1 million apples
- 936,000 bananas
- 312,000 oranges
- 684,000 carrots
- Nearly 24 tons of onions
- 50,000 pounds of mushrooms
- 57,000 pounds of cheese
- 190,000 loaves of bread
- 5,500 pounds of butter
- 16,000 pounds of tofu
- 20,000 heads of lettuce

All those ingredients will create a rotating menu of:

- 320 hot main entrée dishes
- 160 vegetable and potato dishes
- 128 rice and pasta dishes
- 400 different dessert, pastry, and bakery items

CHAPTER 13

Technology and Integrated Supply Management

LEARNING OBJECTIVES

1. Describe the role of technology in improving operations/ supply chain management. In particular, identify and describe key types of service technologies and key types of manufacturing technologies.
2. Identify and describe key types of supply chain information technologies. Explain the bullwhip effect and how to minimize it.
3. Explain typical benefits and challenges of new technologies.
4. Describe factors that support technology development and implementation.

American Express Pushes the Electronic Payment Envelope

More than half of the Fortune 500 use one of American Express's commercial card products, and the company is seeking to use this dominance to make inroads into the electronic invoicing market. In December 2006, American Express announced a deal to buy Harbor Payments Inc., an Atlanta company that specializes in electronic invoicing and electronic payment capabilities. The objective is to help companies eliminate paper processing. Brenda Blake, general manager of electronic invoicing and payment services for American Express, said that even when a company places orders electronically, it receives paper invoices 80 percent of the time and is forced to pay for orders by physical check 66 percent of the time. This leads to numerous inefficiencies, with the result that it can take weeks, and sometimes months, to make standard payments. Electronic billing offers the ability to automate the entire purchasing cycle and make it paperless by connecting directly with suppliers and customers. This service is expected to be especially attractive to firms doing business in multiple countries. According to Ms. Blake, "With electronic invoice payments, they're [companies] able to fully audit and have control over their purchasing." Mr. Phillip J. Philliou, an independent payments consultant, stated that this

Unallocated American Express credit cards await new owners.

move will help American Express differentiate itself because "all the Fortune 1000 companies are hell-bent on automating the way they procure. Business-to-business (B2B) sales is a core strength of Amex, and this would be another great service to offer their current base of clients. I think it will allow them to compete even more aggressively with other purchasing card businesses."[1] ■

Advances in technology are the foundation for productivity and quality improvements in business. The industrial revolution of the nineteenth and twentieth centuries was fueled by technological advances in transportation, communication, and power. Transportation technologies progressed from sailboats to steamboats, railroads, automobiles, and airplanes. Each new advance allowed people to ship goods faster and over greater distances. Communication technologies progressed from mail to the telegraph, to the telephone, and to the Internet and mobile communications technologies. Table 13.1 provides a chronological overview of some

TABLE 13.1 Key Inventions of the Eighteenth to Twenty-First Centuries

Date	Technology/Concept	Developer/Inventor
1769	Steam engine	James Watt
1776	Division of labor	Adam Smith
1790	Interchangeable parts	Eli Whitney
1807	Steamboat	Robert Fulton
1814	Steam locomotive	George Stephenson
1885	Internal combustion engine	Gottlieb Daimler
1911	Principles of scientific management	Frederick W. Taylor
1913	Moving assembly line	Henry Ford
1951	Commercial digital computers	Sperry Univac, IBM
1958	Integrated circuit	Jack Kilby and Robert Noyce
1969	Internet	U.S. Department of Defense Advanced Research Projects Agency
1989	World Wide Web	Timothy Berners-Lee, European Organization for Nuclear Research (CERN)
2003	Hybrid car	Toyota

For a more extensive timeline of key technologies and inventions, go to http://inventors.about.com/.

[1] Source: H. Michael Jalili, "Amex Vendor Acquisition Aims at B2B," *American Banker* 171, no. 133 (2006), 1.

Automobile engineer Wilhelm Maybach sits in the driver's seat with Paul Daimler (son of Gottlieb Daimler) and two other men in an 1886 Daimler automobile.

of the key technologies that have shaped business operations over the last three centuries.

Often it is hard to imagine life without computers, yet the advances in computers have been enormous and incredibly fast. ENIAC, short for Electronic Numerical Integrator and Computer, was the first large-scale, electronic, digital computer that was capable of being reprogrammed to solve a full range of computing problems. This computer was so large (27 tons) that it occupied an entire room and had less computing power than a cellular phone has today. Fortunately for us, the technology behind this product (and all others) improved substantially over time.

To focus the discussion of technology for business, it is helpful to define three general types of technology. **Product technology** consists of the features and characteristics of a particular product or service. Products such as cars, computers, and televisions are continuously being improved and changed. In terms of operations and supply chain management, we are more interested in **process technology**, or the methods, procedures, and equipment associated with producing goods or services. Process technology, such as Henry Ford's moving assembly line for the Model T automobile, is the fundamental driver for improvements in business productivity. New process technologies lead to operational improvements such as lower costs, faster delivery, and better quality. **Information technology** involves the use of computers and other electronic equipment to collect, store, process, and send information. Information technology is an essential component of modern operations. Examples include the use of bar codes and radio frequency identification (RFID) to identify and track goods, electronic data processing, e-mail, instant messaging, and the Internet.

- **Product technology** the features and characteristics of a particular product or service
- **Process technology** the methods, procedures, and equipment associated with producing goods or services
- **Information technology** the use of computers and other electronic equipment to collect, store, process, and send information

TECHNOLOGY AND ITS ROLE IN IMPROVED OPERATIONS/SUPPLY CHAIN MANAGEMENT

There is no doubt that technological advances have played a huge role in decreasing costs, improving capabilities, and improving quality in every type of business. Sometimes it seems as if there are new technologies coming out every day. While many technologies are useful in a wide variety of settings, there are some fundamental differences between the use of technology in primarily service-oriented businesses and manufacturing-oriented businesses. Therefore, we examine the use of technology in each of these sectors separately.

Technology in Services

The role of technology in service businesses is substantially different from that in manufacturing. In general, services require much more generalized technology because products tend to be less general and less amenable to automation. Services have historically not experienced efficiency gains of the same magnitude as those experienced by manufacturing because of the difficulties involved in applying new technologies and the greater need for human interaction between service providers and customers. However, there are always innovative businesses that find new ways to do things. In particular, the Internet is radically changing many service businesses through its ability to create a buffer between service providers and customers without compromising the ability to customize the service experience.

Although services generally are less tangible than manufactured goods and require greater contact between provider and customer, these businesses frequently have a substantial need for production technologies to process physical goods. Restaurants provide a good example of the range of technologies needed. Most restaurants employ primarily general-purpose technologies such as ovens, refrigerators, dishwashers, grills, and other such equipment. However, fine restaurants such as Charlie Trotter's in Chicago utilize specialized equipment, such as a dedicated bread oven, to facilitate their highly customized, high-quality products. Similarly, fast-food restaurants such as McDonald's also employ specialized technology, only the goal here is to reduce costs by standardizing processes. In fact, since the mid-1950s, McDonald's and other fast-food restaurants have been phenomenally successful at utilizing technology to speed up food production and reduce costs. Examples of McDonald's innovations include automated French fry cookers that automatically sense when the fries are done (by measuring the increase in oil temperature, *not* by timing the process) and raise them out of the cooking oil, drink dispensers that automatically pour the exact amount of soda per cup, and cash registers that transmit orders to a television screen in the food preparation area. A more recent innovation is the development of a "flash" toaster that can toast a hamburger bun in 11 seconds. This innovation was necessary to allow sandwich production to switch from a make-to-stock to a make-to-customer-order system. The secret of developing a fast toasting system actually lies in changing the ingredients in the bread so that it doesn't burn at the higher temperatures required to toast it quickly.

It is helpful to think of service technologies as relating to either back-office or front-office procedures. Many service businesses have a line of customer visibility that separates **back-office activities**, which the customer does not directly interact with or see, from **front-office activities**, which directly involve the customer and require the customer's presence. Banks provide a good example; front-office activities include such things as opening new accounts, handling deposits and withdrawals, and answering customers' questions. The primary technology used to support these activities is a bank's information system, which tracks account and customer information. The development of the automated teller machine (ATM) has greatly increased banking efficiency because it allows banks to reduce the number of cashiers, as customers do much of the work themselves when making deposits and withdrawals at an ATM. What ATMs have done is shift much of the front-office work to the back office. Instead of the customer needing to interact directly with a teller, the customer performs his or her ATM transaction, and bank employees then process these transactions in batches. Bank employees must still open every deposit, verify that the check is for the stated amount, cancel the check, and process some paperwork, but these activities can now be done in one continuous batch instead of waiting for customers to arrive and having large periods of inactivity. Back-office activities in a bank include posting checks and deposits to customer accounts, printing monthly statements, and returning canceled checks. Customers have no idea how these activities are carried out, nor do they particularly care. Because these activities do not involve direct customer interaction, they can be aggregated in one central location and performed with specialized equipment. Large banks such as Citigroup, Bank of America, Chase, Wachovia, Wells Fargo, and HSBC utilize computer-controlled conveyors, sorters, readers, and check cancelers to process and sort more than a half million checks per day.

- **Back-office activities** activities in services that the customer does not directly interact with or see
- **Front-office activities** activities in services that directly involve the customer and require the customer's presence

Similarly, the U.S. Post Office utilizes optical character recognition systems to electronically capture the zip code on letters and sort letters in extremely high volumes (over 6 million per day in the main Chicago post office). Average citizens never see most of this back-office technology, but they do see mail carriers delivering mail to their houses on a daily basis.

The separation between back- and front-office processes occurs at the line of visibility, which is the point at which customers lose physical sight of the steps in a particular process. In general, it is easier to automate back-office processes, which occur behind the line of visibility and which customers cannot see. However, many of the improvements in information and communications technology over the past few years have altered the line of visibility. For example, consider booking tickets for a concert or show. Ten years ago, this required a telephone call to the arena or theater, as well as the participation of both the customer and a representative of the company offering the concert or show. Today, tickets can usually be bought online or via cellular phone. This is because technology has been used to push the line of visibility backward. Customers can now "see" whether tickets for a particular show are still available. This provides greater convenience for customers while also cutting labor costs for the provider. Similar examples can be found in booking airline tickets, paying bills online, purchasing items online, and many other situations.

TECHNOLOGY IN OPERATIONS MANAGEMENT

McDonald's Technology Evolution

McDonald's has long been a leader in technology. From the first days of the restaurant chain, it proactively sought to develop technology suited to its specific purposes, as illustrated by the following passage describing the first McDonald's restaurant after the founders, Dick and Mac McDonald, converted it from a drive-in with carhops that served meals to people in their cars in 1949:

The brothers had defined a totally new food service concept, but to make it work they realized they badly needed unique kitchen tools. Since the kitchen equipment of the day was not designed for their assembly line production, the McDonalds began inventing the first implements of the fast-food industry. For example, Dick McDonald designed a portable stainless steel lazy Susan that could hold twenty-four hamburger buns. In a staging area away from the grill, the buns were "dressed" with condiments by two crewmen as the lazy Susan rotated. Attached to the mobile platform, the lazy Susan was then rolled to the grill, loaded with hamburgers and rolled back to an area where the burgers could be wrapped.[2]

This quote illustrates two key principles of technology. First, the technology does not need to be complicated or fancy—just effective. Second, the most valuable technology is usually produced, designed, or conceptualized by the company using it. Off-the-shelf technology is available to everyone and is less likely to provide an enduring competitive advantage.

In the years since, McDonald's has continued to refine its process technology with simple yet effective tools, such as the ring to make the eggs for Egg McMuffins round, the French fry scoop, and cash registers with buttons for value meals that reduce the need for extensive training for a cashier. In recent years, McDonald's has implemented numerous computer-based technologies for scheduling, ordering, planning, and other such functions. These efforts have included the use of distant call centers to manage drive-up orders (i.e., the operator taking the order may be hundreds or thousands of miles away from the customer), as well as changes in product technology such as offering wireless service at restaurants. Table 13.2 and the online videos illustrate some of the changes in technology over the years. Can you identify and describe technologies that McDonald's currently uses and how they make the business run more efficiently or effectively?

[2] John F. Love, *McDonald's Behind the Arches*, 1995, Bantam Publishers, Revised Edition, p. 17.

TABLE 13.2 Technologies at McDonald's Through the Years

Type of Technology	1960	2009
Product technology	10 products, very limited—hamburger or cheeseburger	More than 35 products including Filet of Fish, Big Mac, Quarter Pounder, salads
Process technology	Lazy Susan for preparing hamburgers Specially designed grill Condiment dispensers	Soft drink machines with automatic cup holders Cash registers with programmed menus Automatic French fry machines
Information technology—communicating orders	Verbal	Electronic link from drive-up to production or from counter to production
Information technology—sourcing/invoicing	Checklists, phone calls, letters	Software system automatically tracks inventory and planned shipments, links with invoicing and bill paying
Information technology—scheduling workers and payroll	Worksheets, pen and paper	Software for scheduling—recommends required staff levels at specific times of the day. Linked to payroll and accounting systems

The course web site has a video of a 1950s/1960s–era McDonald's and a 2007-era McDonald's. Can you identify clear differences in the technology?

Service businesses make extensive use of self-sourcing, which includes customers in the process in a way that reduces the resource demands on the organization providing the product or service while also providing the customer with improved service. Examples of self-sourcing technology include allowing customers to fill their own cups at a fast-food restaurant, order tickets to a show online, pay bills online, check themselves in for an airline flight, and check themselves out at a grocery store. Technology is a critical facilitator of such self-sourcing, whether it is the soda machine, the web site that allows purchases, or the checkout machine that processes customer purchases at a grocery store. The topic of self-sourcing is examined in Chapter 3, "New Product Development."

Manufacturing Technologies

Technological changes have occurred in almost every industry, with many tools having highly specialized applications to a single industry. For example, car manufacturers have progressively improved the quality of parts in their engines, making the

Machining of a rotor for a power plant turbine using a computer numerically controlled (CNC) machine tool.

engines more efficient, reliable, and consistent in production. Similarly, advances in material composition, as well as production tools, have allowed electronics manufacturers such as Sony, Hewlett-Packard, and Apple to make smaller and smaller devices that perform a range of functions—combining phones, music players, video, cameras, and calendar activities, among many others. While individual technological advances can be identified in almost any industry and discussed in terms of how they have led to improved products or processing, we will focus more on a set of more general technologies that have been applied in a wide range of situations. Manufacturing technologies can be grouped into three broad groups: **processing technologies**, which physically move, shape, form, cut, or assemble products; **design technologies**, which assist in developing plans for producing products or designing the products themselves; and **administrative technologies**, which assist in tracking information related to the manufacturing process.

- **Processing technologies** technologies that physically move, shape, form, cut, or assemble products
- **Design technologies** technologies that assist in developing plans for producing products or designing the products themselves
- **Administrative technologies** technologies that assist in tracking information related to the manufacturing process
- **Computer numerically controlled (CNC) machines** machines that combine two components: (1) a traditional machine tool such as a lathe or a grinder that is used to turn, drill, or grind different parts into shape, and (2) a computer that controls the type and sequence of operations performed by the machine
- **Industrial robots** programmable machines that are designed to handle materials or tools in the performance of a variety of tasks
- **Automated materials handling systems** systems that use computer-controlled equipment to move, package, and store products

Processing Technologies

Since the 1960s, **computer numerically controlled (CNC) machines** have combined two components: (1) a traditional machine tool such as a lathe or a grinder that is used to turn, drill, or grind different parts into shape, and (2) a computer that controls the type and sequence of operations performed by the machine. The machine typically has a single tool belt with numerous tools attached. When a new tool is required, the computer controls turn the tool belt until the proper tool is positioned, and the tool changer attaches that tool to the spindle. The photo shows a basic CNC machine tool. The advantage of this type of equipment is that it is very flexible in terms of the speed with which it can perform setups to produce various parts or products. Rather than requiring a human operator to laboriously change the settings on the machine after each operation or part, the machine runs a software program that chooses the proper tool, positions the tool, and performs the appropriate operation. CNC machine tools were originally controlled by cumbersome, tape-read computers that were very difficult to program and operate. More recently, advances in computer software have paralleled those in popular operating programs such as Windows or Macintosh, and CNC machine tools are now controlled by built-in personal computers that are much easier to program and operate.

Industrial robots are programmable machines that are designed to handle materials or tools in the performance of a variety of tasks. Robots are often used to replace workers in repetitive manual activities that are dangerous, uncomfortable, or dirty. Robots are used in automobile factories to weld components together, in food processing plants to remove defective items, and in numerous other applications. Robots typically have an arm that can be manipulated to reach different positions and an end effector or hand. Examples of end effectors include paint sprayers, welders, or grippers to pick things up. Robots are generally limited in the work they can perform because their dexterity does not come close to that of a human, and thus they cannot handle fragile objects well. However, recent advances have extended their capabilities by adding vision, tactile sensing, and better coordination of movement.

Automated materials handling systems use computer-controlled equipment to move, package, and store products. Examples of this technology include computerized conveyors and **automated storage and retrieval systems** (AS/RS), in which computers direct automated loaders to pick and place items from a storage rack. **Automated guided vehicle** (AGV) systems utilize embedded wires in the factory floor to guide driverless vehicles from location to location.

A **flexible manufacturing system** (FMS) consists of a combination of several individual pieces of equipment that allows materials to be automatically loaded, unloaded, and shaped at machining centers equipped with CNC machine tools that can perform multiple operations. These systems can produce a very large variety of parts with almost no loss of production time due to tooling setups or changeovers. The equipment is very expensive, costing from $1 million to $20 million to install. Figure 13.1 shows an example of an FMS layout manufactured by Makino, Inc., of Mason, Ohio.

Automated production and assembly—two robots working in tandem.

● **Automated storage and retrieval systems** systems in which computers direct automated loaders to pick and place items from a storage rack

● **Automated guided vehicle** a system that utilizes embedded wires in the factory floor to guide driverless vehicles from location to location

● **Flexible manufacturing system** a combination of several individual pieces of equipment that allows materials to be automatically loaded, unloaded, and shaped at machining centers equipped with CNC machine tools that can perform multiple operations

● **Computer-aided design** the use of computers to interactively design products and prepare engineering documentation

● **Computer-aided engineering** a system used to evaluate the engineering characteristics of a part or product by computing stresses, manufacturing parameters, and other technical information

● **Computer-aided process planning** software that helps plan manufacturing processes by analyzing different routing alternatives to streamline the flow of work in process through the plant

Design Technologies

Computer-aided design (CAD) is the use of computers to interactively design products and prepare engineering documentation. CAD has several advantages over hand-drawn plans, including the ability to model plans in three dimensions instead of two, to catalog existing parts so that designers can quickly look for a part that fits their needs rather than having to design one, and to track revisions to existing drawings. Large manufacturing corporations have historically had a difficult time ensuring that parts were built to the correct revision of a drawing (parts or products sometimes went through scores of revisions) because different people within a plant might have two or three different plans for a part or product. CAD stores all the part information electronically, so another advantage is the ability to transfer the information directly to production equipment such as an FMS or CNC machine tool. The term *factory of the future* has been applied to a few leading-edge facilities where much of the work is now paperless, with plans being developed and catalogued using CAD, then transferred electronically to an FMS for production. CAD has been one of the most commonly utilized advanced manufacturing technologies since the early 1980s, both because of its relatively low cost (a top-notch CAD system costs a few thousand dollars, and very basic systems can be bought for as little as $50 to $100) and because of its ease of use.

Computer-aided engineering (CAE) is used to evaluate the engineering characteristics of a part or product by computing stresses, manufacturing parameters, and other technical information. CAE has led to huge improvements in many areas, such as bridge and skyscraper construction, because it allows engineers to model the stresses placed on a building or bridge in a much simpler and quicker fashion. **Computer-aided process planning** (CAPP) is software that helps plan manufacturing processes by analyzing different routing alternatives to streamline the flow of work in process through the plant. CAPP is used to develop the programs that run processing equipment such as FMS, as well as to sequence and schedule various operations so as to maximize the efficiency of the overall production facility. The Best Practices in Operations Management feature on Ford's use of virtual modeling and avatars is an application of CAPP.

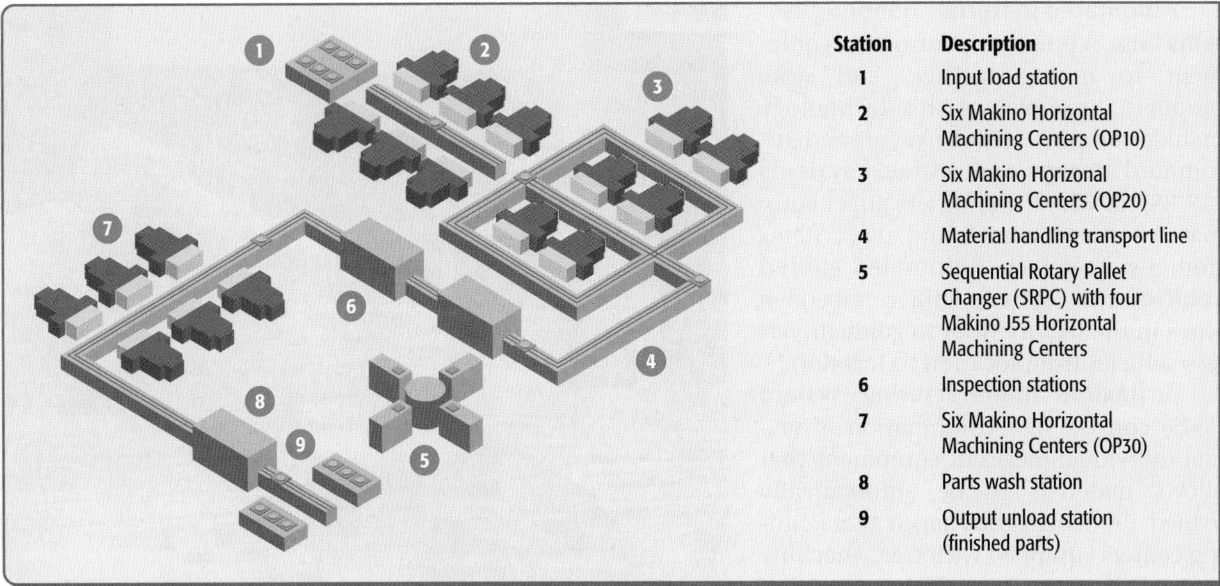

Station	Description
1	Input load station
2	Six Makino Horizontal Machining Centers (OP10)
3	Six Makino Horizonal Machining Centers (OP20)
4	Material handling transport line
5	Sequential Rotary Pallet Changer (SRPC) with four Makino J55 Horizontal Machining Centers
6	Inspection stations
7	Six Makino Horizontal Machining Centers (OP30)
8	Parts wash station
9	Output unload station (finished parts)

FIGURE 13.1 FMS System Produced by Makino, Inc.

Source: Courtesy of Makino.

BEST PRACTICES IN OPERATIONS MANAGEMENT

Computer Testing of Work Methods at Ford

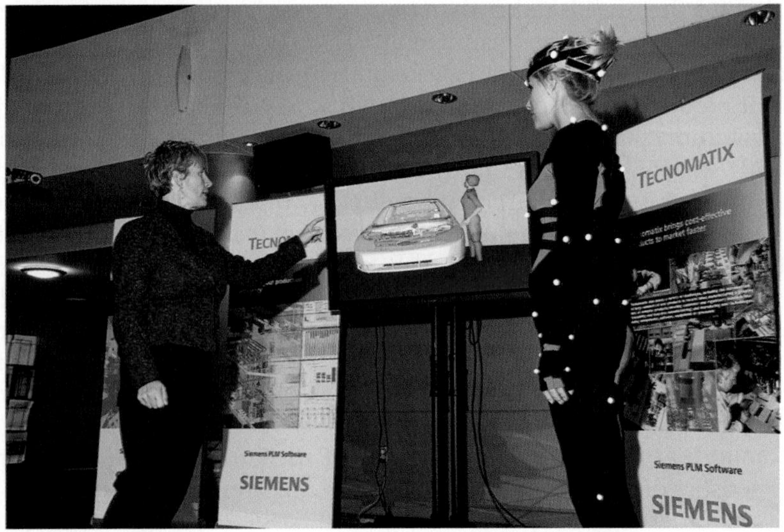

Ford's digital human ergonomics.

Ford uses a sophisticated computer program to test and evaluate working conditions prior to actually setting up an assembly line. The technology is used to create virtual factories, parts, and cars that are lifelike so that virtual workers or avatars can assemble them and identify problems during the computer simulation rather than after the facilities have been built and equipped. The virtual software was developed in collaboration with German supplier Siemens AG and uses a digital human model or smart avatar to record critical data for designing the process of building a car or truck. Data collected include stress on joints when moving a heavy part or the distance a worker must reach to install a bolt or wire.

(continued)

BEST PRACTICES IN OPERATIONS MANAGEMENT

Computer Testing of Work Methods at Ford (*continued*)

According to Allison Stephens, Ford's ergonomics technical specialist with vehicle manufacturing engineering: "Our digital employees—Jack and Jill—are helping us predict the ergonomic effect of long-term repetitive motions. The impact on health and safety metrics, as well as on quality, has been tremendous." The more physically difficult a job is, the less likely it is to be completed properly. Thus Ford uses the data to make tasks easier to perform during the allotted cycle time, with the goal of reducing both injuries and employee turnover. The automaker has been using this approach to digital ergonomics (or CAPP) since 2000 and credits it in part with an 11 percent improvement in quality for 2007 versus the industry average of 2 percent, according to a 2007 study by the Global Quality Research System.

Source: Sarah Webster, "Computer Models Ease Ford Workers' Tasks, Raise Quality," *Detroit Free Press,* March 26, 2008, p. E1.

Administrative Technologies

Administrative technologies are those that track, record, and analyze the information that is required for manufacturing activities. **Manufacturing requirements planning** (MRP) consists of interconnected software packages that may include forecasting, master scheduling, order entry, engineering data, bills of material, maintenance, purchasing, and receiving/distribution capabilities. MRP systems help in planning production and tracking inventory by forecasting and calculating order sizes and quantities. These systems were first developed in the 1970s, when mainframe computers were necessary to handle the computational challenges. Most MRP systems started off as a series of isolated programs—e.g., one for forecasting, one for production planning, and one for inventory control—and businesses worked to integrate the outputs from one system to be read into another. Unfortunately, many of these so-called legacy systems are run with different computer languages and have a very difficult time speaking to one another—almost as if a meeting involved people speaking multiple languages without any interpreters. As computers have rapidly developed greater data processing capabilities, a new type of system called enterprise resource planning (ERP) has been developed that uses a large, integrated information system that can support most enterprise processes and data storage needs across the entire organization. Leading ERP providers include SAP, Peoplesoft, and Baan. ERP packages are very expensive to install ($1 to $10 million), but they offer the ability to truly integrate all of a business's functions in one system.

● **Manufacturing requirements planning** interconnected software packages that may include forecasting, master scheduling, order entry, engineering data, bills of material, maintenance, purchasing, and receiving/distribution capabilities

SUPPLY CHAIN INFORMATION TECHNOLOGIES

One of the biggest changes in the past 10 to 15 years has been the ability to use information technology to virtually integrate companies across the supply chain so that they can exchange information on orders and transactions more quickly and efficiently. Figure 13.2 provides a simplified view of some of the many information transfers that occur between various partners in the supply chain. These include purchase orders, manifests, invoices, electronic payments, forecasts, and receiving/acknowledgment. Organizations use a variety of software programs to coordinate and exchange this information.

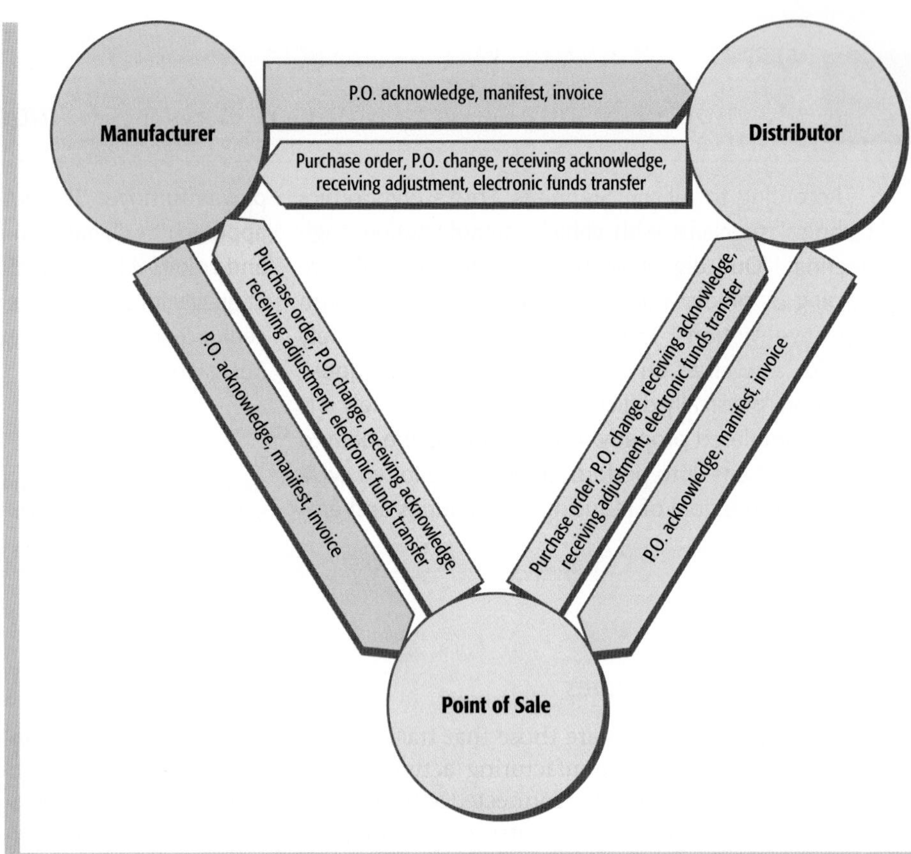

FIGURE 13.2 Information Flow Model

Linking Across Organizations

An overview of supply chain information systems is provided in Figure 13.3. This overview was first developed by Steven Kahl, a software industry analyst at Piper Jaffray. The overview was then refined in a textbook by Chopra and Meindl. Figure 13.3 examines three levels of a generic supply chain: suppliers, internal supply chain, and customers. A separate column is added for logistics to deal with transportation issues such as network design, warehouse and transportation planning, and warehouse management and transportation.

Enterprise resource planning systems were defined earlier in this chapter. They pull together a variety of basic business functions, including finance, accounting, marketing, sales, and various operational systems such as inventory and materials management, purchasing, and scheduling. Figure 13.4 provides an overview of the various functions and areas of a company that are typically integrated in an ERP system.

When an ERP system is implemented properly, it connects all areas of a business and can be used to connect the business directly with its suppliers and customers. Manufacturing can see orders as soon as they are received. Purchasing gets an up-to-the-minute report of what manufacturing requires. Sales can track the exact and current status of a customer order. The accounting system is immediately updated as relevant transactions occur. This type of integration has substantial benefits, with savings that can be in the millions of dollars. Redundant jobs can be eliminated and double entry of information reduced.

To illustrate the power of ERP systems, let's consider what information systems for a particular company looked like prior to ERP systems. First, there would be many different software packages for different computer platforms, none of

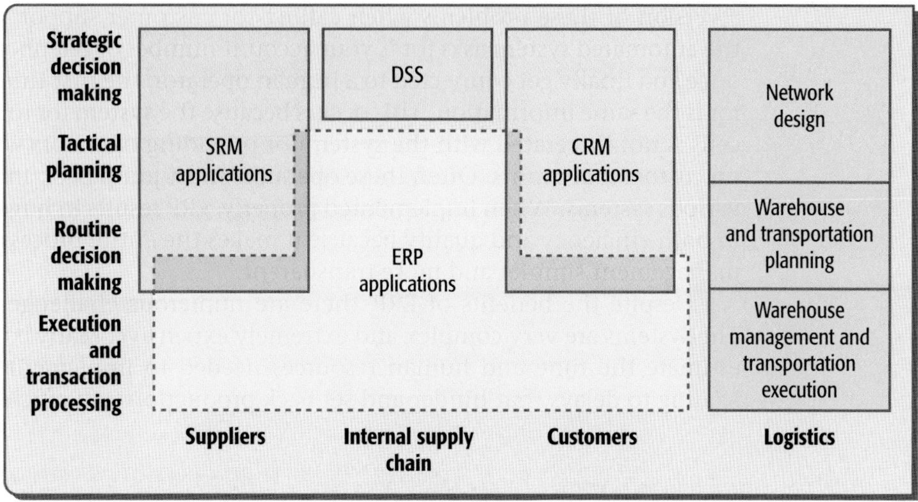

FIGURE 13.3 Supply Chain Technologies

Source: S. Kahl, Bozarth, Cecil, and Robert B. Handfield. *Introduction to Operations and Supply Chain Management,* 2d ed. Electronically reproduced by permission of Pearson Education, Inc., Upper Saddle River, New Jersey.

which talked directly with the others. For example, an order might come into sales and need to be posted to the sales accounting system. Because the sales system was not integrated with the manufacturing planning system, the order data would have to be reentered into this system, taking extra time and creating an opportunity for quality problems. Similarly, when the order was completed and delivered to the customer, data would need to be entered into the accounting system in order to initiate and monitor the billing cycle. Finally, if a product was returned for any reason, this initiated a whole new series of transactions in sales, manufacturing planning, and accounting. You have probably experienced

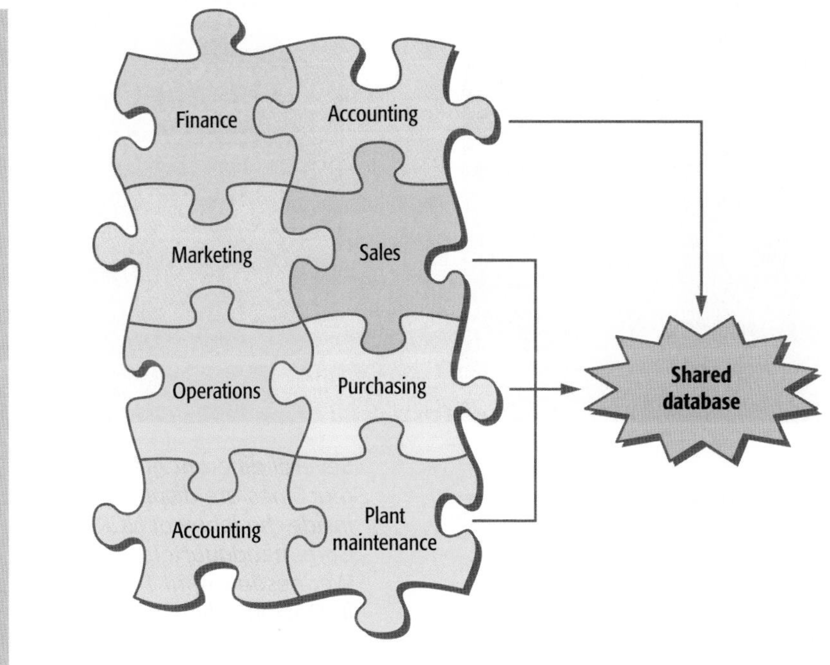

FIGURE 13.4 An ERP System

a version of these problems when calling for customer support—the first thing the automated system asks for is your account number or telephone number, and once you finally get connected to a human operator, the first thing he or she asks for is the same information. This occurs because the system for routing the phone calls is not integrated with the system for providing operators with information on customer accounts. Often these operators must jump back and forth between various systems. When implemented properly, ERP results in huge improvements in both efficiency and quality because it makes the entire process of information management simpler and more transparent.

Despite the benefits of ERP, there are numerous challenges and obstacles. The systems are very complex and extremely expensive. Many companies underestimate the time and human resources needed to implement such a system, leading to delays that hinder and set back production and efficiency.

TECHNOLOGY IN OPERATIONS MANAGEMENT

ERP for Medical Equipment and ATMs

Manufacturing catheters and ATMs may seem like very different processes, but the ERP systems powering the information behind the manufacturing process are very similar. Both C. R. Bard, a manufacturer of heart catheters and stents, and NCR, a maker of ATMs, point-of-sale systems, and data warehouse technology, began long-term overhauls of their business information systems by standardizing on a single ERP platform. Results have been positive at both companies, with a reduction in the number of distribution centers and an improvement in accurate and on-time shipments to customers.

Several different ATM machines are displayed inside the lobby of NCR Corp. headquarters, Wednesday, April 11, 2007, in Dayton, Ohio.

At Bard, implementation began in 2001, with the goal of getting better control of inventory, eliminating third-party distribution centers, and centralizing the company's 400,000-square-foot global distribution center. Prior to the new ERP system, a single product would pass through two or three facilities, with no one system having a global view of the business and information being spread out over several local databases. When a product was manufactured, each facility managed its

(continued)

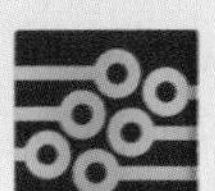

TECHNOLOGY IN OPERATIONS MANAGEMENT

ERP for Medical Equipment and ATMs (*continued*)

particular part of the process, with the information in the corporate system being updated when the product was ready to send to the next facility. Because the majority of processes required manual data input, there were many chances for information errors.

Since ERP implementation, work on a catheter is tracked and reviewed by one system. Production of a catheter may begin in a facility in Monks Corner, South Carolina, with the catheter then being sent to Nogales, Mexico, for packaging. Finally, it is shipped to Covington, Georgia, for sterilization. The manufacturing components of ERP direct the products among work stations within each facility, while the system also routes products between facilities and updates each order's progress in near real time. After the sterilization and quality assurance processes at the Covington facility are complete, the product is loaded onto a shuttle truck that delivers it to the global distribution center. There, the ERP system sends a signal to the warehouse management system to receive the product. At the distribution center, operators scan bar codes to update the warehouse management system, and the product is assigned to stocking locations, where it is available to fill orders. This quick overview leaves out several steps in the process but gives an idea of the magnitude of the information exchanges that must take place. A very similar sequence of events is followed at NCR or in a supply chain where each facility is owned and operated by a different company.

NCR's implementation began in 2000. The company had 20 different order management systems, 3 different warehouse management systems, and over 166 distributed applications spread throughout the company. The implementation of the ERP system allowed NCR to consolidate redundant distribution centers into regional centers, with greater visibility of inventory across the facilities. This allows different divisions to share common inventory, thus improving inventory turns. By the end of 2005, NCR had rolled out ERP to over 90 percent of the company, with great success. The photo on the previous page shows production of ATMs similar to the type produced by NCR.

Source: B. Trebilcock, "A Tale of Two ERP Systems," *Modern Materials Handling* 60, no. 13 (2005), 27.

The focus of ERP systems is primarily on the daily transactions at a very tactical level. **Decision support systems** (DSS) are information systems that assist users in analyzing, manipulating, and presenting data in a way that aids higher-level decision making. These systems are used to help with decisions like facility design, product design, product portfolio management, and other decisions where a great deal of data is needed, yet the decision involves a strategic and expensive investment.

● **Decision support systems** information systems that assist users in analyzing, manipulating, and presenting data in a way that aids higher-level decision making

Supplier relationship management (SRM) and customer relationship management (CRM) systems are computer-based information systems that focus on external linkages with suppliers and customers. These are the systems that must interface with the systems and people at upstream suppliers and downstream customers. An example of an SRM is the computer system that a company such as Wal-Mart, Kroger, or Tesco uses to send orders to its various suppliers. The SRM must be able to send out the information in a standard format that the supplier's systems (often ERPs themselves) can read and integrate with easily. SRM applications include activities such as design collaboration, sourcing decision analysis, negotiation, purchase order and bid transmittal, and supply collaboration. In a sense, CRM systems are the opposite of SRM systems; they link the firm with its customers by providing applications such as market analysis, selling transactions such as invoices, order management, and call/service center management.

Amazon provides an excellent example of both an SRM and a CRM in practice. The book retailer employs an SRM to manage transactions with book wholesalers, which aggregate book titles from numerous publishers, individual publishers, logistics providers, and packaging providers. Amazon has thousands of order transactions and shipments from each of these suppliers or partners on a daily basis. Similarly, Amazon uses its CRM system to focus downstream—on customers. Amazon is well known for developing custom web pages, e-mails on books of interest, and other features that are designed to serve customers and entice them to make additional purchases from the retailer. This CRM system is also the tool that allows customers to track their orders from the time they click on the famous "one click order" to the time the product lands on their doorstep.

- **Network design applications** systems that analyze long-term strategic questions such as facility location/sizing and the design of transportation networks
- **Warehouse and transportation planning** systems that facilitate tactical planning by allocating static logistics capacity in an optimal manner based on business requirements
- **Warehouse management and transportation management systems** systems that manage, track, and control transactions and movement of materials between supply chain partners

The final group of IT systems we will examine focuses on logistical decisions. **Network design applications** analyze long-term strategic questions such as facility location/sizing and the design of transportation networks. Common components of such systems include simulation software such as Arena or Flexsim and optimization modeling software such as Lindo or ILOG. One of the challenges that many supply chains face is the evolution of facilities over time. For example, a smaller company or supply chain may start out with one distribution center that is located centrally in the company's primary sales region (say, east of the Mississippi for an eastern U.S. company). As the company's sales grow, it may need to add a second facility. The decision on where, how, and what size facility to add is complicated by many factors that need to be analyzed simultaneously. Similarly, a company such as Sony has a network consisting of numerous manufacturing plants, distribution centers, suppliers, and customers. The prospect of expanding or contracting this network requires fairly complex analysis to capture the many interactions between facilities and partners within the supply chain.

Warehouse and transportation planning systems facilitate tactical planning by allocating static logistics capacity in an optimal manner based on business requirements. These systems also make use of simulation and optimization modeling. For example, decisions need to be made concerning which units or parts to carry in a particular distribution center and how many units to ship from each distribution center to each demand point. An optimization or simulation model would make use of data on distribution center capacities, demand levels, location of demand, and shipping costs in order to find a low-cost solution.

A pick-to-light fulfillment system. The computer system sequentially paces workers through a sequence of items to fill an order. Lights show which item(s) to pick and the quantity.

Warehouse management and transportation management systems manage, track, and control transactions and movement of materials between supply chain partners. Warehouse management systems control the flow of work in a warehouse by telling workers where to store materials, where to pick them up, where to send them to, and what quantity to pick. Much of this work is facilitated by technologies such as the bar code or RFID, automatic conveyor belts, and pick-to-light systems. The photograph shows a worker using a pick-to-light system in a distribution center. Transportation management systems plan and manage flows between companies. In the last 15 years, changes in communication technology such as the Internet, mobile phones, tracking technology, and global positioning systems have radically changed the amount of information generated and the speed with which this is done. Most companies can track a particular shipment to its exact location within minutes or seconds and can provide real-time status updates to customers or suppliers.

Despite the increased emphasis on logistics systems over the past 15 years, the level of integration with the other supply chain technologies in Figure 13.3 is still relatively low. This is due to the fact that logistics systems have largely been seen as an outside-the-company or at-the-end-of-the-shift type of thing. In other words, historically, businesses worried most about getting products produced and purchased, and then figured out where and how to ship them. In the current age of increasingly integrated supply chains, this approach is outmoded. Thus, firms should work to integrate these logistics systems with other supply chain systems. One primary hurdle is technical: Getting different systems to work together increases complexity and makes it more challenging to optimize the entire system rather than individual components within the system. The second primary hurdle is organizational: Logistics personnel need to be involved earlier in the decision-making process and must have a major voice in planning shipments and production.

The Bullwhip Effect

We turn now to an examination of interactions between supply chain members involving the exchange of information and inventory. This is a critical area in which information technology has greatly enhanced the ability of companies to exchange information quickly, accurately, and inexpensively in ways that really create the ability to manage a true supply chain rather than simply operations within a single company. The link between computer technologies, information technology, and supply chain management is the fundamental reason for the tremendous growth in interest, application, and development of the wide field of supply chain management and the associated tools and techniques.

Supply chains are very dynamic because of their interorganizational nature and their complexity. Every firm in a supply chain is linked to other firms upstream and downstream. The flow of goods, services, materials, and information is complex because firms are owned and operated in an independent manner rather than as a supply chain. The decisions and actions of one partner in a supply chain can affect the operations of both upstream and downstream partners. Upstream members of a supply chain must react to orders and other transactions from downstream members. For example, Wal-Mart has a reputation for being a challenging customer, often demanding that its suppliers provide specific packaging types or sizes. While having Wal-Mart as a customer can provide a great deal of business, it can also bring many challenges. Typically there will be increasing variability in order quantities as you proceed upstream. The **bullwhip effect** is the situation in which variance in demand increases from downstream to upstream in a supply chain. The term gets its name from the motion of a bullwhip—the handle starts the action with a small motion, while the tip has a large range of motion.

● **Bullwhip effect** the situation in which variance in demand increases from downstream to upstream in a supply chain

Figure 13.5 illustrates the bullwhip effect for a variety of packaged goods, such as cookies made by Kellogg's or toilet paper made by Kimberly Clark. Daily demand for particular types of cookies is fairly consistent at the store level, but retailers' orders (such as those from Tesco, Wal-Mart, or Target) are much more variable. In turn, the variation in the manufacturer's weekly orders for packaging materials from its supplier is much higher than the variation in retailer orders. Finally, the package supplier, the furthest upstream link in this supply chain, has

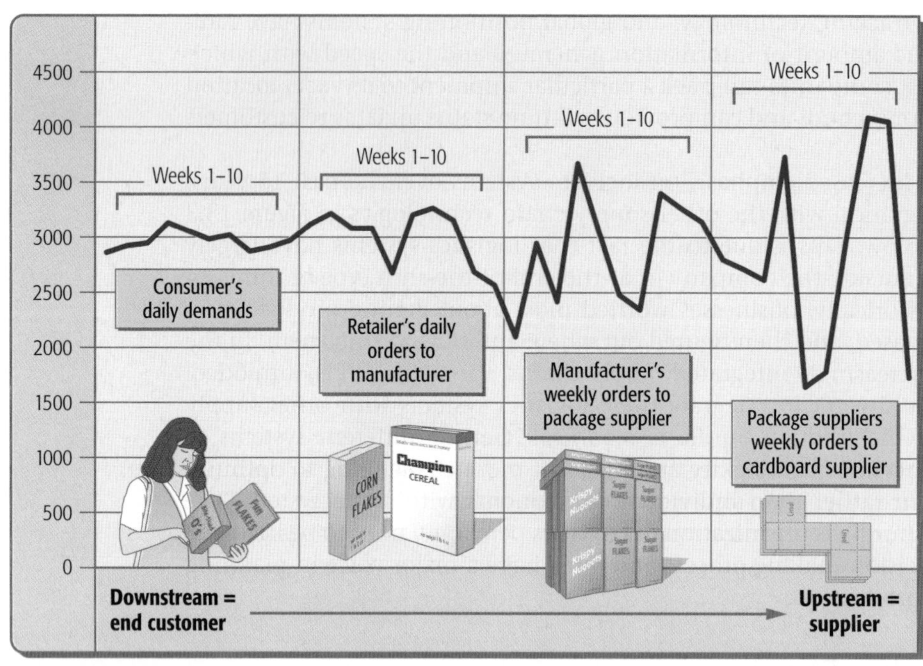

FIGURE 13.5 Bullwhip Effect for Packaged Goods Such As Cookies or Toilet Paper

the greatest variability. Because of the mismatches between levels of the supply chain, inventories accumulate in some companies while shortages occur elsewhere. Firms with too much inventory reduce their ordering, and those with shortages seek to expedite or increase their orders. The end result is a great deal of variance and frustration caused by processes that are quite well thought out at the firm level but do not work well across the overall supply chain. The causes of the bullwhip effect come from both outside the individual firm (i.e., the supply chain) and inside the firm itself. Examining these causes provides a first step toward reducing the damaging effects.

External Causes

A company cannot directly control the actions of its customers or suppliers. These parties will often make decisions that appear to be in their own best interests but can cause challenges for other parties in the supply chain. However, while companies cannot directly control other members of the supply chain, they can often find ways to subtly alter those members' behaviors or to hedge against uncertainties introduced by other parties. Some of the major external causes of the bullwhip effect include the following.

Variable Delivery Times. The delivery times for components and parts often vary from what the supplier quotes. Late deliveries of key parts or components can cause delays in production. Firms may switch from producing one product to another because a key component is missing. Suppose Sony is faced with a shortage of a particular circuit board for TV Model 100. To accommodate this shortage, Sony may switch production to TV Model 200. This necessitates changes in the required parts, resulting in changed order quantities.

Incorrect Shipment Quantities. When an order comes in with fewer units than expected—because of either poor quality, a miscount, or a problem in production—this can cause disruptions in the production of the items using that component. Incorrect shipments have a ripple effect similar to that caused by late shipments.

Volume Changes. Customers often demand a change in the quantity ordered for a product or service. This necessitates a fast reaction from the manufacturer, which may in turn require changes from suppliers. For example, an unusually cold winter will lead to increased sales of snow blowers, which in turn will lead to increased demand for engines, rotors, handles, and the other component parts of a snow blower.

Service and Product Mix Changes. Changes in the mix of goods in an order from customers can cause a ripple effect. For example, a grocery store such as Kroger might change the composition of its Oreos order from 60 percent 16-ounce packages and 40 percent 24-ounce packages to a 40/60 mix. This decision can lead to changes in the production schedule at the Oreo plant. Similarly, the companies that supply Nabisco with the packaging and raw materials for Oreos will need to change their schedules.

Internal Causes

Many supply chain disruptions are the result of an organization's own behavior. While the decisions at the company level may seem logical, the effects of those decisions can have a large ripple effect. Companies have direct control over many of these internal causes and can reduce their effect by communicating and coordinating with customers and suppliers. Internal causes include the following.

Service or Product Promotions. Service or product promotions, while good for increasing sales, lead to spikes in demand. Typically, companies will offer price discounts to spur the sales of a product or service. Consumer packaged goods manufacturers such as Kellogg's, Nabisco, Coca-Cola, or Campbell's are particularly prone to problems resulting from promotions. A company like Coca-Cola will often discount its product during periods of slow demand (such as the winter). Retailers may take advantage of these discounts to forward-buy products well in advance of expected sales. This practice creates excess inventory at the retailer, and the spike in demand from large orders may force the manufacturer to use overtime production.

From a supply chain point of view, pricing policies should be structured to facilitate steady demand and lower costs across the supply chain. For example, the Campbell Soup Company introduced a strategic pricing plan that provided financial incentives for customers to place orders that were more efficient for the supply chain as a whole. This program included incentives for placing electronic orders, accepting direct-to-store deliveries, and buying full pallets or truckloads of a particular product. Campbell's shares the savings with customers in order to create a win-win situation that minimizes total supply chain costs.

Information Errors. Forecast errors and incorrect information within the company's ERP system can cause large variations in the upstream supply chains. Faced with a forecast that turns out to be significantly low or high, companies will try to expedite or cut the quantity of an order. Such changes come with little notice, forcing suppliers and other upstream partners to react quickly. Incorrect information such as miscounts of physical inventory can cause shortages (leading to expedited or increased purchases) or excess inventory (leading to order cancellations or reductions). Incorrect or delayed information flow between buyers and suppliers also affects supply chain dynamics. Companies that share data with their suppliers can cause confusion if the data are updated too often or too sporadically. Information can get distorted when it is passed through multiple links in the supply chain, just as a rumor gets started by being passed from one person to another. Supply chain managers should look to minimize information errors wherever possible.

New Service/Product Introductions. New service and product introductions have a large effect on the supply chain because of the increased uncertainty as to how the new offering will sell. A wildly successful product such as a Sony Playstation 3 can face extreme shortages in demand. Alternatively, a product that is forecast to sell well but falls flat can create major stores of excess inventory throughout many levels and locations in the supply chain. New products and services often require new production techniques, systems, and supply chains. If the new systems do not ramp up production as quickly as expected, there can be dramatic shortages throughout the supply chain.

Engineering Changes. Changes to the design of products or services can have a large impact on suppliers. An effort to streamline the design of a bicycle so that it requires fewer parts may make the end product less expensive, but it will also alter relationships with the suppliers of the parts. Similarly, adding features such as an icemaker on a refrigerator creates more supply relationships to manage, and also more opportunities for errors to occur.

Internally Generated Shortages. Internal shortages of parts can occur for a number of reasons, including machine breakdowns, inefficient or new workers, strikes, sickness, or quality problems in production. As companies scramble to correct one shortage, another shortage may be created in another area or the problem may be passed on to suppliers. High turnover or excessive demands placed on the work force can also result in quality problems or shortages.

Minimizing the Bullwhip Effect

Once the causes of the bullwhip effect are understood, there are several steps that can be taken to reduce its impact on the supply chain. These steps involve a combination of information technology to help coordinate information exchange across organizations, changes in inventory practices, and greater cooperation between supply chain partners.

Coordinating Information. Sharing sales information with other supply chain members is one of the key ways to reduce the bullwhip effect. Managers should look to minimize the cycle time in receiving and updating demand information. One technique that is common is vendor-managed inventory (VMI), where vendors monitor sales at the retailer and replenish inventories when supplies are low. In the 1990s, Procter & Gamble had major bullwhip problems with one of its bestsellers: Pampers diapers. Despite relatively constant customer demand, Procter & Gamble was faced with substantial variability in the orders from retailers. The variability was amplified further when it was transmitted upstream to Procter & Gamble's suppliers. Among the primary causes were order batching, where distributors ordered on an infrequent basis, and frequent price changes by Procter & Gamble. One of the solutions was to employ vendor-managed inventory starting with the supplier 3M managing inventory for Procter & Gamble, which in turn managed inventory for its key customer, Wal-Mart.

Inventory Policies. One of the best tools involves the use of everyday low pricing, which consists of offering constant prices and removing price promotions that encourage customers to place large orders. Reducing lead time is another effective tool because it allows both suppliers and customers to reduce their levels of safety stock and place smaller orders. Postponement occurs when a manufacturer delays completing the final features of a product until a firm customer order is received. Postponement allows companies to hold inventory in a general form and change it to a specific form demanded by customers through assembly or manufacturing. For example, Hewlett-Packard can forecast overall demand for printers fairly accurately, but because it sells printers in scores of countries and the power requirements and languages vary, there is huge variability at the country level. Hewlett-Packard redesigned its manufacturing process so that the printers were produced separately from the power cords and user manuals, which are then added to the final package at regional distribution centers that serve particular countries. The use of postponement allowed Hewlett-Packard to better forecast the demand for printers and adjust this core product through the addition of less expensive and easier to manage power cords and user manuals, leading to a dramatic reduction in cost and improvement in responsiveness.

Cooperation Among Supply Chain Members. Sharing information and cooperating to set policies that benefit the entire supply chain involves the development of a high degree of trust between partners. Coordinating forecasts and ordering policies is very effective, but it requires the sharing of sensitive information. Partners must also communicate frequently and understand the challenges that each organization faces. Often, purchasing contracts will be structured so that a customer or supplier can share in the benefits realized by its trading partner resulting from changes that it made within its organization.

BEST PRACTICES IN OPERATIONS MANAGEMENT

Using RFID to Combat Counterfeit Drugs

Patients usually assume that the drugs they purchase in their local pharmacy are the ones that their physician prescribed and are the correct ones. Yet drug counterfeiting is a huge problem worldwide, with the World Health Organization estimating that global sales of counterfeit drugs were $32 billion in 2003, or 10 percent of all drugs sold worldwide. Drug counterfeiting is rampant for two primary reasons. First, drugs have a very high value-to-weight ratio. Second, the lengthy supply chain among producer, wholesalers, distribution, and retailers involves numerous parties and is open to substitution, switching, and/or false labeling.

The U.S. Food and Drug Administration (FDA) and its counterparts in other countries are looking to radio frequency identification (RFID) as a key technology for combating counterfeiting. Pharmaceutical manufacturers have for a long time generated their own ID codes for raw materials, ingredients, and finished products. These codes are applied to the interim containers and packaging throughout the production process. The problem with counterfeiting occurs once the drugs leave the manufacturer's facility and enter the wider market, where tracking becomes very difficult. To address this issue, the FDA passed a law requiring drug distributors to provide a complete pedigree or chain of custody for all products passing though their system as of December 1, 2006. This is an enormous challenge because the big three wholesalers move about 2.5 million bottles of drugs a day through the supply chain, each of which has to be tracked at every step. RFID is seen as a way

(*continued*)

BEST PRACTICES IN OPERATIONS MANAGEMENT

Using RFID to Combat Counterfeit Drugs (continued)

to provide unique serialization, meaning that every bottle, package, or container of medicine at any point in the supply chain has a unique ID number assigned. Existing methods of bar coding are too easy to counterfeit. RFID is much more difficult to duplicate because the information is burned into the chip at the manufacturer. RFID is seen as the solution because it is difficult to copy and does not require line of sight reading, as bar codes do.

Sources: B. Brewin, "FDA Wants Prescription Drugs Tracked with RFID," *Federal Computer Week* 20, no. 20 (2007), 14; H. Forcinio, "Cracking Down on Counterfeiting," *Pharmaceutical Technology* 30, no. 8 (2006), 46–48; R. W. Buzzeo, "Counterfeit Pharmaceuticals and the Public Health," *Wall Street Journal,* October 4, 2005, A20.

EVALUATING TECHNOLOGY INVESTMENTS

While new technologies can certainly lead to improvements, the decision as to whether and when to invest in a new technology is a very challenging one. There are scores of techniques for evaluating investments in new technology. Here the focus is on providing an overview of the factors that should be considered, rather than describing one or more specific techniques for making a decision as to whether to invest.

Companies have historically evaluated technology investments primarily on the basis of financial analysis; for example, a net present value calculation may be performed and the decision to install a new technology may be made if the return is positive. However, innovative technologies are difficult to evaluate purely quantitatively for several reasons. First, the potential benefits and costs of unproven technologies are often difficult to estimate accurately because there is so little experience with their use. Second, many of the potential benefits are not associated with greater productivity, but rather with the ability to achieve economies of scope, greater production flexibility, or more service for the customer. Many computer-based technologies, such as FMS, CAD, or a new piece of software for web site administration, are difficult to evaluate because their benefits are often more strategic in nature and difficult to quantify. Traditional financial analysis tends to focus primarily on the costs of implementation and the resulting reductions in production cost. Yet the benefits of many computer-based technologies often involve increased product variety, improved product quality, and faster cycle times. These types of benefits are very difficult to quantify or place a precise financial value on. The approach most businesses have taken is to combine traditional financial analysis, such as cash flow or net present value, with a more subjective analysis of the intangible benefits of a given technology. Thus, the evaluation process for new technologies is often more subjective than objective.

There are two key things to remember when evaluating new technologies. The first is that there is a strong first mover advantage. Developing a new technology is one of the few ways to build a truly sustainable competitive advantage. There is a great deal of empirical evidence showing that firms that experiment and are the first to adopt new technologies generally have better financial performance than firms that play follow the leader. While many technologies fail, generally the business learns even from its failures. If a business chooses to wait until a technology has been "proven" safe, then it is difficult for that business to gain an advantage from what has become a commodity product.

The second key thing to remember when evaluating new technologies is that the cost of hardware is generally only the tip of the iceberg. Numerous companies have discovered the hard way that the costs of software, training, and the learning time required to fully master a new technology can be several times the up-front hardware costs. The lesson here is that it is important to allocate a sufficient budget for training and development, and also to set reasonable goals for a new technology. A new technology will not radically change a business by itself. Instead, new technologies are best thought of as catalysts for change—the employees and the organization must change with the new technology.

Typical Benefits of New Technologies

New technologies come with both benefits and challenges. A key to maximizing the value of these technologies is finding ways to exploit the beneficial aspects, while minimizing the challenges and hurdles faced during implementation. Many companies have had catastrophic results because they emphasized the wrong aspects of a new technology and/or rushed to implement a new technology without a good understanding of the issues.

Cost Reductions

The easiest benefit to quantify is reductions in cost resulting from the ability of new technology to either replace workers entirely or speed up the rate of production. Prior to the development of widespread computer applications in the early 1970s, the term *automation* most often meant fixed automation, where tools were developed for a specific application. These technologies would apply to only a single product or a few products, but would greatly speed up production. For example, at many fast-food restaurants, such as Panchero's, tortillas are rolled fresh from dough when a customer orders food. This is done to keep the tortilla as fresh as possible; however, each tortilla may take 30 to 60 seconds to make. In contrast, a commercial bakery will have an automated rolling machine that can make 10,000 or more tortillas per hour at considerably less cost per unit.

Cost reductions can also result from changes in materials, reductions in inventory, improved distribution, or increased quality. Cabinet manufacturers such as Merillat or Kraftmaid use patterning software to maximize the percentage of each foot of lumber used in cutting parts for cabinets. Information technologies have played a key role in reducing inventory and transportation costs. One of the primary reasons for holding inventory and having multiple distribution centers is as a buffer against the unpredictability of demand. The earlier discussion of the bullwhip effect highlighted the need for supply chain partners to carefully manage information exchange across the supply chain.

While many technologies lead to substantial cost reductions, it is important to also consider the skill level of the employees operating the equipment. More advanced equipment often requires much more highly skilled or educated employees to properly operate, set up, and maintain the equipment. It is also very important to realize that new technologies generally have other, less tangible benefits. In fact, the primary benefits of many technologies are based more on economies of scope or the ability to efficiently increase variety or product quality, as described in the next sections.

Increased Product Variety

New technologies typically offer ways to increase product variety. Computer-based technologies offer the ability to capitalize on **economies of scope**, which allow many products to be produced cost-efficiently using the same equipment. The LEGO® Factory example shown in Figure 13.6 (on page 499) illustrates the value of economies of scope: By developing a system to offer a completely customizable

● **Economies of scope** the ability to produce many products cost-efficiently using the same equipment

LEGO set, the company attracts new customers and can charge a price premium. Another example of increased product variety is Lands' End, which offers custom-manufactured pants. The customer goes to Lands' End's web site and answers a few questions regarding his or her pants size and dimensions, and the order is then transmitted to the manufacturer. A computerized pattern maker is employed to cut the specific pattern for that pair of pants, and the final product is sewed and assembled, then mailed to the customer.

BEST PRACTICES IN OPERATIONS MANAGEMENT

LEGO® Custom Building Blocks

The LEGO Group has been making plastic blocks that can be assembled into a huge variety of shapes since 1932, but customization occurred only when the child (or adult) took standard sets of LEGO pieces and put them together in his or her own unique way. Starting in 2005, The LEGO Group introduced a new computer application called LEGO Factory that lets customers design their own products; however, the cost of these products is relatively similar to that of "made to stock" products without customization. The company allows this mass customization by utilizing a Digital Designer software package that customers can download for free and use to design their unique LEGO product. The LEGO Group then assembles the product for shipping to the customer by making several minor modifications to the normal five-step LEGO production process. Figure 13.6 provides an overview of the process for fulfilling a custom order.

The five steps in the normal process are

1. *Granules.* Plastic granules of different colors are melted, dumped into a high metal silo, and then fed into molding machines.
2. *Molding.* The plastic granules are then heated and fed into molds. Pressure is applied to the blocks, and then they are cooled.
3. *Transport.* The molding process is completely automated, with finished pieces rolling down conveyor belts and then being sorted into boxes by color and shape. When a box is full, the molding machine sends a radio signal to one of the several robot trucks that are guided by grooves in the floor. The trucks pick up full boxes and dump them onto another conveyor belt that takes them to the next step.
4. *Decorating and assembly.* The bricks are then decorated, if necessary (some bricks get additional details, such as painting of eyes and lips on a face).
5. *Packaging.* In this stage, LEGO kits are created. Boxes, called cassettes, travel on a conveyor belt underneath the bins that hold each type of piece. The bins automatically feed the correct number of pieces into each box: An individual kit might contain 20 big blue blocks, 15 little blue blocks, 25 big red blocks, and so on. In the final step, packing operators fold the boxes, add additional pieces (oddly shaped or one-of-a-kind pieces) by hand, and watch for any machine-caused mistakes.

To create customized sets, LEGO Factory alters the process just described only in Step 5. In this step, the software takes an inventory of the pieces the customer has selected for his or her design and sends the order to the LEGO warehouse. There, in a small corner of the warehouse, The LEGO Group has set up a manual fulfillment center. The company simplifies the process by offering a limited selection of bricks for the custom orders, thus keeping fulfillment costs only slightly higher than those for standard sets of bricks. According to Michael McNally, The LEGO Group's senior brand-relations manager, "We've already produced these elements. So it's just a matter of rejiggering our fulfillment process and packing process." The results have been well received by customers, with over 77,000 models designed by the software in the first month of availability. Some of the most complex models have included the Danish Parliament Building and M. C. Escher's "Another World."

To design your own custom model or to see how it works, go to http://factory.lego.com/.

Source: M. A. Prospero, "Brick by Brick: Lego's New Building Blocks," *Fast Company,* issue 98 (2005), 35.

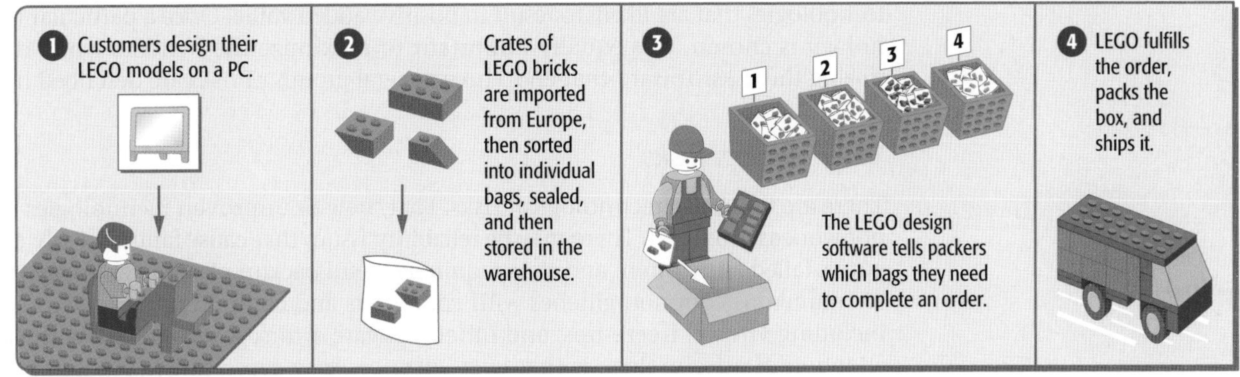

FIGURE 13.6 Illustration of LEGO® Factory Customization Process

Source: From *Fast Company* by Prospero, M. A.,. Copyright 2005 by Mansueto Ventures LLC. Reproduced with permission of Mansueto Ventures LLC in the format Textbook via Copyright Clearance Center.

Improved Quality

Technology is often used to improve quality. Automated equipment reduces variability by removing human labor from the system. Process technology is designed to perform the same task repeatedly, and when it is properly done, it leads to much higher quality. In the LEGO example, technology is used heavily to both reduce costs and improve quality. The molding machines are highly automated and are designed to deliver LEGO blocks with no more than 0.01-inch variations. Conveyor belts are used to move pieces between stations. Automatic sorting equipment is used to build packets of LEGO blocks and is substantially more accurate and faster than human labor would be at doing this job.

Jumeirah Essex House LEGO model. The 8.5-foot replica is built to scale and is the world's largest free-standing hotel model built from LEGO bricks, created by Master Model Builder from LEGOLAND California, Eric Hunter, on display in the lobby of the Jumeirah Essex House—Monday, December 17, 2007, in New York.

Faster Cycle Times

Manufacturing technologies such as the automated LEGO molding machine, CNC machines, or FMSs typically lead to reduced cycle times because setup times are greatly reduced. An important part of equipment design is making it easy and fast to change from one part to another. Plastic injection-molding machines of the type used by The LEGO Group have been engineered over the years to allow quick changeovers from one mold to another. Electronic communication, such as instant messages, electronic orders, e-mail, and the Internet, also leads to faster exchange of information. Reduced cycle times are beneficial because they facilitate shorter order delivery times, allow smaller orders to be produced, and also allow companies to respond more quickly to changes in market demand.

Technology Adoption Risks

Unfortunately, technology is not a magical solution to a company's problems. Most new or unproven technologies come with a high degree of risk and uncertainty. In order to manage and implement operating technologies successfully, it is critical to carefully evaluate the relative benefits versus the risks and to seek to choose only those technologies that are likely to result in positive added value. Once a particular technology is chosen, it is equally important to maximize the benefits while minimizing the risks. Toward that end, three general groups of risks are described here.

Technological Risks

There are two basic technological risks. First, new or unproven technologies may not work as promised. There may be reliability issues that cause failures. Early computers failed fairly often, and thus required careful backup plans. Even today there are numerous common glitches with computers and computer-based technology, including viruses, freeze-ups, and other software errors. A second risk with early adoption of a technology is that later advances may cause earlier versions to become obsolete. The advantage of being the first with a technology is very powerful (it is difficult for a company to be a leader if it waits until a technology is established and successful before adopting it), but latecomers often can leapfrog competitors by implementing later versions of the technology. Global positioning system (GPS) software is an excellent example of both types of technological risk. Early adopters struggled with maps and coordinates that were inaccurate, while also finding that the software helped them improve route efficiency. More recently, FreshDirect, an online grocer based in New York City, had a different problem. The routing software worked well in two dimensions for developing routes and maps across the city. However, the third dimension, building height, was problematic. The software was unable to account for the difference in travel time for the delivery person between an apartment or condominium on the first floor and an apartment on the eighth floor of a building with no elevator. The travel time and effort required to go up seven flights of stairs is fairly substantial and has a large effect on the timeliness of the delivery. For other users, as later versions of software were developed, early adopters also struggled with when and how to upgrade their systems.

BEST PRACTICES IN OPERATIONS MANAGEMENT

UPS Improves Routing

Robin Walker, dispatch planning supervisor for United Parcel Service's Eugene, Oregon, distribution center, can look at a computer screen and see how UPS's fleet of trucks is scheduled with packages. When a truck becomes overloaded, she can move some packages to a neighboring route with a lighter load. Alternatively, if a truck is short on packages, she can move packages from a busier route in order to balance the load. The software uses precise maps generated by GPS systems to forecast travel times and generate a turn-by-turn route map for every driver. The software compares alternative routes to find the ones that are lowest cost in terms of mileage and travel time. The particular routing technology was implemented in July 2002 and has shaved 299,000 miles per year off routes in the Eugene area. When the technology is fully implemented throughout the state, it is expected to cut 1.1 million miles from the 18.5 million miles accumulated by UPS drivers each year—a saving of 112,000 gallons of gasoline.

Sophisticated routing programs offered by companies such as Descartes Inc. and Micro Analytics are used by delivery companies around the world to cut costs, save time, and deliver a variety of products in a timely manner. Larger companies such as UPS, FedEx, and Airborne utilize programs developed in-house. The programs combine sophisticated mapping techniques, including GPS, with calculation algorithms to develop detailed routes—the software even helps monitor the location of each truck at any specific time to avoid congestion and traffic delays. Figure 13.7 provides an illustration of multiple routes developed by a routing system sold by Descartes Inc.

Source: S. B. McDonald, "UPS Is Driving Hard to Optimize Technology," *Knight Ridder Tribune Business News,* September 24, 2006, p. 1. Route picture courtesy of Descartes Inc.

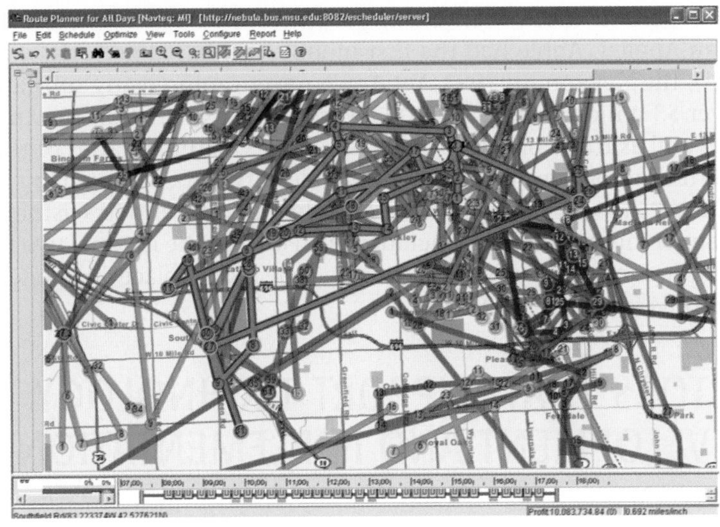

FIGURE 13.7 Routing Map from Descartes Route Planner Software (Detroit, Michigan Area)

Organizational Risks

Many firms do not adapt their organizations to make the most of a new technology. The employees using the technology must be trained to use the technology properly, and the ways in which particular activities are carried out often need to be changed. Many newly implemented technologies fail because workers have not been properly trained or given time to become familiar with new equipment. People tend to be uncomfortable with change, and many technologies feel threatening. Thus, it is critical that employees be provided with ample learning time to adapt to new technologies. If a company pushes too hard and workers become frustrated, they will simply go back to the old way of doing business and refuse to try new technologies. Adopting a new technology is similar to getting a new cellular phone. Many users will use the phone just to make phone calls, either because this is what they are used to or because they will not take the time to learn new features. However, the cell phone can do much more than that—take pictures, act as a calendar, text message, play games, and so on. Companies must create an environment that encourages workers to experiment with and try new features of a technology.

New technologies are often most valuable when they act as a catalyst for change, and businesses must be careful to embrace rather than avoid that change. For example, despite the promise that computer technologies would lead to paperless factories and offices, most businesses are swimming in more paper today than ever before. This is because businesses have not adapted their organizations to accept the electronic storage of records or the formal recognition of electronic communication. To truly progress toward a paperless workplace, organizations need to adapt their business processes.

Market Risks

Investments in technology are subject to the perceptions of customers and the general marketplace. Often a company will invest in a given technology, only to discover over time that changes in the market have made that technology obsolete or unprofitable. Apple Computer is a great example of a company that has very innovative products but often encounters a market that is not sufficiently receptive to its products. From 1994 to 2004, Apple was issued 1,300 patents (almost 50 percent more than Dell), yet Microsoft's earnings were 145 times larger than Apple's. Apple had the first mobile, pen-based personal digital assistant (PDA), the Newton, in 1993. Yet Apple never captured any substantial stake in the over $3 billion market for PDAs. Part of the explanation for Apple's difficulties, as well as those of many other companies, is the vagaries of the marketplace. The technology must not only be feasible but also be accepted by consumers, who by nature are very unpredictable. Luckily for Apple and its customers, its recent stream of innovations also includes the iPod and the iPhone, two fabulously successful products that have revolutionized the marketplace and generated substantial profits for Apple.

FACTORS THAT SUPPORT TECHNOLOGY DEVELOPMENT AND IMPLEMENTATION

Technology should be viewed as a means to an end, not as an end in itself. The most successful business applications of new product or process technology are those that incorporate and match well with changes in the "softer" side of the organization. It is imperative that organizations that are implementing cutting-edge technology invest as much or more time and effort in their work force. Technology is fundamentally a tool to facilitate the work that humans can accomplish. A good rule of thumb is that a company should spend two times as much on the soft side of a technology (i.e., training and support) as it does for the hardware or physical technology itself.

Worker Training and Empowerment

Many companies experience difficulties because they underinvest in training and providing time for employees or customers to learn a new technology. The true potential of most technologies lies not in replacing the work force, as many companies blindly seek to do, but in supplementing workers' capabilities. Shoshanna Zuboff[3] provides a persuasive description of this phenomenon by contrasting alternative approaches to implementing and managing technologies based on the roles assigned to workers within the organization. **Automating** primarily seeks to replace workers and preserve the status quo by retaining managerial control over knowledge. In contrast, an **informating** approach focuses on learning as a continuous process, seeking to transform the organization and add value through learning. An informating approach seeks to break down barriers within the organization and share knowledge freely. In providing workers with more responsibility, greater autonomy to make decisions, and more training to develop skills that can be used to tap the full potential of new technologies, an informating approach is more strategic than an automating approach. New technologies force management into a new role, that of managing intellectual capital, not equipment. Once a technology is in place, management's job is to nurture the intellectual capabilities of workers in order to create a competitive advantage.

- **Automating** an approach to technology that seeks to replace workers and preserve the status quo by retaining managerial control over knowledge
- **Informating** an approach to technology that focuses on learning as a continuous process, seeking to transform the organization and add value through learning

Strategic Emphasis

Many organizations experience disappointing results with new technologies because they do not have a clear strategic reason for implementing them. Too often a technology is implemented because it seems like an easy solution, competitors

[3] S. Zuboff, *In the Age of the Smart Machine: The Future of Work and Power* (New York: Basic Books, 1988).

are all using it, or it sounds really impressive. This is similar to the reasoning of George Leigh Mallory when he was asked why he sought to climb Mt. Everest in 1924: "Because it is there." Like Mallory, who died on the ascent of Everest, many companies with unclear strategies also fail. It wasn't until 1953 that Edmund P. Hillary and Tenzing Norgay successfully climbed the mountain—using a new technology (bottled oxygen) that didn't exist in Mallory's time.

Organizations should consider their strategy carefully when implementing a new technology and look at the long-term benefits rather than focusing primarily on the short-term payback. Often technologies get adopted in order to reduce costs, but their primary benefits are more likely to come from improved quality, greater flexibility, or faster delivery. For example, many proponents of RFID chips argue that they will greatly reduce supply chain costs. Yet at present there is little evidence to support this proposition, particularly because plain old bar codes work so well. Instead, much of the potential for RFID is tied to offering new choices, such as a grocery cart that automatically checks for items on your grocery list and recommends additional items that you may want.

SUMMARY

1. Describe the role of technology in improving operations/supply chain management. In particular, identify and describe key types of service technologies and key types of manufacturing technologies.

- Technology has always played a major role in making operations faster, more consistent, lower cost, and higher quality. From the moving assembly line for Model Ts to computers and the Internet today, technological advances offer new capabilities for operational processes.
- Service technology needs to be more generalized because of the greater need for human interaction between service providers and customers. Service technologies can be classified as either back office or front office.
  - (1) Back-office activities are those that the customer does not directly interact with or see. There is more opportunity for standardization and the use of technology to automate back-office activities. The Internet allows customers greater insight and value from back-office activities.
  - (2) Front-office activities are those that directly involve customers. There is less opportunity for standardization and automation. Computer-based technologies have provided customers with greater access and convenience while reducing costs for companies providing the services. Computers also shift the line of visibility, allowing customers to see and use information from back-office activities.
- Manufacturing technologies have some distinct differences from service technologies.
  - (1) Processing technologies physically move, shape, form, cut, or assemble products. Examples include CNC machine tools, industrial robots, and automated materials handling systems.
  - (2) Design technologies assist in developing plans for producing products. Examples include computer-aided design (CAD) and computer-aided process planning (CAPP).
  - (3) Administrative technologies assist in tracking information related to the manufacturing process. Examples include manufacturing requirements planning (MRP) and enterprise resource planning (ERP).

2. Identify and describe key types of supply chain information technologies. Explain the bullwhip effect and how to minimize it.

- Supply chain information technologies allow greater information tracking and availability both across a single organization and among multiple partners within a wider supply chain. Information on purchase orders, manifests, invoices, electronic payments, forecasts, and receiving/acknowledgment is routinely exchanged between organizations in a fast, accurate, and low-cost manner.
- Enterprise resource planning systems pull together a variety of basic business functions, including finance, accounting, marketing, sales, and various operational systems, such as inventory and materials management, purchasing, and scheduling. When an ERP system is implemented properly, it connects all areas of a business and can be used to connect directly with suppliers and customers.

- Key supply chain information technologies include decision support systems (DSS), network design applications, and warehouse and transportation planning systems.
- The bullwhip effect occurs in a multilevel supply chain when variance increases from downstream to upstream. There are a variety of external causes (variable delivery times, incorrect shipment quantities, volume changes, and service and product mix changes) and internal causes (service/product promotions, information errors, new service/product introductions, engineering changes, and internally generated shortages). The bullwhip effect has negative consequences for managing inventory across the supply chain.
- The bullwhip effect can be reduced through the application of information technology and a few alterations in supply partner behaviors. Key steps include coordinating information, adjusting inventory policies, and increasing cooperation among supply chain members.

3. Explain typical benefits and challenges of new technologies.

- Typical benefits of new technologies include cost reduction, increased product variety, improved quality, and faster cycle times. Companies must be careful not to place too much of a premium on cost reduction because the primary benefit of many technologies comes from increased product variety or improved quality. There is a tendency for companies to focus on cost because it is the easiest benefit to quantify, yet subjective methods of estimating benefits should also be employed.
- Common risks in adopting new technology include technological risks (the technology doesn't work as expected or is soon made obsolete by newer technologies), organizational risks (the company and its employees are not able to fully capitalize on all the benefits of a technology), and market risks (customers may not fully appreciate or buy the new technology).

4. Describe factors that support technology development and implementation.

- Worker training and empowerment is a critical foundation for implementing new technologies. A tool is only as good as the person utilizing it. Many companies fail with new technologies because they underinvest in training or expect employees to learn a new technology too quickly.
- Carefully defining the strategic emphasis of a new technology is critical. Many technologies are implemented using a "me too" approach—i.e., a competitor has the technology or it is widely seen as the "next big thing"—and so a company implements the technology without a clear plan for how it will be used. A company should have a clear set of priorities for what it is trying to accomplish with a particular technology and should take a long-term outlook rather than simply expecting a quick payback.

QUESTIONS

1. Pick a single business organization and make a list of the technologies it utilizes in its daily operations. Which of these are less than five years old? Which are less than ten years old? More than ten years old? Describe how each technology facilitates smoother or better-quality operations. Label each technology as either specialized or general-purpose.
2. Describe the information systems that a typical restaurant might use and the tasks these systems perform. How might such systems differ between a low-cost restaurant such as a McDonald's and a high-quality, five-star restaurant such as Le Cinq in Paris? How must these systems interact with the systems of suppliers, vendors, and customers?
3. Give three examples of organizations that have acquired or developed new technologies to support the following objectives:
   a. Reducing cost
   b. Reducing lead time or lead time variability
   c. Improving quality
   d. Increasing flexibility and the ability to customize
4. Go online to a web site like Google Video or YouTube. Search for terms such as "manufacturing technology," "manufacturing robot," "food manufacturing," and similar terms. See if you can find a few videos that show manufacturing technology in use. Describe the technology—what are its key benefits? What are the challenges? How expensive or difficult do you think it is to buy or implement this technology? What skills do workers need to have in order to operate or utilize this technology?
5. Give three examples of recent process technology innovations. Are these particular to a specific business, or are they more generally applicable?
6. Give three examples of a disruptive technology—one that forces or facilitates a radical change in the way a company conducts its business.

CASE STUDY

Online Purchasing at McDonald's

In 2002, when McDonald's offered to put an extra strip of bacon on any hamburger for 35 cents, it encountered drastic forecasting problems. The promotion turned out to be so popular that the company had to increase its order for pork bellies, which sent a bullwhip effect across the economy, resulting in shortages and increased costs. The source of the problem? Thousands of franchisees, each of them operating somewhat independently, using largely manual ordering systems that did not feed information to corporate headquarters on a timely basis.

The company responded by developing an online ordering system to help it plan its purchases and shipments. The system was first implemented in European stores in 2003, leading to a 30 percent reduction in raw waste, a 30 percent reduction in store inventory, and a decrease in store transfers (i.e., shipments of bacon between stores because of shortages) from 8 percent to 4 percent. In addition, order times for each store were cut in half, saving 60 minutes per week. Annual savings per store were $5,585, which equates to $11.5 million for the 2,072 restaurants in France and Germany.

McDonald's is leading a shift to "demand chain planning" by fast-food restaurants. In 2003, the National Restaurant Association estimated that only 12 percent of restaurants ordered food supplies electronically, and only 10 percent ordered nonfood supplies electronically. With more than 31,000 restaurants serving more than 46 million customers per day in 119 countries, McDonald's has thousands of trucks on the road delivering food and supplies to its franchisees. With its Happy Meals promotions, McDonald's is one of the largest toy distributors in the world. Each store receives supplies one to three times per week.

McDonald's has several major challenges in integrating its supply chain. First, the majority of its restaurants are owned by franchisees, limiting the company's ability to control the adoption and implementation of new technologies. According to Robert Bauer, information technology director for McDonald's global supply chain, "It's difficult to get the restaurants to give us information. They look at us as a big brother: 'you are going to do bad things to me.'" The franchisees do not have to agree to use the software. Thus, while there are about 13,000 restaurants in the United States, only 12,100 use the online system. Second, the entire supply chain is outsourced, from hamburger and French fry production to warehousing and transportation. The company began revamping its supply chain in 1996 with software and technology from Manugistics, Oracle, and Sun. Several years were spent primarily collecting and organizing data. McDonald's worked closely with its two major distribution contractors, Martin-Brower and Perseco. The technology works well for everyday projects but hits snags with limited-supply items like Happy Meal toys, where the promotions run for 28 days, yet the toys must be produced 12 months in advance. There is no chance to correct for poor forecasts once the promotion has started.

QUESTIONS

1. Getting franchisees to adopt the online ordering system is a major challenge. What techniques would you use to encourage adoption?
2. Draw a supply chain map showing the various parties in McDonald's supply chain: food growers, manufacturers, distributors, corporate headquarters, and restaurants. Describe the type of information that needs to be exchanged between the partners in each pair of partners. What is each organization looking for in its information systems?
3. Describe differences in how McDonald's should handle information and planning for (1) regular food items, (2) nonfood items like wrappers or napkins, and (3) promotional or one-time items like Happy Meal toys.

Source: K. Hickey, "McDonald's Tall Order," *Traffic World,* January 5, 2004, pp. 1–4.

CHAPTER 14

Global Supply Chain and Service Integration

LEARNING OBJECTIVES

1. Explain the meaning of globalization.
2. Describe why firms globalize and establish international production facilities. Discuss various strategies for international production.
3. Evaluate the positives and negatives associated with outsourcing and offshoring.

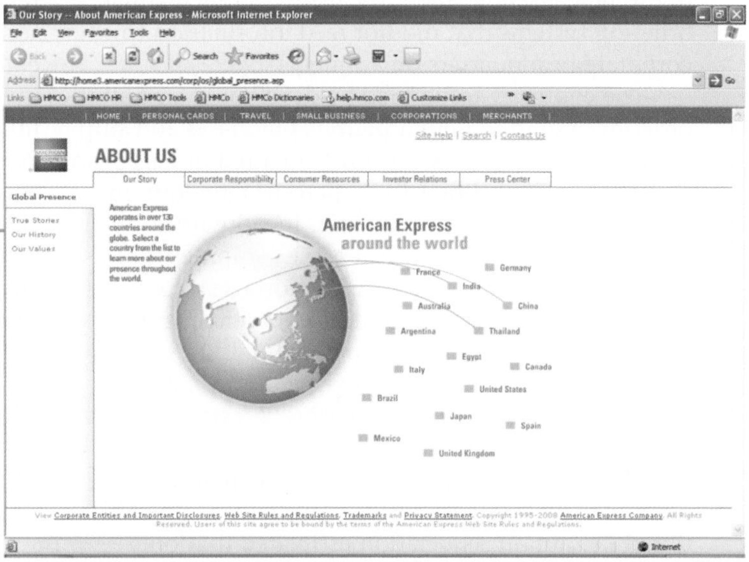

American Express—A Global Corporation

Throughout this textbook, we have described many examples of the operations management practices of American Express, Kellogg's, and Sony. These three companies operate in very different industries: American Express delivers a variety of financial services, Kellogg's primarily produces breakfast cereals, and Sony manufactures a range of electronics and entertainment products.

While there are many differences among the operating environments of the three companies, they also face similar challenges as global corporations. All three companies operate in multiple countries as both producers and marketers of their products and services. Therefore, many of the operational challenges faced by the three companies are quite similar. For example, all three have to constantly evaluate the effectiveness of their supply chains; fluctuations in currency exchange rates; changing international laws and tariffs; production and labor costs; and the hiring, training, and retention of high-skill employees. A brief description of the global operations of American Express is provided in Table 14.1.

AMEX now operates in 130 countries around the globe, with large operations in at least 15 countries. As a result, AMEX needs to maintain a highly secure financial information system to keep track of millions of financial transactions worldwide. Because the organization of banks and financial institutions is quite different in different parts of the world, AMEX needs to maintain highly skilled financial and information system analysts in several different countries to provide secure transactions and customer service to combat fraud.

TABLE 14.1 Early Globalization of American Express

Country	Event
United States	American Express was founded in 1850 in New York.
Mexico	American Express first established a presence in Mexico in 1852, represented by agents in Acapulco through Wells, Fargo & Company. It opened a second office in Mexico City in 1880, but ceased all activities in 1910 because of the Mexican Revolution. It restarted its activities in Mexico in 1925, launching a campaign to promote tourism in Mexico, mainly from the United States and Cuba.
Canada	AMEX expanded its operations into Canada by opening two offices in Toronto and Hamilton in 1853. By the end of the 1850s, American Express was well established in Canada. Now, Canada has the second largest American Express card member base in the world, after the United States.
United Kingdom	It was in the United Kingdom in 1881 that AMEX launched its first business venture in Europe, authorizing the British firm of Meadows & Co. to receive £200 annually to "look after the management of American Express Company's freight between Liverpool, London and other places where they have offices." Fifteen years later, in 1896, the company opened its first exclusive office, in London.
Spain	American Express's history in Spain goes back to the late 1880s, when American Express established a chain of agents throughout Europe for the cashing of its money orders, which were launched in 1882. By the 1950s, Spain was rapidly increasing in popularity with American tourists and American Express opened an office in Madrid. Its activities included travel, financial services, and shipping services.
France	The very first exclusive American Express office outside North America was opened in Paris in 1895. Five years later, American Express established its current office at 11, rue Scribe, Paris, an address that was to become legendary to tourists in Europe. It is estimated that more than 35 million travelers have passed through the doors of the company's Paris office since it opened, making it the best known American Express office in the world.
Germany	At the turn of the twentieth century, Hamburg was a major world port, closely associated with the movement of goods, money, and people, and it was there that, in 1898, American Express chose to open one of its first two offices in Germany.
Italy	American Express opened its first Italian office in 1901 in the port city of Genoa, where the thriving shipping business complemented the company's growing international express activities.
China	American Express's involvement in China dates back to 1916, when it first conducted banking and travel operations in Hong Kong. The company was among the first companies to establish ground support in China for its customers from all over the world.
Argentina	American Express opened its first Latin American offices in Buenos Aires in 1916.
Japan	In 1917, just two years after American Express officially entered the travel business, it opened an office in Yokohama dedicated to travel, shipping, and limited banking. Recent years have brought many partnerships with major Japanese companies, including Toyota and Shinsei Bank.
Egypt	American Express's presence in Egypt dates back to 1919, when the Cairo Express Agency became the company's official correspondent in Egypt.

(continued)

TABLE 14.1 Early Globalization of American Express (*continued*)

Country	Event
India	American Express has been offering travel-related services in India since 1921, when, seeking to complete its chain of offices around the world, American Express opened an office in Calcutta (now Kolkata), which was then one of the most important and liveliest business centers between Europe and Asia. A second office was opened in Bombay (now Mumbai) a year later. American Express is now the largest travel network in India.
Brazil	American Express's presence in Brazil dates from 1923, when, by agreement with Sociedade Anonimo Viagens Internacionale (SAVI), representatives of American Express in Rio de Janeiro began to offer travel services, sales of travelers cheques, and general financial business.
Australia	American Express opened its first travel office in Australia in Sydney in 1954, with offices opening in many other cities in the ensuing years.

Source: http://home3.americanexpress.com/corp/os/global_presence.asp

Furthermore, AMEX credit cards and travelers cheques need to be securely manufactured and shipped to customers around the world. Similarly, customer service needs to be provided to the end users of credit cards and travelers cheques and also to merchants (e.g., retailers, hotels, restaurants, and other establishments where AMEX cards and travelers cheques are used).

In many countries, AMEX sells only travelers cheques and credit card services and has only a small number of employees. However, in about 15 countries, AMEX's operations are quite diverse. Although the company was founded in the United States in 1850, it became an international corporation very soon afterward when it opened an office in Mexico in 1852 and two in Canada in 1853. Table 14.1 shows the opening years for offices around the world as AMEX evolved into a truly global corporation. ■

GLOBALIZATION

We live in a globally connected world now. Political, economical, cultural, and naturally occurring events around the world affect each of us, even though we may not realize it. Thanks to advances in efficient production and distribution systems, we get the benefits of using goods manufactured at locations around the world that have been delivered to us in a cost-effective manner. Also, advances in information and communications technology are now allowing companies to deliver a wide range of services, from financial transactions to customer service to medical diagnostics, to customers all around the world. This interconnected production system also means that any disruption propagates through nations at a very rapid rate. For instance, any unscheduled blockage of ships at one of the world's major ports, such as Hong Kong, Amsterdam, Singapore, or Dubai, can affect the availability and prices of many essential goods in rural towns in the United States. Similarly, any changes in currency exchange rates (e.g., the U.S. dollar against the euro, the Japanese yen, the Indian rupee, or the Chinese yuan) can affect both the demand for and the supply of goods and services across the world.

This chapter provides an overview of topics related to global production. We will provide a background and history of globalization and also discuss the advantages and challenges associated with international production. The chapter also discusses many emerging trends related to globalization, such as outsourcing and offshoring.

What Is Globalization?

The *Encyclopaedia Britannica* defines **globalization** as "the process by which the experience of everyday life, marked by the diffusion of commodities and ideas, can foster a standardization of cultural expressions around the world."

Globalization the process by which the experience of everyday life, marked by the diffusion of commodities and ideas, can foster a standardization of cultural expressions around the world

Essentially, the term *globalization* refers to increasing global connectivity, integration, and interdependence in the economic, social, technological, cultural, political, and ecological spheres. For example, globalization of industries allows for worldwide production and broader access to goods and services for consumers, and globalization of financial institutions allows better access to funds and credit for consumers, companies, and government agencies. Similarly, the globalization of transportation and communication systems allows for better flow of goods, people, and information among nations.

Why Globalize?

A company explores global production for a variety of reasons. While there are costs associated with managing and operating a multinational organization, many companies pursue global production because it offers several benefits:

- Access to *cheaper labor and operating costs* is one of the most common reasons for locating production facilities overseas. Labor rates vary considerably among nations; therefore, for many specific types of production activities, it is cheaper for companies to produce overseas than to expand in their home countries. For example, many manufacturing facilities have been set up in China and Bangladesh to take advantage of those countries' lower labor costs. Similarly, many telephone and Internet-based customer support centers have been established in India during recent years because of lower operating costs.
- Sometimes, companies locate their facilities in another country to get access to the *knowledge and skills* of people in that country. For example, many information technology–based operations have recently been established in several eastern European countries and in India because of the vast pool of highly skilled workers in those areas. It should be noted that access to knowledge and skills does not necessarily come at a lower cost. Switzerland, Germany, and Japan are examples of countries where companies locate facilities to get access to populations who are highly skilled in financial services, engineering, and technology, even though the labor costs are higher.
- Yet another reason for globalization of industries involves access to *resources*. Certain parts of the world are rich in natural resources. For example, many of the minerals-based industries are based in South American countries, which have some of the world's largest mining industries.
- Globalization also allows companies access to *new markets*. By locating facilities in new countries, firms can market their products and services to a new set of customers. Therefore, firms always look for growth opportunities abroad. For example, we can see the outlets of many well-known American brands (e.g., McDonald's, Marriott, and Starbucks) around the world.

- Facilities at strategic international locations can also reduce *logistics and distribution costs*. A foreign location can become a hub for distribution of a firm's products to markets in the neighboring region. For example, Apple, Sony, and other electronics producers operate distribution and warehousing facilities at various strategic locations in North America, Europe, Asia, and the rest of the world.
- Sometimes firms locate their facilities internationally to take advantage of *tax and financial incentives* provided by local governments. To encourage development, many emerging nations have established "tax-free production zones" within their borders. The companies operating within these zones get significant tax rebates and access to cheaper capital. For example, the software development facilities of many international firms are located in SEEPZ, Mumbai (India), because of very attractive tax incentives provided by the local government.
- Finally, firms also locate internationally for *political and industry-specific reasons*. For example, by locating a production facility in a country, providing employment, and participating in various community activities, a firm can slowly become "local" rather than stay a "foreign" entity. For example, Holden cars are commonly considered to be Australian, but they have been part of the General Motors family since the 1920s.

- **Adaptation** boosting revenue and market share by maximizing local presence in a country
- **Aggregation** achieving economies of scale by creating regional or global operations
- **Arbitrage** the exploitation of differences among national or regional markets, often by locating separate parts of supply chains in different places

According to Ghemawat (2007), when firms globalize, they need to consider three approaches to global integration. A firm uses the first approach, known as **adaptation**, to boost revenue and market share by maximizing its local presence in a country. The second approach, known as **aggregation**, is used to achieve economies of scale by creating regional or global operations. The third approach, **arbitrage**, is the exploitation of differences among national or regional markets, often by locating separate parts of supply chains in different places. The differences among the three approaches based on different criteria are described in Table 14.2.

While companies follow many different paths, as described in Table 14.2, Farrell (2004) suggests a five-stage model for globalization, shown in Figure 14.1.

Brief History of Globalization

While globalization has received increased attention in the news media during the last few decades, it has been a long process spanning the last several centuries. Earlier forms of globalization existed during the Mongol Empire, and global integration continued through the expansion of European trade in the sixteenth and seventeenth centuries, when the Portuguese and Spanish Empires reached to all corners of the world. During the seventeenth century, the Dutch East India Company was established as a shareholder-owned corporation. The nineteenth century is often called "the first era of globalization," a period characterized by rapid growth in international trade and investment among the European countries, their colonies, and, later, the United States. However, globalization

McDonald's and Starbucks can now be found in many countries around the world.

TABLE 14.2 Differences Among the Three Approaches to Globalization

	Adaptation	Aggregation	Arbitrage
Competitive Advantage Why should we globalize at all?	To achieve local relevance through national focus while exploiting some economies of scale	To achieve scale and scope economies through international standardization	To achieve economies through international specialization
Configuration Where should we locate operations overseas?	Mainly in countries that are similar to the home base, to limit the effects of culture, administrative, geographic, and economic distance		In a more diverse set of countries, to exploit some elements of distance
Coordination How should we connect international operations?	By country, with emphasis on achieving local presence within borders	By business, region, or customer, with emphasis on horizontal relationships for cross-border economies of scale	By function, with emphasis on vertical relationships, even across organizational boundaries
Controls What types of extremes should we watch for?	Excessive variety or complexity	Excessive standardization, with emphasis on scale	Narrowing spreads
Change Blockers Whom should we watch out for internally?	Entrenched country chiefs	All-powerful unit, regional, or account heads	Heads of key functions
Corporate Diplomacy How should we approach corporate diplomacy?	Address issues of concern, but proceed with discretion, given the emphasis on cultivating local presence	Avoid appearance of homogenization or hegemonism (especially for U.S. companies); be sensitive to any backlash	Address the exploitation or displacement of suppliers, channels, or intermediaries, which are potentially most prone to political disruption
Corporate Strategy What strategic levers do we have?	Scope selection Variation Decentralization Partitioning Modularization Flexibility Partnership Recombination Innovation	Regions and other country groupings Product or business Function Platform Competence Client industry	Cultural (country-of-origin effects) Administrative (taxes, regulations, security) Geographic (distance, climate differences) Economic (differences in prices, resources, knowledge)

Source: Reprinted by permission of *Harvard Business Review.* From "Managing Differences: The Central Challenge of Global Strategy," by Ghemawat, P.

The Five Stages of Global Restructuring				
Industries and companies tend to globalize in phases; at each stage, there are different opportunities for creating value. In the first three stages, value comes from basic improvements to typical business practices. In the last two stages, it comes from true process innovations and market expansion. The stages are not necessarily sequential.				
1. Enter new markets	**2. Move production abroad**	**3. Disaggregate the value chain**	**4. Reengineer the value chain**	**5. Create new markets**
Companies use production models similar to the ones they deploy at home to enter new countries and expand their customer bases.	Companies relocate their entire production processes to take advantage of cost differentials; they export finished goods globally.	Companies' individual product components are manufactured in different locations or regions; countries may specialize in component manufacturing, assembly, or both.	Companies redesign their production processes, taking local factors into account, to maximize efficiencies and cost savings.	Given lower costs due to globalization, companies can offer new products at lower prices and can penetrate new market segments or geographies, or both.
Less global ◄				► Highly global

FIGURE 14.1 Globalization Stages

Source: Reprinted by permission of *Harvard Business Review.* From "Beyond Offshoring: Assess Your Company's Global Potential" by Farrell, D.

began to slow down at the beginning of the First World War and almost collapsed during the late 1920s and early 1930s.

Globalization during the period after World War II has been driven by advances in technology, communication, and transportation, all of which have reduced the costs of trade and international production. International organizations and cooperative agreements such as the World Trade Organization (WTO), General Agreement on Tariffs and Trade (GATT), International Organization for Standardization (ISO), and North American Free Trade Agreement (NAFTA) have played a significant role in removing various obstacles and facilitating the process of globalization.

During recent years, globalization has continued to move ahead despite worldwide economic and political instability. However, it is advancing on different paths in different nations, according to the 2006 A. T. Kearney/*Foreign Policy* Magazine Globalization Index™, an annual study that assesses the extent to which nations accounting for the majority of the world's population are becoming more or less globally connected.[1]

The 2006 A. T. Kearney/*Foreign Policy* Magazine Globalization Index ranks 62 countries representing 85 percent of the world's population and 96 percent of the world's GDP based on 12 variables grouped into four categories: economic integration, personal contact, technological connectivity, and political engagement. The index quantifies economic integration by combining data on trade and foreign direct investment. Technological connectedness is gauged by counting Internet users, Internet hosts, and secure servers. Political engagement is assessed by taking stock of the number of selected international organizations that each country belongs to and the number of selected international treaties that each country signs, as well as each country's financial and personnel contributions to U.N. peacekeeping missions and levels of governmental transfers. Personal contact is charted by looking at a country's international travel and tourism, international telephone traffic, and cross-border transfers, including remittances. The current rankings of the most globalized nations are presented in Table 14.3. One can argue that a foreign-based corporation is more likely to be successful in a more globalized nation. One can also

[1] *Foreign Policy,* November–December 2006, pp. 75–81.

argue, however, that a higher globalization index also means a higher level of competition for the foreign operators. Therefore, when considering international expansion, it is essential that, at the minimum, the organization consider the level of globalization within the target country and of the region within the nation.

GLOBAL PRODUCTION AND MULTINATIONAL CORPORATIONS

A **multinational corporation** (MNC) is a corporation or business enterprise that manages production establishments or delivers services in at least two countries. Very large multinationals have budgets that exceed those of many countries. A key feature of a multinational is the inclusion of back-office functions (e.g., supply,

● **Multinational corporation** a corporation or business enterprise that manages production establishments or delivers services in at least two countries

TABLE 14.3 The World's Most Globalized Nations

Rank	Country
1	Singapore
2	Switzerland
3	United States of America
4	Ireland
5	Denmark
6	Canada
7	Netherlands
8	Australia
9	Austria
10	Sweden
11	New Zealand
12	United Kingdom
13	Finland
14	Norway
15	Israel
16	Czech Republic
17	Slovenia
18	Germany
19	Malaysia
20	Hungary

Source: Reproduced with permission from *Foreign Policy,* www.foreignpolicy.com, #157, November/December 2006. Copyright © 2007 by A.T. Kearney and the Carnegie Endowment for International Peace.

procurement, and customer support) in each of the countries in which it operates. Multinational corporations can be divided into three broad groups according to the configuration of their production facilities:

- **Horizontally integrated multinational corporations** corporations that use production establishments located in different countries to produce the same or similar products
- **Vertically integrated multinational corporations** corporations that use production establishments in a certain country or countries to produce products that serve as inputs to their production establishments in one or more other countries
- **Diversified multinational corporations** corporations that use production establishments located in different countries but are neither horizontally nor vertically integrated

- **Horizontally integrated multinational corporations** use production establishments located in different countries to produce the same or similar products. For example, McDonald's restaurants around the world serve almost identical products. Hotels operated by Marriott, Hilton, and other companies operate using similar standards.
- **Vertically integrated multinational corporations** use production establishments in a certain country or countries to produce products that serve as inputs to their production establishments in one or more other countries. For example, while Apple sells many of its products (e.g., iMac computers and iPods) in the United States, some of its production facilities are located in other countries where labor costs are lower (e.g., China). Similarly, Nokia produces its mobile phone in facilities around the world to serve a global customer base.
- **Diversified multinational corporations** use production establishments located in different countries but are neither horizontally nor vertically integrated. For example, corporations such as Microsoft, IBM, and Siemens operate various production facilities around the world and fit the description of a diversified multinational corporation. It is hard to pinpoint the exact reason for the final structure of a large diversified multinational corporation because it evolves over many decades.

What Production Functions Are Globalized?

As mentioned earlier, the presence of multinational corporations and the approach of global production has now become a very common phenomenon in the interconnected business world. In the process, many production functions that have crossed international boundaries are performed at locations far from the home country of the business organization.

- *Manufacturing* products and their components at locations far from the home country is perhaps the most common function of a global firm. To remain competitive, firms often locate their factories close to cheap labor or raw materials. Therefore, during recent decades, many manufacturing plants and factories have been established in China, Taiwan, and other countries around the world.
- *Procurement* is another activity that is increasingly becoming global. In a non-globalized environment, a firm often bought raw materials and components from suppliers located close to its production facilities. However, the ease of transportation and the reduction in other associated costs in a global economy make it possible for companies to purchase their supplies from vendors located far from their home countries. As discussed in Chapter 2, ISO 9000 standards are often used in this situation to evaluate the quality of the suppliers located in different countries.
- *Maintenance and monitoring.* Because of advances in information technology, it is becoming possible to remotely monitor and maintain manufacturing equipment that is located far from the monitoring/maintenance provider. For example, much industrial automation equipment costing several millions of dollars provided by Siemens can be monitored and maintained by engineers located in Germany and other places around the world. Similarly, in many

organizations, computer systems are often monitored by technicians in remote locations. These technologies are allowing doctors, for example, to monitor critical indicators of their patients' condition, such as remote monitoring of pacemakers for heart patients.

- Because products are manufactured in factories located around the world, *logistics and distribution services* have also become extremely globalized. It is often the case that a component manufactured by Company A in Country X is shipped to Country Y, where it is picked by Company B and shipped again to Country Z, where Company C assembles the finished product. International ports such as Hong Kong, Singapore, Dubai, and Amsterdam are increasingly playing an extremely important role in facilitating global production and maintaining the supply chain without disruptions.
- *Customer service and support* provided by telephones or via the Internet (chat, talk, instant messaging, e-mails) has seen an explosion in globalization during the last decade. It is now very common to talk to a service agent in India, Ireland, or Australia even when the customer tries to contact his or her company in the United States.
- With the advances in information technology and the spread of education worldwide, it is now possible to locate facilities for complex and *knowledge-based business processes* internationally. For example, using the Internet, healthcare facilities can make patients' records available to medical experts who might be located far from the home country. Similarly, many complex financial and legal functions can also be performed remotely.
- Increasingly, many companies are also locating their own facilities or outsourcing production activities in foreign countries to facilitate *product development and innovation.* As mentioned in Chapter 3, product development in goods and services industries is a very complex and long-term process. However, effective product development is essential for a firm's long-term success. Globalization has allowed many firms to locate product development activities abroad. For example, Microsoft, IBM, Oracle, and many other western companies have located their facilities in several different countries to take advantage of the local talent pool for their product development efforts.

BEST PRACTICES IN OPERATIONS MANAGEMENT

Made in the World by Toyota

Toyota Motor Corporation (TMC) is one of the world's leading auto manufacturers, offering a full range of models. Global sales of its Toyota and Lexus brands, combined with those of Daihatsu and Hino, totaled 8.81 million units from January 1, 2006, to December 31, 2006. Besides its own 12 plants and a number of manufacturing subsidiaries and affiliates in Japan, Toyota has 52 manufacturing companies in 26 countries and regions, which produce Lexus- and Toyota-brand vehicles and components. As of March 2007, Toyota employed approximately 299,400 people worldwide and marketed vehicles in more than 170 countries. Its diversified operations include telecommunications and prefabricated housing.

Figures 14.2 and 14.3 describe Toyota's global production network. Clearly, it is not an exaggeration to say that a Toyota car is "Made in the World."

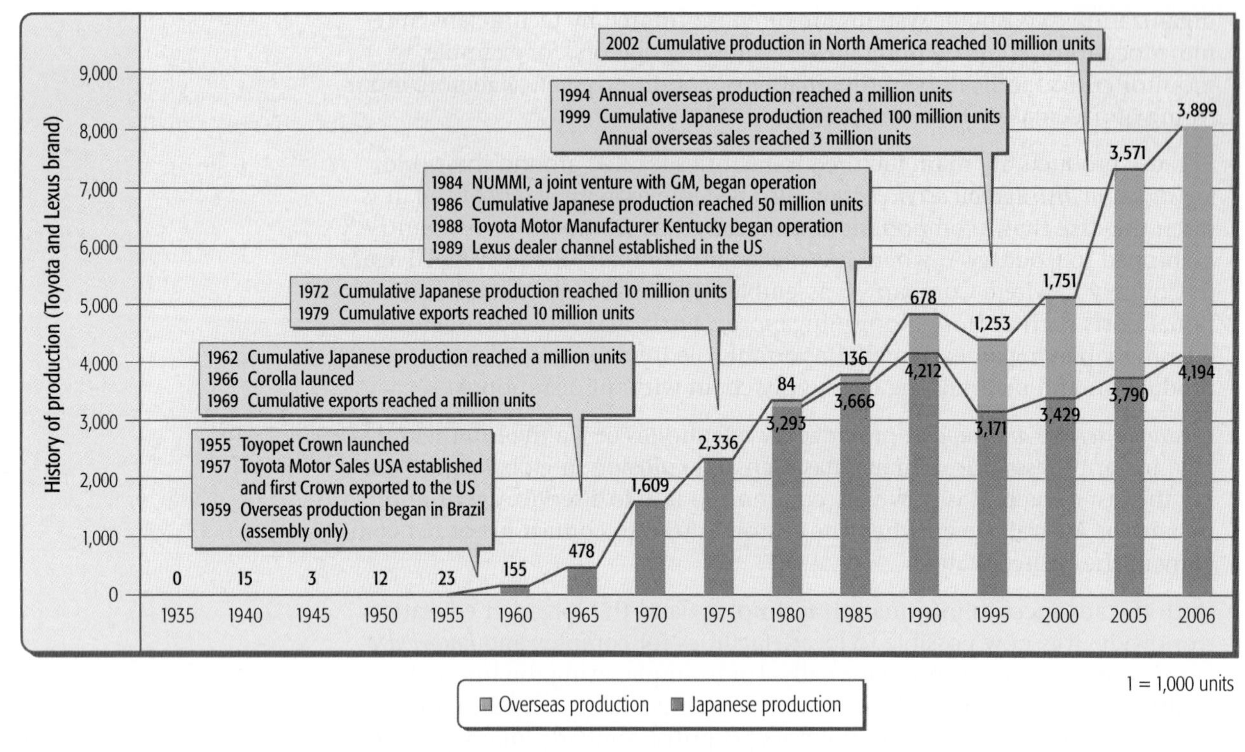

FIGURE 14.2 Historical Timeline for Toyota's Global Production

Classification of International Production Facilities

Professor Kasra Ferdows (1997) has developed a classification scheme to explain the various roles that international production facilities play for a multinational corporation. He classifies international production facilities into six distinct categories:

- **Offshore factory** a factory established to produce specific items at low cost

- **Offshore factory.** An offshore factory is established to produce specific items at low cost. These items are exported to markets outside the country for additional work (i.e., for additional processing or for use as components of another product) or for direct sales. Investments in technical and managerial resources are kept at the minimum required for production. Little development or engineering occurs at the site. Local managers rarely choose key suppliers or negotiate prices. Accounting and finance staffs primarily provide data to managers in the home country. Outbound logistics are simple and beyond the control of the plant's management. Customer service call centers located in India by companies such as American Express are examples of offshore factories.

- **Source factory** a factory whose primary purpose is low-cost production but whose strategic role is broader than that of an offshore factory

- **Source factory.** The primary purpose for establishing a source factory is low-cost production, but its strategic role is broader than that of an offshore factory. Its managers have greater authority over procurement (including the selection of suppliers), production planning, process changes, outbound logistics, and product customization and redesign decisions. A source factory has the same ability to produce a product or a part as the best factory in the company's global network. Source factories tend to be located in places where production costs are relatively low, infrastructure is relatively well developed, and a skilled work force is available. For example, many manufacturing firms have production or assembly facilities in Mexico, known collectively as *maquiladoras*.

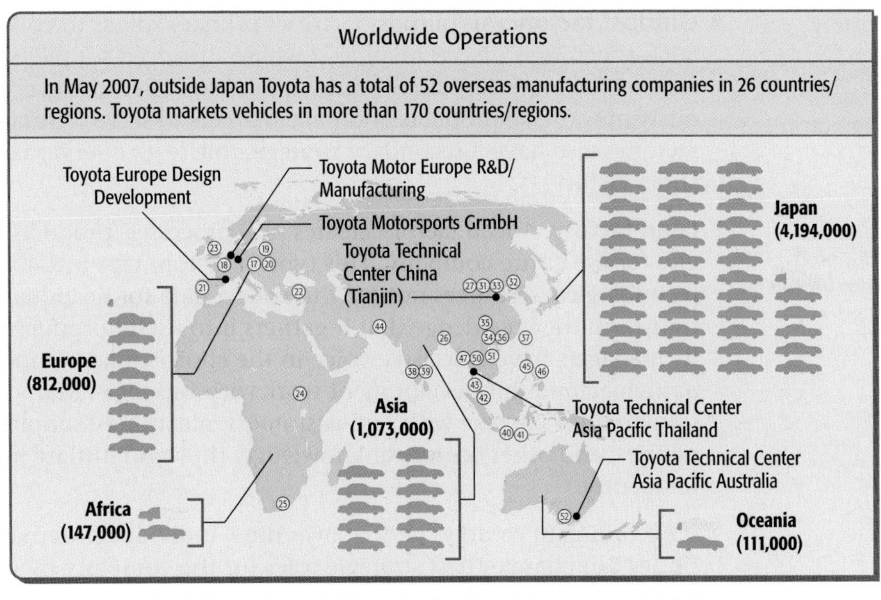

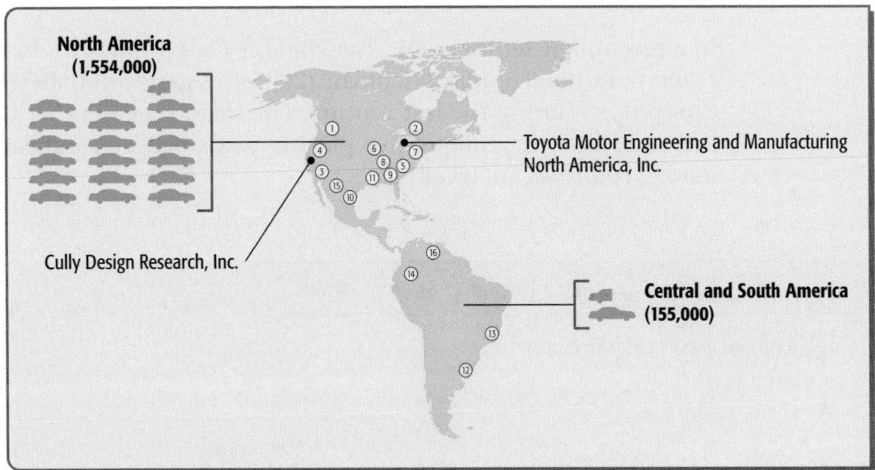

FIGURE 14.3 Toyota's Production Facilities Outside Japan

Source: © 1995–2008 TOYOTA MOTOR CORPORATION. All Rights Reserved. Reprinted with permission.

- **Server factory**. A server factory supplies specific national or regional markets. It typically provides a way to overcome tariff barriers and to reduce taxes, logistics costs, or exposure to foreign exchange fluctuations. Although a server factory has relatively more autonomy than an offshore factory to make minor adjustments in products and production methods to fit local conditions, its authority and competence in this area are very limited.

- **Contributor factory**. A contributor factory also serves a specific national or regional market, but its responsibilities extend to product or process engineering and to the development and choice of suppliers. A contributor factory competes with the company's home plants to be the testing ground for new process technologies, computer systems, and products. It has its own development, engineering, and production capabilities. A contributor factory also has authority over procurement decisions and participates in the choice of key suppliers for the company.

- **Server factory** a factory that supplies specific national or regional markets; it typically provides a way to overcome tariff barriers and to reduce taxes, logistics costs, or exposure to foreign exchange fluctuations

- **Contributor factory** a factory that also serves a specific national or regional market, but whose responsibilities extend to product or process engineering and to the development and choice of suppliers

● **Outpost factory** a factory whose primary role is to collect information

- **Outpost factory**. An outpost factory's primary role is to collect information. Such a factory is placed in an area where advanced suppliers, competitors, research laboratories, or customers are located. Because every factory obviously must make products and have markets to serve, virtually all outpost factories also have a secondary strategic role (e.g., a server factory or an offshore factory).

● **Lead factory** a factory that creates new processes, products, and technologies for the entire company

- **Lead factory**. A lead factory creates new processes, products, and technologies for the entire company. This type of factory taps into local skills and technological resources not only to collect data for headquarters, but also to transform the knowledge that it gathers into useful products and processes. Its managers have a decisive voice in the choice of key suppliers and often participate in joint development work with suppliers. Many of its employees stay in direct contact with end customers, machinery suppliers, research laboratories, and other centers of knowledge; they also initiate innovations frequently.

According to Ferdows (1997), over time, individual international production facilities can change their strategic roles for the company by gaining additional competence, eventually becoming lead factories (Figure 14.4).

The World Is Flat

In a recent best-selling book, *The World Is Flat: A Brief History of the Twenty-First Century,* author Thomas Friedman (2005) presents an analysis of the globalization process during the last century. Friedman suggests that the world is flat in the sense that the competitive playing fields between industrial and emerging market countries are leveling.

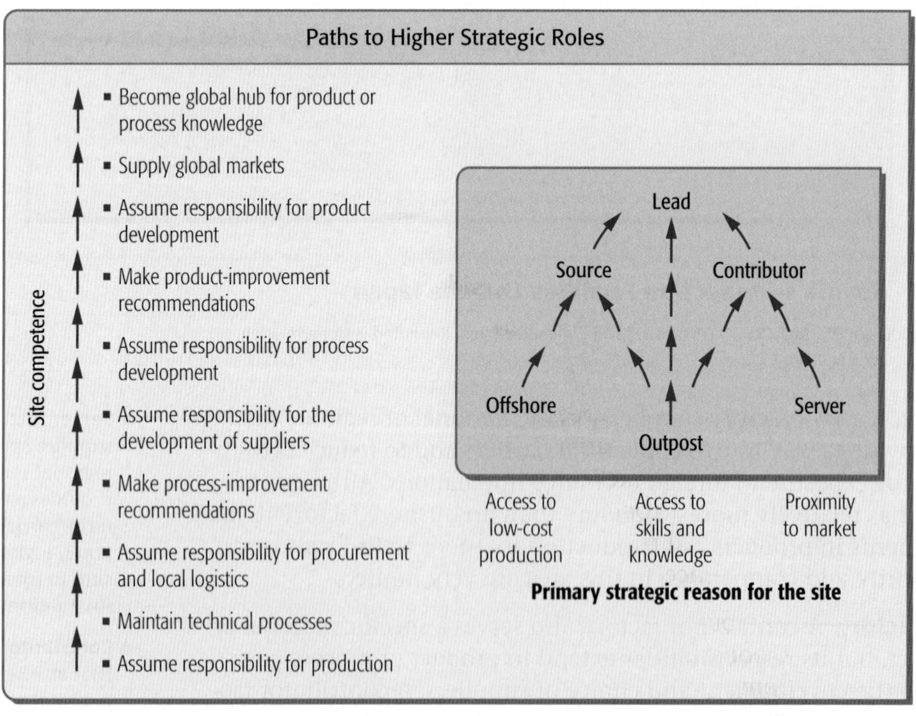

FIGURE 14.4 Evaluation of the Strategic Role of an International Production Facility

Source: Reprinted by permission of *Harvard Business Review.* From "Making the Most of Foreign Factories" by Ferdows, K.

In his book, Friedman describes many examples to illustrate how companies in India and China are becoming part of large, complex global supply chains that extend across oceans through a process called outsourcing, providing everything from service representatives and x-ray interpretation to component manufacturing. He describes how these changes were made possible through intersecting technologies, particularly the Internet, fiber optics, and the use of computers.

Friedman lists 10 "flatteners" that have contributed to the development of supply chains and services across national borders (Figure 14.5).

- *Collapse of the Berlin Wall.* Friedman sees the collapse of the Berlin Wall as the starting point for the leveling of economic playing fields across countries, which facilitated the fast development of global production. The event not only symbolized the end of the Cold War but also allowed people from both sides of the wall to join the economic mainstream.
- *Rise of the Web browser.* Netscape and the Web broadened the audience for the Internet from its earlier role as a communications medium used primarily by scientists and universities.
- *Workflow software.* This type of software gives machines the ability to exchange information with other machines without any human involvement. Friedman believes that these first three forces have become a "crude foundation of a whole new global platform for collaboration."
- *Open source collaboration.* Collaboration of communities and individual users on online projects has led to open source innovation. Examples of such collaboration include open source software, blogs, Wikipedia, and social networking web sites such as Facebook and MySpace.

FIGURE 14.5 Drivers for the "Flattening" of the World

- *Outsourcing.* Friedman argues that outsourcing functions has allowed companies to split service and manufacturing activities into components, with each component being performed in the most efficient, cost-effective way anywhere in the world.
- *Offshoring.* Offshoring means the relocation of business processes from one country to another. This includes any business process, such as production, manufacturing, or services. While offshoring of manufacturing increased significantly during the 1970s and 1980s, the offshoring of services has rapidly increased in recent years. Examples of manufacturing offshoring include manufacturing facilites owned by Apple, Sony, General Motors, and Toyota in China. Examples of service offshoring include the software development and R&D facilities of Google, IBM, and Microsoft in India.
- *Efficient supply chain.* Friedman compares the modern retail supply chain to a river and points to Wal-Mart as the best example of a company that uses technology to streamline item sales, distribution, logistics, and shipping.

● **Insourcing** an operations strategy in which a distribution company performs a variety of services on behalf of another company

- *Insourcing.* **Insourcing** refers to an operations strategy in which a distribution company (e.g., UPS) performs a variety of services on behalf of another company. This approach requires close cooperation between the manufacturer and the distributor but also makes the supply chain more responsive to customer needs.

● **In-forming** the ability to build and deploy one's own supply chain for knowledge, information, and entertainment

- *In-forming.* According to Friedman, **in-forming** is the ability to build and deploy one's own supply chain for knowledge, information, and entertainment. Internet search engines such as Google and community sites such as Yahoo!, MSN, Second Life, FaceBook, and numerous others are allowing an individual to become a self-directed, self-empowered researcher and selector of products and services.
- *High-tech personal gadgets:* Personal digital equipment like mobile phones, iPods, personal digital assistants, instant messaging, and voice over Internet Protocol (VoIP) is becoming a backbone for offering many new products and services.

In addition to his 10 flatteners, Friedman also offered the concept of the triple convergence, which created a new, flatter global business environment.

- *Convergence I.* Up until the year 2000, the 10 flatteners were semi-independent from one another. However, around the year 2000, all the flatteners converged with one another.
- *Convergence II.* After the emergence of the 10 flatteners, a new platform had to be built in order to do business. Businesses had to begin collaborating horizontally, which meant that companies and people had to start working with other departments or companies as peers in order to add value or to develop product and service innovation. However, the convergence occurred when horizontal collaboration and the 10 flatteners began to reinforce each other.
- *Convergence III.* After the fall of the Berlin Wall, countries that had followed a Soviet economic plan—such as China, India, Russia, and the countries of eastern Europe, Latin America, and central Asia—began to open up their economies to the world. When these new players converged with the rest of the global playing field, they added new brainpower to that field. Therefore, the convergence enhanced horizontal collaboration across the globe. In turn, this convergence was the most important force in shaping politics and economics in the early twenty-first century.

OUTSOURCING AND OFFSHORING

Outsourcing can be defined as turning over all or part of an organizational activity to an outside vendor. Empirical evidence suggests that carefully crafted outsourcing strategies increase the overall performance of the firm. Outsourcing is generally considered to be a very powerful tool for cutting costs and improving performance. Since the early days of industrialization, manufacturing companies have increasingly outsourced part of their production functions to their suppliers.

● **Outsourcing** turning over all or part of an organizational activity to an outside vendor

For example, while Henry Ford's early automobile plant was completely vertically integrated, modern automobile companies outsource a large percentage of their component manufacturing to their suppliers and focus their own resources on the design, assembly, and perhaps production of selected proprietary components. A similar trend is observed in other industries: Dell, Hewlett-Packard, Sony, Apple, and a majority of other large companies outsource a large portion of their work to their suppliers.

Types of Outsourcing and Offshoring Activities

During the last 25 years or so, we have also begun seeing many functions in service industries, such as financial services, healthcare, retail, and so on, being outsourced to suppliers. For example, large hospitals often outsource diagnostic testing services to specialized laboratories. Similarly, banks often outsource the processing of home mortgage applications to several local companies around the country.

While the concept of outsourcing is quite old, large-scale global outsourcing is a relatively new phenomenon. Starting in the 1970s, many large western corporations started outsourcing the manufacturing of components and subcomponents to suppliers in China, Taiwan, Singapore, Mexico, and other countries where production costs were lower. More recently, a similar trend has occurred in the service sector. For example, many information systems–related functions are outsourced to Infosys, Wipro, and Tata Consulting Services, which are based in India.

Outsourcing of work can bring diversity into the work force. There will be an influx of new ideas, which can create much-needed momentum within the company. However, there needs to be an established intellectual property protocol, documenting concepts and ideas to appropriately protect the intellectual rights of both the company and the work force. The company to which work is outsourced should be made to feel that it is a required and useful member of the organization as a whole so that the vendor and its employees will be better motivated to perform. Traditional outsourcing focuses on achieving higher performance, greater flexibility, and reduced costs. Outsourcing offers the possibility of imposing control on the process, allows the conversion of the fixed costs into variable costs, and creates the opportunity for increased profitability and expanded flexibility. Rapid innovations are probable in technology outsourcing,

Infosys facility in Bangalore, India.

so attention should be paid to estimating the needs of the industry at least three years in advance.

● **Offshoring** transferring production from one country to another, with or without outsourcing to a supplier organization

Offshoring means transferring production from one country to another, with or without outsourcing to a supplier organization. In other words, it is possible for a firm to offshore its production to another country without outsourcing the work to another company. Similarly, it is possible for a company to outsource production to a supplier located in its home company (i.e., outsourcing without offshoring). The four combinations are described in Figure 14.6.

As mentioned earlier, commonly offshored functions include manufacturing, information technology, facilities, or applications within a firm (such as its communications equipment) and other firm services (also known as business process outsourcing) in such areas as finance and accounting, human resources, marketing and sales, customer support centers, and other industry-specific processes. Among the fastest-growing aspects of global outsourcing is **business process outsourcing** (BPO). BPO began as the outsourcing of routine financial and accounting operations, such as payroll, accounts payable and receivable, insurance, and property accounting, to another company. More sophisticated BPO work includes credit collection, benefits administration, pension administration, insurance claims processing, and computer-aided tomography. Two areas that have been retained until recently are research and development activities. But lately, even these activities have been moving offshore.

● **Business process outsourcing** the outsourcing of routine financial and accounting operations, such as payroll, accounts payable and receivable, insurance, and property accounting, to another company

Offshoring can be broadly divided into four types. The first is a traditional kind of outsourcing, which could include component manufacturing and basic training courses. The second type includes peripheral activities, such as warehousing, subassemblies, customer care services, and similar support mechanisms. Activities like secure data backup and data processing would fall under critical activities and processes, the third type. The fourth classification is strategic problem-solving activities like new product development, research and development, design management, and total management of information technology.

Contrary to popular belief, outsourcing does not always arise out of cost considerations. It can also arise out of a shortage of skilled workers. Particularly in the information technology (IT) area, but elsewhere as well, it is a way of solving skill shortages—not just immediate vacancies, but areas where there is constant pressure as a result of technological advances and great external demand for people with the requisite skills and expertise.

When outsourcing a particular product or service, the goals are to focus on core business strategy, to reduce or control costs while improving functionality, to improve competitiveness, to provide better management control, to improve flexibility, and to free up resources for core functions, among others. One of the

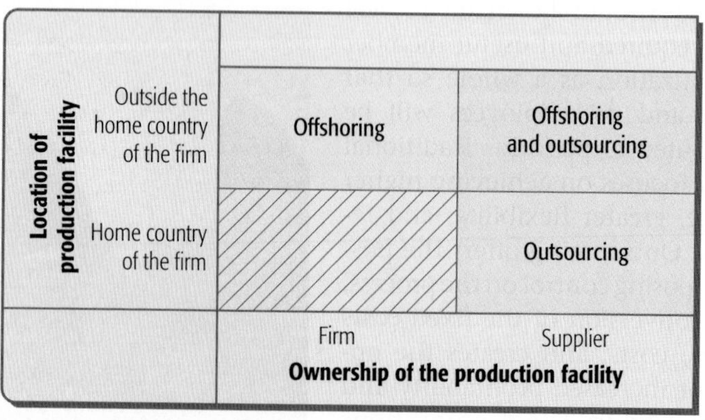

FIGURE 14.6 Outsourcing and Offshoring

strongest decision drivers toward outsourcing is concentrating on the company's priorities. A useful example is customer service telephone call centers. A technical company like Sony or a financial services company like American Express would rather focus on doing what it does best rather than using up resources and time on customer service. The offshore units still need to be monitored and the feedback implemented, but the burden of actually managing the call center has been passed on to another organization. Not only has the burden been passed on, but there is usually a cost-cutting incentive as well because of differences in labor costs. Also, the supplier of the outsourced service or product has to deal with the costs and resources involved in labor turnover, which include temporary replacements and hiring and training of new recruits.

Outsourcing noncore activities allows firms to focus on the activities that they do best and improve their overall performance. Transferring noncore activities to specialized vendors can help reduce costs and improve the performance of those activities. Important soft criteria include a good cultural fit, a commitment to continuous improvement, flexibility, and a commitment to developing long-term relationships and trustworthiness.

A good contract is essential to outsourcing success because the contract helps to establish a balance of power between the client and the vendor. Among the best business practices is outsourcing the correct activities after carefully considering different vendors and selecting the right one, writing a meaningful contract, paying attention to personnel issues, reducing labor turnover, maintaining control over the outsourced activity, carefully reviewing the hidden costs of outsourcing, and planning an exit strategy.

Turnover of labor in general, as well as high-tech and executive labor in particular, can affect a company the most. The migration of labor to a competitor can sometimes be devastating for a company because of the movement of intellectual property with the employee. Strict policies on labor turnover should be adhered to. This might include imposing fines on the vendor if it exceeds a set level of labor turnover every year.

Risks Related to Offshoring and Outsourcing

There are many challenges associated with maintaining operational excellence with offshore operations. Ensuring that the employees of the offshore company understand the organization and the business it performs is a key element. There needs to be an appropriate structure in place that takes the interface between the two organizations into account. There is also a need for two partially overlapping management teams, which have to be set up in such a way that an active coordination and feedback structure exists. This management team will also need to be aware of the constant technological changes that might occur. There should be an effective channel of open communication between the parent company and its offshore partner. This approach will enable problems to be identified and solved in an effective manner.

A number of models for effective global outsourcing and offshoring have been proposed. One model, developed by Aaron and Singh (2005), is particularly useful within the context of operations management. The authors have developed a framework that describes both structural and operational risks associated with offshoring different types of business functions. Furthermore, they also describe approaches for choosing the location of international production facilities and organizational forms to minimize the impact of these risks. The risks and their proposed operations strategies are summarized in Figure 14.7.

The risks of outsourcing are many and complex. They vary from minimal to very high, depending on the type of service or knowledge business that is being outsourced. The major risk that can arise out of outsourcing is the loss of quality.

Evaluating Operational Risk

To evaluate operational risk (the risk that processes won't operate smoothly after being offshored), companies should classify processes by how precise their metrics for quality are, as well as the extent to which work can be codified. We've listed some processes that our research shows fall into each category.

Codifiability of work	Imprecise/Subjective	Precise/Objective
Easy	**MODERATE RISK** *(opaque processes)* ▪ Insurance underwriting ▪ Invoice management ▪ Cash-flow forecasting	**LOW RISK** *(transparent processes)* ▪ Transaction processing ▪ Telecollection ▪ Technical support
Moderate	**HIGH RISK** *(codifiable processes)* ▪ Equity research ▪ Yield analysis ▪ Litigation support	**MODERATE RISK** *(codifiable processes)* ▪ Customer service ▪ Account management
Difficult	**HIGHEST RISK** *(noncodifiable processes)* ▪ Pricing ▪ Working capital management	**HIGH RISK** *(noncodifiable processes)* ▪ Supply chain coordination ▪ Customer data analysis

Precision of metrics used to measure process quality

Evaluating Structural Risk

To ascertain structural risk (the risk that relationships with service providers may not work as expected), companies should look at how precise their quality metrics are as well as the extent to which the execution of processes can be monitored. Most processes fall into one of four catagories.

Ability to monitor work	Imprecise/Subjective	Precise/Objective
Easy	**HIGH RISK** ▪ Equity research ▪ Litigation support ▪ R&D support	**LOW RISK** ▪ Transaction processing ▪ Insurance claims processing ▪ Customer service
Difficult	**HIGHEST RISK** ▪ Pricing ▪ Product design	**MODERATE RISK** ▪ Supply chain coordination ▪ Customer data analysis

Precision of metrics used to measure process quality

FIGURE 14.7 Risks and Operations Strategies Associated with Offshoring

Source: Reprinted by permission of HARVARD BUSINESS REVIEW. From "Getting Offshoring Right" by Aron, Ravi and J. V. Singh, December 2005.

Choosing the Right Location and Organizational Form

Once a company has determined the operational and structural risks of outsourcing its processes, it can use this grid to choose the best locations and organizational forms for those tasks. The nine cells in this table show the optimal offshoring responses to different levels of risk.

Operational risk	Structural risk: Low	Structural risk: Moderate	Structural risk: High
High	**Outsource to service provider located nearby** *(nearshore)* ▪ Litigation support	**Set up captive center nearby or onshore** ▪ R&D ▪ Design	**Execute process in-house and onshore** ▪ Pricing ▪ Corporate planning
Moderate	**Offshore and outsource to service provider over time** ▪ Insurance claims processing ▪ Customer support	**Use extended organization offshore, but monitor closely in real time** ▪ Supply chain coordination ▪ Bioinformatics	**Set up captive center offshore** ▪ Equity research
Low	**Offshore and outsource to service provider** ▪ Data entry ▪ Transaction processing	**Use extended organization offshore** ▪ Telecollection ▪ Technical support	**Use extended organization offshore, but conduct frequent process audits** ▪ Customer data analysis ▪ Market research analysis

FIGURE 14.7 Risks and Operations Strategies Associated with Offshoring (*continued*)

Usually this arises because of a lack of extensive knowledge of what the supplier actually deals in. Or the vendor's employees might work mechanically, without any emotion or passion for the parent company. Dell's recent decision to move some of its call centers back to the United States is an example of how corporate customers, angered by the poor quality of customer service, influenced Dell to make the decision to un-outsource. Outsourcing can be used to save money, but when it degrades critical business attributes such as quality, reliability, integrity, and security, it can become a public relations disaster.

In supply chain situations, there could be risks such as shipping delays, unavailability of shipping capacity, and customs issues while physically transporting goods. Also, there could be variations in costs as a result of foreign exchange fluctuations, closing down of factories as a result of local labor strikes, and other such issues.

When companies enter into technology licenses with offshore vendors, they may be creating a contractual risk. As technology changes rapidly, these long-term contracts might leave the company stuck with outdated and mediocre technology that makes it tough to compete in the market. Outsourcing in the manufacturing industry could potentially lead to counterfeit products, which can eat into the market share of brand owners.

Most IT organizations have business knowledge that resides within the developers of applications. In some cases, this expertise may be a proprietary or competitive advantage. Companies must carefully assess this business knowledge and determine whether moving it either outside the company or to an offshore location will compromise company practices. When outsourcing research and development activities, there is the obvious risk that patents might be filed in the individual employee's name. The employee could take this information to a competitor, with the result that the organization would lose its intellectual property.

Rapid growth among outsourcing vendors has created a dynamic labor market. Key personnel are usually in demand for new, high-profile projects, or even at risk of being recruited by other offshore vendors. While offshore vendors will often quote overall turnover statistics that appear relatively low, the more important statistic to manage is the turnover of the key personnel on an account. Common turnover levels are in the 15 to 20 percent range, and creating contractual terms based on those levels is a reasonable request. Liabilities are being placed on the vendor for any personnel that must be replaced. High turnover is an indirect cost to the organization because it must increase the amount of time spent on knowledge transfer and training new individuals.

Organizations that are evaluating any kind of outsourcing should question whether vendors have sufficiently robust security practices and whether they can meet the internal security requirements of the parent company. While most organizations find offshore vendors' security practices impressive (often exceeding internal practices), the risk of security breaches or lack of intellectual property protection is inherently raised when working in international business. Privacy concerns must be completely addressed. Although these issues rarely are major impediments to outsourcing, the requirements must be documented and the methods of integration with vendors defined. Also, when dealing with sensitive customer information like tax information, social security numbers, and credit card numbers, care must be taken to ensure that these data are not compromised by the employees working for the vendors. There have been recent articles in the news about how employees have tried to misuse such data. The notable problem with such misuse of data is that the parent company cannot influence the decision of the judiciary system in the vendor's country. For example, while the laws concerning privacy violations in the United States are very strict, those in India might not be equally vigorous and punitive.

The cultural differences between countries can also be perceived as a major limitation, especially in the customer service industry. Even though most customer service is outsourced to countries where the majority of the population is English-speaking, pronunciation and accents can vary tremendously. Many vendors put call center employees through accent training. In addition, cultural differences include religions, modes of dress, social activities, and even the way a question is answered. Most leading vendors have cultural education programs, but executives should not assume that difficulties with cultural alignment will be insignificant or trivial.

The time and effort involved in transferring knowledge to the vendor is a cost that is rarely accounted for by IT organizations. Most IT organizations experience a 20 percent decline in productivity during the first year of an agreement, largely because of the time spent transferring both technical and business knowledge to the vendor. Many offshore vendors are deploying videoconferencing (avoiding travel) and classroom settings (creating one-to-many transfer) to improve the efficiency of knowledge transfer. In addition, employee turnover often places a burden on the IT organization because it must provide additional information for new team members.

A number of problems that emerge from outsourcing stem from a loss of direct control over the outsourced activity. Loss of control produces risks that often do not seem to be accounted for when the outsourcing decision is under consideration. Outsourcing leads to fragmentation of a long-established and effective system. There could be a loss of employee morale and internal coherence in the organization. The efficient management of personnel issues is crucial because employees generally view outsourcing as an underestimation of their skills. Outsourcing has a negative impact on employees' sense of job security and loyalty, even when they keep their positions within the firm.

Therefore, the decision to outsource and offshore business functions should be evaluated very carefully. A very useful managerial checklist has been developed by scholors for the firms that are considering outsourcing decisions (see Table 14.4). It suggests that each company must take these issues seriously for successful implementation of any outsourcing decisions.

A number of factors contribute to a successful offshoring relationship. These include people factors such as workers' general knowledge skills, workers' language skills, workers' cultural awareness, project management, and labor cost; technical infrastructure, which includes infrastructure, workers' technical skills, project management, and control processes; client interface, which includes a knowledgeable client, trust, language skills, a problem resolution process, time differences, and client/outsourcer travel; and business infrastructure, which includes a plan, cost control measures, advertising, payment processes, and legal representation. The final critical success factor is intellectual property protection, tax laws, banking laws, customs laws, travel laws, and telecom regulations.

TABLE 14.4 An Outsourcing Checklist

1	A firm should make its outsourcing decision based on long-term strategic goals and not short-term tactical urgency
2	The firm should retain its core domain knowledge
3	An exit strategy should be in place
4	There should be full communication with current employees
5	Joint teams between the firm and its outsourcing supplier should be created for implementation
6	The firm should invest time, money, and effort in the selection of an outsourcing vendor
7	Appropriate performance measures should be decided early
8	The right incentives should be provided to all concerned
9	The firm should take appropriate insurance coverage

Source: Reprinted by permission of *Harvard Business Review*. From "An Outsourcing Checklist" by Michelman, P. Copyright © 2005 by the Harvard Business School Publishing Corporation; all rights reserved.

SUMMARY

1. Explain the meaning of globalization.

- Globalization of industries means movement of production facilities from a firm's home country to other locations around the world.
- A number of countries around the world can be considered to be highly globalized. They include Singapore, Switzerland, and the United States, among others.

2. Describe why firms globalize and establish international production facilities. Discuss various strategies for international production.

- Firms globalize to take advantage of lower labor and operating costs, to get access to skilled employees and natural resources, to get financial and tax-related incentives, and to achieve political and industry-specific goals.
- Many production functions can be globalized. These functions include manufacturing, procurement, logistics and distribution, customer service and support, knowledge processes, and new product innovation.
- A firm's international production facilities can be divided into six categories: offshore factory, source factory, server factory, contributor factory, outpost factory, and lead factory. With the passage of time and increases in competence, the role of an international production facility can change, until it eventually becomes a lead factory.

3. Evaluate the positives and negatives associated with outsourcing and offshoring.

- Outsourcing and offshoring offer a number of advantages to a company, such as cost reduction, knowledge increases, and efficiency gains.
- A number of things must go right for the execution of an offshoring or outsourcing relationship to be successful.
- A firm needs to carefully evaluate the risks associated with offshoring to mitigate the negatives of this approach.

QUESTIONS

1. Why do firms globalize? Give examples of both manufacturing and service firms that have used adaptation, aggregation, and arbitrage as their approach for globalization.
2. Table 14.3 shows the list of the most globalized nations for the year 2006. Locate the most recent list of most globalized nations. Explain the observed changes.
3. Find examples of sets of companies that have chosen to (1) globalize and (2) not globalize the following functions:
   a. Manufacturing
   b. Procurement
   c. Maintenance
   d. Logistics
   e. Customer service
   f. Knowledge-based business processes
   g. Product development
4. Discuss the main reasons why the companies identified in Question 3 have chosen to globalize or not globalize particular functions.
5. Find examples of an offshore factory, source factory, server factory, contributor factory, outpost factory, and lead factory.
6. Do you agree with Friedman's description of the "flat world"? Why or why not?
7. Explain the differences between outsourcing and offshoring. When is it appropriate for a firm to outsource and/or offshore its production functions?

CASE STUDY

Customer Support Outsourcing @ eBay

"Why are we to continue outsourcing, and even consider expanding it? In other words, why should we keep paying someone else to do what we can do for ourselves?"

Kathy Dalton leaned forward in her chair. She read the message on her computer screen and let the words sink in. "Why had I not anticipated that?" she asked herself. "After all, I am adept at asking insightful questions."

Several leading consultants were claiming that offshoring had lost much of its cachet in recent years, as companies were coming to grips with the real costs, logistics, management commitment, and service quality associated with the use of third-party partners in India, the Philippines, and elsewhere. In her proposal, Dalton had reinforced the benefits to eBay of continuing to outsource outside the United States and to weave more "nearshoring" alternatives into her new strategy as well.

eBay's Customer Support Organization

Worldwide, eBay's customer support staff consisted of an estimated 3,000 full-time equivalents (FTEs), accounting for roughly two-thirds of the corporate work force. eBay operated major service centers in Salt Lake City, Omaha, Vancouver, Berlin, and Dublin. Smaller company-owned customer support groups were located in Sydney, Hong Kong, London, and Seoul. The majority of these employees spent their workdays responding to customer e-mails. In 2004, eBay answered more than 30 million customer inquiries, covering everything from questions about selling, bidding, product categories, billing, and pricing to thornier issues involving illegal or prohibited listings and auction security (Table 14.5).

Leading companies like American Express, GE, and Citibank had been outsourcing some of their customer service functions domestically for 10 to 15 years and offshore for at least half that time before eBay felt comfortable in considering outsourcing. By mid-2001, outsourcing had surfaced as a viable way for eBay's customer support operation to scale to demand, avoid capital outlays, reduce unit costs, and leverage its investment in technology and management talent.

But the senior staff in San Jose, including then-CEO Meg Whitman, was concerned about the potential reaction of the eBay community. If you traded on eBay, you were not just a customer. You were a member of a passionate and vocal community of users who felt strongly (and rightly so) that eBay's success was directly attributable more to them than to the business savvy of headquarters staff in San Jose. How would the community react to having some customer support inquiries answered by people who not only were not employed by eBay, but did not even reside in the United States?

The outsourcing pilot program begun in Fort Lauderdale in February 2002 had been relatively seamless. The plan had been to run the pilot for six months before attempting to route volume offshore to one of the service centers in Bangalore, India. However, the service quality and e-mail productivity results from the vendor were on a par with those of eBay's own staff after only three months. The customer support team decided to cut the pilot short and sent the first e-mails to India in June 2002.

TABLE 14.5 eBay Customer Support Volumes by Channel (in millions)

	2001	2002	2003	2004
General Support				
E-mail	8.1	12.1	14.6	16.1
Phone	0.1	0.3	0.4	0.8
Chat	NA	NA	0.4	0.4
Total	8.2	12.4	15.4	17.3
Trust and Safety				
E-mail	4	6.8	9.8	12.6
Phone	0	0	0	0
Chat	NA	NA	0.1	0.6
Total	4	6.8	9.9	13.2
Combined GS and T&S				
E-mail	12.1	18.9	24.4	28.7
Phone	0.1	0.3	0.4	0.8
Chat	NA	NA	0.5	1
Total	12.2	19.2	25.3	30.5

The eBay community's reaction to outsourcing portions of its customer service was essentially only a small ripple in a big pond. There were some issues with the written English of the agents in India. A handful of complaints found their way to Whitman's desk. Still, the service quality and productivity metrics of the outsource providers, both domestic and foreign, rivaled and frequently surpassed the same measurements for eBay's own employees (Table 14.6). Dalton wondered, "What are the limits?"

New Outsourcing Strategy

When she was given the responsibility for outsourcing in July 2004, Dalton dug deeply into the existing operation to understand both the issues and the opportunities and threats facing the department.

The first opportunity she saw was to increase the percentage of outsourcing from 30 percent of overall volume to at least 50 percent. She calculated that this would save an incremental $3.9 million a year. The second opportunity would help her to accomplish the first. It was to target for the first time specific volume types within Trust and Safety and demonstrate that these could be successfully handled by a third-party outsourcer. The third area of opportunity was to seek a new outsourcing partner. Dalton was concerned that for two years, eBay had used only one outsourcing vendor. She reasoned that adding a second vendor would benefit eBay by instilling competition in both pricing and performance metrics between the two vendors, as well as providing a measure of redundancy in the event of system outages.

In order to increase the outsourcing to 50 percent of total volume, and at the same time take advantage of the opportunity for including Trust and Safety volume in the mix, Dalton had devised a strategy with three levels or tiers. Each tier represented a progressively more complex type of work, in terms of both the nature of the customer inquiry and the channel through which it accessed customer support (Table 14.7).

Tier 1. This tier included only e-mails involving the most basic general support–type questions. These were typically simple questions concerning bidding and selling that could be answered using a template of responses from the automated system. Because these were less complex customer inquiries, training for the service representatives was less demanding and could be conducted over a three-week period. Most of eBay's tier 1 volume was already being handled by the two outsourcing facilities in India. Dalton analyzed all the remaining inquiry types to try to identify an additional 260,000+ e-mails that could be safely offloaded to India as well. If these volumes could be found, she thought she might be able to negotiate with the vendor for a volume discount from $0.81 per e-mail to $0.72.

Tier 2. This tier was made up of general support e-mail volume that was considered a bit more complex than tier 1 work. It included more billing-related and account adjustment questions, for which more in-depth training of the service representatives was needed. eBay had outsourced a small portion of this volume, but only to the Florida center, where English was the workers' native language. Now, Dalton proposed utilizing locations in Canada as another option for handling this

TABLE 14.6 Metric Comparison for eBay In-house and Outsourcing Vendors (Comparison for Similar Volume Types)

	Jul-02		Dec-02		Jul-03		Dec-03		Jul-04		Dec-04	
	In	Out	In	Out	In	Out	In	Out	In	Out	In	Out
E-mails Productivity/Hr	14.8	13.1	15.2	14.7	15.5	15.4	15.7	16.1	15.8	16.3	15.8	16.3
E-mails per FTE/Month	2,050	1,963	2,181	2,095	2,202	2,189	2,240	2,255	2,250	2,291	2,250	2,285
E-mail Quality %	94%	88%	95%	94%	95%	95%	94%	95%	93%	95%	93%	96%
Customer Satisfaction %	87%	83%	87%	86%	87%	88%	88%	88%	87%	88%	87%	89%
E-mail Unit Cost ($)	1.59	0.87	1.55	0.86	1.56	0.85	1.49	0.82	1.48	0.81	1.48	0.81

TABLE 14.7 Proposed Outsourced Volume and Unit Cost by Tiers

	Current (Dec. 2004)			Proposed (Dec. 2004)		
	Monthly Volume	% of Total Volume	Unit Cost	Monthly Volume	% of Total Volume	Unit Cost
Tier 1						
General Support	510,000	21.30%	$0.81	775,000	32.40%	$0.72
Tier 2						
General Support	68,000	2.80%	$1.45	186,000	7.80%	$1.15
Tier 3						
General Support	20,000	0.80%	$1.48	25,000	1.04%	$1.33
Trust and Safety	NA	NA	NA	210,000	8.80%	$1.33
Total	598,000	24.20%		1,196,000	50.00%	

volume. These locations could satisfy the requirement that the workers be native English speakers and could prove very effective from a cost standpoint. Though Canada was not as low-cost an environment as India, the Canadian tier 2 locations were on average 22 percent more economical in cost per e-mail than the domestic outsourced facilities and eBay's wholly owned service centers.

Tier 3. This tier was reserved for more complex general support questions, those that required flexibility and some judgment on the part of the service employees. Also, it was in this tier that Dalton proposed that some simple Trust and Safety inquiries be handled. She was careful not to select work that was overly sensitive in terms of customers' personal information or that necessitated detailed investigative work. Types of inquires that qualified included reports from eBay users on spam or potential scam sites and those listing violations or member misbehavior, such as not paying for items received and shill bidding. This tier consisted mainly of e-mail volume, yet Dalton designed it so that some simple phone and chat inquiries were included as well.

To BOT or Not to BOT

Dalton had also done some research on the subject of developing eBay-owned and managed sites offshore, although not in real depth. She opened her file drawer and pulled out a folder labeled across the top with the letters "BOT." It had been several months since she had gathered the contents. Before she knew it, an hour had elapsed and she remained focused on sifting through the packet of information, occasionally pausing to run several scenarios through a quickly composed Excel spreadsheet. After another 45 minutes of analysis, she was ready. She printed the spreadsheet and quickly surveyed it for clarity. It was not as detailed as it would need to be in the coming days, but it would help her frame a conversation with her boss about the question she had been asked in her e-mail:

"Why should we keep paying someone else to do what we can do for ourselves?"

In her spreadsheet, Dalton outlined and quantified three alternatives (Table 14.8). The first alternative involved only tier 1 of her proposed three-tiered strategy: maintain the relationships with eBay's offshore outsourcing partners, continue to improve the operation in India, and identify incremental volume to outsource in order to drive e-mail costs lower. She viewed this scenario as the least risky of the three alternatives.

The second alternative was to eliminate the outsourcing vendors altogether. In this option, she proposed that customer support not renew its contracts with the vendors, but instead purchase or lease land or an already established facility in India and build its own operation. Dalton knew that this alternative presented the most risks to eBay, including capital outlay, real estate commitments, governmental compliance, communications infrastructure, and in-country management resources. Yet, according to her spreadsheet assumptions, this alternative promised the biggest potential long-term payoff in unit cost reduction, something that eBay's executive staff prized highly.

She believed that her third alternative, called "Build, Operate, and Transfer," or "BOT" for short,

TABLE 14.8 Dalton's Spreadsheet

		Cost/Hr/Seat (250 Seats)	Cost/Hr/Seat (500 Seats)	Cost/Hr/Seat (1,000 Seats)	Avg. Initial Investment/Seat (One-Time Cost)	Avg. Transfer Cost/Seat (One-Time Cost)
Scenario I Outsourcing to third-party vendors	E-mail, phone, chat	$10.17	$9.56	$8.60	NA	NA
	E-mail only	$6.24	$5.38	$4.66	NA	NA
Scenario 2 Build eBay-owned center	E-mail, phone, chat	$9.73	$8.85	$7.77	$12,000	NA
	E-mail only	$5.30	$4.68	$4.14	$11,000	NA
Scenario 3 Build, Operate, Transfer (BOT)	E-mail, phone, chat	$9.88	$9.03	$8.10	NA	$3,500
	E-mail only	$5.34	$4.96	$4.40	NA	$2,900

was the most creative and represented a hybrid of the first two. She recommended that eBay contract with a third-party vendor that would acquire or build an operations center, staff and manage it, and then, after a specified period of time of perhaps a year or two, transfer full ownership to eBay. This option appealed to her more than the second one because the vendor would bear the initial risks during the start-up phase, which she considered the most challenging and expensive. eBay could limit its cost exposure up front until the operation had been ramped up and was running. She planned to tell her boss that the most critical points of the BOT alternative were to negotiate the appropriate level of management fees with the outsourcing vendor and to work out the intricacies of the actual transfer of ownership down the road.

Dalton's biggest concern, however, was the fact that she had so far been unable to find any example of a domestic company utilizing a BOT approach with a vendor in India. To her knowledge, eBay would be the first customer service operation attempting such a strategy. As she prepared to pick up the phone and dial her boss's number, she was haunted by eBay's well-entrenched mantra of not being on the "bleeding edge" with any new, unproven experiments.

QUESTIONS

1. What are you (in the role of Kathy Dalton) going to present at the outsourcing strategy meeting, and why?
2. When companies like Dell are contracting outsourcing in some areas, should eBay consider expansion?
3. What are the limits to outsourcing Trust and Safety correspondence?
4. What are the advantages and disadvantages of the BOT strategy, and how does it stack up against the other two options that Dalton outlines in her Excel spreadsheet?
5. What will eBay's senior management do with Kathy Dalton's proposed three-tiered outsourcing strategy?

Source: This case is adapted from Newman, Grikscheit, Verma, and Malapati (2006). A detailed version of this case is available from Case Collection of Indiana University CIBER or the European Case Clearinghouse (case # 606-043-1).

Appendix

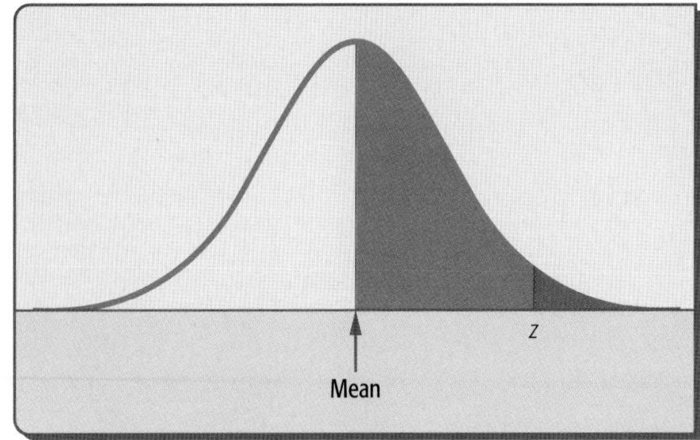

Normal Distribution: Probability Content from Mean to Z

Z	0.00	0.01	0.02	0.03	0.04	0.05	0.06	0.07	0.08	0.09
0.0	0.5000	0.5040	0.5080	0.5120	0.5160	0.5199	0.5239	0.5279	0.5319	0.5359
0.1	0.5398	0.5438	0.5478	0.5517	0.5557	0.5596	0.5636	0.5675	0.5714	0.5753
0.2	0.5793	0.5832	0.5871	0.5910	0.5948	0.5987	0.6026	0.6064	0.6103	0.6141
0.3	0.6179	0.6217	0.6255	0.6293	0.6331	0.6368	0.6406	0.6443	0.6480	0.6517
0.4	0.6554	0.6591	0.6628	0.6664	0.6700	0.6736	0.6772	0.6808	0.6844	0.6879
0.5	0.6915	0.6950	0.6985	0.7019	0.7054	0.7088	0.7123	0.7157	0.7190	0.7224
0.6	0.7257	0.7291	0.7324	0.7357	0.7389	0.7422	0.7454	0.7486	0.7517	0.7549
0.7	0.7580	0.7611	0.7642	0.7673	0.7704	0.7734	0.7764	0.7794	0.7823	0.7852
0.8	0.7881	0.7910	0.7939	0.7967	0.7995	0.8023	0.8051	0.8078	0.8106	0.8133
0.9	0.8159	0.8186	0.8212	0.8238	0.8264	0.8289	0.8315	0.8340	0.8365	0.8389
1.0	0.8413	0.8438	0.8461	0.8485	0.8508	0.8531	0.8554	0.8577	0.8599	0.8621
1.1	0.8643	0.8665	0.8686	0.8708	0.8729	0.8749	0.8770	0.8790	0.8810	0.8830
1.2	0.8849	0.8869	0.8888	0.8907	0.8925	0.8944	0.8962	0.8980	0.8997	0.9015
1.3	0.9032	0.9049	0.9066	0.9082	0.9099	0.9115	0.9131	0.9147	0.9162	0.9177
1.4	0.9192	0.9207	0.9222	0.9236	0.9251	0.9265	0.9279	0.9292	0.9306	0.9319
1.5	0.9332	0.9345	0.9357	0.9370	0.9382	0.9394	0.9406	0.9418	0.9429	0.9441
1.6	0.9452	0.9463	0.9474	0.9484	0.9495	0.9505	0.9515	0.9525	0.9535	0.9545
1.7	0.9554	0.9564	0.9573	0.9582	0.9591	0.9599	0.9608	0.9616	0.9625	0.9633
1.8	0.9641	0.9649	0.9656	0.9664	0.9671	0.9678	0.9686	0.9693	0.9699	0.9706
1.9	0.9713	0.9719	0.9726	0.9732	0.9738	0.9744	0.9750	0.9756	0.9761	0.9767
2.0	0.9772	0.9778	0.9783	0.9788	0.9793	0.9798	0.9803	0.9808	0.9812	0.9817
2.1	0.9821	0.9826	0.9830	0.9834	0.9838	0.9842	0.9846	0.9850	0.9854	0.9857
2.2	0.9861	0.9864	0.9868	0.9871	0.9875	0.9878	0.9881	0.9884	0.9887	0.9890
2.3	0.9893	0.9896	0.9898	0.9901	0.9904	0.9906	0.9909	0.9911	0.9913	0.9916
2.4	0.9918	0.9920	0.9922	0.9925	0.9927	0.9929	0.9931	0.9932	0.9934	0.9936
2.5	0.9938	0.9940	0.9941	0.9943	0.9945	0.9946	0.9948	0.9949	0.9951	0.9952
2.6	0.9953	0.9955	0.9956	0.9957	0.9959	0.9960	0.9961	0.9962	0.9963	0.9964
2.7	0.9965	0.9966	0.9967	0.9968	0.9969	0.9970	0.9971	0.9972	0.9973	0.9974
2.8	0.9974	0.9975	0.9976	0.9977	0.9977	0.9978	0.9979	0.9979	0.9980	0.9981
2.9	0.9981	0.9982	0.9982	0.9983	0.9984	0.9984	0.9985	0.9985	0.9986	0.9986
3.0	0.9987	0.9987	0.9987	0.9988	0.9988	0.9989	0.9989	0.9989	0.9990	0.9990

References

Chapter 1

Boyer, K. K., and M. Lewis. "Competitive Priorities: Investigating the Need for Trade-offs in Operations Strategy." *Production and Operations Management* 11, no. 1 (2002): 9–20.

Boyer, K. K., M. L. Swink, and E. Rosenzweig. "Operations Strategy Research in the POMS Journal." *Production and Operations Management* 14, no. 4 (2005): 442–449.

Chase, R. B., and D. A. Garvin. "The Service Factory." *Harvard Business Review* 67, no. 4 (1988): 61–69.

Hayes, R. H., and G. P. Pisano. "Beyond World Class: The New Manufacturing Strategy." *Harvard Business Review* 72, no. 1 (1994): 77–86.

Hayes, R. H., and S. C. Wheelwright. *Restoring Our Competitive Edge: Competing Through Manufacturing.* New York: John Wiley & Sons, 1984.

Hill, T. J. *Manufacturing Strategy: Text and Cases,* 2nd ed. Burr Ridge, IL: Irwin, 1994.

Holcomb, T. R., and M. A. Hitt. "Toward a Model of Strategic Outsourcing." *Journal of Operations Management* 25, no. 2 (2007): 387–402.

Rudberg, M., and B. Martin-West. "Global Operations Strategy: Coordinating Manufacturing Networks." *Omega* 36, no. 1 (2008): 91–106.

Schmenner, R., and M. Swink. "On Theory in Operations Management." *Journal of Operations Management* 17, no. 1 (1999): 97–113.

Skinner, W. "Manufacturing: Missing Link in Corporate Strategy." *Harvard Business Review,* 47, no. 3 (1969): 136–145.

Chapter 2

Ahire, S. L., D. Y. Golhar, and M. A. Waller. "Development and Validation of TQM Implementation Constructs." *Decision Sciences* 27, no. 1 (1996), 23–56.

Anderson, S. W., J. D. Daly, and M. F. Johnson. "Why Firms Seek ISO 9000 Certification: Regulatory Compliance or Competitive Advantage." *Production and Operations Management* 8, no. 1 (1999), 28–43.

Cook, L. and R. Verma. "Exploring the Linkages Between Quality System, Service Quality, and Performance Excellence: Service Providers' Perspectives," *Quality Management Journal,* 9, no. 2 (2002), 44–56.

Corbett, C. C., M. J. Montes-Sancho, and D. A. Kirsch. "The Financial Impact of ISO 9000 Certification in the United States: An Empirical Analysis." *Management Science* 51, no. 7 (2005), 1046–1059.

Crosby, P. B. *Quality Is Free: The Art of Making Quality Certain.* New York: McGraw-Hill, 1979.

Deming, W. E. *Out of the Crisis.* Boston: MIT Press, 1982.

Evans, J., and W. M. Lindsay. *The Management and Control of Quality,* 7th ed. Mason, OH: South-Western Cengage Learning, 2007.

Flynn, B. B., R. G. Schroeder, and S. Sakakibara. "A Framework for Quality Management Research and an Associated Measurement Instrument." *Journal of Operations Management,* 1994.

Garvin, D. "Competing on the Eight Dimensions of Quality." *Harvard Business Review,* 1987.

Hendricks, K. B., and V. R. Singhal. "The Long-Run Stock Price Performance of Firms with Effective TQM Programs." *Management Science* 47, no. 3 (2001), 359–368.

Hendricks, K. B., and V. R. Singhal. "Does Implementing an Effective TQM Program Actually Improve Operating Performance? Empirical Evidence from Firms That Have Won Quality Awards." *Management Science* 43, no. 9 (1997), 1258–1274.

Pande, P. S., R. P. Newman, and R. R. Cavanagh. *The Six Sigma Way: How GE, Motorola and Other Top Companies Are Honing Their Performance.* New York: McGraw-Hill, 2000.

Parasuraman, A., V. Zeithaml, and L. L. Berry. "A Conceptual Model of Service Quality and Its Implications for Future Research." 49, no. 4 (1985), 41–50.

Pyzdek, T. *The Six SIGMA Handbook: The Complete Guide for Greenbelts, Blackbelts, and Managers at All Levels.* New York: McGraw-Hill, 2003.

Tague, N. R. *The Quality Toolbox,* 2nd ed. Milwaukee, WI: ASQ Quality Press, 2005.

Chapter 3

Alam, I., and C. Perry. "A Customer-Oriented New Services Development Process." *Journal of Services Marketing* 16, no. 6 (2002), 515–534.

Booz Allen Hamilton. *Management of New Products.* New York: Booz Allen Hamilton, 1968.

Booz Allen Hamilton. *New Products Management for the 1980s.* New York: Booz Allen Hamilton, 1982.

Christenson, C. *The Innovator's Dilemma.* Boston: Harvard Business School Publishing, 1997.

Cooper, R. G. "Third-Generation New Product Process." *Journal of Product Innovation Management* 11, no. 1 (1994), 3–14.

Cooper, R. G., S. J. Edgett, and E. J. Kleinschmidt. "Optimizing the Stage-Gate Process: What Best-Practice Companies Do: II." *Research Technology Management* 45, no. 5 (2002), 21–27.

Fine, C. H. *Clockspeed: Winning Industry Control in the Age of Temporary Advantage.* New York, Basic Books, 1998.

Gupta, S., and M. Vajic. "The Contextual and Dialectical Nature of Experiences." In *New Service Development—Creating Memorable Experience,* edited by J. A. Fitzsimmons and M. J. Fitzsimmons. Thousand Oaks, CA: Sage Publications, 1999, 33–51.

Hendricks, K. B., and V. Singhal. "Does Implementing an Effective TQM Program Actually Improve Operating Performance? Empirical Evidence from Firms That Have Won Quality Awards." *Management Science* 43, no. 9 (1997), 1258–1274.

Johnson, S. P., L. J. Menor, A. V. Roth, and R. B. Chase. "A Critical Evaluation of the New Service Development Process: Integrating Service Innovation and Service Design. In *New Service Development—Creating Memorable Experience,* edited by J. A. Fitzsimmons and M. J. Fitzsimmons. Thousand Oaks, CA: Sage Publications, 1–32.

Kim, W. C., and R. Mauborgne. *Blue Ocean Strategy: How to Create Uncontested Market Space and Make the Competition Irrelevant.* Boston: Harvard Business School Publishing, 2005.

Louviere, J. J., D. Hensher, and J. Swait. *Stated Preference Methods: Analysis and Applications.* Cambridge, United Kingdom: Cambridge University Press, 2000.

Menor, L. J., M. V. Tatikonda, and S. E. Sampson. "New Service Development: Areas for Exploitation and Exploration. *Journal of Operations Management* 20, no. 2 (2002), 135–157.

Pine, B. J., and J. H. Gilmore, "Welcome to the Experience Economy." *Harvard Business Review* 76, no. 4 (1998), 97–105.

Scheuing, E. E., and E. M. Johnson. "A Proposed Model for New Service Development." *Journal of Services Marketing* 3, no. 2 (1989), 25–35.

Stalk, George, Jr. "Time—The Next Source of Competitive Advantage." *Harvard Business Review,* Vol. 66, no. 4 (July–August 1988), 41–51.

Tsai, W., and T. Klastorin. "New Product Introduction: Timing, Design and Pricing." *Manufacturing and Service Operations Management* 6, no. 4 (2004), 302–320.

Tsai, W., G. Schmidt, and R. Verma. "New Service Development," in *Handbook of New Product Development.* Oxford, United Kingdom: Elsevier, September 2007.

Urban, G. L., and J. R. Hauser. *Design and Marketing of New Products.* Malden, MA: Blackwell Synergy, 1980.

Verma, R. "Unlocking the Secrets of Customer Choices." *Cornell Center for Hospitality Research Managerial Report,* January 2007.

Verma, R., Z. Iqbal, and G. Plaschka, "Understanding Customer Choices in e-Financial Services." *California Management Review* 46, no. 4 (2004), pp. 43–67.

Womak, J. P., D. T. Jones, and D. Roos. *The Machine That Changed the World.* New York: Rawson Associates, 1990.

Chapter 4

Chase, R. B., and D. M. Stewart. "Make Your Service Fail-Safe." *Sloan Management Review* (Spring 1994), 35–44.

Ettlie, J., and H. Stoll. *Managing the Design-Manufacturing Process.* New York: McGraw-Hill, 1990.

Fitzsimmons, J. A., and M. J. Fitzsimmons. *Service Management: Operations, Strategy and Information Technology,* 4th ed. New York: Irwin/McGraw-Hill, 2004.

Francis, R. L., L. F. McGinnis, and J. A. White. *Facility Layout and Location: An Analytical Approach,* 3rd ed. Upper Saddle River, NJ: Prentice Hall, 2001.

Goldratt, E. M., and J. Cox. *The Goal: A Process of Ongoing Improvement,* 2nd ed. Croton-on-Hudson, NY: North River Press, 2002.

Hyer, N., and U. Wemmerlov. *Reorganizing the Factory: Competing Through Cellular Manufacturing.* Portland, OR: Productivity Press, 2002.

Karmarkar, U. "Will You Survive the Services Revolution?" *Harvard Business Review* (May–June 2004), Vol. 82, No. 6, 99–107.

Shunk, D. L. *Integrated Process Design and Development.* Homewood, IL: Business One Irwin, 1992.

Upton, D. "What Really Makes Factories Flexible." *Harvard Business Review* (July–August 1995), 73, no. 4, 74–84.

Verma, R., and G. Plaschka. "Predicting Customer Choices." *Sloan Management Review* 47, no. 1 (2005), 7–10.

Chapter 5

Duray, R., P. T. Ward, G. W. Milligan, and W. L. Berry. "Approaches to Mass Customization: Configurations and Empirical Validation." *Journal of Operations Management* 18, no. 6 (2000), 605–625.

Fisher, M. L. "What Is the Right Supply Chain for Your Product?" *Harvard Business Review* 75, no. 2 (March–April 1997), 105–116.

Greene, J. H. *Production and Inventory Control Handbook,* 3rd ed. New York: McGraw-Hill, 1997.

Ireland, R. "ABCs of Collaborative Planning, Forecasting and Replenishment." *Journal of Business Forecasting* 24, no. 2 (2005), 3–5.

Krupp, J. A. G. "Are ABC Codes an Obsolete Technology?" *APICS—The Performance Advantage* (April 1994), 34–35.

Lapide, L. "RFID: What's in It for the Forecaster," *Journal of Business Forecasting Methods & Systems* 23, no. 2 (2004), 16–19.

Onwubolu, G. C., and B. C. Dube. "Implementing an Improved Inventory Control System in a Small Company: A Case Study." *Production Planning and Control* 17, no. 1 (2006), 67–76.

Silver, E. A., D. E. Pyke, and R. Peterson. *Inventory Management, Production Planning and Scheduling,* 3rd ed. New York: John Wiley & Sons, 1998.

Vollmann, T. E., W. L. Berry, D. C. Whybark, and F. R. Jacobs. *Manufacturing Planning and Control Systems for Supply Chain Management: The Definitive Guide for Professionals,* 5th ed. New York: McGraw-Hill, 2004.

Chapter 6

Callioni, G., X. de Montgros, R. Slagmulder, L. N. Van Wassenhove, and L. Wright. "Inventory-Driven Costs." *Harvard Business Review* 83, no. 3 (2005), 35–37.

Clarke, R. H., D. Twede, J. R. Tazelaar, and K. K. Boyer. "Radio Frequency Identification (RFID) Performance: The Effect of Tag Orientation and Package Contents." *Packaging Technology and Science* 19, no. 1 (2006), 45–54.

De Toni, A. F., and E. Zamolo. "From a Traditional Replenishment System to Vendor-Managed Inventory: A Case Study from the Household Electrical Appliances Sector." *International Journal of Production Economics* 96, no. 1 (2005), 63–77.

Galbreth, M. R., and J. D. Blackburn. "Optimal Acquisition and Sorting Policies for Remanufacturing." *Production and Operations Management* 15, no. 3 (2006), 384–392.

Greene, J. H. *Production and Inventory Control Handbook,* 3rd ed. New York: McGraw-Hill, 1997.

Hendricks, K. B., V. R. Singhal, and J. K. Stratman. "The Impact of Enterprise Systems on Corporate Performance: A Study of ERP, SCM, and CRM System Implementations." *Journal of Operations Management* 25, no. 1 (2007), 65–82.

Katz, J. "Reaching for ROI on RFID." *Industry Week,* February 1, 2006.

Kelle, P., and A. Akbulut. "The Role of ERP Tools in Supply Chain Information Sharing, Cooperation and Cost Optimization." *International Journal of Production Economics* 93 (2005), 41–54.

Krupp, J. A. G. "Are ABC Codes an Obsolete Technology?" *APICS—The Performance Advantage,* April 1994, pp. 34–35.

Onwubolu, G. C., and B. C. Dube. "Implementing an Improved Inventory Control System in a Small Company: A Case Study." *Production Planning and Control* 17, no. 1 (2006), 67–76.

Silver, E. A., D. E. Pyke, and R. Peterson. *Inventory Management, Production Planning and Scheduling,* 3rd ed. New York: John Wiley & Sons, 1998.

Vollmann, T. E., W. L. Berry, D. C. Whybark, and F. R. Jacobs. *Manufacturing Planning and Control Systems for Supply Chain Management: The Definitive Guide for Professionals,* 5th ed. New York: McGraw-Hill, 2004.

Waller, M., M. E. Johnson, and T. Davis. "Vendor-Managed Inventory in the Retail Supply Chain." *Journal of Business Logistics* 20 (1999), 183–197.

Chapter 7

Aghazadeh, S. M. "MRP Contributes to a Company's Profitability." *Assembly Automation* 23, no. 3 (2005), 257–265.

Bendoly, E., and T. Schoenherr, "ERP System and Implementation-Process Benefits: Implications for B2B E-procurement." *International Journal of Operations and Production Management* 25, no. 4 (2005), 304–319.

Cotteleer, M. J., and E. Bendoly, "Order Lead-Time Improvement Following Enterprise Information Technology Implementation: An Empirical Study." *MIS Quarterly* 30, no. 3 (2006), 643–660.

Davenport, T. H. "Putting the Enterprise into the Enterprise System." *Harvard Business Review,* July–August 1998, 121–131.

Jacobs, F. R., and T. W. Weston. "Enterprise Resource Planning (ERP)—A Brief History." *Journal of Operations Management* 25, no. 2 (2007), 357–363.

Krajewski, L. J., B. E. King, L. P. Ritzman, and D. S. Wong. "Kanban, MRP and Shaping the Manufacturing Environment." *Management Science* 33, no. 1 (1987), 39–57.

Kreipl, S., and M. Pinedo. "Planning and Scheduling in Supply Chains: An Overview of Issues in Practice." *Production and Operations Management* 13, no. 1 (2004), 77–92.

Melnyk, S. A., R. Sroufe, F. Montabon, R. Calantone, L. Rummala, and T. J. Hinds. "Integrating Environmental Issues into Material Planning: 'Green' MRP." *Production and Inventory Management Journal,* 3rd Quarter 1999, 36–45.

Orlicky, J. *Material Requirements Planning: The New Way of Life in Production and Inventory Management.* New York: McGraw-Hill, 1974.

Pinedo, M. L. *Planning and Scheduling in Manufacturing and Services.* New York: Springer, 2005.

Plossl, G. W., and O. W. Wight. *Production and Inventory Control: Principles and Technique.* Englewood Cliffs, NJ: Prentice Hall, 1967.

Sridharan, V., W. L. Berry, and V. Udayabhanu. "Freezing the Master Production Schedule Under Rolling Planning Horizons." *Management Science* 33, no. 9 (1987), 1137–1149.

Vollmann, T. E., W. L. Berry, D. C. Whybark, and F. R. Jacobs. *Manufacturing Planning and Control for Supply Chain Management,* 5th ed. New York: McGraw-Hill, 2004.

Wu, J. H., and Y. M. Wang, "Measuring ERP Success: The Ultimate Users' View." *International Journal of Operations and Production Management* 26, no. 8 (2006), 882–903.

Yen, H. R., and C. Sheu, "Aligning ERP Implementation with Competitive Priorities of Manufacturing Firms: An Exploratory Study." *International Journal of Production Economics* 92, no. 3 (2004), 207–220.

Zhao, X., F. Lai, and T. S. Lee, "Evaluation of Safety Stock Methods in Multilevel Material Requirements Planning (MRP) Systems." *Production Planning and Control* 12, no. 8 (2001), 794–803.

Chapter 8

Dilts, D. M., and K. R. Pence. "Impact of Role in the Decision to Fail: An Exploratory Study of Terminated Projects." *Journal of Operations Management* 24, no. 4 (2006).

Gary, L. "Managing Project Risk." Harvard Management Update (Oct. 1, 2005), www.harvardbusiness.com.

Goldratt, E. M. *Critical Chain.* Great Barrington, Mass: North River Press, 1997.

Murray, K. "Risk Management: Beyond the Textbooks." *Project Management Network* 12, no 6 (1998).

Pinto, J. K., and O. P. Kharbanda. "How to Fail in Project Management (Without Really Trying)." *Business Horizons,* July–August 1996.

Project Management Institute. *A Guide to the Project Management Body of Knowledge (PMBOK® Guide).* Newtown Square, PA: Project Management Institute, 2004.

Slywotzky, A. J., and J. Dryzek. "Countering the Biggest Risk of All." *Harvard Business Review,* March–April 2005.

Tate, K., and P. Martin. *Project Management Memory Jogger.* Salem, NH: GOAL/QPC, 1997.

Wheelwright, S. C., and K. Clark. "Creating Project Plans to Focus Product Development." *Harvard Business Review,* September–October 2003.

Chapter 9

Armacost, A. P., C. Barnhart, K. Ware, and A. M. Wilson. "UPS Optimizes Its Air Network." *Interfaces,* January–February 2004.

Beis, D. A., P. Loucopoulos, Y. Pyrgiotis, and K. G. Zografos. "PLATO Helps Athens Win Gold: Olympic Games Knowledge Modeling for Organizational Change and Resource Management." *Interfaces,* January–February 2006.

Blake, J. T., and J. Donald. "Mount Sinai Hospital Uses Integer Programming to Allocate Operating Room Time." *Interfaces,* March–April 2002.

Brown, G., J. Keegan, B. Vigus, and K. Wood. "The Kellogg Company Optimizes Production, Inventory, and Distribution." *Interfaces,* November–December 2001.

Thompson, G. M., and R. Verma. "Computer Simulation in Hospitality Teaching, Practice, and Research." *Cornell Quarterly,* 2003.

Chapter 10

Bakke, N. A., and R. Hellberg. "The Challenges of Capacity Planning." *International Journal of Production Economics* 31 (1993), 243–264.

Hammesfahr, R., D. Jack, J. A. Pope, and A. Ardalan. "Strategic Planning for Production Capacity." *International Journal of Operations and Production Management* 13, no. 5 (1993), 41–53.

Jain, A. "Value of Capacity Pooling in Supply Chains with Heterogeneous Customers." *European Journal of Operational Research* 176, no. 2 (2007), 794–808.

Klassen, K. J., and T. R. Rodleder. "Combining Operations and Marketing to Manage Capacity and Demand in Services." *Service Industries Journal* 21, no. 2 (2001), 1–30.

Rauner, M. S., M. Kraus, and S. Schwarz. "Competition Under Different Reimbursement Systems: The Concept of an Internet-based Hospital Management Game." *European Journal of Operational Research* 185, no. 3 (2008), 948–963.

Upton, D. "What Really Makes Factories Flexible." *Harvard Business Review,* July–August 1995, pp. 74–84.

Chapter 11

Andersen, B., and T. Fagerhaug. *Root Cause Analysis: Simplified Tools and Techniques,* 2nd ed. Milwaukee: ASQ Quality Press, 2006.

Brassard, M., and D. Ritter (eds.). *The Memory Jogger II: A Pocket Guide of Tools for Continuous Improvement and Effective Planning.* Salem, NH: Goal/QPC Press, 1994.

Heskett, J. L., T. O. Jones, G. Loveman, W. E. Sasser, Jr., and L. A. Schlesinger. "Putting the Service Profit Chain to Work." *Harvard Business Review,* March 1994.

Pande, P. S., R. R. Cavangh, and R. P. Neuman. *The Six Sigma Way.* New York: McGraw-Hill, 2000.

Tague, N. R. *The Quality Toolbox,* 2nd ed. Milwaukee: ASQ Quality Press, 2004.

Verma, R. "Unlocking the Secrets of Customer Choices." *Center for Hospitality Research Report,* January 2007.

Chapter 12

Abernathy, F. H., J. T. Dunlop, J. H. Hammond, and D. Weil. "Control Your Inventory in the World of Lean Retailing." *Harvard Business Review,* November–December 2000.

Bowen, D., and W. E. Youngdahl. "Lean Service: In Defense of a Production Line Approach." *International Journal of Service Industry Management* 9, no. 3 (1998).

Goldratt, E. M., and J. Cox. *The Goal: A Process of Ongoing Improvement.* Great Barrington, Mass: North River Press, 1986.

Karmarker, U. "Getting Control of Just-In-Time." *Harvard Business Review,* September–October 1989.

King, A. A., and M. J. Lenox. "Lean and Green? An Empirical Examination of the Relationship Between Lean Production and Environmental Performance." *Production and Operations Management* 10, no. 3 (2001).

Lee, S. M., and M. Ebrahimpour. "Just-in-Time Production System: Some Requirements for Implementation." *International Journal of Operations and Production Management* 4, no. 4 (1984).

Miller, J. G., and T. E. Vollmann. "The Hidden Factory." *Harvard Business Review,* September–October 1985.

Schonberger, R. J. *Japanese Manufacturing Techniques: Nine Hidden Lessons in Simplicity.* New York: The Free Press, 1982.

Schonberger, R. J. *World Class Manufacturing Casebook: Implementing JIT and TQC.* New York: The Free Press, 1987.

Shah, R., and P. Ward. "Defining and Developing Measures of Lean Production." *Journal of Operations Management,* vol. 25, no. 4 (June 2007): 785–805.

Womack, J. P., and D. T. Jones. *Lean Thinking: Banish Waste and Create Wealth in Your Corporation.* New York: Simon & Schuster, 1996.

Womack, J. P., D. T. Jones, and D. Roos. *The Machine That Changed the World: The Story of Lean Production.* New York: Harper Perennial, 1991.

Chapter 13

Boyer, K. K. "Evolutionary Patterns of Flexible Automation and Performance: A Longitudinal Study." *Management Science* 45, no. 6 (1999), 824–842.

Boyer, K. K., G. Leong, P. T. Ward, and L. Krajewski. "Unlocking the Potential of Advanced Manufacturing Technologies." *Journal of Operations Management* 15, no. 4 (1997), 331–347.

Chopra S. and P. Meindl. *Supply Chain Management,* 2nd ed. Upper Saddle River, N.J.: Prentice Hall, 2004.

Forrester, J. W. "Industrial Dynamics." *Harvard Business Review,* July–August 1958.

Goldhar, J. D. and M. Jelinek. "Plan for Economies of Scope." *Harvard Business Review* 61 no. 6 (1983), 141–148.

Hawn, C. "If He's So Smart . . . Steve Jobs, Apple and the Limits of Innovation." *Fast Company,* issue 78 (2004), 68.

Hendricks, K. B., V. R. Singhal, and J. K. Stratman. "The Impact of Enterprise Systems on Corporate Performance: A Study of ERP, SCM, and CRM System Implementations." *Journal of Operations Management* 25, no. 1 (2007), 65–82.

Lee, H. L., V. Padmanabhan, and S. Whang. "The Bullwhip Effect in Supply Chain." *Sloan Management Review* 38, no. 3 (1997), 70–77.

Lummus, R. R., L. K. Duclos, and R. J. Vokurka. "The Impact of Marketing Initiatives on the Supply Chain." *Supply Chain Management: An International Journal* 8, no. 4 (2003), 317–323.

Metters, R. and V. Vargas. "A Typology of De-Coupling Strategies in Mixed Services." *Journal of Operations Management* 18, no. 6 (2000), 663–682.

Chapter 14

Aaron, R., and J. V. Singh. "Getting Offshoring Right." *Harvard Business Review,* December 2005.

Farrell, D. "Beyond Offshoring: Assess Your Company's Global Potential." *Harvard Business Review,* December 2004.

Farrell, D. "Smarter Offshoring." *Harvard Business Review,* June 2006.

Ferdows, K. "Made in the World: The Global Spread of Production." *Production and Operations Management* 6, no. 2 (1997), 102–109.

Ferdows, K. "Making the Most of Foreign Factories." *Harvard Business Review,* March–April 1997.

Friedman, T. *The World Is Flat: A Brief History of the Twenty-First Century.* New York: Farrar, Straus and Giroux, 2005.

Ghemawat, P. "Managing Differences: The Central Challenge of Global Strategy." *Harvard Business Review,* March 2007.

"The Global Top 20." *Foreign Policy* and A. T. Kearney, Inc., November–December 2006, pp. 74–81.

Linder, J. C. "Transformational Outsourcing." *MIT Sloan Management Review,* Winter 2004.

Michelman, P. "An Outsourcing Checklist." *Harvard Management Update,* 2005.

Newman, S., G. Grikscheit, R. Verma, and V. Malapati. "eBay Customer Support Outsourcing." Indiana University CIBER and European Case Clearinghouse, case # 606-043-1, 2006.

Quinn, J. B. "Outsourcing Innovation: The New Engine of Growth." *Sloan Management Review,* Summer 2000.

Quinn, J. B. "Strategic Outsourcing: Leveraging Knowledge Capabilities." *Sloan Management Review,* Summer 1999.

Youngdahl, W., R. Verma, and K. Ramaswamy. "Exploring New Research Frontiers in Offshoring Knowledge and Service Processes," *Journal of Operations Management,* March 2008.

Photo Credits

Chapter 1: p. 2, AFP/Getty Images; p. 3, Lou-Foto/Alamy; p. 4, Used with permission.

Chapter 2: p. 28, Tetra Images/Corbis; p. 29, © 1992–2008 The Ritz-Carlton Hotel Company, L.L.C. All rights reserved. Reprinted with the permission of The Ritz-Carlton Hotel Company, L.L.C.; p. 45, Chad Ehlers/Alamy; p. 47, National Institute of Standards and Technology; p. 49, AFP/Getty Images; p. 50, George Steinmetz/Corbis

Chapter 3: p. 68, M. Taghi/Zefa/Corbis; p. 69, Apple Handout/epa/Corbis; p. 70, Legoland, California; p. 72: Herman Miller, Inc.; p. 72, Tony Cordoza/Alamy; p. 72, Synthetic Alan King/Alamy; p. 72, media-blitzimage (UK) Limited/Alamy; p. 73, Courtesy of IDEO; p. 82, José Manuel Ribeiro/Reuters/Corbis; p. 83, Copyright © 2008 Joie de Vivre. Reprinted with permission; p. 84, Courtesy of Timbuk2 Designs, Inc.; p. 85, Phototake, Inc./Alamy; p. 87, Motoring Picture Library/Alamy; p. 87, Courtesy of Dell. Used with permission; p. 89, Myrleen Ferguson Cate; p. 89, Time & Life Pictures/Getty Images; p. 90, Car Culture/Corbis; p. 90, Transtock, Inc./Alamy

Chapter 4: p. 102, Courtesy of Kellogg's; p. 106, Richard Levine/Alamy; p. 108, Roger Bamber/Alamy; p. 109, Lou Linwei/Alamy; p. 110, Getty Images; p. 111, AP Photo; p. 116, AP Photo; p. 127, Charlie Schuck/Stock This Way/Corbis; p. 127, Vario Image GMBH & Co. KG/Alamy

Chapter 5: p. 145, Ramin Talaie/Corbis; p. 164, Moodboard/Corbis; p. 164, Jeff Vanuga/Corbis

Chapter 6: p. 195, Najlah Feanny/Corbis; p. 200, Kevin Foy/Alamy; p. 201, dbimages/Alamy; p. 216, Detroit News archives; p. 220, Alamy; p. 222, Jim Zuckerman/Corbis

Chapter 7: p. 233, Alamy; p. 233, AP Photo/Mark Bialek; p. 256, Silver Spring Foods, Inc.; p. 263, Alex Segre/Alamy; p. 265, Sven Hagolani/Zefa/Corbis; p. 276, Alamy

Chapter 8: p. 279, Walt Disney Pictures/Pixar/The Kobal Collection; p. 280, Jorge Ferrari/epa/Corbis; p. 297, Getty Images; p. 310, IT Stock International/Jupiter Images

Chapter 9: p. 324, AP Photo/Dale Atkins; p. 336, © 2008 Microsoft Corporation. All rights reserved; p. 338, Yiorgos Karahalis/Reuters/Corbis; p. 344, AFP/Getty Images

Chapter 10: p. 363, cardcow.com; p. 370, AP Photo/Laurent Rebours; p. 372, © Jim Block; p. 387, Najlah Feanny/Corbis; p. 389, Image Source Black/Jupiter Images

Chapter 11: p. 405, Michael Newman/PhotoEdit, Inc.; p. 406, James L. Amos/Corbis; p. 409, Alamy; p. 411, Creatas Images/Jupiter Images; p. 418, AP Photo/Matt Slocum

Chapter 12: p. 447, AFP/Getty Images; p. 451, Alamy; p. 455, Alamy; p. 456, Alamy; p. 458, Holger Hollemann/epa/Corbis; p. 460, Everett Kennedy Brown/epa/Corbis; p. 463, Alamy; p. 465, Wikipedia Commons

Chapter 13: p. 476, Alamy; p. 478, Hulton-Deutsch Collection/Corbis; p. 482, Phototake, Inc./Alamy; p. 483, Phototake, Inc./Alamy; p. 484, Courtesy of Ford and Siemens, Inc.; p. 488, AP Photo; p. 490, KNAPP; p. 499, AP Photo; p. 501, Route picture courtesy of The Descartes Systems Group, Inc. Reprinted with permission.

Chapter 14: p. 508, Used with permission; p. 512, Alamy; p. 523, Alamy

Index